# THE GOVERNANCE OF COMPLEMENTARY GLOBAL REGIMES AND THE PURSUIT OF HUMAN SECURITY

Series Supranational Criminal Law: Capita Selecta, Volume 21

Published in the series:

1. *Supranational Criminal Law: a System Sui Generis*, Roelof Haveman, Olga Kavran and Julian Nichols (eds.)
2. *Double Jeopardy Without Parameters: Re-characterization in International Criminal Law*, Olaoluwa Olusanya
3. *Harmonization of Criminal Law in Europe*, Erling Johannes Husabø and Asbjørn Strandbakken (eds.)
4. *Sentencing and Sanctioning in Supranational Criminal Law*, Roelof Haveman and Olaoluwa Olusanya (eds.)
5. *Application of International Humanitarian and Human Rights Law to the Armed Conflicts of the Sudan: Complementary or Mutually Exclusive Regimes?*, Mohamed Abdelsalam Babiker
6. *Supranational Criminology: Towards a Criminology of International Crimes*, Alette Smeulers and Roelof Haveman (eds.)
7. *Individual Criminal Liability for the International Crime of Aggression*, Gerhard Kemp
8. *Collective Violence and International Criminal Justice – An Interdisciplinary Approach*, Alette Smeulers (ed.)
9. *International Criminal Law from a Swedish Perspective*, Iain Cameron, Malin Thunberg Schunke, Karin Påle Bartes, Christoffer Wong and Petter Asp
10. *The Implementation of the European Arrest Warrant in the European Union: Law, Policy and Practice*, Massimo Fichera
11. *The Principle of Mutual Recognition in Cooperation in Criminal Matters*, Annika Suominen
12. *The European Public Prosecutor's Office*, Martijn Willem Zwiers
13. *Victimological Approaches to International Crimes: Africa*, Rianne Letschert, Roelof Haveman, Anne-Marie de Brouwer, Antony Pemberton (eds.)
14. *The United States and International Criminal Tribunals*, Harry M. Rhea
15. *EU Sanctions: Law and Policy Issues Concerning Restrictive Measures*, Iain Cameron (ed.)
16. *Whose Responsibility?* Malin Thunberg Schunke
17. *Genocidal Gender and Sexual Violence*, Usta Kaitesi
18. *Addressing the Intentional Destruction of the Environment during Warfare under the Rome Statute of the International Criminal Court*, Steven Freeland
19. *Individual Criminal Liability for the International Crime of Aggression*, Gerhard Kemp
20. *Selective Enforcement and International Criminal Law: The International Criminal Court and Africa*, James Nyawo

# THE GOVERNANCE OF COMPLEMENTARY GLOBAL REGIMES AND THE PURSUIT OF HUMAN SECURITY

## The interaction between the United Nations and the International Criminal Court

Andrea Marrone

intersentia
Antwerpen – Cambridge

Intersentia Ltd
Sheraton House | Castle Park
Cambridge | CB3 0AX | United Kingdom
Tel.: +44 1223 370 170 | Fax: +44 1223 370 169
Email: mail@intersentia.co.uk
www.intersentia.com | www.intersentia.co.uk

*Distribution for the UK and Ireland:*
NBN International
Airport Business Centre, 10 Thornbury Road
Plymouth, PL6 7PP
United Kingdom
Tel: +44 1752 202 301 | Fax: +44 1752 202 331
Email: orders@nbninternational.com

*Distribution for Europe and all other countries:*
Intersentia Publishing nv
Groenstraat 31
2640 Mortsel
Belgium
Tel.: +32 3 680 15 50 | Fax: +32 3 658 71 21
Email: mail@intersentia.be

*Distribution for the USA and Canada:*
International Specialized Book Services
920 NE 58th Ave Suite 300
Portland, OR 97213
USA
Tel.: +1 800 944 6190 (toll free) | Fax: +1 503 280 8832
Email: info@isbs.com

The Governance of Complementary Global Regimes and the Pursuit of Human Security. The interaction between the United Nations and the International Criminal Court

Cover illustration: Francisco DE GOYA (1746-1828), Etching, Plate 47 from 'Los desastres de la guerra'



ISBN 978-1-78068-402-4
D/2016/7849/151
NUR 828

British Library Cataloguing in Publication Data. A catalogue record for this book is available from the British Library.

# PREFACE

In 1998 the State Parties to the Rome Statute established a treaty-based organization of universal character dealing with humanitarian crimes of international concern committed against civilians in conflict and post-conflict situations. The Rome Statute institutions are complementary to the United Nations system but independent from such an established international regime, whose aims are to facilitate the cooperation in the field of international security, international law and human rights. The emerging regime of international criminal justice constitutes arguably the most significant reform of international law, but there is still a long way ahead for systemic changes in the governance of humanitarian affairs centralizing individual rights in intra-state conflict and post-conflict situations. It remains to be seen how the concept of human security would have an impact *a)* on the transition of international law and international security; *b)* on the measures applied on the ground by complementary international mandates; *c)* on the role of the Security Council, State sovereignty and the international governance of humanitarian escalations; and *d)* on the creation of new norms and the place of non-state actors in international law. Moreover, it is also important to assess the evolution of universal jurisdiction, including the policy formulations of global threats and further definitions of serious crimes of common concern such as the crime of aggression, including their controversial governance and the application of double standards in the selection of inter-state conflict situations resulting from acts of aggression. Another aspect requiring attention is to avoid the use of the emerging regime of international criminal justice as an instrument of coercive diplomacy in the context of peace and security maintenance by those permanent members of the UN Security Council (China, Russia and the US), which so far rejected the Rome Statute partnership, but still use it occasionally when this favors their own political interests. In other words, we will look at the ingredients required and the recipe wished, if any, while advocating for democratic governance systems based on the principles of *global justice* and the role of public international law and its institutions consolidating human security. In this study the intersection between politics, law and institutions complementary in their nature, receives an accurate analysis proposing integrated governance models of peace, justice and security to be applied globally.

The multidisciplinary approach of important fields such as law and globalization, the politics of justice and international law, including the developments in the field of human security, are absolutely required when exploring the construction of a global society. Much more important then is to preserve what remains of the concept of the nation-state, its sovereignty and governance, in the turmoil of regimes and sub-regimes led by criminal groups and conflicting political factions. The undemocratic and violent political transitions and the complete absence of law and order characterize the disintegration of many domestic systems unwilling or unable to carry out genuinely their duties towards their citizens. The shorter distance between the concept of the nation-state, its domestic governance systems, and the international community monitoring internal affairs during civil wars, becomes for many stakeholders problematic, but it still represents an important opportunity to preserve fundamental individual rights. The efforts to safeguard universal values on the side with individuals and communities devastated by war and crime through governance structures fostering international peace, justice and security are absolutely worth it. The advocacy of human security measures, including monitoring, reporting and fact finding activities to reveal severe violations of international humanitarian law, represents a paradigm shift challenging international relations. Such an advocacy is contrary to state-centric security policy including governance models keeping the impunity regime of international crimes unchanged in several situations.

In general terms human security measures prioritize the needs of individuals and communities as important guarantors of sustainable peace, development and stability. Unfortunately, in multiple and inter-linked situations, the failure of preventive strategies of mass atrocity crimes severely compromised the safety of civilians, including their fundamental individual rights. In several countries, such as in Libya, Syria, Sudan, Democratic Republic of Congo, Uganda, Kenya, Central African Republic, Ivory Coast and Mali, civilians have severely paid the consequences of such failure. The costs of human lives after the humanitarian disaster in Rwanda, Sierra Leone, Somalia and Cambodia are well known and indicate serious problems dealing with the causes and effects of war and crime. Besides, the sometimes claimed *right* of humanitarian intervention of the international community is challenged now and qualified by the responsibility to protect civilians in situations of mass atrocity crimes. Such an international norm represents an unfinished business in global politics and is considered by many far from capable of preserving the rule of international law. The current practice of governing the international order deserves analysis between the *liberal* vision of normative frameworks in the view of pluralism and its theories, and a *supranational* capacity from the perspective of constitutionalism. The preservation of the rule of law as a principle of governance in a world of multilevel jurisdictions requires discussions, as well as the advocacy of global values in international relations, such as multilateralism, collective responsibility, global solidarity and mutual accountability.[1] As clearly described by Delmas-Marty, "complementarity does not separate national from international criminal jurisdiction, nor does it put them in conflict with each other...".[2] The grey-zones of the complementarity principle, however, clearly arise in the governance of justice functioning outside the arrays of peace and security maintenance in conflict and post-conflict situations. This study deals with the impact, challenges and possible solutions in such governance. It proposes other options rather then the use of military means or military coalitions when intervening in situations of war and crime.

This study offers an overview of the challenges occurring in the emerging regime of international criminal justice as a tool of sustainable peace. It illustrates the impact of such regime in international relations focusing on the obstacles and concerns of its governance in the context of the maintenance and restoration of international peace and security. It advocates for an appropriate interaction strategy between the United Nations and the Rome Statute institutions as a matter of international mutual concern and for the sake of human security. The responsibility to protect cannot be considered as the evolution of human security. Further progress is required in the frameworks of governance dealing with it. In accordance with this study the political compromise reached in Rome contains the same controversial issues not yet resolved in the international legal and political order. The review conference of the Rome Statute in Kampala (Uganda) confirmed the challenges for such emerging regime to find a place in the arrays of peace and security. The political selectivity of the Security Council responding to mass atrocity crimes, the political criteria to reach the resolutions of international criminal justice, and the application of double standards when dealing with them, are the main factors undermining the credibility of the so-called "narrowed" international responses during intra-state conflicts. Some would even consider the use of international legal processes to replace or complement acts of war mandated by the Security Council. With the Rome Statute, such limitations confronting the pursuit of peace and justice are not completely alleviated. In accordance with a broad and idealistic interpretation of the Rome Statute, however, the governance of international criminal justice could be defined as the response to safeguard individuals and communities in extreme conflict situations through the rule of law, multilateralism, collective responsibility, global solidarity

---

1 For an overview of the debate and the extensive literature on the issue of legal pluralism and globalization see R. Michaels, 'Global Legal Pluralism', Duke Law School Faculty Scholarship Series, Paper 185, 2009, accessible at: http://lsr.nellco.org/duke_fs/185 See also A. S. Sweet, 'Constitutionalism, Legal Pluralism, and International Regimes', Yale Law School Faculty Scholarship Series, Paper 1295, 2009, accessible at: http://digitalcommons.law.yale.edu/fss_papers/1295.

2 See M. Delmas-Marty, "Interactions between National and International Criminal Law in the Preliminary Phase of Trial at the ICC", Oxford Journal of International Criminal Justice, Volume 4, Issue 1, March 2006, at 2–11.

and accountability, fighting against the regime of impunity of serious crimes at local, regional and international levels.

Since 1945 the discourse around the international legal order has been dominated by the political role of the United Nations and its institutions. It needs to be noted that while the UN has been the object of significant criticism, it has nevertheless played a remarkable role both in the progressive development and codification of international law. The Preamble of the UN Charter reads in part: "We the peoples of the United Nations determined to save succeeding generations from the scourge of war [...] and to establish conditions under which justice and respect for the obligations arising from treaties and other sources of international law can be maintained, and to promote social progress and better standards of life in larger freedom [...]". Although the Preamble is an integral part of the UN Charter, it does not set out any of the rights or obligations for its member States. Rather, its purpose is to serve as an interpretative guide for the provisions of the UN Charter through the highlighting of some of the core motives of the founders enforcing the organization.[3] In 2005 the member States of the UN General Assembly embraced the responsibility to protect civilians in paragraphs 138–139 of the Outcome Document of the so-called World Summit. In the historic gathering of world leaders in New York for the High-level Plenary Meeting of the General Assembly, the heads of States and governments reached consensus on the formulation of the responsibility to protect populations from genocide, war crimes, ethnic cleansing and crimes against humanity. When States are 'manifestly failing' to protect their population from mass atrocity crimes and peaceful means are inadequate, the international community would take collective action in a 'timely and decisive manner' through the Security Council and in accordance with the UN Charter and with the cooperation of regional organizations as appropriate.[4] The emerging regime of international justice and leadership accountabilities, the preservation of human rights and international inquiries and the rehabilitation of victimized civilians are important tools to establish the truth and create the premises to *protect*, *react* and *rebuild* in situations of war and crime. The good governance of such tools contributes to sustainable peace. Obviously, such an important shift in the international politics of mass atrocies deserves attention at the present and in the years to come. The governance of global regimes of complementary character and the dilemma of human security are concepts requiring analysis and debate.

---

3 For an illuminating overview of such an approach see the Report of the Rapporteur of Commission I/1 UNICO VI, 1945, at 446–7, Doc. 944 I/1/34(1). See also L. Gross, 'The Charter of the United Nations and the Lodge Reservations', 41 AJIL 3, 1947, at 531.

4 UN General Assembly, Sixtieth Session, 2005 World Summit Outcome, UN Doc. A/RES/60/1, 2005, para. 138 and 139.

# STUDY OUTLOOK

This study explores the governance of global regimes fostering peace, justice and security in extreme situations of war and crime. It examines the quest of *complementarity* between international frameworks of governance and the dilemma of human security measures applied in the practice on the ground in conflict and post-conflict situations. It debates the challenges, obstacles and concerns in the governance of peace operations, law enforcement and civilian protection duties. It argues about the meaning of international humanitarian escalations of *last resort* under the flag of civilian protection duties. It debates the requirement of a political *road map* centralizing civilian protection duties in collapsed societies. It examines the governance of international mandates in the field operations not being appropriately integrated between them, and which obviously lose part of their effectiveness. The analysis of the humanitarian escalations of *last resort* between complementary global regimes and their impact in the field operations is central for new policy orientations. The presence of both the United Nations and the International Criminal Court; the configuration of international mandates on the ground; the deployment of peace enforcement operations; the investigations and prosecutions of mass atrocity crimes are interdendent resources. They deserve accurate risk assessments for the sake of civilians in multiple situations. These global tools have the potential to improve human security expectations in situations of war and crime. There is, however, a long way ahead. After a decade of the Court's existence and activity the practice demonstrates the needs for integration, harmonization and consolidation between global regimes of complementary character.

The preliminary part of this study addresses serious concerns in the institutional and normative decentralization characterizing the emerging regime of justice falling under the Rome Statute. It also emphasises the theories of 'statehood', 'sovereignty' and 'governance' and the urgent requirement of political convergence on sensitive issues. The introduction argues that due to the absence of a *supranational* organization for an implementation of the emerging regime of justice at domestic, regional and international levels the harmonization between so defined multilateral, global, universal, complementary international governance institutions involved in conflict and post-conflict situations is fundamental. The global interactions based on the rule of law, multilateralism, collective responsibility, global solidarity and mutual accountability wait to be translated in governance mechanisms at disposition of the international community, finding remedies for a consistent evolution of international relations in the post-cold war. In order to reach democratic standards in such interactions the independence and authority of justice is a basic requirement for human security. It should be time for the nation-states to choose between maintaining the Charter of the United Nations as drafted after WWII, or to consider radical changes regulating human security issues. The main challenge which unfortunately will remain unanswered is whether consensus can be found on a *road map* fostering peace, justice and security dealing with the criminal accountability of States and individuals during armed conflicts. The aspects of *protective*, *retributive* and *restitutive* justice require further application at domestic, regional and international levels. In order to verify the current evolution or devolution of these aspects, the first part of this study debates the quest of *complementarity* and the dilemma of human security in conflict and post-conflict situations. The second part elucidates some of the challenges, obstacles and concerns in the governance of complementary global regimes and the necessity of political convergence. The third part deals with the humanitarian escalations of last resort and their governance in the field operations and offers the concluding assessment deriving from the case studies selected.

The introduction of this study clarifies the statement of the problem, the research questions, the purpose of the research and the methodology used. It debates on the nature of the current architecture of governance and the limits of complementary global regimes dealing with international threats and crimes. It is of fundamental importance to question the impact of international humanitarian escalations and the role of the United Nations and the International Criminal Court responding to mass atrocities and crime prevention, firstly verifying theories, principles, current practice, and secondly, finalizing recommendations useful to maximize the results with defined mechanisms upholding the human security doctrine. The principles and theories upholding the expectations of human security characterize the journey of this study. However, this work does not solve the grey-zones still prevailing in the conceptualization of human security. This concept requires policy implementations and governance models between global regimes of complementary character. The theoretical uncertainties in the concept of human security could be solved by concrete actions in the governance of complementary global regimes. For such governance it is important to remind the background information of the causes of war and crime which have devastating consequences on nation-states, regional and international organizations, communities and individuals. The complementary character of the UN and the Rome Statute institutions should be based on the human security doctrine. In order to clarify the meaning of this concept the study examines the Rome Statute institutional framework and the interaction background between the United Nations and the International Criminal Court, answering questions related to the interdependence of peace, justice and security in the field operations, and the necessity to improve measures of human security such as protection, relocation, reparation and rehabilitation of civilians victimized by serious crimes of common concern. This study demonstrates that further efforts are required by decision-makers for the conceptualization of human security and its expectations. Political convergence is further required about jurisdictional extensions and complementarity for the governance of international threats and crimes destabilizing peace and security.

There is a significant amount of evidence to suggest that both internal instability and State fragility significantly increase the commission of atrocity crimes such as genocide, war crimes and crimes against humanity, including the flight of refugees spreading from single to multiple States, causing regional and large scale instability. However, the policy approach about international humanitarian interventions in fragile States are fragmented, decentralized and the priorities not harmonized with early warning and early action. Obviously, the current international legal frameworks reflect such discrepancies and need to be challenged with political convergence. Besides, the global governance of war and crime requires reliable models, systems and institutions updated to the challenges of the time. The judicial outcomes pointing out crimes and perpetrators are not used for the configuration of international mandates of law enforcement on the ground. The accountability system of international crimes does not receive sufficient support in order to strengthen its deterrent effect in conflict and post-conflict situations. In situations of conflict breaking out since the end of the bipolar world order, which left unresolved the main causes in the majority of such conflicts, civilians have been the greatest victims of warfare. In particular women and children, who are often the targets in times of violence and have been severely used as a weapon of war. In such context, law enforcement and civilian protection duties wait to receive a place in the fight against the impunity of international crimes and within the arrays of peace and security maintenance keeping alive the links of reconstruction and development.

The country-situations in Sub-Saharan Africa, Middle East and East Asia are impressive examples where ethno-political conflicts show dramatic statistics. In the African Great Lakes Region for instance, the political crisis and the continuing violence between different factions involved in political transitions, the establishment of a war economy and militarized regimes and the impunity of serious crimes of common concern are the only realities identified through reliable empirical data. The analysis of such data demonstrates that global regimes are not yet entirely able to cure the causes of warfare. However, they can have an impact at least on the effects in the short and middle terms, while developing the capacity to act on the causes in the long term. In order to accomplish such a model of governance an expansion of *complementarity* between established and emerging global regimes is absolutely required for the sake of the human security doctrine. The UN deployment of robust peacekeeping in the field operations for instance, should perform civilian protection duties hosting and complementing the investigative activities of the International Criminal Court in both referrals and non-referrals activities of the Security Council. The States non-parties to the Rome Statute should be bound and be engaged through their UN membership. In the current reality of humanitarian escalations the regime of international criminal justice falling under the Rome Statute functions without any power of police and law enforcement on its own, but depends from the cooperation from its States Parties and relevant stakeholders, such as the United Nations. Therefore, global strategies are absolutely required to *prevent*, *react* and *rebuild* situations of war and crime in accordance with the rule of law, multilateralism, collective responsibility, global solidarity and mutual accountability. This study approaches the politics of international law and the views of future law, or *de lege ferenda*, as opposed to *de lege lata*, or the law as it currently exists. It examines the controversial debate between the consolidation of global values in the constitution of the world community against pluralistic legal frameworks based on decentralized laws and institutions far from offering sustainable peace in situations of war and crime.

This study focuses on the longstanding debate to manage, maintain and restore peace and justice centralizing the protection of civilians in situations of war and crime. It advocates for solutions in the shortcomings of interaction between complementary global regimes fighting against the impunity of crimes of international concern, while offering sustainable peace in extremely violent conflict zones, before, during and after civil wars. It emphasizes the priority of implementing measures of human security in conflict and post-conflict situations with an integrated approach of governance of peace and justice. It clarifies the concept of global justice and its *retributive*, *protective* and *restitutive* aspects which are undermined by the shortcomings of political engagements, international responsibilities and constitutional adjustments reflecting international, regional and national realities. This study explores the nexus between law and politics in the emerging regime of justice debating models of governance to secure the rule of law in a system of multilevel jurisdictions. It emphasizes the international political convergence required, and still missed, and the role of international law promoting the consolidation between complementary global regimes based on cooperation. It proposes an insight of international criminal justice and the role of public international law to promote it. It debates feasible solutions on structural, normative and operational issues implementing the governance of justice in conflict and post-conflict societies in accordance with the human security doctrine. The purpose of this study is to verify the progress of public international law and its multilateral premises dealing with war and crime according to the challenges of the time. It offers an extensive analysis of the paradigms in the making of complementary international governance institutions fostering human security in multiple situations, providing some direction on the way to formulate *de lege ferenda*.

The rise of the Rome Statute system represented a shift from State-centric political positions to the claims coming from civil society organizations. However, it still struggles to find its place in the system for the maintenance or restoration of international peace and security. The establishment of a permanent International Criminal Court was pressured by civil society to decision-makers in order to centralize the role of the victims during judicial proceedings fighting against the impunity of serious crimes. The political compromise that has been reached so far in regard to the Court's position in peace and security mandates still characterizes its limits. The governance of international criminal justice requires risk assessments which cannot be limited only to the Court's activities. Such governance requires global considerations on the ways international regimes would become complementary. The main considerations are listed and examined in this work. From a broader perspective this study clarifies the main challenges and opportunities of regulatory frameworks fostering human security. The interaction between complementary global regimes is seen as an important tool in order to build up the basic premises of *global justice* for the advancement of sustainable peace, human development and for the protection of human rights. It is fundamental to define preventive measures between global regimes of complementary character before mass atrocity crimes would occur. It is important to reflect on reliable response mechanisms applicable during the humanitarian escalations of *last resort* characterized by extreme violence and violations falling under international law, including measures applicable in the context of rehabilitation, reparation and humanitarian assistance to the victims of war and crime.

The human security doctrine which has developed in the last couple of decades deserves further application of its concept even with the difficulties incurred in our globalized world.[5] The rule of international law would profit from such an approach evolving in the centralization of individuals.[6] It is important to measure the standards of complementary interactions between the relevant actors centralizing individuals in global matters. The member States of multilateral treaties have still the *protective* responsibility towards civilians in their own territories and jurisdictions, while the international community is in charge of preventing, reacting, and rebuilding situations of war and crime. Models of capacity-building are required in the absence of the nation-state and its disintegration, including the nation-state formation moved by political oppositions based on violence and controversial domestic governance such as corruption, autocracy and armed conflicts and the constant risk that the

5 For an overview of the debate and literature on human security see T. Owen, "Human Security – Conflict, Critique and Consensus: Colloquium Remarks and a Proposal for a Threshold-Based Definition", Security Dialogue, September 2004, vol. 35, no. 3, at 373–387.

6 See G. Oberleitner, "Human Security: A Challenge to International Law?", Global Governance, Vol. 11, No. 2 (Apr.–June 2005), at 185–203.

perpetrators of serious crimes would offend the dignity of human lives. Besides, that the basic rights of civilians would be violated, or they would be taken as the hostage during violent political transitions, and with the range of crimes committed by the perpetrators simply remaining unpunished. The governance of peace, justice and security is examined in the three parts of this study providing an assessment of law enforcement, civilian protection and other urgent issues waiting for solutions. This study attempts to define the meaning of complementary global regimes in accordance with the UN Charter and the Rome Statute. The progress of international law and its institutions centralizing fundamental individual rights requires with no doubts further political convergence and advocacy. The many and real challenges to reach sustainable peace in situations of war and crime demonstrate the necessity of a political *road map* to define, design and manage global regimes of complementary character. In this study the search and formulation of political convergence on these issues is considered a very good opportunity for decision-makers.

# CONTENTS

# LIST OF ABBREVIATIONS

| | |
|---|---|
| ADT | Darfur Atrocities Documentation Team |
| AJIL | American Journal of International Law |
| AMIS | African Union Mission in Sudan |
| ASIL | American Society of International Law |
| ASP | Assembly of States Parties to the Rome Statute |
| ASP Res. | Assembly of States Parties to the Rome Statute Resolution |
| AU | African Union |
| AU Dec. | African Union Decision |
| AUPD | African Union Panel on Darfur |
| AUO | African Union Organization |
| BYIL | British Yearbook of International Law |
| CARICOM | Caribbean Community and Common Market |
| CAT | Convention against Torture and Other Cruel, Inhuman or Degrading Treatment or Punishment |
| CIA | Central Intelligence Agency |
| CICC | Coalition for an International Criminal Court |
| CPA | Comprehensive Peace Agreement in the Sudan |
| CPPCG | Convention on the Prevention and Punishment of the Crime of Genocide |
| EJIL | European Journal of International Law |
| EU | European Union |
| ESIR | English School of International Relations |
| GA Res. | General Assembly Resolution |
| HRQ | Human Rights Quarterly |
| ICC | International Criminal Court |
| ICCPR | International Covenant on Civil and Political Rights |
| ICESCR | International Covenant on Economic, Social and Cultural Rights |
| ICISS | International Commission on Intervention and State Sovereignty |
| ICJ | International Court of Justice |
| ICLQ | International and Comparative Law Quarterly |
| ICRtoP | International Coalition for the Responsibility to Protect |
| ICTY | International Criminal Tribunal for the Former Yugoslavia |
| ICTR | International Criminal Tribunal for Rwanda |
| ICG | International Convention on Genocide |
| IHL | International Humanitarian Law |
| ILC | International Law Commission |

| | |
|---|---|
| IMTFE | International Military Tribunal for the Far East |
| IRF | International Refugee Law |
| IR | International Relations |
| ISAF | International Security Assistance Force in Afghanistan |
| JPR | Journal of Peace Research |
| LAS | League of Arab States |
| LJIL | Leiden Journal of International Law |
| LRA | Ugandan Rebel Lord's Resistance Army |
| NILR | Netherlands International Law Review |
| MINURCAT | United Nations Mission in the Central African Republic and Chad |
| MoU | Memorandum of understanding |
| MONUC | United Nations Organization Mission in the Democratic Republic of Congo |
| MONUSCO | United Nations Organization Stabilization Mission in the Democratic Republic of Congo |
| NATO | North Atlantic Treaty Organization |
| NGO | Non-governmental organization |
| ONUC | United Nations Operation in the Congo |
| POC | Protection of Civilians |
| PRIO | Peace Research Institute Oslo |
| RtoP | Responsibility to protect |
| R2P | Responsibility to protect |
| SC Res. | Security Council Resolution |
| SCSR | Special Court for Sierra Leone |
| SIPRI | Stockholm International Peace Research Institute |
| STL | Special Tribunal for Lebanon |
| SWGCA | Special Working Group on the Crime of Aggression |
| SRSG | Special Representative of the Secretary-General |
| SSR | Security Sector Reform |
| TAL | Transitional Administrative Law |
| TI | Transcend International |
| TRI | Transcend Research Institute |
| UN | United Nations |
| UNAMID | African Union/UN Hybrid operation in Darfur |
| UNCOI | United Nations Commission of Inquiry |
| UNDP | United Nations Development Programme |
| UNDPKO | United Nations Department of Peacekeeping Operations |
| UNGA | United Nations General Assembly |
| UNHRC | United Nations Human Rights Council |
| UNMIS | United Nations Mission in the Sudan |
| UNMIC | United Nations Interim Administration Mission in Kosovo |
| UNOCHR | United Nations Office of the Commissioner of Human Rights |
| UNSC | United Nations Security Council |

| | |
|---|---|
| UNSG | United Nations Secretary-General |
| TFV | Trust Fund for Victims |
| VRS | Army of the Republika Srpska |
| WW | World War |
| YIHL | Yearbook of International Humanitarian Law |

"I observed that men rush to arms for slight causes, or no cause at all, and that when arms have once been taken up there is no longer any respect for law, divine or human. It is as if, in accordance with a general decree, frenzy had openly been let loose for the committing of all crimes".

Hugo Grotius, *On the Law of War and Peace*, 1625

# INTRODUCTION

# 1. THE GLOBAL REGIMES DEALING WITH INTERNATIONAL THREATS AND CRIMES

## PRELIMINARY REMARKS

This study debates the ways *complementary* global regimes are currently empowered and governed in the field operations, and emphasizes the constant risk of reducing the effect of their respective peace and justice efforts, if appropriate interactions are not settled and political convergence is not finally found. This study argues that the emerging regime of international criminal justice is still missing the support of regional and international organizations, which are important at the same extent of nation-states for the sake of human security. The good governance of such sensitive issues might shorten the links in the preservation of individual rights. The civilian protection measures entail additional competence, which requires further institutional design, including resources and know-how about the victims of war. Besides, the priority should be given to sensitive issues waiting for solution, offering a well-defined place of the Rome Statute regime in global governance systems dealing with individual rights in conflict and post-conflict situations. Both the States and the complementary tools at disposition of the international community need substantial reforms in order to respect, protect and fulfil the right of the victims of human rights violations to an effective civilian protection remedy. In the end, the establishment of an independent international judiciary is only a halfway step to *prevent*, *react* and *rebuild* conflict and post-conflict situations, including the range of crimes deriving from them.

This study is very cautious about the claim that nation-states would have a legal 'right' to intervene with military operations under the 'flag' of civilian protection duties. After all, the use of force is essentially prohibited under international law and this is not the only tool to stop mass atrocity crimes. But how does the emerging regime of international criminal justice falling under the Rome Statute, currently receive a place in the arrays of peace and security maintenance? How are violent internal political transitions governed at global scale? Is the international society more human, more secure, and more peaceful with the complementary tools currently at disposition? And which is its current ability to take care of serious breaches of human rights? This work approaches the distinction between the concepts of legality and power in the absence of *checks and balances* systems monitoring the 'right' of humanitarian intervention, and the paradigm shift of civilian protection duties. It offers reflections on the important role of *complementary* global regimes to mitigate such fields when intervening with their activities in the domestic jurisdictions of 'failed' States. The advocacy expressed in this study is that statehood, sovereignty and governance deserve to remain central in the current debates dealing with the fight against international threats and crimes and the developments of human security.

In the context of intra-state and inter-state conflicts, or also referred as armed conflicts of international and non-international character, the question is how the international community develops the capacity-building to deal with both these conflict categories. In situations of war and crime the causes and the disastrous effects on civilians require reliable deterrent tools. In the past two decades most wars have taken the form of intra-state conflicts. Some of their causes derived from the competition to patronize resources and lands, have been triggered by political and economic transitions, by ineffective governance and by corruption and undemocratic inequalities. In broad terms, the main cause of the disintegration of the nation-states and their struggle to retain a place in the global society are not self-sufficient elements to prevent the commission of mass atrocity crimes. The majority of intra-state conflicts are still holding the causes and effects of the post-colonial formation of nation-states at the expenses of civilians.[7] The cruelty and brutality with which intra-state conflicts are fought and the difficulties to have deterrent systems in place against them are partly due to the use of child soldiers and gender crimes, the privatization of warfare, and the presence of non-state actors such as the use of paramilitary forces. The frameworks of governance in place dealing with them are characterized by a myriad of gaps. The causes rooted in societies devastated by war and crimes have as the negative effects: the regime of impunity, the unstable and unrepresentative political institutions, the poor infrastructure in domestic governance systems and the abundance of cheap weapons and porous borders.

The view expressed in this study is that violent intra-state transitions require models of capacity-building rather than support with military operations, which should remain neutral and focus on civilian protection duties. The military intervention in Libya represents a bad example of the practice of civilian protection measures applied collectively. Bad decisions and bad governance destabilise the tools at disposition by the international community and deserve to be challenged. The problem is not only what makes accountability more or less feasible and what strategies are deployed by *complementary* global regimes to achieve visible results

---

7 On the legal and political distinction between tribes and races, see, M. Mamdani, *When Victims Become Killers: Colonialism, Nativism and Genocide in Rwanda*, 2001.

on the ground. Another requirement is the recognition of the responsibility to constantly review and reform, enhancing the role of regional institutions in the formulation of peace and security policies, which still focus on State security, rather than human security. Another requisite refers to the constitutional adjustments in order to maximize the results of humanitarian interventions on the ground in conflicts and post-conflict situations, while also preserving the international legal and political order centralizing fundamental individual rights in global affairs and civilian protection measures. The UN Charter needs amendments including a democratization process of its institutions. This is a fragmentary process that still requires solutions. It has been advocated for too long and deserves at least to remain at such, particularly in the context of conflict prevention, use of force and large scale escalations of serious violations of international humanitarian law.

## 1.1. THE DETERMINATIONS REQUIRED BY INSTITUTIONS, POLICY AND LAW

In this study, the following issues are extensively discussed from several legal and political perspectives: the design, definition and the governance of global regimes in the post-cold war era; the international governance institutions deriving from such global regimes; the transition of international security, the preservation of human security globally, and the responses to global threats based on collective efforts; the governance of international threats, and the challenges for international criminal justice in the arrays of peace and security, namely about the measures for its maintenance and restoration. This analytical work measures the standards of effectiveness of the tools already at disposition of the international community, assessing the governance gaps and the priority to maximize their impact at domestic, regional and international levels. The approach in this study is that *complementary* global regimes fostering human security have to be prepared to respond to *a)* the abuses of fundamental individual rights and freedoms compromised by the coercions of political leaders and warlords; *b)* the exploitations of children and women in times of violence and war; *c)* the trafficking of weapons and drug trade; including *d)* all other dysfunctions of domestic governance such as abuse of power and corruption. These international threats, and the crimes deriving from them, characterize the reality in several countries in the complete absence of domestic governance systems able to respond to severe violations of international humanitarian principles and laws. With regard to the formulation of international security policies for instance, there are serious doubts about the approach of the US, as permanent members of the Security Council, and Israel, that *failed* States are the source of the most serious international threats and crimes. Such an approach by the decision-making in peace and security maintenance is contested in this study. After all, it is evident that fragile, or so-called 'failed' States are mainly a real threat for their own citizens, and that State 'failure' and international security, are not necessarily the two faces of the same coin.[8] In order to offer some background useful for the reader, and further clarify the analysis performed in the several parts of this study, both preliminary remarks and section outlines will appear in every chapter and sections. The purpose is to shed some light on the conceptual orientations expressed in the topics and the theoretical tools used in the argumentations.

In the international political circles the approach of the responsibility to protect norm diverges between the search of mechanisms of prevention and early warnings and military response, and the use of force in case of mass atrocity crimes. A wider reflection is that the Security Council would remain in charge of nearly all mechanisms of enforcement available, while from a theoretical perspective multilateral forces should be used for emerging regimes attempting to stabilize law and order in situations of mass atrocity crimes such as the Rome Statute. As far as premature it could be considered, this study debates whether there would be harmonization of such issues in the UN Charter as the constitution of the world community, and if, there would be ever a role of international criminal justice in humanitarian interventions, and if yes, how such role would be. It is important to examine the progress of *complementary* global regimes and the intersection between world politics and international law, including possible measures of human security to be found in the interaction strategies of international governance institutions. This study recalls the necessity of an appropriate strategy, combining the responsibility to protect civilians in conflict and post-conflict societies with the determination to put an end to the impunity of mass atrocity crimes. Several documents have been analysed to verify the *status quo* of such a strategy at governmental, regional and global levels especially with regard to the armed conflicts occurring in the African Great Lakes Region and the concerns of the African Union during the instability of peace and security spreading in the African continent, including the political unrest and the violence on civilians spreading in the Middle East and Asia, and further political support required by the EU and the Latin America group of States to the emerging regime of international criminal justice falling under the Rome Statute.

The empowerment and public authority of international governance institutions dealing with global threats and crimes persist to be problematic for the reasons examined in this study. Therefore, the ways global actors interact with each other deserve to be questioned. If we only consider the minimal resources allocated to them, the expectations to respond to the current breakdowns in domestic jurisdictions affected by war and crime are very high. First, the international governance institutions have to rely on the support and cooperation

[8] See P. M. Stewart, *Weak Links. Fragile States, Global Threats, and International Security*, Oxford University Press, May 2011.

of governments. Second, in order to maximize the results in conflict and post-conflict situations the interaction between them is central for democratic governance, but not less problematic. A political *road map* represents an important opportunity finding suitable solutions fostering peace and justice in the context of human security. The interaction between the accountability mechanisms and the responsibilities to protect individuals require further international efforts from the relevant political actors. When the International Commission on (Humanitarian) Intervention and State Sovereignty defined the responsibility to protect, identified a responsibility to *'prevent'*; a responsibility to *'react'*; and a responsibility to *'rebuild'*. Thus, specific responsibilities before, during, and after the humanitarian escalations would occur.[9] Unfortunately, the interaction between complementary global regimes does not reflect sustainable model of prevention, international assistance and capacity-building applicable during intra-state conflict. The political forces engaged in the implementation of the regime of international justice are still delaying to prioritize the law enforcement of judicial decisions and the civilian protection duties in the field. The ability to *'prevent'*, *'react'* and *'rebuild'* situations affected by war and crime requires comprehensive programs of reconstruction, support of electoral systems, rule of law and justice sector reforms (army, police and judiciary). Therefore, all possible donors have to be mobilized as well as academics and civil society.

The occurrence of the emerging regime of justice in the context of peace and security and the potential, whether still latent, to stimulate the modernization of the tools (and mechanisms) at disposition by the world community, such as the UN system, will need further investigation. It is too soon to speculate on these sensitive governance issues of the international society and their transition. At this moment in time, however, the initiation of the public administration of international criminal justice simply struggles to find its place in the arrays of peace and security. The outcome deriving from such initial struggle should not be delayed any longer and receive visibility through primary (UN Charter, Rome Statute) and secondary law (UN-ASP legislation) including arrangements and agreements in the field missions. This study indicates that the current political discussions are characterized by some degree of theoretical shortcomings, constraints and speculations at national level, including *ultra vires* interpretation of the treaty-law, which received extensive legal research since the establishment of the Rome Statute. The global governance issues which are at the core of these

9 In 2005 the political imperatives of the UN World Summit Outcome declared that "each individual State has the responsibility to protect its populations from genocide, war crimes, ethnic cleansing and crimes against humanity. This responsibility entails the prevention of such crimes, including their incitement, through appropriate and necessary means. *We accept* that responsibility and will act in accordance with it. The international community should, as appropriate, encourage and help States to exercise this responsibility and support the United Nations in establishing an early warning capability". See the Report of the UN Secretary-General, *Implementing the responsibility to protect*, UN doc. A/63/677, (2009).

arguments do not receive any progress if we also consider the weak shift and decentralization of the treaty-based bodies preserving human rights under the UN umbrella and their liaison with the Rome Statute regime. It is agreed that the UN Charter represents the crystallization of an era that does not apply well to the contemporary international society. Its institutions reflect such dissoluteness instead of evaluating the needs of the time and responding to them. In any case, the UN democratization should be considered as a process that would in the first place enhance its capacities, tasks, duties and responsibilities.[10] The purpose of such process should avoid any possibility for some of its members to profit or acting far away, or shaping at their own advantage universal premises fostering peace, justice and human security. In this way, the interaction between complementary global actors would bring innovation in their competence, duty and knowledge sharing.

## 1.2. CONFLICT GOVERNANCE, HUMANITARIANISM AND GLOBAL JUSTICE

The responsibility of the international community to intervene in domestic jurisdictions of *failed* States, unable or unwilling to fight against the impunity of serious crimes, has been established by the Rome Statute in accordance with the Charter of the United Nations. Such important accomplishment is absolutely not an end to itself. Much more needs to be done. Of primary importance is the search of a *complementary* place such regime would receive within the international legal and political order. The legal and political challenges of global humanitarianism need the attention by the decision-making enforcing *complementary* global regimes and their international governance institutions.[11] The main assumption is that the relationship between *complementary* global regimes should have been settled by primary law (UN Charter and Rome Statute) and not by separate 'relationship' agreements which limit the necessary implementation of governance at global level of sensitive humanitarian issues. The evolution of the human security doctrine will need to solve such limitations in the years to come. The effectiveness of the Court remains to be determined and may well be hampered by having just slightly more than half of the members of the United Nations as signatories. The fact that such a tribunal was established is in itself a major accomplishment. Hopefully, its presence will bring the States and

[10] See J. Muravchik, The Future of the United Nations: Understanding the Past to Chart a Way Forward, 2005. See also N.J. Schrijver, "The Future of the Charter of the United Nations", Max Planck Yearbook of United Nations Law, 2006, 10: 1–34.

[11] For the debate see the book review by T. M. Shaw of *Fragile Peace: State Failure, Violence and Development in Crisis Regions*, T. Debiel, A. Klein (eds.), 2002. The book review is to be found in T. M. Shaw, *Journal of Contingencies and Crisis Management*, 2005, Volume 12, Issue 3, at 128–135, accessible at: www.politicalreviewnet.com/polrev/reviews/JCCM/R_0966_0879_077_1004614.asp.

the world community closer to prosecuting international crimes and closer to the preservation of victim rights. There are valid reasons to explore the meaning of global regimes intended to be the governance tools of the international society and the evolution of international law for the sake of individuals. In other words, the progress achieved and achievable by concrete human security measures and human rights law. For the first time in the history of an international tribunal the Rome Statute centralizes the roles of victims and witnesses in the judicial proceedings. The security concerns of investigation and prosecution still remain and especially in the field operations. The fight against international threats and crime deserve the support by the UN presence on the ground and by the political circles sponsoring it. The deployment of peace operations should complement the investigative activity on the ground and engage in civilian protection duties. But this is not the case.

This study requires multidisciplinary assessments and preliminary analysis before formulating pragmatic recommendations. It highlights the necessity to clarify the meaning of complementary duties particularly in the configurations of mandates and multidimensional operations in the field in extreme conflict situations, and in case of serious violations of international humanitarian law. It focuses on the verification of global strategies of relationships and partnerships in order to raise a democratic architecture fostering human security, using the 'old' and the 'new' established global tools such as the United Nations and the Rome Statute institutions. This chapter clarifies further the main theoretical approach characterizing this work, before the study embarks on the respective analytical assessments dealing with the intersection between international law and global politics. It clarifies the unresolved issues in the construction of a global architecture of governance dealing with intra- and inter-state conflicts and with serious violations of international humanitarian law. Moreover, it contains the statement of the problem, the research questions, the purpose of the research, the topics to be debated and the methodology used, including a summary of the multidisciplinary approach performed in this study. It also offers further clarification of the meaning of *complementary* global regimes fostering peace and justice and the possible progress in their governance. It discusses the investigation required in order to formulate conclusions and recommendations to be addressed to the political organs enforcing *complementary* global regimes dealing with intra- and inter-state armed conflicts.

The fundamental rights of individuals in situations of war and crime deserve to be central. The emerging regime of international criminal justice is in need of a consolidated strategy of engagements at political, institutional and normative levels, not only *vis-à-vis* the States but also with regional and international stakeholders. There are no doubts that the efforts undertaken by the States must build up an acceptable law enforcement strategy that would improve the regime of justice and human rights protection in their own domestic reality. Besides, international governance institutions of universal character need to be modernized according to the challenges of the time. Another argument is whether individual rights, specifically victim rights, are at the centre of such sensitive systemic issues, or the interests of the States are exclusively central. In other words, the attempt of this study is to verify whether the rule of law functions as a principle of governance in modern societies in both constitutional and pluralistic approaches. This study also underscores the political convergence required fostering peace and justice in the current transition of the world order.

## 1.3. INTEGRATED OR DISCONNECTED GLOBAL ARCHITECTURE OF GOVERNANCE?

With the end of the cold war intra-state conflicts, regional instability and serious breaches of human rights have received significant international attention. This has strengthened the promotion of *complementary* global regimes as preventive tools of war and crime. The inter-state conflicts are concerned with regional competition and distribution of natural resources, among other reasons of nation-state formation, while the intra-state conflicts are the result of civil wars rooted in ethnic, religious, and violent political transitions, including bad governance, autocracy and corruption. Every conflict situation has a particularly history and background. However, they share some of the same causes generating war and crime. The constant risk is that the devastating effects in such situations would spread at larger scale, if not properly dealt with. In Sub-Saharan Africa the quest for nation-building occurred during the independence explosion of the 1960s aimed at developing nation-states, was followed by the neo-liberal reforms of the 1980s and 1990s, which left behind significant capacity gaps at the domestic level, where civic engagement in public governance had been inexistent and civil wars were spreading all over the continent.[12] During the past two decades, governance has become a key concept in the international development debate and policy discourse over these countries. In Africa, there has been an historical record of bad governance and improving it must place the African continent on a path of sustainable development encompassing good governance and prosperity with a consolidation of peace, security, and stability.[13]

---

12 See M. Mamdani, 'Political Violence and State Formation in Post-Colonial Africa', International Development Centre Working Paper Series, Paper No.1, October 2007 accessible at: http://idc.open.ac.uk/files/Resource/20090911_031601_2192.pdf.

13 For an overview of the UN projects and research findings see K. R. Hope, *The UNECA and Good Governance in Africa*, Harvard International Development Conference: Governance and Development in a Dynamic Global Environment, 2003, Boston, accessible at: www.uneca.org/dpmd/Hope_Harvard.doc For an overview of participation in public governance, civic engagement, and decentralization of government in the process of policy development, service delivery, and public accountability of institutions in Sub-Saharan Africa see

In both cases of *inter-* and intra-state conflicts the lasting process of militarization has been the cause of armed conflicts in the majority of such domestic regimes. The militarization in underdeveloped countries became the substitute of possible progress of domestic governance institutions other than army.[14] So said, which are the opportunities to recur to the rule of law in such life-threatening situations for civilians during armed conflicts? Which are the models of governance proposed in this particular moment of shortcomings and failure of monitoring systems of war and crime at domestic, regional and international levels? Are the actual 'paradigms in the making' of *complementary* governance combined with the 'work in progress' of global values (such as the rule of law, multilateralism, collective responsibility, global solidarity and mutual accountability), contributing further to the development of the international society dealing with global threats and crimes? Besides, how should a universal jurisdiction be enforced, in order to have an impact simultaneously on the causes and effects of mass atrocity crimes in domestic and regional realities? And last but not least, how are the current humanitarian escalations dealt with by international governance institutions of universal character? Obviously, finding the responses to such sensitive questions requires looking at the transition of the institutional contours of international law, including the political convergence required by the formulation of a *road map* of governance fostering peace diplomacy, justice and human rights. This study performs such a task, among other tasks.[15]

The political agenda to fight against international threats and crimes reflects a couple of important aspects which may influence the current international legal and political order according to the challenges of the time. Such an agenda would primarily depend on the determination of the political organs enforcing *complementary* global regimes fostering peace, justice and security, and secondly depend on the implementation of norms universally recognized in domestic jurisdictions and national constitutions, including the important role of regional political entities and civil society. The fight against threats and crimes needs further implementation in domestic, regional and international frameworks, which require assistance by international governance institutions in accordance with the politics of transition in conflict and post-conflict societies. The problem

---

E. Armstrong, "Integrity, Transparency and Accountability in Public Administration:", in *Ethics, Transparency and Accountability*, United Nations source: DESA, UN Department of Economic and Social Affairs, 2005, accessible at: http://unpan1.un.org/intradoc/groups/public/documents/un/unpan020955.pdf.

14 See R. Luckham, 'The Military, Militarization and Democratization in Africa: A Survey of Literature and Issues', in *African Studies Review*, Vol. 37, No. 2 (Sep., 1994), at 13–75.

15 For relevant studies providing some conceptual definition of governance see M. Bevir, *Key Concepts in Governance*, 2009. See T. Weiss, "Governance, good governance and global governance: Conceptual and actual challenges", *Third World Quaterly*, Volume 21, Issue 5, 2000, at 795. See also R. Falk, *On Humane Governance: Toward a New Global Politics: The World Order Models Project Report of the Global Civilization Initiative*, 1995.

is that the governance of global threats, such as the intra-state warfare, the spreading of regional conflicts and mass atrocity crimes, the military exploitation of humans and resources, the bad governance and corruption, the drug trafficking, the terrorism and the use of weapons of mass destruction, suffers from systemic breakdowns at social, economic and political levels, including the shortcomings of nation-states to comply with international law and multilateral approaches. Besides, some of these global threats do not receive any crime definition and are still in the way of being digested by global politics. It is required to look at the ways international regimes have been enforced and are currently governed, focusing on the meaning of their *complementary* role and their possible evolutions in the fight against international threats and crimes. Now that serious violations of international humanitarian law are categorized as disturbing international peace and security, they require further responsibilities at domestic, regional and international levels. Further legal research is also required on common and shared responsibilities of intergovernmental entities, their competence and know-how, including the transition of the responsibilities of international organizations and the implementation of new fields of law such as international administrative law.

In theory, the governance of international regimes fighting against war and crime is based on the principles of the rule of law, multilateralism, collective responsibility, global solidarity and mutual accountability. There are no doubts that these principles of governance promote social progress, human rights, and the achievement of world peace. Within the current international legal and political order urgent solutions are required in the short, middle and long term balancing the 'right' of humanitarian intervention and its transition to the 'responsibility' to protect civilians with every means. Legal frameworks are required preserving fundamental individual rights, while extending the criminal accountabilities equally when dealing with the international crimes characterizing conflict and post-conflict situations. The preservation of the rule of law has the potential to impact order and stability in transition societies, while also retaining universal values shared by the world community. However, the ways international humanitarian law and human rights law may provide a relevant legal framework applicable in situations not qualifying as an armed conflict is still not clear, including the accountability mechanisms, law enforcement, and civilian protection measures in conflict and post-conflict situations. The historical, political and legal factors of such lacuna are extensively examined in the struggle to achieve a democratic architecture based on human security. In order to measure the aspects of democratic governance, further research would still be required per situation, keeping in mind that a perfect analytical formula does not exist, while the theory offers valuable principles for the policy formulation to *prevent*, *react* and *rebuild* in conflict and post-conflict situations.[16]

## 1.4. STATEMENT OF THE PROBLEM

The establishment of an international judicial institution responsible to verify on a case by-case basis when serious international humanitarian crimes committed by individuals would fall within the competence of domestic judicial authorities, and when an international judiciary would be required, is a visible accomplishment advocated for ages. The important paradigm shift refers to governing the transitional challenges characterizing massive humanitarian escalations in conflict and post-conflict situations, between the responsibility to protect civilians and the fight against the impunity of international crimes. In the current legislation of the United Nations, the civilian protection duties are associated to the maintenance of peace and security and to the right of intervention in the domestic affairs of sovereign States for humanitarian reasons, extending further the reach of a criminal jurisdiction to punish the perpetrators of serious crimes of common concern. The shift throughout the humanitarian intervention doctrine, including the *ex-post* capacity of international judicial institutions and *ad hoc* tribunals established by the Security Council, and the transition to the notion of the responsibility to protect and human security doctrine, including the *ex-ante* capacity of the International Criminal Court using its *proprio motu* powers, requires reliable models of governance. Empirical verifications indicate that the humanitarian intervention by States or military coalitions, if not occasionally illegal, was often attributable to political or economic interests, rather than human rights, or based on global solidarity. The political responsibilities and the legal accountabilities of such actors wait to be further fulfilled. This explicitly means that the architecture of governance of *complementary* global regimes simply depends on the political convergence of several important issues which

[16] According to the Secretary-General Ban Ki Moon and the report released by the International Commission of on Intervention and State Sovereignty (ICISS), these are the three pillars of the R2P. The responsibility to protect (R2P or RtoP) is a UN initiative established in 2005. It consists of an emerging norm, or set of principles, based on the idea that sovereignty is not a right, but a responsibility. R2P focuses on preventing and halting four crimes: genocide, war crimes, crimes against humanity, and ethnic cleansing, which it places under the generic umbrella term of, *Mass Atrocity Crimes*. The Responsibility to Protect has three pillars. 1. A State has a responsibility to protect its population from mass atrocities; 2.The international community has a responsibility to assist the State to fulfil its primary responsibility; 3. If the State fails to protect its citizens from mass atrocities and peaceful measures have failed, the international community has the responsibility to intervene through coercive measures such as economic sanctions. Military intervention would be considered as the last resort option. See the *Report of the ICISS and State Sovereignty*, 2001, accessible at: http://responsibilitytoprotect.org/ICISS%20Report.pdf For relevant positions in this debate see also T. Weiss, 'The Sunset of Humanitarian Intervention: The Responsibility to Protect in a Unipolar Era', *Security Dialogue*, 2004, Vol. 35, issue 2.

are discussed in this study. The most important of which is the extension of accountabilities when fundamental individual rights are violated, including the implementation of civilian protection duties.

The legal frameworks based on cooperation are characterized by several shortcomings of compliance and require responsibilities in the political configurations of mandates deployed in the field operations including their legal accountabilities. The *complementarity* principle intended to delimit domestic and international responsibilities is not applied in the delimitation of competence between international public authorities involved in the humanitarian escalations of so-called *'last resort'*. The international responsibilities and the forms of accountabilities of non-state actors are not yet defined when intervention in mass atrocities occurs and since international crimes are committed. In many situations, the political configuration of mandates on the ground takes in consideration, on the one hand, only the compromised position of the local government without even verifying whether the peace negotiations are taking place with the individuals most responsible of the crimes. On the other hand, the judicial activity in the field should not be paralyzed by peace processes and negotiations. In the majority of these situations the right timing and the unity of intents of such global actors involved in mass atrocities are seriously compromised. Moreover, victim rights and civilian protection duties are still waiting for reliable models applicable on the ground. Another issue, which is not considered a marginal one, refers to the internal regime of accountabilities in the UN when peace forces deployed would also commit unlawful acts. Thus, international political responsibilities and legal accountabilities are in transition and require both legal and political debate based on accurate findings provided by research projects in the field of international law, international relations and peace and security studies.

From an empirical perspective, it is still not verified whether international criminal justice would have an impact on the maintenance and restoration of international peace and security, while its complementary role with political global regimes is in transition and deserves attention. It is important to provide assessments of the peacekeeping operations and the configuration of security mandates on the ground, considering the presence of complementary global actors which are responsible at the same extent to preserve acceptable standards of human security, such as the United Nations and the Rome Statute institutions. Another aspect relates to the challenges of peace enforcement, collective security and humanitarian interventions, including their accountabilities in democratic governance systems. In order to govern such issues substantive reforms are required, if not, such governance would only be based on legal controversy and political *impasse*. This study looks at the political dilemma deriving from the past, which shaped the formulation of the legal frameworks visible in the present. Policy formulation and legal issues characterize the governance of *complementary* global regimes which still function without international governance institutions updated to the challenges of the time, while acting in a decentralized system of governance. Many analysts, throughout the verification of empirical data, proved that "democracy is the form of government least likely to kill its citizens, and that democracies do not wage war against each other".[17] Thus, in which ways are *complementary* global regimes able to contribute to the theory of democratization of societies, at domestic, regional, and international levels?

In the last decade, the inquiries of legality of the '*right*' of humanitarian intervention in international law received valuable and extensive scholarly analysis. The risk of 'unilateral' humanitarian intervention for instance, derived from the failure of the collective security system established after the WWII and was characterized by the delegating role of the UN Security Council to military *ad hoc* coalitions as the only alternative to the inaction in case of mass atrocity crimes. In the post-cold war era and with the adoption of the Rome Statute, the shift of civilian protection duties deserves discussion in order to centralize individuals in conflict and post-conflict situations, extending the accountabilities of the criminal leaderships and major perpetrators, while monitoring the impunity regime of domestic jurisdictions in the conflict and post-conflict phases. The paradigm shift between the concept of international security and human security is in transition and deserves attention, including the serious shortcomings of law enforcement after the judicial outcomes based on supranational rules. The practice of the responsibility to protect civilians on the ground deserves assessments, not only for the military responses authorized and for the forces deployed in the field such as peacekeepers, but also for other *complementary* actors of the United Nations such as the International Criminal Court, which also struggles with protection measures of witnesses and victims of serious humanitarian breaches of international law. For the International Criminal Court, and in accordance with its *ex-ante* character, the ideal would be receiving support before, during, and after the human security concerns would arise in violent conflict and post-conflict situations. But this is an idea not realised, and probably it will never do. If we look at the political distance taken by some relevant States and regional entities from the Rome Statute, it would be accurate to refer to an *impasse* in the design of a governance structure of complementary character. This study analyzes the strengths and weaknesses of *complementary* international regimes and proposes reforms in order to respond to the spreading of intra-state conflicts, and the commission of serious crimes deriving from them, including the international responses in inter-state armed conflicts which governance is still in a state of uncertainty (e.g. aggression).

---

[17] R.J. Rummel, *Power Kills: Democracy as a Method of Nonviolence*, 1997, at 11.

There are no doubts that national jurisdictions have the first responsibility fighting against the impunity of mass atrocity crimes. If we only consider the first decade of existence of the Rome Statute and the outcomes of its first review, the concern is not only related to finding remedies of cooperation by implementing national legislations, but also on the way the Rome Statute institutions and the UN interact and work together. In order to clarify the obstacles in the interaction between the United Nations and the International Criminal Court, this study also reports *a)* on the institutional and normative decentralization and fragmentation of the international legal order; *b)* on the current status of the governance of international criminal justice complementing the maintenance of peace and security at global level; and *c)* on the multidimensional character of international mandates, including the operational gaps on the ground, where both organizations are involved. In theory, when intervening in the domestic affairs of 'failed' States the collective effort to implement the effectiveness of *complementary* global regimes refers to the nexus between politics and law in the field of human security and humanitarian protection. The concept of *complementary* global regimes, one based on the evolution of world politics and the other exclusively legal based on its judicial character, deserves analysis and discussion. The legal and political analysis of their interaction offers valid considerations for the governance of peace and justice and threats and crimes. In other words, the opportunities for further progress of international law, finding applicable measures of human security and law enforcement cooperation in case of serious violations of international humanitarian law during armed conflicts all of them require debate. With the advent of the Rome Statute it is acknowledgeable that there is the opportunity for States without armed forces to rely on the rule of law contributing to the transition of security in their domestic governance, which undeniably requires a deeper humanitarian perspective. The regime of justice falling under the Rome Statute is a vital component of this transition. However, considering the political standpoints of relevant States opting out from such multilateral regime, there seems to be hardly any determination to design a system of governance based on the accountabilities of the States and individuals at the same extent. At structural level and for the purpose of capacity-building, it would be important to establish a ministerial network of support for the Court either linked at domestic or at regional and international levels with specific institutional liaisons. The networks already in place should receive appropriate implementation. Another aspect is that in the current reality of its governance a capacity-building model for the emerging regime falling under the Rome Statute is still under construction.

While especially less powerful States enlarged the emerging regime of justice, giving the impression of the success of the Rome Statute campaign, its place within the regional and international realities is characterized by shortcomings of political convergence, and by a serious political *impasse* undermining its credibility. If the political support by the EU and Latin America to the Rome

Statute system requires further political determinations, other regional entities such as the AU, Asian groups of nation-states and the League of Arab States take political distance from important interactions in the governance of political instability, violence against civilians and the commission of mass atrocity crimes. The non-parties to the Rome Statute system such as the US, China and Russia do not show the political willingness to finally becoming part of it. The fact that the Court obtains requests from the Security Council, for instance, does not mean receiving appropriate operational support during its operations on the ground. Furthermore, the outcomes of the inquires of serious breaches of human rights by the UN Human Rights Council should also engage the Security Council to *refer* dangerous situations for civilians to the Court, providing support on the ground with the configuration of its mandates. The Rome Statute regime simply struggles to find its *complementary* role within established international governance systems. The question is whether its existence and activities would stimulate the political convergence required for the democratization process of international governance institutions fostering peace, justice and security.

## 1.5. RESEARCH QUESTIONS

This study examines the emerging architecture fostering peace, justice and security looking at *complementary* global regimes, including the decision-making of intergovernmental organizations and the political forces responsible of their empowerment. It recalls the unresolved issues in the sequence of peace and justice between international governance institutions. This is the case of the interaction between the UN Security Council and the International Criminal Court (ICC) as an outsider from, but not stronger then to the UN system. Such interaction represents the opportunity for further implementation of international law and for the progress in the politics of justice. In several situations the so-called 'interests of peace' and 'interests of justice' do not coincide, even if they represent in theory the two faces of the same coin. The cooperation of the Security Council with the Court is not compulsory. It is exclusively based on political engagements not able to guarantee sustainable peace on the ground in situations of war and crime. The Security Council should consider law enforcement measures to support further the concept of accountability, thus strengthening the role of the International Criminal Court in the current international legal and political order. The Rome Statute institutions should be part of the peace-building process, especially with regard to the victims and witnesses undertaking their protection, relocation and rehabilitation. In order to promote the domestic autonomy of judicial proceedings *in situ*, the emerging regime of international criminal justice should receive resources to rehabilitate domestic judicial systems in the post-conflict phase, with the UN supporting the reform of security sectors and rule of law of domestic institutions (police, army and judiciary). From a wider perspective, democratic interaction strategies are required to contribute to the transition of international law dealing with different legal systems and traditions. The analysis performed in this study concentrates on political, legal and institutional frameworks respectively dealing with international threats and crimes in conflict and post-conflict situations, and the way those frameworks interact with each other. This study attempts to verify their *complementary* roles dealing with the political responsibility of the States and the legal accountability of the individuals committing international humanitarian crimes, and the efforts to maximize the results to prevent and reduce them while making sure they are not left unpunished. This study explores the advent of global humanitarianism and the international interventions under the flag of the responsibility to protect civilians and the possible links with the emerging regime of international criminal justice fighting against the impunity of genocide, crimes of war, crimes against humanity, and possibly at a later stage, of the crime of aggression, under the treaty-based 'opt-out' clauses based on the nation-state consent. This study advocates for interactions developing the role of *complementary* global regimes in the establishment of an 'open' society where the domestic, regional and international realities would contribute in the governance of international threats and crimes.

In the scholarly debates the principles and visions of 'internationalism' favoring the policy of cooperation among nation-states have been argued between several approaches in the context of balance of power, democratic governance, and institutional reforms of universal premises. Current areas of discussion include national and ethnic conflict regulation in intra-state warfare, the fight against the impunity of serious breaches of human rights, and civilian protection measures during large scale humanitarian escalations. The common element in the current debates is the relevance of international regimes and their *complementary* roles. From a legalistic perspective the cooperation between them is still devoid of any compulsory character. The paradigm shift dealt with in this study is about the ways these regimes are *complementary* to each other, particularly considering the necessity of a global architecture fostering peace, justice and security and its governance. The question is: at which extent such architecture is feasible and desired in the current break downs of governance systems at domestic, regional and international levels? Are *complementary* global regimes developing legal frameworks based on further international political responsibilities and legal accountabilities? Is there a chance to centralize human security concerns and the fundamental rights of individuals affected by war and crime? Moreover, is the political convergence required possible, without the consent of relevant stakeholders such as some of the permanent members of the Security Council? And last but not least, does the pessimistic view that underscores the risks of conflicting international regimes, including conflicting laws, conflicting mandates and multilevel jurisdictions represent a real threat for the preservation of the rule of international law and the progress of an 'open' global society able to monitor human security measures internationally? The sensitive challenges in the international legal order are characterized by competing conceptual approaches dealing with them. There is disagreement between the views to control power politics towards a legal order of supranational character and the alternatives of dealing with normative conflicts between multiple legal frameworks based on pluralism. The several issues dealt by constitutionalism and pluralism represent the current politics of international law dealing with the disintegrations of the nation-states and their failure towards their own citizens. The concern behind relates to the political will of a constitution of the world community retaining such sensitive issues or just relying on multiple legal frameworks dealing with several approaches of governance.[18]

In our globalized world the question is whether international governance institutions, or so defined 'sister' organizations, are able to interact according to the principle of interdependence between peace, justice and security, or the idea of such 'relationships' and 'partnerships' are left in doubt by several overlaps at structural, normative and functional levels. After all, the threats to peace and security and the commission of international crimes in conflicts and post-conflict societies are strictly interrelated, if we look at the current legislation of the Security Council. But how is such principle of interdependence translated in the practice? How are the international responses to threats and crimes taking shape in multilateral political engagements? Are such responses governed in accordance with the rule of law as a tool of governance and in accordance with the challenges of the post-cold war era, or political realism simply prevails? For some observers it seems that the Court would constantly be jeopardized in extreme conflict situations in the context of *peace v. justice* including several human security issues. In any case, granted amnesties neutralizing the accountability of serious humanitarian breaches need to be out-of-the-way from peace talks and negotiations, while coercive diplomacy needs to find back the preventive approach of international threats and crimes. As eminent commentators would suggest on such controversial issues, amnesties for mass atrocity crimes, whether explicit or *de facto*, have no legal validity at international level. Now that there is an independent international judiciary it should be allowed to the application of the law impartially, targeting alleged crimes by warlords, as well as any potential unlawful act committed by military alliances or other non-state actors. In other words, all global players involved have to feel responsible for their actions.[19] But is this really the case?

---

18 See the suggestions of M. Delmas-Marty, *Ordering Pluralism. A Conceptual Framework for Understanding the Transnational Legal World*, 2009.

19 See C. Bassiouni, "Advancing the Responsibility to Protect through International Criminal Justice", in H. Cooper and J. Voïnov Kohler (eds), *Responsibility To Protect. The Global Moral Compact for the 21st Century*, 2009 at 31.

In order to find responses this study assesses the current interaction between *complementary* global regimes including the requirement of an accountability system that would retain political responsibilities and legal accountabilities at the same extent for all parties involved in conflict and post-conflict situations. Emphasis is given to finding measures to maximize the results in the preservation of law and order at global level and in the field operations. The issues are addressed through the following questions:

*Do we witness the emergence of an international architecture of governance fostering peace and justice, including measures of human security applicable in conflict and post-conflict situations?*

*What kind of challenges, obstacles and concerns characterize the governance of complementary global regimes?*

*How do the referrals to the International Criminal Court and their governance in the field operations currently work?*

A global architecture fostering peace, justice and security embodies the idea that the rule of international law as a principle of governance and its institutions, would focus on the accountabilities of individuals, nation-states and non-state actors in case of severe violations of common concern. In the current 'testing' environment visible in the responses to peace and security threats the application of this idea of the rule of law present several issues which nearly neutralize the enthusiasm about the enforcement of a global architecture of governance dealing with international threats and crimes. The political configuration of *complementary* global mandates fostering peace, justice and security on the ground present serious shortcomings in the civilian protection duties, including the engagement of law enforcement against criminal perpetrators, once the judicial outcomes have been released by the Court (see the case of Uganda and Democratic Republic of Congo, Kenya, Sudan, Libya and Mali).[20] The concern would be whether the persuasion of the permanent members of the Security Council in support of the referrals to the Court represents only the means of political pressure marginalizing respectively the criminal regime in the Sudan, or neutralizing the totalitarian Libyan regime, or even protecting the aggressive regime in Syria, rather than a real political determination to raise human security

20 In 2013, the Office of the Prosecutor opened an investigation into alleged crimes committed on the territory of Mali since January 2012 after the referral coming from the Government. The United Nations Multidimensional Integrated Stabilization Mission in Mali (MINUSMA) takes over the authority from the African-led International Support Mission in Mali (AFISMA). The robust peacekeeping mandate in Mali is not configured to support the quest of justice in the country. French forces deployed in Mali have been authorized to intervene in support of MINUSMA when under imminent and serious threat upon request of the Secretary-General, see UN doc. S/RES/2100 (2013).

and civilian protection duties on the ground. As several observers emphasize, the contradiction in such positions undermines the pursuit of international criminal justice falling under the Rome Statute and the UN Charter. The main concern is the expression of militarization ignoring the basic principle of neutrality when intervening in the hostilities, including a weak system of accountability *vis-à-vis* non-state actors. Another concern refers to the double standard characterizing the international humanitarian escalations with the last situation left ignored being Syria.

These are only some of the aspects characterizing the international political divisions to intervene in transition societies and domestic security systems during massive humanitarian crisis deriving from intra-state conflicts. Complementary global regimes should prioritize a strategy of interaction in the field operations and also at global level, in order to marginalize the non-cooperation of a criminal regime such as the government of the Sudan. The analysis of the 'situation' in the Sudan, as referred by the Security Council to the Court, and the judicial 'case' as initiated by the Court after the referral by the Security Council S/RES/1593 (2005), require attention on the breakdowns of the peace enforcement configurations by the Security Council, including the involvement in mass atrocities by other actors in Africa, such as the African Union and civil society organizations. In other words, the negative political repercussions received by the emerging regime of international criminal justice established under the Rome Statute. The same view is valid in the case of the tribal structure and the complete absence of the State in Libya, and the sensitive governance issues for the Libyan transitional council, which is dealing with the challenges of the vacuum of power after the regime of its tyrant, including the reconstruction of domestic security sectors still in transition, and which deserve to be further monitored by international governance institutions. In regard to Syria, the absence of any international response and civilian protection measures so far is a matter of serious concern considering the outcome of the UN commission of inquiry on the serious breaches of human rights committed in the country. The double standards in the selection of situations by the Security Council are once more confirmed. The regime of international criminal justice falling under the Rome Statute does not have any jurisdiction in Syria. The political pressure of the Arab League on the Syrian authorities should be result-oriented. The presence of its observers on the ground is still a weak action considering the extreme violence on civilians protesting against the totalitarian regime. Thus, how is the doctrine of civilian protection duties currently working in such extreme situations?

A principal question addressed in this study is whether the Court is marginalized in its tasks to fight against the impunity of serious crimes, or if there is the political will to implement relations with the United Nations mandates in the field operations. The main concern is whether there is sufficient cooperation to monitor domestic channels while respecting the *complementarity* principle and State sovereignty. It also needs to be verified whether the current legal status of international cooperation is sufficient to destabilize criminal regimes compromising sustainable peace. The Rome Statute institutions need to be prepared to influence the rule of law with the jurisprudence of its Court. There are no doubts about the importance of such role. The problem is still the resistance of the Court's decisions by powerful States, domestic jurisdictions, and the lack of multilateral cooperation in respect to the 'interests of justice'. These obstacles, combined with the UN negotiations and political involvements in peace-talks with criminal regimes, characterize at the present the humanitarian crisis escalated to the Court as the *last resort* option (see the case of the Sudan and Libya). The main assumption expressed in this study is that multilateral institutions, and the complementary regimes deriving from them, should not miss the opportunity to centralize individuals in international affairs. Models of governance of international threats and crimes are required at domestic, regional and international levels. The Rome Statute explicitly declares the need to bring its institutions into relationship with the United Nations. In this phase of its existence the Court needs to build up a strong identity becoming a result oriented judicial institution, responding positively to the critics, rejections and huge expectations, delivering best standards of public administration of international criminal justice. The Court however, cannot do this alone. The presence of the UN in the field where the Court is involved needs collective efforts in the conflict and post-conflict phases. The Court's role is to bring justice into the ex-colonial reality of remote communities with possible proceedings on the ground, to restore the regime of terror and the suffering of victims of severe human rights offences contributing to sustainable peace and stability. In the first phase of its existence the Court focused on the mass atrocity crimes as a priority to bring justice in some regimes of terror prosecuting the perpetrators. This is common to the DRC, CAR, Uganda, Kenya, and Ivory Coast, Libya and Darfur investigations and prosecutions, where some of its judicial outcomes are still waiting to be enforced. The next important duty of the Court's judiciary is to repair the pain of the victims by providing justice. The overview of the lesson learned by the UN *ad hoc* tribunals, including the evolutionary path of international criminal law, is complemented by the substantial and very extensive literature of scholars and practitioners noted in this study. The findings of this study verify that the implementation of human security measures between *complementary* global regimes would allow the universality of supranational rules, enhancing their credibility as international governance institutions fostering peace, justice and security at domestic, regional and international levels.

## 1.6. PURPOSE OF THE RESEARCH

In this study the complementary role of the Rome Statute institutions to the United Nations system is explored not exclusively with regard to the important interaction between the judicial organ, the International Criminal Court and the UN bodies, but between all actors involved in building networks in the emerging treaty-based architecture: the Assembly of the States Parties to the ICC and the UN political organs, as well as the UN specialized agencies, regional intergovernmental and non-governmental organizations. This includes the important role of academics and civil society offering their recommendations, guidelines and fact-findings of human rights violations addressed to such international governance institutions of universal character. The determination of this work is to examine the debate around the governance of complementary global regimes and the dilemma of human security. This study questions the place of the emerging regime of international criminal justice in the arrays of peace and security maintenance and restoration. It attempts to define their complementary roles and the idea of a global architecture dealing with peace and justice in the context of human security centralizing and serving the rights of individuals in times of war and crime. Unfortunately, this study cannot be considered exhaustive. The topics and the issues examined will need further multidisciplinary research.

Against the backdrop of the peace and justice debates, many have questioned the impact of the Rome Statute in real terms against an international judicial institution not ready for a performance appraisal, instead, prepared for more jurisdiction, authority and resources. The aim of this study wants to fill the gap in existing literature on the creation of a global architecture towards the interaction of universal organizations mandated of fostering peace, justice and security through complementary judicial and political mechanisms, involving the domestic, regional and international realities. It focuses on the interaction between the United Nations system and the Rome Statute institutions responsible of democratic governance in their complementary field of expertise arguing on the current status of their cooperation. The subjects of such interaction also include the promotion of the universality of the Rome Statute, the status of implementing national legislations, and various aspects of law enforcement, cooperation and operational assistance to the Court. The legislative history of the Rome Statute institutions since their establishment, and the UN longstanding presence in enduring conflicts, have been extensively analysed in order to detect global strategies and concrete objectives fostering peace, justice and security towards their interaction. This study considers the reasons of the delay and the obstacles in finding remedies implementing a system of international criminal justice, which can be found *a)* in the conflicting ideas of peace and justice in conflict and post-conflict situations; *b)* in the *impasse* of the reforms of the UN peace operations incorporating justice in the peace-building phase; *c)* in the international responses of law enforcement following judicial decisions in on-going conflicts; and *d)* in the search of civilians protection duties. In order to empower the system of international criminal justice, national implementation and judicial reforms at domestic level are important in the same way as for global actor reforms such as the UN and the Rome Statute institutions.

As underlined by Köchler "only a multipolar international system with a fair distribution of power and resources can credibly serve the causes of world peace, justice and human rights as proclaimed in the UN Charter. It is for this reason that a democratic reform of the United Nations, and in particular of the Security Council, has come to be urgently required in this transitory phase of a post-cold war order, where the paradigm of power politics still prevails".[21] The main theoretical assumption motivating this study is that democratic governance of international threats and crimes must also include less or non-democratic States. Such integrative approach will act as a strong stimulus to their ongoing or future democratization process of domestic governance, and also preserve their basic right of self-determination and autonomy. After all, the policy approach generating political fracture between categories and sub-categories of States needs to be neutralized with all means as it may cause conflict.

This study offers an assessment of the impact of the Rome Statute institutions in the global order, emphasising the importance of an interaction strategy between relevant complementary actors. It analyses the evolution of the rule of law, multilateralism, collective responsibility, global solidarity and mutual accountability as principles of global governance in the international society, and their impact on the ground in conflict and post-conflict situations.[22] This study debates the current transition of *complementary* global regimes and their interaction for the sake of peace diplomacy and negotiations offering sustainable stability, combined with the fight against the impunity of crimes of common concern, upholding human rights standards, including the search of measures of human security applicable on the ground in the field operations. In other words, it offers an assessment of the necessary measures applicable in situations of war and crime in accordance with universal values. It promotes the link between

21 For the debate see H. Köchler, 'Summary: A "New World Order" of Transnational Democracy versus the "Old World Order" of Superpower Rule', in *The United Nations and International Democracy: The Quest for UN Reform*, IPO Research Papers, 1996, accessible at: www.hanskoechler.com/unid.htm See also H. Köchler, *Global Justice or Global Revenge? International Criminal Justice at the Crossroad*, 2003.

22 The intent is also to contribute to the theoretical debate on global governance issues between global politics, international law and international relations, see L. S. Finkelstein, 'What is Global Governance?, in *Global Governance* 1 (1995), at 367. See also F. Nuscheler, 'Global Governance, Development, and Peace: On the interdependence of Global Regulative Structures', in P. Kennedy, D. Messner, F. Nuscheler (eds.), *Global Trends and Global Governance*, 2002, accessible at: www.sef-bonn.org/download/publikationen/sonderbaende/sb-12-Feb-2000_zusammenfassung_en.pdf.

international criminal justice and the concept of sustainable peace in conflict and post-conflict situations towards the configuration of mandates on the ground. This study recalls the legal aspects regulating peace enforcement operations, the UN institutional reforms expected and not yet performed, including the legal and political determinations enforcing treaty-based organizations and their public links necessary for an international architecture dealing with global threats and crimes. This study measures the level of public authority of the Court as new international institution considering its jurisdictional reach in domestic realities, and the need of support from relevant actors involved on the ground in enduring conflicts. Attention is given to the judicial institution dealing with supranational criminal proceedings for the most responsible individuals of mass atrocity crimes centralizing human security measures. This study, which cannot be considered as exhaustive, also examines the interaction between the Rome Statute institutions (Assembly of States Parties, Trust Fund for Victims and the Court) and the United Nations system on sensitive governance issues. It considers the importance of their independence and delimitation of competence on one side, and the necessary cooperation, resource and knowledge sharing, on the other.

The purpose of this study is to fill a gap in the existing literature about the interaction of universal organizations mandated of fostering human security through political and judicial mechanisms, namely the United Nations system and the Rome Statute institutions. The interaction of such complementary global regimes in conflict and post-conflict situations, including the implementation of strategies supporting their partnership and relationship is the main object of this study. Moreover, the motivation is to offer an analysis of the emerging regime of international criminal justice towards the implementation of multilateral institutions and their consolidation. After all, the interaction between the United Nations and the Rome Statute institutions takes place at several levels, but most importantly it represents the nexus of global politics and the rule of law, interacting with several branches of international law, respectively humanitarian, criminal and the emerging law of human rights. The idea to promote the rule of law as a principle of global governance in the international society, receives assessment on the ways it currently works and eventually evolves. This study debates the current humanitarian escalations of last resort between *complementary* global regimes and their impact in the field operations. It measures the *status quo* of human security between theory and practice. By way of case studies it examines the multidimensional operations fostering peace and justice, the issue of cooperation in the Democratic Republic of Congo (DRC) and the humanitarian escalation of severe violations in the Sudan referred by the UN Security Council to the International Criminal Court. In other words, this study discusses the meaning of complementary roles of international regimes dealing with human security in conflict and post-conflict societies and the opportunity of an integrated approach of governance.

The evolving concept of universal jurisdiction and international criminal law; the modern doctrine of humanitarian intervention and protection duties of civilians; the challenges faced by the legal theory in addressing issues on the sovereignty of nation-states and the responsibilities of global actors including the governance of complementary global regimes in the international society require further research. These contested concepts represent the central dilemmas facing governments, international organizations, civil society and civilians. The meaning of complementary global regimes fostering human security such as the United Nations system and the Rome Statute institutions needs clarification. It is fundamental to build up consensus on further international efforts to manage international humanitarian escalations of *last resort*. The delimitation between sovereignty and international governance, the concept of nation-state and its self-determination, and the international responsibilities centralizing fundamental individual rights deserve constant attention by legal and political theorists. The search of governance systems centralizing human security and its challenges, obstacles and concerns are the main parameters used to explore the current humanitarian escalations between global institutions of complementary character.

## 1.7. THE TOPICS SELECTED/PROPOSED

The analysis of global matters challenging the international legal and political order includes often the risk of being merely abstract, if it does not offer pragmatic recommendations on specific problems. This study wants to avoid such a risk. It explores the asymmetry of international legal and political relations manifested in the governance of complementary global regimes fostering peace, justice and security at global scale. The purpose of this work is to find solutions using appropriately the knowledge acquired in the field of study proposed, setting the priorities in the governance of threats and crimes between complementary global regimes. The first priority is finding applicable measures of human security in situations of serious violations of international humanitarian law. The findings of this study provide recommendations to policy makers on global governance issues, enhancing the ability of the international society to respond to large scale humanitarian crisis during internal civil wars, and eventually in armed conflicts of international character. The purpose is to preserve the rule of law in a globalized world and multilevel jurisdictions. This is only possible through substantial progress of political convergence, institutional reforms, and systemic changes in the governance of international threats and crimes. After all, only through such actions there would be the contribution of complementary global regimes to the principles of open society and further definition of *global justice*.

This study offers a clarification of the limited statutory provisions regulating the ICC and the UN interaction; it considers the complementary duty of the Rome Statute with the UN Charter; the Court's independence from the UN framework; the controversial relationship with the Security Council and the political agenda of the conference review of the Rome Statute still far from solving the several issues of cooperation between States Parties and international organizations of complementary character. With regard to the Rome Statute the political impasse between the signature and the ratification of key players is well known and needs solutions for the substantive support the Court needs from States Parties and non-States Parties and with regard to the cooperation with the Security Council. This study also approaches the debate on the amendment proposals of the Rome Statute and the impasse of further jurisdictional progress of the judicial institution. It also analyses the cooperation between the United Nations and the Assembly of States Parties to the Rome Statute in the formulation of legal and political frameworks of governance. It attempts to verify the potential of the rule of law among other values and principles of governance, sustaining the human security doctrine among international governance institutions dealing with war and crime. The emphasis is given to developments programs, social equality, and capacity-building activities at domestic, regional and international levels. After all, in order to retain models of governance for devastated domestic realities by war, crime and famine, the feasible interactions between global actors require political convergence of expectations, which are emphasised in this study. The Rome Statute system is based on important aspects of human security, such as the interests of victims and witnesses. Their protection, relocation and rehabilitation require deeper responsibilities upholding such human security measures. The interaction between the United Nations and the Rome Statute institutions is extremely important. It gives rise to the protective, reparative and retributive meanings of *global justice* throughout measures for peace, justice and security to restore individual rights, and the dignity of human lives offended in situations of war and crime.

This study offers an analysis of the nexus between humanitarian protection and justice with an integrated and comprehensive approach towards conflict prevention, stabilization and reconstruction. Complementary global regimes have the function to balance the distribution of powers in international relations throughout compliance of international law. For the sake of the principles of accountability and compliance, the International Criminal Court and the United Nations have a central role to play. The purpose of their interaction is to end the impunity regime of severe violations of human rights, towards global deterrent mandates, getting closer to the real concerns of civilians in fragile and disintegrated States not able or unwilling to bring sustainable peace and justice on their own ground. In the field of human rights and for their preservation once treaty-based organizations, including the bodies deriving from the UN Charter, would prove a lack of compliance by their States parties, the Security Council and other political organs should immediately open inquiries and also referrals about individual criminal accountabilities. In these situations, the cooperation with the Rome Statute system should be mandatory. The case studies selected and proposed offer an overview of the practice applied in the field operations where complementary international mandates are involved. The findings of this study demonstrate that a normative harmonization is necessary if the vision of constitutionalism would be materialized. The functional implementation of relationship agreements advocated by the theoretical approach of pluralism is only a timid instrument of cooperation. Further evolution of international law would mean to focus on governance at multilateral scale, finding appropriate adjustments in the normative and institutional tools of the international community as a whole, or the so defined community obligations. The rules of cooperation between complementary global mandates are having an impact on the lives of individuals, while public power will need further implementation of legal techniques in new fields of public international law, regulating global governance and administration, according to the principles of transparency and accountability. The international community needs a model replacing progressively old methods of peace and security maintenance at global scale. The interaction between human security and transnational justice at national, regional and global levels needs the attention by the decision-making either from the perspective of constitutionalism or pluralism. Human security and the preservation of human rights should be the priorities in both these approaches involved in the design of global governance frameworks.

## 1.8. METHODOLOGY

The research methods applied in this study refer in summary respectively to: *a)* the multidisciplinary approach of the theories of international regimes based on human security and complementing with each other, and *b)* the legal and political solutions required to fill the gaps of governance fostering peace and justice. These research methods emphasise the institutional, normative and functional analysis of *complementary* global regimes and the legal and political sources to verify their *status quo*. From a theoretical perspective the approach in this study tries to bring some light on the difficulties to reinforce the doctrine of human security which has been lost in the academic discourse. The interaction between complementary global regimes fostering peace, justice and security would preserve the idea of human security in international society.

### 1.8.1. MULTIDISCIPLINARY APPROACH

This study brings together an assessment made from the perspective of international law, international relations, political science and legal philosophy. It attempts to verify the governance of justice and the transition of international peace and security in conflict and post-conflict situations characterized by mass atrocity crimes. It provides an extensive analysis of the new trends in modern international relations between mutual responsibilities of States combined with the individual accountabilities of criminal perpetrators. It offers an analytical tool about legal and political ramifications of the Rome Statute and its role in the emerging regime of justice *vis-à-vis* the States, the United Nations and the international community as a whole. It contains explanatory, qualitative and constructive research methods applied for an implementation of the basic principles of international relations and international law. These principles represent interdependent targets to govern peace, justice and security and symbolize the tools for setting the global priorities of democratic international regimes dealing with:

1) *Rule of law*
2) *Multilateralism*
3) *Collective responsibility*
4) *Global solidarity*
5) *Mutual accountability*

This study will extensively approach the first three, the international rule of law, multilateralism, and collective responsibility, but it will still refer to all basic principles of international relations regulated by the UN and recently by the Rome Statute system. Sharing knowledge to develop global values in the international society is the function of public international organizations and this is common either to the United Nations and the Rome Statute institutions as multilateral tools of governance. The scope is the protection of human rights, the promotion of human security, combining political consensus to an appropriate lawmaking process for the implementation of more democratic international regimes of complementary character. An extensive literature review has been performed considering both policy and legal aspects in the field of international criminal justice, and the ways new crimes would be considered for future reviews of the Rome Statute. In order to propose a consolidation model between the United Nations and the Court's regimes, the UN missions from peacekeeping to peace building, especially in the African Great Lakes Region where the Court is involved since the beginning of its investigative and prosecutorial activities, have been extensively examined. The intent is to promote democratic standards of interactions only achievable throughout concrete institutional reforms, which would also allow the extension of a universal jurisdiction to other serious crimes of common concern and wider design of an architecture governing international threats and crimes.

### 1.8.2. THE THEORIES OF EMERGING INTERNATIONAL REGIMES BASED ON HUMAN SECURITY

This study navigates the main international regime theories focusing on a variety of theoretical and methodological approaches used to explain and analyse the content, formation and effectiveness of international law and its institutions and to suggest improvements. The most common definition of international regimes found in the literature comes from eminent scholars as "institutions possessing norms, decisions, rules and procedures facilitating a convergence of expectations".[23] The liberal view of regime theory argues that international regimes are instances of international cooperation and that international governance institutions are regimes which affect the behaviour of States. On the one hand, for liberal scholars cooperation is indeed possible despite anarchy. The realists on the other hand, do not mean that cooperation never happens, but that it is not the norm in the global order. The realist view of regime theory assumes that cooperation makes a difference of degree between anarchy and conflict in international relations. The question of the idealists is whether international cooperation can be better matched by a corresponding system of international responsibility, shared responsibility, and compliance, as the main issues characterizing the emerging regime of international criminal justice. The main argument is whether the current interaction between the United Nations and the Rome Statute institutions creates the prerequisite of a global democratic 'system', or a global 'architecture' fostering international criminal justice in the context of human security in conflict and post-conflict situations.

From a theoretical perspective this study considered the several approaches in the global governance of international humanitarian escalations. The *realists* complain that States pursuing utopian moral visions through intervention and humanitarian aid do their subjects harm and destabilize the international system. The majority of such interventions have been based on economic or political interests and not in the domain of human rights. The *particularists* object the destruction of traditional cultures by cultural colonialism under the guise of economic liberalism or defense of human rights. The *nationalists* deplore the fact that so many people are stateless or live under inefficient and tyrannical regimes that monitoring them at international level represent only utopia.

[23] See S.D. Krasner, *International Regimes*, Cornell University Press, 1983. S. Haggard, "Theories of International Regimes", 41 *International Organizations*, 1987, at 491. See also A. Hasenclever, P. Mayer, V. Rittberger, *Theories of International Regimes*, 1997, at 2.

The advocacy of the society of States, or *cosmopolitans* is concerned about the disintegration of nation-states and about the imperial ambitions of the powerful. The *cosmopolitans* believe that the contemporary world badly fails to guarantee equal social, economic, and political standards. Such equal standards would require considerable changes in the actions of wealthy individuals and States. They might, for instance, require the transfer of capacity-building with every means in fragile States. They might require building international institutions able to limit, or even replace, the self-interested action of powerful States and corporations. They might require global governance systems based on collective responsibility, global solidarity and mutual accountability.[24]

The meaning of *complementary* international regimes is explored focusing on the effectiveness of the policy trend of 'institutionalism' emerging in the current world order, including the intersection of the three schools of thought within the study of international regimes, such as: the *realists*, focusing on power relationships; the *neoliberals*, analysing the constellation of interests; and the *cognitivists*, emphasizing knowledge dynamics, communications, and interactions.[25] The emerging regime of international criminal justice represents the determination to harmonize legal systems around the preservation of human rights and universal principles and norms, fighting against the impunity and inaction of serious crimes of common concern. The methods applied in this study verify whether such regime finds its place in global governance issues of peace and security, while focusing on the intersection between international humanitarian law, human rights law and international criminal law. The methods applied also focus on the verification of governance and capacity-building of such complementary global mandates in conflict and post-conflict situations. Furthermore, these methods (normative, structural and functional) verify whether complementary roles of international governance institutions offer political and legal inputs for the definition of crimes internationally recognized, contributing to further progress of an *ex-ante* jurisdiction dealing with serious recognized international crimes. The methodology applied also clarifies to a certain extent the implementation required in the immediate, middle and long terms in order to enhance the relationship and partnership between complementary global governance

24 See M. Griffiths, *Fifty Key Thinkers in International Relations*, 1999. See also I.B. Neumann, O. Waever (eds), *The Future of international Relations: Masters in the Making*, 1997. J. Kruzel, J.N. Rosenau (eds), *Journeys Through World Politics: Autobiographical Reflections of Thirty-four Academic Travellers, 1989.* M. Smith, *Realist Thought from Weber to Kissinger*, 1986. D. Thürer, The "failed State" and international law, *Revue Internationale de la Croix-Rouge/International Review of the Red Cross*, Volume 81, Issue 836 / December 1999, at 731–761. See T.M. Franck, *Fairness in International Law and Institutions, 1995.* N.J. Schrijver et al, *The United Nations of the Future. Globalisation with a Humane Face*, 2006. See also O. Spijkers, *The United Nations, the Evolution of Global Values and International Law*, 2011.

25 For inspiring theoretical approaches on the creation of global values in the international legal and political order see M. Griffiths, N.J. Schrijver, O. Spijkers, *supra*.

institutions. The legislative history of these organizations is extensively analysed, including the inputs of all relevant stakeholders. The poor arrangements and agreements in the field operations where complementary mandates are currently deployed receive analysis and critics. The suggestion is to overcome the lacuna in protection, relocation and rehabilitation of victims and witnesses with an institution cooperating with the Court and other relevant stakeholders.

### 1.8.3. LEGAL AND POLICY SOURCES

The main primary sources used for this research are the treaties and the legislative history, respectively of the United Nations and the Assembly of the States Parties of the International Criminal Court. The Rome Statute and the declarations of interpretation by its States Parties, the UN Charter, the Vienna Convention on the Law of Treaties; the relationship agreement between the UN and the ICC and the cooperation agreements with regional organizations, most notably the EU, the AU, the League of Arab States and with the specialized agencies of the UN family, in particular the agreements with the UN peace operations in situations where the Court is involved, all of them receive appropriate analysis. The institutional 'contours' of international law are debated between 'old' and 'new' tools of governance fostering peace, justice and security. It needs to be noted that since this study deals mainly with relatively new concepts in international law, customary international law is hardly relevant to it.

In order to offer an overview of the legal environment of the International Criminal Court, the general principles of international law, the principles of fairness and justice, which are applied universally in legal systems around the world (e.g. good faith, *res judicata*, impartiality of judges), have been found in decisions of international tribunals and national courts and in references in writings and teachings of eminent scholars. These conceptual sources frequently involve procedural matters and the international tribunals rely on these principles when they cannot find authority in other sources of international law. Another category of sources are related to the policy formulations at national and regional levels and the intersection between peace, justice and security applied globally. Apart from the treaties the judicial decisions of the ICJ on immunities[26] and its extensive jurisprudence have been consulted, such as its judgment on the Application of the Convention on the Prevention and Punishment of the Crime of Genocide which provided authoritative guidance on the concept of genocide and

26 For the debate over the immunity see S. Wirth, "Immunity for Core Crimes? The ICJ's Judgment in the Congo v. Belgium Case", 4 *European Journal of International Law* 13, 2002, at 877.

the duty of States Parties to prevent genocide.[27] Other primary materials include: the Security Council and General Assembly resolutions, such as the Security Council referrals; the referrals from the States parties (DRC, Uganda, CAR and Ivory Coast) and non-parties to the Rome Statute (e.g. Occupied Palestinian Territories); the autonomous judicial activity of the Court in Kenya; and the official reports of the UN Commission of Inquiry on Darfur.[28] The dynamics of peace enforcement and the international duty to protect civilians have been examined in situations where both the UN and the ICC are involved (DRC and Sudan). Of particular importance for this research are also the ASP resolutions concerning the Special Working Group on the Crime of Aggression (SWGCA) including also the outcomes of the working group on cooperation which settles the main channels of cooperation and the main problems thereof between the Rome Statute institutions and the States, and between the Rome Statute institutions and the United Nations.[29] The controversial issue of the definition of aggression will be approached using primary sources as the results of the meetings of the Special Working Group on the crime of aggression.[30] Furthermore, important sources are: the work of the Preparatory Commission for the ICC,[31] the institutional documents and outcomes of reports and studies of working groups of the ASP and the UN.[32] The negotiated relationship agreement[33] and the ICC-UN interaction[34] have been extensively analyzed, taking in consideration the latest developments. The so called *Dutch Proposal* pursuant to "Resolution E", adopted at the Rome

---

27 Application of the Convention on the Prevention and Punishment of the Crime of Genocide (*Bosnia and Herzegovina v. Serbia and Montenegro*) *(Judgment)* [2007] ICJ at 18 October 2007 (*'Application of the Convention on Genocide'*) www.icj-cij.org For the background of the case, genocide and State responsibility and the ICJ jurisprudence see D. Turns, "The Court's Judgment on the Merits: The Jurisdictional Question" in "Application of the Convention on the Prevention and Punishment of the Crime of Genocide: Bosnia and Herzegovina vs. Serbia and Montenegro", (2007) in 398 *Melbourne Journal of International Law* 8(2), accessible at: www.austlii.edu.au/au/journals/MelbJIL/2007/22.html.

28 Available at: www.un.org/News/dh/sudan/com_inq_darfur.pdf.

29 Available at: www.icc-cpi.int/library/asp/ICC-ASP-4-SWGCA-1-_FINAL_English.pdf.

30 The complete overviews of the ASP sessions and the latest Report of the SWGCA are accessible at: www.icc-cpi.int/asp/aspaggression.html.

31 As with the Rome Conference, all States were invited to participate in the Preparatory Commission. Among its achievements, the Preparatory Commission reached consensus on the Rules of Procedure and Evidence and the Elements of Crimes. These two texts were subsequently adopted by the Assembly of States Parties. Together with the Rome Statute and the Regulations of the Court adopted by the judges, the two documents comprise the Court's basic legal texts, setting out its structure, jurisdiction and functions.

32 For an overview of the Complete Report of the Preparatory Commission to the Assembly of States Parties and the resolutions of the General Assembly see list of document available at: www.un.org/law/icc/prepcomm/prepfra.htm.

33 The Relationship Agreement, concluded on 4 October 2004 by the President of the Court and the Secretary-General of the United Nations on behalf of their respective institutions, affirms the independence of the Court while establishing a framework for cooperation. See the *Negotiated Relationship Agreement between the UN and the ICC*, accessible at: www.icc-cpi.int/library/asp/ICC-ASP-3-Res1_English.pdf.

34 See the CICC Team on the UN-ICC Relationship Agreement and ICC liaison office at the UN, ICC-ASP/4/6, accessible at: www.iccnow.org/documents/NYoffice_TeamPaper.pdf.

Conference in 1998, seeking to codify a definition of the crime of terrorism in the Rome Statute has been reported, including the proposals of States according to Article 124 of the Rome Statute and the amendments and debates approached during the review conference of the Rome Statute in Kampala.

# PART I

# THE QUEST OF COMPLEMENTARITY AND THE DILEMMA OF HUMAN SECURITY

# 2. THE LEGAL AND POLITICAL FRAMEWORKS FOSTERING HUMAN SECURITY

## PRELIMINARY REMARKS

This part explores the quest of *complementarity* trying to fix the margins between statehood, sovereignty and international governance of mass atrocity crimes and the pursuit of human security. It offers an overview of the tools at disposition by the international community in societies in transition from conflict to reconstruction offering reliable models of governance and based on the advocacy of human security. In this chapter the following topics have been comprehensively debated: the legal and political frameworks of governance fostering human security, the discussions around the rule of international law, the function of multilateralism versus unilateral interests, and the risk of opportunistic policy formulations. The last section concludes the assessment provided in the whole chapter about the transition of the concept of security and the paradigms in the making between the conceptualization, the applicability, and the critics of the human security doctrine. In other words, it highlights the formulation of human security systems of complementary character fighting against war and crime and the requirements thereof. The contribution in this debate underscores the needs of democratic governance of humanitarian affairs throughout institutional reforms, strengthening the partnerships and relationships of governance institutions of complementary character with measures of human security.

This chapter clarifies where the emerging regime of international criminal justice comes from, and where it should go within the arrays of the governance of international peace and security and its role in the maintenance and restoration of sustainable peace. The main assumption articulated in this chapter is that the architecture of global governance systems reflecting the world as it existed in 1945, has not kept pace with the fundamental changes taking place in the world community. We face an incredible amount of shortcomings in the governance systems fostering human security at national, regional and international levels. The paradigm shifts include the spread of global threats, the commission of serious crimes of common concern during violent political transitions, and the devastating consequences of intra-state armed conflicts. The military interventions for humanitarian reasons and the protection duties of civilians are inconsistent, while the interaction strategies to prevent mass atrocity crimes with timely intervention are not sufficient. The influence of non-state actors involved in armed conflicts has repercussions in the transition of human security and humanitarian intervention in conflict and post-conflict situations, including the problem of their accountabilities. Therefore, it is required to identify the policy and the normative requirements for an effective governance system centralizing human security, when dealing with intra-state and inter-state warfare and with the violations of international humanitarian law and human rights law.

This chapter argues that there are some opportunities to progress with human security measures between the emerging regime of international criminal justice and the established regime fostering sustainable peace in conflict and post-conflict situations of the United Nations. It debates the transition of global regulatory frameworks fostering human security, considering the intersection between international politics and laws, including the paradigm shift of global *complementarity* between established global regimes and emerging sub-regimes, the purpose of which is to solve the political impasse crucial for the progress of *global justice* and its architecture of governance. The approach in this chapter is complementary to the broad concept of human security originally articulated by the United Nations Development Programme (UNDP) in its *Human Development Report* delivered two decades ago,[35] and its annual analytical reports which followed next, including the theoretical and empirical findings of NGOs and relevant think tanks, in accordance with the current changes occurring in the international society.[36]

From the valuable assessments performed in the past by legal and political theorists we learn that human security focuses on the protection of individuals, rather than defending the physical and political integrity of States from external military threats, which represents the traditional goal of national security. Ideally, national security and human security should be mutually reinforcing, but in the last hundred years far more people have died as a direct or indirect

---

35 See UNDP Human Development Report 1994, *New Dimensions of Human Security,* accessible at: http://hdr.undp.org/sites/default/files/reports/255/hdr_1994_en_complete_nostats.pdf.

36 Important references are the empirical findings of think-tanks and their programming activities such as The Hague Global Justice Institute (IGJ) dealing with the 'judiciary and global justice'; 'international affairs, peace diplomacy and global justice'; 'environment, development and global justice'. Such programming activity is dedicated to the promotion of knowledge of law and justice as the basis of, and in relation, to peace, security and social and economic development, using a comprehensive approach. The analysis of theory and practice and a network organization facilitates cross-fertilization towards global challenges such as failing States and governance systems, resource conflicts, climate change and its multiple consequences, the changing international architecture, the effectiveness of international judicial institutions and the increasing importance of non-state actors. See the mission of The Hague Global Justice Institute (IGJ) accessible at: http://thehagueinstituteforglobaljustice.org/index.php?page=Mission&pid=121.

consequence of the actions of their own governments or rebel forces in internal civil wars, more than have been killed by invading foreign armies during inter-state conflicts. Acting in the name of national security we have seen that the governments themselves can pose profound threats to human security. This was the case in Syria, Libya, Iran, Tunisia, Egypt including any other aggressive and criminal regime where the army easily turned against its own populations. In such countries the reforms of the security sectors such as the army, police and the judiciary depend on the outcomes of political transitions and democratic reforms. The same requirement is valid for the States committing the crime of aggression characterizing inter-state conflicts. The crime of aggression had been included in the Rome Statute in 1998 while its definition and implementation were deferred to a review conference. The amendments adopted in 2010 define the crime of aggression and provide for the conditions for the exercise of jurisdiction over this crime. The Court may exercise jurisdiction over the crime of aggression once thirty States have ratified the amendments, and subject to a decision to be taken after 1 January 2017 by the States Parties.[37]

The States have the primary responsibility to protect civilians and the ways the international community deals with civilian protection measures, is definitely questionable. The human security policy focuses its attention on the threats stemming from violence to individuals and to collapsed societies where the absence of the rule of law could lead to political, military, social or economic instability and inequality. The emerging regime of international criminal justice falling under the Rome Statute is interpreted as a tool of human security and as such deserves global support. This chapter discusses the limits of such emerging international regime and its transition centralizing human security. It supports the idea of an integrated approach of governance able to offer capacity-building on the ground for the sake of humanitarian protection and human development through reparation measures, rehabilitation programs and social re-integration of the victims of war. Therefore, the interaction between complementary global regimes advocated in this study is based on the concept of *global justice*, respectively its *retributive*, *protective* and *restitutive* aspects. The human security doctrine deserves further consideration by the political actors enforcing complementary global regimes, and this of course, for the several reasons outlined in this chapter.

In order to have a complete overview, this chapter recalls what has been accomplished in the past in the context of multilevel criminal jurisdictions dealing with the serious violations of international law, which received a pluralist

---

37 See Handbook *Crimes of Aggression and War Crimes* published by the Liechtenstein Institute on Self-Determination. Part I of the handbook is based on a workshop on the ratification and implementation of the Kampala amendments on the Crime of Aggression that took place at New York University on 25 June 2012. The handbook is accessible at: http://crimeofaggression.info/documents/1/handbook.pdf.

approach by primary and secondary laws in the global legal order. The attention also goes to the interaction between pluralist regulatory frameworks respectively dealing with the accountability of the States and of the individuals as in the case of the crime of aggression which is not yet politically agreed. This chapter clarifies the lacuna of human security measures between complementary global regimes, including the political impasse of multilateralism between the theories of constitutionalism and pluralism of international legal systems. It contributes to the views of the international legal world moving from the relative and the universal "to build order without imposing it, to accept pluralism without giving up on a common law".[38] The struggle remains: how far is it really possible to measure such transitions?

## 2.1. INTERNATIONAL CRIMINAL JUSTICE: THE EVOLUTION OF HUMAN SECURITY?

### SECTION OUTLINE

The historical overview of the definition of multilevel jurisdictions, including the establishment of judicial institutions enforced by political organs after the scourge of world wars, is important to measure the progress already achieved at global level fighting against the impunity of international crimes. The Court today is a major international institution securing justice for victims when it cannot be delivered at the national level. Investigations in nine country situations concern shocking allegations such as mass murder, rape, torture and the use of child soldiers. The prosecutor is currently conducting preliminary examination in ten situations including Palestine, Afghanistan, Georgia, Guinea, Colombia, Honduras, Korea, Nigeria and Ukraine.[39] The Court, however, does not have jurisdiction on individuals responsible in case of aggression during inter-state conflicts. Such jurisdictional pillar received postponement during the first review conference of the Rome Statute in Uganda (Kampala) and waits for further consensus and resources in 2017. In order to verify the reasons of such an impasse it is required to look in the past. The main theory promoted in this section is that on the one hand, for an understanding of the effects deriving from the political determinations enforcing international governance institutions, it is required to look at the causes placed in the past by the decision-making. On the other hand, if we want to understand the effects that might appear in the future, it is required to focus on the causes currently laid down by the decision-making. The question

38 M. Delmas-Marty, *Ordering Pluralism. A Conceptual Framework for Understanding the Transnational Legal World*, 2009. M. Delmas-Marty, *Les forces imaginantes du droit: Tome 1, Le relatif et l'universel*, 2004.

39 See ICC website » Structure of the Court » Office of the Prosecutor » Policies and Strategies » ICC – Policy Paper on Preliminary Examinations, November 2013.

is whether the international governance institutions deriving from such political process would be able to simultaneously have an impact on the causes and effects of war and crime. The main concern is if there would be human security measures during humanitarian escalations of *last resort* between the complementary global regimes fostering peace and justice. So said, in which direction evolve the policies of global 'humanitarianism', global 'solidarity', collective 'responsibility' and mutual 'accountability'? This section briefly recalls the historical background of multilevel criminal jurisdictions, the UN judicial activity, and the progress of international criminal justice surely requiring further research.

### 2.1.1. THE HISTORICAL BACKGROUND OF MULTILEVEL CRIMINAL JURISDICTIONS

With regard to the inter-state conflicts (intended as international conflicts, or conflicts between States) the world community has sought to prevent war and eliminate aggression for ages. After World War I the efforts to limit international warfare resulted in the establishment of the League of Nations. The Treaty of Versailles of 1919 called for the prosecution of Kaiser Wilhelm II for waging unjust war but efforts to carry out this provision were fruitless since he found refuge in The Netherlands. The Kellogg-Briand Pact of 1928 provided for the formal renunciation of war as an instrument of any national policy.[40] This renunciation became the basis of the London Charter of 8 August 1945, which established in Nuremberg the International Military Tribunal for the prosecution of the major Nazi war criminals, and of the 1946 Charter for the International Military Tribunal for the Far East (IMFTE) establishing a similar war crimes trial in Tokyo.[41] These charters, the indictments and judgments of the tribunals, and the 1947 United Nations resolutions embodying the 'Nuremberg Principles', are among the legal sources for considering aggression a 'crime against peace'.[42]

In 1945, the United Nations Charter in Article 2(4) and Article 39 prohibited aggression but no definition of the crime was established.[43] No real consensus on the meaning of aggression was reached until the United Nations' definition

40 The Kellogg-Briand Pact served as the legal basis for the creation of the notion of crime against peace. It was for committing this crime that the Nuremberg Tribunal and Tokyo Tribunal sentenced a number of people responsible for starting World War II.

41 For an historical overview of the International Military Tribunal for the Far East (IMTFE), commonly called the Tokyo trial see Y. Totani, *The Tokyo War Crimes Trial. The Pursuit of Justice in the Wake of World War II*, Harvard University Press, 2008. See also N. Boister, R. Cryer, *Documents on the Tokyo International Military Tribunal. Charter, Indictment and Judgements*, Oxford University Press, 2008.

42 UN doc. General Assembly Resolution 177 (1947).

43 For an overview see "International Criminal Law. Defining International Crimes", in *Law Library, American Law and Legal Information, Free Encyclopedia*, accessible at: http://law.jrank.org/pages/1392/International-Criminal-Law-Defining-international-crimes.html.

of aggression was agreed upon on 14 December 1974.[44] The definition states in rather general terms that "aggression is the use of armed force against the sovereignty, territorial integrity, or political independence of another State, or in any manner inconsistent with the Charter of the United Nations". The definition also enumerates, not exhaustively, other specific examples of aggression and sets forth their legal and political consequences. The definition does not cover acts by non-state actors. The two key military alliances at the time of the definition's adoption, the NATO and the Warsaw Pact, were non-State parties and thus were outside the scope of such legal considerations. Moreover, such definition did not deal with the responsibilities of individuals for acts of aggression but only with the State responsibility. Aggression was widely perceived as an insufficient basis on which to ground individual criminal prosecutions.[45] Those jurisdictional issues have been discussed in multilateral negotiations for decades, with the last event being the review conference of the Rome Statute in Kampala in 2010 which is approached in the next paragraphs. But before looking into the latest outcomes, it is required to recall the UN political role in the advent of international criminal justice.

### 2.1.2. THE UN JUDICIAL ACTIVITY AND INTERNATIONAL CRIMINAL JUSTICE

Throughout history, the United Nations has adopted, or at least considered the adoption, of a number of variations on the definition of international crimes. In 1948, only a few years after the Nazi Holocaust ended, the General Assembly adopted the text of the Genocide Convention.[46] Among these there are also the resolutions endorsing the standards of the Nuremberg Charter, the International Law Commission's Draft Code of Crimes against the Peace and Security of Mankind, and the Statutes of the two *ad hoc* international criminal tribunals established by the Security Council. In the past however, the relations between threats and crimes, intra-state and inter-state conflicts and individual accountabilities have been resolved in the absence of an established regime of international criminal justice which were only based on *ad hoc* Security Council resolutions. The international criminal tribunals for the former Yugoslavia (ICTY) and for Rwanda (ICTR) were established by the Security Council to punish violations of international law during the Yugoslavia conflict and the Rwanda genocide. The United Nations also administered the domestic criminal justice system of Kosovo. Likewise, Sierra Leone and the United Nations concluded an agreement to establish a Special Court to prosecute both international and

---

44 UN doc. General Assembly Resolution 3314 (1974).

45 L. F. Damrosch, "Enforcing International Law through Non-forcible Measures", *Recueil De Cours/Collected Courses*, Académie de Droit International de La Haye, 1998, at 202.

46 UN doc. General Assembly Resolution 260 (1948).

domestic crimes committed during the conflict in the country. A similar tribunal for prosecution of Khmer Rouge has been established in Cambodia. The Special Tribunal for Lebanon (STL) was established by an agreement between the United Nations and the Lebanese Republic.[47] The United Nations Security Council, acting under Chapter VII of the Charter of the United Nations, endorsed the agreement on 30 May 2007.[48] The STL marks the first time that the UN-based international criminal court tries a 'terrorist' crime committed against a specific person. According to the United Nations it is a "tribunal of an international character based on the highest international standards of criminal justice".[49]

Thus, as discussed above and taking in consideration the analytical contributions of eminent experts in the field of international law such as Arsanjani and Reisman, if we look at the evolution of international criminal justice in the course of history, two types of international criminal tribunals have emerged.[50] The first category exemplified by the tribunals at Nuremberg and Tokyo, may be called *ex post* tribunals. They were established after the acute and violent situations in which the alleged crimes occurred, and had been resolved by military victory and new political settlement after WWII. As a result, the tribunals' judicial activity did not affect international security concerns. Even if some conditions of instability were still present, these were not likely to be dealt with, as the victorious parties patronized the political momentum. The second generations of *ad hoc* tribunals established by the Security Council also has an *ex post* nature and were based on international security considerations settled by the political and executive organ of the United Nations.

Another category of international tribunals may be called *ex ante* tribunals. They are established before an international security problem had been resolved or even manifested itself, or established in the middle of the conflict in which the alleged crimes were taking place. In these circumstances authoritative political entities such as the Security Council and its operations in the field, if any, would have only been initiating the re-establishment of order in these situations, triggering the negotiations with the governments responsible of conflict resolution, or just addressing the threats of peace and security, or better say the severe humanitarian violations, to the appropriate judicial channels, which also require the involvement of human rights treaty-based bodies within the UN system (UNHCHR).[51] In

47 UN doc. Security Council Resolution 1664 (2006).

48 UN doc. Security Council Resolution 1757 (2007).

49 For an overview of the current proliferation and insight of international criminal tribunals see R. Zacklin, 'The Failings of *Ad Hoc* International Tribunals', in *Journal of International Criminal Justice* (2004) 2 (2), at 541.

50 See H. Arsanjani, W. M. Reisman, "The International Criminal Court and the Congo: From Theory to Reality", in L. N. Sadat, M. P. Scharf (eds.) *The Theory and Practice of International Criminal Law. Essays in Honor of M. Cherif Bassiouni*, 2008, at 325.

51 See S/RES/1970 (2011) which provides jurisdiction to the International Criminal Court over the situation in Libya since 15 February 2011. See A/HCR/16/20 (2010), "Combating Impunity

such context the *ex-ante* judicial decisions may in theory influence the political configuration of peace enforcement by the Security Council depending on the willingness of further international engagements, while the Security Council may still suspend prosecutions for the benefit of peace negotiations. It is clear that the interests of justice and the discretion settled in article 53 of the Rome Statute (initiation of an investigation) is part of such *ex-ante* activity of the International Criminal Court which *ratio* is also valid in the referral activity of the Security Council. In the practice, however, the Court is not an *ex-ante* judicial institution. It is a tool of *last resort* and witnesses serious crimes allegedly committed in conflict and post-conflict situations in accordance with the principle of complementarity. Article 53 provides that the Prosecutor may desist from acting either in relation to opening an investigation or in continuing with an investigation that has been opened, if it appears that the decision to desist would be in the interests of justice. The decision of the Prosecutor not to investigate or not to prosecute based on these grounds may be reviewed by the Pre-Trial Chamber on its own initiative, or at the request of the referring State or the Security Council, and, in such a case, the decision of the Prosecutor will only be effective upon confirmation by the Chamber. The text of Article 53 reflects another aspect of the compromise reached during the first conference in Rome.[52]

The Court could be rather seen as an *ex ante* tribunal without police and law enforcement capabilities.[53] In the longstanding *peace v. justice* debate some observers would even see the Court as an *ex ante* tribunal which "may create conflicting pressures on both the domestic tribunals and the actors responsible for resolving the security problem in the country in question. A unique challenge falls on the judiciary and other domestic security sectors such as conventional army and police. Such actors determine whether and how to set priorities among their curial responsibilities and the inevitable political consequences of their actions". Such pragmatic approach of the "law in action" would only be feasible under important conditions.[54] First of all, in respect of the judicial impartiality and independence from the political compromise with criminal domestic regimes; second, with a judicial institution able to monitor multinational law enforcement interventions, holding humanitarian interventions accountable when necessary;

---

and Strengthening Accountability, the Rule of Law and Democratic Society", in the 2010 Annual Report of the United Nations High Commissioner for Human Rights, at 62.

52 See C. Gallavin, 'Article 53 of the Rome Statute of the International Criminal Court: In the Interests of Justice', 14 *KCLJ*, 2003, at 179–198. See also C. Gallavin, 'The Security Council & the ICC: Delineating the Scope of Security Council Referrals and Deferrals', 5 *New Zealand Armed Forces Law Review*, 2005, at 19–38.

53 See H. Arsanjani, W. M. Reisman, *supra*.

54 See H. Arsanjani, W. M. Reisman, "The Law in Action of the International Criminal Court", 99 *The American Journal of International Law* 2, 2005, at 385. See also R. Gerber, "Mass Atrocities and the International Community: The Multilateral Framework for Prevention and Response", *The Stanley Foundation Articles*, April 2011, accessible at: www.stanleyfoundation.org/articles.cfm?ID=678.

and third, through balancing public powers between international executive and judicial authorities towards configurations of mandates on the ground, institutional liaisons and resource sharing. Such idealistic assumptions however, depend on the willingness of the international community to give more credibility to the Court and to its public authority *vis-à-vis* international political bodies such as the Security Council. One example of such reasoning would simply be that human security waits for reliable mechanisms requiring political configurations of mandates assisting investigations and prosecutions on the ground with protection, relocation and rehabilitation of victims and witnesses. What we currently see, instead, are political organs compromising with warlords the end of violence in the countries in question at the expenses of international criminal justice. These and other issues are extensively dealt with in this study.

### 2.1.3. A UNIVERSAL OR A CUSTOMIZED JURISDICTION?

A frail accomplishment after post-cold war is the fact that the supremacy of the Security Council monitoring international threats and crimes such as rebuilding societies after conflict; setting *ad hoc* tools of international criminal justice with politicised judicial mandates; rehabilitating the access of justice in post-conflict realities; initiating legal reforms, including domestic institutional empowerment and rule of law sectors, among other things, are currently challenged by the independence of a permanent judicial institution dealing with the most serious breaches of international humanitarian law and human rights. The Rome Statute, however, did not challenge such 'supremacy'. The UN peacekeeping operations should serve with law enforcement operations following the judicial decisions of the Court. Moreover, a key question is to what extent non-state actors would be accountable for acts attempting human rights. The major concern in the current practice is to fill the accountability and responsibility gaps at all levels. If such lacuna is not solved serious risks would attempt the universal project of international criminal justice and its global institutions.

We all agree that the jurisdiction of the Court cannot be defined as universal as yet.[55] As a young institution the Court ought to expand the highest international standards of international criminal justice, representing an example to be followed by any tribunal of international character, while complementing domestic

[55] For an extensive legal analysis of some provisions of the Rome Statute see C. Stahn, M. El Zeidy, H. Olasolo, "The International Criminal Court's Ad Hoc Jurisdiction Revisited", 99 *American Journal of International Law,* 2005, at 421. For an historical overview after the invitation given to the International Law Commission by the United Nations General Assembly to study the 'desirability' and 'possibility' of establishing a judicial organ as "a Criminal Chamber of the International Court of Justice (ICJ)" see Vespasian V. Pella, "Towards and International Criminal Court", 44 *American Journal of International Law,* 1950, at 37. See also UN doc. A/760 (1948); UN doc. A/AC.48/4 (1951).

jurisdictions on criminal proceedings. The ideal would be to achieve universality of such international judicial institution dealing with the accountability of individuals in domestic judicial systems. Its presence requires strengthening relations between and within courts and tribunals of States involved in the preservation of international humanitarian law. The presence of the Court represents an historical opportunity. It offers a new direction to the evolution of international relations, international law and international criminal justice. Its impact in devastated domestic realities however, still needs to be verified by social scientists. The Court cannot operate alone. Reconciliation and human security need a re-engagement of higher political priority. The responsibility relies on the actors involved and primarily on the nation-states, including the UN system, international and regional organizations, civil society and other stakeholders. This section promotes further research on the legal responsibilities of global actors and constitutional strategies of universal character according to the UN Charter and the Rome Statute.

## 2.2. THE TRANSITION OF GLOBAL REGULATORY FRAMEWORKS

### SECTION OUTLINE

In this section the attention goes further to the evolution of the rule of law and the human security expectations in global regulatory frameworks of governance dealing with intra- and eventually inter-states conflicts. In theory, these frameworks are interdependent and complementary in their nature and reflect the global politics of international responses in mass atrocities. Looking further into the past, and for an understanding of the present, while avoiding speculations in regard to the future, it can be said that the establishment of the International Criminal Court is the result of longstanding negotiations and a legal discourse which took place in the United Nations as a forum for its 193 Member States to express their views, through the General Assembly, the Security Council, the Economic and Social Council and other bodies and committees involved in the preservation and evolution of international law. The International Law Commission presented a draft statute in 1993 which was examined by a committee appointed by the UN General Assembly in 1995. The Rome Statute was adopted on 17 July 1998. The Statute became a binding treaty, and came into force after it received its 60$^{th}$ ratification, which was deposited at a ceremony at United Nations Headquarters on 11 April 2002. As a result of many years of negotiations aimed at establishing a permanent international tribunal to punish individuals who commit genocide and other serious international crimes, the UN General Assembly convened a conference in Rome on the establishment of an International Criminal Court.[56] This section provides an overview of the transition of global regulatory frameworks dealing with *inter*- and intra-state conflicts, and the triggering mechanism of jurisdiction deriving from them.

### 2.2.1. THE PATH OF UNIVERSALITY AND INTEGRITY: FROM ROME TO KAMPALA

After a longstanding diplomatic compromise, the Rome Statute was rapidly adopted by a vote of 120 to 7, with 21 countries abstaining. The seven countries that voted against the treaty were Iraq, Israel, Libya, China, Qatar, the United States, and Yemen. With the rejection of the United States and China, and with Russia abstaining, three permanent members of the UN Security Council are still not parties, while as of today 123 States ratified the Rome Statute.[57] The important elements of such revolutionary international treaty are without any doubt of historical character for modern international legal and political relations, first of all, as a response to the shortcomings of domestic jurisdictions in the fight against the impunity of serious crimes, and second, for the independence of such permanent judicial institution from the political and executive organ of the United Nations. The establishment of the Rome Statute represents the substantive alternative to the practice of the Security Council establishing *ad hoc* tribunals whose judicial mandates are currently under completion. Distant from reaching the *trias politica* or separation of powers in international relations, the Rome Statute represents the evolution of supranational criminal law, humanitarian and human rights law, pacing effectively the arena of international criminal justice mandates. Nevertheless, a new horizon arises for the emerging 'contours' of international criminal justice in the field of international institutional law, international administrative and constitutional law, including the law of international organizations. These pluralist contours require legal tools to counterbalance conflicting laws and the gaps in the preservation of the legal order in the absence of a constitutional strategy.[58]

56 UN doc. A/CONF.183/10, 17 July 1998, Final Act of the United Nations Diplomatic Conference of Plenipotentiaries on the Establishment of an International Criminal Court, accessible at: www.un.org/icc/index.htm.

57 For an overview of the ratification chart by region of the Rome Statute see CICC, *A Universal Court with Global Support*, accessible at: http://iccnow.org/?mod=romeratification See also the ICC States Parties chronological list updated in 2013 and accessible at: www.icc-cpi.int/en_menus/asp/states%20parties/Pages/states%20parties%20_%20chronological%20list.aspx.

58 For an interesting overview of new fields of public international law and the theories of the potential and problems of global administrative law enhancing the accountability of global governance, see N. Krisch and B. Kingsbury, 'Introduction: Global Governance and Administrative Law in the International Legal Order', in *European Journal of International Law*, (2006), Vol. 17 No. 1, 1–13, accessible at: www.ejil.org/pdfs/17/1/64.pdf.

The first review conference of the Rome Statute in Uganda (Kampala) in 2010 gathered over 2000 delegates of States Parties and non-State Parties such as the US from all corners of the globe. At provisional level, the States Parties discussed the following amendment proposals: the revision of Article 124 of the Rome Statute; the crime of aggression; the inclusion of the use of 'certain' weapons as war crimes in the context of an armed conflict not of an international character, such as the amendments of Article 8. In accordance with the treaty provisions, any future amendment to the Rome Statute requires the support of a two-thirds majority of the States Parties, and an amendment will not enter into force until it has been ratified by seven-eighths of the States Parties. Any amendment to the list of crimes within the jurisdiction of the Court will only apply to those States Parties that have ratified it, with the possibility of an *opt- out* clause by the States not endorsing such amendments.

The international legal order is still characterized by the absence of a *supranational* organization monitoring compliance of universal norms. However, some gaps should be filled according to the high expectations of a world constitution of the international community. With regard to the issue of public authority it would be extremely important also to define the parameters between multilateral approaches of governance and the bilateral engagements as for *non*-members, or only observers within the emerging multilateral regimes of complementary character. This is the case of some permanent members of the Security Council such as the US, China and Russia as well as other States (India, Pakistan, Israel, Iran and Syria). In addition to such policy issues the institutional and constitutional matters of the United Nations and the Rome Statute institutions will be part of the discussions. The Security Council for instance should refrain from the use of the veto in situations of mass atrocity crimes, namely genocide, war crimes, and crimes against humanity as proposed in the policy formulation of the 'Small five' (Costa Rica, Jordan, Liechtenstein, Singapore and Switzerland). Their proposal and policy formulations will need to be discussed in the General Assembly. If such proposal would pass, the civilians in Syria would at least have a better chance to be served by international justice and accountability.

### 2.2.2. LEGALIZING AGGRESSION FROM THREAT TO CRIME

The Statute of the International Criminal Court (ICC) adopted in Rome in 1998, lists aggression as a crime within the jurisdiction of the Court. Negotiations leading to the adoption of the Rome Statute produced consensus on a very narrowly defined core concept of crimes to be applied under the treaty, such as genocide, crimes against humanity and crimes of war. In the first instance, political consensus was not reached on aggression under the Rome Statute negotiations. Although a definition of the crime of aggression has finally been agreed, the jurisdiction of the Court will need more than that.[59] Resource sharing is fundamental, including appropriate triggering mechanisms between the governance institutions of universal character. It needs also to be noted that during the review conference of the Rome Statute in Kampala the States Parties agreed that no sooner than 2017, the Security Council may refer aggression to the Court for prosecution of aggressive leaders from any nation, regardless of whether it has joined the Court. Alternatively, if a State party or the Court's Prosecutor refers aggression to the Court, then the Prosecutor must see if the Security Council has determined that an act of aggression by the accused nation has occurred.[60]

In the past, the Security Council rarely determined that acts of aggression occurred. It has been much easier for the political and executive organ of the United Nations to determine a threat to or breach of international peace and security. This is one of the reasons why most governments pressured some means for the Court proceedings, in the absence of an explicit Security Council decision on aggression. The compromise reached in Kampala requires that if the Security Council fails to reach any such decision on acts of aggression after six months from any referral, the Court's pre-trial judges can deliberate on the issue. If the chambers authorise the Prosecutor to investigate aggression however, the Security Council can still block the inquiry by adopting a mandatory resolution. Such ultimate decision given to the Security Council was essential to bring the UK and France on board, as permanent members of the UN political body, while also appealing the American observer delegation in Kampala, which exerted influence

[59] Although article 5(1) of the Rome Statute, the founding treaty of the International Criminal Court (ICC), included in its jurisdiction the crime of aggression as one of the core crimes, the Court cannot exercise its jurisdiction with regard to this crime until the adoption of a definition and jurisdictional conditions was agreed upon. The negotiations in this regard have stirred considerable debate among States. In 1998 when the Rome Statute was formally adopted, States decided to continue with the longstanding legal debate. In 2002, the subsequent Preparatory Commission concluded its work with a Discussion Paper proposed by the Coordinator of the Working Group on the Crime of Aggression which reflected the status of the negotiations. In September 2002, the Assembly of States Parties (ASP) established a Special Working Group on the Crime of Aggression (SWGCA), open to all States including non-States Parties, to continue discussions on the crime. Since 2003, the SWGCA has met both formally during ASP sessions and informally at Princeton University. A revised Discussion Paper was proposed by the Chairman in January 2007 and new version was issued for the resumed sixth ASP session in June 2008. In February 2009 the Group agreed on a set of proposals on aggression that left only a few questions open, mainly related to the role of the Security Council. Finally the proposal was ready for the review conference in Kampala as described above. For an overview and analysis of such intersection between international law and politics see, S. Barriga, W. Danspeckgruber, C. Wenaweser, *The Princenton Process on the Crime of Aggression*, Liechtenstein Institute on Self-Determination, 2009. See also M. Gillett, "The Anatomy of an International Crime: Aggression at the International Criminal Court", *International Criminal Law Review*, Volume 13, Issue 4, at 829, accessible at: http://booksandjournals.brillonline.com/content/journals/15718123/13/4.

[60] See ICC-ASP/1/Res.1; ICC-ASP/8/Res.6; ICC-ASP-RC/Res.6, 2010, accessible at: www.icc-cpi.int/iccdocs/asp_docs/Resolutions/RC-Res.6-ENG.pdf.

despite the fact that the United States is not a party to the Rome Statute. Another particular aspect of such compromise is that the nationals of non-States Parties are excluded automatically from the jurisdictional liability of the Court.

Thus, it can be said that the interaction frameworks between institutional premises preserving peace, justice and human security in international conflicts, and the fight against the impunity of serious breaches committed during military aggression still wait to be universally enforced. The jurisdictional regime of the crime of aggression is currently on hold, if we consider the outcome of the first review of the Rome Statute in Kampala.[61] The review conference based the definition of the crime of aggression on the UN General Assembly resolution 3314 (XXIX) of 14 December 1974. In this context, if agreed, to qualify aggression as a crime committed by a political or military leader which, by its character, gravity and scale constituted a manifest violation of the UN Charter. As regards the Court's exercise of jurisdiction, the conference agreed that a situation in which an act of aggression appeared to have occurred could be referred to the Court by the Security Council, acting under Chapter VII of the UN Charter, irrespective as to whether it involved States Parties or non-States Parties. Moreover, while acknowledging the Security Council's role in determining the existence of an act of aggression, the conference agreed to authorize the Prosecutor, in the absence of such determination, to initiate an investigation on his own initiative or upon request from a State Party. In order to do so, however, the Prosecutor would have to obtain prior authorization from the Pre-Trial Division of the Court. Also, under these circumstances, the Court would not have jurisdiction in respect to crimes of aggression committed on the territory of non-States Parties, or by their nationals, or with regard to States Parties that had declared that they did not accept the Court's jurisdiction over the crime of aggression.

The most contentious issue relates once again to the relationship between the Security Council and the Court. In particular, the controversy exists regarding the situations where the Security Council would not yet have determined that

61 The 8th session of the Assembly of the States Parties (ASP), which took place on 18–26 November 2009, was foreseen to serve as a filtering mechanism of the issues that were discussed at the Review Conference in Kampala, Uganda (31 May to 11 June 2010). The ASP decided to forward to the Review Conference for its consideration only the proposals for amendments concerning the revision of Article 124 of the Rome Statute, the possible adoption of provisions for the crime of aggression and the first of the proposals put forward by Belgium to extend the jurisdiction of the Court to cover the use of certain weapons in the context of armed conflicts not of an international character. In addition, discussions were held regarding other proposals presented by Belgium, Belize and Trinidad and Tobago, Mexico, the Netherlands and South Africa. None of those proposals gathered sufficient support for their consideration at the upcoming Review Conference. Nevertheless, the ASP agreed to create an ASP Working Group on Amendments that will serve as a mechanism to continue discussions on all of the submitted proposals and any other future proposal toward the next ASP in 2010 and ahead.

a State committed an act of aggression.[62] Some States have expressed the view that under Article 39 of the UN Charter, the Security Council has exclusive competence to determine an act of aggression committed by a particular State. Under this view, the Court would not be able to proceed with a case in the absence of a Security Council determination to declare a State aggressor by specific acts against another State. This was simply the view expressed by the permanent members of the Security Council.[63] Other States have argued that the Security Council has primary, but not exclusive authority to determine an act of aggression, and that the absence of a Security Council determination should not preclude the Court from proceeding with a case. Under the revised 'green light' option, the Security Council could make a decision not to object to the investigation of the crime of aggression instead of making a determination of an act of aggression. Other governments have insisted that since the Security Council may already *refer* a situation to the Court and *defer* an investigation in accordance with article 13 and 16 of the Rome Statute respectively, no additional provision on a prior determination of an act of aggression, or other prior decision would be necessary by the Security Council. Overall, many States have expressed the view that the conditions for the exercise of jurisdiction must reflect a careful balance between the independence of the Court as a judicial body, and the fundamental role of the Security Council in maintaining peace and security under the UN Charter.

The journey to find consensus on such sensitive governance issues appears to be a long one. Only a couple of years ago the States clarified their agreement exclusively on due processes and the way they would proceed on these several issues. The independence of the Court has been promoted by the majority of the States Parties and such view is more than welcome. However, the way such view would be accomplished in the practice is still unclear and remains to be seen. In any case, the prior determination by the Security Council, or another UN organ, would not be prejudicial to the Court's own determination on its jurisdictional substance. The Court has to make its determination in accordance with the definition under the Rome Statute and in accordance with the rights of the accused. During the sixth session of the Assembly of the States Parties, the

---

62 Article 39 of the UN Charter provides that the Security Council shall determine the existence of any act of aggression and "shall make recommendations, or decide what measures shall be taken in accordance with Articles 41 and 42, to maintain or restore international peace and security". The act of aggression is the use of armed force by one State against another State without the justification of self-defence or without authorization by the Security Council.

63 The ideal formula for the crime of aggression expressed by the permanent members of the Security Council has simply been the opt-in jurisdictional procedure left to the discretion of the States. In order to bridge the gap between the permanent members and a considerable number of other States seeking some alternative to an exclusive filter by the Security Council on aggression, other options have been proposed. For an overview of additional proposed options see D. Scheffer, "A Pragmatic Approach to The Crime of Aggression", in R. Bellelli (ed.) *International Criminal Justice: Law and Practice from The Rome Statute to Its Review*, 2010, at 609.

States welcomed the clarification that the jurisdictional triggers of article 13 of the Rome Statute would remain applicable independently of the question of additional preconditions. With regard to other preconditions, the special working group on the crime of aggression (SWGCA) focused in particular on the revised 'green light' option and on the option to enlarge the role of the Pre-Trial Chamber.[64] Nevertheless, both proposals were met with more reluctance than support by the permanent members of the Security Council. Following long negotiations during the Review Conference of the Rome Statute in Kampala (Uganda), the States Parties finally adopted provisions governing the terms of the Court's ability to investigate and prosecute individuals for the crime of aggression.[65] The States Parties to the Rome Statute agreed upon a jurisdictional regime for the crime of aggression, which provides separate procedures depending on whether the situation was referred by the UN Security Council, or whether it came before the Court through a State referral or upon the ICC Prosecutor's initiative. The review conference determined that the activation of jurisdiction is still subject to a positive decision by the Assembly of the States Parties which cannot be taken before 1 January 2017 and one year after the ratification or acceptance of the amendments by 30 member States.[66] The regime of Article 16 of the Rome Statute is once again confirmed, while the provisional change appears in the Article 15 of the Rome Statute.[67]

In conclusion, another element to be emphasized is that the emerging regime of international criminal justice is not able to regulate the cluster of humanitarian interventions and counter terrorism actions by individuals in a position to exercise control, or empowered to direct political-military actions against another State. In the practice, the unilateralism of the national security policy of some States to affirm military supremacy in international relations still takes place at the expense of the citizens of fragile and disintegrated States. In the military operations in Iraq, and later in Afghanistan, the international community witnessed that the national security policy of a couple of States (US and UK) might take the proportions of military coalitions involving multinational forces causing humanitarian casualties and human rights violations including the risk of a crash of international stability.[68] These breaches of international humanitarian law

---

64 See International Criminal Court, Assembly of the States Parties (ASP), *Report of the Special Working Group on the Crime of Aggression*, ICC-ASP/7/SWGCA/2, 20 February 2009.

65 See ICC Press Release, *Review Conference of the Rome Statute concludes in Kampala*, ICC-ASP-20100612-PR546, accessible at: www.icc-cpi.int.

66 For a provisional overview see the Amendments to the Rome Statute of the International Criminal Court on the Crime of Aggression, Annex I, ASP/RC/Res.6, 28 June 2010, accessible at: www.icc-cpi.int/iccdocs/asp_docs/Resolutions/RC-Res.6-ENG.pdf.

67 Article 15 *bis*: Exercise of jurisdiction over the crime of aggression (State referral, *proprio motu*), Article 15 *ter*: Exercise of jurisdiction over the crime of aggression (Security Council referral).

68 See P. Shiner, A. Williams, *The Iraq War and International Law*, 2008.

represent serious violations but do not fall under any supranational jurisdiction.[69] Moreover, such military interventions rely on old mechanisms of conflict management, while reflecting an unlawful concept of international security and a distortion of international law which is still weak *vis-à-vis* non-state actors.[70]

## 2.2.3. THE TRIGGERING MECHANISMS OF JURISDICTION

In this study the complementary role of the Rome Statute institutions with the United Nations system receives clarifications, as well as the controversial challenges characterizing their interaction. Such interaction was compromised by the provisions of the Rome Statute setting the initial stage of 'triggering mechanisms' of jurisdiction during intra-state armed conflicts. As we have seen, the crime of aggression characterizing inter-state conflicts has been extensively delayed for political reasons.[71] Hopefully such jurisdictional mechanisms will receive appropriate re-configurations depending on the evolution of the Court's jurisdiction and the universal ratification of the Rome Statute. In any case, the ways public authorities interact with each other sharing their specific insight in devastating conflicts, deserve discussions for the sake of entire communities. It is important to review some of the initial assessments in the formation of the Court's jurisdiction. Right after the Rome Statute came into force and with regard to the debate on the lacuna of law enforcement in the treaty-based and brand new judicial institution, the *American Society of International Law* clarified its scholarly standing point that what emerged from the diplomatic compromise during the Rome Conference, which shaped the provisional nature of the treaty, was a Court with a 'two-track' system of jurisdiction. Scharf in his '*Results of the Rome Conference for an International Criminal Court*' described that 'track one' would constitute situations referred to the Court by the Security Council. This track would create binding obligations on all States to comply with orders of evidence or surrender of indicted persons under Chapter VII of the UN Charter. Track one would be enforced by Security Council "imposed embargoes, the

69 Besides, during the investigation by the ICTY and its prosecution strategy, when the NATO forces intervened in the former Yugoslavia, atrocities were allegedly committed by its forces and the resultant investigations by the UN on the allegations were damning. The NATO forces escaped indictment only by a single vote in the UN Security Council. This has functioned to discourage the western powers to be hesitant at including the crime of aggression in the Rome Statute.

70 See P. W. Singer, 'War, Profits, and the Vacuum of Law: Privatized Military Firms and International Law', *Columbia Journal of Transnational Law,* 42:2, Spring 2004, at 521.

71 The crime of aggression is a crime forming part of customary international law, therefore can be prosecuted by any State. The problems it currently faces are purely political manipulations by nations manifesting their political intent to frustrate the ICC. This was the case of the policy orientations by the US, especially during the previous administration under George W. Bush, including the distant positions taken by China and Russia as the permanent members of the UN Security Council.

freezing of assets of leaders and their supporters, and/or by authorizing the use of force". In other words, the possible authorization of military enforcement by the Security Council under the flag of international criminal justice, humanitarian interventions and the duty to protect civilians.

According to Scharf it is indeed the 'track one' that the US favoured during the Rome Statute negotiations. With all respect to this theory, the question is whether such primary 'law enforcement track' falling under Chapter VII of the UN Charter is translated in concrete actions, considering the practice in the case of Sudan, against President Al Bashir, since the International Criminal Court received jurisdiction by the Security Council.[72] With the Court's arrest warrants to the Sudanese leaders, the pressure for an international action grows, but there is no agreement in the Security Council on what this action should be. Due to unilateral economic interests in Sudan, China is even contrary to the isolation of the government in Sudan. While the US is supporting the arrest warrants, the Security Council may give priority to such political standpoints and even freeze the charges against the President of Sudan. Moreover, the negative political reactions became visible from the African Union against the judicial decisions of the Court in the Darfur's case. The credibility of the Court's judicial deliberations is at a crossroad between double standards and politicized positions of nation-states not cooperating with the Court, including a distortion from the Security Council authorizing the use of military force under the flag of the responsibility to protect civilians, which characterizes also the situation and the referral addressed from the Security Council to the Court in Libya.

The 'second track' described by Scharf would constitute situations referred to the Court by individual countries (States Parties), or initiated by the ICC Prosecutor (*proprio motu* powers). This track would have no potential for any law enforcement action, but rather would rely on the good-faith cooperation of the States Parties to the Rome Statute. Thus, it was widely understood according to such theory that for the US "the real power was in the first track". The US however, still demanded protection from the second track of the Court's jurisdiction. As a consequence, the Court is facing serious difficulties regarding the judicial assistance, law enforcement and cooperation in situations unable to end the impunity of gross violations of human rights. An example would be the case in Uganda where peace and justice were not seen as the two sides of the same coin. The peace processes would neutralize and freeze the arrest warrants, including the necessary cooperation to enforce the judicial decisions of the Court. In addition to the political rejection and the controversial relation between peace,

72 UN Doc. S/RES/1593 (2005), Referral to the International Criminal Court of the situation in Darfur (Sudan). For an overview of the lack of support received in Sudan, see ICC-02/05 the situation in Darfur, Sudan, ICC reports to the UNSC, accessible at: www.icc-cpi.int/cases/Darfur/s0205/s0205_un.html.

justice and reconciliation, the investigations of the Court are all characterized by serious security problems, especially reaching and protecting witnesses and victims in the field.[73] Moreover, another security issue refers to the fact that for the ICC staff and the field offices, the assistance of the UN peacekeeping operations is extremely vital but still insufficient. In the DRC, several violations have been committed by the parties involved in the field including peacekeepers, which requires an internal UN justice system dealing with such matters, as the Court does not have jurisdiction over it.

According to Scharf and in order to address the US concerns during the negotiations of the Rome Statute, the following protective mechanisms were incorporated into the Court's Statute pressured by the US: first, the Court's jurisdiction under the second track which only relies on the cooperation of the States, would be based on a concept known as *complementarity* which was defined "as meaning the Court would be a *last resort* tool which comes into play only when domestic authorities are unable or unwilling to prosecute".[74] At the insistence of the US, "the delegates at the Rome Conference added an additional clause to the concept of *complementarity* by providing in Article 18 of the Rome Statute that the Prosecutor has to notify States with a *prosecutive* interest in a case of intention to commence an investigation. If, within one month of notification, such a State informs the Court that it is investigating the matter, the Prosecutor must defer to the domestic investigative activity, unless it can convince the Pre-Trial Chamber that such investigation is unlawful. The decision of the Pre-Trial Chamber is subject to interlocutory appeal to the Appeals Chamber (e.g. the Appeals Chamber deliberation on the situation in Kenya). Article 8 of the Court's Statute specifies that the Court would have jurisdiction only over 'serious' war crimes that represent a 'policy or plan'. Thus, random acts of personnel involved in a foreign peacekeeping operation would not be subject to the Court's jurisdiction.

Article 15 of the Court's Statute monitors complaints addressed to the Prosecutor by requiring the approval of a three-judge pre-trial chamber before the prosecution can launch an investigation, as in the situation addressed by the Prosecutor in Kenya and Ivory Coast after the post-election violence. The decision of the chamber is subject to interlocutory appeal to the Appeals Chamber. Article 16 of the Statute allows the Security Council to affirmatively vote to postpone an investigation or case for up to twelve months, on a renewable basis. "While this does not amount to the individual veto the US had sought, this does give them and the other members of the Security Council a collective control over the Court, if no permanent member 'vetoes' the resolution calling for postponement.

---

73 UN doc. Security Council Resolutions 1422/2002 and 1487/2003.

74 M. P. Scharf, 'Results of The Rome Conference for an International Criminal Court', August 1998, *ASIL Insights*, accessible at: www.asil.org/insigh23.cfm.

These measures were considered sufficient for other major powers, including the United Kingdom, France and Russia, which voted in favour of the Rome Statute. But without what would amount to any veto of jurisdiction over US personnel and officials, the US felt bound to vote against the Rome Statute".[75]

Even no experts of international relations and international law are aware of the devastating consequences of such rejection of the Rome Statute under the Bush administration. On the contrary the 'agendas' of the current Obama administration focusing on 'repair', 'resume', 'renew' contain pragmatic new policy elements for international law considering what President Obama has called a "new era of engagement" in his remarks addressed to the UN General Assembly. The Rome Statute institutions however, are still waiting for such global engagements.[76]

### 2.2.4. THE IMPACT AND PROGRESS OF THE REVIEW CONFERENCE

Regarding the jurisdictional progress of the Court in terms of article 123 of the Rome Statute the review conference in Uganda (Kampala) has so far been the only statutory one. As a result of discussions at the sessions of the Assembly of States Parties (ASP), a number of proposals did not gather sufficient support for their consideration at the review conference, such as terrorism, the use of weapons of mass destruction and other serious threats in the sense of receiving crime definition globally recognized. Nevertheless, the ASP agreed to create a working group on specific amendments, which will serve to continue discussions on the submitted proposals and any other future proposal.[77]

Participation in the conference was open to representatives of States Parties to the Rome Statute, observer States, States not having observer status, representatives designated by intergovernmental organizations and other entities that received a standing invitation from the UN General Assembly, representatives designated by regional intergovernmental organizations or other international bodies

[75] See M. P. Scharf *supra*.

[76] See H. Koh, S. J. Rapp, *The US Engagement with the ICC and the Outcome of the Recently Concluded Review Conference*, Special Briefing to the US Department of States, June 15 2010, accessible at: www.state.gov/s/wci/us_releases/remarks/143178.htm.

[77] The eighth session of the ASP of November 2009 (ICC-ASP/8/20) was foreseen to serve as a filtering mechanism of the issues to be discussed at the Review Conference in Kampala, Uganda (31 May to 11 June 2010). Thus, the ASP decided to forward to the Review Conference for its consideration only the proposals for amendments concerning the revision of Article 124 of the Statute, the possible adoption of provisions for the crime of aggression, and the first of the proposals put forward by Belgium to extend the jurisdiction of the Court to cover the use of certain weapons in the context of armed conflicts not of an international character.

invited to the Rome Conference, representatives of subsidiary bodies of the Assembly of States Parties (ASP), officials and staff of the Court, officials and staff of the United Nations, non-governmental organizations invited to the Rome Conference, and other persons accredited or invited to attend the conference. The States Parties officials, national judicial and prosecutorial authorities, NGOs and other members of civil society, reported on the status and impact of international criminal justice and the Rome Statute regime.

The initiation of a 'stocktaking' process of the Court's presence in the international legal order and its impact in mass atrocity situations, including the perspective of victims and communities affected by the Court's work on the ground, was proposed as an important topic by numerous States, by the ASP, NGOs and other members of civil society. With regard to the case-law and its jurisprudence, the main task for the Court is to guarantee fair trials, giving back the voice to the victims of crimes with participation and reparation programs. The review conference included assessments to consider the holistic success and impact of the Rome Statute to date, with a particular focus on the following areas: a) the impact on victims and affected communities; b) the principle of complementarity; c) the status of cooperation; and d) the dilemma of peace and justice.[78]

Political and legal challenges on the role of complementary global regimes complementing domestic governance institutions for the fight against the impunity of international crimes are important preconditions for decision-making. Only time will prove if such 'systemic' assessments during the review conference in Kampala will raise the standards of policy making and strategy building, fostering peace, justice and security altogether. The role of parliamentarians and the legislative implementation at national level remains the key. At international level measuring the effectiveness of such a 'system' of governance should not preclude the basic requirement to harmonize the treaty law in the Rome Statute and the UN Charter, strengthening the political consensus on structural and substantial reforms. These are considered essential topics before any other future 'systemic' assessment would take place.

An important aspect that limits the current progress of the emerging regime of international criminal justice, is the distance taken by political standpoints on global threats in the way of being defined as crimes falling under international law. Some proposals on terrorism have been put on the table of the negotiations and addressed to the political premises of the Assembly of the States Parties but there seem to be an impasse in the decision making about the international regime

---

78 ICC RC/WGOA/1/Rev.2, RC/WGOA/2, RC/ST/V/INF.1, RC/ST/V/INF.2, Review Conference of the Rome Statute, Kampala, Uganda, 31 May – 11 June 2010. For an overview of the official documents see: www.icc-cpi.int/Menus/ASP/ReviewConference/Review+Conference.htm.

under which such global threat would fall. In general, the current exercise of the powers of the Security Council relating to the maintenance of international peace and security can directly affect individual rights. This is in particular true for targeted sanctions. In this case, the respect due to human rights requires that the affected individuals enjoy certain procedural safeguards, including an effective remedy against a listing decision. The Security Council Committee established pursuant to paragraph 6 of resolution 1267 (1999) concerning Al-Qaida and the Taliban and associated individuals and entities (hereafter referred to as the "Al-Qaida and Taliban Sanctions Committee") oversees the implementation by States of the three sanctions measures (freeze of assets, travel ban and arms embargo) imposed by the Security Council on individuals and entities associated with the Taliban and the Al-Qaida organization.

It needs to be noted that the 1267 Sanctions Committee maintains a Consolidated List of individuals and entities subject to the sanctions measures in the context of counterterrorism. By Resolutions 1267 (1999), 1333 (2000), 1390 (2002), as reiterated in resolutions 1455 (2003), 1526 (2004), 1617 (2005), 1735 (2006) and 1822 (2008), the Security Council has obliged all States to: freeze without delay the funds and other financial assets or economic resources, including funds derived from property owned or controlled directly or indirectly; prevent the entry into or the transit through their territories; prevent the direct or indirect supply, sale, or transfer of arms and related material, including military and paramilitary equipment, technical advice, assistance or training related to military activities, with regard to the individuals, groups, undertakings and entities placed on the Consolidated List. In accordance with paragraph 13 of Resolution 1822 (2008), the Al-Qaida/Taliban Sanctions Committee makes accessible a narrative summary of reasons for the listing for individuals, groups, undertakings and entities included in the Consolidated List.[79] After the terrorist attacks of 9/11 the last decade has been characterized by an approach against terrorism which created serious issues for human rights law including serious violations of humanitarian principles.[80] Real consensus is still required in the fight against terrorism including its definition as international crime. Unfortunately, the advent of the first review of the Rome Statute did not progress on terrorism and we will discuss later some of the political reasons behind such an impasse.

---

79 For an overview of the narrative summaries of reasons for listing, see www.un.org/sc/committees/1267/narrative.shtml. See also M. Bothe, "Security Council's targeted sanctions against presumed terrorists: The need to comply with human rights standards" 6(3) *Journal of International Criminal Justice* (2008), at 541–555. See also I. Cameron, 'UN Targeted Sanctions, Legal Safeguards and the ECHR', 2006 *Nordic Journal of International Law* 72, 1 at 56. See C. Warbrick, 'The European Response to Terrorism in an Age of Human Rights', (2004) 15 EJIL, at 989. See also J. Farrall, K. Rubenstein (eds), *Sanctions, accountability and governance in a globalised world*, 2009.

80 See the US *National Strategy for Counterterrorism*, White House, June 2011, accessible at: www.whitehouse.gov/sites/default/files/counterterrorism_strategy.pdf.

## 2.3. THE NORMATIVE AND POLICY ORIENTATIONS

### SECTION OUTLINE

The previous section addressed the lacuna of human security measures between legal and political frameworks preserving international order, peace and security and fundamental individual rights. It pointed out the role of the emerging regime of international criminal justice in multiple situations of war and crime; the jurisdictional nature deriving from previous *ad hoc* models based on double standards; the rule of law as a principle of governance in extremely violent political transitions, aggressive domestic regimes and political élites far from preserving human security. It examined the transition of global regulatory frameworks and the intersection between policy and law about international interventions in intra- and inter-state conflicts. It demonstrated the limits of complementary global regimes dealing with international threats and crimes and their democratic governance. This section debates the missing priorities of normative and policy orientations securing individuals in times of turmoil and violations of international law. It examines the concept of human security in international law and world politics serving the quest of peace and justice. First of all, it needs to be verified whether civilian protection measures would ever be applied to victims and witnesses of genocide, war crimes, ethnic cleansing and crimes against humanity, during both security operations and judicial activities, when at least the international community decides to intervene with *last resort* investigations and prosecutions of States parties and/or not parties to the Rome Statute. This is only one of the reasons why the complementary role of the Rome Statute regime to the United Nations system deserve clarification in order to define the governance of justice during humanitarian interventions in 'failed' States. Moreover, it is also important to understand the possible evolution of the Court's jurisdiction and its public authority once the judicial outcomes have been released. In other words, the ways *complementary* global regimes would translate in practice reliable measures of *protective* justice towards the proceedings of security systems, law enforcement and sustainable order, including capacity-building of domestic governance systems dealing with *retributive* and *restitutive* justice. This section discusses the missing priorities in the governance of peace, justice and security. It offers some observations about the dilemma of human security in international law and global politics and the importance of regimes of complementary nature governing sustainable peace towards justice and accountability and possible capacity-building.

## 2.3.1. THE MISSING PRIORITIES

The analysis of empirical data shows that the major constraint detected in the governance of peace and justice is the lacuna of human security measures. Human security depends on an understanding of preventive measures capable of preventing international threats and crimes, and on the willingness of the actors involved to apply those measures, especially by the States themselves and their political will to follow such measures, but also by international governance institutions in accordance with their roles to provide applicable models to be followed by domestic governance structures, including regional and international realities. The problem of 'stateless" territories, their sensitive statehood issues, and the conflicts and violations deriving from them, are still left out of any support by global governance systems. These systems are still correctly defined as state-centered, even if lately the harm suffered by the individuals in conflict zones characterized by severe human rights violations requires regulatory frameworks of governance. In this study the governance model proposed is based on the principle that the proper referent for security should be the individual rather than the State. Human security holds that a people-centred view of security is necessary for national, regional and international stability. It advocates that more efforts and resources need to be invested in an accurate knowledge of early warning, identifying the fragility of the situation and the risks associated with it, in order to anticipate a possible attempt to peace and serious violations of international humanitarian law. Unfortunately, such an approach did not materialize in the practice and methods applied in the referrals of the Security Council to the Court in the Sudan and Libya, while still keeping the Court far from ending the impunity of the mass atrocity crimes committed in Syria, Palestine, Iraq, Afghanistan and other country-situations where jurisdiction, support and cooperation are required.

The establishment of an international judicial institution, advocated for decennia, dealing with individual perpetrators outside the UN premises, while fighting against the impunity of serious crimes internationally recognized, represents a revolutionary development for the promotion of global values, such as integrity and universality. However, the creation of a reliable architecture and mechanisms fostering peace, justice and security is characterized by important challenges which are related to the absence of separation of powers between legislative, judicial and executive international mandates and by the negative repercussions on the creation of a state-building apparatus applicable in 'failed' States for the sake of human security. The lack of political support of the judicial decisions of the Court in the Sudan, Uganda and the Democratic Republic of Congo (DRC), for instance, show that the comprehensive efforts of the United Nations to stop conflicts and atrocities visible in peace negotiations, peace enforcement operations, and escalations of humanitarian disasters are not taking part in support of the regime of international criminal justice. Besides, in the debate on the normative provisions that led to the adoption of Article 16 of the Rome Statute relating to the possible tensions or disconnection between peace and justice and their governance, including real-life experience to govern international humanitarian escalations, were indeed underestimated. The lacuna of human security measures still persists when preventive diplomacy would fail, while the links between justice, human development and sustainable peace are weak and inconsistent in the majority of the conflict and post-conflict situations assessed in this study.

## 2.3.2. HUMAN SECURITY AND INTERNATIONAL LAW

The questions addressed in this section relate to the lack of protection measures of civilians during intra-state conflicts. The Court is expected to receive appropriate consideration in the configuration of peace enforcement mandates including the findings of inquiry commissions of the UN Human Rights Council. It is essential to focus on the ways the policy of the responsibility to protect (RtoP), and the fight against domestic criminal regimes would centralize fundamental individual rights and the universality of human rights principles when dealing with escalations of mass atrocity crimes. The preventive efforts of armed conflicts wait for concrete accomplishments of global governance. It needs to be noted that in accordance with the principle of proportionality, the incidental and unintended harm caused to civilians, or civilian property, must be proportionate and not excessive in relation to the concrete and direct military advantage anticipated by an attack on a military objective. Under international humanitarian law (IHL) and the Rome Statute indeed, the death of civilians during an armed conflict, no matter how grave and regrettable might be, does not in itself constitute a war crime. International humanitarian law and the Rome Statute permit belligerents to carry out proportionate attacks against military objectives, even when it is known that some civilian deaths or injuries will occur.[81] With the war in Iraq some important features of international law have been compromised. Unfortunately, the establishment of the Rome Statute institutions would not signify the solution of

81 Article 52 of the Additional Protocol I to the Geneva Conventions provides a widely-accepted definition of military objective: "In so far as objects are concerned, military objectives are limited to those objects which by their nature, location, purpose or use make an effective contribution to military action and whose total or partial destruction, capture or neutralization, in the circumstances ruling at the time, offers a definite military advantage", see L. Moreno-Ocampo, OTP letter to senders re Iraq, 9 February 2006, page 4–5, footnote 11, accessible at: http://www2.icc-cpi.int/NR/rdonlyres/F596D08D-D810-43A2-99BB-B899B9C5BCD2/277422/OTP_letter_to_senders_re_Iraq_9_February_2006.pdf See also H. E. Shamash, "How Much is Too Much? An Examination of the Principle of Jus in Bello Proportionality", in Israel Defense Forces Law Review, Vol. 2, 2005–2006, accessible at http://ssrn.com/abstract=908369.

longstanding issues in the realm of compliance of international law. If some of its branches received consistent jurisprudence in the criminality domain, including the fact that international law is no longer solely concerned with relations between sovereign States, there is much less progress about possible alternatives that could further preserve the international legal order by the foundational and systemic changes occurring in the world society.

### 2.3.3. HUMAN SECURITY AND WORLD POLITICS

Another problem is that the 'responsibility to protect' (RtoP) 'norm' does not have as yet a firm legal character but is left to the fluctuations of global politics. The Protection of Civilians (POC) and the Responsibility to Protect (RtoP or R2P) for instance, are distinct but very closely linked from a theoretical perspective. The POC has its roots in universal principles of international humanitarian law (IHL) as well as human rights and refugee law. The POC constitutes the full range of activities that intergovernmental organizations, States, international NGOs, and individuals can pursue to advance the legal and physical protection of civilians, particularly in the context of armed conflicts. This notion of protection can be understood to include: physical protection from immediate harm; satisfaction of the needs essential for the sustenance of life, and freedom to exercise fundamental human rights. The RtoP calls on national authorities, regional organizations and global institutions to cooperate in the protection of civilians from genocide, war crimes, ethnic cleansing and crimes against humanity. Much work needs to be done to identify the scope of civilian protection, the measures needed to protect civilians and the best practices applicable. The RtoP is a framework for realizing the POC in the most egregious cases, such as the prevention of, and the protection from mass atrocity crimes. The whole POC agenda is substantially wider than that one covered by the RtoP, and aspects of the preventive components of the RtoP extend beyond the POC. So said, what kind of interrelation can be found between the two, and how this would be applied by complementary global regimes? How did the RtoP work in situations of war and crime such as in the DRC, in the Sudan and in Libya, whereas the humanitarian assistance on the ground was constantly compromised by the military operations deployed in the field and by the lack of cooperation by criminal regimes?

Unfortunately, apart from providing some definitions of volatile international policies, the operational relationship between the POC and the RtoP remains unclear. More work is needed to understand what protection activities contribute to preventing the escalation, or constitute an effective response to the commission of mass atrocity crimes, and hence, how and where the two concept are symbiotic. In the Horn of Africa for instance, there is clearly a drought but the reason why thousands of people are leaving their homes in search of food is also because a violent insurgency in Somalia, along with the forced recruitment of youths, which is making things worse. Much of southern and central Somalia is controlled by *al Shabaab* Islamist militants linked to al Qaeda who imposed a ban on food aid in 2010.[82] These *al Shabaab* militants have since maintained the embargo on the World Food Program (WFP), calling the world food aid program a 'spy agency'. *Al Shabaab* accused the United Nations of invasion and determined not to allow humanitarian agencies with 'hidden agendas' to return on the ground. Part of the problem according to reliable analytical reports is that much of the fundings for WFP and some other humanitarian aid agencies come from the United States, opening them to charges of controversial objectives which again relate to security policy and its anti-terrorism agenda, much more than humanitarian assistance to the population starving to death.[83] Furthermore, it needs to be noted that with East Africa facing its worst drought in 60 years affecting more than 11 million people, the United Nations has declared a famine in the region for the first time in a generation. The overcrowded refugee camps in Kenya and Ethiopia are receiving some 3,000 new refugees every day, as families flee from famine-stricken and war-torn areas. The situation of East of Africa is characterized by the slow response of Western governments, local governments to terrorist groups blocking access, terrorist and bandit attacks, including anti-terrorism laws that restrict who the aid groups can deal with, not to mention the massive scale of the current humanitarian crisis. The unfortunate information is that in the Sudan as well both the POC and the RtoP agendas have constantly failed, and are still in the hands of controversial international political engagements which are compromising the stability in the country, and with the criminal and violent leaderships, undermining the credibility of the international judicial outcomes falling under the Rome Statute. So said and avoiding speculations, the substantial progress in the normative and policy frameworks centralizing individuals in international affairs, and the governance institutions dealing with them, needs to be verified. In fact, the involvement of the Court in mass atrocity crimes in the African continent could be interpreted as the hope of having a deterrent effect of the serious violations of individual rights committed in several countries, and which hopefully would take full ownership of their fight against the regime of impunity of international crimes of common concern.

---

82 See Abdisaid M. Ali, *The Al-Shabaab Al-Mujahidiin: A profile of the first Somali terrorist organisation,* Institut für Strategie Politik Sicherheits und Wirtschaftsberatung (ISPSW), Berlin, Germany, June 2008, accessible at: www.isn.ethz.ch/isn/Digital-Library/Publications/Detail/?id=55851.

83 See B. Malone, 'Horn of Africa aid caravan too late, again', *Somalia on msnbc.com,* 26 July 2011, accessible at: http://msnbc.msn.com/id/43900689/ns/world_news-africa/ For an insight into the struggle against terrorism in the Horn of Africa, in the situations in Djibouti, Eritrea, Ethiopia, Kenya, Somalia, Sudan, and Yemen, see R. I. Rotberg, *Battling terrorism in the Horn of Africa,* Brookings Institution Press, 2005.

Since the early 1990s the African Great Lakes Region, politically and geographically defined as the Democratic Republic of Congo (DRC), Burundi, Rwanda, Uganda and Tanzania, has been convulsed by genocide, civil wars, inter-state conflict and flawed democratic transitions. The conflicts of the last decade across this region must be understood in the context of ethnic and religious conflict, the struggle of State formation and the role of natural resources originating such conflicts. Three factors have been identified as key contributors to conflict and mass atrocities in the region: ethnicity, absence of domestic systems of governance and exploitation of natural resources (pillage). Peace-building strategies and post-conflict recovery have increasingly sought to address both political and economic issues, incorporating the national, regional and the international dimensions. The empirical results regarding African countries point out that in the majority of these situations, conflicts returned to be the reality after a very short break through from war to peace. This is the reason why the governance of complementary global regimes requires attention. Such governance represents the opportunity to maximize both actions and results fostering peace, justice and security. However, it requires to be challenged in the right direction with a strong political *road map*.

## 2.4. THE PARADIGM SHIFT OF GLOBAL 'COMPLEMENTARITY'

### SECTION OUTLINE

The political determination to establish an independent, permanent, universal, International Criminal Court in 'relationship' with the United Nations system, "with jurisdiction over the most serious crimes of concern to the international community as a whole", was settled in the preamble of the Rome Statute. The preamble of the treaty recognizes the link between peace and justice, stating that "grave crimes threaten the peace, security, and well-being of the world" and affirming that States Parties are "determined to put an end to the impunity for the perpetrators of these crimes and thus, contribute to the prevention of such crimes". Considering the practice of the last decade, the pursuit of peace and justice in conflict and post-conflict societies presents some controversial challenges. Several problems occur in the coordination of efforts of independent political and judicial mandates, particularly between the configuration strategies of international peacemakers and peacekeepers, and the interests of victims and witnesses of international crimes on relocation, protection and reparation in the context of human security.

Even if peace and justice complement each other in the long term, in the short term tensions have arisen between efforts to secure peace, and efforts to ensure accountability of international crimes. In theory, the principle of the interdependence between peace, justice and security at global level should focus on strengthening relationships and partnerships between complementary international mandates, such as the Rome Statute institutions and the United Nations system, particularly considering the main characteristic of the emerging regime of international criminal justice, based on cooperation networks at domestic, regional and global levels. In practice, the interdependence between peace, justice and security is compromised by the obstacles on balancing powers at international level. In my view this is particularly true looking at the interaction between political, executive and judicial mandates and the 'governance' that derives from such compromise.

At structural level, none of the Rome Statute institutions is formally part of the United Nations system, however their mandates are complementary. Such global governance institutions are involved respectively on international threats, peace and crime control, but their partnership is not sufficiently defined, while the Court's jurisdiction is limited to the most serious crimes of international concern. The legal relationship between the Court and the United Nations is governed by the relationship agreement.[84] Any amendment of such agreement shall be approved by the UN General Assembly and by the Assembly of States Parties (ASP) in accordance with article 2 of the Rome Statute.[85] Several basic principles, such as discretion and confidentiality, preside over the cooperation between the Court and the United Nations, which is also based on specific arrangements regulating such poor interaction in the field missions.

### 2.4.1. THE CHALLENGES IN GLOBAL REGIMES

Since the Court's establishment several States Parties referred to the Court their inability to investigate and prosecute serious crimes on their own (e.g. Democratic Republic of Congo, Uganda, Central African Republic, Ivory Coast and Mali), while preliminary assessments are performed by the Court to verify whether investigations should be opened in Afghanistan, Colombia, Palestine, Guinea, Georgia, Honduras, Nigeria, Democratic Republic of Korea and Ukraine. A preliminary assessment is the first phase of the Court's Prosecutor activities. It is a phase during which the office of the Prosecutor first examines the jurisdiction

84 As reported in the addendum to the note of the Secretary-General, UN doc. A/58/874/Add. 1, the draft relationship agreement was approved by the Assembly of States Parties to the Rome Statute on 7 September 2004 at The Hague. The Netherlands recommended the adoption of the draft resolution by the General Assembly without a vote, thereby approving the draft relationship agreement between the UN and the ICC. Because the several concerns about the ICC, the United States rejected the consensus on the draft resolution. See UN doc. General Assembly, A/58/PV.95, 13 September 2004, Agenda item 154, at 5.

85 UN Doc. A/RES/58/79, UN doc. A/58/874 (2004).

of the Court, whether crimes falling under the ICC jurisdiction may have been, or are committed in a given situation.[86] If the conditions are met, whether genuine investigations and prosecutions are being carried out by the competent authorities in relation to these crimes and, as a third step, whether the possible opening of an investigation by the Prosecutor would not go against the interests of justice.[87] During this phase, and in accordance with Article 15 of the Rome Statute, the Office of the Prosecutor proactively evaluates all information on alleged crimes from multiple sources, including communications from individuals, non-governmental organizations and other parties concerned. The triggering of a preliminary examination does not imply that an investigation will be opened. The extensive literature existent since the first phase of existence of the Court on such policy orientations, which fall under the normative framework of the Rome Statute, is the result of a longstanding scholarly debate on issues such as the selection of situations and admissibility, the complementarity and the impact on affected communities, including public outreach and witnesses and victims' rights.

## 2.4.2. THE CHALLENGES IN POLICY AND LAW

It should be clear at this stage that this study explores practical steps in furthering the international rule of law as a principle of governance. It offers an analysis of the challenges characterizing the emerging regime of international criminal justice arguing on the imperfect interaction between the International Criminal Court and the United Nations, particularly during the operations on the ground fostering human security. The rule of law as a principle of governance centralizing human rights and justice is extensively argued by scholars and practitioners, while international governance institutions struggle with the preservation of such fundamental principle according to their respective mandates. The supranational lacuna characterizing the international legal order is not resolved by the presence of institutions of universal character. A legal framework regulating such interactions does not contain a defined strategy or *road map* and it is considered very poor. Political deadlocks slow down the transition of humanitarian interventions, use of force, protection duties of civilians, reconciliation and reconstruction, which should create the premises of *global justice*. Appropriate interaction strategies between independent and complementary mandates for the sake of individuals are an opportunity to preserve further the rule of law. After all, such public

86 Office of the Prosecutor, *Draft Policy Paper on Preliminary Examinations*, 2010, accessible at: www.icccpi.int/Menus/ICC/Structure+of+the+Court/Office+of+the+Prosecutor/Policies+and+Strategies/Draft+Policy+Paper+on+Preliminary+Examinations.htm.

87 Office of the Prosecutor, *Policy Paper on the Interests of Justice*, 2007, accessible at: www.icc-cpi.int/NR/rdonlyres/772C95C9-F54D-4321-BF09-73422BB23528/143640/ICCOTPInterestsOfJustice.pdf.

authorities operate in accordance with the constitution of the international community and need democratic 'triggering mechanisms' monitoring serious international threats and crimes. The precondition of appropriate triggering mechanisms however, depends on real consensus in balancing powers between such complementary global entities. In other words, the intersection between international law and global politics by the research community is further required.

The domestic jurisdiction of any sovereign State includes the right to define and punish crimes. Every State decides for itself, according to its legal traditions and within the limits of international law.[88] International law does not determine which point of view is to be preferred between monism and dualism. International law only requires that its rules are respected, and that States are free to decide on the manner in which they want to respect these rules and make them binding on their citizens. In theory, the supremacy of international law is a rule in both dualist and monist legal systems, while in practice if a treaty is accepted for purely political reasons, and States do not intend to fully translate it into national law, or to take a monist view on international law, then the implementation of the treaty is very uncertain. The impasse of a treaty depends indeed on the combination of several factors. The institutions deriving from such treaties need to be proactive in preventing whatever impasse. The institutional design established by the treaties may limit the level of uncertainty, firstly proposing a model of harmonization between the international legal systems of the world, and secondly enhancing definitions of crimes of serious common concern, offering assistance in the implementation of national legislations. The theory applicable in this doctrinal context is balancing public powers to maximize results. The precondition is a good delimitation of competences, working methods and good relationships between complementary actors especially on the ground. The policy of cooperation between such independent, and most importantly complementary institutions, is extremely important and needs to be visible in their respective legislations.

88 For an overview of the debate regarding the substantive criminal matters, international cooperation and implementing solutions of the Rome Statute, R. S. K. Lee, *States' Responses to Issues Arising from the ICC Statute: Constitutional, Sovereignty, Judicial Cooperation, and Criminal Law*, (2005), at 215. This is a comparative study focusing on the legislative methods and techniques used in 12 countries to give effect to the ICC, which covers both common law and civil law countries: Argentina; Brazil; South Africa; The Netherlands; Liechtenstein; France; Sweden; Germany; Norway; Italy; Canada; and the UK. The practice of each State forms a chapter focusing on constitutional, sovereign, and criminal issues. Two additional chapters discuss such issues now facing Japan and Mexico. The contributors focus on real issues encountered and methods and techniques actually employed with the purpose of serving as a practical guide to those countries still looking for methods to give effect to the Rome Statute. In each case the authors explain why certain legislative approaches were used and why others were not selected. The authors are all experts with years of experience in the field; most of them participated in preparing the relevant domestic laws and in the making process of the Rome Statute.

It is still argued by many policy observers that the extent of such cooperation preserving peace, justice and security is treated as matters of common concerns. In my view, only towards an accurate interaction between complementary global regimes it would be possible to maximize the results with the use of minimal resources. Such interaction depends of course on a defined strategy settled by the decision-making enforcing global governance institutions towards democratic reforms, which are still pending. The political convergence on such issues does not receive any progress, if we consider the positions of the permanent members of the Security Council in regard to the situation in Syria.

## 2.5. THE POLITICAL IMPASSE OF MULTILATERALISM

### SECTION OUTLINE

The analysis of the legislative history of the United Nations and the Rome Statute institutions during the first decade of their existence shows that there have been delays for the International Criminal Court to enter into a substantive relationship with the United Nations. In addition to such delays the relationship between the United Nations and the African Union (AU) failed to design a *road map* for the peace process in the Sudan. The Darfur's peace talks by the UN, which called on all parties to cease hostilities and prepare for forthcoming negotiations, did not work. As a result, the humanitarian disaster in the whole Sudanese region considerably increased. The Court would then receive the first referral from the UN Security Council as massive humanitarian escalation of last resort, where serious crimes falling under its jurisdiction had been committed.[89] Right after the opening of an independent investigation in Darfur the Court's officials declared that such an investigation "will require sustained cooperation from national and international authorities. It will form part of a collective effort, complementing African Union and other initiatives to end the violence in Darfur and to promote justice".[90] The Court however, remained completely isolated. Not any political and diplomatic support was ever provided by the Security Council, by the Assembly of the States Parties and by the other relevant organs in order

89 UN doc. S/RES/1593 (2005).

90 See Report of the former Prosecutor of the International Criminal Court Luis Moreno-Ocampo to the Security Council Pursuant to UNSCR 1593 (2005), 29/06/2005 accessible at: www.icc-cpi.int/nr/exeres/2386f5cb-b2a5-45dc-b66f-17e762f77b1f.htm On 25 May, 2010, Pre-Trial Chamber I of the International Criminal Court (ICC) ordered the ICC Registrar to transmit the decision informing the United Nations Security Council about the lack of cooperation by the Republic of the Sudan in the case of *the Prosecutor v. Ahmad Muhammad Harun (Ahmad Harun) and Ali Muhammad Ali Abd-Al Rahman (Ali Kushayb)*, in order for the Security Council to take any action it may deem appropriate. See ICC-02/05-01-07 accessible at www.icc-cpi.int/iccdocs/doc/doc868180.pdf.

to re-shape the relations between the Court and the several members of the African Union which, as States Parties to the Rome Statute, took severe distance from the judicial institution. In this collapse of cooperation, the discrepancy of law enforcement and the lack of engagement in such humanitarian escalations became visible very soon. The Court would not receive any support right after the extension of its jurisdiction to a non-State party by the UN Security Council in Darfur. Its judicial outcomes did not receive any follow up. The cooperation between the Security Council and the Court shows the lacuna of political and diplomatic support and the complete absence of law enforcement engagements. The consensus in the UN political organs resulted to be weak. The unilateral interests of China with regard to Sudan and also the abstention of the US characterized the vote of the Resolution 1593 (2005). Even referring the situation to the Court in light of the findings of the International Commission of Inquiry on violations of international humanitarian law and human rights law in Darfur, the so-called Cassese Commission, the collective efforts have been neglected compromising further the authority of the international judicial institution. The same controversial political trends characterized the involvement in the situation in Libya and the inaction with regard to Syria.

### 2.5.1. ENGAGING IN RELATIONSHIPS AND PARTNERSHIPS?

This section argues not exclusively on the relationship between the Security Council and the Court but refers to deep-rooted systemic issues still waiting for political convergence and democratic solutions. The actual overlaps obviously point out the absence of the separation of powers in international relations and the failure of democratic reform of the political and executive organ of the UN empowering the voice of less represented States. In the case of the African States and their obligations falling under the Rome Statute including the controversial position of the African Union (AU), the political solution would be to avoid with every means the distance between the AU Peace and Security Council and the UN Security Council. In accordance with the UN Charter the regional dimension is extremely important. In my view, such dimension should receive a specific role in any systemic change of democratic governance. The interaction between the Security Council and the Court is characterized by the inexistence of law enforcement solutions between executive and judicial, and by the absence of a supranational judicial organization which should monitor the accountability regime at global level. The 'triggering mechanisms' regulating humanitarian escalations of last resort need attention.

In the presidential statement issued by the Security Council on the rule of law, the Council notes that "the fight against the impunity for the most serious crimes of international concern has been strengthened through the work of the International Criminal Court" and "it intends to continue to fight impunity and uphold accountability with appropriate means...".[91] The question is at which extent there is genuine political determination to establish global 'partnerships' between such complementary global mandates dealing with humanitarian escalations of last resort in conflict and post-conflict societies. So said, which is the extent decision-makers are committed to build up a credible international state-building apparatus, assisting 'failed' States and societies in transition from mass atrocities to rehabilitation? What kind of strategy or *road map* will characterize such 'system' of interventions in mass atrocity escalations? How such interventions would comply with the standards of legality in international law? Furthermore, the interaction between the Court, the Security Council and the General Assembly involves clusters of assistance at legal, political and operational levels. Issues such as law enforcement of judicial decisions, protection of witnesses and victims, security of field offices on the ground, security of personnel and threat assessments of country-specific situations, including resource sharing, seem to remain under discussion in the years to come.[92] The first step currently dealt with, involves logistics, communication channels and information exchange, while such 'relationship-building' is currently in the 'work in progress' phase on legal assistance, institutional liaison and cooperation. This study merely clarifies where the Court comes from and how far it can go in the absence of the necessary conditions implementing its public judicial authority.

## 2.5.2. INTERNATIONAL GOVERNANCE INSTITUTIONS AND THE RULE OF LAW

The extensive literature on the disintegration of the nation-states in modern society points out that one unequivocal aspect of globalization is that any of the problems afflicting the world today compromise domestic, regional and international stability at the same extent. Poverty, armed conflicts and violations of international humanitarian law are some of the problems originating the dilemma of human security. These global problems are increasingly transnational in nature, and cannot be dealt only at the national level, or by "state to state" negotiations. The comprehensive approach of this study considers the symptoms of the current shifts in the international order, including the necessity of political decision-making to find concrete remedies of democratic global governance of humanitarian affairs. Whilst today with the use of modern technology the

91 UN doc. SC/9965, 29 June 2010, accessible at: http://un.org/News/Press/docs/2010/sc9965.doc.htm.

92 For the debate see M.H. Arsanjani, W.M. Reisman, "The Law in Action of the International Criminal Court", *The American Journal of International Law*, Vol. 99, No. 2 (April 2005), at 399.

outcome of international criminal judicial proceedings in a fair trial against a 'war lord', has at some point the chance to circulate around the planet providing the signal of fairness, truth and deterrence, the impact of globalization on the breakdown of the nation-states in war-torn societies are the main causes of serious humanitarian violations, including instability and serious attempts to peace and security.[93]

Globalization pressures on democratic global governance of international threats and crimes requiring the implementation of the rule of law and *global justice*. Such motivations have indeed forced "international governance institutions to redefine their role of universal provider as one that encompasses the roles of catalyst, enabler, gatekeeper, consensus builder, mediator and negotiator".[94] The view of globalization is a "process of essentially increasing intense interconnectedness, interactions, interdependence, and integration across borders, State and communities, local, national, global, and in different spheres of human life. This process is leading to the emergence of one world, a *global society*. Consequently, it is often reduced to a process reducing the power and the importance of nation-state, increasing the idea of a global world ruled by global rules and global organizations. The point that divides scholars, involved in theories about globalization, is indeed if globalization announces the death of the modern nation-state.[95] The evident disintegration of the nation-states in conflict and post-conflict situations, or so defined in the policy circles 'failed' States, causes a crisis of the governance institutions and public powers at domestic level in the majority of such situations. Such breakdowns at national level challenge the tools of democratic governance at international level for the preservation of security and their competence to rehabilitate law and order complementing such complex domestic realities. This study does not discuss such globalization theories. They have been extensively dealt by relevant literature but emphasizes however, the required process of democratization of global governance institutions fostering peace, justice and security towards further definition of their complementary roles and responsibilities one another.[96]

---

93 For some useful research findings on the impact of globalization on the nation-states, including the role and evolution of universal organizations in democratic governance processes in the last decade, see G. Bertucci, A. Alberti, 'Globalization and its impact on the State: The role of the State in domestic and international governance' in *World Public Sector Report: Globalization and the State*, ST/ESA/PAD/SER.26, 2001, United Nations, Department of Economic and Social Affairs, at 29, accessible at: http://unpan1.un.org/intradoc/groups/public/documents/UN/UNPAN012761.pdf.

94 See A. Bertucci, *supra*.

95 See A. M. Slaughter, *A New World Order: Government Networks and the Disaggregated State*, (2004). For the debate see also K. Choudhary, 'Globalisation, Modernity and Nation-building', in K. Choudhary (ed.), *Globalisation Governance Reforms and Development in India*, (2007), at 523.

96 See also K. H. Ladeur, *Public Governance in the Age of Globalization*, (2004).

The rule of law is one of the most important components of public democratic governance at the same extent of political processes. The basic principles of the rule of law are found in the authority of the judiciary, human rights, freedom of information, civil society participation and human development. The preservation of the rule of law at domestic and international levels relates to processes of democratization and maintenance of human rights, extending issues of mutual concern towards multilateral approaches. States and non-States parties of international governance institutions need to comply with norms universally recognized, while being flexible and open to democratic reforms. International governance institutions, which share complementary universal mandates, have to be prepared to assist domestic realities with all their means, especially in extreme conflict and post-conflict situations identifying the right choice of international intervention on each case, while being able to interact and serve other complementary actors on the ground. For the fight against the impunity of serious breaches of human rights, even non-member States should prepare themselves to such a process of democratization, but is this the case considering the position taken by the permanent members of the Security Council?

The question is whether international governance institutions give yet momentum to a universal system in respect of international humanitarian law and human rights, and thus "contributing to freedom, security, justice and the rule of law, as well as to the prevention of armed conflicts, the preservation of peace and the strengthening of international security, including the advancement of post-conflict peace-building and reconciliation...".[97] The number of international regimes, as a form of governance coordinating behavior among countries around an issue, has increased dramatically since WWII, and today international regimes cover almost all aspects of international relations that might require coordination among countries and other international actors, from security issues (such as weapons non-proliferation, conflict management or collective security), human rights (international criminal justice, humanitarian assistance), development, environment, information and communication, just to name a few. The emerging regime of international criminal justice has its fundaments to fight against the impunity gap worldwide. It offers deterrence, reconciliation and jurisprudence on victims' rights. The argument is that such regime cannot function in isolation from peace and security, but should be part of it for the sake of human security and *global justice*.[98]

97 Resolution ICC-ASP/9/Res.3, Strengthening the International Criminal Court and the Assembly of States Parties.

98 For an overview of the legal struggle creating the premises of an emerging world system of justice in which individual rights will be enshrined in laws secured by both States and the world community see G. Robertson, *Crimes Against Humanity: The Struggle for Global Justice*, (2002).

## 2.5.3. INTERNATIONAL HUMANITARIAN POLICIES, NORMS AND PRINCIPLES

Since its establishment, the role of the United Nations institutional design is confronted with the main challenges occurring in conflict and post-conflict societies and the necessary adjustments required by the international features fostering peace, justice and security. As Kofi Annan stressed in the Millennium Report addressed to the UN institutions and Members States, "a new understanding of the concept of security is evolving. Once synonymous with the defence of territory from external attack, the requirements of security have to embrace the protection of communities and individuals from internal violence".[99] The former Secretary-General in his important report underlined that "while the post-cold war multilateral system made it possible for the new globalization to emerge and flourish, globalization, in turn, has progressively rendered its institutional designs antiquated".[100] While democratic institutional reforms seem to receive a political impasse and peace operations are in danger of systemic failure, the achievement of the UN's 2005 World Summit was the adoption of the 'responsibility to protect' principle.[101] That year, the UN General Assembly voted unanimously in favour of a major new concept of international protection duties of civilians. The responsibility to protect norm represents a major paradigm shift for the protection of victims of international crimes worldwide. But does this mean that the emerging regime of international criminal justice would receive a specific place in such global policy formulation?

Despite the fact that during the UN World Summit outcome in 2005 the heads of State and government unanimously affirmed that "each individual State has the responsibility to protect its populations from genocide, war crimes, ethnic cleansing and crimes against humanity", the parties explicitly referred to the duty to protect civilians in conflict and post-conflict situations, stating that "when a State manifestly fails in its protection responsibilities, and peaceful means are inadequate, the international community must take stronger measures including Chapter VII measures under the UN Charter, including but not limited to the collective use of force authorized by the Security Council".[102] Such duty

---

99 UN Doc. A/54/2000, Fifty-fourth session Agenda item 49 (b), The Millennium Assembly of the United Nations, Report of the UN Secretary-General, Kofi Annan.

100 K. Annan, *We the peoples: the role of the United Nations in the twenty-first century*, 2000, at 11, accessible at: www.unmillenniumproject.org/documents/wethepeople.pdf.

101 For an overview of the UN peace operations debate see, A. J. Bellamy, P. Williams (eds.), *Peace Operations and Global Order*, 2005. See B. Jones, R. Gowan, and J. Sherman, "Building on Brahimi Peacekeeping in an era of Strategic Uncertainty", *NYU Centre for International Cooperation*, April 2009, accessible at: www.alnap.org/resource/11243 See UN doc. A/63/677, Report of the Secretary-General, "Implementing the Responsibility to Protect", 12 January 2009. See also A.J. Bellamy, "The Responsibility to Protect and the problem of military intervention", in *International Affairs*, Volume 84, Issue 4, July 2008, at 615–639.

102 Paragraphs 138–139 of the 2005 UN World Summit Outcome Document.

did not provide sufficient elements, either at strategic, normative levels, or a comprehensive review of existing United Nations capacities to prevent or halt genocide, war crimes, ethnic cleansing and crimes against humanity. There is still the need to develop strategies, standards, processes, tools and practices to implement the ways such responsibility can best encourage States to live up to their duty to protect their populations, and discourage States or groups of States from misusing the responsibility to protect for inappropriate purposes, as a dangerous version of military humanitarian intervention. In accordance with the rule of law, as the basic principle of governance such duty does not provide any additional basis for the use of force under international law. On the contrary, it reinforces the prohibition of the use of force, and the limited exceptions to that prohibition set out in the UN Charter in the case of self-defence, or authorisation by the Security Council.[103]

Right before the adoption of the norm of the 'responsibility to protect' there have been some new trends in the establishment of treaty-based international public authorities which are complementary to the holistic duty of the UN, namely, the establishment of an independent international judiciary dealing with individual criminal responsibility and based on the principles of universality and integrity. In other words, a legal framework that might serve as a deterrent of war and mass atrocity crimes, infringements of the Geneva Conventions, its protocols, and serious violations of humanitarian and human rights law. Such framework received the setting up of the International Criminal Court by the Rome Statute outside the institutional system of the United Nations. Just more than a decade ago, the Rome Statute paved the way for the establishment of a Court capable of prosecuting individuals allegedly responsible for serious breaches of international humanitarian law (IHL) and with jurisdiction over crimes internationally recognized.

Human rights and international criminal justice advocates have emphasised the importance of such emerging regime to help achieve justice for all, by filling a gap in the international legal system by dealing with individual responsibility as an enforcement mechanism of the rule of law. The *ratio* behind is to end

[103] The traditional legal issues that advocates of the 'responsibility to protect' must confront are similar to those concerning whether there currently exists an international legal right of humanitarian intervention in the absence of a Security Council authorization. For a general review of the various perspectives within the legal debate useful previous references include A. Boyle, "Kosovo: House of Commons Foreign Affairs Committee 4th Report, June 2000", *International and Comparative Law Quarterly* (2000) Vol. 49, at 876; L. Henkin, "Editorial Comments: NATO's Kosovo Intervention Kosovo and the Law of 'Humanitarian Intervention'", *American Journal of International Law* (1999), Vol. 93, at 824; C. Greenwood, "International Law and the NATO Intervention in Kosovo", *International and Comparative Law Quarterly* (2000), Vol. 49, at 927; S. Chesterman, *Just War or Just Peace: Humanitarian Intervention and International Law*, 2001.

the impunity of serious crimes by establishing the principle of individual criminal accountability for all who commit crimes against international law as a cornerstone of international criminal law; to help end conflicts, since violence often leads to further violence, by providing the deterrent that at least some perpetrators of war crimes or genocide may be brought to justice; to remedy the deficiencies of *ad hoc* tribunals, which immediately raise the questions of 'selective justice', by establishing a Court that can operate in a more consistent way and regardless of the time and place in which atrocities occurred; to take over when national criminal justice institutions are unwilling or unable to act in times of violent conflict, when institutions collapse or national judicial systems lack of the political will to pursue their own perpetrators; to deter future war criminals by establishing more clearly that mass atrocities will not go unpunished any longer.

### 2.5.4. CONCLUSIONS

In conclusion, some commentators of the outcomes of the Review Conference of the Rome Statute in Kampala would argue "whether the Court will ever be truly universal in its ability to protect individuals from the worst forms of abuse" in conflict zones, without the support of the Security Council. For these analysts "the Court, like any international mechanism intended to promote human rights, faces the impossible task of acting morally in a political world characterized by power inequalities, domination and violence. Because the Court lacks of an independent law enforcement capacity, it must often accommodate itself to political powers instead of challenging it".[104] Hopefully, democratic interaction strategies between complementary global regimes will neutralize such extreme assumptions or speculations. Only through initiating an appropriate interaction strategy there will be a real chance of more public authority for the Court not only *vis-à-vis* the States, but also between the Court and the UN. In any case the Court as an *ex-ante* tribunal is only one aspect of the features in the governance of justice falling under the jurisdiction of the Rome Statute, while the parallel activity of the Security Council promoting *ex post* mixed courts and tribunals on crimes falling outside the Rome Statute is still active, although the historical *ad hoc* tribunals are in the completion phase of their activities (ICTY, ICTR).

The fact that a political outline characterizing the *ex-ante* international security situations in a specific country will impact both the Security Council and the International Criminal Court, the configuration of their mandates in the field operations need to be based on a specific strategy of interactions, including the implementation of legal responsibilities of cooperation. It has been argued that just

---

104 S. Al-Bulushi, A. Branch, *In Search of Justice: The ICC and Power Politics*, 2010, at 4, accessible at: www.almasryalyoum.com.

as the international military intervention in modern warfare has been destructive in fighting an enemy, so also can the use or better say the abuse, of laws dealing with perceived or an actual political enemy in the name of humanitarianism. It has further been argued that the conduct of the Security Council so far has worked to legitimize these fears from States and within their regional political realities. Many countries therefore, fear that the Court could be used by powerful nations to intimidate weaker opponents. This is the reason why the emerging regime of international criminal justice will need a specific role within the arrays of peace and security maintenance, including the States and regional entities which have been marginalized even if the peace and security concerns regard closely their own territories and their own domestic jurisdictions.

The civilian protection duties need to be associated to the emergencies of relocation and protection of witnesses and victims. With the advent of the Rome Statute it is also important to verify in the long term the impact on affected communities by the new features offering participation, reparation and rehabilitation, in other words the mechanisms implementing the rights of the victims. The examples that are of main interest for us are those that witnessed courts and tribunals operating in the absence of powers of law enforcement and in the majority of the situations, even against the executive power, as in the case of the UN *ad hoc* tribunals. As many observers have emphasized, "although international laws and tribunals are devoid of enforcing powers, they still serve a decisive function in forcing major players to assume more virtuous behaviour".[105] In agreement with such doctrinal approach, further clarification of the assessment performed in this chapter follows in the next section.

## 2.6. THE PARADIGMS IN THE MAKING OF HUMAN SECURITY

### SECTION OUTLINE

This section reflects on the human security doctrine and its paradigms in the making between peace-building, civilian protection duties and the links of cooperation with investigations and prosecutions of serious international crimes. It concludes the assessment of the sensitive transitions in the legal and political world order of the post-cold war era and the adjustments required by complementary global tools. It examines some of the national, regional and international approaches governing international threats and crimes and the concept, application and the critics of the human security doctrine. In this chapter

[105] See D. Archibugi, 'The Rule of Law and Democracy', in *European Journal of International Relations*, 2004, Vol. 10(3), at 462.

the limits encountered by legal and political frameworks centralizing human security have been extensively discussed. In conclusion this section supports the idea of an integrated approach of governance offering capacity-building on the ground for the sake of human security and human development. After all, the interactions between complementary global regimes advocated in this study endorse the main aspects of global justice, respectively its *retributive*, *protective* and *restitutive* aspects. A greater and amplified *complementarity* between global regimes fostering human security would be beneficial for their own evolution. It would unlock any political impasse of multilateral tools of global governance, including the universal aspirations dealing with peace, justice and security in comprehensive and effective manners. This section demonstrates that for an international architecture of governance fostering peace and justice, the human security measures applicable in conflict and post-conflict situations require an integrated approach of governance.

The global humanitarian policy formulation and the transition of governance systems concern the evolution of security at domestic, regional and global levels. Security is a concept in transition. The word security itself comes from the Latin etymology *securus*, which literally means 'free from care'. Its concept remains volatile if we consider the several approaches in the chronological formulation of humanitarian policy and law, including the treaties and conventions deriving from them. There are valid reasons to formulate appropriately the different aspects of the concept of security and the interrelation between human security, domestic security and international security. What we have seen in the course of history is that at international level the concept of security centred mainly on the issues of war and peace between States, or inter-state conflicts. In particular, it focused on the question of the nature of conflict and the use of military force. Today, the intra-state failure in the governance of domestic security sectors (army, police and judiciary), their inexistence in several undeveloped countries, and their political transitions are central for the governance of international conflicts and humanitarian crimes. Such failure in domestic security perturbs the minimal requirements of human security and requires both national and international responsibilities which go beyond State sovereignty. This is a good reason to advocate for reliable governance systems centralizing individuals, challenging behaviours in trafficking weapons, avoiding the militarization of corrupted regimes and the mentality of armed groups using child soldiers, which are constantly violating the basic requirements of the rule of law and fundamental individual rights. There are no doubts of the global responsibilities in such governance which wait for further accountabilities of non-state actors.

The inter-state insecurities are also in transition. Although there is today a definition of the crime of aggression, as the traditional component of regional and international security, its governance is still in a sort of political deadlock waiting for consensus. The important theoretical and unifying aspect, valid either for domestic, international or regional human security approaches, is to neutralize the risks of militarization in the policy formulation for each of them. In such context, it is fundamental to provide assessments of the governance of complementary global regimes reacting to a governance crisis in 'fragile' or so-called 'failed' States responding to threats and crimes on individuals. The question is whether complementary global regimes adjust their roles in the current transition of international security with an appropriate interaction strategy between them. In other words, it is important to verify whether there is a common search of human security measures towards their complementary and universal nature. The legislation of the last decade by the political organs (e.g. by the UN institutions and the Assembly of States Parties to the Rome Statute) shows a lacuna of civilian protection measures on the ground while serious crimes are committed. Once the selection of situations would bring complementary international mandates on the same ground of war and crime, they should allocate protection measures at least of the groups of individuals selected as victims and witnesses. Such complementary mandates should work together for the protection, relocation and rehabilitation of individuals affected by war and crime. Furthermore, the inter-state insecurities require the extension of multilateral action against international crimes.

### 2.6.1. NATIONAL, REGIONAL AND INTERNATIONAL APPROACHES

The policy formulation regarding international threats and crimes is an important paradigm in the making. It remains to be seen how it evolves in global governance systems of complementary character. If on one side it can be affirmed that since the terrorist attacks on 9/11 the international community *a)* deepened the legal framework that provides grounds for going after terrorists; *b)* increased the obligations of the UN Member States to undertake concrete efforts to fight against terrorism; and *c)* launched a framework of actions to overcome the financing to terrorist organizations;[106] on the other side, there are still divisions on the multilateral governance of such international threat including the legal problems to define terrorism as a recognized international crime. After 9/11 the US, for instance, focused on some improvements after the failure of communication and

[106] See the UNSC approach in the resolution on 'Threats to international peace and security caused by terrorist acts' which criminalize terrorist activities, UN doc. S/RES/1373 (2001). Including over 16 UN conventions on terrorism and the UNSC resolution on the 'Non-proliferation of weapons of mass destruction' which also constitute a threat to international peace and security and in which the Security Council "*decides that* all States shall refrain from providing any form of support to non-State actors that attempt to develop, acquire, manufacture, possess, transport, transfer or use nuclear, chemical or biological weapons and their means of delivery…", see UN doc. S/RES/1540 (2004) accessible at: http://daccess-dds-ny.un.org/doc/UNDOC/GEN/N04/328/43/PDF/N0432843.pdf?OpenElement.

intelligence between the expensive apparatus of internal security in the country, while its public authorities currently struggle on rebuilding approachable security policies in the international sphere, which have been reluctant to human security, if we evaluate the devastating effects of the security policy of the 'global war against terror', and its impact incurred and reflected at global scale.

With regard to the fight against al Qaeda, the US, under the first Obama administration, opposed the use of the words 'global war on terror' to describe much of George Bush's hazardous national security policy and embracing the White House's legalistic approach to terrorism, defining instead the conflict an 'overseas contingency'. Before taking office for the first presidential round Obama clarified to the audience of voters his intention to revise the prevailing policy on terrorism. Obama made clear he would seek 'to use the language more precisely and to bring actions in line with intentions'. But this did not mean the end of the global war on terror. He only rephrased using the term war 'against a far-reaching network of violence and hatred'. Hopefully, the slogan of such global 'war' would not only change in the language used. Within hours of taking office, the new president ordered the closure of the Guantánamo detention facility which still waits to be dismantled, and in the following days he outlawed detainee torture and re-established the binding force of the Geneva Conventions on the US. The new president also went on Arab television to begin reversing the perception that the US is engaged in a conflict against all Muslims or Islam, and announced that the US has 'a stake in the well-being of the Muslim world'. The new president declared, too, that his administration would refrain from using the familiar Bush phrase 'global war on terror', but maintained that it 'is very important to recognize that the US has a battle or a war against some terrorist organizations'. Obama's words and actions aimed to puncture the inflated drama that has characterized international relations' scholarship and literature on peace and security studies. Rather than 'a battle to the death between the forces of good and evil' as expressed by his predecessor, the war was to become 'a human-sized conflict between States pledged to act in accordance with agreed rules of warfare and a reasonably well-defined adversary'.[107]

Such new approach however, would currently lack of concrete actions taking in considerations international governance institutions able to take the lead on such global security issues, influencing the deterrence of targets by the adversary at global scale, namely the UN and the Rome Statute institutions. The multilateral perspective of such actions is still not measurable. The UN premises for instance, are a constant target worldwide of attacks in the last couple of decades. Instead,

---

107 See the President Obama's Speech, *A New Beginning*, Cairo University, Egypt, June 4 2009, accessible at: www.whitehouse.gov/the_press_office/Remarks-by-the-President-at-Cairo-University-6-04-09 See also L. van den Herik, N. Schrijver (eds.), *Counter-terrorism Strategies in a Fragmented International Legal Order. Meeting the Challenges*, CUP, 2013.

according to former US Secretary of Defense Robert Gates 'president Obama has made it clear that the situation in Afghanistan should be a top overseas military priority. The ideology the US face was incubated there when Afghanistan became a 'failed' State, and the extremists have largely returned their attention to that region in the wake of their reversals in Iraq. As we have seen from attacks across the globe, on 9/11 and afterwards, the danger reaches far beyond the borders of Afghanistan or Pakistan'. The consequence being NATO's main role in Afghanistan, pressuring again its allies through its UN-mandated International Security Assistance Force (ISAF) which for some analysts became a protectorate of the corrupted Afghan State.[108] So said, if we try to measure the accomplishments of importing democracy in the region, delusion would be the right word.

The situation of terrorist recruitment training in Yemen, the situation in Afghanistan and the struggle for other countries in the region not to become a new refuge for Al-Qaeda (as the jihadists' franchise in the impoverished Arabian peninsula which urge new attacks against Western targets), is a matter of mutual concern and needs an international approach, with a detailed jurisdiction, intelligence and resources. As Galtung asserts, on the necessity of policy change needed on terrorism, in his article *"To End Terrorism, End State Terrorism"*, he explains that "Hitler's success can be explained by the humiliating 1919 Versailles treaty, which called Germany alone responsible for WWI and imposed huge reparations for 50 years. Of course, nothing can justify what Hitler did. Understanding is not forgiving. But without understanding, we are condemned to repeat history".[109] In the Middle East civilians are expressing on their own the readiness and the courage for a democratic change, against the autocracy and dictatorship of lasting criminal regimes. They need solidarity and support during and after such difficult political transitions. In other words, they will deserve to

---

108 For an overview of the US military strategies in the region, see R. Gates, 'Submitted Statement to the Senate Armed Services Committee' January 27, 2009, accessible at: http://armed-services.senate.gov/statemnt/2009/January/Gates%2001-27-09.pdf For an extensive political analysis challenging the US policy on terrorism since Clinton's administration, later Bush and currently Obama, and the quest of the global war on terror as a military strategy, see A. Zalman, J. Clarke, 'The Global War on Terror: A Narrative in Need of a Rewrite', 2009, 2 *Ethics & International Affairs* Vol. 23, accessible at: www.cceia.org/resources/journal/23_2/essays/002#_footnote16 For an analysis of the statements of President's Obama released to the media and his communication strategy adjusting policy wordings, see L. C. Baldor, 'Obama: US Choosing Words Carefully in Terror War', *Associated Press*, 2009, February 3, accessible at: http://abcnews.go.com/Politics/wireStory?id=6798802 For scholars' views considering the war on terror as a symptom of current shifts in the international order shaped by globalization, rather than as a consequence of political decision-making, see P. Bobbitt, *Terror and Consent: The Wars of the Twenty-First Century*, (2008). For an early historical perspectives analyzing the roots of the resentments that dominate the Islamic world today and that are increasingly being expressed in acts of terrorism, see B. Lewis, *The Crisis of Islam: Holy War and Unholy Terror*, (2004).

109 See J. Galtung, D. Fisher, To End Terrorism, End State Terrorism, in Transcend Research Institute, 2002, accessible at: www.transcend.org/tri/.

raise their voice in domestic governance. But are we really able and prepared to provide tools and assistance to raise their domestic governance? Or weapons and military arsenals would remain the only exchange and option?

After the multiplicity of terrorist attacks in western societies, Galtung addressed important issues for policy makers in the US which are still on the table considering the failure of current national security and intelligence in the US to prevent such attacks. Galtung clarifies that "there are serious flaws in foreign policy formulations, however well intended. We create enemies through our insensitivity to the basic needs of the peoples around the world, including their religious sensitivities. Suggesting democratic policy steps to the US, Galtung clearly highlights to "withdraw the military bases from Saudi Arabia; recognize Palestine as a State; enter into dialogue with Iraq to identify solvable conflicts; resolve the tensions with Iran; pull out militarily and economically from Afghanistan; stop the military interventions and reconcile with the victims". With such resolutions Galtung clarifies that the same day such actions would be taken by the decision-makers "1.3 billion Muslims would embrace America; and the few terrorists left would have no water in which to swim. It would take a speech-writer of half an hour, and ten minutes to deliver it; as opposed to, say $60 billion for the Afghanistan operation. This is not easy for the national security policy, says Galtung, "but the benefits would be immeasurable".[110] While this may be somewhat considered as a demagogical assessment, it clearly suggests that the solution must be shown by multilateral actions in contrast with unilateral interests and national security approaches, which have resulted to be inappropriate in the policy formulations and resulted in devastating consequences at national, regional and international levels.

### 2.6.2. THE GOVERNANCE OF INTERNATIONAL THREATS AND CRIMES

In theory, the role of international criminal justice has also the potential to play an important role in the realm of terrorism and organized crime. For such

[110] With a very pragmatic approach in his peace study work, Galtung underlines that the State system is yielding to regionalization and globalization. State foreign policies can no longer be based on (dominant) nation interests only, but have to be aligned with regional and nature-human-global interests towards action for peace, education and training for peace, dissemination of knowledge for peace, based on research which goes beyond empirical and critical studies of past and present, into constructive studies of the future, focusing on problems of peace studies proposing concrete actions. For suggestions to policy maker on terrorism see J. Galtung, D. Fisher, *To End Terrorism, End State Terrorism,* in Transcend Research Institute, 2002, accessible at: www.transcend.org/tri/ For the debate on globalization policy issues see J. Galtung, B. Gosovic, A. Khosla, A. Zammit, 'The Millennium Development Goals: Missing Goals and Mistaken Policies' in *MDGs: A Costly Diversion from the Road to Sustainable Development,* 2008, 20 at 37, accessible at: www.transcend.org/tri/downloads/the_mill.pdf.

governance the policy making of the permanent members of the Security Council does not seem to be appealing, however, the interaction between threats and crimes can surely serve for the maintenance of peace and security globally under important conditions of multilateral governance. In addition to the legal, political and jurisdictional obstacles in the definition of urgent threats, waiting to be internationally recognized as serious crimes, such as terrorism, the international community will need to take concrete strategic steps preserving democratic governance towards an institutional design of global interactions between complementary mandates, which will need to share intelligence, resources and best practices in their respective fields of expertise, which are without any doubt complementary. In 2010, the States Parties to the Rome Statute institutions met for the possible adoption of some provisions in the Rome Statute defining the crime of aggression and reviewed the transitional provision in Article 124 of the Rome Statute. A proposal has been tabled by the Belgian delegation regarding the addition of the use of specific weapons to the definition of War Crimes in Article 8. A proposal offered by the Netherlands, in accordance with 'Resolution E' regarding the adoption of the crime of terrorism as a distinct crime under the Rome Statute, has been addressed to the Assembly of the States Parties to the Rome Statute. Trinidad and Tobago has put forward a proposal on the crime of international drug trafficking for inclusion in Article 5, which concern also proposals received regarding terrorism.[111] For such global threats in the way of being defined as international crimes the jurisdiction of the Court has not been considered by the Assembly of the State Parties to the Rome Statute, and the discussions are on-going. This is the sign that the political organs are well aware of the gaps in such governance. After all, without political convergence, systemic change, and a reliable structure of cooperation, the current architecture would not be ready to deal with any extension of the Court's jurisdiction. As previously discussed, the same view is also applicable to the crime of aggression, including terrorism and the use of weapons of mass destruction.

The priority would be first to challenge the approach of policy making on such sensitive issues. Nobody knows how long this process will take. Since the beginning of the new century persistent terrorist activities (9/11 in the US, 2004 in Madrid and attacks in some other parts of the world) forced the UN General Assembly to maintain its focus on the ways to eliminate the scourge of international terrorism, stressing the need of a multilateral approach for the suppression of such crimes. Over the past decade, terrorism has been a global challenge underscoring the imperative of effective multilateralism. The literature and the views of scholars

[111] See the reports of the Review Conference in Kampala, 11/02/2011: RC/11, annex IV, Report of the Working Group on other amendments; RC/WGOA/1/Rev.2, Draft resolution amending article 8 of the Rome Statute; RC/WGOA/2, Draft resolution on article 124 of the Rome Statute, accessible at: www.icc-cpi.int/en_menus/asp/reviewconference/Pages/review%20conference.aspx#officialdoc.

also highlight the weaknesses of multilateralism in its current form. The so-called 'war on terror' needs a different approach. In my view, even the word "war" has been indeed inappropriate since the beginning of such policy formulation.[112]

The concept of 'effective multilateralism' emerged as the basic doctrinal foundation of the EU deliberations in the past decade. Since 2003, it has also been the basis for the EU's external relations, with the aim of expressing the global need for effective international institutions and decisive international action. In order to offer an updated version of the implementation necessary by governments of the legislative instruments listed in the Declaration on terrorism of the European Council of 25 March 2004, and subsequent major instruments identified by the United Nations, the EU Counter-Terrorism Coordinator, Gilles de Kerchove addressed a couple of years ago to the European Council, the document in the context of an EU Action Plan on combating Terrorism. The first version of the EU Action Plan to Combat Terrorism is contained in 7233/1/07 REV 1. This report is a response to the European Council's request to the EU Counter-Terrorism Coordinator for a report every six months on the implementation of the Action Plan to combat terrorism adopted in June 2004. In 2005, the EU decision-makers established a high level political dialogue on counter-terrorism, between the European Council, the Parliament and the Commission, meeting once per EU Presidency to ensure inter-institutional governance on these sensitive security threats. The main strategic commitment of the EU is based on the political determination "to combat terrorism globally, while respecting human rights, and make Europe safer, allowing its citizens to live in an area of freedom, security and justice". The strategic elements characterizing the EU policy are "prevent, protect, pursue, and respond".[113] Although such policy developments as global threat, it is still not possible to refer to terrorism as a crime under the Rome Statute and international law. It remains to be seen whether such policy formulations at European level would help. Limited as it is at regional scale. Multilateralism is in any case the key and complementary regimes have a specific call, which requires further efforts in order to reach the global dimensions.

---

112 For valid contributions on such debate see H. Duffy, "Harmony or Conflict? The interplay between human rights and humanitarian law in the fight against terrorism", in L. van den Herik, N. Schrijver (eds.), *Counter-terrorism Strategies in a Fragmented International Legal Order. Meeting the Challenges*, CUP, 2013.

113 For a detailed overview of the EU Counter-Terrorism Strategy established since 2005, see 14469/4/05 REV 4, accessible at: http://register.consilium.eu.int/pdf/en/05/st14/st14469-re04.en05.pdf For an updated overview of concrete actions to be fulfilled by EU delegations at legal and policy level on the implementation of the Strategy and Action Plan to Combat Terrorism, see last Report 9715/1/09 REV 1 accessible at: http://register.consilium.europa.eu/pdf/en/09/st09/st09715-re01.en09.pdf.

## 2.6.3. THE CONCEPTUALIZATION OF HUMAN SECURITY

The short outline of the challenges characterizing complementary global regimes deserves some reflections on the principles from which they derive. There seem to be the shared view that the human security doctrine points out both the causes and the long-term implications of conflicts instead of simply reacting to problems, as the traditional international security approach is often accused of doing. The preventive efforts should focus on reducing, and hopefully eliminating, the need of (military) intervention altogether, while an investment in rehabilitation or rebuilding should ensure that past conflicts do not increase future violence acting on the causes of such conflicts. We look at the gaps between the theory and the practice of such governance approach. The first responsibility to apply human security parameters bears on the domestic jurisdictions themselves, and only at a secondary stage an international community concern, which still struggles with the basic measures applicable *when*, *where* and *how* to intervene. Such international concern became visible during the escalations of severe humanitarian crisis characterized by mass atrocity crimes and after the failure to act in a timely and decisive manner, holding the promise which the States made to each other of 'never again' with regard to genocide and other mass atrocity crimes.

The human security theories influencing the agenda in the new century conclude that such concept of security stands for a 'paradigm in the making' as exemplified by the main organizations established around such policy orientations, as for instance the Rome Statute institutions.[114] For the first time with a multilateral treaty international governance institutions received provisions centralizing *restitutive* justice for the victims of mass atrocity crimes. In fact, human security ensures that a better knowledge of the rapidly evolving large-scale threats has respectively a major impact on individuals and communities, and also strengthening mobilization of the wide array of actors actually involved in participative policy formulation in the various fields of the rule of law and democratic self-determination. So said, what characterizes concretely the emerging paradigm of human security in the governance of complementary global regimes fostering peace and justice? The question is whether the knowledge, advocacy and policy

114 The concept of human security, which emerged in the 1994 *UNDP Development Report*, is on its way to changing the practice and institutions of global governance. The underlying issues of human security, a focus on the individual, the waning of State sovereignty and the rise of new actors, the shift in our understanding of security, the need and risks of humanitarian intervention, the reform of the Security Council, the conduct of complex peace missions, and the adequate reaction to new threats, pose a challenge to international law. As a value-based and people-centered approach to security, human security will contribute to normative changes in the international legal order. For an overview of this approach see G. Oberleitner, 'Human Security: A Challenge to International Law?' In *Global Governance: A Review of Multilateralism and International Organizations*, Apr.-June 2005, Vol. 11, No. 2, at 185–203.

formulation of human security have been translated in governance systems for the sake of individuals in situations of war and crime. Otherwise, what else do we need?[115]

## 2.6.4. THE APPLICABILITY OF HUMAN SECURITY

We have seen that the human security conceptual framework embraces the transition from past restrictive notions of security tending to identify it solely with defensive, aggressive or retributive behaviours, to a much more comprehensive multidimensional concept based on the respect for all human rights and democratic principles. It contributes to sustainable development and especially to the eradication of extreme poverty, which is a denial of all human rights. It reinforces the prevention at the root of different forms of violence, discrimination, conflict and internal strife mainly on civilian populations in all regions of the world and without exception. It provides a unifying theme for multilateral action to the benefit of the populations most affected by interrelated political, social and economic insecurities in the context of global solidarity. This revolutionary unifying concept stands for strategic approaches adopting an interdisciplinary intersection between development goals, including a domestic, regional and global humanitarian approach and the empowerment of civil society. For the UN Secretary-General Dag Hammarskjöld, the United Nations had a primary responsibility to do everything within its means to protect successive generations from the ravages of war. In his final Annual Report to the General Assembly, Dag Hammarskjöld argued that this objective was to be progressively achieved via the international community's realization of four fundamental principles, namely: *(i)* equal political rights, both in terms of sovereign equality and individual respect for human rights and fundamental freedoms; *(ii)* equal economic opportunities, thereby promoting higher standards of living through the creation of conditions conducive to development and economic and social advancement; *(iii)* a firm rule of law framework underlying the actions and activities of the international community; and finally *(iv)* the prohibition of the use of force contrary to the common interest of the international community.[116] A strategy based on human security anticipates and prioritizes international threats, focusing on the preventive actions of the actors needed, or involved on the ground, for the preservation of law and order.[117] The question is whether

115 See M. Goucha and C. Maresia, *What Agenda for Human Security in the Twenty-first Century?* Published by UNESCO, second edition, 2005. See also O. Richmond, 'Human Security, the Rule of Law, and NGOs: Potentials and Problems for Humanitarian Intervention' in *Human Rights Review*, Vol. 2, No. 4 (July–September 2001).

116 For an overview of this legacy, see Kofi Annan, *Dag Hammarskjöld and the 21st Century*, Uppsala, 6 September 2001, accessible at: www.un.org/Depts/dhl/dag/legacy.htm.

117 In examining the development of international law, it becomes apparent that the goals of international law are not distinct from those of human security. The principles underlying

nation-states and global actors are prepared and equipped to follow some of the recommendations formulated in the field of legal and political sciences, creating governance systems based on the human security doctrine.

The centralization of decision-making of international humanitarian intervention exclusively in the domain of the Security Council risks undermining the human security expectations to intervene in situations of mass atrocity crimes. In order to maximize the multidimensional character of human security a strategy of interactions between complementary global actors is fundamental. An example would be whether the protection measures of civilians in conflict zones are currently taken care of, or the establishment of other treaties and international governance institutions are required. Moreover, are victims and witnesses of serious humanitarian violations falling under such protection measures? In order to respond to such issues the interaction of complementary global regimes on the ground in the last decade is extensively analysed. In situations of war and crime only a deep understanding of the causes may have an impact on the effects. The emerging paradigm is to challenge the traditional notion of national security by arguing that the proper referent for security should be the individual rather than the State. Human security holds that a people-centred view of security is necessary for national, regional and global stability. The United Nations and the Rome Statute institutions are based on such view of security which is supposed to centralize fundamental individual rights. The question is whether their contribution to the 'paradigm in the making' of human security is really measurable according to the current interaction between them, including their necessary reforms still waiting to be fulfilled.

In the struggle of shaping a consistent policy at global level harmonizing human security measures in conflict and post-conflict societies with development programs, the former UN Secretary-General and current Chair of the Advisory Board of the Coalition for the International Criminal Court (CICC) Kofi Annan, in his report *Larger Freedom*, clarified that "the protection and promotion of the universal values of the rule of law, human rights and democracy are ends in themselves. They are essential for a world of justice, opportunity and stability. No security agenda and no drive for development will be successful, unless they are based on the sure foundation of respect for human dignity".[118] In the African Great Lakes Region, in Central African Republic, Kenya, Ivory Coast, cross-

human security have been latent in international law and are evolving with increasing dynamism to encompass many of the basic principles of human security. For an overview see H. Owada, 'Human Security and International Law', *United Nations Audiovisual Library of International Law*, 2011, accessible at: http://untreaty.un.org/cod/avl/faculty/Owada.html See also H. Owada, "Human Security and International Law", in U. Fastenrathat et al (eds.), *From Bilateralism to Community Interest: Essays in Honour of Judge Bruno Simma*, 2011, 505.

118 Report of the Secretary-General A/59/2005, *In Larger Freedom: Towards Development, Security and Human Rights for All*, 2005.

related programs for justice, institutional building, reconciliation and victims rehabilitation should be able to anticipate and complement the model proposed by the United Nations Development Program (UNDP), its strategic plan on the rule of law, and domestic access to justice, falling within the areas of both democratic governance, crisis prevention and recovery in societies in transition. The policy shaped through the last decades over 'failed' States is to destabilize criminal and corrupted regimes with militarized peace enforcements before development programs and security sector reforms (army, police and justice systems) would take place. Such policy trends deserve attention.

### 2.6.5. THE CRITICS TO THE HUMAN SECURITY DOCTRINE

The critics of the human security concept argue that its vagueness undermines its effectiveness;[119] that it has become little more than a vehicle for activists wishing to promote humanitarian causes, that it does not help the research community to understand what security means; or help decision makers to formulate good policies.[120] This chapter critically questioned the progress of complementary global regimes fostering the centralization of individuals in situations of war and crime. In other words, it offered an assessment of international regimes fostering peace, justice and security and their complementary role to be seen on the ground in conflict and post-conflict situations. International security relies on political processes and in the long term the tools at disposition by the international community have to create the premises of *global justice* focusing on reconciliation and reconstruction. In one word: sustainability. These tools should focus, in particular, on the transition of societies from conflict and crime, to stability and order. The current resolutions of the UN Security Council contain targeted sanctions against identified groups of individuals responsible of serious crimes, including the responsibility of the actors on the ground to protect civilians. The UN Security Council, emphasizing 'all necessary measures'in certain specific country-situations, also relies on the referrals to the emerging regime of international criminal justice. The question is whether in such context, the counterbalance of centralizing specific human security measures of protection, relocation and rehabilitation of individuals in conflict zones is part of a strategy of interaction between complementary global regimes and whether peace diplomacy would not neutralize judicial decisions. In one simple word: the truth as recognition of the human suffering of individuals.

---

119 See R. Paris, 'Human Security. Paradigm Shift or Hot Air?' in *International Security*, Vol. 26, No. 2, 2001.

120 For a comprehensive analysis of all definitions, critiques and counter-critiques, see S. Tadjbakhsh, A. M. Chenoy, *Human Security. Concept and implications*, 2007.

This chapter concludes anticipating the importance of the requirement of an integrated approach of governance which is dealt in the next one more extensively. The search of a model of governance of peace and justice as tools of human security deserve attention by the decision-making. With particular regard to the justice responses at domestic level, research findings are extremely necessary to address appropriate methodologies of external interventions, firstly measuring the societal impact of international criminal proceedings in domestic jurisdictions on a case by case basis, and secondly influencing the institutional capacity-building and the rule of law in such difficult conflict and post-conflict situations. Only the use of such knowledge, fostering local adaptation of governance institutions in shifting criminal and dictatorial regimes, would ultimately allow these countries to profit of development and cooperation programs. The scholars promoting such an idea in the context of the politics of transitions would prioritize: the political pressure on governments reluctant to prosecute perpetrators; the assistance required in building legal frameworks and training legal officials; the support provided for investigations, including forensic analysis and security sector reform; and at last but not least, creating trust in the justice system among the local population. With regard to further research required in the field of the human security sectors, the impact of international governance institutions on communities and individuals also needs empirical assessments. The approach on lessons-learned studies based on the experience of other international and hybrid criminal courts of relevance to the International Criminal Court, may only be useful in some areas and might result partly to be insufficient, considering that the Court's challenges "are and will remain unique".[121]

---

121 For an overview of the US foreign policy orientations provided by the Council on Foreign Relations, see D. Kaye, *Justice Beyond The Hague. Supporting the Prosecution of International Crimes in National Courts,* Council on Foreign Relations Press, June 2011. This report provides important insights into the strengths and limitations of current international justice mechanisms. It makes a clear case for increasing support to national legal systems and outlines a variety of ways that the US government can improve and coordinate its aid with others. While there will always be a place for international courts in countries that cannot or will not prosecute perpetrators themselves, this Council Special Report argues that domestic systems can and should play a more meaningful role, the report is accessible at: www.cfr.org/international-criminal-courts-and-tribunals/justice-beyond-hague/p25119?co=C009603 See also G. Boas, G. Oosthuizen, 'Suggestions for Future Lessons-Learned Studies: The Experience of Other International and Hybrid Criminal Courts of Relevance to the International Criminal Court', January 2010, *International Criminal Law Services*, at 1, accessible at: www.icisfoundation.org.

# 3. THE GOVERNANCE OF PEACE AND JUSTICE AS TOOLS OF HUMAN SECURITY

## PRELIMINARY REMARKS

The previous chapter wanted to shed some light on the transition of global regulatory frameworks fostering human security. It clarified the construction, meaning and subject matter of global regimes of legal and political nature dealing with international threats and crimes. It offered some background information of the emerging regime of international criminal justice and the foundation of its jurisdiction. It examined the normative and policy orientations of human security based on both the rule of international law and world politics. It focused on the paradigm shift of complementarity between global regimes and the interpretation of its meanings. It attempted to clarify the challenges and opportunities and the expectations of human security from different perspectives and views. It indicated that in order to progress with the architecture of governance fostering human security in conflict and post-conflict situations multilateral engagements are absolutely required. The multilateral perspective should expand further the principle of complementarity between statehood, sovereignty and the tools of international governance in accordance with the constitutions of the world community. This chapter examines the governance of peace and justice as tools of human security. It wants to stimulate further progress in accordance with the expectations of human security and the policy formulations required at domestic, regional and international levels responding to mass atrocity crimes. It underscores the prospects and the lasting debate of peace, justice and security, the unresolved governance issues, and the requirement of an integrated approach of governance of peace and justice.

This chapter explores the lasting debate between peace and justice and the unresolved governance issues between peace operations, law enforcement and civilian protection duties. It argues about the importance of interactions between complementary global regimes and underscores the preventive strategy of mass atrocity crimes required at global level. It recalls the background of the emerging regime of international criminal justice after decades of political efforts to reach consensus for the ratification of an international treaty, which would finally regulate the jurisdiction of a permanent criminal tribunal. As previously clarified, the Court was established with the scope to generate further jurisprudence after the judicial activity of the *ad hoc* UN tribunals, and among other purposes such as the preservation of the rule of law and human rights. Its potential to become a global tool of human security depends, however, on many factors. Some of them have already been debated in the previous chapter. This chapter recalls the necessity to find an integrated model of governance that would have sustainable results on the ground in conflict and post-conflict situations. Such model of governance requires appropriate reforms, capacity-building and a greater complementarity. The governance model proposed would centralize the rights of individuals, including their protection, safety and security in situations of war and crime. All actors involved in such policy formulations (States, international and regional organizations and civil society) have to take complete ownership of their responsibilities towards individuals. In this way the evolution of international law preserving the fundamental rights of individuals in situation of war and crime would absolutely progress.

## 3.1. RENEWED RESPONSIBILITIES TO RESPOND TO MASS ATROCITY CRIMES?

### SECTION OUTLINE

This section points out some of the issues characterizing the intersection between legal and political regimes of complementary nature based on cooperation, and the practice of delivering justice in conflict and post-conflict societies devastated by mass atrocity crimes. It underscores further the importance of an integrated approach of governance fostering peace, justice and security in conflict and post-conflict situations realizing the *protective, retributive* and *restitutive* principles of *global justice*. In the last years, the unresolved tensions between peace and justice resulted in a long and open debate between scholars, practitioners, representatives of governments and civil society, including officials of international organizations. It needs to be noted that an analytical framework to properly understand the positive and negative effects of accountability during or after conflicts combined with peace processes and peace negotiations is weak and somewhat unreliable. The debate over whether pursuing international criminal justice is helpful or harmful to peace processes during political violence has become a *mantra* in the realms of international relations and international law.[122] The lessons learned from the interaction between peace and justice in conflict and post-conflict societies

[122] See L. Arbour, *Doctrines Derailed?: Internationalism's Uncertain Future*, Global Briefing 2013 opening speech from the International Crisis Group's President & CEO Louise Arbour, accessible at: www.crisisgroup.org/en/publication-type/speeches/2013/arbour-doctrines-derailed-internationalism-s-uncertain-future.aspx See also M. Kersten, "The ICC and its impact: more known unknowns", *Open Democracy*, 5 November 2014, accessible at:

indicate that the occurrence of short term methods to secure peace, incorporating individuals with records of past abuses into local governments, caused negative long-term effects on affected communities by war and crime. The analysis of the UN missions and the activities in the field operations confirm this unfortunate trend in several situations such as in the Sudan and in the DRC. In extreme conflict situations the amnesties on the table of peace negotiations produced a dangerous message that abuses would be tolerated encouraging more violence. The clusters of peace and justice, including the issues of victims, cooperation and complementarity, have been debated during the stocktaking exercise of international criminal justice during the Review Conference of the Rome Statute in Kampala. Such debates concluded that in conflict and post-conflict situations "the negative consequences that had been predicted would occur on peace processes from pursuing international criminal justice, had fortunately not materialized".[123] Thus, are there renewed responsibilities responding to mass atrocity crimes in sustainable ways? Are we finally able to respond internationally to the political violence against civilians in conflict and post-conflict situations?

### 3.1.1. THE ONGOING DEBATE

The complementary nature of legal and political regimes, and the way they interact for the sake of human security in conflict and post-conflict situations is extremely important. In particular, the controversial relations between global politics and the rule of international law deserve discussions between the responsibility to protect civilians and the fight against the impunity of mass atrocity crimes. In other words, the idea of an architecture governing international relations towards a comprehensive international strategy establishing the primacy of the law, while using it as a fundamental tool of global governance, is the paradigm shift deserving attention. This study proves that the political expectations centralising individuals in global matters require first of all the clarification about the use of justice involving the lives of civilians in situations of war and crime, and those legal frameworks prioritizing the rule of law and the universality of their provisions, challenging the criticism of what Koskenniemi defined in *The Politics of International Law* "the corruption of the rule of law either in the narrow chauvinism of diplomats, or the speculative utopias of an academic elite".[124] In 1848 Lacordaire rightly noted that "between the strong and the weak, between the rich and the poor, between master and servant, it is freedom that oppresses

https://www.opendemocracy.net/openglobalrights/mark-kersten/icc-and-its-impact-more-known-unknowns.

123 Review Conference of the Rome Statute. Stocktaking of International Criminal Justice: *Peace and Justice*. Draft Moderator's Summary: Introduction by Kenneth Roth. RC/ST/PJ/1, 7 June 2010.

124 See M. Koskenniemi, 'The Politics of International Law', in 4 *EJIL*, 1990.

and the law that sets free".[125] Arbour would emphasise that "the purpose of law in a free and democratic society is to liberate, not to restrain. It is to create a safe and just environment in which human conduct is regulated, and power is constrained so that maximum freedom and safety is attained by all".[126]

When observing the dynamics characterizing the formulation of international regimes it is clear that the political process comes before the supremacy of legal frameworks dealing with international disputes and international humanitarian affairs. The *protective*, *retributive* and *restitutive* aspects of *global justice* require some important decisions to be taken by the relevant decision-makers, considering the political convergence of expectations projected in contemporary governance systems. According to the principle of *complementarity* and the policy of the responsibility to protect civilians recalled in several UN fora, the Court will monitor national judicial proceedings, offering assistance as appropriate on the ground to end the impunity regime of international crimes. The simple question is *how*? The hope is that many States as soon as possible would become parties to such a system. The accession to the Rome Statute would mean for the nation-state a concrete option to protect its citizens from the danger of authoritarianism of its own leadership or criminal regime. At global level, in the field of international criminal law there will finally be a permanent standard and a reference institution in the context of the proliferation of international tribunals. However, there seem to be little chances to centralize the *trias politica* balancing the legislative, executive and judicial powers in the international order. The Court's presence, after all, does not solve the absence of the *trias politica* in international relations including the killings by dictators to retain their power such as in the Sudan, Syria and Lybia, just to name a few situations. Besides, the African Union is taking serious political distance from the Court. The risk is that some of the African States would neglect their legal obligations as States Parties to the Rome Statute expressing the wish to withdraw their memberships.[127] From a legal perspective and ignoring political standpoints the Court will have to continue its fight against the impunity and go ahead with its judicial proceedings. This section recalls the responsibilities of cooperation between the States, regional and international organizations.

---

125 See H. Lacordaire, *Conférences de Notre-Dame de Paris*, éd. Sagnier et Bray, 1848, at 246.

126 See L. Arbour, *supra*. See L. Arbour, 'The Rule of Law', in *The New York Time*, 26 September 2012.

127 The African Union (AU) has accused the ICC of singling out Africans for prosecution and has previously called for the Court to drop the Kenya cases. Kenyatta and Ruto, as well as Joshua Arap Sang, face crimes against humanity charges for their alleged roles in planning ethnic violence after disputed 2007 elections in Kenya. The violence between their respective Kikuyu and Kalenjin communities left at least 1,100 dead and more than 600,000 homeless. See *AU to discuss ICC trials of Kenyan leaders*, Aljazeera, 20 September 2013, accessible at: www.aljazeera.com/news/africa/2013/09/20139209543865471.html.

Obviously with regard to the collective security and global threats there will be plenty of limits in defining the legal link between the State and the individual responsibility. This must be the ambition of the UN-ASP political and institutional interactions. The Court's responsibility is to ensure the quality of criminal justice, to be a well-understood and well-supported institution and to become an outstanding model of public administration. The question is if the Court's jurisdiction is able to end the impunity regime of international crimes. Like the *ad hoc* tribunals for Yugoslavia and Rwanda, the ICC is not essentially set up to deal with international conflicts, but rather to provide and administer "international justice" to internal conflicts, in countries too weak to perform justice. The difference with the *ad hoc* tribunals is that the ICC is institutionally independent from the Security Council and power politics. But is this assumption true considering the provisions of the Rome Statute such as Article 13 and 16 and the power of the Security Council to defer investigation or prosecution? Besides, are the States willing to find consensus on the reform of the UN Charter applying a constitutional approach, or pluralism would continue as the liberal ideology applicable to international normative frameworks?[128]

### 3.1.2. THE RULE OF LAW ADVOCATES

In this study the views of the rule of law advocates are absolutely welcome. Some important aspects determining the evolution of international law are the policy formulation and law-making process of its institutions, and their capacity-building to interact with each other to maximize the results, and further preserving the concept of international society. In regime theory international governance institutions are by definition instances of international cooperation with legal personality which derive from international treaties. Their enforcement depends on the political process supporting particular sets of ideas and values expressed in political convergence of expectations, legal provisions and normative frameworks. Their rules of cooperation may create governance functions which might result not appealing by a particular policy, political interest and further formulation of laws.[129] This is the case of the cooperation regime of not binding

---

[128] For an extensive contribution and analysis of the legal requirements of the United Nations and the future of the Charter see, N. Schrijver, "Applying, Interpreting and *de facto* Modifying the Charter", *The Future of the Charter of the United Nations,* (2006) Max Planck Yearbook of United Nations Law, at 13. See also N. Schrijver 'et al', *The United Nations of the Future. Globalisation with a Human Face*, (2006), at 304. For an overview of the discussion on the constitutional character of the UN Charter and the legal consequences arising from that characterization, see B. Fassbender, *The United Nations Charter as the Constitution of the International Community*, (2009).

[129] See E. C. Luck and M. W. Doyle (eds.), *International Law and Organization: Closing the Compliance Gap*, 2004.

character settled between the United Nations and the emerging regime of the Rome Statute.

The current paradigm shift is at which extent the interaction between the United Nations and the Rome Statute system is important for the governance of peace, justice and human security. This interaction represents a responsibility of both the nation-state and the international community to implement constitutional standards for a universal jurisdiction protecting fundamental individual rights. The view expressed in this study is that the complementary character of such regimes represents the key for further progress: *a)* in the regime of human rights (rehabilitation, reconstruction and victim rights, including humanitarian and socio-economic issues,); *b)* in the regime of international peace and security maintenance and restoration, or better say supporting the main purposes and tools at disposition for humanitarian interventions in conflict and post-conflict societies (civilian protection duties, including conflict prevention and peace enforcement, peace-making, peace-keeping and peace-building); and *c)* in the emerging regime of international criminal justice (jurisdictional matters and the reference of the jurisprudence, harmonization of domestic judicial channels with appropriate assistance to national implementation of laws, and for the preservation of fundamental individual rights). The rule of law has a fundamental task defining the complementary character of international regimes. However, the practice displays the difficulties in keeping the compliance of legal frameworks based on cooperation.

### 3.1.3. THE GAPS OF THE GLOBALIST APPROACH

The examination of the theory and the practice of international regimes points out the sensitive gaps of complementary governance based on international cooperation. The disintegration of the nation-states contains the idea that the international community could do something about the issues listed above preserving law and order at global level. This study simply underscores the politics of international criminal justice in the context of maintaining peace and security which governance indicates serious gaps of human security measures, among other serious problems of legal, institutional and political nature. It debates the challenges, obstacles and concerns in the governance of complementary global regimes based on cooperation by the relevant stakeholders. The case studies argue about the potential to maximize the results on the ground by using the limited 'arrangements and agreements' between international governance institutions without challenging the primary law. What is simply argued is the absence of a political *road map* to govern peace, justice and security at global scale. In the preamble of the Rome Statute, its members, or so-called States Parties, expressed their political determination to establish an independent permanent International Criminal Court in relationship with the United Nations system. The purposes and principles of the Charter of the United Nations were reaffirmed once again in the Rome Statute over national sovereignty, territorial integrity and the use of force, as crystallized in the UN Charter since the end of WWII. Today, situations in which one or more crimes appear to have been committed can be referred to the International Criminal Court by the Security Council, acting under Chapter VII of the UN Charter, by a State Party to the Rome Statute, or by the Court itself, under specific conditions.

This section points out, among other problems, the unresolved governance issues of mass atrocity crimes considering the lasting debate between peace and justice, respectively, between the political determinations and the legal frameworks fostering peace, justice and security at domestic, regional and global levels. In the complex scenario of international relations, the rule of international law as a principle of governance is undergoing a substantial impasse between the *constitutionalist* and the *pluralist* different theoretical approaches of the international legal order. Between a centralized normative framework able to assume the existence of a constitution of the world community, and the liberal view of the pluralistic approach of complementing global mandates, able to respond to the challenges of the time. In other words, the assumption that the rule of law, conceived at domestic level, would be also applicable in the organization of the international society depends by the relationship and partnership between complementary global mandates. As Delmas-Marty correctly points out "we must therefore go beyond models to find a flexible relationship between law and politics that will make the future European and world orders at least sustainable, if not entirely stable".[130] I would say that in order to accomplish such important goal we need a clear *road map* alongside the uncertain future of internationalism and its doctrines.[131]

### 3.1.4. THE PRACTICE OF DELIVERING JUSTICE

The concern is that the idealistic prospects to establish an appropriate architecture, dealing with the causes and the effects of mass atrocity crimes, in accordance with the challenges of the time, is for many an unrealistic vision, while for others this requires consensus and political convergence about institutional reforms and systemic changes. The humanitarian escalation of *last resort* in the conflict in the Sudan, including the following inaction after the judicial outcomes of the Court by the executive and political organs of the United Nations and by the Sudanese authorities, indicate ample discrepancy in the politics of international criminal

130 See M. Delmas-Marty, "Models of Transformation: in the Land of Orderly Clouds", in *Ordering Pluralism*, 2009 at 164.

131 See L. Arbour *supra*.

justice and its governance. Moreover, the compromised provisions of the Rome Statute between the Security Council and the Court, which give the priority to peace processes on investigations and prosecutions, also produced sensitive consequences in the effort to destabilize the criminal and still active regime of the LRA in Uganda, or the leadership of the Sudanese government responsible of mass atrocity crimes. Among other natural resources Uganda has oil, and the unilateral action by the US to send a few military advisers to fight against the LRA in 2011, has been heavily criticised as the typical resource addiction of the US, characterizing the interests of the global economy, instead of acting under the flag of humanitarian solidarity. The appropriate action should be pressuring the Ugandan government to enforce the arrest warrants against the LRA rebels. The Ugandan government has a specific responsibility fighting against the impunity of international crimes, and if military action would be authorized, it should come from the multilateral premises in accordance with the rule of international law. The US should promote multilateral action against the LRA and become a member of the Rome Statute system. Until that moment, the risks of unilateral interests in Africa would always receive as many critics as possible, including the unfortunate reaction of China and Russia in regard to the situation in Syria, and their interests to keep the Syrian regime in place. In summary of these arguments, the criteria for humanitarian intervention in the wake of regime change in Libya, and the on-going humanitarian crisis in Syria, including the law enforcement capacity of the Court's involvement and its judicial decisions in the DRC, Central African Republic, Kenya, and Ivory Coast, including the new investigative situations of the Court, need an integrated approach of governance.

It is a decade that the international judicial institution is operational, however, no solution has been found in the law enforcement dilemma of its judicial decisions. In regard to the situation in the Sudan on 1 March 2012, Pre-Trial Chamber I issued a warrant of arrest against Mr. Abdel Raheem Muhammad Hussein ("Hussein") for 41 counts of crimes against humanity and war crimes allegedly committed in the context of the situation in Darfur (Sudan). Mr Hussein is currently Minister of National Defence of the Sudanese Government and former Minister of the Interior and former Sudanese President's Special Representative in Darfur. In the situations where criminal domestic regimes and their leaders still in power would use the civilians as hostages, the criteria to guarantee civilian protection measures are not defined by governance systems based on international cooperation. The three aspects of *global justice*, namely, the *protective*, *retributive* and *restitutive* aspects are not satisfactorily fulfilled by complementary global regimes. The links between humanitarian intervention, law enforcement and reconstruction in conflict and post-conflict situations wait to find a place in complementary governance systems. Unfortunately, even with the advent of the Rome Statute system a preventive strategy of mass atrocity crimes is still required. The current challenges, obstacles and concerns, including the debate deriving from them, require appropriate attention by the decision-making in the short, middle and long terms. Let us proceed further with the analysis of this sensitive debate and the prospects of peace and justice.

## 3.2. THE PROSPECTS OF PEACE AND JUSTICE

### SECTION OUTLINE

This section examines the quest of civilian protection and some of the challenges, obstacles and concerns in the governance of peace and justice. It advocates for further progress of the rule of international law to regulate the complementarity character of global regimes fighting against war and crime and intervening in situations of political violence against civilians. The maintenance of international peace, justice and security after the cold war indicates that the international community became soon powerless to the new international threats and massive crimes spreading at local, regional and global scale. In these conflicts the civilian population is targeted more than ever before. Dictatorship and despotism cause instability, disrupt economic activity, and reduce opportunities for civilians. In many countries, bad governance, authoritarian regimes, opportunistic political élites and the availability of weapons have led to weak States and their domestic governance structures to undermine fundamental individual rights. Corruption, abuse of power, weak institutions and the lack of accountability corrode States from within and contribute to regional insecurity. Intra-state conflict not only destroys infrastructure but also encourages further criminal behaviours making governance activities impossible. A number of decolonized regions, like the African Great Lakes, became soon caught in a downward spiral of conflict and serious violations of international humanitarian law. The rhetoric, however, that the Court would be against the African continent is groundless and this section demonstrates some of the reasons why.

### 3.2.1. THE QUEST OF CIVILIAN PROTECTION

Soon after the cold war a renewal of ethnic conflicts in Africa resumed into a state of anarchy and political violence in many countries. In addition, international terrorism and proliferation of weapons of mass destruction remain important threats to peace and security among nations worldwide, including the transition of Arab politics and the risk that autocratic regimes could hijack pro-democracy movements, as it happened in Iran in 1979, in Libya or currently in Syria. Looking back to the historic transition which occurred in Iran at the end of the 1970s, the uprising against the *shah* was led by pro-democracy youths who took the streets. In the end the regime created a closed and an autocratic society. Across the Middle East the common phenomenon is that authoritarian regimes try to stop unprecedented peaceful protests with brutality and unacceptable violence. These countries struggle between liberation and enormous bloodshed, including the protesters' ability to reach the eyes of the world, not really able to determine the outcomes of difficult political processes, which are all characterized by the potential of authoritarian regimes. The approach by the international community in these situations characterized by serious humanitarian escalations is extensively examined by scholars in the field of international law and international relations. They are supposed to work hand in hand in order to advise policy makers about feasible solutions in the short, middle and long term.

If it could be said that the transition of the Arab region has similarity with the events occurred in Eastern Europe in 1989 following the decline of the Soviet bloc, the situation in the Arab region is characterized by other concerns.[132] However, it is not possible to predict what happens next. What is well known is that the authoritarian regimes in these countries kept control giving rewards to supporters and punishing opponents, military and police power, redirecting hostility toward targets in the West and other means. The majority of these countries are not States Parties to the Rome Statute. This means that the Court could receive jurisdiction by the Security Council as it happened for the situation in Libya. The Court, however, has a limited place in the preservation of peace and security as shown by the challenges also debated in the next paragraph.

For many observers the sponsor of the doctrine of the Muslim Brotherhood could intensify revolutionary Islamist terrorism and also attacks on the West. Despite the existence of the risks in such political transitions, people in the Arab world have expressed their democratic wishes with courage and determination. There are new opportunities to combine democracy and Islam but also threats of conflicts of intra-state nature. In Egypt for instance, the power given to the army and police in the transition after Mubarak's regime, requires political balancing between religion, Islam and the formation of the State. In this uncertain context the question is whether complementary global regimes and the political forces empowering them will focus on a prevention strategy of mass atrocity crimes by fighting against serious violations of human rights. These countries will need support in their transitions giving the priority to the security sector reforms (army, police and judiciary). There are moments in history in which the impossible

132 The pressure of the international community to probe human rights violations is growing, see N. Pillay, High Commissioner of Human Rights, *Egypt: Change system that bred rights abuses*, 1 February 2011, accessible at: www.ohchr.org/en/NewsEvents/Pages/DisplayNews.aspx?NewsID=10695&LangID=E See also for an extensive statement addressed to the government, *UN High Commissioner for Human Rights urges Government restraint and respect for human rights in Egypt*, 28 January 2011, accessible at: www.ohchr.org/EN/NewsEvents/Pages/DisplayNews.aspx?NewsID=10688&LangID=E.

becomes unavoidable to challenge political violence. The changes occurring in the Middle East were unimaginable to nearly everyone like the dissolution of the Soviet Union just before its fall. But the power of people movements has a logic and timeline on its own. In the Middle East, the hopes of its people are interrelated with those of the world. In moments like these, it is inspiring to know that global solidarity, in hope and in action, can play a small part in such difficult political transitions. The international community is called upon deeper responsibilities if we also consider the political, economic and social disintegration of regional organizations and their unity of intents based on the policy of global solidarity.

### 3.2.2. CHALLENGES

Right at the beginning of the new century the world's first permanent international tribunal became a reality. Its establishment will be preserved in some form as an historical record of global proportions for the sake of civilians in conflict and post-conflict societies. The Court has jurisdiction over the most responsible individuals accused of committing serious international crimes. This is to some extent considered by social scientists as the result of the 'failure', 'collapse' or 'disintegration' of the nation-states unable to protect civilians namely their own citizens, while for human rights activists the governance of justice is responding to a crisis in international democracy and to the unilateral security policy of some nation-states neglecting human rights. Others would refer to the national security and criminal policies applied in the last decade in many countries. Namely the classic, liberal 'rule of law' concept as a tool for regulating globalization and security threats in modern information societies. This type of criminal law "parades legislatively in the guise of security law, intervention and occupation law, and, most recently, in the development of a special criminal law solely applicable to the 'enemy'. Such unilateral approach goes hand in hand with a dismantling of human rights, first gradually, but now with increasing rapidity, which frequently occurs in the name of human rights".[133] There are no doubts that the emerging international criminal justice and the Rome Statute regime neutralize such unilateral approaches for the sake of the preservation of human rights standards in international criminal proceedings. The question is whether such emerging regime is governed as sub-regime complementing the United Nations system preserving human rights, and if both would create an architecture fostering peace, justice and security applicable on a case-by-case basis in situations of war and crime with early warning and prevention strategies including law enforcement.

133 For an overview of the debate on the erosion of the human rights protection see, J. Arnold, "Protection of Human Rights by Means of Criminal Law: On the Relationship between Criminal Law and Politics" in W. Kaleck. M. Ratner, T. Singelnstein (eds.), *International Prosecution of Human Rights Crimes*, (2007), 3 at 12.

The way justice is governed is an important matter for all of us. The purpose of the governance of justice is to reach affected communities unable to see justice on the ground, to be the judiciary evidence that the dignity of life has been violated, influencing the change in disintegrated nation-states, where the civilians do not have any right left, and even no fundamental right for their own life. The aim of the governance of justice is to repair the harm caused on civilians. They could finally see justice prevail in their communities despite the inability or unwillingness of their own State. For the first time in history victims will be recognized in the judicial proceedings according to the Rome Statute of the International Criminal Court, however the obstacles these reparation programs are facing are also a matter of mutual concern (insufficient funds, victims threatened and withdrawing and considerable delays in the prosecution of perpetrators). The first decisions of the ICC demonstrate that child applicants for victim status are confronted with particular difficulties: children struggle with the proof of their identity and age; uncertainties exist about their ability to submit an application for participation on their own behalf among other issues.[134]

In accordance with the challenges approached in this study and from a pragmatic approach, as Richard Goldstone notes, "international law cannot exist in isolation from the political factors operating in the sphere of international relations".[135] This is the reason of the multidisciplinary approach required in this field to prove that there is a substantial evolution of public international law which has evolved in use and importance vastly over the twentieth century, due mainly to the increase of human rights violations in armed conflict. New threats in modern society allow the laws and customs of war, or the law of armed conflict to regulate the conduct and responsibilities of belligerent leaders, referring to individuals engaged in warfare, in relation to each other, and against protected witnesses, usually meaning civilians. The Rome Statute reflects the positive evolution of international (criminal) law and the humanitarian policy in case a State is unable or unwilling to do otherwise centralizing victim rights. The problem for the Court is that it does not receive sufficient support in the collective responsibility to protect victims and witnesses.[136] The implementation of such responsibility

134 For an overview, see C. Ferstman, M. Goetz and A. Stephens, *Reparations for Victims of Genocide, War Crimes and Crimes Against Humanity: Systems in Place and Systems in the Making*, (2009). See also C. Chamberlain Bolaños, *Children and the International Criminal Court : analysis of the Rome Statute through a children's rights perspective*, Leiden University, Series of the E.M. Meijers Institute (2014).

135 See R. Goldstone, "International Criminal Court and Ad Hoc Tribunals", *The Oxford Handbook on the United Nations*, in T. Weiss, S. Daws (eds.), (2007), 463 at 474. See also R. Goldstone, A. Smith, *International Judicial Institutions: The Architecture of International Criminal Justice at Home and Abroad*, (2008).

136 On the debate between security and human rights and the features of international law protecting civilians, see O. A. Hathaway, 'Looking Ahead: Can Treaties Make a Difference?' 2002 111, *The Yale Law Journal* 8, at 1935. Three months before Kenya's deputy president is due to go on trial at the International Criminal Court several victims of violence that followed

depends on several factors. In the current architecture of the governance of peace, justice and security the creation of a new institution responsible for the protection of victims and witnesses is recommended to the decision-making responsible of such lacuna.

### 3.2.3. OBSTACLES

The problem is that the principle of inter-dependence between peace, justice and security, characterizing complementary global regimes is not applied in the practice. The decisions of the Court have been undermined in many fronts in Darfur,[137] in the DRC and in Uganda.[138] The Court urges an appropriate governance strategy with the United Nations in conflict and post-conflict societies. In Uganda for instance, the political orientation of the Security Council diluted the judicial decisions of the Court. Uganda served a two-year term in the Security Council just a few years ago. According to the diplomatic channels of the country representatives in the Security Council, Uganda had to be the most prominent voice of Africa, as the Security Council focused on several African issues, including *a)* violence in the DRC, Central African Republic, chaos in Kenya and the absence of State in Somalia; *b)* the war in the Sudanese region of Darfur; and *c)* the worsening violence on Uganda's own doorstep in the eastern DRC. The position of the government of Uganda was to bring closer international attention on African conflicts, which might warrant the Security Council to approve international intervention, safeguarding the international security dimension of international relations in other African countries more than on the Ugandan territory. On the other hand, the expectation to have the Court dealing with the last resort escalations of humanitarian crises, as it happened in Darfur, is characterized by the political uncertainties in the current transitional phase of law and order. The African States, under the premises of the newly established African Union, pressure the decision-making process regarding peace and

---

a disputed election in late 2007 have pulled out of the proceedings, see T. Maliti, "Dozens of victims write to ask to withdraw from trial, says victim's lawyer", *ICC Kenya Monitor*, Open Society Justice Initiative, 13 September 2013, accessible at: www.icckenya.org/.

137 Following the referral from the United Nations Security Council on 31 March 2005, the Prosecutor received the document archive of the International Commission of Inquiry on Darfur. In addition, the Office requested information from a variety of sources, leading to the collection of thousands of documents. The Office also interviewed over 50 independent experts. After thorough analysis concluded that the requirements for initiating an investigation were satisfied. See ICC-OTP-0606–104 accessible at: www.icc-cpi.int/menus/icc/situations%20 and%20cases/situations/situation%20icc%200205/.

138 In December 2003 the President Yoweri Museveni of Uganda took the decision to refer the situation concerning the Lord's Resistance Army to the Prosecutor of the International Criminal Court. The Prosecutor determined that there was a sufficient basis to start planning for the first investigation of the International Criminal Court. See the case ICC-02/04–01/05 accessible at: www.icc-cpi.int/menus/icc/situations%20and%20cases/situations/situation%20 icc%200204/related%20cases/icc%200204%200105/uganda.

justice, the governance of threats and crimes, the monitoring deferral activity of criminal proceedings giving priority to the role of the Security Council in peace processes and negotiations, thus neutralizing the truth and the judicial outcomes of the Court. In other words, the regime established under Article 16 of the Rome Statute is at a crossroad. In the situation in Darfur, the Security Council should guarantee an increased force on the ground to protect civilians, stabilize the deteriorating security situation, and follow up on the arrest warrants of the Court according to the reports received by the Court on the Sudanese cases against the leaders of the country.[139] In the past, international criminal justice has been managed by the Security Council with selective enforcement and this still remains a problem, as it did the "victor's justice" of post-WWII.

At normative level, Cryer points out that one solution would have been having the Rome Statute ratified as part of the UN Charter. Alternatively the Security Council might impose duties upon all member States.[140] The point is whether the States are ready to compromise such a universal codification regulating the public authority of humanitarian violations and law enforcement capacity, while combining the accountability of measures of humanitarian intervention.[141] A pragmatic approach underscores the fact that for an implementation of the governance of justice, structural and normative adjustments are necessary. Such adjustments would create the background of crime control at global scale allowing progress of the treaty law on terrorism, fraud and corruption, trafficking of drugs and weapons and other 'globalized' crimes. This step however is far to be reached if we look at the features of the governance of justice and the struggle between ownership, independence and public authority between political, executive and judicial international mandates. The promotion of a 'systemic change' is necessary for an empowerment of the Court in the peace and security regime, with the purpose of balancing powers in the international legal and political order. This issue is very

139 See ICC-CPI-20091009-MA49, *The Prosecutor v. Bahr Idriss Abu Garda*, Case ICC-02/05-01/07 Pre-Trial phase, The Prosecutor v. Ahmad Muhammad Harun ("Ahmad Harun") and Ali Muhammad Ali Abd-Al-Rahman ("Ali Kushayb") accessible at: www.icc-cpi.int/cases/Darfur/c0205.html See, ICC-02/05-01/09, tthe warrant of arrest for Al Bashir lists seven counts on the basis of his individual criminal responsibility under Article 25(3)(a) of the Rome Statute as an indirect (co) perpetrator including: five counts of *crimes against humanity*: murder, Article 7(1)(a); extermination, Article 7(1)(b); forcible transfer Article 7(1)(d); torture Article 7(1)(f); and rape Article 7(1)(g); two counts of *war crimes*: intentionally directing attacks against a civilian population as such or against individual civilians not taking part in hostilities -Article 8(2)(e)(i); and pillaging – Article 8(2)(e)(v) accessible at: www.icc-cpi.int/Menus/ICC/Situations+and+Cases/Situations/Situation+ICC+0205/Related+Cases/ICC02050109/ See also Sixth Report of the Prosecutor of the International Criminal Court, to the UN Security Council pursuant to UNSC 1593 (2005) accessible at: www.icc-cpi.int/otp/otp_events/RP_20071205.html.

140 See R. Cryer, *Prosecuting International Crimes: Selectivity and the International Criminal Regime*, (2005), at 237.

141 See N. D. White, Empowering Peace Operations to Protect Civilians: Form over Substance? (September) 13 J*ournal of International Peacekeeping* (2009) 3–4, at 327.

delicate considering the negative impact of the Court's arrest warrants on several members of the African Union and the Arab League. The Security Council has a specific responsibility with regard to these very sensitive political issues before escalating situations to the Court, or freezing them using Article 16 of the Rome Statute. Even with a serious lack of resources received by the Security Council, the Court delivered its judicial decisions remaining detached from political compromises. However, the Court needs a more structured support by the UN institutions, *a)* especially under the General Assembly which should consider the governance of justice as a matter of mutual concern mandatory for all States; *b)* by the Security Council and possibly by the UN judicial channel before the UN political organs; *c)* by the International Court of Justice which would be the most appropriate dealing with disputes between States and the UN Charter obligations.

In the long term, the promotion of a 'systemic change' of governance would have a positive impact on the project of universal jurisdiction, making the Rome Statute institutions, especially its political organ (the Assembly of the States Parties), able to monitor aggression, terrorism, drug trafficking and other crimes in the Court's jurisdiction. Considering the obstacles in the regulation of humanitarian escalations, it is however not feasible to see the Court's jurisdiction implemented, if such obstacles in the governance of justice are not solved. There are still several limits in the governance of justice dealing with both humanitarian crises and collective security in the absence of a supranational organization and separation of legislative, executive and judicial powers in the international legal order. The escalation of humanitarian disasters in times of war under the premises of the maintenance of peace and security, and the judicial outcomes of serious human rights breaches do not receive appropriate follow up. The risk of such discrepancies is compromising the future of international criminal justice.[142] Moreover, the current status of the governance of international criminal justice reflects the reality characterizing the project of universal jurisdiction between theory and practice. The emerging practice of a permanent International Criminal Court dealing with the accountability of individuals responsible of serious crimes is still too weak, comparing its jurisdiction with the international humanitarian crises occurring in Africa, Middle East and other regions. The intra-state African conflicts are all characterized by severe violations and abuses of human rights and by old models of conflict management. These conflicts destabilize peace and security, as also shown by the Security Council resolution on Darfur, where protections duties of civilians under the R2P norm did not work. Another challenge deriving from such humanitarian escalations is that the Court's jurisprudence will need to keep alive the rights of the victims.

142 For research contributions, in the area of international crime, law, and criminal justice which considers the globalization of international criminal justice see, M. Deflem, 'Review of Governing Through Globalized Crime: Futures for International Criminal Justice', 2009 38 *Contemporary Sociology*, at 153.

### 3.2.4. MATTERS OF INTERNATIONAL MUTUAL CONCERN

The jurisprudence of the Court will need to confirm the contribution of the Rome Statute to the rule of international law and the fulfilment of obligations by the States Parties on matters of international mutual concern. The Rome Statute represents a carefully drawn compromise between two ideas: countries should be first of all responsible for administering their *état de droit* within their territory, and respect the assumption that holding people accountable for the most serious crimes under international law is ultimately an international, but firstly a domestic concern.[143] The Court is intended to complement national justice systems, not to replace them, as the Preparatory Ad Hoc Committee for the Court and the ILC discussions made clear.[144] From an historical perspective, the Rome Statute became operational while the struggle of the international community determined concrete and fair reforms of the United Nations, specifically: over the use of force, after decades of Security Council resolutions about security,[145] peace operations, humanitarian intervention and about the institutional struggle of the General Assembly to receive an empowered role for the protection of human rights and collective security.[146] The United Nations reform, specifically the enlargement of the Security Council, has been an issue under discussion in the General Assembly for a long time. The issue of reform also figured prominently in the Assembly's debate in the last decade, but consensus is far to be reached. The discussions, however, contributed to improving the transparency of the Council's work and also clarified its role by developing policies and doctrines for the prevention of conflicts, managing increasingly complex crises, identifying the needs of peacekeeping and peacebuilding, and dealing with new threats such as the fight against terrorism. Many observers would believe that the political impasse in international relations currently manifesting under the UN premises, would receive a new input through the Rome Statute. The question is whether the empowerment of the Court's mandate really becomes a matter of international mutual concern, or it remains in the hands of just a few stakeholders. The responsibility to protect civilians between peace enforcement and the protection

143 For an extensive overview on the problems related to implementing legislation and cooperation on the Court in domestic regimes, see C. Stahn, "The International Criminal Court and the Shortcomings of Domestic Legislation: Introductory Note", (2007) LJIL 20, at 165. For a legal analysis of the Court's relationship with domestic jurisdiction see C. Stahn and G. Sluiter, *The Emerging Practice of the International Criminal Court* (2009), 208 at 400.

144 For the discussion within the ILC see Report on the work of its forty-seventh session, 2 May – 21 July 1995, GA, official records, fiftieth session, supplement No 10 (A/50/10), par. 47.

145 For reference reports and materials on the UN reform see the web portal accessible at: www.un.org/reform/peace_security.shtml.

146 See *Certain Expenses Case*, ICJ Reports (1961) at 166. See also UN doc. A/RES/377(V) A (1950), the "Uniting for Peace" resolution.

measures of victims and witnesses among other governance issues still require solutions.

In the Resolutions ICC-ASP/6/Res.2 and ICC-ASP/11/Res.8, *Strengthening the International Criminal Court and the Assembly of States Parties*, the Assembly of States Parties declared:

> "*Mindful* that each individual State has the responsibility to protect its population from genocide, war crimes, and crimes against humanity, that the conscience of humanity continues to be deeply shocked by unimaginable atrocities in various parts of the world, and that the need to prevent the most serious crimes of concern to the international community, and to put an end to the impunity of the perpetrators of such crimes, is now widely acknowledged; *Convinced* that the International Criminal Court is an essential means of promoting respect for international humanitarian law and human rights, thus contributing to freedom, security, justice and the rule of law as well as to the prevention of armed conflicts, the preservation of peace and the strengthening of international security and the advancement of post-conflict peace-building and reconciliation with a view to achieving sustainable peace, in accordance with the purposes and principles of the Charter of the United Nations; *Convinced* also that there can be no lasting peace without justice and that peace and justice are thus complementary requirements; *Convinced* further that justice and the fight against impunity are, and must remain, indivisible and that in this regard universal adherence to the Rome Statute of the International Criminal Court is essential [...]

This resolution points out the importance to strengthen the Rome Statute system and refers to the following important factors: a) the Rome Statute and the relation with other multilateral organisations; b) institution-building; c) cooperation and implementation; d) the role of the Assembly of States Parties. The Annex I and II deal respectively with the "Recommendations on the Plan of Action for achieving universality and full implementation of the Rome Statute of the International Criminal Court" including the "Recommendations on international cooperation". In delivering the Court's annual report to the UN in 2014, ICC President Song acknowledged the fundamental partnership that exists between the UN and the ICC, as both organizations are "based on the ideals of peace, security and respect for human rights, and the realisation that these goals can only be attained through the rule of law and international cooperation". He called upon all States to join the ICC, stressing that "the values of the Rome Statute reflect global solidarity and commitment to peace, security and international law".[147]

[147] See Judge Sang-Hyun Song, *Annual Report to the United Nations General Assembly*, 30 October 2014, accessible at: www.icc-cpi.int/iccdocs/presidency/UNGA-PS-30-10-2014-Eng.pdf.

### 3.2.5. THE UNRESOLVED GOVERNANCE ISSUES

The previous observations referred to the United Nations and the Court's role in the governance of international criminal justice since the Court's establishment, considering the referrals received by multiple States from the volatile and strategically important region for its natural resources: the African Great Lakes Region, including the first referrals from the Security Council (Sudan and Libya and the missing referral of the situation in Syria).[148] In general, the exchange of expertise, study and working groups to keep international complementary mandates alive would promote their relationship as expected in the Preamble of the treaty establishing the Court, which is complementary to the UN Charter. The purpose of this analysis is to improve the ways the UN, together with the Court's judicial mandate, would influence the contemporary international legal order on the creation of a capacity-building apparatus applicable in conflict and post-conflict situations. The international governance of justice is based on compliance of treaty obligations and accountability of serious breaches of human rights; nevertheless, there are still gaps of law enforcement capabilities, protection duties of civilians including victims and witnesses, and the rehabilitation of communities affected by war and crimes. The ideal would be that when mass atrocity crimes would be referred to the Court under the premises for the preservation, restoration and maintenance of international peace and security, the Court would receive binding support and cooperation by complementary stakeholders such as the UN institutions.

In order to offer sustainable peace in fragile States, while fighting against the impunity of serious international crimes, preserving and restoring order requires reforms of the army, police and judicial systems. Such efforts respond to the challenges of domestic security sectors. The consolidation of the rule of law at domestic and international levels is among the priorities of the United Nations. In the emerging regime of international criminal justice the States empower mechanisms to put an end to the impunity of serious crimes which also requires compliance and accountability through national implementation of legislations. In peace operations mandates for instance, the Security Council increasingly included the improvement of security institutions and legal systems in fragile States. The wide range of institutional reforms proposed in the UN brought as limited result a new approach in the configuration of the Security Council

148 The term Great Lake African Region is likewise somewhat loose. It is used in a narrow sense for the area lying between northern Lake Tanganyika, western Lake Victoria, and lakes Kivu, Edward and Albert. This comprises Burundi, Rwanda, north-eastern Democratic Republic of Congo, Uganda and north-western Kenya and Tanzania. It is used in a wider sense to extend to all of Kenya and Tanzania, but not usually as far south as Zambia, Malawi and Mozambique nor as far north as Ethiopia, though these four countries border one of the Great Lakes. See www.wikipedia.com.

mandates unifying peacekeeping and the rule of law. The only institutional restructuring process occurred in the last decade concerns the unification of peacekeeping entities (DPKO) and the Office of the Rule of Law and Security Institutions (OROLSI) with the scope to provide an integrated and forward-looking approach to the UN post-conflict assistance. The Office of the Rule of Law and Security Institutions (OROLSI) brings together the following entities of the Department of Peacekeeping Operations (DPKO): the Police Division (PD), the Disarmament, Demobilization, and Reintegration Section (DDR), the UN Mine Action Service (UNMAS), the Security Sector Reform Unit (SSR) and the Criminal Law and Judicial Advisory Service (CLJAS).[149]

As Arbour points out the "rule of law institutions are important and the development agenda has long neglected them even under the heading of governance. In most conflict-prone areas we spend, for example, more money and political capital on elections and support for the executive than on the establishment of a competent, professional and independent judiciary. This is true from Afghanistan, the DRC and Somalia to Guatemala, Sri Lanka and the Central Asian republics: weak or corroded judicial systems are both a product of crisis and a sign of crises to come".[150] With regard to the rule of law discourse in peace and capacity-building operations and as a tool of governance, Hughes and Hunt would emphasize that "although the rule of law is now widely recognized as indispensable to effective peace operations, its delineation remains elusive. Researchers contest its substance, while those most responsible for its implementation, as for instance the United Nations promulgate only abstract notions needed to disseminate detailed decisions. At its worst, this means that competing reform activities undermine each other, making long term success less likely". The questions addressed by scholars are about the deficiencies in how the rule of law is conceived between States and non-states actors.[151] Either at conceptual or operational levels there should be space for more engagement in the configuration of peace operations offering assistance and resources to complementary international mandates.

When addressing to the Rome Statute Conference to create a permanent Court, Benjamin B. Ferencz resumed his speech with the following remarks: "human rights must prevail over human wrongs. International law must prevail over international crime".[152]

---

149 For an overview of such internal governance structure in the UN Peacekeeping operations see: www.un.org/en/peacekeeping/orolsi.shtml.

150 See L. Arbour, *supra*.

151 See B. Hughes, C. Hunt, "The Rule of Law in Peace and Capacity Building Operations: Moving beyond a Conventional State-Centred Imagination", 2009 (September) 13 *Journal of International Peacekeeping*, 3–4, at 267.

152 B. Ferencz, former Nürnberg prosecutor at Pace Peace Center, June 16, 1998, accessible at: www.un.org/icc/speeches/616ppc.htm.

## 3.3. PEACE AND JUSTICE: THE LASTING DEBATE

### SECTION OUTLINE

The lasting debate in the international political circles on peace and justice has an important function for the promotion of the broad concept of *global justice*. It is important to emphasize that such concept would shed some light on the dichotomy between peace and justice in devastated societies by war and crime. This standpoint clarifies the position taken in world politics by some nation-states, regional and inter-governmental organizations on the formulation of the humanitarian policy, human rights and international law. So said, are international governance institutions able to handle peace and justice as the two faces of the same coin?

The tensions between peace and justice have long been debated. Both legal theory and policy must be refined for practical application in situations emerging from violent conflict or political repression. Some formative research addresses these dilemmas through an overview of the legal obligations and the implications of the coming into force of the International Criminal Court on the following issues: *a)* as a deterrent tool of judicial and legal nature influencing law and order at domestic level; *b)* for a holistic approach including sustainable peace and development; and *c)* throughout 'hard' case studies regarding the tensions between peace and justice in conflict and post-conflict situations. This section offers some direction on the way forward to build a future on peace and justice between accountability versus conflict stabilization, international responses based on peace sustainability expanding further the concept of *global justice*.

### 3.3.1. THE CENTRALIZATION OF INDIVIDUALS IN GLOBAL AFFAIRS

In the past, the topic of peace and justice would have been approached exclusively as peace *versus* justice, instead of being considered as interdependent and complementary factors. Despite the new trend in approaching the peace and justice debate there still are, however, real tensions and issues that need to be addressed. The important policy element of human security as sustainable catalyst of domestic stability in conflict and post-conflict situations waits to be implemented. International humanitarian escalations between political, executive and judicial mandates, characterized by severe humanitarian atrocities need an appropriate configuration of law enforcement mandates centralizing civilian protection and victims' rights. The question is whether such idealistic approach would be feasible in conflict situations fulfilling the expectations of *global justice*, which purpose is to centralize individual rights in global matters. Between the sensitive priorities in conflict and post-conflict situations the interactions of complementary public authorities present specific responsibilities. International governance institutions need to keep abreast of appropriate communication channels and focal points, including institutional liaisons. The question is whether such level of interaction is sufficient, or much more would be required in order to maximize the results on the ground. For many observers, the solutions need to be found in the political forces empowering complementary global regimes and such an approach is absolutely right.

### 3.3.2. ACCOUNTABILITY VS. CONFLICT STABILIZATION?

In the wake of intervention in serious intra-state conflict spreading at larger scale, as the situations in the African Great Lakes Region, controversial debates often arise between those who advocate for 'justice' through domestic or international prosecutions, and those who prioritize 'peace' and argue that efforts to provide criminal accountability may impair or undermine the fragile post-conflict settlement. This debate became more evident regarding Uganda, where peace negotiations between the Lord's Resistance Army (LRA) and the Ugandan government took place while the International Criminal Court had indicated the senior rebel leadership responsible for the crimes. The sequence of peace and justice and the interaction between the Security Council and the judicial institution resulted to be quite controversial for several reasons.[153] This situation was referred by the Ugandan government to the Court in January 2004. The Office of the Prosecutor (OTP) opened its investigation in July 2004. Five arrest warrants had been issued against top leaders of the Lords Resistance Army (LRA): Joseph Kony, Vincent Otti (allegedly killed in 2007 on order of Kony), Okot Odhiambo, Raska Lukwiya (killed on 12 August 2006, whose arrest warrant has been withdrawn), and Dominic Ongwen. These four arrest warrants are outstanding.[154] Over the last two years reliable sources confirm that the LRA

[153] Uganda has twice previously been chosen for a Security Council seat, in 1966 and 1981. Some critics sought unsuccessfully to block the country's return to the prestigious position in the UNSC with a two year mandate until 2010. The US reporter Georgianne Nienaber noted that Uganda has been accused of wanton human-rights violations and resource plundering in the eastern part of the DRC. Her posting was headlined: "Uganda does not deserve seat on UN Security Council; it's time to pay attention." Nienaber's commentary cited remarks by a leader of the US-based advocacy group Friends of the Congo who described Uganda as "certainly an agent of the US wreaking havoc on the African continent, particularly in Congo." See G. Nienaber, "Uganda does not deserve seat on UN Security Council. It's time to pay attention", *The Huffington Post*, 1 October 2008, accessible at: www.huffingtonpost.com/georgianne-nienaber/uganda-does-not-deserve-s_b_130853.html.

[154] For an overview of the situation in Uganda see W. Burke-White, "Reconciling Peace and Justice: The International Criminal Court in Uganda" 2007 (July). Paper presented at the annual meeting of the The Law and Society Association, TBA, Berlin, Germany, accessible at: www.allacademic.com/meta/p182030_index.html See also the report of the Office of the Prosecutor, "Investigations and Prosecutions", 2009 (Weekly Numbers) published by the office in the *OTP*

killed more than 1,250, abducted more than 2,000 and displaced close to 300,000 in the DRC alone. In addition, there have been substantial numbers of killings and abductions by the LRA in both the South of Sudan and in the Central African Republic. Thus, accountability is required, but how does accountability work between domestic, regional and international structures of governance?

### 3.3.3. THE INTERNATIONAL RESPONSES

While the maintenance of peace, justice and security in conflict and post-conflict societies has been challenged drastically since the end of the bipolar world order, old models of conflict management and military features of civilian protection duties might undermine the safeguard of human rights, if not appropriately governed. The evolution of the human security policy at domestic and global scale, the legal mechanisms to centralize individual rights, and the interaction of universal mandates fostering peace and justice in conflict and post-conflict situations, play a central role in defining objectives, setting standards and monitoring compliance of States and non-States actors. These interdependent factors of governance can be evaluated by measuring their impact on devastated communities with the use of empirical data according to each situation where international governance institutions are involved. The ideal would be to have appropriate configurations between peace operations and direct protection mechanisms of witnesses and victims of international crimes, while enforcing judicial arrest warrants of warlords at large. After all, the legislative chronology of the Security Council indicates that humanitarian violations have to be handled as threats to peace and security in accordance with the UN Charter requiring measures under Chapter VI and Chapter VII.[155] Despite the new orientations in humanitarian policy and the legal frameworks applicable in armed conflicts on violations of international humanitarian law, the international responses include on the one hand the risk of enforcement practices moved by strategic and political interests of military coalitions. On the other hand, a communitarian-oriented approach is based towards building a community of *global justice* rehabilitating societies unable or unwilling to do it themselves. The simple question between these different approaches is: *how to proceed?*

---

*Weekly Briefing*, issue 6, accessible at: www.icc-cpi.int/Menus/ICC/Structure+of+the+Court/Office+of+the+Prosecutor/Weekly+Briefings/.

155 For an overview of the different approaches between prevention and response to mass atrocity crimes see D. Kuwali, 'Old Crimes New Paradigms: Preventing Mass Atrocity Crimes' in R. I. Rotberg (ed.), *Mass Atrocity Crimes. Preventing Future Outrages*, 2010, at 25. See S. Sewall, 'From Prevention to Response: Using Military Force to Oppose Mass Atrocities', in R. I. Rotberg (ed.), *Mass Atrocity Crimes. Preventing Future Outrages*, 2010, at 159. See also G. Evans, 'During the Crisis: The Responsibility to React', in G. Evans (ed.), *The Responsibility To Protect. Ending Mass Atrocity Crimes Once and For All*, 2008, at 105.

The concern is whether communitarian approaches are currently applied in the practice in the field operations. The failure of the African Mission in Sudan (AMIS) on the protection of civilians in Darfur is one of the examples of the emerging controversy of the responsibility to protect (R2P). Scholars as Barber argue that while the existence of the responsibility to protect has been widely endorsed in the Sudan, there has been relatively inadequate attention paid to its content. The treaty on the founding of the African Union stipulates that the Union has the right to intervene on humanitarian grounds in a member States that 'gravely and massively violates human rights'.[156] In the context of the AMIS intervention in Darfur it is important to clarify the question of "what the responsibility to protect actually entails: for peace-support operations, for the States that send them, and most importantly, for the civilian population that expects to be protected by the soldiers sent to protect them". Because the responsibility to protect, as described by the International Commission on State Sovereignty (ICISS) and endorsed by the UN Secretary General, by the General Assembly and by the Security Council, says little as to positive obligations such as might require peace support operations to actively protect civilians, solutions are expected refining such legal framework. It is suggested by Barber, emphasizing the peacekeeping failure in Darfur, "that it is in the law of occupation that we come closest to finding a legal responsibility to protect, more than other features of international law".[157] This important standpoint found in the literature considers whether there are obligations that can be drawn from international human rights or international humanitarian law that may assist in locating a substantive content for the responsibility to protect. Some scholarship would emphasize the gaps in monitoring humanitarian interventions under the flag of the responsibility to protect in armed conflicts, including the fact that there are any legal parameters of jurisdiction in case of violations and abuses. In fact, the emerging regime of international criminal justice did not receive any place in the configuration of such mandates, neither can use such civilian protection forces, nor monitoring or indicting them in case of serious human rights breaches. Peacekeepers have been simply left out from the 'independent' judicial regime of the Rome Statute. Thus, how does the global fight against impunity works and evolves, and which are the issues on the table waiting for solutions by the decision-makers?

---

[156] See article 4 (h) of the founding treaty of the African Union (2000) on the right of the AU to intervene in a Member State pursuant to a decision of the Assembly in respect of grave circumstances, namely: war crimes, genocide and crimes against humanity. See also A. A. Yusuf, 'The right of intervention by the AU: A paradigm shift in regional enforcement action?', *African Yearbook of International Law*, vol. 11 (2003), pp. 3–21.

[157] See R. Barber, "Reflections on the Peacekeeping Failure in Darfur: Is There Any Substance to the Responsibility to Protect?" (2009) 13 *Journal of International Peacekeeping* 33, at 294. See also G. Evans, *The Responsibility to Protect. Ending Mass Atrocity Crimes Once and For All*, 2008.

### 3.3.4. THE CONCEPT OF GLOBAL JUSTICE

A couple of years ago, 60 years after the famous judgement of the International Military Tribunal at Nuremberg, a distinguished gathering in the same courtroom launched a conference entitled *Building a Future on Peace and Justice* addressing the causes of sensitive issues. The outcome was a political document called the *Nuremberg Declaration on Peace and Justice* which was addressed to the United Nations General Assembly in 2008 (A/62/885). The promoters believed that such document may be useful to the United Nations, its members, including those involved at the local, national and international levels in all phases of conflict transformation, including mediation, post-conflict peace-building, development, and the promotion of transitional justice and the rule of law, and thus, being able to influence the future practice of making and building "just and lasting peace". Although this is not a legal document, it contains definitions, principles and recommendations on issues of peace, justice and impunity, and making peace and dealing with the past, as well as promoting development. In this document 'peace' is understood as meaning sustainable peace. Sustainable peace goes beyond the signing of an agreement. Sustainable peace requires a long-term approach that addresses the structural causes of conflict, and promotes sustainable development, rule of law and governance, including the respect for human rights, making the recurrence of violent conflict less likely. The cessation of hostilities, restoration of public security and meeting basic needs are urgent and legitimate expectations of people who have been traumatized by armed conflict, 'Justice' in such debates is understood as meaning "accountability and fairness in the protection of rights, and the prevention and redress of wrongs". Justice must be administered by institutions and mechanisms that enjoy legitimacy, comply with the rule of law, and are consistent with international human rights standards. Moreover, justice combines elements of criminal justice, truth-seeking, reparations and institutional reform, as well as the fair distribution of, and access to, public goods, and equity within society at large.[158] The next sessions of this chapter debate the prospects of justice governance; the interaction between complementary legal and political regimes; and the preventive strategy required of mass atrocity crimes.

[158] See K. Ambos; J. Large; M. Wierda (eds.), *Building a Future on Peace and Justice: Studies on Transitional Justice, Peace and Development The Nuremberg Declaration on Peace and Justice*, (2009). See also C. Bassiouni, D. Rottenberg, "Facing Atrocity: The Importance of Guiding Principles on Post-Conflict Justice", in *The Chicago Principles on Post-Conflict Justice*, 2008 at 9.

## 3.4. THE GOVERNANCE OF PEACE AND JUSTICE

### SECTION OUTLINE

There are no doubts that the governance of peace and justice as tools of human security requires further political efforts to maximize the results of complementary global regimes involved in conflict and post-conflict situations. The rule of law and multilateralism, including the policy formulations regarding collective responsibility, global solidarity and mutual accountability require further evolution. This section explores the prospects of the governance of peace and justice considering the different views to preserve the international legal and political order. In addition to the principle of complementarity with domestic jurisdictions international criminal justice has been associated to the maintenance of peace and security and its enforcement tools. Its governance requires specific responsibilities, political determinations and legal frameworks defining measures of humanitarian protection in conflict and post-conflict situations. The young regime of international criminal justice can only be effective if all actors are committed to contribute to the universal goal of ending the impunity of serious crimes. The cooperation frameworks offering sustainable peace in conflict and post-conflict situations is now complemented by the regime of justice. Such regime seems to be customized by dealing with a defined category of serious humanitarian breaches, while it is nearly paralyzed about further jurisdictional progress. These doctrinal assumptions derive from a middle ground between the *pluralist* and *solidarist* (or *constitutionalist*) international relations theories and foreign policy principles of States members and non-members of both organizations (the UN and the Rome Statute institutions), which are explored in this section. Let us proceed per steps exploring the governance of justice in world politics between the maintenance of international peace and security, and the preservation of the rule of law and human rights. In other words, the diplomatic compromise resumed in the legal provisions which characterize the nature of the Rome Statute based on *soft-law* of cooperation with the UN system.

### 3.4.1. GOVERNANCE OF JUSTICE AND WORLD POLITICS

The emerging regime of justice provides the moral basis for very different types of international responses on humanitarian grounds. At doctrinal level international 'solidarism', or 'monism' in legal theory, is a political and legal process in which sovereignty is transferred from domestic governance institutions to be held by an independent and 'supranational' jurisdiction. Legally, the 'solidarist' approach stands on the assumption that "the more closely international law approximates to national law, the more the individual has the chance to become the direct bearer of legal rights and duties".[159] International pluralism, or 'dualism' in legal theory, refers to public power held to remain at the disposal of a government authority after the enumeration or delegation of specified powers to other public authorities or multilevel jurisdictions. Such trends in world politics divided the approach of the nation-states on the Rome Statute and its provisional codification. The 'solidarist' approaches of the EU members, for instance, became visible in the establishment, assistance and support to the Rome Statute institutions, as well as towards their relation with some members of the African Union (AU), in particular the African, Caribbean and Pacific States (ACP) and some members of the Arab League.[160] Linklater and Suganami argued on defined humanitarian responsibilities for minimizing harm to the members of vulnerable societies. Subject to UN approval such 'solidarist' States can exercise a collective right of humanitarian intervention when gross violations of human rights occur. In their views the solidarists would have a *prima facie* duty to avoid complicity in human rights violations in other societies. The basic assumption of the 'solidarist' approach is that the 'pluralist' commitment to sovereignty and sovereign immunity should be replaced by the notion of personal responsibility and accountability for infringements of the laws of war. For the 'pluralists' the breaches of the laws of war should be punishable in both domestic and international courts. The assumption of this foreign policy is that the sovereignty of States is conditional on compliance with international law and human rights, and that States have responsibility as custodian of human rights everywhere.[161]

In theory, there are no doubts of the relationship between global solidarity and universality of the humanitarian policy of the 'solidarist' group. The critics to the majority of the EU members as States Parties of the Rome Statute, however, refer to the delay in implementing national legislations including their *soft* political approach taken during the Review Conference in Kampala on the peace and justice debate, and all the sensitive governance issues deriving from it, which are still waiting for pragmatic solutions. Moreover, the EU encourages

---

159 See G. Schwarzenberger and E. D. Brown, *A Manual of International Law*, 1976, at 65.

160 EU Member States support the International Criminal Law Network's annual conference on the ICC and Arab States. In 2007 this was supported by the United Kingdom, Germany and Ireland. In 2006 by the United Kingdom, Belgium and Ireland. In 2005 it was supported by Denmark, Germany and Ireland (together with other non-EU States). Further information is available at www.icln.net see also General Secretariat of the EU, Council Consilium, *The EU and the ICC*, February 2008, accessible at: www.consilium.europa.eu/uedocs/cmsUpload/ICC_internet08.pdf.

161 See A. Linklater, H. Suganami, *The English School of International Relations*, 2006. For discussions on how these principles were debated and/or ignored within different States (US, UK and France) and international institutions (Security Council) in relation to Darfur see D. R. Black, P. D. Williams, *The International Politics of Mass Atrocities: The Case of Darfur*, 2010, at 5. See also R. Jackson, *Solidarism or Pluralism? Political Ideas of the American Union and the European Union*, McGill University-Université de Montreal Research Group in International Security (REGIS), October 10, 2008, accessible at: www.cepsi.umontreal.ca/uploads/gersi_chronicles.file/WP28RobertJackson.pdf.

the group of ACP to be part of the regime of international criminal justice and implementation of human rights through the clause settled in the cooperation agreement for development and trade relations, the EU-ACP (or so-called *Cotonou Agreement*).[162] These clauses inserted in 2005 on the occasion of the first revision of the agreement regulate the steps towards ratifying and implementing the Rome Statute and related instruments. Other novel provisions of the revised *Cotonou Agreement* include reinforcing political dialogue and rendering the provisions on good governance, human rights, democratic principles and the rule of law, more constructive and operational.[163] The governance of justice depends on the different and controversial political positions between support and rejection, either by some permanent members of the Security Council, or by the African Union and the Arab League, including the political distance of the Asian continent. The important assumption in this study is that the democratization processes and reforms in the international system delayed for too long, and thus, the consequences deriving from such a delay deserve further debate in order to reach the political convergence of expectations required. The political convergence found at global level should be able to influence and interact with the regional and domestic realities offering autonomy and capacity-building, overcoming in some ways, the current crisis of governance systems at all levels fostering peace, justice and security.

### 3.4.2. GOVERNANCE OF JUSTICE AND PEACE AND SECURITY

Through the findings of this study there should be awareness of the main challenges arising in the governance of international criminal justice as a tool of peace and security. The absence of police and law enforcement after supranational judicial decisions of the International Criminal Court is only one example of such governance controversy. The United Nations established the first generation of

162 The Cotonou Agreement entered into force in 2003 and was subsequently revised in 2005 and 2010. It innovates with obligations to ensure prosecution of the most serious crimes at the national level and through global cooperation. Additionally, article 11.6 of the Agreement includes a clear-cut provision that obliges States parties to: "(a) share experience on the adoption of legal adjustments required to allow for the ratification and implementation of the Rome Statute of the International Criminal Court and (b) fight against international crime in accordance with international law, giving due regard to the Rome Statute. The parties shall seek to take steps towards ratifying and implementing the Rome Statute and related instruments". The consolidated version of the second revision in 2010 is accessible at: http://ec.europa.eu/europeaid/where/acp/overview/cotonou-agreement/index_en.htm.

163 See document of the European Commission (EU-ACP), Second Revision of the *Cotonou Agreement*, Agreed Consolidated Text, 11 March 2010. Regarding the organization of the negotiations, three thematic negotiation groups were set up: i) political dimension, institutional issues and sector specific policies; ii) economic cooperation, regional integration and trade; iii) development and finance cooperation, accessible at: http://ec.europa.eu/development/icenter/repository/second_revision_cotonou_agreement_20100311.pdf.

special international criminal tribunals in Yugoslavia, Rwanda and Sierra Leone to prosecute those responsible for mass atrocity crimes which mandates are under completion. Judicial convictions of political and military leaders were meant to bring justice to victims and to deter others from committing such crimes in the future. These special or *ad hoc* tribunals established by the political and executive organ of the United Nations gave jurisprudential impetus to the formation of an independent International Criminal Court, as a judicial institution making individuals accountable of serious crimes outside the political realm or 'selective justice' of the Security Council, which nevertheless, remains still active in the establishment of a second generation of mixed courts or tribunals, while tasking peacekeeping with comprehensive mandates in conflict and post-conflict situations characterized by serious humanitarian violations. Such multidimensional activity on the ground by the Security Council in peace enforcement mandates excludes any assistance to the judicial decisions of the Court. In some cases, as in the DRC, the unpreparedness of troops on the ground represented a serious risk aggravating serious violations of human rights, after obtaining weak and unreliable commitments during peace processes and negotiations with domestic criminal regimes.

The occurrence of public international authorities involved in investigations and prosecutions of the most responsible perpetrators of serious crimes internationally recognized is not new, as well as the shortcomings of domestic jurisdictions dealing effectively with such crimes in different legal and institutional systems of the world. The past failure of the international community to prevent, halt and punish genocides, war crimes, ethnic cleansing and crimes against humanity, currently stands for global regimes based on international cooperation, which can be seen as setting responsibilities at domestic, regional and international levels. International cooperation, including the harmonization or integration of international complementary mandates working for peace and justice in conflict and post-conflict environments, are sensitive issues waiting to be explored by theoretical and empirical research in the field of public international law. Further research is necessary, revealing the extent and the nature of the problem of dispersing international responsibilities of States and international organizations as a result of international cooperation. One of the struggles for international law is that when the responsibility for policies is shared among several actors, the responsibility of every individual actor is likely to diminish proportionately. Legal accountabilities and responsibilities are further expected in the current process of legal and political theorizations.

### 3.4.3. GOVERNANCE OF JUSTICE AND HUMAN RIGHTS

According to recent judicial proceedings occurring in Dutch courts about the role of the UN peacekeeping force in Srebrenica, whose mandate was to prevent mass atrocities, the immunity of the United Nations seems to prevail.[164] In determining whether the immunity of the United Nations was in conflict with other rights under international law, the Dutch District Court addressed the standards set out in the International Covenant on Civil and Political Rights, the European Convention on Human Rights and the Genocide Convention. The domestic court in The Netherlands concluded that its inquiry into the possible conflict between the absolute immunity of the UN and other standards of international law did not lead to an exception to the immunity, and determined that it was therefore not competent to hear the case, which could ultimately end up before the European Court of Human Rights. The exclusion of the UN to appear in national courts restricts the right of access to domestic courts. It is clear that the responsibility of the UN needs to be refined, before any changes are likely to occur in national courts on the UN immunity. In fact, as the Dutch Court of Appeals stated correctly, the UN is the international organization with the most far-reaching powers, but with the recent rulings national courts would have no jurisdiction even to hear civilian cases brought against the UN. According to the claim of the representative of the Dutch Foundation Mothers of Srebrenica, "human rights should prevail as it is the ultimate objective of human rights to provide protection against the strong powers of public authorities. If the UN is the only organization in the world that stands above the law, human rights lose their fundamental function. How credible is the UN as the foremost human rights organization if the organization itself severely disregards these fundamental rights?"[165] In this study such sensitive issue arises with regard to the UN peace operations and the role of justice, emphasizing the necessity to redefine the accountability of peacekeeping forces in the UN, while revisiting the regime of immunities which seems to be only at its initial stage and only dealt internally in the organization.

---

164 Court of Appeal The Hague, Case Number District Court: 07-2973, *Mothers of Srebrenica et al. v. State of the Netherlands and United Nations*, Judgement of 30 March 2010. Supreme Court of The Netherlands, Final appeal judgment, LJN: BW1999; ILDC 1760 (NL 2012), 12 April 2012. For the analysis of the judgement see, R. van Alebeek, *Oxford Reports on International Law in Domestic Courts*, ILDC 1760 (NL 2012), 1 May 2012.

165 For discussion see A. Hagedorn, "UN-immunity disregards fundamental human rights: A decision by the Court of Appeals at The Hague in the case of the Mothers of Srebrenica", *The Hague Justice Portal*, 2010, accessible at: www.haguejusticeportal.net/eCache/DEF/11/659.html See B.E. Brockman-Hawe, "Questioning the UN's Immunity in the Dutch Courts: Unresolved Issues in the Mothers of Srebrenica Litigation", 10 *Washington University Global Studies Law Review* 727 (2011), accessible at: http://openscholarship.wustl.edu/law_globalstudies/vol10/iss4/3 See also T. Henquet, "The Jurisdictional Immunity of International Organizations in the Netherlands and the View from Strasbourg", 10 *International Organizations Law Review* 2 (2014), at 538.

### 3.4.4. THE RULE OF LAW AND INTERNATIONAL COOPERATION

The nature of modern warfare is in constant transition, while conflicts are increasingly interrelated, involving non-state actors and including the deliberate targeting of civilians. This has led some observers to question the relevance, or at the least the applicability of international humanitarian law (IHL) while others would see the challenge to have those legal frameworks respected and put into practice by all actors dealing with modern warfare. Others would refer to a sort of 'new law' which undermines the binding character of legal frameworks based on cooperation. In international law, however, the responsibility to hold individuals accountable of serious crimes lies with the States as well as with the international community as a whole. If appropriate consideration is not given to the challenges of the time with appropriate reform, the concept of legal responsibilities of international governance institutions would remain volatile. Another important aspect characterizing such debates is that the rule of law would be considered as the main drive of global governance systems. This is contested by the fact that the rule of law relies on political principles when dealing with mass atrocity crimes such as fighting against the impunity of international crimes. Despite cooperation is a legal obligation of States according to the regime established by the Rome Statute there are still no mechanisms to enforce it. The only formal possibility for the International Criminal Court to deal with non-cooperation issues is to refer to political organs (the Assembly of States Parties to the Rome Statute, the United Nations Security Council).

The concern addressed is how the regimes based on international cooperation currently function, according to the universal purpose of creating a global 'system' of international criminal justice. New perspectives are necessary on the question how international cooperation can be better matched by a corresponding system of international responsibility, which would facilitate compliance and accountability, as the fundamental prerequisite of a global 'system' of international criminal justice. The challenge is still to convert broad political proclamations and engagements into policy, law and practice for the creation of such a 'system'. The dominant principle of individual responsibility of States and international organizations, and the scholarship based on it, provide neither the concepts nor the perspectives for addressing shared responsibilities between States and other actors involved in humanitarian interventions in conflict and post-conflict situations. Now that the International Law Commission concluded its longstanding project to develop principles and doctrine on international responsibility of IOs,[166] without even having addressed the problem of shared

[166] UN Doc. A/CN.4/L.778, *Responsibility of international organizations*, International Law Commission Sixty-third session, Geneva, 26 April–3 June and 4 July–12 August 2011. See

responsibilities, there is a critical need to move beyond such an impasse. Until such responsibilities are not clearly set and defined, either compliance or accountability in the international legal order remain both a distant and complex ambition of the international community and its global governance institutions. After all, the lasting peace and justice debate could only be resolved embracing such responsibilities, especially on the ground in the field operations.

### 3.4.5. POLITICAL DETERMINATIONS AND LEGAL FRAMEWORKS

In conclusion, it needs to be noted that the legislation of the UN political organs is very poor with regard to the Court's presence and activity in the field missions and operations, including diplomatic and political pressure to the States in question offered by the UN. The triggering mechanisms between such organizations of universal character will need further attention in the near future. Further evolution will depend on the jurisdictional progress of the Court, and hopefully on the universal ratification of the Rome Statute. The Assembly of the States Parties to the Rome Statute (ASP), as the political and legislative organ, has specific responsibilities in this regard. In theory, the principle of universality is not limited to the number of States that become parties to the Rome Statute but to the universal obligation of any State to fight against the impunity of serious crimes. As it is understood by the analysis of the Rome Statute regime, universality is definitely implemented when States execute their obligation to investigate and prosecute the most serious crimes under international law at the national level, in their national courts. Nevertheless, the obligation of domestic justice systems to fight the impunity of crimes of common concern is essential at the same degree of insisting on compliance in the political and executive bodies of the United Nations. The issue of cooperation of binding character deserves to be put on the table in political fora and finally resolved in order to maximize the results in the field operations.

The policy approach of some powerful States divided very soon the positions over the authority of the International Criminal Court, particularly on the notion of the rule of international law, its preservation, implementation and institutions. The rejection of the Rome Statute by some relevant members of the United Nations

---

ILC, "Draft Articles on the Responsibility of International Organisations" in *Yearbook of the International Law Commission*, 2011 vol. II, Part Two, accessible at: http://legal.un.org/ilc/texts/instruments/english/draft%20articles/9_11_2011.pdf See also J. Wouters, J. Odermatt, "Are all International Organisations created equal? Reflections on the ILC's Draft Articles on the Responsibility of International Organisations" (DARIO), *Global Governance Opinions* March 2012, accessible at: https://ghum.kuleuven.be/ggs/publications/opinions/opinions13-wouters-odermatt.pdf.

would be in their view a reason of their strong commitment to the rule of law and *not* an opposition to it. Political standpoints would refer to the discourse over the rule of international law, including constitutional and legal matters at domestic level. The success of the Rome Statute institutions on the other hand, is directly related to the will of the States and intergovernmental organizations to support it, either at bilateral or multilateral levels, with the unique role of the Assembly of States Parties (ASP) ensuring adequate assistance to the independent judicial institution on one side, and to the States on the other in order to harmonize their legislations to the Rome Statute which activity, of course, also faces quite a few challenges. The institutional design of the Rome Statute still needs to determine the evolution of the emerging regime of international criminal justice. Such 'contours' are extremely important for the preservation of the rule of international and domestic law between compliance and accountability.

With regard to the enforcement dilemma and the 'observer' status of the Rome Statute by the US, some political analysts have noted that the danger for the Court is to compromise itself with a government that not only refuses the role of international law, but that has also been accused of aggression in Iraq as a situation outside of the Court's jurisdiction. The indirect requests of political engagement addressed to the US to assist in apprehending criminal suspects have been lately discussed. The Obama administration has declared its interest in working more closely with the Court, not with the intent of becoming a party to the Rome Statute, but executing arrest warrants. In any case, "an alliance between the US and the Court that fails to demand the US ratification of the Rome Statute is a perfect example of the risk for the Court accommodating itself to political power, and risks providing justification for the direct use of US military force under the guise of capturing war criminals".[167] Such policy trends will need to be seriously and effectively dealt by the Assembly of States Parties to the Rome Statute in the immediate, middle and long terms in order to avoid opportunistic and unilateral advantages of whatever States, jeopardizing the independence and multilateral character of the International Criminal Court.

---

167 See S. Al-Bulushi, A. Branch, *Review Conference of the Rome Statute. In Search of Justice: The ICC and Power Politics*, 23 June 2010, Egypt, accessible in Arabic at: www.almasryalyoum.com See also B. Willson, 'US Aggression Against Iraq: Historical and Political Context', 1st January 2000, accessible at: www.brianwillson.com/u-s-aggression-against-iraq-historical-and-political-context/ For some controversial legal basis see W. H. Taft, T. F. Buchwald, "Preemption, Iraq, and International Law", 97 *The American Journal of International Law* 3, (Jul., 2003), at 557, accessible at: www.jstor.org/stable/3109840 See also L. Everest, "Oil Power and Empire: Iraq and the US Global Agenda", *Common Courage Press*, 2004, accessible at: www.worldcantwait.net/materials/OPE-CHAPTER%20ONE.pdf R. C. Kramer, R. J. Michalowski, "War, Aggression and State Crime. A Criminological Analysis of the Invasion and Occupation of Iraq", 45 *The British Journal of Criminology* (2005), at 446, accessible at: http://homepages.wmich.edu/~kramerr/BJC.pdf.

# 3.5. AN INTEGRATED APPROACH OF GOVERNANCE

## SECTION OUTLINE

This last section underscores the necessity to find an integrated model of democratic governance between complementary global regimes fostering peace, justice and security. It suggests interactions challenging domestic realities affected by war and crime, and also for the preservation of the rule of law at regional and international levels. It reflects on the principles, the requirements, and the search of governance models universally applicable. It questions the status of the rule of law as a principle of governance and the model of governance proposed fostering peace and justice. There is awareness that while the 20th century brought the development of international norms and agreements, the 21st century opened with an abundance of international law (and treaty-based organizations) but a problem of compliance by the States became more evident. The compliance in the areas of arms control, justice and human rights has become a major challenge of the new millennium for international law and its institutions. The States do not always live up to the standards they set for themselves in international treaties. The explosion of international provisions has not been followed by a complementary development of international institutions able to monitor States' efforts to implement these norms and to facilitate their compliance, especially towards individual rights. On the other hand, to illustrate the prominent ways in which norms, law enforcement, and national interests inseparably interact in world politics, it suffice to think about the US political rejection of the International Criminal Court, including the controversial position of other permanent members of the Security Council.[168] It is clear that for an integrated approach of the governance of peace and justice it is fundamental the political convergence between the actors empowering complementary global regimes. In this section it is emphasized that human security requires systemic reforms. This section debates an integrated approach of governance to reach the domestic realities with preventive strategies of war and crime.

New responsibilities are common to 'sister' organizations such as the UN and the Rome Statute institutions. In order to influence the domestic sphere in situations of war and crime their interaction is important and needs attention in the years to come. Effective strategies of cooperation between universal mandates are necessary to create the precedents of deterrence destabilizing criminal regimes, while assisting national courts and domestic systems for the sake of fundamental

[168] See for the debate E. Luck, M. Doyle (eds), *International Law and Organization. Closing the Compliance Gap*, (2004). See J. R. Katalikawe, H. M. Onoria, B. G. Wairama, 'Crises and Conflict in the African Great Lakes Region: The Problem of Non-Compliance with Humanitarian Law', in *International Law and Organization: Closing The Compliance Gap*, (2004), 121 at 152.

rights (victims' rights). Global institutions reforms are extremely important for the implementation of such strategies preserving the rule of law at micro and macro levels. The interaction of universal institutions complementing domestic realities recall the necessity of implementing new rules regulating mandates involved in complex international affairs, while policy makers need to promote human security measures, incorporating justice in all stages of such interventions with programs and projects focusing on institutional capacity building.

### 3.5.1. THE SEARCH OF MODELS OF GOVERNANCE

Today, universal organizations have an important monitoring function for the sake of the rule of law at national and international levels complementing domestic realities. Global institutions came about to preserve the international order with global norms and values, mandated to preserve compliance by States and non-States actors during and after civil wars. The prohibition of the use of force contrary to the common interest of the international community through the remedy of accountability should characterize the progress of collective security. *Making War and Building Peace* for instance, examines the peacekeeping missions before and after civil wars, among other important issues. Doyle's work compares peace processes that received the UN involvement, to those that did not. Considering the failure of humanitarian interventions, Doyle and Sambanis argue that in order to optimize the results on the ground, each UN mission must be designed to fit the conflict, with the right authority and adequate resources being able to initiate projects of reconstruction, while serving other actors involved in the field.[169] Between such relevant actors the International Criminal Court should receive an integrated position in the arrays of peace and security. However, for such an integrated approach of governance to take place, political convergence and institutional reforms are required. According to the existing binding treaties and in respect with the pillars of the modern international legal order (international human rights law, international humanitarian law, international criminal law and international refugee law) finding remedies of governance of today's international society must reflect the institutions of the twenty-first century, which need more than further legislative implementation at domestic, regional and international levels. The search of political convergence making systemic reforms is the right priority.

[169] See M. Doyle, N. Sambanis, 'War-Making, Peacebuilding, and the United Nations', in *Making War and Building Peace: United Nations Peace Operations*, (2006), at 23.

### 3.5.2. THE REFORMIST APPROACH

The reform of global institutions and a new approach of mandate configurations on the ground are central for the governance of peace, justice and security at national, regional and international levels. According to the UN institutional sources, laying down strong legal foundations for transparent, accountable and efficient democratic institutions is crucial for the success of the establishment of lasting and sustainable peace. With the purpose to challenge policy making not yet sufficiently focusing on such interactions, an outline of the institutional contours preserving the rule of law at national and international levels for peace, justice and security is fundamental. In order to identify areas of interaction in respect of the delimitation of competences and complementary intervention between different mandates, the debate needs to engage on a prevention strategy of mass atrocity crimes including the reconstruction of disintegrated nation-states and institution building, monitoring, advising, planning, and assisting domestic realities in both conflict and post-conflict situations.

First of all, appropriate structural and normative adjustments are the important prerequisites for the creation of a system of international criminal justice. The adjustments and the reforms of modern institutions are necessary in order to optimize the results on the ground. In practice their interaction depends on: *a)* the determination to define appropriate political strategies and objectives to maximize the results in conflict and post-conflict situations towards accountability, integrity, effectiveness and transparency; *b)* the creation of a legal pillar of global institutional interactions and their responsibilities, complementing the compliance of international humanitarian law and human rights, thus contributing to freedom, security and justice and regulating further the international legal order preserving the rule of law as the basic prerequisite of democratic governance, towards the accountability of all actors involved in accordance with basic principles, such as legality and equality in the eyes of the law; *c)* further legislation at national, regional and international levels implementing democratic governance of justice and human rights *d)* and by making international justice locally relevant towards the awareness of victims' rights in domestic judicial systems.

The causes of the commission of serious crime in Africa are argued to be more of a capacity-building concern rather than a law enforcement issue during difficult political transitions. However, weak institutional capacity for effective policing, coupled with scarce basic information of criminal justice systems such as prosecutorial, courts and detention data, hamper efforts to make appropriate diagnostic solutions. The clear indication is a lack of efficiency and effectiveness of their criminal justice system including the main security sectors. Since 2004, the World Bank emphasized the need to focus on the security of developing countries.

Security was defined as a public good that was conditional for development. The main concern is indeed State repression and ineffective security and justice systems. Development in Africa thus, requires a secure environment summarized by the so-called 'security first' or 'security and development' approach. Human security requires, first and foremost, an appropriate functioning of the State. Some current projects aim to encourage greater focus on State responsibility and capacity building to provide security. Such projects focus on the efficacy of the criminal justice system in these countries. This means offering the capacity building to deal with the nature of mass atrocity crimes with army, police and judiciary including the safeguard of victims and witnesses. In doing so, the implementation of such projects offers respect for human rights and the rule of law as key requirements for security and development. In order to build confidence among the public and the political leadership in countries where respect for human rights and the rule of law have been largely absent, the benefits of these actions have to be demonstrated from an empirical perspective on a case by case basis. The countries selected by the relevant global actors should receive sufficient support from electoral processes to domestic judicial systems preserving law and order.[170]

### 3.5.3. THE PRINCIPLES

The rule of law as a principle of governance of complementary mandates needs attention. The interaction between the UN and the Rome institutions is extremely relevant and it is without any doubt a reflection of finding remedies preserving further the rule of law. The concept of the rule of law found in the UN reports has been defined as a principle of governance in which all persons, institutions and entities, public and private, including the State itself, are accountable to laws that are publicly promulgated, equally enforced and independently adjudicated, and which are consistent with international human rights norms and standards. It requires, as well, measures to ensure adherence to the principles of supremacy of law, equality before the law, accountability to the law, fairness in the application of the law, separation of powers, participation in decision-making, legal certainty, avoidance of arbitrariness and procedural and legal transparency.[171] The rule of

---

170 For a good example of such assistance provided to Sub-Saharan countries and further implementation, see the project of the *African Human Security Initiative* (AHSI) 2 *Country Assessment on Crime and Criminal Justice*, 2001, accessible at: www.africanreview.org/docs/background/masterquest.pdf.

171 See UN doc. S/2004/616, Report of the Secretary-General on "The Rule of Law and Transitional Justice in Conflict and Post-Conflict Societies". In this report the Secretary-General invited all States Members of the United Nations to move towards the ratification of the Rome Statute at the earliest possible opportunity. See S/2004/616 para. XIII. See also UN doc. A/RES/66/102 (2012) and A/66/749 (2012). For an extensive assessment of the future of accountability and the struggle of defining international crimes, see S. R. Ratner, J. S. Abrams, and J. L. Bischoff,

law as a principle of governance represents the tool for measuring democracy.[172] In order to approach the debate of global interactions the theory of the rule of law and its necessary re-conceptualisation in a global environment, is fundamental. In relation to global law and its application in new and existing institutions of global governance, Zifcak points out primarily that "the values that should underlie the rule of law globally are legality, equality, legitimacy, accountability and a commitment to fundamental human rights". The impact of globalization upon the rule of law is a fundamental value within liberal democratic sovereign States. Not many scholars have focused on studies to relate globalization exclusively to law.[173] The rule of law in the globalization process is important not only to influence domestic realities but also to regulate interactions between global mandates with regard to security, law enforcement and crime control in conflict and post-conflict societies. In 2006, the UN General Assembly adopted a resolution on "the rule of law at the international and national levels". The resolution noted that many organs, departments, bodies, offices, funds and programmes within the UN system are currently devoted to the promotion of the rule of law at international and national levels. It requested the Secretary-General to prepare an inventory of all the activities, as well as a report on how to strengthen and coordinate them".[174] As anticipated earlier "although the rule of law is now widely recognised as indispensable to effective peace operations, its delineation remains elusive". Researchers contest its substance while those most responsible for its implementation (*e. g.* the United Nations) promulgate only abstract notions needed to inform detailed decisions".[175] Some views underscore the current limits of the rule of law as a principle of governance. A report of the UN Secretary-General A/66/749 in preparation of the High-level Meeting on the Rule of Law was submitted to the General Assembly in March 2012, as requested in the Resolution A/RES/66/102. In order to galvanize collective efforts to strengthen the rule of law at the national and international levels, the Secretary-General proposed in his report that the General Assembly adopt a programme of action for the rule of law, agree to a process to develop clear rule of law goals and adopt other key mechanisms to enhance dialogue on the rule of law. The Secretary-

*Accountability for Human Rights Atrocities in International Law: beyond the Nuremberg Legacy*, 2009.

172 See G. L. Munck and J. Verkuilen, 'Conceptualizing and Measuring Democracy: Evaluating Alternative Indices', February 2002, *Comparative Political Studies* Vol. 35, N° 1, 5 at 34.

173 Regarding security and human rights and the new ways of thinking about global law and its application in new and existing institutions of global governance see, S. Zifcak, 'Globalizing The Rule of Law: Rethinking Values and Reforming Institutions', *Globalization and the Rule of Law*, (2006), 32 at 62.

174 See UN doc. A/RES/61/39, 18 December 2006.

175 For an overview of the current debate see, B. Hughes, C. Hunt, 'The Rule of Law in Peace and Capacity Building Operations: Moving beyond a Conventional State-Centred Imagination', September 2009 *Journal of International Peacekeeping*, Volume 13, Numbers 3–4, pp. 267–293 (27).

General also encouraged Member States to take the occasion of the High-level Meeting to make individual pledges related to the rule of law.[176]

## 3.5.4. THE REQUIREMENTS

The current debate on the impact of the Rome Statute system on victims and affected communities, the issues of positive *complementarity* and cooperation, the impact of international justice on peace processes and peace building, are all related to interaction strategies and to the rule of law at national, regional and international levels centralizing the rights of the victims.[177] Attention is necessary on finding remedies of interactions between the UN and the Court's mandate in peace building operations and the necessary reforms thereof in order to have in place prevention strategies of mass atrocity crimes. This is an important requirement for the creation of a global justice system. The prerequisite of such a system interacting with the UN refers to solving the legislative lacuna between the responsibility to protect, peace operations and the empowerment of the Court's authority in law enforcement.

In recent years, with regard to democratization processes of global governance, a number of the resolutions of the United Nations General Assembly and its Economic and Social Council have called upon both the member States and the UN itself to gather information on governance innovations that hold promise for overcoming the challenges of exclusion, and that contribute positively to improve public governance systems and procedures. Such remedies should not only become transparent, but should foster and sustain accountability and, most importantly, participation. In response, several divisions, departments and

---

176 See UN doc. A/66/749, 16 March 2012, *Delivering justice: programme of action to strengthen the rule of law at the national and international levels: Report of the Secretary-General*, accessible at: www.unrol.org/files/SGreport%20eng%20A_66_749.pdf See also UN doc. A/RES/67/1, 30 November 2012, *Declaration of the High-level Meeting of the General Assembly on the Rule of Law at the National and International Levels.*

177 For an extensive overview of the debate on reparations for victims see C. Ferstman, M. Goetz, A. Stephens, *Reparations for Victims of Genocide, War Crimes and Crimes Against Humanity: Systems in place and Systems in the Making*, (2009). On the current debate over complementarity and the practice of the Court during the first year of its activity, see W. A. Schabas, C. Sthan and M. M. El Zeidy, 'The International Criminal Court and Complementarity: Five Years On', 2008 *Criminal Law Forum*, at 3, accessible at: www.springerlink.com/content/n86h134236147107/ For other contribution see also H. Takemura, *A Critical Analysis of Positive Complementarity*, accessible at: www.defensesociale.org/xvcongreso/pdf/cfp/16)_A_critical_analysis_of_positive_complementarity_Takemura.pdf For an overview of the discussions on the key strategic and policy issues facing the Office of the Prosecutor see a description of the first three years of the OTP's work; (Three Year Report June 2006); as well as to the strategy for the coming years (Prosecutorial Strategy September 2006) and the Interest of Justice paper. See Report on Prosecutorial Strategy (2006, 2007, 2008, 2009, 2010, 2011), accessible at: www.icc-cpi.int/Menus/ICC/Structure+of+the+Court/Office+of+the+Prosecutor/.

sections of the UN institutions have launched several initiatives to support such participatory governance. The same trend of participatory governance should follow the activity of the Assembly of the States Parties of the Rome Statute which needs to be institutionally engaged for the assistance required to the States implementing legislation at national level, providing support for governmental processes and institutional capacity-building, comparative policy research and analysis, information sharing, training programmes, including advisory services. The legislative activity of the Assembly of States Parties including the yearly resolutions of the UN General Assembly on the Rome Statute system of institutions should support such implementation profiting the domestic harmonization of legislations according to the Rome Statute provisions. Such participatory governance need to include support also for non-State Parties, civil society organizations, research institutions and academics.

### 3.5.5. THE MODEL OF GOVERNANCE PROPOSED

Recent general reports on peace operations conclude how failed States can be helped to pave the road to peace after violent conflicts avoiding the risks of going back to the regime of war which characterize international crimes and mass atrocity scenarios.[178] New models are proposed to governments which are responsible of reviewing their policy work. At international level, as extensively clarified by Voorhoeve in his report *From War to the Rule of Law*, the role of the UN and the ICC in the peace building operations needs a systematic 'case by case' approach considering the following tasks: ending violence, emergency assistance, disarmament, economic reconstruction, transnational justice and reconciliation. The UN should ensure that the Court's activity is integrated into the strategic and operational planning of peace operations (peace-building). In his pragmatic book Voorhoeve underlines that "in order to succeed, each task is often dependent on the effective execution of the others". International organizations are called upon to specific responsibilities, consolidating complementary regimes with a result-oriented approach in all stages of peace operations.

With regard to the dilemma of peace and justice in conflict societies, Voorhoeve makes clear that "it is particularly bitter to the population if war criminals are given amnesty as part of a cease-fire agreement or peace deal. This is one of the harshest examples of the trade-off between peace and justice. Distant theoreticians believe that peace and justice are basically the same. Making such compromises is one of the hardest tasks of the diplomatic mediators, political leaders and peacemakers,

178 In his report "In Larger Freedom" Secretary General Kofi Annan prefaced his proposal for the creation of a United Nations Peacebuilding Commission with the alarming estimate that "roughly half of all countries emerging from civil war lapse back into violence within five years", Kofi Annan, *In Larger Freedom*, UN Doc. 59/2005.

which often get them into trouble afterwards, once the situation has stabilised".[179] Peace and justice operations have to meet in the middle somewhere in order to maximize the results on the ground. Regarding the peacekeeping operations in Darfur, Barber's legal assumption is that "because the responsibility to protect[180] says little as to positive obligations, such as might require peace support operations to actively protect, it is important to assess whether there are obligations that can be drawn from international human rights or international humanitarian law that may assist in locating a substantive content for the responsibility to protect.[181] Considering the research findings on the failure of the African Mission in Sudan (AMIS) to provide protection to civilians in Darfur, and of the emerging doctrine of responsibility to protect, Barbers's argument is that "while the existence of the responsibility to protect has been widely endorsed, there has been limited attention paid to its content".[182]

The success of global institutions involved in peace, justice and security will depend on a number of critical factors. Among them there is the need to ensure a common basis in international norms and standards and to mobilize the necessary resources for a sustainable investment in justice. As underlined by Ryngaert "the casual link between international criminal justice and a durable peace, political reconciliation, and the entrenchment of the rule of law has not yet been conclusively proven".[183] In order to have a reliable evaluation of the effectiveness of international criminal justice in various post-conflict situations, empirical research by social scientists is necessary. In the context of sequencing peace and justice, however, it is well proved that sacrificing justice in the hope of securing peace is often projected as a more realistic option to end conflict and bringing about stability than holding perpetrators to account. Such option does not work, because crime would be committed over again, and stability further compromised. International law and humanitarian policy should evolve to the point where both peace and justice should be the objectives of negotiations aimed at ending a conflict where the most serious crimes under international law

179 See J. Voorhoeve, 'From War to the Rule of Law. Peace Building after Violent Conflicts', 2007, WRR, *Dutch Scientific Council for Government Policy*, accessible at: www.wrr.nl/content.jsp?objectid=4143.

180 As described by the International Commission on State Sovereignty (ICISS) and endorsed by the UN Secretary General, the General Assembly and the Security Council.

181 For peace-support operations, for the States that send them, and most importantly, for the civilian population that expects to be protected by the soldiers sent to protect them.

182 See R. Barber, Reflections on the Peacekeeping Failure in Darfur: Is There Any Substance to the "Responsibility to Protect"? September 2009 *Journal of International Peacekeeping*, Volume 13, Numbers 3–4, pp. 294–326 (33).

183 For an exhaustive overview of the case studies contributing to the rule of law and structural peace, towards the creation of a global criminal justice system, including models of post-conflict and restorative justice since the work of the international military tribunals, see C. Ryngaert, *The Effectiveness of International Criminal Justice*, Introduction, (2009), at vii-xvii.

have been committed. At the very least, peace agreements should not foreclose the possibility of justice at any stage of the negotiations.[184] Arbour's suggestion that "we need to be more strategic about the convergence of justice with the resolution of armed conflicts" is absolutely right. This cannot be done by either peace or justice trumping the other, she clarifies, "as in effect it would through sequencing one before the other, but rather by seeking in every case an outcome that maximises both. This in turn requires compromise both sides have to give".[185] The second part of this work offers an in-depth analysis of complementary global institutions and the politics of justice. Particularly, between the responsibility to protect civilians and the fight against the impunity of international crimes, which should progress towards the implementation of human security measures advocated in this study.

## 3.6. CONCLUDING REMARKS

It is now time to summarize and conclude the first part of this study dealing with the dilemma of human security and the quest of complementary global regimes fostering it. It can be concluded that human security requires an integrated approach of governance of international regimes of complementary character dealing with international criminal justice and peace enforcement, civilian protection duties and the responsibility to protect civilians, and the rule of international law and comlementarity with domestic jurisdictions. War and crime are frequently manifesting in modern societies. The danger is constantly what history defines as a repetition of the spiral of war, if no action will influence domestic and international criminal regimes. There is no chance of achieving peace without justice. After Rwanda we are still witnessing to genocide, alleged crimes against humanity, crimes of war and extreme violence against civilians during difficult political transitions. Extreme tyranny and dysfunction of power bring both civil society and institutions to refer situations where the dignity of life of the human being seems to be forgotten. The international community is deeply concerned by the chaos characterizing modern societies, this considering the large regional inter-state conflicts which represent a grave threat to peace and security. Human rights offences are presently taking place in the Middle East, Africa, South America,[186] Asia, and even in some parts of Europe, with the

---

184 See for a very useful overview of fact-findings, informing the debate on *justice v. peace* specifically over accountability and peace, Human Rights Watch, *Selling Justice Short. Why Accountability Matters for Peace*, Report July 2009, accessible at: www.hrw.org.

185 See L. Arbour, *Doctrines Derailed?: Internationalism's Uncertain Future*, Global Briefing 2013 opening speech from the International Crisis Group's President & CEO Louise Arbour, 28 Oct 2013, accessible at: www.crisisgroup.org/en/publication-type/speeches/2013/arbour-doctrines-derailed-internationalism-s-uncertain-future.aspx.

186 See Human Rights Watch, *Child Soldier Global Report 2010*, Bolivia, Colombia, Ecuador, Chile, Paraguay, Peru, accessible at: http://hrw.org/doc?t=south_america&document_limit=300,20.

Security Council politicizing intervention with resolutions creating merely some *ad hoc* tribunals under its own regime of selective justice which started decades ago.

At the beginning of the 21st century some critical developments took place and suggested that the world was getting ready to make individuals accountable for violations of human rights. Ethnic and religious micro-conflicts, aggression between nations, crises of domestic governance systems, constitutional disregarding of regional and global organizations, new threats to peace and security, and severe violation of international humanitarian law, are some of the fundamental causes and effects of international crimes. Providing *retributive* and *restorative* justice after violent conflicts has received more attention by the international community. Since 1945 there have been some 250 conflicts in almost every region of the world which have caused, at the low end, an estimated 70 million casualties, and at the high end, 170 million human lives. Yet, only a few of those responsible for such atrocities have been prosecuted. Most of the perpetrators have benefited from impunity, in part due to the absence of post-conflict justice mechanisms.[187] On the top of strengthening accountability it is absolutely necessary to implement the emerging norms and practices associated with the protection of individuals in situations of genocide, crimes against humanity, and war crimes; including the international criminal prosecution of such crimes; and the provisions of humanitarian interventions under the flag of the responsibility to protect. Such an approach would help to understand the interactions and trade-offs associated with these various international responses and the conditions under which one or more of the responses may be used by the international community. In this part of this study the protection, relocation and rehabilitation of civilians is considered as a shared responsibility between the two regimes, UN and ICC, during armed conflicts and in the post-conflict stages.

The universal principles regulating the UN and the ICC are respectively expressed in the UN Charter and in the Rome Statute. These principles represent the moral values for the promotion of international criminal justice and the foundations of public international law. They are applicable either for member States or for international governance institutions. This assumption refers to the interaction between complementary global regimes and their shared responsibilities when dealing with the accountability of States and individuals. Such interaction permits to evaluate the evolution of governance in peace and justice issues. The

187 For an extensive overview of the rise of international criminal law principles see, C. Bassiouni, "Accountability for Violations of International Humanitarian Law and Other Serious Violations of Human Rights" in *Post-Conflict Justice*, (2002), at 3. For some reports on Armed Conflicts and Conflict Management see www.sipri.org. See also T. B. Seybolt, "Controversies about Humanitarian Military Intervention" *Humanitarian Military Intervention: The Conditions for Success and Failure*, (2007), at 294.

rule of international law and the human security policy are the tools to determine a global constitutional strategy of the world community. New legal techniques are necessary for international lawyers in the innovative field of public international law enhancing also the accountability of governance. The question is whether such legal approaches would regulate the interactions of complementary public mandates and their shared responsibilities in the current state of affairs of international relations. The argument is based on the urgent priority to keep alive the constitutional struggle of the international community for international criminal justice, while national implementation of legislations would progress at domestic level.

The fight against serious crimes of common concern of the international community is an important aspect preserving the human security doctrine. It requires strategies of prevention, retribution and restoration strengthening the international legal and political order dealing with conflict and post-conflict societies. This part discussed the importance of complementary global regimes fostering peace and justice for the sake of human security at domestic, regional and global scale. In order to verify if there is a preventive strategy in place between the maintenance of peace and security and the emerging regime of international criminal justice, normative, political and institutional mechanisms applied at domestic, regional and at international level, either for humanitarian protection or collective security, received reflections.[188] This part offered some legal and political considerations in respect to the responsibility to protect civilians promoted by the United Nations. It recalled the discrepancies characterizing the humanitarian intervention regime in conflict scenarios without following and enforcing the judicial outcomes of the International Criminal Court.[189] Obviously, this analysis focuses on the dichotomy of the administration of justice of *last resort* of the Court on one side, and the conflict management, including humanitarian intervention and peace operations of the United Nations, on the other. It advocates the necessity of an effective preventive strategy, deepening the determination of States to put an end to the impunity regime of international crimes and human rights violations. Such a strategy would reconcile the fight against international crimes for peace, justice and deterrence in conflict and post-

188 For an overview of the debate to enforce international criminal law by the use of universal jurisdiction in national courts, see C. K. Hall, "Universal Jurisdiction: Developing and Implementing an Effective Global Strategy" in W. Kaleck, M. Ratner, T. Singelnstein, (eds.), *International Prosecution of Human Rights Crimes*, 2007, at 85.

189 "Humanitarian intervention," defined simply, is military action taken to prevent or terminate violations of human rights that is directed at and is carried without the consent of a sovereign government. In the last decade this manifested in authorizing military intervention in the affairs of sovereign States for "humanitarian reasons." For an analysis of the controversiality of such intervention, see L. S. Sunga, "The Role of Humanitarian Intervention in International Peace and Security: Guarantee or Threat?" in H. Köchler (ed.), *The Use of Force in International Relations*, 2006, 41, at 83. See also G. Evans, *Rethinking Collective Action*, 2004 CASR, edited excerpts, accessible at: www.casr.ca/ft-evans1.htm.

conflict societies. The target is to prove in the end that this very basic theory to be sustained in both policy and law making processes, recalls the interdependence between the administration of conflicts, warfare, peacekeeping and post-conflict justice.[190]

The current status of the Court's jurisdiction; its lack of law enforcement resources; the current interaction with the UN; and the weak cooperation pillar established with the States Parties and non-parties to the Rome Statute are further characterized by the following concerns: are complementary global regimes focusing on the implementation of a preventive strategy of mass atrocity crimes in place? Is the regime of the Rome Statute sufficient and self-reliant in the application of human security measures, such as relocation, and rehabilitation, while broadening victims' protection in situations of mass atrocity crimes? Besides, observing the political standpoints and the legal obligations of the African States in accordance with the Rome Statute, is there space for a preventive strategy of mass atrocity crimes? The African Union requires a clear and well defined working relationship between the Security Council and the Court.[191] From a legal perspective, the AU decisions against the Court with regard to the Bashir case in the Sudan, and the Kenyan situation granted under Article 15 of the Rome Statute, point out issues such as: *a)* the ability of the Security Council to refer matters to the ICC under Article 13 of the Rome Statute; *b)* the Security Council's exclusive deferral powers under Article 16; *c)* the role of regional bodies such as the AU with respect to ICC decisions on prosecutions and investigations; *d)* the position of immunities for individuals from non-ICC member States; *e)* the relationship between Articles 27 and 98, which respectively place a requirement on States to arrest individuals and a requirement to observe other international obligations, including international customary law arising from immunities.[192]

This part reflected the controversial debate of authority in humanitarian intervention, the maintenance of peace and security by the Security Council, and the possible role of international criminal justice, which seems to be considered as a deterrent tool without receiving a *road map* of governance between peace, justice and applicable measures of human security on the ground in the field operations. The analysis of complementary global regimes indicates the lack of progress about the theory of checks and balances in the international legal order. The controversial debate between the choice of peace processes and

190 See for an extensive overview, C. Bassiouni, *Post-Conflict Justice, International and Comparative Criminal Law Series* (2002), at 286.

191 See D. Akande, M. Du Plessis, C. Chernor Jalloh, Position Paper, *An African Expert Study on the AU concerns about Article 16 of the Rome Statute of the ICC*, Institute for Security Studies, 2010.

192 See D. Akande, "The African Union takes on the ICC Again: Are African States Really Turning from the ICC?" Blog of the *European Journal of International Law*, 2011, accessible at: www.ejiltalk.org/the-african-union-takes-on-the-icc-again/.

criminal proceedings needs to be re-opened. Article 16 of the Rome Statute immediately follows several provisions (Articles 13–15) establishing how situations can be referred to the ICC for investigation and prosecution. Entitled, "Deferral of investigation or prosecution," Article 16 reads, "No investigation or prosecution can be commenced or proceeded with under this Statute for a period of 12 months after the Security Council, in a resolution adopted under Chapter VII of the Charter of the United Nations, has requested the Court to that effect; that request may be renewed by the Council under the same conditions". In order to provide reliable answers, institutional, legal and political settings deserve analysis, including the part of the Rome Statute linked to the authority of the Security Council and to the Charter of the United Nations on peace and security maintenance. Strategically, and hopefully in the short term, the UN and the ICC need the African Union on their side in order to have a fundamental contribution on a prevention strategy and early warnings of mass atrocity crimes. Testing the political convergence required by the African continent would open the door to further regional support, and hopefully, also coming from other intergovernmental organizations, such as the League of Arab States. This remains the expression of the genuine wish of advocacy for these groups of States to protect their own citizens in their own territories. Hopefully their political reality would not turn out their position in the opposite direction of human security.

The second part of this study deals with the challenges, obstacles and concerns in the evolution of democratic governance of complementary global regimes fostering peace, justice and security universally, and the political convergence required between different legal systems and traditions injured by the disintegration of nation-states. It examines the challenges, the structure and the political convergence required in the governance of complementary global regimes, including the global responsibilities preventing and responding and also rebuilding situations affected by mass atrocity crimes. These global responsibilities are considered as important opportunities to further progress and neutralize any impasse in such governance. The definition of the complementary character of global institutions for the sake of human security is without any doubt an important opportunity. The governance systems centralizing the rights of individuals towards their institutional structures, operational mandates, judicial proceedings and rehabilitation programs will require further attention in the years to come. The next part provides the views about: *a)* the place that the emerging regime of international criminal justice should receive in the arrays of peace and security, and *b)* the meaning of complementary regimes governing peace, justice and security at global scale. The evolution of an institutional architecture dealing with international threats and crimes and the possible extension of universal jurisdiction require political convergence of expectations, policy definitions and complementary policy requirements. Before exploring the current practice applied on the ground in the peace operations, the second part of this study offers an overview of the frameworks involved in peace enforcement, including the *protective*, *retributive* and *restorative* aspects of justice based on international cooperation. It emphasizes the challenges to preserve further the rule of law and human rights as important prerequisites of democratic global governance of complementary global regimes involved in conflict and post-conflict situations.

# PART II

# THE GOVERNANCE OF COMPLEMENTARY GLOBAL REGIMES: CHALLENGES, OBSTACLES AND CONCERNS

# 4. THE CHALLENGES IN THE GOVERNANCE OF COMPLEMENTARY GLOBAL REGIMES

## PRELIMINARY REMARKS

The governance of complementary global regimes dealing with war and crime requires significant efforts from relevant stakeholders, such as States, regional and multilateral organizations and civil society, just to name a few. There are still several obstacles to centralize individuals in situations of war and crime. The accomplishment of sustainable peace in many of them is problematic. The deterrent impact deriving from the fight against impunity is not self-sufficient in such situations. The previous part of this study explored the global values and the requirement of an integrated approach of governance between frameworks fostering human security. Such an approach requires systemic changes at structural, normative and functional levels. The interaction between international governance institutions of complementary character is not configured by primary but only by secondary law. The secondary law regulates the operational activities in the field, or so-called arrangements and agreements, where international governance institutions of complementary nature are both involved. In such context, an integrated approach of governance based on compulsory cooperation is required. These issues will also be extensively discussed in the case studies dealt with in the third part of this study. The purpose of this part is to promote the idea of an effective interaction strategy between complementary global regimes according to the human security doctrine and the rule of law in international relations. Before the recommendations addressed to the decision-makers would take place in the last section of this chapter, the attempt now is to explore the main challenges, obstacles and concerns in the governance of complementary global regimes at structural, normative and functional levels.

This part underscores the fact that the key to solve some of the relevant gaps governing war and crime is seen in the interaction between global regimes of complementary character. Hopefully, political convergence will be found in the immediate, middle and long terms with mandatory cooperation in both *referral* and *non-referral* activity coming from the Security Council to the Court. Unfortunately, the transition of governance systems fostering human security is compromised by several factors. The three chapters of this part deal respectively with the challenges in the governance of complementary regimes, the structure and competence of their institutions, and the requirement of political convergence to become complementary in accordance with the constitution of the world community. This part will focus respectively on the governance of humanitarian escalations of *last resort* in the context of international peace and security, including the possible extention of jurisdiction of international crimes, and the gaps of law enforcement and civilian protection duties. It concludes that further evolution of global regimes governing war and crime depends from the policy formulations of their complementary character. The ideology and the political determination to end the impunity of serious crimes of common concern deserve some progress in the policy-making establishing human security measures at domestic, regional and international levels. Joint efforts between the UN and the Rome Statute institutional system should also help national capacities coping with mass atrocity crimes, while strengthening their national justice systems. A political *road map* of interactions for the sake of good governance is still not defined and in transition. Such a *road map* is considered an important opportunity. It would solve the gaps in the current legal and political frameworks upholding governance structures of complementary and universal character.

This part demonstrates that the supranational character of pluralistic legal frameworks and multilevel jurisdictions require further efforts for the preservation of the world order and the rule of law as an important principle of governance. The question of whether a global constitution exists or is emerging, and if so, what form it takes, is one of the most intriguing and controversial topic of recent international theory and has been extensively studied by several legal and political theorists.[193] Since in our globalized society the realization of an immutable world order is impossible and considered utopia, Delmas-Marty suggests policy adjustments that would preserve diversity. The rule of law "must be called upon to invent a flexible process of harmonisation that leaves room for believing we can agree on, and protect, global values".[194] In line with such considerations this part explores the new practice of international humanitarian escalations and the reach of universality of global institutions, including the first generation of referrals of the Security Council to the emerging regime of justice falling under the Rome Statute. The lacuna of civilian protection mechanisms calling for a 'culture of civilian protection' reminds the actors involved the importance to understand how their responsibilities for the protection of civilians during armed conflicts should be translated into action. Such view is also valid in regard to the *non-referral* activity when complementary actors function on the same grounds in the same situations. This part concludes that the

193 See C. E. J. Schwöbel, *Global Constitutionalism in International Legal Perspective*, 2011.

194 M. Delmas-Marty, *Ordering Pluralism. A Conceptual Framework for Understanding the Transnational Legal World*, 2009.

design of a supranational global architecture fostering peace, justice and security lacks political convergence on the following clusters: *a)* collective security and the use of force based on humanitarian purposes and civilian protection duties; *b)* peace enforcement and peacekeeping deployed with mandates integrating and supporting law enforcement; and *c)* post-conflict peace-building measures to guarantee sustainable peace in situations affected by war and crime.

In this part Chapter IV provides an analysis of global regimes and their transition in the new world order dealing respectively with the responsibility of the States and the accountability of the individuals. The ways these regimes are governed is important to preserve further the rule of law and its reach of universality. Their complementary character deserves clarifications and appropriate policy formulations in the direction of integrated governance systems. This chapter discusses some of the unresolved issues in the frameworks of international governance dealing with collective and human security and the important requirement of political consensus on such issues. Chapter V offers an overview of the governance structure of complementary global regimes including their competence and relationship, and points out the requirement of political convergence to reach global regimes of complementary character. These chapters indicate that systemic changes are required at structural, normative and functional levels in accordance with the constitution of the world community. There are uncertainties and instabilities about *last resort* international escalations based on humanitarian grounds. Justice is disconnected from peace. Security operations, civilian protections duties and law enforcement failed in regard to peace sustainability in several country-situations. This part also discusses the current political impasse in the formulation of international threats and crimes and the possible extension of their complementary governance (aggression, terrorism, weapons of mass destruction, etc.). The important requirements rewarding the idealistic view of an architecture fostering peace, justice and security based on further responsibilities (and against the practice currently applied when dealing with the international escalations of serious violations of international humanitarian law and human rights) is debated taking in consideration the theoretical dichotomy between *constitutionalism* and *pluralism* and further preservation of the world order. Thus, is it time for a change?

## 4.1. THE REACH OF 'UNIVERSALITY'

### SECTION OUTLINE

This section makes the point about the reach of universality between double standards in the selection of situations devastated by war and crime, and the challenges and opportunities in the application of civilian protection measures.

The global support to the investigation and prosecution of serious crimes of common concern is absolutely required, including any monitoring and capacity-building activity for the use of police, army and judiciary supposed to protect civilians in situations of war and crime. The impact of international governance institutions on criminal behavior of States and individuals in situations of war and crime has been extensively dealt by valuable observers, while the complementary interaction between them is still open for debate. In spite of their small sized character and the very few resources allocated outside the constellation of the UN entities, the institutions established under the Rome Statute have the potential to re-propose new approaches for the preservation of the international legal and political order. Such influence depends on several factors, and the most important of them require discussions. This section debates the gaps in the civilian protection measures detectable on the ground, as a reflection of the global humanitarian policies currently in place, the current practice of humanitarian escalations, and the dynamic of intervention in several situations of war and crime against the principles of universality and sustainability.

There are no doubts of the potential for the UN to play a key role in the strengthening of national justice systems by increasing the importance of the Rome Statute in the rule of law programming and development aid, including the security sector reforms of shattered domestic systems. The establishment of inquiry commissions by the UN Human Rights Council (UNHRC) in the situations where the Court is investigating would also benefit the collection of information and evidence useful for its judicial activities, while providing the Security Council with fundamental inputs regarding its referrals. Another important role for the UN would be the configuration of mandates on the ground supporting the activities of the Court as a prerequisite of an architecture fostering peace and justice in the context of human security. The current challenge is to provide real protection and halt the enduring violence in multiple situations of war and crime, while following judicial decisions enforcing the rule of law. The ideal would be that judicial decisions would not be neutralized by political approaches, but instead supported by legal and political responsibilities fulfilling the gaps in the relocation, rehabilitation and reparation as the main civilian protection measures, including law enforcement measures authorized, configured, and deployed on the ground in conflict and post-conflict situations.[195]

[195] See M. W. Brough, J. W. Lango, H. van der Linden (eds.), *Rethinking the Just War Tradition*, 2007.

### 4.1.1. THE LIMITATIONS OF CIVILIAN PROTECTIONS

An extension of capacity-building in situations of war and crime towards law enforcement and civilian protection measures is required. The simple question is: *how?* An initial step for the regime of international criminal justice would be to receive immediate support in the field operations by the political configurations of the peace-building mandates of the Security Council. The problem is that the responsibility to protect civilians in conflict zones with 'all necessary measures' (RtoP or R2P), and its language used in addition to the 'right' of humanitarian intervention with military means, are characterized by flawed decision-making based on the interests and alliances within political organs, and not upon an established legal procedure of compulsory character, as a prerequisite of democratic governance. In contrast with the R2P, the doctrine of humanitarian intervention may be referred as military intervention in a State without the approval of its domestic authorities, and with the purpose of preventing widespread suffering or death among the inhabitants. This differs from the R2P on at least three grounds. First, the remit of humanitarian intervention which aims at preventing large scale suffering or death, whether artificial or not, is far broader than that of the R2P which focuses on the prevention of four crimes: genocide, war crimes, crimes against humanity and ethnic cleansing. Second, the right of humanitarian intervention automatically focuses on the use of military force, by a State or a group of States against another State without its consent. As such, humanitarian intervention overlooks the arrays of preventive and non-coercive measures that are essential for the R2P. Last but not least, to the extent that the doctrine of humanitarian intervention is predicated on the basis of the right to intervene, it can proceed without the need to secure legal authorization by the Security Council, whereas any R2P action involving military force is not.[196] It is clear that the problem of delimiting the responsibility to protect, between sovereign nation-states, international governance institutions, and between them, shaping the legal frameworks in accordance which such norm, still remains.[197]

The same limitation applies to the humanitarian escalations referred to a treaty-based organization dealing with crimes internationally recognized, the jurisdiction of which struggles to hold accountable non-states actors without reliable law enforcement measures. Besides, the support and cooperation falling under such referrals precludes any mandatory character of political organs

196 See E. Passarelli Hamann, R. Muggah (eds.), *Implementing the Responsibility to Protect: New directions for international peace and security?* Igarapé Institute, 2013, accessible at: http://igarape.org.br/wp-content/themes/igarape_v2/pdf/r2p.pdf.

197 For an extensive overview see E. Gareth, *The Responsibility to Protect: Ending Mass Atrocity Crimes Once and for All*, 2008. A. J. Bellamy, *Responsibility to Protect: The Global Effort to End Mass Atrocities*, 2009. J. Pattison, *Humanitarian Intervention and the Responsibility to Protect: Who Should Intervene?* 2010.

including their responsibility. The same limits apply in the configuration of mandates on the ground where peace enforcement operations do not follow up the international judicial activities and their outcomes. In other words, are we simply dealing with the arrays of 'symbolic politics' of law enforcement, or can we refer to a 'paradigm in the making' of governance systems dealing with sensitive human security issues in situations devastated by war and crime? In order to strengthen the role of complementary global regimes fostering human security towards civilian protection measures, further debate on such sensitive issues is required.

### 4.1.2. THE PRACTICE OF HUMANITARIAN ESCALATIONS

The complexity of universality and a sustainable impact of complementary global regimes in difficult situations affected by war and crime are evident for several reasons. Some of them have been approached in the first part of this work and are further examined in the case studies selected. The memberships of the nation-states and the territoriality issue are only a couple of them, including the constitutional, legislative and institutional adjustments to be applied in their domestic capacity. There are currently 193 Member States in the United Nations.[198] Each member has a seat in the UN General Assembly. At the present 123 States joined the membership of the International Criminal Court. Out of them 34 are African States, 19 are Asia-Pacific States, 18 are from Eastern Europe, 27 are from Latin American and Caribbean States, and 25 are from Western European and other States.[199] Afghanistan for instance, is part of both regimes of the UN and the Rome Statute as well as the Republic of Korea; 34 African States are parties to the Rome Statute as well as 18 Asian States; 18 are from Eastern Europe, 27 from Latin America and Caribbean States, and 25 are from Western European and other States. Libya, Bahrain, Egypt, Yemen, Iran, Saudi Arabia, Somalia and other States of the Arab League including some North African States such as Morocco and Algeria, are part of the UN system but not parties to the Rome Statute. Palestine struggles to become a party of both systems but its sensitive statehood issue still waits for solution. Israel is also not a State party to the Rome Statute nor is China, Russia and the US, as permanent members of the UN Security Council. The current practice in the humanitarian escalations of *last resort* in the maintenance of peace and security, the absence of law enforcement after the

198 The Republic of South Sudan formally seceded from Sudan on 9 July 2011 as a result of an internationally monitored referendum held in January 2011, and was admitted as a new Member State by the United Nations General Assembly on 14 July 2011.

199 See for updates the chronological list of States Parties with the membership of Palestine recorded on 02 January 2015, accessible at: www.icc-cpi.int/en_menus/asp/Pages/asp_home.aspx.

Court's judicial outcomes, and the gaps in civilian protection duties represent the main challenges in the governance of complementary global regimes.

As we know, the Sub-Saharan African situations are characterized by the recent formation of nation-states in the post-colonial phase between serious shortcomings of domestic systems dealing with ethnic and religious conflicts, gender crimes, corruption, resource exploitation and State's failure investigating and prosecuting serious breaches of international humanitarian law. Dangerous political transitions are characterized by one characteristic: the presence of warlords and criminal regimes profiting and abusing of the weakness of communities to express their political choice in a democratic context. The common issue characterizing such situations is the absence of the nation-state securing basic rights and the protection of individuals. Some of the national regimes in place prioritize militarization and autocracy in their own domestic governance systems, while political transitions are in place and criminality is the main threat for civilians struggling for democratic governance and the respect of their fundamental individual rights. The question is simple: how are different situations of war and crime governed by complementary global regimes and which are the current expectations deriving from their complementary character?

Targeted sanctions centralize the individual responsibilities during sensitive political transitions, all of them characterized by severe violations of international humanitarian law. With regard to the responses of the international community fighting against war and crime we have seen that the escalation of the situation in Libya delayed the attention required by the violence spreading in Ivory Coast, including Kenya, Uganda, Central African Republic, Democratic Republic of Congo and Mali, particularly during the ectremely violent political transition in these countries. The commission of serious crimes spreads at regional scale. The option of international diplomacy by the United Nations, the US, France and the European Union for instance, represented a severe test to avoid that Ivory Coast would be dragged back into a more violent civil war as the consequence of the post-election violence. The so-called Security Council 'targeted measures' pressed the President Laurent Gbagbo to end months of post-election violence and finally transfer power to his rival Alassane Ouattara who won the presidential election earlier. Laurent Gbagbo had refused to step down even though the United Nations helped organise earlier the election and recognized the political victory of Alassane Ouattara. In the end, a military operation of the UN pressured by France became part of a neutralization campaign against heavy weapons that Gbagbo used against the civilian population. The most serious crimes, including alleged widespread sexual violence, were committed in 2002–2005. The International Criminal Court has jurisdiction over the situation in Ivory Coast by virtue of an Article 12(3) declaration, submitted by the Ivorian government on 1 October

2003. The country accepted the jurisdiction of the Court as of 19 September 2002 and became a State Party to the Rome Statute in 2013.[200]

The former president Gbagbo allegedly bears individual criminal responsibility, as indirect co-perpetrator, for four counts of crimes against humanity: *a)* murder, *b)* rape and other sexual violence, *c)* persecution and *d)* other inhuman acts, allegedly committed in the context of post-electoral violence in the territory of Ivory Coast between 16 December 2010 and 12 April 2011.[201] Currently, the post-election crisis seems to be over, but the struggles remain: reconciliation and reconstruction, including the restoration of security sectors and basic governance systems. The situation and the violence characterizing the political transition of this country seems to be similar to the one occurred in Kenya during and after the general elections,[202] where the security sectors including a reliable judicial system collapsed, and will surely need the support of international governance institutions in accordance with the findings of the accountability system falling under the Rome Statute. When Kenya was preparing itself for the elections in 2007 the State completely failed its own national reform and the justice agenda initiated years earlier ended in the disputed presidential elections. The violence and chaos following the 2007 elections led to the displacement of more than 600,000 people, the deaths of more than 1,200 citizens, the cruel destruction of property and ethnic polarization that is unprecedented in Kenyan history. This paved the way for the negotiations led by a team of eminent African personalities and chaired by Kofi Annan around the *Four Agenda Items*, which negotiations resulted in the Kenya National Dialogue and Reconstruction Agreement to which the government bound itself to implement.[203] The willingness and ability to deal with the post-electoral violence of Kenya were soon seriously compromised.

200 See Statement of the Office of the Prosecutor, 6 April 2011, *Widespread or systematic killings in Côte d'Ivoire may trigger OTP investigation,* accessible at: www.icc-cpi.int/nr/exeres/2386f5cb-b2a5-45dc-b66f-17e762f77b1f.htm.

201 According to the sources quoted by the ICC prosecution in the application to the Judges to open an investigation in Ivory Coast, at least 3000 persons were killed, 72 persons disappeared and 520 persons were subject to arbitrary arrest and detentions during the post election violence. There are also over 100 reported cases of rape, while the number of unreported incidents is believed to be considerably higher. See ICC-02/11, *Situation in the Republic of Côte d'Ivoire* in the pre-trial phase; see also ICC-02/11-3, 23 June 2011, *Request for authorization of an investigation pursuant to Article 15,* accessible at: www.icc-cpi.int/iccdocs/doc/doc1097345.pdf With regard to Kenya on 30 August 2011, the Appeals Chamber of the ICC confirmed Pre-Trial Chamber II's decisions of 30 May 2011 on the admissibility of the cases *The Prosecutor v. William Samoei Ruto, Henry Kiprono Kosgey and Joshua Arap Sang* and *The Prosecutor v. Francis Kirimi Muthaura, Uhuru Muigai Kenyatta and Mohammed Hussein Ali* and dismissed the appeals filed by the Government of Kenya. See ICC-01/09–02/11 OA, 30 August 2011, accessible at: www.icc-cpi.int/iccdocs/doc/doc1223134.pdf.

202 See Kenya background information accessible at: www.icc-cpi.int/NR/rdonlyres/26D853E3-83A6-45F1-BEE9-8B64E3723C55/0/BackgroundNoteKenyaJanuary2012.pdf.

203 The Kenya Human Rights Commission (KHRC), The Kenyan Section of the International Commission of Jurists (ICJ-K) and International Centre for Policy and Conflict (ICPC) presented in 2010 the *Transitional Justice in Kenya: A Toolkit for Training and Engagement*

The proposals by the commission of inquiry into the post-election violence (CIPEV, or so called Waki Commission) establishing a local tribunal with an alternative for pursuing the Court to investigate and try those responsible for the post-election violence were not feasible, considering the findings of the Court to end the impunity regime. The judicial proceedings are currently held in The Hague.[204] In Kenya and Ivory Coast the Court would settle down the limits and main responsibility of national sovereignty prosecuting violence against civilians during political transitions. There is, however, a long way ahead to undermine the limits between statehood, sovereignty and international governance. The problem is to strengthen the global support necessary for such determinations, upholding the importance of the rule of law to the volatile peace processes influencing complementary actions for peace and stability. Besides, the political threat to the Court in the Africa region started because it was simply doing its job. It charged Kenya's Deputy President for killing people who assembled against him during an election, and Sudan's President for murdering women and children in Darfur. Kenya and Sudan are lobbying in the AU to pull out the Court and destroy its chance for success. But in Darfur, DRC, Uganda, Ivory Coast, Kenya and lately in Mali, the Court plays a key role in bringing hope to those terrified by the armies, militias and warlords that have waged war against innocent civilians. The main argument of some leaders with a guilty conscience and blood-dirty hands is that the Court is a Western witch-hunt as most of the investigations focus on Africa. This is not the truth. The Court is an institution created by many African countries, 5 of the Court's 18 judges are Africans, and the chief prosecutor is also African, including the president of the Assembly of the States Parties.[205] The Court represents a light in the darkness of war and crime in Africa and everywhere. It cannot be allowed to end. The African drama of serious attempts to the dignity of civilian lives is not the only concern. Unfortunately, its involvement in other regions is also somewhat compromised by political standpoints, by the limits of its jurisdiction and by the lack of global support.

---

which is both an information source on transitional justice, as well as a training manual for engagement with the on-going TJ processes in Kenya that were restarted in the aftermath of the 2007/8 post-election violence.

204 The Second Vice President of the International Criminal Court (ICC) has informed the top leadership of the African Union (AU) that the Court can only consider suspending the Kenya cases before it if an application is made to the Court. See T. Maliti, "ICC asks AU to address concerns on Kenya cases through legal channels', *ICC Kenya Monitor*, 20 September 2013, accessible at: www.icckenya.org On 19 September 2014, Trial Chamber V(b) vacated the trial commencement date in the case *The Prosecutor v. Uhuru Muigai Kenyatta*, which had been provisionally scheduled for 7 October 2014. On 3 December 2014, ICC Trial Chamber V(b) rejected the Prosecution's request for further adjournment and directed the Prosecution to indicate either its withdrawal of charges or readiness to proceed to trial. Subsequently, on 5 December 2014, the Prosecutor filed a notice to withdraw charges against Mr. Kenyatta.

205 See ICC-ASP-20141002-PR1047, *Minister of Justice of Senegal, H.E. Mr. Sidiki Kaba, endorsed for the position of President of the Assembly, meets with States Parties in New York*, Press Release: 02/10/2014.

What we currently see in other parts of the globe is that the autocracy of regimes in the Middle East twisted revolutions in some of them, or civil wars in others, after 'peaceful' protests of their citizens. In Libya, according to reliable sources, the situation had since 2011 the typical grounds of mass atrocity crimes including the risk of a political transition posing serious global threats to the peace and security in the region. The UN General Assembly resolution of 1 March 2011 unanimously suspending Libya's membership from the United Nations Human Rights Council (UNHRC) was the first sign of the position taken by the international community. According to the UN and the ICC sources, the actions taken by the regime in Libya were clear violations of all norms governing international behaviour and serious transgressions of human rights and international humanitarian law.[206] Libya holds important natural resources as well as weapons and military arsenals acquired in the course of the years by the traffic in the Mediterranean, and which reached the hands of the rebel groups and a tyrant that for too long was tolerated by the world community for several reasons, one of them being the mitigation of North African migration in the South of Europe and another interest of western multinationals for its natural resources. After the Darfur referral of the situation in the Sudan by the Security Council to the Court, the situation in the *Libyan Arab Jamahiriya* followed. Therefore, let us further examine in the next paragraph the humanitarian escalations occurred between international governance institutions and the referral activities so-called of *last resort* by the Security Council to the Court.

### 4.1.3. THE FIRST GENERATION OF REFERRALS FROM THE SECURITY COUNCIL: SUDAN AND LIBYA

In the past and from a legalistic approach, the Security Council acted as a legislator even if the UN Charter did not give such powers to act in that way. The reform of the collective security system did not succeed.[207] The Security Council addressed situations through legislative resolutions that, as a matter of principle, should have been regulated by international treaties. With the Rome Statute it does not seem that the distortion of constitutionalism dealing with peace, justice

---

206 See ICC-01/11 Situation in the Libyan Arab Jamahiriya, Prosecutor's Application Pursuant to Article 58 as to Muammar Mohammed Abu Minyar Gaddafi, Saif Al-Islam Gaddafi and Abdullah Al-Senussi, 16 May 2011, accessible at: www.icc-cpi.int/iccdocs/doc/doc1073503.pdf See also I. Vetrhus, 'Gaddafi: Game Over?', *New Africa Analysis*, 1st of August 2011, accessible at: http://newafricaanalysis.co.uk/index.php/2011/08/gaddafigame-over/ See also All Africa Reports, *Libya: Gaddafi Killed*, 20 October 2011, accessible at: http://allafrica.com/stories/201110201410.html.

207 For the discussions and contributions of effective multilateralism and the importance of policy formulation and institutional reforms see N. Pirozzi, N. Ronzitti, 'The EU and the Reform of the UN Security Council: Toward a New Regionalism?', in *IAI Working Papers*, 12–12, May 2011, at 9, accessible at: www.iai.it/pdf/DocIAI/iaiwp1112.pdf.

and security is definitely solved, but it becomes more complex. When the Court received the referral from the Security Council and the extension of jurisdiction in the Sudan, a non-State party to the Rome Statute, it should have been defined a clear strategy of support from the Security Council during and after the Court's judicial activities.[208] In response, the government of Sudan, supported by Russia, China, Libya, the African Union (AU), and the League of Arab States, argued that the Security Council should exercise its authority under Article 16 to request the suspension of the proceedings in Darfur, claiming that the issuance of an arrest warrant against President al-Bashir would undermine ongoing efforts to find a peaceful resolution of the conflict in Darfur. Soon it became very clear that the Court would not receive any space in the maintenance of peace and security with law enforcement measures. On the contrary, there is still uncertainty of support in the referral activity coming from the Security Council. The risk is to undermine the credibility of global regimes of complementary character governing war and crime.

Although Article 16 permits the Security Council to act in exceptional circumstances, the situation in Darfur did not present such exception for the Security Council to exercise its deferral power. All promises by al-Bashir of ceasefires and peace negotiations had been broken. Therefore, the deferral of the proceedings against al-Bashir could not be seen as a means to *maintain* peace and Article 16 of the Rome Statute was definitely inapplicable. The same approach of the Security Council is repeated in Resolution 1970 (2011) referring the situation of Libya to the Court. The Security Council demands an end to the violence and decides to refer the situation to the Court. This time the resolution has been adopted unanimously under Chapter VII of the UN Charter (Article 41). Although the situation has the main characteristic of an intra-state conflict, the Security Council used the legal provisions of Chapter VII emphasizing the necessity of civilian protection duties. It needs to be noted that in paragraph 8 of the Resolution 1970 (2011) addressing the referral to the Court, the Security Council '*recognizes* that none of the expenses incurred in connection with the referral, including expenses related to investigations or prosecutions in connection with that referral, shall be borne by the United Nations and that such costs shall be borne by the parties to the Rome Statute and those States that wish to contribute voluntarily'. Such an approach is of course very far from a democratic and supportive interaction strategy, if we only consider the complementary nature of the emerging regime of international criminal justice in the context of peace and security in the region. This view deserves some clarification through a quick interpretation of the international military response authorized by the Security Council in Libya.

208 See UN doc. S/RES/1593 (2005).

## 4.1.4. THE INTERNATIONAL MILITARY ENGAGEMENT IN LIBYA

The military intervention in Libya had partly the same political motivations of the situations in Kosovo and ex-Yugoslavia at the time of Slobodan Milošević, or by Saddam Hussein in Iraq. Apart from preventing mass atrocities they meant to destabilize regimes no longer desired by the political circles characterizing international relations. This time in particular in Libya, the intervention was characterized by a controversial mandate by the Security Council oriented on civilian protection duties as expressed in the Resolution 1973 (2011) with a voting record of 10–5 and recalling the Resolution 1970 (2011). These modalities resulted already to be compromised in the Sudan and in the Democratic Republic of Congo as will be proven in the third part of this work.

The Libyan territory is characterized by a larger area not easily accessible on the ground similar to Afghanistan and Iraq. The risk is that the same crimes under international humanitarian law are common to all situations in the Middle East, where unarmed citizens protest against autocratic and criminal domestic regimes. The so-called *Arab Spring* and its hot-blooded situations in the quest of democracy are only at their initial stage. Several violations under international law characterized the civilian protests in Yemen, Bahrain and Syria. The domino effect of political, economic, and humanitarian crisis proceeds in the main region, with Israel being in the middle of them and ready to defend its borders with any (military) means. A couple of years ago, thousands of Palestinians passed from Syria and Lebanon reaching the Gaza Strip and the West Bank toward Israeli border positions, hurling rocks and surging across one frontier before the Israeli army opened fire, killing and injuring hundreds of them. On the top of that, the tensions and the diplomatic fracture in the region become more and more visible in particular with Iran, and at the borders between Syria and Turkey, with the NATO debating again about military action.

The question is whether the selectivity and double standards of referrals from the Security Council to the Court under Chapter VII of the UN Charter, would not only transfer jurisdiction to the complementary regime of the Rome Statute, but also cooperation and resources, including accountability of potentially unlawful actions under international humanitarian law. The political responsibility of the Security Council has a local and regional impact with the League of Arab States (or Arab League) as the important interlocutor in peace and security matters in the region, including the African Union. It is unfortunate to note that such political impact does not profit the regional support to the Rome Statute regime. Another issue was also to verify the standards of humanitarian support to migrants fleeing from the Libyan coast to Italy by the NATO, which had obligations on civilians according to the responsibility to protect (RtoP) including other international obligations. The Council of Europe, which is not an EU institution, but charged with monitoring compliance with the European Convention on Human Rights within the 49 Member States, conducted an investigation to find out why so many people died in 2011 in the Mediterranean despite monitored more closely than ever before.[209] The same humanitarian tragedy regards the current situation of many deaths in the Mediterranean fleeing from Syria and other countries and the poor compliance by the EU and Turkey to refugee law.

When intervening in the situation in Libya the priority was given to the military operations and the delusion of quick fix under the flag of humanitarian global solidarity. For many observers entering a war in Libya, while the international community was still involved in one in Afghanistan, and while Iraq appeared far from stable, was a very bad choice. After referring the situation in Darfur, Sudan (which situation receives assessment in the case study), the UN Security Council voted unanimously Resolution 1970 (2011) to impose sanctions against the Libyan regime, slapping the country with an arms embargo and freezing the assets of its leaders, while referring the on-going violent repression of civilian protesters to the Court.[210] With the Resolution 1973 (2011) the Security Council approved the no-fly zone and the civilian protection mandate trying to involve the Arab League in 'all necessary measures' against the Libyan regime. The military command of the operations in Libya was similar to the mission in Afghanistan (ISAF – International Security Assistance Force) enlarged to the non-parties of the NATO but still part of the military coalition, as for instance Qatar and the Arab Emirates. In any case, the absence of any Arab involvement during the first air strikes on Libyan air defence systems underlined the Western nature of the mission. It was very important for the public opinion in the Arab world to know that this was not simply the West acting against the violent regime in Libya. But was this really the case? Furthermore, it needs to be noted that for the first time

---

209 During the month of August 2011 the Italian coastguards have found death bodies of men on a boat crowded with refugees fleeing Libya, see for the reports BBC, 1st of August, article accessible at: www.bbc.co.uk/news/world-europe-14363905 See also 'NATO does not respond to humanitarian SOS: verifications required by the Italian Ministry of Foreign Affairs', 4 of August, accessible at: http://palermo.repubblica.it/cronaca/2011/08/04/news/nave_nato_non_risponde_a_sos_umanitario_la_lega_non_possono_solo_bombardare-20039567/?ref=HREC1-1 See also the recent jurisprudence of the ECHR, *Hirsi and others v. Italy*, which judgment unambiguously upholds the right of persons intercepted at sea not to be pushed back and to request asylum. For the legal details see the Submission by the Office of the United Nations High Commissioner for Refugees in this case, March 2010, available at: www.unhcr.org/refworld/docid/4b97778d2.html See Council of Europe report, *Lives lost in the Mediterranean Sea: who is responsible?* 29 March 2012, accessible at: http://assembly.coe.int/CommitteeDocs/2012/20120329_mig_RPT.EN.pdf.

210 See ICC-CPI-20110504-PR659, 4 May 2011, *First Report of the Prosecutor of the International Criminal Court to the UN Security Council pursuant to UNSCR 1970 (2011)*. See also *Statement to the United Nations Security Council on the situation in the Libyan Arab Jamahiriya, pursuant to UNSCR 1970 (2011)*, the full version is accessible at: www.icc-cpi.int/NR/exeres/DCBD3E2C-C592-4FB8-B7CB-E18E67F692D1.htm.

Europe would take the lead of the NATO military operations in such explosive area albeit US air support was indispensable.

### 4.1.5. THE ABSENCE OF CIVILIAN PROTECTION MEASURES IN LIBYA AND SYRIA

A quick interpretation of the Resolution 1973 (2011) indicates that the use of military force authorized under Chapter VII of the UN Charter results from the mandate of the responsibility to protect civilians (RtoP). Does then the RtoP also means to take sides during armed conflict, with the rebel groups deserving military support even prior a civil war would take place in a particular country? France was behind this military strategy with other European States ready to provide weapons to the rebel groups. The military operations in Libya engaged initially France, the UK, the US and Canada, with Italy, Spain and Qatar (and other States) possibly joining at a later stage. With this military engagement the RtoP becomes controversial as in the Sudan, where the partial mandate of the Security Council was swapped in the hands of the African Union and then back to the UN operations in the field. The Arab League immediately took political distance, as some of its leaders feared the same treatment reserved to the Libyan regime. The same political reserve was previously taken by the African Union after the indictments against the Sudanese leaders. The nature of the resolutions in Libya, being quite different from the language of peace and security maintenance in the region, authorize to protect civilians prioritizing the military operations, which again raises issues of proportionality, double standards and a willingness of regime change under the premises of dubious and hassled civilian protection measures.

It needs to be also noted that with the enforcement of the no-fly zone in Libya the European countries engaged in the civil war were likely to confront some of their own weapons previously purchased to the Libyan regime. The NATO air strikes had the scope to quickly destroy the major weapons of the Libyan regime. The situation is very similar to what happened in the case of Kuwait and Iraq in 1990. The Resolution 1973 (2011) was adopted in the Security Council by a vote of 10 in favour, to none against, with 5 abstentions (Brazil, China, Germany, India, Russian Federation) with the mandate to protect civilians and civilian populated areas. The main concern about the political preferences by the permanent members of the Security Council is once more confirmed if we look at the positions of China in regard to Sudan, and with Russia blocking global action for the humanitarian intervention in Syria.[211]

---

211 China, which has major oil interests in the Sudan did not arrest Sudanese President Omar al-Bashir during his visit to Beijing on 29 June 2011. See S. Ho, 'China Pledges Lasting

There have been obvious negative consequences creating the precedent of militarization in Libya. The intervention force in Libya was not allowed to occupy the territories and required several stages of interaction between the UN operations on the ground and the International Criminal Court, in case a reliable judicial system would not be in place, and also to protect relocate and rehabilitate victims and witnesses of international crimes, including the enforcement of judicial decisions against the individuals most responsible of such crimes. In any case, the fact that the rebels in the country received weapons outside the arms embargo confirmed the willingness of regime change in the country. Hopefully, the domestic system established by the National Transitional Council (NTC) will receive other forms of assistance oriented to a civil formation of a democratic State and its constitution. After the arrest and killing of former President Gaddafi, the National Transitional Council, which by then controls the whole territory of Libya, declared the country liberated. The NTC has issued a constitutional declaration which sets out a plan for a transitional process that would lead to the drafting of a new constitution and the holding of legislative and presidential elections.[212]

Despite the several critics of *politicization* the Court remained out of the way from the political dynamics of international relations and their compromise. After all, the *bad guy* (Gaddafi) who was left for more than a generation at his place by the international community had been neutralized in a way absolutely not comparable with court's room or any judicial system. A simple question arises: if in Libya the devastating attacks on civilians required the 'protective' mandate by the Security Council, why the attacks on civilians in the Gaza Strip during the Israeli operation Cast Lead have been ignored? After all, as Schabas emphasized on his blog "the Gaza war occurred in 2008 after the R2P norm was taking shape, the conflict resulted in between 1,166 and 1,417 Palestinian and 13 Israeli deaths, and was not far away from where the Libyan regime was currently executing his own people".[213] The same political controversy would also apply to the repressive and violent regime on civilians in Syria, which in my opinion represents the 'Pandora's box' compromising peace and security in the region, if we only consider the vicinity to the regimes in Iran and Lebanon and with Israel in the middle of them. The risk is that the Syrian authorities would use the support from Iran to repress

---

Friendship with Sudan', in *Voice of America*, 29 June 2011, accessible at: www.voanews.com/english/news/africa/China-Pledges-Lasting-Friendship-with-Sudan-124701259.html.

212 For an extensive overview of the fragmented security landscape in Libya see International Crisis Group, *Holding Libya Together: Security Challenges after Kadhafi*, in Middle East/North Africa Report N°115 – 14 December 2011.

213 V. Tsilonis, "Interview with Professor William Schabas. International Protection of Human Rights and Politics: an Inescapable Reality", *Intellectum* 7, (2010), at 46–61. On 11 August 2014, the United Nations Human Rights Council appointed William Schabas to chair the Gaza commission of inquiry, see more at: www.un.org/apps/news/story.asp?NewsID=48459#.VC7LOfmSxws.

civilians with the same brutal methods previously used by the Iranian regime. It all started when the Syrian security forces sent troops to the south of the country firing on unarmed protesters. The rebels claim that thousands of civilians have already died since the initial clashes with the troops in the South and in the North of the country. This stage seems to be only the beginning of extreme violence on civilians escaping in the south of Turkey and Lebanon, compromising the fragile diplomatic relations between Turkey, Israel, Syria and Lebanon on the top of the sensitive and unresolved EU governance issues concerning the refugees.[214] The Syrian authorities on their side claim that the troops have been sent at the request of civilian residents with the scope to protect them against armed criminal groups. According to human rights organizations this undermines further the truth of severe violations of international humanitarian law committed in the country. The statistics of the brutal attacks against civilians confirm the trend that Syria is taking the same devastating large scale proportions of political violence as the situation in Kosovo.[215]

The current disturbing information disclosed by reliable sources operating on the ground in Syria is that the government shoots, poison, and gas, its own people. In the meanwhile, the Security Council failed to agree on a resolution. It is clear that there is international division over condemning the violence in Syria. A draft proposal prepared by France, UK, Northern Ireland, Germany and Portugal was opposed by several States within the 15 members of the Security Council.[216] Russia and China are using their veto powers opposing a resolution falling under the maintenance of peace and security in the region including a referral to the International Criminal Court.[217] The US requests the UN Human Rights Council to start an independent investigation. In the speech-making of the OHCHR, the former High Commissioner for Human Rights Navi Pillay emphasizes that

214 See M. Chulov, 'Syrian refugees in Turkey: People see the regime is lying. It is falling apart', *The Guardian*, 9 June 2011, accessible at: www.guardian.co.uk/world/2011/jun/09/syria-turkey-refugees-denounce-regime Early this year the NATO members convened in Brussels to consider a response to the cross border attack by Syria on Turkey as a member of the organization with France offering the military lead. After the mortar rounds fired from Syria the NATO discusses the military stra tegy. The United Nations Secretary-General voiced growing concern over the risk that the confrontation might have on the regional peace. See the article 'Nato will defend Turkey from Syria attacks', *The Telegraph*, 12 November 2012, accessible at: www.telegraph.co.uk/news/worldnews/europe/turkey/9672199/Nato-will-defend-Turkey-from-Syria-attacks.html.

215 H. Guindy, 'Mass Atrocities Across Syria', in *Al-Ahram Weekly On-line*, 2–8 February 2012, accessible at: http://weekly.ahram.org.eg/2012/1083/re2.htm.

216 See UN doc. S/2011/612 (Draft resolution not approved).

217 Despite repeated appeals by senior United Nations officials for accountability for crimes being committed in Syria, the Security Council was unable to adopt a resolution that would have referred the situation in the war-torn nation to the ICC, due to vetoes by permanent members Russia and China. See UN News Centre, *Russia, China block Security Council referral of Syria to International Criminal Court*, 22 May 2014, accessible at: www.un.org/apps/news/story.asp?NewsID=47860#.VOxSp3zF_RA.

"the Syrian government has an international legal obligation to protect peaceful demonstrators and the right to peaceful protest. The first step is to immediately halt the use of violence, then to conduct a full and independent investigation into the killings, including the alleged killing of military and security officers, and to bring the perpetrators to justice".[218] Simple questions arise: why the Security Council did not use the remedy of international criminal justice falling under the Rome Statute referring the situation of Syria to the International Criminal Court?[219] And independently from the *last resort* option of international criminal justice, where have been left the *solidaristic* civilian protection measures falling under the RtoP? In order to provide a comprehensive response the next section clarifies further the concerns characterizing the difficult reach of universality in its *dark* side, including some of the challenges and opportunities.

## 4.2. THE GLOBALIST APPROACHES OF GOVERNANCE SYSTEMS

### SECTION OUTLINE

The concerns regarding the transition of global security systems, the legal and political responsibilities of their governance, and the unresolved statehood issues denote the globalist approaches of governance dealing with the accountabilities of States and individuals at the same extent, including the accountabilities of non-state actors in situations of war and crime. Even if the criteria to isolate violent and criminal regimes by the international community seem to be the current political trend, reliable models of governance are still waiting to be defined. It needs to be noted that the globalist approaches can have at least two different and opposing meanings. One meaning refers to the policy formulations placing the interests of the world community above those of single nation-states towards a constitution of the world community. Another view perceives the entire world community as a proper sphere for one powerful nation or a group of leading nations to project political influence globally. In both cases there seem to be any agreement about alternative theories that could make sense of systemic changes

---

218 The OHCHR provides a forum for identifying, highlighting and developing responses to contemporary human rights challenges, and act as the principal focal point of human rights research, education, public information, and advocacy activities in the United Nations system. See OHCHR Media Center, *Pillay urges Syria to halt its assault on its own people*, 9 June 2011, accessible at www.ohchr.org/EN/NewsEvents/Pages/Media.aspx?IsMediaPage=true.

219 After months of deadlock, the Security Council finally responded to the escalating violence in Syria which escalated with the use of force against civilians in the city of Hama, 130 miles (210 kilometers) north of the capital Damascus, condemning President Bashar Assad's forces for attacking civilians and committing human rights violations. See UN News and Media Division, SC/10352, *Security Council, in Statement, Condemns Syrian Authorities for Widespread Violations of Human Rights, Use of Force Against Civilians*, 3 August 2011, accessible at: www.un.org/News/Press/docs/2011/sc10352.doc.htm.

in the global legal and political order. In the policy formulation and the creation of normative frameworks deriving from it, the advocates of constitutionalism or pluralism still do not find common grounds. Such dichotomy is easily detectable when we look at the empowerment and institutional design of global regimes and the international governance institutions deriving from them, which complementary nature is still not applied in the practice. This section recalls some of the lessons deriving from the past, before the transition of global security systems would receive further analysis and debate in accordance with the human security doctrine and the quest of *complementarity* already approached in the first part of this study.

The fact that there is not a world government but rather multilateral settings to debate issues and determine collective course of actions, does not mean that the international community is not responsible to improve democratic legitimacy of international governance institutions. On the contrary, such legitimacy depends on democratization processes balancing powers between complementary public authorities, while also defining policies and legal responsibilities. In order to explore the current standpoint of such democratic processes the controversial long-running debates *a)* on peace and justice priorities; *b)* on the law enforcement and cooperation dilemmas; *c)* on the human rights defence and implementation of human security measures; *d)* on the preservation of the rule of law at domestic, regional and global levels; *e)* on the political determinations to implement democratic interactions in conflict and post-conflict situations where complementary global actors are currently involved, require all of them appropriate solutions. In other words, the nature of the responsibilities of cooperation those complementary governance institutions might share in the middle and long terms, require further debate in international political *fora*, on the nature, identification, prevention and prosecution of mass atrocity crimes. The expectation is that from the debate in the General Assembly and in the Security Council and other stakeholders, such as the Assembly of the States Parties to the Rome Statute, a political *road map* would be translated into action, not only limited to the support of pluralistic frameworks based on cooperation, but implementing and integrating a constitution of the world community able to unify global efforts and values. After all, the fight against impunity and accountability for the most serious crimes of international concern has been strengthened throughout the Rome Statute, in ad *hoc* and *mixed* tribunals, as well as specialized chambers in national tribunals. In this regard, the General Assembly and the Security Council should engage not only in situation-related forms of commitment but as mandatory obligation for all UN member States, thus for both categories of States Parties and non-Parties to the Rome Statute. After all, the call for such political *fora* should promote the global engagement in the fight against impunity and also draw attention to the full range of justice and reconciliation mechanisms, including truth and reconciliation commissions, national reparation programs, guarantees of non-recurrence, while promoting institutional reforms, rule of law and security sector reforms in domestic jurisdictions. In other words, the international community and its tools of governance should be prepared to adopt appropriate measures aimed at those who violate international humanitarian law and human rights law.

### 4.2.1. THE GLOBAL CONCERNS

In my opinion, and considering the chronology of the current humanitarian escalations between political and judicial international mandates, the first argument is the lack of preventing mass atrocity crimes towards timely intervention, as well as finding an integrated approach of governance. To clarify the concerns the following may be helpful. What we currently see is that national constitutions and domestic governance institutions are collapsing even in modern democracies such as in Greece, Italy, Spain and Portugal and not exclusively in the so defined 'failed' States. The problem is that such phenomena compromise much deeper the national legislations and the separation of powers of public authorities at local, regional and international levels centralizing the fundamental rights of individuals in constitutional frameworks. We all know that the preservation of universal values depends on the ways they are enforced and governed. The potential that multilateral premises would further contribute to the implementation of a world constitution according to the challenges of the time deserves discussions. A political strategy of interactions between law enforcement institutions is still pending, while there are discrepancies between domestic, regional and international responsibilities. The global solidarity, and the moral advent of humanitarianism to govern issues such as the humanitarian interventions under the flag of civilian protection duties (R2P or RtoP), mass atrocity crimes, terrorism, drug trafficking, migration and refugees, proliferation of weapons of mass destruction, are characterized by serious political deadlocks. Besides, the lack of a global strategy challenging the traditional concept of international security compromised in several occasions human rights and the rule of law (e.g. the wide scale conflict during the Iraq War encompassing a military campaign by a multinational force led by troops from the United States and the United Kingdom, or the policy formulation after the terrorist attacks launched by the Islamist terrorist group al-Qaeda upon the United States in New York City and the Washington DC areas). The governance of humanitarian crisis in conflict and post-conflict situations is characterized by serious controversy. If on one side States and global actors refer to the international responsibility to intervene in case domestic systems collapse and are not 'able' or 'unwilling' to protect civilians, on the other side an architecture of such governance represents a problematic 'paradigm in the making'.

There are no doubts that the emerging regime of international criminal justice gives authority to the two bodies of international law dealing with the treatment of individuals, such as human rights and international humanitarian law. We can easily acknowledge that international law has evolved in its use and importance due to the increase in armed conflict and mass atrocity crimes, but it still struggles to regulate criminal behaviors of States and non-state actors, including the civilian protection measures in conflict zones. Further progress of the rule of law seems to depend on the development of effective and complementary treaty regimes centralizing fundamental individual rights. Previous assessments of the international legal order suggest that the solutions depend on the international governance institutions, which deserve further constitutional parameters by the political actors enforcing them *in* and *out* their own governance systems. In the current system of international governance, however, the problem of the absence of a supranational system and *trias politica* in international relations is not solved by the existence of complementary international governance institutions. The lacuna of *checks and balances* systems between international public authorities dealing with peace, justice and security is not solved and still remains. The paradigm shift of complementary global regimes is that they try to find possible solutions through cooperation but an interaction strategy between them is still to be found. Their respective relationship *vis-à-vis* the States receives priority with the consequence of tensions between peace and justice mandates, which also derive from the absence of a well-defined interaction strategy between international regimes and emerging sub-regimes. The consequence is well known in the gaps of civilian protection measures either in the context of peace processes and justice mandates in conflict and post-conflict situations and the difficult task to provide sustainable peace.

### 4.2.2. THE GLOBAL RESPONSIBILITIES

The multilateral frameworks under the UN premises of preventive diplomacy, crisis prevention, early warning and accountability are absolutely considered an important part of the interaction strategy advocated in this work. This study promotes the predictability of assessments and legal definition of collective or shared responsibilities between international regimes which will need further legal research. This work focuses on the complementary role of international regimes fostering peace diplomacy, without compromising judicial proceedings of legal institutions such as the International Criminal Court. It denotes the importance of justice, intended as the restoration of the rule of law considered as centralizing individual rights during humanitarian crisis in conflict zones. This study emphasizes the necessity of joint solutions promoting the development of 'accountable' and 'democratic' governance, which is critical to building the capacity to manage conflicts, violence and crime in conflict and post-conflict situations.

There seem to be new opportunities after the failure of international security systems and the shortcomings in the fight against the impunity of mass atrocity crimes in Bosnia, Rwanda, Somalia and Angola. Such opportunities require reliable interaction strategies. In Srebrenica for instance, the UN peacekeepers were the witnesses of massive ethnic cleansing. They had to leave the truth of the Bosnian *enclave* behind. The events included the killing of thousands of Bosnian Muslims as well as the mass expulsion of millions of them, in and around the town of Srebrenica in Bosnia and Herzegovina. In July 1995 the United Nations Protection Force (UNPROFOR), represented on the ground by a few hundreds of Dutch peacekeepers, failed to prevent the town's capture by the Serbian army and the subsequent massacre. The protection mandate by the UN did not work, the alliances did not respond, the configuration of the international mandate did not have solutions to the Srebrenica massacre, which became the largest mass murder in Europe since WWII.[220] These serious humanitarian crimes of common concern were committed by the units of the Army of Republika Srpska (VRS) under the command of General Ratko Mladić, who has evaded arrest by the ICTY and remained at large for 16 years just remaining in Serbia under an assumed name. His capture was considered as one of the pre-conditions for Serbia to join the European Union. According to the lessons learnt from the past in Rwanda, Sierra Leone and in the Balkans, an assessment is required on the ways the international community would 'prevent', 'react', and 'rebuild' conflict and post-conflict situations affected by mass atrocity crimes in multiple conflict zones enforcing appropriately complementary governance institutions. The question is whether we learn enough from the past experience deepening our shared responsibilities.

In general terms, the international governance institutions decide on cooperation agreements and arrangements providing some structure to their mutual interests. Notwithstanding this field of law is mostly underestimated in the advancement of a world constitution, it gives at least some weight to the definition of complementary global regimes and their transition. The ideal would be to merge constitutional provisions of a humanitarian character dealt by the Rome Statute in the UN Charter, perhaps combined with the amendments of the UN Charter advocated for years. We are all aware that this depends on several factors, the most important of which would be the universal ratification of the Rome Statute. In any case, the resource and knowledge sharing between the United Nations and the Rome Statute institutions remains an important *conditio sine qua non* of good governance, but such fundamental step is only at its initial stage and still waiting for visible engagements. With the Rome Statute, the emerging regime operating in the field of *retributive* and *restitutive* international criminal justice

---

220 See S. Perkins, 'The Failure to Protect: Expanding the Scope of Command Responsibility to the United Nations at Srebrenica', 62 *University of Toronto Fac. L. Rev.* 193:2004, accessible at: http://heinonline.org/HOL/Page?handle=hein.journals/utflr62&div=14&g_sent=1&collection=journals.

would be based on the cooperation with relevant partners, such as the United Nations institutions and its specialized agencies. Such cooperation is still in the implementation phase and is not legally binding for the UN political institutions such as the Security Council. The practice indicates that the interaction between complementary global regimes depends on political processes enforcing international mandates on the ground, combined with jurisdictional triggering mechanisms in accordance with the treaty provisions. The challenges occurring in the context of statehood, sovereignty and international governance deserve attention measuring how far complementary global regimes centralize individual rights, with the States and the criminal perpetrators being in the middle of them. Once judicial proceedings would find out about the truth there should not be any political approach able to neutralize it. Besides, only a judicial institution would be able to define the degree of inhumanity, or better say criminality, considering the range of crimes committed, while offering valid justifications for the 'right' of humanitarian intervention. And last but not least, this right should be appropriately used in civilian protection measures for the victims and witnesses of international crimes of common concern upholding the important *protective* aspect of international criminal justice.

## 4.2.3. THE UNRESOLVED STATEHOOD ISSUES

In the context of jurisdictional matters including the sensitive statehood issues and the pressure of referral activities from the UN to the Court, a valid controversial example is that the UN Human Rights Council (UNHRC) adopted a resolution (A/HRC/RES/22/25) as a follow-up to the report of the UN fact-finding mission on the Gaza conflict, which contains the recommendation to the UN General Assembly to submit the previous report on the human rights violations in the Gaza war to the UN Security Council for its consideration and appropriate action. The Human Rights Council explicitly recommends the referral of the situation in the Occupied Palestinian Territory to the International Criminal Court, pursuant to article 13(b) of the Rome Statute.[221] It also recommends that the General Assembly remain apprised of the matter until it is satisfied that appropriate action has been taken at the domestic or international level to ensure justice for the victims and accountability for the perpetrators, and also remain ready to consider whether additional action within its powers is required in the interests of justice.[222] The real matter waiting for solutions is still the issue of statehood

221 Article 13(b) of the Rome Statute. "The Court may exercise its jurisdiction with respect to a crime referred to in article 5 in accordance with the provisions of this Statute if…a situation in which one or more of such crimes appears to have been committed is referred to the Prosecutor by the Security Council acting under Chapter VII of the Charter of the United Nations…".

222 See UN doc. A/HRC/12/48 (2009), Report of the United Nations Independent Fact-Finding Mission on the Gaza Conflict. See also UN doc. A/HRC/16/72 (2011), Report of the Special

of the Occupied Palestinian Territory and the admissibility of the violations occurred against civilians during the Gaza war. This confirms the unresolved issue by the UN legal and political institutions about the public international authority recognizing Palestine as a State, which seems unlikely that would be the International Criminal Court and neither the United Nations.[223] The recognition of a new State or government is an act that only other States and governments may grant or withhold. It generally implies readiness and ability to assume diplomatic relations. The United Nations is neither a State nor a government, and therefore does not possess any authority to recognize either a State or a government.

On 1 January 2015, the Government of Palestine lodged a declaration under article 12(3) of the Rome Statute accepting the jurisdiction of the ICC over alleged crimes committed "in the occupied Palestinian territory, including East Jerusalem, since June 13, 2014". On 2 January 2015, the Government of Palestine acceded to the Rome Statute by depositing its instrument of accession with the UN Secretary-General. Upon receipt of a referral or a valid declaration made pursuant to article 12(3) of the Rome Statute, the Prosecutor, in accordance with Regulation 25(1)(c) of the Regulations of the Office of the Prosecutor, and as a matter of policy and practice, opens a preliminary examination of the situation at hand. Accordingly, on 16 January 2015, the Prosecutor announced the opening of a preliminary examination into the situation in Palestine in order to establish whether the Rome Statute criteria for opening an investigation are met. Specifically, under article 53(1) of the Rome Statute, the Prosecutor shall consider issues of jurisdiction, admissibility and the interests of justice in making such determination.

Over 140 nations from the Middle East, Africa, Asia, Latin America and Europe have already endorsed the initiative of the UN recognition of the State of Palestine, but Israel's right-wing government and the US vehemently oppose it. Europe is still hesitant, but a massive public push brought them to vote for this momentum to end 40 years of military occupation. While the roots of the Israeli-Palestinian conflict are complex, most analysts agree that the best path to peace would be the creation of two States as also endorsed by the UN Security Council. However, repeated peace processes have been undermined by violence on both sides, extensive Israeli settlement-building in the West Bank, the humanitarian blockade on Gaza and Israeli strike on civilians, as well as rockets from Gaza on South Israel. The Israeli occupation has fragmented the territory for a Palestinian State and made daily life misarable for the Palestinian people. The UN, the World

Rapporteur on the situation of human rights in the Palestinian territories occupied since 1967, Richard Falk.

223 For an overview of the military occupation and the limits of the Court's jurisdiction see M. Glasius, 'The ICC and the Gaza War: legal limits, symbolic politics', 28 March 2009, accessible at: www.opendemocracy.net/article/the-icc-and-the-gaza-war-legal-limits-symbolic-politics.

Bank and the IMF have all recently announced that Palestinians are ready to run an independent State, but confirm that the main constraint to success is the Israeli occupation. The US President has called for an end to settlement expansion and a return to the 1967 borders with mutually agreed land-swaps, but Israeli Prime Minister Netanyahu has furiously refused to cooperate. The UN resolution to upgrade Palestine from its status as an observer *entity* to an observer *State* does not change the Palestinians lives on the ground. Most important, the UN resolution shapes the urgent need for the resumption and acceleration of negotiations within the Middle East peace process.[224] That remains the key according to both Israel and the Palestinian authority to a real two-state solution. As correctly point out by Stork "the argument that Palestine should forego the International Criminal Court because it would harm peace talks rings hollow when 20 years of talks have brought neither peace nor justice to victims of war crimes. People who want to end the lack of accountability in Palestine and deter future abuse should urge President Abbas to seek access to the ICC".[225]

The legal and political determinations of the UN Human Rights Council addressing issues in the legal framework of governance and referral activity between the UN institutions and the Court confirm the necessity to establish the complementary character of both global regimes preserving the rule of law and human rights. There are no doubts that complementary organizations, such as the UN Human Rights Council and the International Criminal Court, have to relate to each other in situations of serious breaches of human rights. Such complementary role is also at its initial stage and also in transition. It needs to be noted that the Human Rights Council is an inter-governmental body within the UN system made up of only 47 States responsible for strengthening the promotion and protection of human rights around the globe. As previously emphasized the Human Rights Council was created by the UN General Assembly on 15 March 2006 with the main purpose of addressing situations of human rights violations and make recommendations on them. For many, and particularly for the permanent members of the Security Council, it accommodates better if the complementary role of the Court to the UN would fall in the peace and security maintenance. But then, can we still simply assume that the UN Security Council is still the predominant authority dealing with serious human rights breaches in conflict and post-conflict situations? If yes, should it not be the case to provide resources to the emerging regime of international criminal justice established under the Rome Statute? This is a matter to be absolutely dealt with by the UN General Assembly and the outcome of it remains to be seen considering the needs for an emerging international regime to accomplish its universality.

---

224 See UN doc. General Assembly, Resolution A/RES/67/19 (2012), recorded vote of 138 for the recognition of observer State to 9 against, with 41 abstentions.

225 HRW, *Palestine: Go to International Criminal Court,* May 8 2014, accessible at: www.hrw.org/news/2014/05/08/palestine-go-international-criminal-court.

## 4.3. THE TRANSITION OF GLOBAL SECURITY SYSTEMS

### SECTION OUTLINE

This section further debates the transition of governance systems in the new order fostering human security and which surely need further accomplishments. The transition deserving attention regards the system of collective security and the nature of civilian protection measures when human security is seriously compromised. Another aspect refers to the policy definition of international threats in international crimes which would enhance the jurisdiction falling under the Rome Statute and its future extension. It needs to be noted that in the context of global order, international regimes simply deal with the governance without a government, depending on their provisions, policy formulation and the cooperation with their stakeholders and partners. The lasting struggle for the legal doctrine delineating domestic and international responsibilities in situations of war and crime brought some results but there is still a long way ahead. Further progress depends on the jurisprudence of legal institutions and by the determination to enforce the rule of law and the standards of human rights at domestic, regional and international levels. The dilemma is the governance of political transitions that are internal to collapsed nation-states and their failure *vis-à-vis* the security of individuals during civil wars. In many situations of war and crime, the engagement in military actions by States and global actors would appear legal but not fully legitimate, while promising unrealistic civilian protection duties during humanitarian interventions. The same concern is valid for the governance of conflicts between States, or inter-state conflicts, as in the case of the commission of the crime of aggression. Such governance also represents a controversial 'paradigm in the making' for complementary global regimes, considering the triggering mechanisms between the UN Security Council and the International Criminal Court respectively dealing with the accountability of States and individuals, and which received further postponement by the political forces responsible of their empowerment.

It needs to be noted that the term *supranational* has sometimes been used in an undefined sense as a substitute of international, transnational, or global decision-making. Both the UN and the Rome Statute institutions are to a large extent not *supranational*. The majority of the nation-states of the world community have dualist systems, meaning that they will only accept international obligations through the process of incorporation, as for instance, by signing, ratifying and adopting international treaties and conventions.[226] In contemporary international

[226] For an overview of the various aspects of crimes against humanity, which unlike genocide and war crimes were never set out in a comprehensive international convention, including

regimes the intergovernmental decision-making still plays a prominent role centralizing individuals in conflict and post-conflict situations. The formulation of the global humanitarian policy and the legal frameworks deriving from it, deserve discussions to verify the meaning and the nature of the governance of complementary global regimes fostering human security, including the *status quo* of the idea of cosmopolitan democracy. The idea of cosmopolitan democracy has been advocated with reference to the reform of international organizations. This includes the implementation of the Rome Statute institutions about victims and witnesses protection, the institution of a directly elected world parliament or world assembly of governments, and more widely the democratization of international organizations such as the UN.[227] This section reflects on the possible transitions from collective security to human security towards appropriate interaction strategies balancing powers between complementary global regimes fostering peace and justice. The purpose is to stimulate the debate in order to find urgent consensus by the relevant decision-making embracing the transition and challenges of human security and the complementary responsibilities of global regimes. Appropriate reforms of working methods should be in line with a political *road map* visible in a defined strategy of interactions.[228]

### 4.3.1. WHAT KIND OF CIVILIAN PROTECTION MEASURES?

It is clear that the role of the UN and the regulation of collective security are in transition given the rise of intra-state conflicts since the end of WWII. The interventions of the world community in such conflicts require systemic changes and adjustments which appear to be partial when we look at the empowerment and interaction between complementary global regimes. Besides, collective security is more ambitious than the systems of alliance security or collective defense. It seeks to encompass the totality of States within a region, or indeed globally, addressing a wide range of possible international threats. While collective security is an idea with a long history, its implementation in the practice has proved to be problematic.

discussions on gender crimes, universal jurisdiction, the history of codification efforts, the responsibility to protect, ethnic cleansing, peace and justice dilemmas, amnesties and immunities, the jurisprudence of the *ad hoc* tribunals, the definition of crimes against humanity in customary international law, the definition of the International Criminal Court, the architecture of international criminal justice, modes of criminal participation, crimes against humanity and terrorism, and the inter-state enforcement regime see L. N. Sadat (ed.), *Forging a Convention for Crimes Against Humanity*, Cambridge University Press, 2011.

227 For an overview of the debate on cosmopolitan democracy and the relation between the governance at local, regional and global levels see D. Archibugi, 'Cosmopolitan Democracy and its Critics: A Review', in *European Journal of International Relations*, 2004, Vol. 10(3), at 437–473).

228 See R. Thakur, *The United Nations, peace and security: from collective security to the responsibility to protect*, Cambridge University Press, 2006.

Several prerequisites have to be met for it in order to have a chance to work in an appropriate way and with an integrated approach of governance.[229] Collective security may have to evolve ensuring stability and a fair international resolution to intra-state conflicts. Whether this will involve more powerful peacekeeping forces or a larger role for the UN diplomatically, will likely be judged from a case to case basis. In any case, according to the outcomes of the studies of four decades of peacekeeping operations, it is proved that "turning peacekeepers into a fighting force erodes international consensus on their functions, encourages withdrawals by contributing contingents, converts them into a factional participant in the internal power struggle, and turns them into targets of attacks from rival internal factions".[230] These are the factors characterizing the practice on the ground in the multidimensional operations in the DRC, and in other peacekeeping operations which meant severe loss of human lives. These forces have to be trained and prepared for humanitarian protection measures and the emerging regime of international criminal justice should profit from such forces deployed on the ground.

First of all, in the context of civilian protection measures it needs to be noted that the Court's victims and witness protection program should help encourage witnesses to be more confident in contributing to the investigation, assisting the goal of accountability that the victims and civil society have been campaigning towards the Rome Statute. As the UK delegation stressed during their contribution to the Special Fund of the Court on relocation of victims and witnesses[231] "we remain concerned about continuing reports of witness intimidation and official interference. Those who attempt to subvert the search for justice should be aware that they also could find themselves accountable for their actions in The Hague, at the Court's premises".[232] The protection duties of civilians in situations of

---

229 See A. Roberts and D. Zaum, *Selective Security: War and the United Nations Security Council since 1945*, International Institute for Strategic Studies, London, Abingdon: Routledge, 2008.

230 See R. Thakur, 'From Great Power Collective Security to Middle Power Peacekeeping' in H. Smith (ed.), *Australia and Peacekeeping*, Canberra, Australian Defence Studies Centre, 1990, at 20. See also R. Thakur, 'From Peacekeeping to Peace Enforcement: The UN Operation in Somalia', in *The Journal of Modern African Studies* Vol. 32, No. 3 (Sep. 1994), at 387–410.

231 The purpose of the Special Fund of the Court on relocation is to assist States Parties that are willing to host witnesses at risk but are not in a position to finance such support, and aims at fostering regional solutions for the relocation of witnesses at risk, thereby reducing the impact of relocations on their life. Using such arrangements, the Court also seeks to galvanize cooperation partners into strengthening national capacity to protect witnesses in regional States such as Kenya. This new modality developed by the Registry of the Court is complementary, and does not replace traditional Framework Agreements on Relocations, which are still very much needed by the Court.

232 See ICC-CPI-20101126-PR601. The Court relies on the cooperation of States for a number of key protection issues. International organizations are also the main stakeholders for the Court; discussions have been initiated with the UN Office of the High Commissioner for Human Rights and the possibility of establishing a joint international authority on protection issues.

conflict and crime by the Security Council should embrace the Court's activities pressuring the States to preserve the right of the victims enforcing the law, while upholding operational measures of protection, relocation and rehabilitation. A joint international institution dealing with victims' protection measures would be absolutely required. It is important to recall the current trends in the practice applied on the ground during difficult political transitions characterized by serious violations of international humanitarian law and human rights, and which disturb international peace and security spreading at regional level, as in the case of the African Great Lakes Region, or in other regions and in the Middle East.

### 4.3.2. THE POLITICS OF TRANSITION IN CONFLICT ZONES

What we currently see is that in many countries national security systems based on oppressive security are no longer tolerated by their own citizens. In situations of war characterized by humanitarian violations, the security sectors, especially armies, might even become a source of widespread insecurity by themselves (see the situations in Egypt, Tunisia, Morocco, Bahrain, just to name a few). In several countries in Africa, Asia and in the Arab world for instance, including countries in Europe and other western societies, the political transitions are characterized by the ambition to accomplish civil States and democratic governance.[233] The civilian revolutions against dictatorial, corrupted and violent regimes require a deep understanding of the local actors in order to provide appropriate support and civilian protection measures, while fighting against the impunity of serious crimes. The international (military) responses focusing on old methods of security, whereas in large-scale humanitarian crisis the security systems have collapsed, or are simply in the hands of autocratic and dictatorial regimes, or have always been inexistent, are controversial and not sustainable in the search of democratic order and stability. The current military engagements characterizing the international responses in internal armed conflicts undermine the credibility of multilateral treaties fostering stability and the rule of law, including the international governance institutions deriving from them. It needs to be noted that international treaties, their codification and the organizational structures deriving from them, suffered from the well-known shortcomings in the policy formulation with regard to the use or misuse of armies, their illicit traffics to dangerous warlords, the constant formation of armed group and a myriad of non-state actors' not politically identifiable, which create chaos and violence exploiting resources and human lives. In several situations the members of the

233 See R. Luckham, 'The Military, Militarization and Democratization in Africa: A Survey of Literature and Issues', in *African Studies Review*, Vol. 37, Number 2, 1994, at 13–75.

Security Council have violated the arms embargos compromising the neutrality of their intervention during violent political transitions (e.g. Libya and Syria). We can acknowledge that the politics of transition in conflict and post-conflict situations have to deal with massive atrocities with the absence or the 'failure' of the State and require appropriate intervention under important conditions.

### 4.3.3. COLLECTIVE SECURITY AND HUMAN SECURITY

The current challenges in the international legal order between statehood, sovereignty and international governance deserve discussion, including the transition of collective security and the use of military force. Collective security can be understood as a security arrangement in which all States cooperate collectively to provide security for all, by the actions of all against any States within the groups, which might challenge the existing order by using force.[234] The NATO was established to provide security for its member States against an external military threat. Since the end of the cold war the NATO has undertaken collective security missions in upholding the principles of the UN Charter on behalf of the UN showing its controversial *modus operandi*. The use of military force upholding the principles of the UN Charter can only be taken up by the UN Security Council under Chapter VII of the UN Charter. In such cases, since the UN does not have a standing army on its own, it can call upon the collective military capabilities of member States or alliances, such as indeed the NATO. As relevant analytical outcomes would emphasize, "the most striking feature of NATO involvement in the management of international crises remains the progressive erosion of the Security Council authority, which culminated with the intervention in Kosovo. The crisis in Iraq also demonstrated that there was no agreement among the members of the NATO on whether obtaining an authorization from the Security Council before resorting to force, was a legal requirement or only a matter of political expediency".[235] So said the collective security system is meant to protect civilians and not to undermine human rights and is also supposed to be accountable for its actions. But is this really the case looking at the practice applied on the ground?

In the situation in Libya, the resolution of the Security Council authorized the military response using the language of the responsibility to protect civilians (RtoP or R2P). We will look at the ways such civilian protection duties have been performed earlier also in the Sudan and in the DRC. The protection of

---

234 For major contributions see N. J. Schrijver, 'Reforming the UN Security Council in Pursuant of Collective Security', in *Journal of Conflict & Security Law*, Vol. 12, No 1, 2007, at 134. See also N. M. Blokker and N. J. Schrijver (eds.), *The Security Council and the Use of Force*, 2005.

235 For an analytical overview see T. Gazzini, 'Nato's Role in the Collective Security System', *Journal of Conflict and Security Law*, Vol. 8, No 2, 2003, at 231.

civilians during armed conflict is not a new concept but relatively established in international humanitarian law.[236] With the advent of the R2P, the international community accepted for the first time the collective responsibility to act, should States fail to protect their own citizens from mass atrocity crimes. The R2P, thus, imposes two obligations: the first upon each State individually, the second on the international community of States collectively. With embracing the responsibility to protect a long and unresolved debate over *whether* to act, became instead, a discussion about *how* and *when* to act. This was certainly progress. Unlike humanitarian intervention, the R2P aspires to ground national and international action in law and institutions of complementary nature. Rather than compromising sovereignty, the R2P aspires to tie together 'responsible sovereignty' and 'international responsibilities' to 'prevent', 'react' and 'rebuild'. In Libya, the arms embargos on the country had been violated prior to the military intervention reported by the Security Council. Even if it was the case that preventive measures had failed with the tyrant in charge and the violent regime in the country, the main concern refers to the political choice to let weapons enter into the country, making sure that they would reach the hands of the rebel groups, and finally taking part into the devastation of the armed conflict. So said, is such expression of militarization and regime change valuing the parameters of human security and the supranational rules enshrined in the UN Charter and the Rome Statute? The idealistic view is that it would have been more appropriate to release arrest warrants against the perpetrators of the range of crimes falling under the R2P, and only after performing the required international police and law enforcement, authorizing the use of force with the determination to catch the most important individuals responsible of the serious crimes disturbing peace and security in the country, and in the region. In this way the credibility of complementary tools would have received another impact globally, especially in regard to the ratification campaign of the Rome Statute.

## 4.3.4. THE RISKS IN THE POLICY FORMULATIONS

The main concern is that the prevention of serious humanitarian breaches and the protection of civilians during difficult political transitions are currently applied towards international security measures of militarization. There are serious doubts that such an approach is a reliable preventive measure able to challenge the mentality of war and crime during armed conflicts of a non-international character or intra-state conflics. Moreover, does global solidarity mean that military coalitions have the potential to challenge the ideology of despotism? The controversial policy issue is also related to the governance of terrorism and

[236] In this regard see the Geneva Convention IV, relative to the Protection of Civilian Persons in Time of War, Geneva 12 August 1949.

the use of weapons of mass destruction, including other serious global threats which have been left aside from any multilateral (legal) system. The fight against terrorism, or 'war on terror' against the worst enemy, characterized the 'fiction' of ideology in the security policy of some modern democracies, with Osama Bin Laden wanted death or alive. Such approaches have undermined universal values shared by the world community. Torture, imprisonment, liquidations and other methods used by secret intelligence have violated the basic requirements of human rights law, creating further extremisms and international fracture. The problem is that terrorism, as an international security threat, including its legal definition as international crime, is only at its initial stage of being considered in multilateral governance systems. Moreover, the raid by US Special Forces in Abbottabad, Pakistan, killing Osama Bin Laden, raised a number of legal questions that are likely to have far reaching implications for future military operations.[237] Particularly, the legal issues that arise in situations where a decision is made to target individuals, potentially outside the hostilities of arm conflicts, using military force. The analysis of these issues requires determination of what legal framework(s) properly regulates such use of force. Respectively, *a)* the legal justifications and counterarguments for military intervention targeting members of armed groups on the territory of another State; *b)* the applicability of international humanitarian law and/or human rights law to such operations; *c)* the implications of such operations for the evolving concept of direct participation in hostilities by civilians; and *d)* whether there is a need for new norms to regulate such operations. In the near future it would be required to see whether there is some space left in the provisional domain of the Rome Statute on terrorism, limiting the extent on which terrorism would only be left to the Security Council's domain.

### 4.3.5. PROTECTING CIVILIANS

In many civil wars combatants target civilians and relief workers with impunity. Beyond direct violence, deaths from starvation, disease and the collapse of public health the number of civilians killed by bullets and bombs increased. Millions more are displaced internally or across borders. Human rights abuses and gender violence are rampant. Under international law, the primary responsibility to protect civilians from suffering in war lies with belligerents, either by State or non-State actors. International humanitarian law provides minimum protection and standards applicable to the most vulnerable in situations of armed conflict,

237 See A. S. Deeks, "Pakistan's Sovereignty and the Killing of Osama Bin Laden", *ASIL Insights*, Vol. 15, Issue 11, May 5, 2011, accessible at: www.asil.org/insights/volume/15/issue/11/pakistans-sovereignty-and-killing-osama-bin-laden J. Rollins, *Osama bin Laden's Death: Implications and Considerations*, Congressional Research Service Reports, May 5, 2011, accessible at: www.fas.org/sgp/crs/terror/R41809.pdf.

including women, children and refugees. Its compliance is an issue. Such laws must be respected. All combatants must abide by the provisions of the Geneva Conventions. All Member States should sign, ratify and act on all treaties relating to the protection of civilians, such as the Genocide Convention, the Geneva Conventions, the Rome Statute of the International Criminal Court and all refugee conventions. Humanitarian aid is a vital tool for helping governments to fulfill this responsibility. Its core purpose is to protect victims, minimize their suffering and keep them alive during the conflict so that when war ends they have the opportunity to rebuild their shattered lives. The provision of international assistance is a necessary part of this effort. Donors must fully and equitably fund humanitarian protection and assistance operations.[238] Models of governance and capacity-building are absolutely required. This section concludes on the problematic intersection between international law and global politics on sensitive matters waiting for political solutions. Once again, political convergence is the key prior whatever institutional design and possible reforms of global governance systems which are explored in the next section and in the last chapter of this part. This paragraph reports the recommendations of the high-level panel on threats, challenges and change protecting civilians. The Secretary-General based this report in part on work undertaken by the United Nations High Commissioner for Refugees and also on the strong advocacy efforts by nongovernmental organizations. The Secretary-General prepared a 10-point platform for action for the protection of civilians in armed conflict. The Secretary-General's 10-point platform for action should be considered by all actors: States, NGOs and international organizations, in their efforts to protect civilians in armed conflict.[239]

From this platform, particular attention should be placed on the question of access to civilians, which is routinely and often flagrantly denied. United Nations humanitarian field staff, as well as United Nations political and peacekeeping representatives, should be well trained and well supported to negotiate access. Such efforts also require better coordination of bilateral initiatives. The Security Council can use field missions and other diplomatic measures to enhance access to and protection of civilians. Particularly egregious violations, such as those which occur when armed groups militarize refugee camps, require emphatic responses from the international community, including from the Security Council acting under Chapter VII of the Charter of the United Nations. Although the Security

238 See Report of the Secretary-General's High Level Panel on Threats, Challenges and Change, Part 3, *A more Secure World: Our Shared Responsibility*, 'Collective Security and The Use of Force', Protecting Civilians, Para. 239, at 74, accessible at: www.un.org/secureworld/report2.pdf.

239 See UN doc. S/2005/740, Report of the Secretary-General on the Protection of Civilians in Armed Conflicts, 28 November 2005, accessible at: www.responsibilitytoprotect.org/files/SGReportPOC.pdf.

Council has acknowledged that such militarization is a threat to peace and security, it has not developed the capacity or shown the will to confront the problem. The Security Council should fully implement resolution 1265 (1999) on the protection of civilians in armed conflict. Of special concern is the use of sexual violence as a weapon of conflict. The human rights components of peacekeeping operations should be given explicit mandates and sufficient resources to investigate and report on human rights violations against women. Security Council resolution 1325 (2000) on women, peace and security and the associated Independent Experts' Assessment provide important additional recommendations for the protection of women. The Security Council, United Nations agencies and Member States should fully implement its recommendations. The current transition of global security systems requires political consensus. Such important requirement is discussed in the next section.

## 4.4. THE REQUIREMENT OF POLITICAL CONSENSUS

### SECTION OUTLINE

In this section it is argued that the structure of governance that has emerged after a series of decisions of the UN and the Rome Statute institutions represent an important step forward, but does not solve the fundamental problems in the global architecture dealing with international threats and crimes. The fact that seventeen years have elapsed since the adoption of the Rome Statute requires taking stock of the developments, assessing the collective achievements that have been made, and reflecting on those areas where action remains inadequate. The protection measures of civilians in conflict and post-conflict situations are still insufficient, while the principle of universality upholding the formulation of human security policy in governance systems is in transition. The following sections provide further clarification throughout the required risk assessments of the global architecture fostering peace, justice and security, which requires political convergence to fight against international threats and crimes, and which is expected to deal with States and individuals at the same extent. The requirement of political convergence is debated in the last chapter of this part dealing with the relationship between the UN regime and the emerging regime of international criminal justice falling under the Rome Statute. This section recalls the necessity to 'prevent', 'react' and 'rebuild' in mass atrocities situations with a constitutional strategy and a political *road map* integrating the governance of peace and justice for the sake of human security. The last paragraph of this section reports the pragmatic recommendations addressed by the UN High Level Panel on *Threats, Challenges and Change* which, in addition to the institutional reform of the UN, focused on the governance of *a)* the collective security and the use of force; *b)* the peace enforcement and peacekeeping capability; *c)* the post-conflict peace-building and *d)* the civilian protection duties. All of these clusters of governance require consensus based on human security expectations. For such sensitive governance issues human security is the most important requirement of the political convergence necessary.

In contrast with the traditional meaning of domestic governance of nation-states, which refers to decision-making defining expectations, granting public powers or verifying performance in domestic governing activities, we are well aware that the term global governance denotes the regulation of international relations between independent and sovereign States in the absence of a *supranational* authority. There is generally agreement between the different schools of governance that the extreme challenges taking place in societies in transition, combined with the shortcomings of domestic jurisdictions, require solid rather than symbolic international governance institutions based on the principles of neutrality, integrity and universality. The United Nations peacekeeping operations have traditionally followed three core principles: the consent among the parties to the conflict, the neutrality and impartiality of the UN forces deployed, and the use of force by UN personnel only in cases of self-defence.[240] The mission of mandates of universal character is to preserve norms and values internationally recognized for the sake of individual rights, while implementing strategies on matters of mutual concern and public good under the premises of 'effective' multilateralism.[241] The last decades have been characterized by several shortcomings of multilateral options. The systemic crisis of governance institutions became more complex with the economic and financial break downs occurred at domestic, regional and global levels. Nevertheless, while new opportunities arise for the governance systems of threats and crimes, on which the States may rely in case of serious domestic shortcomings, we are still far from the realization of any *supranational* system, which current interaction is only based on the early formation of mutual interests, including agreements and arrangements of cooperation based on secondary law, e.g. the relationship agreement between the United Nations and the International Criminal Court. The risk is the distance between governance systems of complementary character dealing with international threats and

240 See for valuable contributions to this debate N. Tsagourias, 'Consent, Neutrality/Impartiality and the Use of Force in Peacekeeping: Their Constitutional Dimension', *Journal of Conflict and Security Law* Volume 11, Issue 3, 2006, at 465–482. See also M. P. Karns, 'The Past as Prologue: The United States and the Future of the United Nations System', in F. A. Chadwick, G. M. Lyons, J. E. Trent (eds.), *The United Nations System: The Policies of Member States*, UNU, 1995, at 410. See for earlier legal contributions, T. Komarnicki, 'The Problem of Neutrality under the United Nations Charter', in *Transactions of the Grotius Society*, Vol. 38, 1952, at 77. See also C. Reith, 'International Authority and the Enforcement of Law', in *Transactions of the Grotius Society*, Vol. 38, 1952, at 109.

241 For an overview of the debate see K. Krause and A. Knight, *State, Society, and the UN System: Changing Perspectives on Multilateralism*, UNU Press, 1995.

crimes. International governance institutions, States and non-States actors should forge a new consensus on a broader and more effective collective security system towards a deeper advocacy of systemic and global reforms centralizing civilian protection measures.

### 4.4.1. THE REQUIRED ACTIONS TO 'PREVENT' 'REACT' AND 'REBUILD' IN MASS ATROCITY SITUATIONS

Simply reflecting on the efforts required by the world community it is obvious that a constitutional strategy at international level has the potential to influence national constitutions and vice versa. Such a strategy would neutralize the risks of undemocratic positions compromising judicial decisions and the important role of justice, which simply deserves a place in the arrays of international peace and security. On the other hand, the visibility of such a constitutional strategy would harmonize universal values in the different legal systems and traditions of the world community. The efforts should focus on keeping pace of the dialogue with local communities and civil society, including regional intergovernmental organizations, approaching the arena of non-state actors, groups, and activists promoting human rights, and also of others, extending the knowledge of political factions, armed groups, mercenaries and rebels characterizing each conflict situations. From another angle, the constant interaction between multilateral political actors enforcing international governance institutions is fundamental. In any case, the main responsibility remains in the hands of modern nation-states approaching such important issues in their constitutions and legal systems, while challenging the international legal order and vice versa. In our case, it is required to observe the constellation of international governance institutions and the necessary requirements of democratic governance of international threats and crimes, which require high standards of preventive diplomacy, mediation, negotiation and good standards of international cooperation preserving the progress of human security. Moreover, the development of capacity-building models of domestic governance are also required, if we also look at the shortcomings even in modern democracies and well established nation-states in western societies, including the collapse of regional governance systems, which are compromising the concept of security and global solidarity due to the disintegration of their unity of intents and their *supranational* character.[242]

It needs to be clarified that the International Criminal Court is not exclusively seen as a criminal and/or a human rights Court, but also as an enforcement

[242] See P. De Grauwe, *The Governance of a Fragile Eurozone*, Centre for European Policy Studies (CEPS), May 2011. See also D. Gros, T. Mayer, *August 2011: What to do when the Euro crisis reaches the core*, CEPS, August 2011, accessible at: www.ceps.eu/book/august-2011-what-do-when-euro-crisis-reaches-core.

mechanism of universal humanitarian principles in modern international relations. The preservation of the rule of law has been perceived as a principle of governance and as an important preventive tool of serious international crimes. In this study, the relationship between the United Nations and the International Criminal Court is interpreted as the opportunity for further inputs for a constitution of the world community.[243] The establishment of norms and compliance mechanisms universally recognized for the sake of stability in conflict situations characterized by extreme violence and by severe violations of international humanitarian law, the extension of multilevel jurisdictions and the way they are governed, are the main societal phenomena deserving detailed analysis. The establishment of global tools serving the domestic capacity-building with an impact on the security sectors in devastated nation-states (army, police and judiciary), including the protection duties of civilians during armed conflicts, violence and crime are interdependent phenomena which centralize the responsibilities of the States towards the international community but also the other way around. The question is whether the international community will centralize human security measures during intra- and inter-state conflicts based on the theory of constitutionalism or pluralism. Or better say the establishment of an international legal order able to control power politics throughout the rule of law, or the alternative ways of dealing with conflicts between legal frameworks in the absence of the political will upholding a *supranational* legal order.

## 4.4.2. THE IMPORTANT REQUIREMENT OF POLITICAL CONVERGENCE

This section debates the issue of political convergence required and not yet found. It should be clear at this stage that the international tools upholding the responsibilities to 'prevent', 'react' and 'rebuild' situations of war and crime need implementations. In the emerging governance of complementary global regimes two main factors require new orientations: the current shift in international relations after post-cold war, characterized by a different nature of political transitions, regime clashes and warfare, and the necessity for global governance institutions to interact with each other on consensus and strategy-building, including resource sharing, exchange of expertise, and lessons learned. The practice applied on the ground, in conflict and post-conflict situations during

[243] For an overview of the debate on constitutional protection of humanitarian rights, the internationalisation of law and transnational constitutional principles see the reports of the conference *From Peace to Justice* organised by The Hague Academic Coalition (HAC) and held on 15 and 16 May 2008 at the Peace Palace in The Hague. The overall theme of the conference was *The Dynamics of Constitutionalism in the Age of Globalisation*, accessible at: www.hiil.org/events/past-events/ See also B. Fassenberg, 'The Meaning of International Constitutional Law', in R. St. John Macdonald, D. M. Johnston (eds.), *Towards World Constitutionalism: Issues in the Legal Ordering of the World Community*, (2005), at 837.

humanitarian escalations deriving from violent political transitions, indicates that the principles of responsibility and accountability wait for configuration and implementation of civilian protection duties, including law enforcement engagements in accordance with the judicial outcomes of an independent international judiciary. The dilemma is whether modern nation-states are willing to adjust their constitutional parameters to universal values, preserving the legal and political order based on national and international responsibilities. After all, nation-states are responsible for the *status quo* of international relations not exclusively based on political realism which prioritizes their national interest and security over ideology, moral concerns, and political and social reconstructions.[244] Therefore, it is important to recall some of the challenges occurred in the post-cold war era in the context of international security;[245] the international humanitarian interventions during violent political transitions; the reach of universal governance institutions, and the efforts to centralize individuals and their fundamental rights in conflict and post-conflict societies. Political consensus on such issues, among other matters, is absolutely required.

### 4.4.3. SUMMARY OF THE RECOMMENDATIONS

In conclusion, it is required to recall again and summarize the recommendations of relevant observers of threats that have emerged since the end of the Cold War, including ongoing conflicts in the Middle East, threats of terroristic attacks, and genocidal intra-states conflicts.[246] Unfortunately, these are still waiting for collective achievements and reflect some areas where actions remain inadequate, very poor, or insufficient. The recommendations focus on: *a)* collective security and the use of force, *b)* peace enforcement and peacekeeping capability, *c)* post-conflict peace-building and *d)* civilian protection.

*a) Collective security and the use of force*

Article 51 of the Charter of the United Nations reads: "Nothing in the present Charter shall impair the inherent right of individual or collective self-defense

---

244 See J. Baylis, S. Smith, P. Owens, 'International and Global Security in the post-cold war era', in *The Globalization of World Politics. An Introduction to International Relations*, IV edition, Oxford University Press, 2008, at 253.

245 While the wide perspective of international security regards everything as a security matter, the traditional approach focuses mainly or exclusively on military concerns. For an overview of the evolution of this field of study see B. Buzan and L. Hansen, *The Evolution of International Security Studies*, Cambridge University Press, 2009.

246 See The Secretary-General's High-level Panel Report on Threats, Challenges and Change, *A more secure world: our shared responsibility*, A/59/565 (2004), Follow-up to the outcome of the Millennium Summit accessible at: www.unrol.org/doc.aspx?n=gaA.59.565_En.pdf See also M. W. Brough, J. W. Lango, H. van der Linden (eds.), *Rethinking the Just War Tradition*, 2007.

if an armed attack occurs against a Member of the United Nations, until the Security Council has taken measures necessary to maintain international peace and security. Measures taken by Members in the exercise of this right of self-defense shall be immediately reported to the Security Council and shall not in any way affect the authority and responsibility of the Security Council under the present Charter to take at any time such action as it deems necessary in order to maintain or restore international peace and security". The Security Council is fully empowered under Chapter VII of the Charter of the United Nations to address the full range of security threats with which States are concerned. The task is not to find alternatives to the Security Council as a source of authority but to make the Council work better than it has, as Kofi Annan often put it. The High-level Panel endorsed the emerging norm that there is a collective international responsibility to protect, exercisable by the Security Council authorizing military intervention as a last resort, in the event of genocide and other large-scale killing, ethnic cleansing or serious violations of humanitarian law which sovereign governments have proved powerless or unwilling to prevent. Such authorization by the Security Council and further escalation to justice should be characterized by compulsory cooperation with the Court, including resources and robust peace-making and peace-building.

In considering whether to authorize or endorse the use of military force, the Security Council should always address whatever other considerations may be taken into account. As discussed by Brough, Lango and van der Linden the following "five basic criteria of legitimacy" should be carefully considered: a) *seriousness of threat*. Is the threatened harm to State or human security of a kind, and sufficiently clear and serious, to justify *prima facie* the use of military force? In the case of internal threats, does it involve genocide and other large-scale killing, ethnic cleansing or serious violations of international humanitarian law, actual or imminently apprehended? b) *proper purpose*. Is it clear that the primary purpose of the proposed military action is to halt or avert the threat in question, whatever other purposes or motives may be involved? c) *Last resort*. Has every non-military option for meeting the threat in question been explored, with reasonable grounds for believing that other measures will not succeed? d) *proportional means*. Are the scale, duration and intensity of the proposed military action the minimum necessary to meet the threat in question? e) *balance of consequences*. Is there a reasonable chance of the military action being successful in meeting the threat in question, with the consequences of action not likely to be worse than the consequences of inaction? The above guidelines for authorizing the use of force should be embodied in declaratory resolutions of both the Security Council and General Assembly.[247] An important additional element should be

[247] M. W. Brough, J. W. Lango, H. van der Linden (eds.), *Rethinking the Just War Tradition*, 2007, at 3.

the appropriate considerations of the commission of international crimes and the violence on civilians spreading in multiple countries with the configuration of peace enforcement mandates supporting international justice activities on the ground (investigations and prosecutions).

*b) Peace enforcement and peacekeeping capability*

The developed States should do more to transform their existing force capacities into suitable contingents for peace operations. Member States should strongly support the efforts of the UN Department of Peacekeeping Operations, building on the important work of the Panel on UN Peace Operations of the UN Secretariat, to improve its use of strategic deployment stockpiles, standby arrangements, trust funds and other mechanisms in order to meet the tighter deadlines necessary for effective deployment. The States with advanced military capacities should establish standby high readiness and self-sufficient battalions that can reinforce UN missions, and should place them at the disposal of the UN. In regard to peacekeeping operations the Brahimi report is a useful tool to evolve with civilian protection duties. In response to criticism, particularly of the cases of sexual abuse by peacekeepers, the UN should take further steps toward reforming its operations. The Brahimi report was the first of many steps to review former peacekeeping missions, isolate flaws, and take steps to delimit mistakes ensuring the efficiency of future peacekeeping missions. The UN has vowed to continue to put these practices into effect when performing peacekeeping operations in the future. However, Brahimi's call that the UN missions have the means commensurate to their mandates has never been fully implemented. Mandates express ambitious protection of civilian agendas, while troop contributing countries are wary of putting their forces in harm's way to do just that.[248]

The technocratic aspects of the UN peacekeeping reform process have been continued and revitalized by the DPKO in its Peace Operations 2010 reform agenda. This included an increase in personnel, the harmonization of the conditions of service of field and headquarters' staff, the development of guidelines and standard operating procedures, and improving the partnership arrangement between the Department of Peacekeeping Operations (DPKO) and the United Nations Development Programme (UNDP) with the African Union and the European Union. Besides, the regional and international support should be complemented through national cooperation at all levels. The 'UN Peacekeeping Operations: Principles and Guidelines', incorporates and build on the Brahimi analysis. This needs further updates about the presence of complementary actors

248 See L. Arbour, *Doctrines Derailed?: Internationalism's Uncertain Future,* Global Briefing 2013 opening speech from the International Crisis Group's President & CEO Louise Arbour, accessible at: www.crisisgroup.org/en/publication-type/speeches/2013/arbour-doctrines-derailed-internationalism-s-uncertain-future.aspx.

on the ground such as investigations and prosecutions of international crimes and the support they would require.[249]

*c) Post-conflict peacebuilding*

Special representatives of the Secretary-General should have the authority and guidance to work with relevant parties to establish robust donor-coordinating mechanisms, as well as the resources to perform coordination functions effectively, including ensuring that the sequencing of United Nations assessments and activities is consistent with the priorities of governments. The Security Council should *mandate* and the General Assembly should *authorize* funding for disarmament and demobilization programs from assessed budgets of United Nations peacekeeping operations. A standing fund for peace-building should be established and finance the recurrent expenditures of a nascent government, as well as critical agency programs in the areas of rehabilitation and reintegration of combatants, child soldiers and the victims and witnesses of international crimes.

*d) Protecting civilians*

All combatants must abide by the Geneva Conventions. All Member States should sign, ratify and act on all treaties relating to the protection of civilians, such as the Genocide Convention, the Geneva Conventions, the Rome Statute of the International Criminal Court and all refugee conventions. The Security Council should fully implement resolution 1265 (1999) on the protection of civilians in armed conflict. The Security Council, United Nations agencies and Member States should fully implement resolution 1325 (2000) on women, peace and security. Member States should support and fully fund the proposed Directorate of Security and accord high priority to assisting the Secretary General in implementing a new staff security system in the short, middle and long terms.[250]

---

249 See USG/DPKO, UN Peacekeeping Operations Principles and Guidelines, 2008, accessible at: http://pbpu.unlb.org/pbps/Library/Capstone_Doctrine_ENG.pdf.

250 See Report of the Secretary-General's High Level Panel on Threats, Challenges and Change, *A more Secure World: Our Shared Responsibility*, Annexes, at 97, accessible at: www.un.org/secureworld/report2.pdf.

# 5. THE GOVERNANCE STRUCTURE OF COMPLEMENTARY GLOBAL REGIMES AND THEIR COMPETENCE

## PRELIMINARY REMARKS

As reported in the previous chapters, at the end of the six-week diplomatic conference held in Rome in 1998, 120 countries voted in favour of the Rome Statute. The political support and the development of the treaty-law meant the establishment of new public institutions committed to end the impunity of the gravest crimes known to humanity and bring justice to the victims. The Rome Statute institutions are: the International Criminal Court with exclusively a judicial mandate, the Assembly of States Parties which is the management oversight and legislative body of the Court, and the Trust Fund for Victims implementing Court-ordered reparations and provide physical and psychosocial rehabilitation or material support to victims of crimes within the jurisdiction of the Court. The US joined China, Libya, Iraq, Israel, Qatar, and Yemen as the only seven countries voting in opposition to the treaty, while twenty-one countries abstained. When looking at: *a)* the rejection of the Rome Statute by powerful States; *b)* the political impasse at the regional level as for instance in the African Union; and *c)* the difficulties of complementarity at international level, we notice that cooperation is very difficult to realize. In order to implement a global architecture fostering peace, justice and security able to influence *'l'état de droit'* and the institutional capacity-building in domestic realities, competence allocation, delimitation of competence, institutional reform, mutual and complementing support between such international institutions, are fundamental preconditions of democratic governance involved in the prevention of mass atrocities, including the importance of their working methods in case of international interventions and judicial referrals in situations of war and crime.[251]

The first section of this chapter focuses on the institutional contours characterizing the emerging regime of international criminal justice responsible of a systemic change promoting the links between human security and justice (Assembly of

---

[251] See F. Bensouda, Prosecutor of the International Criminal Court, *Statement to the United Nations Security Council on the Subject of "Working Methods of the Security Council"*, New York, United States, Thursday, 23 October 2014.

States Parties, Trust Fund for Victims and the Court). In order to build a model of international criminal justice it is important to start with strong fundaments at institutional, administrative and legislative levels complementing an independent international judiciary. Such institutional contours dealing with human rights and justice represent the indicator of public authority and the resources allocated in these fields of global governance. In the previous chapter it has been concluded that balancing powers in the international legal order will require the implementation of new fields of law and further political consensus enforcing the Rome Statute regime. For the political promotion of the Assembly of States Parties (ASP) the representation of such institution in regional and global organizations is recommended. In the last years the ASP adopted resolutions on several issues, including the Review Conference of the Rome Statute, the establishment of an independent oversight mechanism, the possible establishment of a liaison office at the African Union Headquarters, the permanent premises of the Court in The Hague, and the programme budget useful for its strategic plan for the next years. During the first Review Conference in Kampala the Assembly adopted resolutions on complementarity; cooperation; aggression; independent oversight mechanism; permanent premises; victims and reparations; amendments to the Rules of Procedure and Evidence; the "omnibus" resolution; and the Court's budget. In the long term the legislative activity of the ASP could have an impact on the maintenance of peace, justice, and security at global level. This section also offers an overview of the Trust Fund for Victims supporting the necessity of a comprehensive strategy for victims' rights, implementing the tools of *restorative* justice.

The second section approaches the legal tools regulating the relationship between the Court and the United Nations, the procedural matters and the agreement provisions, including the inter-institutional liaison between the Court and the UN. It emphasizes the inevitability of further implementation of such legal and institutional tools creating the premises of international criminal justice and its place in the peace and security regime executing *protective* justice with civilian protection measures. The third section offers some conclusions on the necessary challenges to implement the interactions between the Court and the UN. It examines the urgent proposals of the UN peacekeeping and peace building reforms, including the general proposals addressed by the Secretary-General on the security sector reform in peace operations, with clarifications on the rule of law sectors incorporating justice. It offers an overview of the efforts integrating *restorative* justice and reconstruction, into the strategic and operational planning of new post-conflict and peace-building operations. The fact findings deriving from the analysis of the current practice in the field operations indicate many gaps in these areas. This section concludes that there is the necessity to harmonize regimes working for peace, justice and security avoiding duplication, competition or inaction. This of course, is only possible if a strong consensus is reached on democratic institutional reforms of the United Nations, including the binding cooperation required by the regime of the Rome Statute.[252]

In order to conclude the topics dealt in this chapter (on the governance structure of complementary global regimes in their respective competence, and their potential to establish an interaction framework), the fourth section specifically debates on the rule of law and justice in conflict and post-conflict societies under the UN premises, the sectors of the rule of law at international level, the coordination of the rule of law activities within the UN, and the criminal accountability of the UN officials and experts on the ground during the field operations. The purpose of such an assessment is useful to identify feasible solutions on the accountability gaps, including the implementation of interactions between complementary global regimes in the short, middle and long terms. After all, laying strong legal foundations for transparent, accountable and efficient democratic institutions is crucial for the fight against mass atrocity crimes in all aspects of peace and security, such as its preservation, maintenance and restoration.[253]

The view expressed in this chapter is that strengthening the International Criminal Court and the Assembly of States Parties needs political consensus on substantive reforms at structural and normative levels, challenging the relationship with the United Nations system with primary law. The report on cooperation for instance, which was submitted by the Court to the States Parties, contains a high number of United Nations related entries in all categories of cooperation. The United Nations is understood in this report as including all principal organs, as well as peacekeeping operations and missions, funds and programs but not the independent specialized agencies such as the World Bank, WHO and UNESCO. The working group on cooperation between the organizations would offer significant progress about their interaction. Given the scope of the Court's cooperation requirements and the States Parties' obligations about cooperation, a working group is more suited to take this interaction forward than a single focal point. A working group could also be composed of a number of States Parties representatives based in key cities, including The Hague, New York, Brussels, Tokyo and Addis Ababa. The geographic reach of such a working group would have the potential to improve cooperation to the Rome Statute system from regional organizations such as the EU, and the AU, among others.[254]

---

252 See ICC-CPI-20141031-PR1057, *ICC President addresses United Nations General Assembly, calls for universal ratification of the Rome Statute,* Press Release : 31/10/2014. Speech, Statement and Report of the International Criminal Court to the United Nations for 2013/2014 are accessible at: www.icc-cpi.int/en_menus/icc/press%20and%20media/press%20releases/Pages/pr1057.aspx.

253 This concept has been underlined by the UN Secretary-General and by any renowned scholars and practitioners, such as Benjamin Ferencz, Cherif Bassiouni, Claus Kress, Antonio Cassese, and William Schabas, including other highly regarded authors.

254 See ICC-ASP/6/21, 2007, p. 16.

Pursuant to paragraph 60 of resolution ICC-ASP/10/Res.5 of 21 December 2011, the Bureau of the Assembly of States Parties submitted for consideration by the Assembly the report on complementarity. The report reflects the outcome of the informal consultations held by The Hague Working Group of the Bureau with the Court and other stakeholders (including the UNDP and other UN specialized agencies). The Assembly of States Parties is the custodian of the Rome Statute system. While the Assembly itself has a very limited role in strengthening the capacity of domestic jurisdictions to investigate and prosecute serious international crimes, it is a key forum for matters of international criminal justice. Combating impunity both at the national and the international level for the most serious crimes of concern to the international community as a whole, is the core objective of the Rome Statute. In this respect the Assembly has an important role in encouraging and promoting capacity-building at the national level and thereby strengthening the States Parties pillar of the Rome Statute system. Assisting States in assuming their primary responsibility to investigate and prosecute through promoting complementarity in new and existing rule of law programmes and other relevant instruments constitutes an important element in the fight against impunity.[255] In this chapter, however, the idea is to extend complementarity between the UN system and the Rome Statute institutions promoting a governance structure in accordance with their respective competence.

## 5.1. THE ROLE OF THE ASSEMBLY OF STATES PARTIES AND THE TRUST FUND FOR VICTIMS

### SECTION OUTLINE

It can be affirmed that an important element arising in the international contours of international criminal justice is the presence of a new forum in the political apparatus of the Rome Statute: the Assembly of the States Parties. The legislative and political organ of the Rome Statute regime would prepare some grounds to the parliamentary activity of the UN General Assembly, either in the fight against the impunity of mass atrocity crimes or stimulate the debate on global threats and crime definitions. It has the potential to be a forum promoting consensus much closer to the intra-state difficult realities of the African Union (AU), the Arab League (LAS), the permanent members of the UNSC, and other regional organizations, while promoting the Rome Statute at universal level in all judicial systems of the world. A comprehensive strategy for victims for instance, needs to be established towards the interaction between the ASP, the Trust Fund for Victims, the Court's organs and the important partners of the Rome Statute institutions, including the UN actors and regional

[255] See ICC-ASP/11/24, 2012, p. 3.

intergovernmental organizations. Unfortunately, the enthusiasm about these liaisons was undermined by the decision of the AU rejecting the Court's presence in the region. This section focuses on the institutional interaction currently in place between the Court and the United Nations since the establishment of the liaison office (New York) and the permanent Secretariat of the Assembly of States Parties (The Hague) which both started their activities since 2004.[256] The report pursuant to the Assembly resolution ICC-ASP/2/Res.7 concluded that the Court and the Secretariat required a permanent presence in New York. This conclusion was shared by the Court and the Secretariat. The liaison office would liaise and have a representative function with: the United Nations; the States Parties and States that are not parties to the Rome Statute; the international and regional organizations; the non-governmental organizations; the media organizations.

This section also offers an overview of the ICC-UN relationship agreement and the role of the Assembly of the States Parties (ASP) in order to establish an interaction strategy between the Rome Statute and the United Nations institutions.[257] Furthermore, it explores the reporting activity of the Court to the United Nations; the general provisions regarding international cooperation between the UN and the Court; the features of judicial assistance, according respectively to Part III of the ICC-UN relationship agreement and Part IX of the Rome Statute; the legislative role of the ASP and the establishment of an independent oversight mechanism, including the operation of the inspection and evaluation functions of the Court within such governance control mechanism currently debated in the ASP. In order to provide an understanding of the necessary implementation, this section examines the institutional interactions including the information exchange, communication channels and resource sharing between the ICC and the UN institutions, including mechanisms measuring their efficiency, transparency and economy. The purpose is to encourage concrete actions finding appropriate legal remedies of harmonization of complementary mandates dealing with international criminal justice, to be applied in both conflict and post-conflict situations. The States Parties should always promote the activities of the Court in regional and international organizations. This can be done through resolutions, declarations and other forms of political support, as well as different forms of technical assistance. These tools may also be used to facilitate arrest and surrender, with a last resort being the use of coercive instruments available within some of these organizations as international actors contributing to the enforcement of law. The second part of this section approaches the activity of the Trust Fund for Victims, the establishment by the Court of a strategy for victims'

---

256 See ICC-ASP/3/6 on the *Establishment of a New York Liaison Office for the International Criminal Court and the Secretariat of the Assembly of States Parties*.

257 See the Statement "*President of the General Assembly meets with the President of the Assembly of States Parties of the ICC*", New York 10 April 2012, General Assembly 66th Session, accessible at: www.un.org/en/ga/president/66/news/PRStatements/ps100412.shtml.

rights, and the necessary elements for the implementation of an effective system of global justice which depends on the interaction between complementary global regimes.

### 5.1.1. GLOBAL INTERACTIONS AND POLITICAL DETERMINATIONS

There are no doubts that international regimes of complementary character have an important role to play safeguarding individual rights in conflict and post-conflict societies, while challenging the traditional concept of national and international security. The political determination of the States Parties to the Rome Statute refers to the specific function of its institutions, monitoring and destabilizing criminal regimes, while contributing to the preservation of peace and security in accordance with the purpose and principle of the UN Charter. Such high expectations depend on the intersection of policy and law on global issues complementing conflict and post-conflict intervention with retributive and restorative justice in domestic realities, reaching victimized communities on the ground according to the principle of *complementarity*. Regarding the future expectations of remedies implementing interactions in the emerging regime of justice, the Assembly of the States Parties in the resolution "*Strengthening the International Criminal Court and the Assembly of States Parties*" declared:

> "*Convinced* that the International Criminal Court is an essential means of promoting respect for international humanitarian law and human rights, thus contributing to freedom, security, justice and the rule of law as well as to the prevention of armed conflicts, the preservation of peace and the strengthening of international security and the advancement of post-conflict peace-building and reconciliation, with a view to achieving sustainable peace, in accordance with the purposes and principles of the Charter of the United Nations...*Convinced* also that there can be no lasting peace without justice and that peace and justice are thus complementary requirements".[258]

For the judicial proceedings national courts have the priority under the Rome Statute system. The States have the opportunity to bring cases to an international judiciary that they might not otherwise pursue. In each of the situations that the Court is investigating policy efforts have been made to improve domestic justice mechanisms for serious international crimes as a result of the Court's involvement (Uganda, DRC, Sudan, Central African Republic, Central African Republic II, Kenya, Côte d'Ivoire, Libya and Mali) including the situations under preliminary analysis (Afghanistan, Colombia, Nigeria, Guinea, Georgia, Honduras, Iraq,

[258] See ICC-ASP/6/Res.2 (2007), *Strengthening the International Criminal Court and the Assembly of States Parties*.

Ukraine).[259] At global level, additional legal mechanisms will be necessary regulating the principle of accountabilities in international legal relations of public organizations and private corporations, limiting the authority and the powers of the Security Council, while reinforcing legal features in the field of human rights. As previously argued the ideal would be a review of the UN Charter and the Rome Statute accordingly, after decennia of paralysis and fragmentation in peace, justice and security governance matters. Political consensus is necessary to balance powers in the international legal relations. This is true considering the question of judicial review of the acts of the Security Council which is one of the most urgent issues facing the United Nations.[260] In order to have an overview of the institutional setting of the Rome Statute system interacting with important global actors, it is important to look at the legislative activity of new institutions (ASP, TFV), including the norms regulating such interactions based on binding cooperation at least for the States being parties of such institutions.

*The Assembly of States Parties*

The Assembly of States Parties (ASP) is the management oversight and legislative body of the International Criminal Court. It is composed of representatives of the States that have ratified and acceded to the Rome Statute.[261] The Assembly of States Parties has a Bureau, consisting of a President, two Vice Presidents and 18 members elected by the Assembly for a three-year term, taking into consideration principles of equitable geographic distribution and adequate representation of the principal legal systems of the world. On its second session in September 2003 the Assembly of States Parties decided to establish the Permanent Secretariat (ICC-ASP/2/L.5). The Assembly of States Parties decides on various items, such as the adoption of normative texts and of the budget, the election of the judges and of the Prosecutor and the Deputy Prosecutor(s). According to article 112(7) of the Rome Statute, each State Party has one vote and every effort has to be made to

---

259 See ICC website » Structure of the Court » Office of the Prosecutor » Preliminary Examinations.

260 See for discussions, H. Köchler, 'The ICC: Signaling a Paradigm Shift in International Criminal Law?' in H. Köchler (ed.) *Global Justice or Global Revenge? International Criminal Justice at the Crossroads*, 2003, 222 at 224. For an overview of the evolution of human rights law which provides a broad political history of the emergence and development of the human rights movement in the 20th century through the crucible of the United Nations, focusing on the hopes and expectations, concrete power struggles, national rivalries, and bureaucratic politics that modelled the international system of human rights law, see R. Normand, S. Zaidi, *Human Rights at the UN The Political History of Universal Justice*, (2007). For other scholars' publications involved on the UN Intellectual History Project see the list accessible at: www.unhistory.org/ For an overview of the scholarly debate on the UNSC started since the nineties, see M. Bedjaoui, *The New World Order and the Security Council: Testing the Legality of Its Acts*, (1994), 56 at 90.

261 See Rules of Procedure of the ASP, *ASP First session, New York, 3–10 September 2002*, accessible at: www.icc-cpi.int/iccdocs/asp_docs/Publications/Compendium/Compendium.3rd.08.ENG.pdf.

reach decisions by consensus both in the Assembly and the Bureau. If consensus cannot be reached, decisions are taken by vote.[262]

The ASP promotes international criminal justice through the Rome Statute and further empowerment of the jurisdiction of the Court. At this stage the Court, with multiple investigations, situation analysis and the issuance of arrest warrants, needs further support by the States Parties and non-States parties. In order to receive it, the ASP engagement is vital. This for two reasons, first, to secure cooperation from States, various agencies of the United Nations and other inter-governmental organizations, and second, to engage the ASP responsibilities allocating sufficient resources to the Court. There can be no doubt that active support by the States Parties will influence the future of the Court and determine whether the permanent judicial institution ultimately reaches the goals of its establishment. Moreover, the long-term success of the ICC depends on the ASP to act as a politically engaged and supportive body of international criminal justice. The ASP has an important role to play in ensuring that the Court is efficient and operates as intended, complementing national courts and making a meaningful contribution to the cause of justice. As a new and unique institution facing enormous challenges, the Court is responsible in developing best practices becoming an excellent model of public administration of criminal justice. The Court needs to benefit from close engagement by the ASP particularly in this early phase of considering reviews of the Rome Statute. Where there are shortcomings in practice, States Parties can point them out. Thus, aside from being essential to secure cooperation, the active involvement of the ASP with the Court is necessary to guarantee the most effective judicial institution possible.[263] The responsibility of the ASP interacting with the UN liaises in the first part of the Rome Statute on the establishment of the Court. Article 2 states: "The Court shall be brought into relationship with the United Nations through an agreement to be approved by the Assembly of States Parties to this Statute and thereafter concluded by the President of the Court on its behalf". The implementation of such interaction with the UN is a responsibility of the ASP.[264] In the next paragraphs we will see how the ASP functions in practice.

---

[262] See the Assembly of States Parties structure on the ICC-ASP Portal, accessible at: www.icc-cpi.int/asp.html.

[263] See Resolution ICC-ASP/3/Res.8, *Intensifying the Dialogue between the Assembly of States Parties and the International Criminal Court*, 10 September 2004, accessible at: www.icc-cpi.int/asp/documentation/doc_3rdsession.html.

[264] See Coalition for the ICC (CICC, Cooperation Team), *Comments and Recommendations to the Tenth Session of the Assembly of States Parties, 12–21 December 2011, New York*, 2 December 2011, accessible at: www.coalitionfortheicc.org/documents/CICC_Cooperation_Team_Paper_(ASP10).pdf.

*Institutional, managerial and political settings of cooperation*

The ASP represents the bridge between the States, the UN institutions and the Court, necessary for the promotion of the regime of justice. In the process of allocating public powers and competences at global level, the judicial empowerment of the Court promoted by the ASP would influence the multilateral system or regime for human rights protection, the national sovereignty and peaceful international disputes, promoting the rule of law at micro and macro level. However, the institutional identity of the ASP is still in progress, as many difficulties arise considering the absence on board of the majority of the States of the Arab League, Israel, the US, Russia and China.[265] Some of these States opposed the Court since the beginning of its existence. At political level a strategic definition of the global fight against international crimes is expected by the ASP, the UN General Assembly, the Security Council an the Secretary-General. The Court's relationship with the UN and the institutional matters will need further implementation, especially considering the impact on the accession campaign of the Rome Statute, the pillar of cooperation, the definition of crimes and universal jurisdiction, the accountability of corporations and the controversial issue of the UN peacekeepers.[266] The Court itself cannot do anything about statutory matters, as the institution is only dealing with judicial assistance at ministerial level. This is an ASP political responsibility. For any review in fact, the Statute provides the involvement of the ASP for whatever revision. Political consensus is indispensable.

Both the ASP and the UN institutions remain the premises where to address decision-making exclusively based on democratic consensus. Regarding the cooperation, since 2007 the working documents of ASP indicate an extensive activity of its working groups (The Hague and New York). The overall aim of the issues dealt by the two Working Groups has been to create and promote an enabling environment for the Court. It was sought to identify problems and barriers in providing cooperation of a general and structural nature, and highlight generic solutions and models dealing with these interactions which were based on the report submitted by the Court on cooperation, The Hague Working Group decided to organise its work in thematic meetings focusing primarily on the role of the States Parties. The New York Working Group decided to organise its work

265 See M. P. Scharf 'Results of the Rome Conference for an International Criminal Court', (August 1998), *The American Society of International Law*, accessible at: www.asil.org/insigh23.cfm See also M. P. Scharf, 'The Politics of Establishing an International Criminal Court', (1996) *Duke Journal of Comparative and International Law* 6 , 167 at 173.

266 For an overview of the debate of human rights protection and criminal proceedings against corporations between the UN and the ICC see, C. Chiomenti, 'Corporations and the International Criminal Court', in O. De Schutter (ed.), *Transnational Corporations and Human Rights*, 2006, 287 at 312. See also L. van den Herik, "Corporations as future subjects of the International Criminal Court: An exploration of the counterarguments and consequences", in C. Stahn, L. van den Herik (eds.), *Future Perspective of International Criminal Justice*, (2010).

around two main themes, namely the relationship between the UN and the Court, and the role of the States Parties with respect to the Court in the UN context, in view of crosscutting nature of the UN related issues. Furthermore both working groups deal with the issue of international and regional organizations.[267] From these reports it is clear that the ASP is engaged on one side on the managerial, institutional and political settings of cooperation creating a system of interactions with important partners, such as the UN, while empowering the public authority of the Court promoting its transparency, economy and efficiency. The problem arising in these reports is a lack of concrete actions or *road map* to be performed in the short, middle and long terms by the actors involved, respectively the Rome Statute institutions, the States Parties and the UN. Provisions should be made to ensure, that there is a platform for taking forward the work on cooperation as well as a general channel of communication between the Court and States Parties. Such clusters of cooperation and the general legal mechanism regulating them will need further implementation (information sharing, national focal points, procedures and structures of cooperation, and sensitive thematic aspects such as witness relocation and enforcement of sentences agreements) including institution-building between the Rome Statute institutions and the UN. The States Parties should ensure that adequate implementing legislation and supplementary agreements are in place to enable cooperation and ensure that appropriate structures and procedures are established to make such cooperation run smoothly. In short, the States Parties should reinforce an enabling environment of interactions creating a global framework of cooperation.[268]

*Transparency, economy and efficiency*

In line with the supervision on the Court's practice and the performance appraisals by the ASP, article 112, paragraph 4 of the Rome Statute gives the authority to the Assembly of States Parties (ASP) to establish subsidiary bodies in addition to the judicial (OTP, Presidency and Chambers) and non-judicial organs of the Court (Registry). The Court is evolving into a fully operational and complex international judicial institution. Institutional matters and resource allocations require the ASP to fully perform its oversight function for enhancing

267 For an overview of the clusters of cooperation and the general legal mechanisms which will need further implementation in ASP see, ICC-ASP/6/21, Report of the Bureau on Cooperation, 19 October 2007, pp. 17–22. See also Resolution on Cooperation, ICC-ASP/11/Res.5, 21 November 2012, accessible at: www.icc-cpi.int/iccdocs/asp_docs/Resolutions/ASP11/ICC-ASP-11-Res5-ENG.pdf.

268 For an overview of the set of recommendations that might further improve the cooperation between the United Nations and the International Criminal Court, bearing in mind the fact that cooperation between the two institutions is a relatively new phenomenon, including the conclusions in the Report of the Bureau on Cooperation, see ICC-ASP/6/21, 19 October 2007, Conclusions, p. 23, accessible at: www.icc-cpi.int/iccdocs/asp_docs/library/asp/ICC-ASP-6-21_English.pdf.

the efficiency, economy and transparency of the Court. This is in fact the scope of an independent oversight mechanism. This supervisory function is to be carried out at various organizational levels relative to the different activities of the Court, including through investigation, inspection and evaluation of administrative, managerial, organizational and budgetary measures, as well as on the implementation of the regulatory framework of governance in the several Court's organs. The implementation of such organ is only at its initial stage but it is important to report on the provisional character of such mechanism.

The Assembly of States Parties establishes, in accordance with a resolution, an independent oversight mechanism. The Registrar of the Court shall enter into a memorandum of understanding with the United Nations Office of Internal Oversight Services to provide support services on an annual cost recovery basis for the *operationalization* of the oversight mechanism.[269] The documents consulted indicate that such organ which reports to the ASP would start with administrative investigative activities inside the Court and at a later stage with inspection and evaluation in the several organs of the judicial institution. The independent oversight mechanism itself will be expected to develop the rules governing its work, with the following recommendations: *a)* the scope of the independent oversight mechanism will cover internal investigation, evaluation and inspection. The establishment of an independent professional investigative capacity will be implemented immediately and additional elements of oversight, such as inspection and evaluation as envisaged in article 112, paragraph 4, of the Rome Statute, shall be brought into operation following a decision of the ASP to be adopted; *b)* it is envisaged that the investigative unit of the newly established independent oversight mechanism will have *proprio motu* investigative powers and incorporate procedures and protection measures for staff; *c)* it is envisaged that the individuals covered by the oversight mechanism will include all Court staff subject to the Staff Rules and the Court, together with elected officials. It is also envisaged that the investigative unit of the oversight mechanism will be utilized for the conduct of investigations of any allegations of misconduct made against contractors retained by the Court and working on its behalf. Such investigations should be carried out in accordance with the terms of the contract. In circumstances where a contract is silent on the manner and/or the modalities of any investigation, the oversight mechanism will conduct its investigation in accordance with its own established procedures and recognized best practice. The findings of any investigation will be used to determine the applicable sanctions, if any, under the existing contractual regime between the Court and the contractor. Within this context, it is recommended that the Court develops and incorporates

---

269 See ICC-ASP/8/2/Add.3, Report of the Bureau on the Establishment of an Independent Oversight Mechanism, 4 November 2009, accessible at: www.icc-cpi.int/NR/rdonlyres/E603F5B0-F342-4A25-A792-8947AAC8ABDC/0/ICCASP82Add3ENG.pdf.

into its procurement contracts a code of conduct and also appropriate disciplinary procedures to be followed in circumstances of alleged misconduct. *d)* In all cases, if criminal activity is suspected in the course of an investigation, the oversight mechanism must notify the relevant national authorities, such as the State where the suspected crime was committed, the State of the suspect's nationality, the State of the victim's nationality, and where applicable, the host State of the seat of the Court.

### 5.1.2. THE TRUST FUND FOR VICTIMS AND A STRATEGY FOR THEIR RIGHTS

The Rome Statute provided that the Court's legislative body, the ASP should create a Trust Fund for the benefit of victims of crimes falling under the jurisdiction of the Court. The Court can order money and other property collected through fines or forfeiture or orders of reparations against a convicted perpetrator to be transferred into and distributed by the Trust Fund for Victims (TFV). The special target groups of the Trust Fund's assistance efforts are the victims of sexual violence, former child soldiers and abducted children, the families of murder victims and victims of other brutal crimes, and victimized villages. The Fund's assets are mainly used for the physical and psychological rehabilitation of victims. The Fund may also pay victims damages or other reparations by virtue of a decision given by the ICC during a trial. Initiatives for assistance projects come directly from target areas approved by the ICC. At present, a number of projects are under way in the Democratic Republic of Congo and in Uganda. The intention is to expand the scope of activities to the Central African Republic and to Sudan (Darfur). The volume of the funds used for assistance comes as voluntary donations from States. The donations can also be made, for instance, by corporations, private individuals and organizations. The Court may also order that fines or other assets obtained would be transferred to the Trust Fund.

The ASP established the Trust Fund in 2002 and a five member Board of Directors to oversee its activities.[270] The States Parties have been grouped into geographical areas, each of which has a representative on the Board of Directors of the Trust Fund for Victims. The Board's principal task is to guide the Trust Fund's activities and allocation of resources and to coordinate and oversee assistance projects. The Board reports to the Assembly of States Parties. In 2004, a Trust Fund Secretariat was created as part of the Court's Registry, funded by the Court's regular budget,

[270] ICC-ASP/1/Res.6. The ASP may, as and when the workload of the Trust Fund increases, create an expanded capacity, including the appointment of an Executive Director, and "as part of such consideration…consider the payment of expenses of the Trust Fund from the voluntary contribution accruing to it. An Executive Director was appointed in 2006.

and not out of the funds it holds for the benefit of victims.[271] In 2005 the ASP adopted the Trust Fund Regulations, and the Trust Fund began its operations in 2007. Since 2006, the Assembly of States Parties requested the Court to work further in the development of the strategic plan with regard to the "position of victims".[272] The Trust Fund has started implementing projects to provide physical and psychological assistance and material support to victims. Over 34 projects in DRC and Uganda were approved by the Pre-Trial Chambers in 2009.[273] According to a recent submission filed with Pre-Trial Chamber II, the Fund also plans to initiate assistance projects in CAR. This assistance is different by the judicial decisions on awards falling under victims' reparations. The ICC-ASP/8/45 is the Report of the Court on the strategy in relation to the victims. The NGOs were critical on the draft strategy prepared in the course of 2008. The NGOs considered that it was a merely descriptive document which failed to set concrete objectives and strategies. Following the recommendations made by the seventh session of the ASP (ICC-ASP/7/Res.3, *Strengthening the ICC and the ASP*), the Court continued to work on the document with a view to its finalization and presentation to the next sessions of the ASP. The political approach given in 2009 is that such a strategy still lacks on security issues and participation of victims into the proceedings, including notification obligations, protection measures and relocation programs. This means the need to establish an additional organ dealing with such matters. With regard to the reparations, which focused mainly on assistance projects implemented by the Trust Fund for some years, this does not address thoroughly how the Court will implement its reparations mandate.

The implementation of these projects has been ongoing in the last years. Victims have seen in the Rome Statute an unprecedented recognition of rights but the development of a comprehensive strategy is still in progress. The ASP will need to support the Court in such important implementation of victims' rights. The Trust Fund faces challenges inherent to a new and *sui generis* institutions working in on-going conflicts. Resuming the recommendations addressed by civil societies organizations during the Eight Session of the ASP in November 2009 three main points amongst others are extremely important: a) ensure greater transparency and visibility of the Trust Fund, both among international actors and potential beneficiaries; b) continue to devise and implement fundraising strategies; c) exercise effective oversight over the Trust Fund Secretariat and ensure

---

271 ICC-ASP/3/Res.7. *Establishment of the Secretariat of the Trust Fund for Victims*, 10 September 2004, paras 2 and 4.

272 ICC-ASP/5/Res.2, Strategic Planning Process of the Court, para. 3.

273 See the Regulation 50 of the Regulations of the Trust Fund for Victims.

appropriate coordination with other organs of the Court, especially considering the preparations that must be undertaken in view of the first reparations awards.[274]

Victims' rights were not fully taken into consideration by previous international criminal tribunals. The lessons learned from those tribunals determined the drafters of the Rome Statute to give a privileged position to victims before the Court (participation and reparation). The consideration of the interest of victims is at the heart of the Rome Statute. The success of the Court will be measured by its ability to develop and fully implement its mandate with respect to victims. Victims continue to show interest in the Court's proceedings and to participate actively in them. The first trial has seen the participation of 105 victims. Over 350 victims will participate in the Katanga and Ngudjolo trial (DRC). For CAR, 34 victims participated in the confirmation of charges hearing against Bemba, and 78 did so in the Abu Garda hearing. While these are exciting developments, the Court must continue to work hard in order to make victim participation truly meaningful. The development of an adequate victims' strategy is essential for that to happen. In addition, meaningful participation of victims in the proceedings requires increased efforts for adequate legal representation.

## 5.1.3. AN EFFECTIVE SYSTEM OF CRIMINAL JUSTICE

The institutional overview offered in this section indicates that the features of international criminal law are only one element moving forward the effectiveness of the emerging regime of international criminal justice centralizing victims' rights. While empirical reports would try to measure such effectiveness, new rules are necessary harmonizing the interactions of international governance institutions in order to maximize the results on the ground in conflict and post-conflict situations. Being effective is generally understood as having the quality of producing a desired or intended result, but the fight against the impunity of mass atrocity crimes is only at its initial stage of delivering results. The empowerment of an independent judicial channel balancing powers in the international legal order requires the implementation of interactions between complementary global regimes. The role of international governance institutions is fundamental in order to define areas of improvement in the institution building of complementary mandates involved in the administration of international criminal justice. Their involvement will need a well defined delimitation of competences, resource allocations and legal harmonization of administrative matters, including objectives and strategies with regard to their respective mandates in conflict and

[274] See FIDH, "Victims and TFV: Providing Physical and Psychological Assistance and Material Support to Victims, and Preparing for the First Reparations Award", in *Recommendations to the Eight Session of the ASP*, November 2009, n. 532a, pp. 12–13.

post-conflict situations. The purpose is to ensure that domestic legal systems, and other regional legal arrangements to which they are party, have the jurisdiction and the capacity to effectively prosecute international crimes or to extradite the suspects of such crimes.

This section clarified the competence and responsibility of the different institutions within the Rome Statute system. In particular, the capacity-building of the political and managerial channel of the Assembly of the States Parties (ASP) supposed to implement measures of assistance in the judicial systems of the member States and the rule of law sectors, profiting of the partnerships with the UN system in order to promote reforms in the post-conflict phase in domestic systems, preserving the security of individuals and the rule of law sectors (army, police and judiciary). In addition to the basic requirement of legal assistance, the ASP should develop a monitoring activity of national implementations of the Rome Statute provisions in national parliaments and constitutions, including their impact in domestic governance systems. Further political reach in regional realities is also required, integrating emerging public authorities and institutions engaged in the fight against the impunity of international crimes. The Trust Fund is the instrument to centralize the rehabilitation and reparation of victims after long judicial proceedings. The Trust Fund needs a stronger commitment from all member States, global actors and relevant stakeholders. The UN remains of course one of the most relevant actors in order to promote country-specific programming activities of development in communities affected by war and crime, especially after the outcomes of an international judiciary assessing the truth in situations on a case-by-case basis, and which would require further assistance in domestic governance systems for the sake of order and sustainable peace. Humanitarian crisis and the impunity of serious human rights breaches have influenced the evolution of the rule of international policy and law developing multilateral tools for *preventive*, *retributive* and *restorative* justice. In order to fulfil the gaps between complementary but independent global mandates dealing with peace, justice and security, legislative adjustments and harmonization of laws are necessary. At this moment in time, the relationship between the United Nations and the Court has been established by secondary law, which is discussed in the next session.

## 5.2. THE INSTITUTIONAL LIAISON AND THE RELATIONSHIP AGREEMENT BETWEEN THE COURT AND THE UNITED NATIONS

### SECTION OUTLINE

In order to approach the causes of international threats and crimes with democratic tools, decision-makers need to focus on interaction strategies between complementary global actors. There are no doubts that the interaction between the United Nations and the Rome Statute system is a new phenomenon which needs implementation at institutional, procedural and operational levels. In order to deliver optimized results in the field where both mandates are involved, the UN operational support during peace operations to the Court needs attention. After the empirical analysis of the UN peacekeeping operations and their transition into peace-building in conflict and post-conflict situations, it can be concluded that the reconstruction phase can be effective in the field only by supporting new actors committed to peace and justice. The domestic realities in phase of reconstruction can only benefit of the UN peace-building when these are able to support other fundamental actors involved in such process of reconstruction improving human security. The Court of course is definitely one of these actors.[275] In order to have an understanding on the further implementation of the interaction necessary between the Court and the United Nations, this section clarifies the legal instruments currently at disposition, including the inter-institutional matters and liaison between the organizations. The purpose is to identify methods for a better relationship, cooperation and partnership in the regime of international criminal justice.

The relationship agreement between the Court and the United Nations envisages a number of ways in which each of the organs of the Court can cooperate with the United Nations and its organs, funds and programmes. Continued and active interface between the Court and the Security Council, *inter alia* with regard to referrals pursuant to article 13 of the Rome Statute, will be necessary. An analysis of the many functional and administrative links envisaged between the organs of the Court and the United Nations system strongly confirms the need to implement such relationship between the two entities. Since the relocation of the ASP Secretariat to The Hague, there can be no doubt that the absence of official and effective contacts, if allowed to continue, between the Court and the United Nations will adversely affect the working relationship between the two entities. The liaison office of the Court to the United Nations represented a positive accomplishment.

### 5.2.1. THE INTER-INSTITUTIONAL LIAISON

With regard to the inter-institutional liaison an important contribution to the ICC-UN interaction came from the establishment of the ICC New York UN Liaison Office, for a number of reasons.[276] The Rome Statute institutions (the

275 For the debate see M. Doyle, N. Sambanis, 'War-Making, Peacebuilding, and the United Nations', *Making War and Building Peace: United Nations Peace Operations,* 2006, at 23.

276 See ICC-ASP/3/6(2004), "Desirability of a New York Office", in *Establishment of a New York Liaison Office for the International Criminal Court and the Secretariat of the Assembly of States*

Court, the ASP and the TFV) sitting in The Hague are geographically remote from the Headquarters of the United Nations in New York. It was crucial to ensure that this geographical distance would not lead to the development of political and legal distance. To prevent the impact of such inter-institutional decentralization, the Court established a presence in New York, not only to keep the Rome Statute and its institutions on the international agenda, but also to reinforce the role of the Rome Statute institutions collectively, as an essential, dynamic and developing element of the international mosaic of peace and justice. In addition to these political reasons, there were strong practical and logistical justifications for having such a presence in New York. New York is and will remain the centre of international relations and diplomatic negotiations. New York-based representatives of States Parties are most likely to continue to be responsible for servicing the ASP meetings in The Hague. Indeed, almost all least developed and developing countries have representation in New York (as opposed to The Hague) at a level that allows them to follow closely the work of the Court. The next achievement for the Court would be to have support offices in regional organizations including the important requirement of focal points at ministerial level within the domestic governance structure by all States Parties.

The value of developing direct contacts in various agencies of the United Nations is an important implementation issue. Now that the Court has entered its operational phase after the first decade of existence, a closer working relationship with the United Nations system is increasingly important. Although the Court is an independent entity, it was born out of the UN system and their interaction will provide a permanent basis for a continuing relationship and information-sharing between the two organizations, while respecting their autonomy and confidentiality regime. Some of the most relevant UN agencies that may assist the Court under a more structured cooperation agreement include the High Commissioner for Human Rights (OHCHR), the High Commissioner for Refugees (UNHCR), the UN Special Adviser on Genocide and the UN Children's Fund (UNICEF). Other partners would be the other offices of the UN responsible for the overall coordination of the rule of law activities at international level such as the Department of Political Affairs (DPA), the Department of Peacekeeping Operations (DPKO), the Office of Legal Affairs (OLA), United Nations Development Programme (UNDP), the United Nations Development Fund for Women (UNIFEM) and the United Nations Office on Drugs and Crime (UNODC). Most importantly, the UN humanitarian and peacekeeping missions, especially in conflict areas where atrocities are being committed, should provide

*Parties*, p. 2, accessible at: www.icc-cpi.int/library/asp/ICC-ASP-3-6_New_York_liaison_office_English.pdf See the Report of the Committee on Budget and Finance on the Work of its Fifth Session, ICC-ASP/4/27, para.104.*Official Records of the Assembly of States Parties to the Rome Statute of the International Criminal Court, Fifth session, The Hague, 23 November to 1 December 2006* (International Criminal Court publication, ICC-ASP/5/32), part II, D.6 (a).

the Court with vital information and services needed to achieve the Court's goals. The cooperation agreement with the peacekeeping should also facilitate Court's requests for testimony from UN officials, although the preference would be to have harmonization of such agreements with more detailed provisions on security issues of the Court's field offices. In the area of information sharing and MONUC, the practice indicates that the UN confidentiality regime brought some issues with consequences on the delay of DRC's proceedings (*Prosecutor vs. Lubanga*).[277]

## 5.2.2. THE ICC-UN RELATIONSHIP AGREEMENT

Pursuant to Article 2 of the Rome Statute in 2004 the Secretary General of the UN and the President of the ICC signed an agreement that provides for the structure of the relationship between these international governance institutions.[278] The UN-ICC Relationship Agreement which entered into force upon signature recognizes the mandates and independence of both institutions, defines the scope of their relationship, and outlines the conditions under which the UN and the ICC cooperate.[279] This relationship, as elaborated in the agreement, deals with both institutional issues and matters pertaining to judicial assistance and institutional cooperation. In this regard, it includes, *inter alia*, issues like the participation of the ICC in the capacity of observer in the UN General Assembly; exchange of information provisions; the obligation to consult each other on matters of mutual interest; exchange of representatives and high officials; administrative cooperation issues; the provision of conference services on a reimbursable basis; financial matters; and the possibility for certain ICC officials to use the UN laissez-passer as a valid travel document to the missions in the field. Concerning judicial assistance, the UN, in accordance with the Agreement and its Charter, agrees to cooperate with the Court whenever the latter requests the testimony of an official of the United Nations or of one of its programs, funds or offices. The Agreement also addresses issues pertaining to the waiver of privileges and immunities of UN officials as well as the protection of the content of documentation rendered to the

277 See Decision on the consequences of non-disclosure of exculpatory materials covered by Article 54(3)(e) agreements and the application to stay the prosecution of the accused, together with certain other issues raised at the Status Conference on 10 June 2008 No. *ICC-01704-01/06*, 13 June 2008, accessible at: www.icc-cpi.int/library/cases/ICC-01-04-01-06-1401-ENG.pdf.

278 See Rome Statute Part I, Establishment of the Court. Article 2, Relationship of the Court with the United Nations. The Court shall be brought into relationship with the United Nations through an agreement to be approved by the Assembly of States Parties to this Statute and thereafter concluded by the President of the Court on its behalf. See Rome Statute accessible at: www.icc-cpi.int/library/about/officialjournal/Rome_Statute_English.pdf.

279 See ICC-ASP/3/Res.1, Negotiated Relationship Agreement between the International Criminal Court and the United Nations, Source: ASP/UN, Adoption: 04.10.2004 , accessible at: www.icc-cpi.int/library/asp/ICC-ASP-3-Res1_English.pdf.

UN by States or intergovernmental organizations on a confidential basis.[280] Article 18 of the Agreement sets out the terms of cooperation between the United Nations and the Office of the Prosecutor (OTP). The UN undertakes to cooperate with the OTP in particular when the Prosecutor exercises his or her duties and powers with respect to an investigation and seeks the cooperation of the United Nations pursuant to Article 54 of the Rome Statute. Such cooperation will consist mainly of the exchange of information for the purpose of generating new evidence, which can be subject to conditions of confidentiality of the information, protection of persons and security of any operation or activity of the UN.

*The procedural matters*

As noted above, Article 1 contains the purpose of the Relationship Agreement "the present Agreement, which is entered into by the United Nations and the International Criminal Court, pursuant to the provisions of the Charter of the United Nations ("the Charter") and the Rome Statute of the International Criminal Court ("the Statute") respectively, defines the terms on which the United Nations and the Court shall be brought into relationship. The agreement contains 23 articles, divided into IV parts.[281] Part III of the ICC-UN relationship agreement refers to the cooperation and judicial assistance, and contains the general provisions regarding cooperation between the UN and the Court. "With due regard to its responsibilities and competence under the Charter and subject to its rules as defined under the applicable international law, the UN undertakes to cooperate with the Court and to provide to the Court such information or documents as the Court may request pursuant to article 87, paragraph 6, of the Rome Statute".[282] Article 17 regulates the cooperation between the Security Council and the ICC. When the Security Council, acting under Chapter VII of the Charter of the United Nations, decides to refer to the Prosecutor "a situation in which one or more of the crimes referred to in article 5 of the Statute appears to have been committed, the UN Secretary General would transmit the decision to the Prosecutor together with documents and any other material that may be pertinent to the decision of the Council. The Court will keep the Security

280 On the issue see P. C. Szasz, T. Ingadottir, 'The UN and the ICC: The immunity of the UN and its Officials', (2001) 14 LJIL 867, at 885.

281 Preamble; I. General provisions (Articles 1–3); II. Institutional relations (Articles 4–14); III. Cooperation and judicial assistance (Articles 15–20); IV. Final provisions (Articles 21–23). See the Relationship Agreement between the ICC and the UN accessible at: www.icc-cpi.int/library/asp/ICC-ASP-3-Res1_English.pdf.

282 See Article 15, Relationship Agreement between the ICC and the UN. Article 87 (6) Rome Statute: "The Court may ask any intergovernmental organization to provide information or documents. The Court may also ask for other forms of cooperation and assistance which may be agreed upon with such an organization and which are in accordance with its competence or mandate".

Council informed in accordance with the Rules of Procedure and Evidence".[283] This cooperation contains also the procedure to apply when the Security Council adopts a resolution requesting the Court not to commence or proceed with an investigation or prosecution under Chapter VII of the UN Charter. The Court will, where a matter has been referred to the Court by the Security Council, communicate any failure by a State to cooperate with the ICC. Article 18 of the agreement regulates the cooperation of the UN with the ICC Prosecutor on exchange of information.[284]

*The Agreement provisions*

The preamble of the relationship agreement between the ICC and the UN recalls the purposes and principles of the Charter of the United Nations. In this light the Rome Statute, also in its preamble, reaffirms both purposes and principles of the UN Charter. The ICC-UN relationship agreement resumes the role assigned to the ICC in "dealing with the most serious crimes of concern to the international community as a whole, as referred to in the Rome Statute and which threaten the peace, security and well-being of the world". Furthermore, it clarifies the independence of the ICC from the UN system, and provides for an institutional interaction between the two organizations. The conclusion is that within the general provisions of the relationship agreement, the obligation of cooperation and coordination of the arrest warrants from the Security Council would be the part that needs some attention in the years still to come.

The second part of the relationship agreement contains the institutional relations between the ICC and the UN. Article 4 refers to the reciprocal representation. The Court "may attend and participate in the work of the General Assembly of the UN in the capacity as observer", while the UN Secretary General shall have a standing invitation to attend public hearings of the Chambers of the Court "that relate to cases of interest to the United Nations and any public meeting of the Court". Listing some areas of mutual interests it would also give more specification to the personnel arrangements and its presence on the ground, which seems to be a matter of concern, due to the fact that this is regulated by an additional treaty. In fact "strive for maximum cooperation in order to achieve the most efficient use of specialized personnel, systems and services" would mean to use specific training of staff involved in the ICC field office operations and in areas where there would be a need of exchange of expertise and intelligence.[285] This would of

283 See Article 17, Relationship Agreement between the ICC and the UN, Cooperation between the UNSC and the ICC.

284 See Article 18, Relationship Agreement between the ICC and the UN Cooperation between the UNSC and the Prosecutor.

285 See Article 8, Relationship Agreement between the ICC and the UN, accessible at: www.icc-cpi.int/library/asp/ICC-ASP-3-Res1_English.pdf.

course facilitate the gathering process of information and evidence and speed up the investigative activity. After all the UN peace operations on the ground and the political affairs department for country and situation specifics, is a useful tool for the ICC situation analysis. This would surely avoid duplications, at least sharing the general country background (statistics, military and factual data in ongoing conflicts), receiving information of the leadership of the specific State monitored under UN premises would be then part of the evidence gathering of the ICC. Administrative cooperation, services and facilities, access to the UN Headquarters and *laissez-passer* procedures fall in the agreement. Article 13 contains no mandatory financial responsibility of the UN. Agreement on costs and expenses resulting from cooperation shall be subject to separate arrangements between the UN and the Court.[286] In brief, the UN needs to provide critical support to the ICC based on its relationship agreement. Member States are encouraged to ratify the Rome Statute without delay and to cooperate with the Court. This relationship will need to be implemented.

## 5.3. THE UNITED NATIONS AND THE PURSUIT OF COMPLEMENTARITY

### SECTION OUTLINE

At this stage the advocacy expressed in this study should be clear. It recalls the necessity of concrete actions incorporating justice between the peace and security operations of the UN and the necessary support needed by the Court (judicial assistance, logistical support, security of field offices, relocation of witness and victims, law enforcement of judicial decisions, including the security of staff and assets). According to the theory that sustainable peace at domestic level is only feasible through justice establishing the truth, the Court's role in peace operations (peace-making, peace-keeping and peace-building) will need to be legally clarified in the years to come. The Court is indeed an important actor deserving such support when investigations and prosecutions are taking place during ongoing conflict situations, including the assistance on security issues for witnesses and victims (protection, relocation, participation, reparation). At institutional and operational levels and in order to provide such support to the Court the interaction between the UN Department of Peacekeeping Operations (DPKO), the UN Development Programme (UNDP) and the political and legal affairs departments of the UN will need to strengthen their cooperation efforts.

---

286 See Part II; Article 4–14, Institutional Relations, Relationship Agreement between the ICC and the UN.

The implementation of the interaction between the Court and the United Nations will only be possible towards a strong political support of State and non-State actors. Although both organizations are currently active in the same situations which are all characterized by judicial referrals, their interaction is left to further normative definition and harmonization in the peace building operations. Attention is needed to avoid duplications, competition and lack of support between these mandates which are currently only shaped in memorandum of understanding between the Court and the UN peace operations in the field. For cooperation in relation to the DRC, a specific memorandum of understanding (MoU) was agreed between the Court and the UN concerning cooperation between the UN mission in DRC (MONUC) and the Court. The MoU was concluded as a supplementary arrangement within the general framework of cooperation set out in the *Relationship Agreement* (ICC/ASP/3/15). The MoU provides for a range of assistance measures to the ICC from MONUC/MONUSCO, including the area of logistical support and judicial assistance.[287] As previously discussed, the reasons of the delay of finding appropriate remedies for such interactions in conflict and post-conflict situations, is to be found in the considerations about the status of reforms in the UN peace operations and the further commitment of the decision makers to optimize results on these sensitive governance issues.[288] In order to offer an overview of the priorities, in the interaction model proposed between complementary global mandates, complementing the Court's regime with the United Nations peace operations, this section recalls the recommendations on the concept of restorative justice in peace building operations; the "lessons learned" addressed to the decision makers of governments in peace operations; the Court's potential, and the indispensable enforcement of its judicial decisions in the field operations. In line with an harmonization model of complementary mandates any State or individual would be responsible of any action in the field, where relocation, protection of refugees, victims and witnesses, security and risk assessments will need a well-defined strategy of interactions between these actors (agencies, funds, programs of the UN system and the Court). General rules respecting statutory matters are necessary to define a normative cluster of support by the UN peace operations to the Court, where interdependent tasks from both sides will need to bring visible results in conflict and post-conflict situations.

[287] See the Report of the International Criminal Court to the UNGA, UN Doc. A/61/217, 3 August 2006, para. 47.

[288] At institutional level the UN Department of Peacekeeping Operations (DPKO) just created in 2007 the Office of Rule of Law and Security Institutions (OROLSI) to provide an integrated and forward-looking approach to United Nations post-conflict assistance in the areas of rule of law and security institutions. Such office brings together the following DPKO entities: the Police Division (PD), the Disarmament, Demobilization, and Reintegration (DDR) Section, the United Nations Mine Action Service (UNMAS), the Security Sector Reform (SSR) Unit and the Criminal Law and Judicial Advisory Service (CLJAS).

Besides, in order to verify the feasibility of the necessary support expected by the UN to the Court in the short, middle and long terms, this section recalls first the controversial issue of peacekeepers and the necessity of implementing internal justice systems related to the UN peacekeeping operations on the ground, solving the lacuna of accountability, transparency and integrity. It also reports about the Court's political rejection on one side, and on the UN efforts incorporating international criminal justice in the context of peace and security maintenance on the other. The legislative and reporting activity between the UN institutions regarding the Court, the Court's reports to the General Assembly and Security Council includes the last developments at institutional level in the area of peacekeeping operations in order to verify the readiness of such tools assisting important actors such as the Court. The last paragraph approaches the theories of eminent scholars about restorative justice in peace building operations. The purpose of this section is to bring attention on the definition of a clear strategy implementing the relationship and partnership of the UN and the Court fostering peace, justice and security.

## 5.3.1. THE BACKGROUND OF PEACE OPERATIONS

The so-called 'right' of humanitarian intervention has been one of the most controversial foreign policy issues of the last two decades both when intervention has happened, as in Kosovo, and when it has failed to happen, as in Rwanda. With the advent of the new century, shortly after the release of the UN-commissioned reports on the 1995 massacres at Srebrenica and on the 1994 genocide in Rwanda, the administrative leadership of the United Nations determined that the peace operations needed serious re-evaluation "with a view to minimizing as far as possible the likelihood of such tragedies occurring again in the future".[289] The Secretary-General, in his report to the General Assembly at the beginning of the new century, challenged the international community to try to forge consensus, once and for all, around the basic questions of principle and process involved, specifically "*when* should intervention occur, under whose authority, and *how*". The same approach and policy trend is visible with regard to the relationship between peace and justice. In the report of the Secretary-General entitled *The Rule of Law and Transitional Justice in Conflict and Post-Conflict Societies* it is emphasized that "the question can never be whether to pursue justice or peace, but rather *when* and *how*".[290] Such controversial issues are still waiting to be clarified. It is hoped that this analysis will contribute not only to the debate about law versus politics, but also on the elevation of law over power politics, against

[289] UN doc. A/55/305, UN doc. S/2000/809, for an overview of the Report of the Panel on United Nations Peace Operations accessible at: www.un.org/peace/reports/peace_operations/.

[290] UN doc. S/2004/616, para. 21.

old models of conflict management, national security and protection of human rights.[291] Many observers would see the Court as an enforcement mechanism to be associated with post-conflict assessments preventing further crimes, violence and instability, taking a specific role into the state-building activity initiated by the reform of domestic security institutions (army, police and judiciary). The problem is that the Court is involved during armed conflicts with poor resources and assistance and only once political transitions have already failed in the way of reaching sustainable stability.[292] This study simply verifies whether the interaction between complementary global regimes would represent the opportunity for a progress of international law in situations of war and crime, with measures and perhaps new institutions dealing with the protection of victims and witnesses. The implementation of the relationship between such complementary global regimes should be settled by the political premises enforcing them, while their partnership further strengthen by agreements and arrangements between international governance institutions on a case-by-case basis. The protection of human rights, the fight against the impunity and the domestic governance of human security are the factors for the preservation of order in difficult political transitions. The links between human development and sustainable models of governance at national, regional and international levels are the keys in accordance with democratic principles and open societies. The basic parameters of civilization have to be preserved at all costs respecting the principle of self-determination, but also the interdependence between regimes at domestic, regional and international levels. The ideal would be the progress in the constitution of the world community and a regulatory framework dealing with peace and justice with an integrated model of governance.

In the theoretical background of peace operations according to the English school and by some other international relations theorists of international conflict

---

[291] For an overview of prosecution of human rights crimes on the national and international level and a new demand for accountability and the universal jurisdiction of the ICC, see W. Kaleck 'et al', *International Prosecution of Human Rights Crimes*, (2006), at 5. See also *An Agenda for Peace,* the report written for the UNSC by the Secretary-General in 1992, introducing the concept of "post-conflict peacebuilding", defined as an "action to identify and support structures which will tend to strengthen and solidify peace in order to avoid a relapse into conflict". See B. Boutros-Ghali, *An Agenda for Peace*, UN doc. A/47/277–S/24111, II.21, 17 June 1992, accessible at: www.unrol.org/files/A_47_277.pdf See also J. S. Sutterlin, "An Agenda for Peace: Fifteen Years Later", in *Disarmament Times*, August 2007, accessible at: http://disarm.igc.org/index.php?view=category&id=59%3Adt2007fall&option=com_content&Itemid=2.

[292] Court's officials constantly underline such lack of international cooperation. Right at the beginning of the Review Conference of the Rome Statute in Kampala the President of the Court stated: "Every year, the Assembly of the States Parties looks at the Court and how it is functioning. But the Court is only a small part of this system. Without cooperation, there will be no arrests, victims and witnesses will not be protected, and proceedings will not be possible". See Judge Sang-Hyun Song, President of the International Criminal Court, *Opening Remarks of the Review Conference*, 31 March 2010, accessible at: www.icc-cpi.int/iccdocs/asp_docs/RC2010/Statements/ICC-RC-statements-JudgeSong-ENG.pdf.

management, the categories of peace support operations have been categorized in conflict prevention, peacemaking, peacekeeping, peace enforcement and peace-building. The first categories of such operations focus on identifying the causes of conflicts and preventing their occurrence, persistence or resumption through military presence, while the second category operates through diplomacy, ceasefire agreement or peace settlement to bring an end to violence. The peacekeeping relies on military forces and police operating with host consent of the national authorities to underpin a peace settlement or ceasefire agreement. The peace enforcement implies force used coercively to get compliance with agreements, impose a peace agreement, or protect civilians from hostilities. Peace-building operations support long term regeneration of war-torn societies establishing sustainable peace through institutional, judicial, military, economic and political capacity-building.[293]

The military role of peacekeeping has once more been dramatically reaffirmed in the last decades. The empirical data resulting from wide ranging conflict study, and the analysis of lessons learnt from past operations such as those in Rwanda and Somalia, in Kosovo, East Timor and in the DRC indicate that either prevention or peace-building strategies repeatedly failed in the context of offering sustainable peace. Another concern is that old models of conflict management by peacekeeping do not receive appropriate configurations in conflict and post-conflict situations in order to serve the emerging regime of international criminal justice dealing with mass atrocity crimes. Such an approach is quite controversial as the peace enforcement resolutions by the Security Council (under Chapter VII) are all characterized by serious breaches of international humanitarian law and human rights law. This political trend represents the evident consequence of the decision-making rejecting the use of multinational forces for the sake of justice; whether from a legal perspective the individuals involved in peace operations would also have immunity status by the emerging regime of international criminal justice.

The independent International Commission on Intervention and State Sovereignty was established by the Government of Canada, shortly after the UN-commissioned reports to respond to the challenges of humanitarian intervention.[294] In regard to the chronology of peace enforcement and the assessments of civil conflicts characterized by ethnic violence as in Kosovo, Somalia, Rwanda and the former Yugoslavia, international humanitarian intervention emphasised the challenges for the UN peacemaking role and the maintenance of collective security. The UN Secretary-General convened an international panel to conduct a major

293 See A. Linklater, H. Suganami, *The English School of International Relations*, 2006, at 8.

294 For an overview of the report see 'The Responsibility To Protect" accessible at: www.iciss.ca/pdf/Commission-Report.pdf.

study on the United Nations peace operations chaired by the Under Secretary-General and former Algerian Foreign Minister Lakhdar Brahimi. The panel was tasked to conduct a wide ranging study and analysis over lessons learnt from past peace and security operations from preventive to post-conflict peace building, including observation missions, peacekeeping and peace enforcement. Confronted with the problems encountered by peacekeeping forces, the Security Council did not establish any operation in the late nineties. The inaction of the Security Council was indeed the consequence of humanitarian disasters and also of military intervention of States or coalitions guided by unilateral strategic interests. Continuing crises in the DRC, the Central African Republic, East Timor, Kosovo, Sierra Leone and Ethiopia-Eritrea, successively led the Security Council to establish six new missions in 1998–2000.[295]

In the practice the UN missions of the last decade, especially in sub-Saharan African countries, have been characterized by comprehensive mandates and multidimensional peacekeeping operations. Lately, the humanitarian protection duties of civilians would allow intervention, peace enforcement and the use of force. A regulatory system of governance of such sensitive issues is nearly inexistent. For some observers the operational character of such interventions should follow configurations and engagements in the form of international police of multinational nature, assisting international investigations and prosecutions of recognized international crimes.[296] In theory, the UN tried to clarify the right of humanitarian intervention through the duty to protect civilians when the States would fail in their own responsibilities, while the practice displays several overlaps. In the Sudan, UNMIS was not able to deploy to Darfur due to the government's steadfast opposition to a peacekeeping operation undertaken solely by the UN as envisaged in Security Council Resolution 1706 (2006). The UN then embarked on an alternative and innovative approach to stabilize the region through the phased strengthening of AMIS, before transfer of authority to a joint AU/UN peacekeeping operation. Following prolonged and intensive negotiations with the government of the Sudan and significant international pressure, the government accepted the peacekeeping operation in Darfur. Successively, the Security Council by its Resolution 1769 (2007), authorized the establishment of the United Nations-African Union Hybrid Operation in Darfur (UNAMID).[297] With regard to the controversial policy issue of civilian protection

295 For an overview see the United Nations Peacekeeping Operations, Background Note, 30 November 2007, accessible at: www.un.org/Dpts/dpko/bnote.htm.

296 G. Day, C. Freeman, "Operationalizing the Responsibility To Protect. The Policekeeping Approach", 11 *Global Governance* 2, 2005, at 139.

297 The African Union/UN Hybrid operation in Darfur, referred to by its acronym UNAMID, was established on 31 July 2007 with the adoption of Security Council resolution 1769 (S/RES/1769, adopted by the Security Council at its 5727th meeting, on 31 July 2007). On 31 July 2008, the Security Council extended UNAMID's mandate for a further 12 months to 31 July 2009 and then again on 6 August 2009, for a further 12 months to 31 July 2010. UNAMID has the

duties, political consensus has been emphasized several times at the UN on the mechanisms of humanitarian interventions, including the issue of public authority of the Security Council to authorize it.[298] The eventual evolution from the 'right' to intervene in intra-state conflicts to the 'responsibility' to protect deserve implementation of policy and law especially with regard to the operations in the field by complementary mandates.

In the DRC, unanimously adopting Resolution 1925 (2010) under Chapter VII of the United Nations Charter, the Security Council decided that MONUSCO, the new version of MONUC's mandate, would be deployed further, authorizing to concentrate its military forces in eastern DRC while keeping a reserve force capable of redeploying rapidly elsewhere. The Security Council decided that MONUSCO would comprise, in addition to the appropriate civilian, judiciary and correction components, a maximum of 19,815 military personnel, 760 military observers, 391 police personnel and 1,050 members of formed police units. Future reconfigurations of MONUSCO would be determined as the situation evolved on the ground, including: the completion of ongoing military operations in North and South Kivu as well as Orientale provinces; improved government capacity to protect the population effectively; and the consolidation of State authority throughout the territory.[299] Emphasizing that the protection of civilians must be given priority, the Security Council authorized MONUSCO to use all necessary means to carry out its protection mandate, including the effective protection of civilians, humanitarian personnel and human rights defenders under imminent threat of physical violence, as well as the protection of UN personnel, facilities, installations and equipment. The UN mission would also support government efforts to fight impunity and ensure the protection of civilians from violations of international human rights and humanitarian law, including all forms of sexual and gender-based violence. The support to the investigations and prosecutions of the ICC is not detectable by the configuration of the peacekeeping mandate in the country, while the agreements and arrangements between peace operations and the Court are not maximizing the results on the ground.

---

protection of civilians as its core mandate, but is also tasked with contributing to security for humanitarian assistance, monitoring and verifying implementation of agreements, assisting an inclusive political process, contributing to the promotion of human rights and the rule of law, and monitoring and reporting on the situation along the borders with Chad and the Central African Republic (CAR). For an overview of the mandate, see Protecting civilians, facilitating humanitarian aid and helping political process in Darfur by UNAMID, accessible at: www.un.org/en/peacekeeping/missions/unamid/.

298 T. G. Weiss, "The Sunset of Humanitarian Intervention? The Responsibility to Protect in a Unipolar Era", 2 *Security Dialogue* 2004, at 135.

299 For an overview of the nature of such comprehensive peacekeeping mandate see www.un.org/en/peacekeeping/missions/monusco/mandate.shtml.

## 5.3.2. PEACEKEEPING REFORMS AND THE ACCOUNTABILITY ON THE GROUND

On the top of the lack of credibility of humanitarian interventions and the issues of coordination, the reform of the UN peacekeeping with the purpose of improving transparency, accountability and integrity is an on-going issue. As pointed out by Schwartz during his testimony before the US House International Relations Subcommittee on Africa (Global Human Rights, and International Organizations), "the United States and other members of the UN Security Council now regularly ask peacekeepers and their civilian counterparts to remake societies coming out of internal conflict: negotiating peace agreements; reforming security sectors and operations; promoting political reconciliation and effective and democratic governance; rebuilding domestic systems of justice. The activity by the DPKO started a process of recent reconstruction with the aim of developing an "exit strategy" for peacekeeping, working closely with partners to ensure a bridge from immediate post-conflict situations towards long-term development. In the years to come the DPKO will need to focus on delivering efficient and effective peace operations by enhancing the partnerships it has established within and outside the UN system. This phase of reconstruction should focus on supporting the Court's field offices.[300] Moreover, in the absence of local capacity, UN troops and international civilian police have been asked to ensure public security in post-conflict environments, responding to threats while mentoring and training local security forces". Schwartz in his capacity of consultant in the US Council on Foreign Relations during his testimony at the Congress in 2005 underlined that the US administration must ensure effective peacekeeping reforms, while sustaining support for UN activities that are critical not only to international peace and security, but also to US national integrity. According to Schwartz it is not possible to discuss seriously peacekeeping reform without addressing the issue of sexual exploitation and abuse by UN peacekeepers in the DRC and in other UN operations. The attention on this issue by the Members of Congress and others is highly appropriate and critically important both because ending victimization is a humanitarian imperative, and because an effective policy of 'zero tolerance' is essential to ensuring the future credibility of the UN peace operations.[301] The ideal should be to consider such forces on the ground as also at the disposition of the Court enforcing its judicial warrants,

---

300 For an overview see the portal of the Office of Rule of Law and Security Institutions (OROLSI) accessible at: www.un.org/en/peacekeeping/orolsi.shtml.

301 See E. P. Schwartz, 'UN Peacekeeping Reform: Seeking Greater Accountability and Integrity', 2005, US Senate, *Council on Foreign Relations*, accessible at: www.cfr.org/publication.html?id=8113 See UN Doc ST/SGB/2003/13, UN Secretary General's *Zero tolerance policy on sexual exploitation and sexual abuse,* in SGB, Secretary Generals Bulletin, Special measures on protection from sexual exploitation and sexual abuse, 2003. For an overview of the debate, see O. Simic, 'Rethinking Sexual Exploitation in UN peacekeeping operations', July-August 2009, *Women's Studies International Forum,* Volume 32, Issue 4, pp. 288–295. See also UN News, *UN*

while being accountable of international crimes falling under the Rome Statute. For an overview of the debate on the mechanisms that need to be established in order to enable peace enforcers to arrest war criminals and of what lessons future peace enforcement missions can learn from the experience of IFOR, SFOR and KFOR, the views expressed by experts in peace, security and justice studies are extremely formative for decision makers.[302]

During his testimony Schwartz recalls the issue of sexual exploitation and abuse by peacekeepers in some field operations in Africa, referring to the report of Prince Zeid Ra'ad Zeid Al-Hussein to the Secretary-General, to advise him on this issue and prepare a public report with urgent recommendations. Prince Zeid's report described a range of shortcomings, including a *mosaic* of rules and regulations that create a lack of clarity such as: *a)* the absence of a system-wide commitment to investigation and, as appropriate, punishment of members of military contingents; *b)* the absence of local enforcement capability for investigation and prosecution of civilian members of the UN missions; *c)* lack of resources, personnel and procedures for effective investigations, training, and interaction with local populations; and *d)* the absence of redress or compensation for victims. Finally, without seeking to excuse sexual exploitation and abuse, the report notes that "absence of organized recreational activities for troops can contribute to aberrant and unacceptable behavior".[303] From the recommendations settled in this report, accountability and integrity must be the two important elements for an appropriate reform of the UN peace operations. The Conduct and Discipline Unit (CDU) was formally established in the Department of Field Support in 2007 following the initial formation of a Conduct and Discipline Team in the Department of Peacekeeping Operations which started its activity only a few years ago. It was launched as part of a package of reforms in UN peacekeeping designed to strengthen accountability and uphold the highest standards of conduct. The new content complies with a General Assembly resolution requesting "the implementation of an effective outreach programme to explain the policy of the UN against sexual exploitation and abuse, and to inform the public on the outcome of all such cases involving peacekeeping personnel, including cases where allegations are ultimately found to be legally unproven."[304]

---

*team looking into alleged sexual misconduct by blue helmets in DRC,* 2009, accessible at: www.un.org/apps/news/story.asp?NewsID=32857.

302 See M. Lyck, 'UN Peace Missions' Involvement in Securing Justice and Transitional Justice', *Peace Operations and International Criminal Justice: Building Peace After Mass Atrocities*, 2009, 35 at 70.

303 See UN doc. A/59/710 (2005).

304 See CDU portal accessible at: http://cdu.unlb.org/.

### 5.3.3. PEACEKEEPERS AND THE COURT

The issue of peacekeepers and the role of the Court have been controversial since the first treaty negotiations. It can be said that this was an explicit reason of the Court's rejection by the US albeit that its resistance related particularly to the American peace soldiers. The Rome Statute contains many safeguards that would prevent the Court from pursuing politically motivated prosecutions against peacekeepers. The Court can only investigate the designated types of very serious crimes that fall within the Court's jurisdiction, including crimes that are unlikely to be authorized or engaged in as part of any peacekeeping mission. The judicial decision by the Court to summon a rebel leader allegedly responsible for the killing of members of the African Union peacekeeping forces in Darfur underscores the gravity of attacks against those deployed to protect civilians. The rebel commander Bahar Idriss Abu Garda appeared voluntarily before the ICC judges to respond to the summons related to such attacks on peacekeeping forces. The US is able to impede the ICC action by investigating any charges against American peacekeepers, even if it does not lead to prosecution. The American Service-Members' Protection Act (ASPA) was a federal law introduced by US Senator Jesse Helms as an amendment to the National Defense Authorization Act and passed in August 2002 by Congress. The stated purpose of the amendment was "to protect the US military personnel and other elected and appointed officials of the US government against criminal prosecution by an International Criminal Court to which the US is not party". Moreover, the UN status of forces agreements including troop contribution agreements applicable to peacekeeping missions, already provide for the US jurisdiction over many criminal offences committed by the US military and civilian members in host countries.[305] This section is not intended to discuss the American national security policy and the reasons of its attacks to the Court, which are well known. However, it should be time to define the US role as non-State Party to the Rome Statute, hopefully characterized by the transition from "rejecting to supporting" the Court with concrete, visible and transparent actions.

[305] For an overview of the practice of UN peacekeeping, in four detailed case studies on El Salvador, Cambodia, Rwanda and the former Yugoslavia, see also, M. Katayanagi, *Human Rights Functions of United Nations Peacekeeping Operations,* (2002). For an chronological overview see, J. Washburn, *Background on Peacekeeping and the ICC*, AMICC, accessible at: www.iccnow.org/documents/FS-AMICC-Peacekeeping.pdf For an overview of the practice of UN peacekeeping, in four detailed case studies on El Salvador, Cambodia, Rwanda and the former Yugoslavia, see also, M. Katayanagi, *Human Rights Functions of United Nations Peacekeeping Operations,* (2002).

## 5.3.4. THE CHALLENGES AND OPPORTUNITIES

The reporting activity of the Secretary-General to the UN institutions, specifically addressed to the Security Council, has been characterized by the necessity of supporting the role of the Court since its establishment. In the report delivered to the Security Council "*The rule of law and transitional justice in conflict and post-conflict societies*" the Secretary-General noted that the Court offers new hope for a permanent reduction in the phenomenon of impunity and the further ratification of its Statute is thus to be encouraged. He stated: "...undoubtedly, the most significant recent development in the international community's long struggle to advance the cause of justice and rule of law was the establishment of the International Criminal Court. The Rome Statute entered into force only on 1 July 2002, yet the Court is already having an important impact by putting would-be violators on notice that impunity is not assured and serving as a catalyst for enacting national laws against the gravest international crimes. It is now crucial that the international community ensures that this nascent institution has the resources, capacities, information and support it needs to investigate, prosecute and bring to trial those who bear the greatest responsibility for war crimes, crimes against humanity and genocide, in situations where national authorities are unable or unwilling to do so".[306]

The Secretary-General continued: "The Security Council has a particular role to play in this regard, empowered as it is to refer situations to the International Criminal Court, even in cases where the countries concerned are not States parties to the Statute of the Court. At the same time, all States Members of the United Nations should move towards the ratification of the Rome Statute at the earliest possible opportunity". Upon receipt of this report from the Secretary-General, the Security Council discussed the matters during the ministerial meeting "*Justice and the rule of law: the United Nations role*".[307] Pleuger (the German representative during the UNSC meeting *5052*) pointed out that the Secretary-General's report, as thorough and thoughtful as it may be, is only the beginning of a long-term global agenda. Pleuger stated: "...important and often difficult questions remain unresolved. Here, I am referring to policy questions such as the proper sequencing and timing of measures to promote peace, justice and reconciliation; to institutional questions such as the cooperation between the UN, notably the Security Council and the ICC; and to resource questions. With regard to the latter, action by the UN must be complemented by assistance that States make available to each other if a State is in need of certain capacities, materials or expertise. The Security Council will urge Member States that are

306 See UN doc. S/2004/616, para. 49, at 16.

307 See UN doc. S/PV.5052 accessible at: www.securitycouncilreport.org/atf/cf/%7B65BFCF9B-6D27-4E9C-8CD3-CF6E4FF96FF9%7D/IJ%20SPV5052.pdf.

able to do so to contribute national expertise and materials". In his statement Pleuger makes clear that "the Secretary-General's report on the rule of law and transitional justice in conflict and post-conflict societies (S/2004/616) is a 'landmark document'. It represents a significant step forward in conceptualizing the rule of law and transitional justice and in explaining their relevance to the work of the UN". Such statement was in line with the position expressed by the representative of the Netherlands on behalf of the EU.

Danforth, the former US representative responded as follows: "...as this Council and the wider membership of the UN know full well, the US has fundamental objections to the ICC created by the Rome Statute. Our problems with the ICC concern the rule of law. We believe the Court should not have jurisdiction over citizens of States that are not parties to the Rome Statute. We believe that the Rome Statute does not reflect due process of law as we understand it, because, among other things, it allows multiple jeopardy and does not provide for jury trials, as our Constitution requires. We believe the ICC runs a high risk of politicization and is not accountable. And we believe the ICC clashes with the international system of the United Nations Charter. It should come as no surprise, therefore, that we do not endorse the report's embrace of the ICC. We can accept the draft presidential statement today because it respects our inability to support the ICC and does not explicitly or implicitly endorse the ICC".

The conclusion would be that the political priority, resource allocations and the determination of the Security Council only focused on the peace operations and security reform for the operational improvements in the African deployments, practically ignoring the Court's presence in the field such as MONUC, UNMIS, UNAMID and MINURCAT.[308] One year later in 2005 the ICC received the first Security Council's referral (Sudan, Darfur). However, the paragraph 7 of the Resolution 1593 (2005) stated that the Security Council "*Recognizes* that none of the expenses incurred in connection with the referral including expenses related to investigations or prosecutions in connection with that referral, shall be borne by the United Nations and that such costs shall be borne by the parties to the Rome Statute and those States that wish to contribute voluntarily; The paragraph 8 "*Invites* the Prosecutor to address the Council within three months of the date of adoption of this resolution and every six months thereafter on actions taken pursuant to this resolution".

[308] For an overview of the last developments in the field missions of the United Nations and the peace operations in Africa see www.un.org/Depts/dpko/dpko/currentops.shtml#africa.

### 5.3.5. RELATIONSHIP AND PARTNERSHIP IMPLEMENTATION

Further consensus will be necessary to provide political support for the Court's work towards concrete actions implementing the relations between the Court and the UN, including the ways the international community would work with the Court. Some fundamental issues on the importance to have a permanent Court operating in the field have been underestimated by some governments, preferring to argue on triggering mechanisms instead of recognizing the public authority of the Rome Statute institutions. The UN General Assembly resolutions supporting the work of the ICC served three main objectives: to provide political support for the Court's work, to underline the importance of the relations between the Court and the UN, and to show the need for the international community to work with the Court.[309] The General Assembly:

> "[...] *Welcomes* the cooperation and assistance provided thus far to the International Criminal Court by States parties as well as States not parties, the United Nations and other international and regional organizations, and calls upon those States that are under an obligation to cooperate to provide such cooperation and assistance in the future, in particular with regard to arrest and surrender, the provision of evidence, the protection and relocation of victims and witnesses and the enforcement of sentences; 6. *Emphasizes* the importance of cooperation with States that are not parties to the Rome Statute [...].

Despite such resolutions the support to the Court is still weak.

### 5.3.6. PEACE BUILDING AND POST-CONFLICT JUSTICE

From the notion of restorative justice the literature reveals that it is possible to generate processes and institutions that can serve the needs of justice during the transition from civil war to the rule of law in domestic realities. These structural and normative international efforts can establish a strong foundation for peace, justice and reconciliation of domestic realities on their own in post-conflict situations. Some scholars emphasize the decentralized policies for the regime formation of restorative justice and the lack of resources on one side, but also the progress through the classic features of international criminal law, for instance in the freezing of assets of criminal perpetrators. Such features represent the income for the reparation of victims but much more will need to be accomplished in the

[309] See UN doc. A/64/356, 17 September 2009, Fifth Report of the International Criminal Court to the United Nations for 2008/2009, accessible at: www.icc-cpi.int/NR/rdonlyres/1BC01710-9C42-44AC-8B18-85EE2A8876EB/281210/A_64_356_ENG2.pdf.

context of sustainable peace and capacity-building. At institutional level, this has been proposed by the UN Secretary General at several stages, bringing as positive outcome the establishment of the UN Peace-building Commission.

> "By establishing the Peacebuilding Commission, Member States of the United Nations have created an important new structure to support fragile societies recovering from the devastation of war" as stated by Secretary-General Ban Ki-moon (SG/SM/11063, 27 June 2007).

The Peacebuilding Commission (PBC) is a new intergovernmental UN advisory body that supports peace efforts in countries emerging from conflict, and is a key addition to the capacity of the international community in the broad peace agenda. The Peacebuilding Commission plays a unique role in *a)* bringing together all of the relevant actors, including international donors, the international financial institutions, national governments, troop contributing countries; *b)* marshalling resources and to *c)* advising on and proposing integrated strategies for post-conflict peacebuilding and recovery and where appropriate, highlighting any gaps that threaten to undermine peace. The concurrent General Assembly and Security Council resolutions establishing the Peacebuilding Commission also provided for the establishment of a Peacebuilding Fund and Peacebuilding Support Office, which together form the UN peacebuilding architecture.[310] The forward-looking orientation of restorative justice is one of the features that render it most attractive to the work of peace building in the post-conflict phase. Therefore while such peacebuilding architecture consolidates itself it is required that it would become an important actor in the field of justice and accountability. The States parties to the Rome Statute should develop a strong relationship within such architecture in order to promote the Court towards such important partnerships.

## 5.3.7. THE CONCEPT OF RESTORATIVE JUSTICE

In conclusion, the *restorative* justice refers to societies seeking to establish, or re-establish, solid institutions and just practices that will sustain and support a peaceful future. It requires capacity-building. Lambourne defines peace-building activities as "strategies designed to promote a secure and stable lasting peace in which the basic human needs of the population are met, and violent conflicts do not recur. Justice and order are important aspects of peace-building in a post-conflict situation where there is a need to end violence, disarm combatants, restore the rule of law, and deal with the perpetrators of war crimes and other

[310] UN doc. A/64/341-S/2009/444, Report of the Peacebuilding Commission on its third session, 8 September 2009, accessible at: www.un.org/peace/peacebuilding/docsandres.shtml.

human rights abuses".[311] Cornwell appraises the potential of *restorative* justice to make "corrections" more effective, civilised, humanitarian, pragmatic and non-fanciful, by looking at "bedrock issues" in contemporary criminology and penology and demonstrates that *restorative* justice offers no "soft options", rather the demands of remorse, acceptance of responsibility, and the repairing of harm done. Cornwell points out that "*restorative* justice makes the case for the radical overhaul of existing approaches on the basis of principle rather than political expediency".[312] Bassiouni clarifies that "a number of different concepts are used to refer to what is sometimes called post-conflict justice, including transitional justice, strategies for combating the impunity, peace-building, and post-conflict reconstruction. These terms have evolved over the past two-a-half decades and, while their definitions and values often overlap, they are rarely used in a consistent manner. Some concepts emphasize the demands of nation-building and democratic governance, while others focus more on institutional development, rule of law, and security". The text of the *Chicago Principles on Post Conflict Justice*, a document that links a theoretical consideration of post-conflict justice with a practical consideration of policy development, was prepared by Bassiouni and Rothenberg. The final draft was presented in the hope that the principles would be integrated into a wider international approach of post-conflict justice.[313] These valid contributions deserve to be mentioned as they represent one of the appropriate voices for a change in policy and law, offering clarity about the implementation of complementarity, linking domestic, regional and international responsibilities in transition societies from conflict, violence and crime, to stability and reconstruction.

---

[311] See W. Lambourne, 'Post-Conflict Peacebuilding: Meeting Human Needs for Justice and Reconciliation', April 2004, *Peace, Conflict and Development Journal* 4, accessible at: www.peacestudiesjournal.org.uk/docs/PostConflictPeacebuilding.PDF See also W. Lambourne 'Transitional Justice and Peacebuilding After Mass Violence', 2010 *International Journal of Transitional Justice* (forthcoming). W. Lambourne 'Justice After Genocide: The Rwandan Experiment with Gacaca Community Justice', 2010 (forthcoming), in proceedings from the conference "Social Justice and Human Rights in the Era of Globalisation: Between Rhetoric and Reality", Katholieke Universiteit Leuven, Belgium, 21–23 August 2006. W. Lambourne (2007), "Peacekeeping and Peacebuilding" in United Nations Association of Australia, *Australia and the United Nations*, UNAA, pp. 27–32.

[312] Restorative justice is a paradigm that was developed over the last twenty years by practitioners working in the field of criminal justice. Because of these modern roots, the concept has been almost exclusively identified with criminal justice. See D. J. Cornwell, 'New Horizons: International Perspectives on Restorative Justice', in *Criminal Punishment and Restorative Justice. Past, Present and Future Perspectives*, (2006), at 108. For an important overview of the debate on restorative justice placing victims of crime at the centre of the criminal justice process see also D. J. Cornwell, *Doing Justice Better. The Politics of Restorative Justice*, (2007).

[313] See the Excerpt from IHRLI's Chicago Principles on Post Conflict Justice: Combating impunity through Prosecution; Truth-Telling and Investigations of Past Violations; Acknowledging Victims' Rights and Providing Remedies of Reparations; Ensuring Accountability through Vetting Sanctions and Administrative Measures; Supporting Memorialization, Education, and the Preservation of Historical Memory; Respecting Traditional, Indigenous, and Religious Approaches to Justice and Healing; Enabling Institutional Reform and Effective Governance.

## 5.4. PRESERVING THE RULE OF LAW TOWARDS PLURALISTIC JURISDICTIONS

### SECTION OUTLINE

The requirements in the policy formulation to extend complementarity between the UN system and the Rome Statute institutions have been debated in the previous sections. The view argued in this section is that the promotion of the rule of law towards complementary global regimes refers to the implementation of a legal framework of interactions advocated in this study, including the constant effort to enhance visibility and accountability of their actions. Such interaction framework, which has still to be found, would enhance both efficiency and credibility of global mandates in the fight against the impunity of international crimes and the quest of sustainable peace. In order to provide a comprehensive assessment on these issues, this section contains an extensive analysis of the UN position concerning the rule of law at international level and the efforts for the creation of an international justice system in conflict and post-conflict societies, including the criminal accountability and the internal justice cluster for the UN officials and experts on mission. The positions of the UN bodies and institutions will be discussed taking into account the reporting activity of the Secretary-General to the Security Council and the resolutions of the General Assembly on these matters. In 2012 the UN members in the General Assembly Rule of Law Declaration explicitly stated "we recognize that the rule of law applies to all States equally, and to international organizations, including the United Nations and its principal organs, and that respect for and promotion of the rule of law and justice should guide all of their activities and accord predictability and legitimacy to their actions".[314]

The involvement of the UN in the promotion and preservation of the rule of law activities at international level is determined by the actors responsible of the overall coordination of the UN efforts in this sensitive area of governance, mainly the Department of Political Affairs (DPA), the Department of Peacekeeping Operations (DPKO), the Office of the High Commissioner for Human Rights (OHCHR), the Office of Legal Affairs (OLA), the United Nations Development Programme (UNDP), the United Nations Children's Fund (UNICEF), the Office of the United Nations High Commissioner for Refugees (UNHCR), the United Nations Development Fund for Women (UNIFEM) and the United Nations Office on Drugs and Crime (UNODC). The rule of law is at the very heart of the UN mission and structure. In the World Summit Outcome Document (2005) the UN members stressed the need for universal adherence to, and implementation

[314] See UN doc. A/RES/67/1, 30 November 2012, accessible at: www.unrol.org/files/A-RES-67-1.pdf.

of, the rule of law at both the national and international levels. The UN is engaged in an on-going process to strengthen its attention to the rule of law. Principal landmarks in this process have included in chronological order: the Millennium Declaration (2000); the Report of the Panel on the UN Peace Operations ("the Brahimi report", 2000); the Report of the Secretary-General: The rule of law and transitional justice in conflict and post-conflict societies" (2004)[315] including the other Reports of the Secretary-General: Uniting our strengths: Enhancing the UN support for the rule of law (2006); Strengthening and coordinating the UN rule of law activities (2008); Annual reports on strengthening and coordinating the UN rule of law activities (2009), Delivering justice: programme of action to strengthen the rule of law at the national and international levels.[316]

At the opening of the general debate of the General Assembly in 2004, following the serious violations of international law and the war in Iraq, the Secretary-General made the following remarks, "we must start from the principle that no one is above the law and no one should be denied its protection. Every nation that proclaims the rule of law at home must respect it abroad, and every nation that insists on it abroad, must enforce it at home. The rule of law starts at home but in too many places it remains elusive. Hatred, corruption, violence and exclusion go without redress. The vulnerable lack effective recourse, while the powerful manipulate laws to retain power and accumulate wealth. At times, even the necessary fight against terrorism is allowed to encroach unnecessarily on civil liberties. It is the law, including the Security Council resolutions, which offers the best foundation for resolving prolonged conflicts, in the Middle East, in Iraq, and around the world. And it is by rigorously upholding international law that we can, and must, fulfill our responsibility to protect innocent civilians from genocide, crimes against humanity and war crimes…".[317]

There are a number of approaches defining the rule of law, or at least identifying the principal elements that constitute such concept. For example, the Secretary-General has defined it in these terms: "the rule of law is a concept at the very heart of the UN mission. It refers to a principle of governance in which all persons, institutions and entities, public and private, including the State itself, are accountable to laws that are publicly promulgated, equally enforced and independently adjudicated, and which are consistent with international human rights norms and standards. It requires, as well, measures to ensure adherence to the principles of supremacy of law, equality before the law, accountability to the

315 See the Secretary-General, Report of the Secretary-General: The Rule of Law and Transitional Justice in Conflict and Post-Conflict Societies, 5, UN Doc. S/2004/616, August 23, 2004.

316 See UN doc. A/66/749 (2012).

317 See K. Annan *The Rule of Law Remains Elusive*, addressed at the opening of the general debate of the fifty-ninth session of the General Assembly New York, 21 September 2004, accessible at: www.un.org/Pubs/chronicle/2004/issue3/0304p4.asp.

law, fairness in the application of the law, separation of powers, participation in decision-making, legal certainty, avoidance of arbitrariness and procedural and legal transparency". As Tolbert asserts, this is a good *black letter* definition of the rule of law because "it covers the principal elements that lawyers expect in terms of how the law is created and applied. An important element is missing from such definition".[318] One area that is repeatedly mentioned both in terms of UN reform and the future role of the organization is in building the rule of law in developing countries, in general, and post-conflict societies, in particular. Both Tolbert and Casper put this in the same way asserting however, that the rule of law is not a recipe for detailed institutional design. The concept of the rule of law does not contain such a prerogative. It is an interconnected cluster of values".[319] In Casper's view "the concept of the rule of law is a fairly empty vessel whose content, depending on legal cultures and historical conditions can differ considerably and, therefore, can give rise to vast disagreements and, indeed, conflicts. One can easily see how differences in the various approaches might lead to conflict. For example, in Iraq there has been considerable debate regarding the extent to which *Shari'a* law, as opposed to secular approaches, should be incorporated into the Iraqi constitution and its legal system". On the other hand, the rule of law at national and international levels as a principle of governance finds deep and solid roots in the UN Charter and in the major declarations adopted by the General Assembly. The rule of law appears as a powerful notion that embraces the most classical and fundamental principles of the international legal order, allowing to face the most urgent and contemporary concerns of the international community, such as the maintenance of peace and security, the respect for human rights and fundamental freedoms, the fight against impunity and universal justice. According to the Charter, the United Nations will need to place "conditions under which justice and respect for the obligations arising from treaties and other sources of international law can be maintained". The intent of this section is to provide an assessment of the last developments in the preservation of the rule of law and justice in the UN.

## 5.4.1. THE RULE OF LAW AND JUSTICE

in the last period of his mandate Secretary-General Kofi Annan pleaded and insisted with the General Assembly that the rule of law is at risk around the world.

[318] See D. Tolbert, A. Solomon, "What is the Rule of Law, Which Rule of Law?", in United Nations Reform and Supporting the Rule of Law in Post-Conflict Societies, 2006 *Harward Human Rights Journal* 19, p. 29, accessible at: www.law.harvard.edu/students/orgs/hrj/iss19/tolbert.shtml#fn10 See also T. Carothers, 'The Rule of Law Revival', 1998 *Foreign Affairs* 77, at 95.

[319] See G. Casper, *Rule of Law? Whose Law?* note Address, 2003 CEELI Award Ceremony and Luncheon, San Francisco, Cal. (Aug. 9, 2003) quoting Martin Krygier, International Encyclopedia of the Social & Behavioral Sciences 13404 (Smelser & Baltes eds., 2001), accessible at: http://iis-db.stanford.edu/pubs/20677/Rule_of_Law.pdf.

He pointed out that there is a framework of fair rules and institutions but "the gaps in applying the rules fairly and impartially is huge".[320] The analysis of the United Nations documents since 2004 contains a common language of justice, incorporating concepts of "justice", "rule of law" and "transitional justice".[321] On 6 October 2004, at the initiative of the United Kingdom, the Security Council held a meeting to discuss *"Justice and the rule of law: the United Nations role"* after the Secretary-General's report of 23 August 2004, entitled *"The rule of law and transitional justice in conflict and post-conflict societies"*.[322] In a statement made on behalf of the Security Council at the conclusion of the meeting, the President of the UNSC stressed the importance and urgency to restore justice and the rule of law in post-conflict societies, not only to come to terms with past abuses, but also to promote national reconciliation and to help prevent a return to conflict.[323] The Security Council later requested the Secretariat to make proposals for implementing the recommendations, set out in paragraph 65 of the Secretary-General's report, aimed at strengthening the efforts of the United Nations system to address the rule of law and transitional justice issues in conflict and post-conflict situations. In the conclusions and recommendations of this document in the Part XIX, *Moving Forward*, the Secretary-General addressed: *a)* the considerations for negotiations, peace agreements and Security Council mandates and *b)* the considerations for the United Nations system.

Paragraph 65 of the report contains the determination of the Secretary-General within his own institutional powers, explicitly addressed to the Security Council and General Assembly. He expressly stated: "I intend to instruct the Executive Committee on Peace and Security, building on the earlier work of its task forces, to propose concrete action on the matters discussed in the present report, for the purpose of strengthening the UN support for transitional justice and the rule of law in conflict and post-conflict countries and to give consideration, *inter alia*, to: *a)* making proposals for enhancing United Nations-system arrangements for supporting the rule of law and transitional justice in conflict and post-conflict societies; *b)* ensuring that rule of law and transitional justice considerations are integrated into our strategic and operational planning of peace operations; *c)* updating the current list of United Nations guidelines, manuals and tools on rule of law topics and supplementing those materials as needed; *d)* proposing new or enhanced United Nations system mechanisms, including common databases

---

320 See UN Press Release SG/SM/9491 GA/10258, Kofi Annan's ground-breaking address at the opening of the 59th session of the UN General Assembly on 21 September 2004. See also Secretary-General's remarks on ringing the Peace Bell, New York, 21 September 2004, accessible at: www.un.org/sg/statements/index.asp?nid=1088.

321 UN doc. S/PV.5052 accessible at: www.securitycouncilreport.org/atf/cf/%7B65BFCF9B-6D27-4E9C-8CD3-CF6E4FF96FF9%7D/IJ%20SPV5052.pdf.

322 UN doc. S/2004/616 accessible at: www.un.org/depts/dpko/dpko/reports.htm.

323 UN doc. S/PRST/2004/34 accessible at: www.un.org/Docs/sc/unsc_pres_statements04.html http://daccessdds.un.org/doc/UNDOC/GEN/N04/539/38/PDF/N0453938.pdf?OpenElement.

and common web-based resources, for the collection and development of best practices, documentation, manuals, handbooks, guidelines and other tools for transitional justice and for justice sector development; *e)* reviewing best practices and developing proposals for workable national-level rule of law coordination mechanisms involving justice sector institutions, civil society, donors and the United Nations system; *f)* developing approaches for ensuring that all programmes and policies supporting constitutional, judicial and legislative reform promote gender equality; *g)* Convening technical-level workshops on the rule of law and on transitional justice experiences from around the world; *h)* establishing arrangements for creating and maintaining an up-to-date roster/ database of justice and transitional justice experts, based upon explicit criteria, reflecting geographic, linguistic, gender and technical diversity, and organized according to particular areas of expertise; *i)* organizing interdepartmental staff-training programmes on the rule of law and on transitional justice; *j)* ensuring systematic debriefing of personnel involved in rule of law and transitional justice operations.

While such institutional policy would take shape with the purpose of strengthening the UN support to justice and the rule of law sectors, the UN political body also deliberated on the situation in Sudan. In 2005 with Resolution 1593 the Security Council refers the situation in Darfur to the Court.[324] On 22 June 2006, the Security Council met to discuss the item entitled *"Strengthening international law: rule of law and maintenance of international peace and security"*.[325] In its preparation for the debate Denmark circulated an informal discussion paper setting out various suggested themes and questions for discussion. Under the broad title proposed for the debate, it was suggested to address three related distinct themes, each critically important for the promotion of the rule of law and human rights: *a)* the promotion of rule of law in conflict and post-conflict situations; *b)* ending impunity for international crimes; and *c)* enhancing efficiency and credibility of UN sanctions regimes. In a presidential statement the Security Council reiterated the need for the Secretariat to provide proposals reported above in paragraph 65 of the Secretary General's report on the rule of law and justice in conflict and post-conflict societies.

In the presidential statement (S/PRST/2006/28), "The Security Council emphasizes the responsibility of States to comply with their obligations to end impunity and to prosecute those responsible for genocide, crimes against humanity and serious violations of international humanitarian law. The Security Council reaffirms that ending impunity is essential if a society in conflict or recovering from

---

324 UN doc. S/RES/1593 (2005). Adopted by Vote of 11 in favour to none against, with 4 abstentions (Algeria, Brazil, China, United States). Other UNSC resolutions are accessible at: www.un.org/ Docs/sc/unsc_resolutions05.htm.

325 See UN doc. S/PRST/2006/28.

conflict is to come to terms with past abuses committed against civilians and to prevent such abuses in the future. The Security Council intends to continue forcefully to fight impunity with appropriate means and draws attention to the full range of justice and reconciliation mechanisms to be considered, including national, international and 'mixed' criminal courts and tribunals and truth and reconciliation commissions". The document does not refer explicitly to the ICC but it only recalls the main responsibility of the UN Member States in a general sense.[326]

## 5.4.2. THE SECTORS OF THE RULE OF LAW

In his report to the General Assembly and Security Council, "*Uniting our strengths: Enhancing United Nations support for the rule of law*" (2006),[327] the Secretary-General points out the normative foundation for legal assistance, namely: the Charter of the United Nations, together with the four pillars of the modern international legal system international human rights law, international humanitarian law, international criminal law and international refugee law; the wealth of United Nations human rights and crime prevention; and criminal justice standards. The rule of law and transitional justice issues must be consistently integrated into the strategic and operational planning of new peace operations and Member States almost universally must recognize the establishment of the rule of law as an important aspect of peacekeeping. As a result, the Security Council should be engaged in including human rights and the reform of policing, judicial, penal and legal systems in peacekeeping mandates. According to the legislative history of the UN on these issues, a stronger political will is necessary in respect to the presence of the ICC in the post-building phase developing specific strategies in countries under investigation. Moreover, the rules of law activities are just about to start in the UN. For purposes of coherence and coordination such rule of law activities of the UN can be grouped into three main sectors. The first one, the *Rule of law at the international level*, includes issues related to the Charter of the United Nations, multilateral treaties, international dispute resolution mechanisms, the International Criminal Court and advocacy, training and education regarding international law. The second, the *Rule of law in the context of conflict and post-conflict situations*, includes two components: transitional justice and strengthening of national justice systems and

[326] For an overview see UNSC Presidential statement "Strengthening international law: rule of law and maintenance of international peace and security" accessible at: http://daccess-dds-ny.un.org/doc/UNDOC/GEN/N06/401/59/PDF/N0640159.pdf?OpenElement.

[327] UN doc. A/61/636, UN doc. S/2006/980, 14 December 2006, Uniting our strengths: Enhancing United Nations support for the rule of law, addressed by the Secretary-General to the Security Council and the General Assembly, the report is accessible at: www.un.org/docs/sc/sgrep06.htm.

institutions. The activities under transitional justice will include the following: national transitional justice consultation processes, truth and reconciliation processes, reparations, international and hybrid tribunals, national human rights institutions, vetting processes and ad hoc investigations, fact-finding and commissions of inquiry. The second component of the rule of law in the context of conflict and post-conflict situations is also the core component of the third sector, on the *Rule of law in the context of long-term development*, and comprises activities in the area of strengthening of national justice systems and institutions (domestic institution building). These include work to strengthen legal and judicial institutions (e.g. prosecution, ministries of justice, criminal law, legal assistance, court administration and civil law), policing, penal reform, the administration of trust funds and monitoring. In addition, the following additional priority areas have been identified: customary, traditional and community-based justice and dispute resolution mechanisms; victim and witness protection and assistance; combating corruption, organized crime, transnational crime and trafficking, and drug control; legal education; public law issues (e.g. land and property, registration, national identification, citizenship and statelessness); interim law enforcement and executive judicial functions performed by the UN; and security support to national police agencies. So as to ensure coherence, the activities in the final sector, the *Rule of law in the context of long-term development,* will closely mirror those activities being undertaken in the context of conflict and post-conflict societies. As the conclusive part of the Secretary-General report points out, the UN human rights standards and norms will be integrated throughout these sectors of the rule of law in all peace operations.

### 5.4.3. THE COORDINATION OF THE RULE OF LAW ACTIVITIES IN THE UN SYSTEM

at the national level, the rule of law activities involve among other aspects, strengthening the constitution, internal laws, institutions of justice, and domestic governance of security sectors (such as army, police and judiciary). Since the rule of law is today at the centre of the UN concerns, the organization needs to deepen and rationalize its rule of law activity, strengthen its capacities, enhance its institutional memory and coordinate more effectively within the UN and with outside actors. To achieve these objectives, a division of labour is being established among the key UN actors. The UN work on rule of law covers a wide area involving a range of themes and sub-topics. Some themes can be described as "cross-cutting" as they are common to the work of most, if not all the UN actors conducting rule of law activities. The organization also supports judicial mechanisms, such as the *ad hoc* criminal tribunals and hybrid tribunals, established mainly to address past international crimes in war-torn societies, and fact-finding-investigatory bodies. Many of these mechanisms are hybrid tribunals or commissions, involving often mixed national and international composition and jurisdiction. They are set up in cooperation with national authorities under the UN auspices and with mandates tailored to the specifics of each situation.[328] To ensure better coordination and adequate capacities across the system, lead entities, designated in accordance with their mandates, will assume clearly defined responsibilities for specific areas of the rule of law activities. Lead entities will be obligated to take action to ensure that required capacities exist upon which the whole system can draw. The designation of lead entities is intended to ensure a much higher degree of coherence, predictability and accountability in the delivery of rule of law assistance to Member States. Many offices within the system are involved in the promotion of the rule of law: an inventory issued by the Secretary-General in 2008 (A/63/64) identified as many as 40 entities active in this field and listed 520 different categories of activities performed for the promotion of the rule of law. In view of the tremendous magnitude and diversity of the UN involvement in this area, the Secretary-General proposed in 2006 to establish a Rule of Law Coordination and Resource Group, chaired by the Deputy Secretary-General and consisting of the main rule of law actors in the system, to ensure the overall coordination of the UN efforts. As already listed in the section outline the membership of the Group consists of the Department of Political Affairs (DPA), the Department of Peacekeeping Operations (DPKO), Office of the High Commissioner for Human Rights (OHCHR), the Office of Legal Affairs (OLA), United Nations Development Programme (UNDP), The United Nations Children's Fund (UNICEF), The Office of the United Nations High Commissioner for Refugees (UNHCR), the United Nations Development Fund for Women (UNIFEM) and the United Nations Office on Drugs and Crime (UNODC).

The Group has prioritized partners to engage in the development and implementation of the Joint Strategic Plan. In developing the Plan, members of the Group and the Rule of Law Unit consulted with the UN system (headquarters and field offices) and external partners. For implementation of the Plan, the Group will draw upon the expertise and cooperation of a wide range of partners depending on the purpose of the partnerships (financial, political, and programmatic) and corresponding to the Plan outcomes. Partners include the wider UN system, Member States, civil society groups, academics and training institutes in donor and recipient countries and international and regional assistance providers. Existing partnerships should be drawn upon to the extent possible. This Group has taken a new strategic and results-based approach to the UN rule of law work, agreeing on a Joint Strategic Plan for 2009–2011 and for the years to come (see *Results Framework*)[329] developing Guidance Notes of the Secretary General on the

328 For an overview of the activities of the UN Rule of Law see the portal accessible at: www.unrol.org/.

329 See Joint Strategic Plan for 2009–2011, Implementation and Partnerships, 2009, pp. 3–4, accessible at: www.unrol.org/doc.aspx?doc_id=2140.

UN Approach to Rule of Law Assistance, Justice for Children and Constitution-making. The Rule of Law Coordination and Resource Group is responsible, under the leadership of the Office of Legal Affairs, for further guidance on the rule of law at the international level. Such activities support the development, promotion and implementation of international norms and standards in most fields of international law. Furthermore, the issues relating to the rule of law at international level are being discussed in different political fora within the UN. The Security Council, for example, has held between 2003 and 2006 several thematic debates on matters relating to the rule of law. Since 2006, on a joint proposal by Liechtenstein and Mexico, the General Assembly has included the item "The rule of law at the national and international levels" on its agenda, entrusting it to the Sixth Committee.[330] In the resolution 62/70 of 8 January 2008 the General Assembly reaffirmed further the need for universal adherence to and implementation of the rule of law at both the national and international levels and its solemn commitment to an international order based on the rule of law and international law, which, together with the principles of justice, is essential for peaceful coexistence and cooperation among States.[331] In the resolution 63/128 of 11 December 2008, the General Assembly has invited Member States to focus their comments at the sixty-fourth session, in October 2009, on the sub-topic of "Promoting the rule of law at the international level". The rule of law is a core principle of governance that ensures justice and fairness, values that are essential to humanity. The rule of law is central to the vision of the Secretary-General for the coming five years, and must guide the collective response to a fast-changing world.[332] The High-level Meeting of the 67$^{th}$ Session of the General Assembly on the Rule of Law at the National and International Levels took place at the UN Headquarters in New York on 24 September 2012. This was a unique occasion for all Member States, non-governmental organisations and civil society represented at the highest level, to discuss and agree a forward looking agenda on strengthening the rule of law.[333]

---

330 The Sixth Committee is the primary forum for the consideration of legal questions in the General Assembly. All of the UN Member States are entitled to representation on the Sixth Committee as one of the main committees of the General Assembly.

331 The General Assembly has considered the rule of law as an agenda item since 1992, with renewed interest since 2006 and has adopted resolutions at its last three sessions. See A/RES/61/39, A/RES/62/70, A/RES/63/128. The Security Council has held a number of thematic debates on the rule of law (UN docs: S/PRST/2003/15, S/PRST/2004/2, S/PRST/2004/32, S/PRST/2005/30, S/PRST/2006/28) and adopted resolutions emphasizing the importance of these issues in the context of women, peace and security (SC res 1325, SC res. 1820), children in armed conflict (e.g., SC res 1612), the protection of civilians in armed conflict (e.g., SC res 1674). The Peacebuilding Commission has also regularly addressed rule of law issues with respect to countries on its agenda.

332 UN doc. A/66/749, 16 March 2012, Report of the Secretary-General, *Delivering justice: programme of action to strengthen the rule of law at the national and international levels*, accessible at: www.unrol.org/files/SGreport%20eng%20A_66_749.pdf.

333 See UN doc. A/RES/67/1 (2012), Declaration of the High-level Meeting of the General Assembly on the Rule of Law at the National and International Levels.

### 5.4.4. CRIMINAL ACCOUNTABILITY OF UNITED NATIONS OFFICIALS AND EXPERTS ON MISSION

From the extensive analysis of the UN documents related to the rule of law at national and international level a couple of points need to be clarified. First of all, that the maintenance of peace, justice and security needs to be based on the principle of accountability of all actors involved in mission operations in the field, and second that a consistent strategy of cooperation between the UN and the Court will need to be implemented in addition to the bilateral agreements with peacekeeping forces. At its sixty-first session, in 2006, the General Assembly decided that the agenda item entitled Comprehensive review of the whole question of peacekeeping operations in all their aspects, which had been allocated to the Special Political and Decolonization Committee (Fourth Committee), should also be referred to the Sixth Committee for discussion of the report of the Group of Legal Experts on ensuring the accountability of the UN staff and experts on mission with respect to criminal acts committed in peacekeeping operations (see A/60/980), submitted pursuant to Assembly resolutions 59/300 and 60/263 and decision 60/563 (decision 61/503 A). At the same session, the General Assembly decided to establish an Ad Hoc Committee, open to all States Members of the UN or members of specialized agencies or of the International Atomic Energy Agency, for the purpose of considering the report of the Group of Legal Experts, in particular its legal aspects (resolution 61/29). At its sixty-second session, the General Assembly strongly urged States to consider establishing to the extent that they had not yet done so jurisdiction, particularly over crimes of a serious nature, as known in their existing domestic criminal laws, committed by their nationals while serving as United Nations officials or experts on mission, at least where the conduct as defined in the law of the State establishing jurisdiction also constituted a crime under the laws of the host State; requested the Secretary-General to bring credible allegations that revealed that a crime might have been committed by United Nations officials and experts on mission to the attention of the States against whose nationals such allegations were made, and to request from those States an indication of the status of their efforts to investigate and, as appropriate, prosecute crimes of a serious nature, as well as the types of appropriate assistance States might wish to receive from the Secretariat for the purposes of such investigations and prosecutions (resolution 62/63).

At its sixty-third session (2008), the General Assembly encouraged States, in accordance with their domestic law or any applicable treaties or arrangements on extradition and mutual legal assistance, to afford each other assistance in criminal investigations or criminal or extradition proceedings, including with regard to evidence; encouraged all States, in accordance with their domestic law, to explore ways and means of facilitating the possible use, in criminal proceedings regarding crimes of a serious nature allegedly committed by UN officials and experts on mission, of information and material obtained from the UN, bearing in mind due process considerations; to provide effective protection to witnesses and others who provide information in respect of such crimes; and to explore ways and means of responding adequately to requests by host States in order to enhance their investigative capacity; decided that the consideration of the report of the Group of Legal Experts on the topic (see A/60/980) should be continued during the sixty-fourth session in the framework of a working group of the Sixth Committee; requested the United Nations to consider any appropriate measures that might facilitate the possible use of information and material for purposes of criminal proceedings initiated by States in respect of such crimes, bearing in mind due process considerations; encouraged the United Nations to take appropriate measures, in the interests of the Organization, to restore the credibility and reputation of officials and experts on mission, in the case of unfounded allegations; urged the UN to continue cooperating with States exercising jurisdiction in order to provide them, within the framework of the relevant rules of international law and agreements governing activities of the UN, with information and material for purposes of criminal proceedings initiated by States; emphasized the importance that no action be taken by the UN that would retaliate against or intimidate UN officials and experts on mission who reported allegations concerning such crimes; and requested the Secretary-General to report to the Assembly at its sixty-fourth session on the implementation of the resolution, as well as with respect to any practical problems in its implementation, on the basis of information received from Governments and the Secretariat, and to include in the report information on the number and types of credible allegations and any actions taken by the UN and its Member States regarding crimes of a serious nature committed by the UN officials and experts on mission (resolution 63/119).[334]

## 5.4.5. CONCLUSIONS

In general, the practice of governing conflict and post-conflict situations shows that the rule of law has been ignored in many cases as a consequence of the accountability gaps and capacity of institutions. The rule of law has been defined as elusive according to UN official reports and by the analytical approaches of many scholars. Acceptable standards of compliance at international level have been weak in the last decades. Under the rule of law national leaders are accountable when committing international crimes. This basic principle,

[334] The item entitled "Criminal accountability of United Nations officials and experts on mission" was included in the provisional agenda of the sixty-fourth session of the General Assembly pursuant to Assembly resolution 63/119 of 11 December 2008. UN doc. A/64/446, 12 November 2009. For an overview of the activity of the Ad Hoc Committee on the Criminal accountability of United Nations officials and experts on mission see information accessible at: www.un.org/law/criminalaccountability/index.html.

ignored in international affairs for decennia, received legal provisions since the establishment of a permanent International Criminal Court. As discussed above, there is less andless space left for the concept of immunities and for norms that belong to an era where the sovereignty of the nation-state was perceived as absolute.[335] The concept of the rule of law expressed by Tomuschat contains a constitutional framework of the international community which includes the basic rules and norms of *jus cogens* and obligation *erga omnes*, but which also permit sovereign action.[336] The individual criminal responsibility, as distinct from the State responsibility, of those who act on behalf of sovereign entities, or on behalf of intergovernmental organizations, must not be left out of the system of international norms and regulations for the protection of human rights. This is the most important prerequisite to preserve the rule of law towards democratic international governance institutions.

The question under what conditions member States of an international organization may be responsible for international wrongful acts committed by international organization has become a question of fundamental importance in modern international law. There has been a continuing transfer of powers to international organizations. At the same time, for injured parties (whether States or private persons) it remains virtually impossible to find a proper remedy against wrongful acts committed by international organizations, *inter alia* due to lack of jurisdiction of international courts, immunity in domestic courts.[337] As a result of these and related factors, in several instances injured parties have tried to pierce the veil of organizations and have attempted to invoke responsibility of Member States in relation to wrongful the acts of international organizations. In 1999 the Former Republic of Yugoslavia brought claims against member States of NATO in regard to the bombardments carried out by NATO in response to the crimes

---

335 In March 2009, the Pre-Trial Chamber (PTC) of the International Criminal Court (ICC) authorized the issue of an arrest warrant in respect of President al-Bashir of Sudan in relation to the alleged atrocities committed in Darfur. The request for the arrest warrant raised the issue of whether a serving head of State may rely upon immunity under international law to shield themselves from proceedings before international criminal tribunals. The decision was the first occasion on which the question of State immunity has been raised before the ICC and the first time an international criminal tribunal has considered the issue in respect of an incumbent head of State. For a legal commentary of head of State immunities in international law and the obligation of States, including Sudan, to comply with the Court's request for cooperation in the execution of the arrest warrant, see S. Williams and L. Sherif, 'The Arrest Warrant for President al-Bashir: Immunities of Incumbent Heads of State and the International Criminal Court', 2009 *Journal of Conflict and Security Law* 14 (1), 71 at 92.

336 See, C. Tomuschat and J. M. Thouvenin, *The Fundamental Rules of the International Legal Order: Jus Cogens and Obligations Erga Omnes*, (2006), 376 at 400.

337 See N. Blokker, "International Organisations: The Untouchables?" in 10 *International Organizations Law Review* 2, 2014/2013, at 259. See also N. Schrijver, "Beyond Srebrenica and Haiti", in 10 *International Organizations Law Review* 2, 2014/2013, at 588.

committed in Kosovo.[338] In 2007, the European Court of Human Rights had to determine whether certain member States of the UN could be held responsible in regard to a failure of the UN to protect civilians from a mined area in Bosnia Herzegovina. The considerable growth of UN activities, as well as the increasing quality demands emanating from the "global rule of law", require a more adequate legal framework for assessing the conduct of the UN.[339]

The rule of international law dealing with the accountabilities of States and individuals waits for further progress in the political convergence of expectations by complementary regimes dealing with war and crime which have to be accountable of their actions. As discussed above, for the implementation of the emerging regime of international justice, which is still under construction, the first step should be to reinforce the accountability mechanisms between States, international and regional organizations, and all parties involved in situations at serious risk during humanitarian interventions. In the long period the practice of accountability would empower the judicial power of the Court in the international legal and political relations. In reality we are still very far from such realization. The problem is that the emerging regime of international criminal justice did not receive any role in the monitoring activity of international humanitarian interventions under the flag of the responsibility to protect. Moreover, as we have seen from the previous assessments, several gaps characterize the governance of civilian protection duties in times of war and crime. Therefore, political convergence is still to be found.

## 5.5. CONCLUSIVE OBSERVATIONS

### SECTION OUTLINE

In order to provide a definition of *complementary* global regimes, it is required to look at the construction of law enforcement intended by established international regimes and emerging sub-regimes, dealing with the criminal accountability of individuals. Those need the determination of the Security Council of unlawful

338 The International Court of Justice (ICJ) ruled that Serbia and Montenegro's claims against NATO members Belgium, Canada, France, Germany, Italy, the Netherlands, Portugal and Britain should be rejected because the Balkan country was not a member of the United Nations at the time the complaint was filed in April1999. The ICJ can only rule on disputes between UN Member States, unless they have signed conventions giving the court jurisdiction or two States agree to let the ICJ consider its dispute or if the UN Security Council refers a case for an advisory opinion. See Legality of the Use of Force Application of the Federal Republic of Yugoslavia (*Yugoslavia v. Belgium*) 1999 I.C.J. 105 (Apr. 29).

339 See UN Secretary-General, *Delivering Justice: programme of action to strengthen the rule of law at the national and international levels*, 16 March 2012, UN doc. A/66/749. See also N. Schrijver, "Beyond Srebrenica and Haiti", in 10 *International Organizations Law Review* 2, 2014/2013, at 592.

acts committed by the States not parties to the Rome Statute, before the Court, in accordance with the principle of territoriality, would determine the criminal behaviour of individual perpetrators during intra- and eventually inter-state armed conflicts. The Security Council authorized an increasing number of diverse international peace operations, ranging from standard peacekeeping deployments to multifaceted peace-making and peace-enforcement operations. Despite rising political support for the strategic use of military presence and force to strengthen the protection of civilians, important aspects of the legal frameworks regulating peace operations remain unclear in support of justice and accountability. This lack of clarity has also raised significant concerns about the impunity for abuses committed in the course of peace operations, especially those established under US Status of Forces Agreements conferring immunity on foreign military personnel (SOFAs).[340] Acting under Chapter VII of the United Nations Charter, the Security Council requested that the ICC, for a twelve-month period beginning on 1 July 2002, refrain from commencing or continuing investigations into personnel or officials from States not a party to the ICC Statute. The Security Council expressed its intention to renew the measure within twelve months for as long as necessary. Obviously, such position of the Security Council was incompatible with the Rome Statute, demonstrated the improper lawmaking use of the Security Council, and contradicted the UN Charter and other international law. In 2004 the Security Council refused to renew the exemption again after pictures emerged of US troops abusing Iraqi prisoners in Abu Ghraib, and the US withdrew its demand.[341] Against the backdrop of recent disagreement about the applicability of international humanitarian law and international human rights law to members of peace operations, the political convergence on such matters is still absolutely required.

This part argued about the shortcomings fostering peace and justice in the field operations, including the lacuna of human security measures and the capacity-building at national, regional and international levels. The topics approached in this part want to emphasize that the deterrent effect of the emerging regime of international criminal justice is identical either in the North or in the South of the world. The culture of accountability is the only catalyst for the legitimacy and compliance in every legal system or constitution. This study addresses recommendations to the leaderships of any government. Such leaders have to be visible, responsible and accountable of their choices having negative consequences on individuals. What we currently see in western societies is that some leaders have been accused, by knowledgeable groups and individuals throughout the world, of complicity in war crimes, crimes against humanity, and other gross

340 See E. Rosenfeld, "Application of US Status of Forces Agreements to Article 98 of the Rome Statute", 2 *Washington University Global Studies Law Review*, 2003 at 273, accessible at: http://law.wustl.edu/wugslr/issues/Volume2_1/p273Rosenfeld.pdf.

341 See UN doc. S/RES/1422 (2002) and UN doc. S/RES/1487 (2003).

human rights abuses. The systemic collapse of legality including the shortcomings of domestic jurisdictions on criminal and corrupted behaviours, require higher standards of accountability. The States Parties to the Rome Statute have accepted obligations going beyond customary law in relation to the immunities of their own officials. In Western society, the return of great recessions is a visible sign that governance systems may even be designed to control over the life of individuals.[342] Rich get richer, and ordinary people are left in a deeper condition of poverty and pressure to perform against corrupted domestic governance systems. For many, the capitalistic system causes a widening gap between the rich and everyone else; constant warfare is justified as necessary to fight 'terrorism'; erosion of personal freedoms; expanding power allocated to the military and police; pervasive control and inequalities; complete lack of accountability by politicians for their fraudulence and crimes; a mass media devoted solely to the establishment of propaganda, and a clash of ethic, social, political and religious values sustaining multicultural differences, are only some of the effects of the systemic crisis of governance. These are some of the reasons why it is important to rely on international governance institutions for the preservation of accountability and compliance of universal values. The political forces empowering them have a specific call to be fulfilled.

### 5.5.1. THE CHALLENGES AND OPPORTUNITIES OF GOVERNANCE SYSTEMS

In this realistic scenario the rule of law, as setting values and as principle of governance, is extremely important as well as multilateralism. The accountability of national leaders combined with compliance mechanisms of the States is the only valid catalyst in this state of affairs, either at domestic, regional, or at international levels. Multilateral and intergovernmental settings have to take concrete measures in order to rebuild weak States in such systemic break downs and transitions, while safeguarding individual rights. In conflict and post-conflict societies of underdeveloped countries the situation is indeed worse. The list of so-defined 'failed' States is growing extensively. The quest for development, cooperation and sustainability in devastated societies is shaped by military enforcement during micro-conflicts, combined with humanitarian interventions involved in the destabilization of criminal and corrupted regimes wasting individual lives. Despite these important reasons for the existence of complementary regimes, there is a lacuna in the accountability and compliance of international entities and

342 M. Chossudovsky, A.G. Marshall, *The Global Economic Crisis: The Great Depression of the XXI Century*, Centre for Research on Globalization, 2010. See also R.C. Cook, 'The Nature of the current Financial Crisis: The System is designed to exert Total Control over the Lives of Individuals', 2009 *Global Research*, accessible at: www.globalresearch.ca/index.php?context=va&aid=13551.

mandates involved in the so-called international humanitarian escalations of *last resort* addressed to multilevel jurisdictions and which are established by political organs. The discourse on the responsibility to protect, for instance, is analogous to the doctrinal and normative frameworks of human rights and democratic governance, but still argued in delimiting multilateral interventions and State sovereignty. It is also argued that powerful nation-states are still a central actor of international governance in peace and in conflict. These are some of the reasons why it is important to asses the extent of which individual rights are kept central in conflict and post-conflict multilateral interventions, according to international criminal justice and human rights standards, including victim rights advocates. The supranational character of a governance system is still absolutely required.

### 5.5.2. THE GLOBAL EFFORT OF INTERACTIONS

The complex interaction between international governance institutions fostering peace, justice and security deserves a detailed analysis at structural, normative and functional levels. The past failures or delays by the international society to respond to mass atrocities discharge important lessons. Protecting civilians in violent conflicts involves understanding the links that the military, political, humanitarian and development aspects entail, as well as recognizing the failure in upholding respect for justice and human rights. The consequences of serious breakdowns in conflict and post-conflict situations determine global responsibilities for complementary governance institutions. There are still gaps when it comes to achieving a wide-ranging protection instrument of individuals in conflict and post-conflict situations, including mechanisms promoting victim rights in domestic judicial systems. These are only some of the reasons why the interaction between complementary international mandates deserves attention from both legal and political perspectives in order to verify feasible ways and further progress centralizing individuals in global matters. Moreover, as we have seen the interaction between the UN bodies and the Rome Statute institutions raises important questions about the project of universal jurisdiction, the enforcement of law and civilian protection duties.

Political consensus will be necessary to determine provisions regulating the relationships, partnerships and operational interactions between complementary global mandates which deal with the reconstruction of societies affected by armed conflicts, towards universal values, such as the rule of law and justice, human rights and democracy, according thus, to the principles of democratic governance. This is the only chance to fulfil the absence of *trias politica* or separation of powers in international relations. This is also the only option for a democratization process which should at least characterize a *road map* for a regime of *checks and balances* of international humanitarian interventions in sovereign States, where the accountability concerns all actors involved, including individuals or States responsible of misconduct. One prerogative of democratic governance is that global governance institutions (UN and Rome Statute institutions) would interact appropriately between them in order to deal with the escalations of humanitarian atrocities, influencing in the short, middle and long terms domestic realities with law and order. The democratisation of such complementary governance institutions through widespread participation is of course a 21st century imperative. Therefore, the quest for democratisation should be pragmatic rather than idealistic and find its place in specific actions and accomplishments.

To that end, and before reporting on the current position of the African Union and other regional organizations, according to the deliberations of the last decade of the EU institutions, it was suggested that the EU should support the expansion of the UN Security Council through the promotion of India, Japan, South Africa and Brazil as permanent members, but that new ways of decision-making should also be explored in parallel in order to avoid the paralysis of the Security Council. Moreover, there should be a greater reliance on those organs and institutions which already reflect a fair measure of democratisation, such as the General Assembly, the Economic and Social Council, the Human Rights Council, the Peace-building Commission, including the Rome Statute institutions which represent fundamental actors for the quest of human rights and for a rule-based international order. The EU systematically pursues the inclusion of an ICC clause in negotiating mandates with third countries. On the initiative of the European Commission, as anticipated earlier, the Cotonou Partnership revised Agreement with ACP countries, in 2005, includes an ICC clause.[343] This is the reason why the Sudan refused to ratify the revised Cotonou Agreement.[344] Under the European Neighbourhood Policy, the European Commission has also negotiated the insertion of ICC clauses into many related Action Plans as well as in association agreements with countries in Latin America. The EU engaged

343 Cotonou Agreement (ICC clause), from the Preamble: *considering* that the establishment and effective functioning of the International Criminal Court constitute an important development for peace and international justice (...) and Article 11 reads, "in promoting the strengthening of peace and international justice, the Parties reaffirm their determination to: share experience in the adoption of legal adjustments required to allow for the ratification and implementation of the Rome Statute of the International Criminal Court; and fight against international crime in accordance with international law, giving due regard to the Rome Statute. The Parties shall seek to take steps towards ratifying and implementing the Rome Statute and related instruments." Furthermore, 16 negotiating directives for agreements under negotiation or to be negotiated include the ICC clause. See European Council, *The EU and the ICC*, May 2010, at 13, accessible at: www.consilium.europa.eu/uedocs/cmsUpload/ICC_may%2010_internet.pdf.

344 See EC, Non-ratification of the revised Cotonou Agreement by Sudan FAQ (August 2009), accessible at: http://ec.europa.eu/development/icenter/repository/sudan_final_non-ratification_faq_200908.pdf.

its support to the Rome Statute institutions with the Common Position in 2003 and an Action Plan immediately after in 2004. The EU can do more in such a process of democratization of governance institutions, promoting the widespread ratification of the Rome Statute towards: *a)* a coordination of EU activities in each of its institutions; *b)* promoting the universality and integrity of the Rome Statute in peace building mandates; and *c)* campaigning for the independence and effective functioning of the ICC supporting the participation of civil society.[345] It is important to analyse the developments in another important regional reality, especially in the African Union but also in the League of Arab States, ASEAN and other political regional realties.

## 5.5.3. THE ADVOCACY OF SYSTEMIC CHANGE

The approach in this part of this study is that with the Rome Statute it can be contested whether any recognition exist of the links between an established system based on individual criminal accountability and the maintenance of international peace and security. The question is whether such links are put in practice during *intra* and inter-state conflicts, and whether they influence further jurisdictional progress for the emerging regime of international criminal justice and its public authority. This study points out that the interaction between the Rome Statute institutions and the UN takes place at several levels, but most importantly represents the nexus between global politics and the rule of law, interacting with several branches of international law, respectively humanitarian, criminal and the emerging law of human rights. There are no doubts that a result-oriented approach empowering the partnerships of universal organizations would replace the unilateral political or legal rhetoric of States for the preservation of individual rights in conflict and post-conflict societies. A strong political consensus or political convergence is necessary to strengthen the relationships and partnerships of complementary global mandates, initiating a democratization process of the international governance of justice, which at the moment excludes law enforcement of binding character of multinational forces, and is not in charge of humanitarian interventions, humanitarian police, and non-state actors. Considering the great expectations of international responses in mass atrocity crimes, while contributing to the formation of a global state-building apparatus dealing with 'failed' States, important solutions have to be

345 For an overview of the EU support to the ICC fostering the creation of a global criminal justice system see J. Wouters, S. Basu, 'A Global Criminal Justice System based on International Cooperation' in *The Effectiveness of International Criminal Justice*, Introduction, (2009), 128 at 140. For an overview of the ICC sub-area of the public international law working party (COJUR ICC) and the implementation of support by the EU in the UN, see Council of the EU (Consilium), "Support to the ICC in UN fora", in *The European Union and the International Criminal Court*, European Communities, 2008, DGF, EU doc. RS/07/2008, p. 15, accessible at: www.consilium.europa.eu/uedocs/cmsUpload/ICC_internet08.pdf.

found in the short, middle and long terms, on collective responsibilities, human security measures, domestic capacity-building and mutual accountability of interventions in conflict and post-conflict situations.

With the Rome Statute, the universal principle of individual criminal accountability of international crimes in domestic jurisdictions has been translated in legal humanitarian frameworks by complementary features and institutions. The purpose of such global architecture is to oppose the culture of impunity of mass atrocity crimes. The intent is to centralize victim rights during fair trials of the most responsible criminal perpetrators. The failure of the nation-state on such responsibilities generates other responsibilities. The concept of complementary regimes is also applicable at international level, considering the humanitarian escalations of violations between the UN and the Rome Statute institutions. Such complementary regimes, and their international governance institutions, deal respectively with the nation-state responsibility and the accountability of individuals. As an outsider from the UN institutional premises the emerging regime of international criminal justice is also being tested in the quest of peace and security for the first time in the Sudan and Libya, receiving jurisdiction under the authority of the Security Council. In accordance with the legal provisions of the Rome Statute, the governments of the Sudan and the Libyan authorities have an obligation to cooperate with the Court even if they have not ratified its founding treaty. The jurisdiction of the Court resulted from the resolutions of the Security Council, and therefore applies to all member States of the UN.[346]

### 5.5.4. INTERNATIONAL CRIMINAL JUSTICE: SHIFTING OR BALANCING POWER?

The Security Council is a political body while the International Criminal Court is a judicial body. They deal respectively with the accountabilities of States and individuals. From a legal perspective and with regard to international conflicts (inter-state, or conflicts between States), the authority given to the Security Council under the UN Charter was not intended for a judicial determination of

[346] See UN doc. S/RES/1593 (2005) which refers to the Report to the Secretary-General of the International Commission of Inquiry on Darfur accessible at: www.un.org/news/dh/sudan/com_inq_darfur.pdf For an Afrocentric outlook of such historic referral by the Security Council see N. J. Udombana, "Pay Back in Sudan? Darfur in the International Criminal Court", *Tulsa Journal of Comparative and International Law*, Vol. 13, 2005–2006. See also Touko Piiparinen, 'The Lessons of Darfur for the Future of Humanitarian Intervention', 13 *Global Governance* 3, 2007, at 365. For an analysis of the conflict in Darfur discussing what the situation reveals about the response of international actors to mass atrocities, see D. R. Black, P. D. Williams, *Security and Governance. The International Politics of Mass Atrocities: The Case of Darfur*, 2010.

the question of aggression for purposes of individual criminal accountability. It was intended to enable the Security Council to take measures to maintain or restore international peace and security. With the Rome Statute, if further agreed, the Court would also receive jurisdiction in the context of peace and security maintenance investigating and prosecuting individuals responsible of aggression. The problem in the maintenance of international peace and security is characterized by the political impasse of the reform of the Security Council, and as counterpart by the presence of the International Criminal Court as a permanent judicial institution functioning through a cooperation pillar between sovereign States and international organizations such as the United Nations. In the words of Cassese, "the UN Security Council has been unable to keep up with increase of violence. No one can contest its inability to react promptly and effectively and to put a stop to massacres amounting to serious threats to the peace or breaches of the peace in Somalia, the former Yugoslavia including Kosovo, Sierra Leone, Ethiopia and Eritrea, Indonesia, the Middle East, and so on".[347] The reform of the Security Council encompasses sensitive democratization issues such as the categories of membership, the question of the veto held by the five permanent members, the regional representation, the size of an enlarged Security Council and its working methods. Currently, no African country has a permanent seat in the Security Council. This is seen as a major political issue negatively influencing the support expected by the African States according to their membership to the Rome Statute and by the African Union in the maintenance of peace and security, including fighting against the impunity of international crimes, enforcing appropriately the emerging regime of international criminal justice. Moreover, considering the past, present and future achievements of international criminal justice both States and non-state actors are responsible of their responsiveness serving the "interests of justice" or so-called community obligations.[348] The simple question is what kind of authority characterizes the emerging regime of international criminal justice in the arrays of peace and security? How such authority would evolve in the future, considering its complementary role with the UN system? In order to provide a complete picture the political standpoints of regional organizations also deserve discussions. After all, they have to be completely involved in finding solutions on peace, justice and security in their own regional realities, upholding the expectations of the human security doctrine and the rule of law. The UN system and the Rome Statute institutions have a specific role on such sensitive issues which deserve further debate. The last paragraph of this section, which ends my conclusive observations, deals with the normative gaps of the Rome

---

347 See A. Cassese, 'et al' "Failure of International Sanctions against Serious State Delinquencies" in *State, Sovereignty and International Governance*, (2004), at 240.

348 On the way the institutional design of the ICC regulates the opportunities of States to shape and strengthen international criminal justice, see S. C. Roach, "Global Governance in Context", *Governance, Order, and the International Criminal Court. Between Realpolitik and a Cosmopolitan Court*, (2009), at 1.

Statute, in particular, its nature as a governance system based on international cooperation of non-compulsory character.

## 5.5.5. THE FEATURES OF JUSTICE GOVERNANCE: THE COOPERATION PILLAR OF THE ROME STATUTE

In conclusion, it needs to be noted that in addition to the relationship between international organizations and their member States, the law of international organizations also covers the interaction between themselves, where the literature is relatively scarce and some is pertinent to the case law. The Darfur case, as first referral to the Court by the UN Security Council, is the case study of such imperfect interaction.[349] According to the provisions of the Rome Statute, the Security Council is not obliged to enforce judicial decisions. The Court simply operates through a judicial pillar, represented by the Court itself, and a cooperation pillar which belongs to the States Parties and through other cooperation agreements with international organizations such as the UN missions in the field.[350] In order to offer an overview of the cooperation regime established by the Rome Statute, Rastan points out that under Article 54 of the Statute the Court may seek the cooperation of any intergovernmental organization or so-called 'arrangements', which refer implicitly to the UN peacekeeping operations, and may enter into specific agreements with the UN, while Article 87 (6) enables the Court to ask any intergovernmental organization to provide information or documents, or other forms of cooperation that are consistent with its judicial mandate. Where the Security Council did not refer a situation, there is nothing preventing the Court from asking the cooperation and assistance of the Security Council pursuant to Article 87 (6) of the Rome Statute and Article 15 of the UN-ICC Relationship Agreement. Obviously, the legal modalities of such forms of cooperation fall outside the regime established by Part IX of the Rome Statute (International Cooperation and Judicial Assistance) which only deals with the State Party obligations. With

[349] In the situation in Darfur, Sudan, three cases are being heard before Pre-Trial Chamber I: The Prosecutor v. Ahmad Muhammad Harun ("Ahmad Harun") and Ali Muhammad Ali Abd-Al-Rahman ("Ali Kushayb"); *The Prosecutor v. Omar Hassan Ahmad Al Bashir and and The Prosecutor v. Bahr Idriss Abu Garda*. On 31 March 2005, The Security Council determined that "the situation in the Sudan continued to constitute a threat to international peace and security", and "decided to refer the situation in Darfur to the Prosecutor of the International Criminal Court", UNSCR 1593 (2005). See, Sixth Report of the Prosecutor of the ICC to the UN Security Council pursuant to UNSCR 1593 (2005) accessible at: www.icc-cpi.int/library/organs/otp/OTP-RP-20071205-UNSC-ENG.pdf See statement of H. Köchler, President of the International Progress Organization after the Darfur referral. H. Köchler, *Double Standards in International Criminal Justice: The Case of Sudan*, (2005), accessible at: http://i-p-o.org/Koechler-Sudan-ICC.pdf See also H. Köchler, *Global Justice or Global Revenge? International Criminal Justice at the Crossroads*, (2003).

[350] For an overview of the legal practice of cooperation and judicial assistance between the ICC and the States, see R. Rastan, "Testing Co-operation: The ICC and National Authorities", (2008) 21 LJIL 431, at 456.

regard to the cooperation with other international organizations, including the UN Security Council, the legal obligation to cooperate with the Court falls under separate arrangements and agreements. In fact, outside the forms of cooperation voluntarily agreed upon these specific legal arrangements, international organizations, namely the UN, are under no legal obligation to cooperate with the Court. Rastan further clarifies that "an international organization cannot be compelled to cooperate in the absence of such consent even when the ICC is acting pursuant to a Security Council referral".[351] In addition to this fragmentation of legal modalities of cooperation, a law enforcement pillar of the governance of justice is inexistent.

In substance, challenging old models of conflict management, intervention in humanitarian crises and ending the impunity of international crimes, requires a defined law enforcement strategy. Sovereign States still have to find the middle ground for an effective governance of justice in conflict and post-conflict situations. The argument in this study refers to the indispensable analysis of emerging complementary regimes working on humanitarian issues and international justice, securing the universality of the rule of law in the international legal order. The findings of this research propose a model of governance (institutional, normative and functional) of multilateral tools based on universal principles;[352] on global values for the protection of fundamental rights; and on the interdependence of international threats and crimes. Only through such considerations of international governance solving the vacuum of law enforcement effectively managed by the sovereign States, by the UN and the ICC, it is possible to challenge the causes of large-scale violations of human rights (due to ethnic conflicts, bad governance and resource exploitation), occurring during internal civil wars (intra-state conflicts), and State aggression (inter-state conflicts). According to the treaty law the States have the responsibility of solving the delay in the harmonization of their domestic legislations. The domestic jurisdiction of the States needs to be monitored according to the principles of universality and accountability. Another problem constantly debated is the deficiency of *checks and balances* regulating the relations between international public mandates and their complementary interaction. In the law of international organizations, *vis-à-vis* the theory of *checks and balances*, their fragmentation and decentralization is constantly a matter of concern in the scholarly or academic literature.

---

351 See R. Rastan, *supra*.

352 See C. Bassiouni and D. Rothenberg , "Facing Atrocity: The Importance of Guiding Principles on Post-Conflict Justice", *The Chicago Principles on Post-Conflict Justice,* (2007) International Human Rights Law Institute, Chicago Council on Global Affairs, Istituto Superiore Internazionale di Scienze Criminali, Association Internationale de Droit Pénal,, at 6, accessible at: www.isisc.org/public/chicago%20principles%20-%20final%20-%20may%209%202007.pdf.

Summarizing the main issues, the emergent features of the governance of justice will need: *a)* to preserve the independence of the judicial pillar of the ICC and the implementation of its jurisdiction; *b)* to extend the further definition of international crimes; *c)* the individual and corporate criminal responsibility; *d)* the criminal responsibility of a State; and *e)* the enforcement of law with States that are not parties to the Statute of the Court. For an evaluation of the possible evolution of the features of justice governance, it will also be important to observe the institutional relations between the General Assembly of the UN, the Assembly of the States Parties to the Rome Statute, the Security Council, the Human Rights Council, the Trust Fund for Victims, the International Court of Justice and the evolution in their relations. A systemic approach, institutional and normative, illustrate this research, which supports the determination of the States expressed in the Rome Statute, establishing a permanent criminal Court in relationship with the UN system with jurisdiction over the most serious crimes of concern to the international community as a whole.[353] In any case, the rule of law should be applied domestically and the main responsibility for it rests with the States themselves.

The next part of this study argues that pressuring the sovereign responsibility of any State on sustainable peace, impunity, meaningful justice to the victims and accountability of criminal perpetrators should be dealt with an integrated approach of governance. It selects two case studies and debates the findings deriving from them. In particular, it provides assessments of the country-specific situation in the Sudan (Darfur).[354] It debates the humanitarian escalations of *last resort* and their governance in the field operations. It argues about the issue of cooperation dealing with serious international crimes and with the fight against impunity while protecting civilian lives. Obviously, this case study cannot be considered as exhaustive. The next and last part of this study advocates for the political will to implement the duty to maintain and restore peace, justice and security according to the human security doctrine. The main requirement would be to develop interaction strategies between legal and political frameworks oriented on the *supranational* perspective of the international legal order and in accordance with the constitution of the world community. Such constitutional drift seems to become more distant in view of the pluralistic approaches taken at

[353] See the Rome Statute provisions in Part II, Jurisdiction, Admissibility and Applicable law, Article 5 (Crimes within the jurisdiction of the Court) until Article 21 (Applicable law), at 3, 16, accessible at: www.icc-cpi.int/Menus/ICC/Legal+Texts+and+Tools/.

[354] In December 2012 the new Prosecutor of the Court informed the Security Council that her office might pursue further investigations of individuals who may be responsible for attacks on civilians, attacks on the United Nations-African Union Mission in Darfur (UNAMID), and the disruption of the delivery of humanitarian relief. See F. Bensouda, *Statement to the United Nations Security Council on the situation in Darfur, the Sudan, pursuant to UNSCR 1593 (2005)*, 13 December 2012, accessible at: www.icc-cpi.int/iccdocs/PIDS/statements/UNSC1212/UNSCDarfurSpeechEng.pdf.

national, regional and international levels. This is particularly true if we look at the developments in the position of the African Union and the relationship with the Security Council and the International Criminal Court, either in the context of peace enforcement operations, or looking at the implications in the context of international criminal justice and human rights obligations of the African States. Moreover, only a minority of States Parties adjusted their internal legislation and constitutional parameters in accordance with the emerging regime falling under the Rome Statute. The lacuna of interaction strategies is also applicable in the bilateral approach of States and global actors implicated in mass atrocity crimes, including the important role of civil society organizations in their collection of fact-findings and reporting activities.

# PART III

# THE HUMANITARIAN ESCALATIONS OF LAST RESORT AND THEIR GOVERNANCE IN THE FIELD OPERATIONS

"Since wars begin in the minds of men it is in the minds of men
that the defences of peace must be constructed".
*From the Preamble of the UNESCO Constitution*

# 6. THE INTERNATIONAL RESPONSES TO MASS ATROCITIES IN AFRICA AND THE CRIMINAL REGIME IN THE SUDAN

## PRELIMINARY REMARKS

The main argument expressed in this part of this study is that without appropriate interaction strategies between complementary global regimes (based on balancing public powers through visible reforms, policy formulation and law-making processes) there would be limits in the creation of a global architecture dealing effectively with the escalations of war and crime. Such interaction strategies are required for democratic governance and for the preservation of the rule of law. The good governance of peace and justice not only depends from the implementation of mutual interests and mutual support applied on the ground between complementary mandates, but also from the developments of governance frameworks and their complementary character at structural, functional and normative levels. The role of the emerging regime of international criminal justice in the arrays of peace and security in Africa is still very weak for several reasons. The formulation of governance frameworks dealing with humanitarian escalations of war and crime is only at its initial stage of realization. The actors involved have to take ownership of their mutual responsibilities of cooperation, law enforcement and civilian protection in situations of mass atrocities. The purpose of this Part III is to introduce the case studies dealing with the humanitarian escalation of *last resort* and their governance in the field operations in the Sudan and in the Democratic Republic of Congo. It debates respectively: *a)* the current place of justice in the arrays of peace and security maintenance, *b)* the political issues around the first generation of international humanitarian escalations of mass atrocity crimes and the governance frameworks dealing with them, *c)* the role of international, regional and bilateral actors in the Sudan and in the Democratic Republic of Congo, and *d)* the management of the intra-state conflict in the Sudan and the lessons learned.

The last years of the century proved to be a period of dramatic transition for the sake of statehood and democratic governance in African States.[355] The inter-state ethnic conflicts had terrible consequences visible in the execution of mass atrocities.[356] In 1989 it seemed that the end of the Cold War heralded far brighter prospects for the African future but good hopes were soon seriously troubled.[357] The continent was devastated by internal conflicts and large scale humanitarian atrocities spreading in multiple countries. It was as if the *Iron Curtain* had been left open releasing the demonic forces of war and crime. Since then, an increasing number of emerging nations have undergone the turning drama of violent conflicts, mass atrocity crimes and the determination of warlords to retain political power at the expenses of civilians. These civil wars have claimed millions of lives, and still do. The list of the so-called *failed* States doubled consistently. In several situations of war and crime the domestic governance systems and institutions are not self-reliant during difficult political transitions, and are exposed to constant failure upholding human security measures. In the majority of such situations the State is replaced by criminal regimes violating fundamental individual rights. Empirical data of mass atrocities demonstrate serious impunity gaps and the powerless or unwillingness of domestic security systems to preserve law and order. The domestic, regional and international responsibilities upholding minimal standards of governance of war and crime are undoubtedly in transition. Although the paradigms of the responsibility to protect civilians in conflict zones and the use of international justice and accountability should be complementary in their governance, this is not the case in the humanitarian escalations of *last resort*. The delimitation between statehood, State sovereignty and the frameworks of international governance requires new policy formulations upholding human security measures. An international architecture of governance fostering human security is absolutely required. There is, however, a long way to go.

The dilemma of human security in the governance of complementary global regimes is still unresolved and waits for visible solutions from the political forces involved in such policy formulations. Besides, the conceptualization of human security upraised already an extensive debate in academic and policy circles. This

[355] See R. H. Jackson, C. G. Rosberg, "Why Africa's Weak States Persist: The Empirical and the Juridical in Statehood", *World Politics*, Volume 35, Issue 1 (Oct. 1982), at 1–24. See also S. Levitsky, L. A. Way, *Competitive Authoritarianism: Hybrid Regimes After the Cold War*, 2010.

[356] For an overview of African conflicts and serious humanitarian breaches currently occurring in several countries, see Human Rights Watch, *CAR/DRC: LRA Conducts Massive Adduction Campaign*, August 11, 2010, accessible at: www.hrw.org/en/news/2010/08/11/cardr-congo-lra-conducts-massive-abduction-campaign For the debate about international interventions and democracies see, W. M. Reisman, 'Humanitarian Intervention and Fledging Democracies', 18 *Fordham International Law Journal*, 1994–1995, at 794.

[357] R. Kaplan, *The Coming Anarchy: Shattering the Dreams of the Post-Cold War*, 2000.

study, however, does not attempt to solve it.[358] If on one side the reality of armed conflicts rendered international protection duties of civilians more complex, on the other there are institutionalized defenders of truth protecting individual rights. This is the vision offered by complementary global regimes such as the UN and the Rome Statute institutions. In the context of the governance of international threats and crimes these regimes represent an opportunity to centralize individuals rather than exclusively prioritizing the interests of nation-states. Obviously, only a *supranational* capacity upholding universal norms would be the satisfactory way dealing with mass atrocity crimes and also fighting against other international threats and crimes. This is of course left to the outcome of political convergence of expectations in global politics, which still depend on the volatile dynamics and fluctuations characterizing international relations and the politics of mass atrocities. The governance debates regarding the breakdowns of domestic jurisdictions, or even worse, about the situations characterized by the complete absence and collapse of nations-states in conflict and post-conflict situations share the same common concerns. Namely, that the international responses in mass atrocities simply depend from fragmented legal and political frameworks based on cooperation requiring further implementation. This is either true in the context of the maintenance, management and restoration of international peace and security, or in the fight against the impunity of serious international crimes. Nevertheless, it is required to assess where feasible opportunities can be found in the humanitarian escalations of *last resort* with an integrated model of cooperation, law enforcement and civilian protection duties in conflict and post-conflict situations. The first section below introduces *a)* the place of justice in the arrays of peace and security as a tool of *last resort*, *b)* the assessment provided by way of case studies and *c)* the outline of the chapters pointing out the practice applied in situations of war and crime before the formulation of the recommendations would take place.

## 6.1. THE PLACE OF JUSTICE IN THE ARRAYS OF PEACE AND SECURITY

### SECTION OUTLINE

The analysis of multilateral perspectives indicates that since the creation of the United Nations system seventy years ago, much of the international law and diplomacy has been developed, shaped, implemented and enforced through the UN bodies and related international organizations dealing with peace and justice.

358 See R. Paris, "Human Security: Paradigm Shift or Hot Air?", *International Security*, Fall 2001, Vol. 26, No. 2, 87–102. See A. Pop, Article Review: Human Security: Paradigm Shift or Hot Air? 2006, accessible at: www.academia.edu/1098843/Article_Review_-_Human_Security_Paradigm_Shift_or_Hot_Air.

Later, with the disintegration of the Soviet Bloc in the early 1990s it emerged a considerably revitalized political determination of the UN to promote a new era of global cooperation. However, the political trend to respond to the challenges of the increasingly interdependent global economy delayed the attention required in the extreme violence occurring in conflict zones and the mass atrocity crimes deriving from them. The international interventions in Africa, particularly in Rwanda and Sierra Leone, did not reduce the misery of civilians.[359] In order to give an idea of the place of justice in the arrays of peace and security this part offers an overview of the conflict management and peace enforcement in the Sudan and the humanitarian escalation of the Security Council to the Court (Darfur). The regime of justice falling under the Rome Statute was generated in the first instance by the determination of civil society organizations advocating for international engagements in mass atrocities preserving fundamental individual rights. Such regime is still far from realizing the expectation of international humanitarian escalations based on the complementary character of global regimes working for sustainable peace. Therefore, the case studies advocate for systemic changes of governance frameworks in order for them to be complementary and maximize the results in conflict and post-conflicts situations.

The Rome Statute system has a limited jurisdiction and does not have police force. The referral of the situation in the Sudan from the Security Council confirms the limitations of its working methods with the Court. In theory, the judicial proceedings against criminal perpetrators not only represent a deterrent tool of international crimes, but most importantly provide the truth in regard to a specific situation requiring political engagement for humanitarian intervention enforcing the law. In the past, such important factor proved not to be reliable in the selection of situations compromising international peace and security. Now, at least, there is a specific tool which still requires a place in the arrays of peace and security for its maintenance and restoration, and also for a well-defined, well-supported and well-visible complementary and comprehensive role in the international operations deployed on the ground. As the case studies will demonstrate, this is not yet the case. The international capacities of law enforcement and the strategies of civilian protection in situations of war and crime require systemic changes at structural, normative and functional levels and an integrated approach of governance fostering human security. In this way the *retributive*, *protective* and *restitutive* aspects of justice and the fight against impunity will serve the quest of sustainable peace in communities affected by war and crime. The attempt of this part is to shed some light on the complementary responsibilities in the humanitarian escalations of mass atrocities, particularly about the so often referred 'African test' of humanitarian interventions under the

[359] See R. Kaplan, *supra*. See also F. Grünfeld, A. Huijboom, *The Failure to Prevent Genocide in Rwanda: The Role of Bystanders*, 2007.

flag of the responsibility to protect and the referrals of *last resort* addressed to the emerging regime of international criminal justice.[360]

### 6.1.1. THE RISK ANALYSIS OF INTERNATIONAL RESPONSES

In general this part examines the governance of international responses in fragile States where 'arrangements and agreements' of cooperation between relevant stakeholders are weak and need implementation. In particular, it emphasizes the necessity to establish 'narrowly focused' mandates and high standards of cooperation based on mutual interests between peace and justice. This trend of governance should be visible in both referral and non-referral activities of the Security Council to the Court. This part examines the dynamics in the case studies dealing with the peace enforcement operations of the Security Council and the judicial activity of the Court providing some recommendations for decision-makers. The first case study gives attention to the first generation of referrals coming from the Security Council to the Court exploring the operationalization of the R2P in the Sudan. The most obvious case for the first application of the new set of mechanisms and guidelines within the duty to protect civilians was Darfur, but we will see that both the Sudanese government and the international community have failed to take the necessary steps to protect civilians in the country. Instead, while the Security Council remained silent to the judicial outcomes addressed by the Court to the Sudanese warlords, the regime of the government in Khartoum and its *janjaweed* militias have conducted a systematic campaign of atrocities in Darfur. The most responsible perpetrators are still at large and there is a political impasse between global and regional actors, namely the UN, the ICC and the AU considering the political unrest and the violence spreading also in South Sudan. Obviously, such an impasse slows down the political *road map* required for an 'architecture' fostering peace, justice and security and the best ways humanitarian escalations should be governed in intra-state, and eventually in inter-state conflicts, upholding the responsibilities to protect civilians.

The Court's jurisdiction is complementary to that of the States that have ratified its Statute while its global mandate is complementary to the UN regime. The Court has no police force and no prisons. Thus, implementing and making effective the obligation of States and other international actors cooperating with the Court's activities has been the most important challenge in the initial period of its existence. Moreover, we have seen that the interaction with the Security

[360] See H. Breakey, "The Responsibility to Protect and the Protection of Civilians in Armed Conflicts: Review and Analysis", *Institute for Ethics, Governance and Law*, Griffith University, May, 2011, accessible at: www.griffith.edu.au.

Council is not characterized by any compulsory cooperation. Paragraph 7 of the Darfur referral by the Security Council to the Court, "*recognizes* that none of the expenses incurred in connection with the referral, including expenses related to investigations or prosecutions in connection with that referral, shall be borne by the United Nations, and that such costs shall be borne by the parties to the Rome Statute and those States that wish to contribute voluntarily".[361] The same trend is confirmed with the referral of the situation in Libya to the Court. An appropriate involvement of the Security Council with resources and law enforcement support does not seem to be the priority. Consensus on such support is expected in the UN General Assembly at least with regard to the referrals addressed to the Court by the Security Council. The *last resort* option of international criminal justice waits for political convergence and for a legal framework based on compulsory cooperation with or without the referrals coming from the Security Council.

### 6.1.2. THE CASE STUDIES ASSESSMENT

*In primis* the case studies reveal several gaps in the international humanitarian escalations and their governance in the field operations. There are no doubts that the conventional (military) methods of conflict management are no longer effective, therefore the configurations of international mandates deployed on the ground require a new approach of governance. The place of justice in the arrays of international peace and security is compromised for several reasons. The governance of the emerging regime of international criminal justice in the context of sustainable peace in intra- and possibly inter-state civil wars requires further decision-making on the ways humanitarian escalations would be performed between complementary global actors. The case studies focus on the operations deployed on the ground and the current restrictions of complementarity, which in some ways reduces the impact of justice and its deterrent effect. In the DRC, for instance, the United Nations invested in multidimensional operations on the ground mandated by the Security Council to assist the country on the road to stability (MONUSCO). The Congolese government referred to the International Criminal Court the investigation and prosecution of serious breaches of international humanitarian law. In the Sudan, the Security Council referred the situation of Darfur to the Court after the shortcomings in peace agreements and peace enforcement.[362] It is clear that peace operations should support the

361 See UN doc. S/RES/1593 (2005).

362 See P. Takirambudde, "UN: Darfur Resolution a Historic Failure", *Human Rights Watch*, September 18, 2004, accessible at: www.hrw.org/news/2004/09/17/un-darfur-resolution-historic-failure See also "Security Council must urgently take action to end impunity in Darfur – ICC Prosecutor", *UN News Centre*, 5 June 2013. See Statement of the Prosecutor of the ICC to the UNSC pursuant to UNSCR 1593 (2005), 05/06/2013, accessible at: www.icc-cpi.int/iccdocs/otp/ICC-OTP-UNSC-Dafur-05June2013-ENG.pdf.

Court *a)* since the referral, *b)* during its investigative activity, and *c)* after its judicial outcomes. In practice, this has not been the case. In the Sudan the law enforcement failed, including the expectations of civilian protection duties and humanitarian assistance. The criminal regime still in power in the country waits to be isolated with concrete international efforts. In the DRC the configurations of peace-keeping and peace-building mandates do not fulfill the requirements of the judicial activities of the Court, including the civilian protection duties of civilians. Hopefully, judicial proceedings will be performed *in situ*, but such trend is not sufficiently detectable in the domestic judicial activity and victims and witnesses still cry for justice. In Mali the configuration of robust peacekeeping operations does not refer to any support to the quest of justice on the ground.[363] In Kenya there is confusion about legal obligations and political positions at domestic and regional levels. The political trend of the AU against the Rome Statute system is absolutely regrettable. In any case, the judicial activities of the Court cannot be compromised by any of its political standpoints.[364] The lack of cooperation with the Office of the Prosecutor by the government of Kenya and the withdraw of the charges of crimes against Kenyatta is deplorable. Justice for victims of the 2007–2008 post-election violence is still an urgent priority.[365]

The case studies indicate that peace and justice mandates are disconnected between them in both categories of referrals to the Court. In regard to Libya, the use of the language in the resolution of the Security Council referred to the responsibility to protect authorizing the military intervention, while extending further the mandate of international criminal justice falling under the Rome Statute. In Libya the national transitional council (NTC) will need to perform reliable domestic governance of both security and rule of law sectors taking care of civilian protection measures, while investigating and prosecuting serious breaches of international humanitarian law.[366] The consensus building in the

---

363 See UN doc. S/RES/2085 (2012). See M. Lankhorst, "Peacebuilding in Mali: Linking Justice, Security, and Reconciliation", *The Hague Institute for Global Justice*, Policy Brief 6, November 2013, accessible at: http://thehagueinstituteforglobaljustice.org.

364 During the yearly speech at the UN General Assembly (31 October 2013) the ICC President Song emphasised that "the Court has the duty to observe the legal framework set by States" and asked the other stakeholders of the system to uphold the integrity of the Rome Statute, respecting the roles assigned to each entity under the Statute. He also stressed that "whereas the Assembly of States Parties can consider legislative issues and discuss political questions, the ICC must remain an independent, judicial institution". See *ICC Annual Report to the United Nations General Assembly*, 31 October 2013, accessible at: www.icc-cpi.int/iccdocs/presidency/Pres-statement-31-10-2013-Eng.pdf.

365 See Amnesty International, "Kenya: Justice for victims of post-election violence still an urgent priority", 5 December 2014, accessible at: https://www.amnesty.org/en/articles/news/2014/12/icc-drops-charges-against-kenyan-president/.

366 See *Sixth Report of the Prosecutor of the International Criminal Court to the UN Security Council pursuant to UNSCR 1970 (2011)*, New York, 14 November 2013, accessible at: www.icc-cpi.int/en_menus/icc/press%20and%20media/press%20releases/Pages/ProsecutorUNSCNov2013.aspx.

Security Council to intervene in Syria totally failed. The dangerous domino effect of the *Arab Spring* characterizing the violence spreading in the entire region of the Middle East still raises serious security concerns. In Syria the international community remains silent and inactive to the commission of serious crimes of common concern. The Court is not able to get involved in Syria. It simply did not receive jurisdiction from the Security Council. In Syria no political convergence has been met in regard to the maintenance of peace, justice and security. The same political *inertia* characterizes the humanitarian crisis exploded in North Korea and the authoritarian nature of its regime, including the gravity, the scale and the nature of the violations committed in this country.[367] The unacceptable nature and magnitude of these crises demand a common position and joint international actions.[368]

If in theory the tools governing multiple situations of war and crime have the role to improve human security expectations centralizing individuals in international affairs, the practice shows serious concerns. There is a long way ahead for further accomplishments of international governance institutions of complementary character. Some of the obstacles, challenges and concerns, including the opportunities upholding multilateral solutions have already been discussed in the previous parts of this study. The case studies conclude this analytical journey which surely requires further research providing solutions to the enforcement of law, civilian protection duties and the models of capacity building in conflict and post-conflict situations characterized by serious violations of international law. The purpose of the case studies is to evaluate the multidimensional capacity of international responses and the efforts maximizing the results on the ground integrating peace, justice and security mandates. Their complementary character requires stronger political determinations strengthening partnerships globally, regionally and on the ground. In order to influence the domestic governance institutions and the accountability system against criminal perpetrators as an important aspect of civilian protection duties, flexible configurations between complementary mandates are strongly recommended in the short and middle terms. In the long term, political convergence should be found by the political forces empowering complementary global regimes on the ways their institutions, and the political processes deriving from them, could work together more effectively.

---

367 See UN doc. A/HRC/25/63 (2014), Report of the commission of inquiry on human rights in the Democratic People's Republic of Korea.

368 The Geneva II Conference on Syria (January 2014) is pursued by UN peace envoy to Syria Lakhdar Brahimi in cooperation with the United States and Russia. The aim of the conference is ending the civil war in the country. See UN Action Group for Syria, Final Communiqué, 30.06.2012, accessible at: www.un.org/News/dh/infocus/Syria/FinalCommuniqueActionGroupforSyria.pdf.

Justice and accountability are fundamental for lasting peace and security in conflict and post-conflict situations. The UN family of institutions, bodies, specialized agencies and donors should support the Court's mandate prioritizing: the *retributive* aspect of justice (investigations, prosecutions, arrest warrants and law enforcement); the *protective* aspect of justice, (relocation, demobilization of ex-soldiers, protection of witnesses of crimes and other civilian protection duties); and the *reparative* aspect of justice (participation of civilians in judicial proceedings, facilitating the reparative measures for the victims of serious international crimes). Besides, the findings of justice should not be left half way deprived of law enforcement capacity, in particular after the failure of preventive diplomacy, peace negotiations and the commission of criminal acts. Once again, justice should receive support with every means in both referrals and non-referrals coming from the Security Council.

### 6.1.3. THE OUTLINE OF THE CHAPTERS

In this part the first chapter points out the humanitarian escalations in mass atrocity and their governance in the field operations exploring the political dynamics of the first referral of the Security Council to the Court in the Sudan, and the political impact at regional level and also for the range of other actors involved. The second chapter deals with the multidimensional operations and the issue of cooperation including the gaps in the coordination, coherence and law enforcement in the DRC as the main obstacles to reach sustainable peace in the country. The third and last chapter provides the concluding assessment about the place the emerging regime of international criminal justice should receive in the arrays of peace and security mandates on the ground. The findings in the case studies underscore the necessity of a political *road map* fostering peace, justice and security with an integrated, democratic and comprehensive approach of governance. The main recommendation addressed to decision-makers on such issues is to re-determine the democratization process of global regimes of complementary character preserving further international law and order. This is considered the fundamental requirement to achieve results in the global fight against international threats, and be prepared to *respond*, *react* and *rebuild* in situations of war and crime in accordance with the challenges of the time and the features of our global society. The progress of democratic governance, or better say, the search of an international architecture fostering peace, justice and security obviously depends on *a)* the evolution of the international politics of mass atrocities, *b)* the cooperation between the actors dealing with humanitarian escalations in extreme situations of war and crime, and *c)* the institutional reforms and reviews of the working methods between them. The definition of complementary global regimes requires a political *road map* at domestic, regional and international levels by the stakeholders investing in them. Despite the critics from a relevant number of observers there seem to be new opportunities fostering peace, justice and security. These opportunities have to rely on the human security doctrine. The complementary character of global regimes deserves the attention from decision-makers in the short, middle and long terms in accordance with the human security doctrine. After all, the approach in accordance with the expectations of human security has the potential "to bring international law better into line with the requirements of today's world".[369]

This part underscores the importance of an interaction strategy between global regimes of complementary character against criminal regimes that destabilize peace and security and violate fundamental individual rights. It offers some observations regarding the international interventions in mass atrocities in Africa. In particular, it explores the challenges of such responses in the African continent and the emerging role of complementary global regimes. It considers the implementation and harmonization as fundamental prerequisites for the definition of the complementary character of such regimes, including the assessments of their legal frameworks based on: *complementarity* (with a particular focus on 'positive complementarity' and the referrals by States to the Court, including the steps that may be taken to encourage and facilitate genuine national judicial proceedings *in situ*); *cooperation* (including implementing legislation, judicial assistance, international actors and regional organizations); *peace and justice* (e.g. the role of the UN, particularly focusing on the law enforcement of the arrest warrants of the Court and the working methods with the Security Council); and the *impact on victims and affected communities* (including outreach, victim participation, reparations and the trust fund for victims).[370] In order to shed some light on the shortcomings of sustainable peace in several situations the next section points out *a)* the dynamics of the international engagements in mass atrocities, *b)* the formulation of humanitarian escalations and the governance frameworks dealing with them, and *c)* the prerequisites for their implementation and harmonization.

## 6.2. THE INTERNATIONAL HUMANITARIAN ESCALATIONS OF MASS ATROCITIES

### SECTION OUTLINE

The idealistic approach in the debate of humanitarian escalations in mass atrocities emphasizes the fact that complementary global regimes should be able to retain either the challenges occurring in international politics, or the global policy

369 G. Oberleitner, "Human Security: A Challenge to International Law?" in *Global Governance* 11 (2005), at 185–203.

370 See ICC-ASP docs., *Stocktaking of International Criminal Justice*, 2010, accessible at: www.icc-cpi.int/en_menus/asp/reviewconference/stocktaking/Pages/stocktaking.aspx.

formulation of humanitarian interventions and mutual accountability, using the rule of law as the most important principle of governance in humanitarian affairs. However, as we have previously discussed, the process of the internationalization of law focusing on the interplay between national, regional and international norms and based on the universalism principle of human rights is a 'work in progress' issue which requires political determination, persistence and time. The intervention in humanitarian matters in sovereign States needs further efforts in accordance with universal values and human rights preservation standards, as well as international governance institutions dealing with civilian protection measures. This is particularly true in this delicate phase of the existing global institutional frameworks which risk not to be further extended by know-how and resources due to the financial constraints and economic breakdowns of many States. The best option should be to benefit from the increased competence and responsibility of the tools already at disposition: the United Nations and the Rome Statute systems. The search of the basic requirements for a global architecture fostering peace, justice and security is fundamental. Such architecture has to be designed in a comprehensive and democratic way and based on the constitution of the world community. Further progress is to be seen in the institutional reforms, in the advancement of global democratization processes, and in the concrete efforts balancing powers between international governance institutions of complementary character. In other words, the applicable ways international global actors would best understand the complex needs of affected populations by war, violence and crime centralizing the rights of civilians. Such an approach, of course, requires political convergence of expectations. Some of the reasons why this is so difficult to realize are examined in this section.

This section examines the emerging regime of international justice as a tool to achieve sustainable peace in intra- and eventually inter-states civil wars. It attempts to define the new concept of humanitarian escalations between complementary global regimes involved in conflict and post-conflict situations and their governance. Such escalations are characterized by the authorizations of the Security Council to intervene in conflict zones with every means in order to maintain and restore peace and security and also to protect civilians. In the African continent and in particular in sub-Saharan Africa in the Great Lakes African region, including Sudan and Chad,[371] the Security Council attempted to leave and authorize the regional involvement in the humanitarian escalations of mass atrocities. This was the case in the Sudan, in the DRC and other situations left to the African Union to intervene with the option of hybrid solutions. In both cases the working methods in regard to the responsibility to protect civilians

[371] See J. Giroux, D. Lanz, D. Sguaitamatti, "The Tormented Triangle: The Regionalization of Conflict in Sudan, Chad and Central African Republic", *Crisis States Working Papers No. 2*, 2009, at 17.

in conflict zones displayed several gaps of governance. In regard to justice the political consensus to extend the Court's jurisdiction has not been reached in several situations of war and crime, with the last one being Syria. The new element about the use of justice as deterrent tool of war and crime and towards the referrals activities of the Security Council to the Court would require, first of all, a place in the arrays of peace and security for law enforcement measures supporting the judicial institution with every means. Instead, the Court is left completely disconnected from the working methods of the Security Council and its involvement falling under the flag of humanitarian interventions. Furthermore, the Court is left quite isolated in regard to the protection, relocation and safety of civilians affected by war and crime. The results of the Court depend on such narrow international cooperation regime and on the legal obligations of its States Parties. The Security Council and the UN members should be supportive before, during, and after the humanitarian escalations so-called of *last resort* would occur. Besides, through the UN political institutions even non-States Parties to the Court should be pressured to cooperate.

### 6.2.1. THE INTERNATIONAL ENGAGEMENTS IN MASS ATROCITIES

From a broad perspective the international engagements in mass atrocities implicated matters of conscience, sense of guilt and helplessness, combined with valuable ethical and universal aspirations to intervene in case of severe violations of international humanitarian law.[372] Despite the psychological, ethical and philosophical aspects, including the political reasons for the creation of the UN *ad hoc* tribunals in the past, a reliable motivation to create a governance system based on individual accountabilities was never part of the political determinations expressed by the permanent members of the Security Council, including many States governed by different legal traditions, and which took political distance from the emerging regime of international criminal justice falling under the Rome Statute. It is clear that the system of accountability proposed by the emerging regime of the Rome Statute needs further political campaign and advocacy from global actors and civil society. Such regime represents the opportunity to centralize the role of the victims of serious international crimes challenging the mentality of impunity of crimes recognised under customary international law. Obviously, the global political engagement of States Parties and non-Parties, international and regional organizations and civil society are absolutely necessary. The risks

[372] See L. E. Fletcher, "From Indifference to Engagement: Bystanders and International Criminal Justice", 26 *Mich. J. Int'l L.* 1013 (2004), accessible at: http://scholarship.law.berkeley.edu/facpubs/598.

of political *impasse*, however, currently persist if we look at the distant political position taken from the African Union against the Rome Statute regime.[373]

The promise made by the international community of '*never again*' in regard to genocide has not been fully maintained. In the early 1990s the UN and the US intervention in Somalia for example, was supposed to be driven by humanitarian concerns, but the subsequent humiliation and improper withdrawal of those forces in 1994 quickly undercut what international engagement there was for intervention on humanitarian grounds. The demands of international humanitarian interventions were enormous and the resources inadequate.[374] Today, from the lessons learned in the situations in Libya, Syria and in the Sudan many have troubles to believe that there is something we can do in the face of the collapse of nation-states and the devastating consequences on civilians. The international responses to the genocide in Rwanda and the Balkans, most notably in Srebrenica, were characterized by weak political engagements. When such interventions did occur, as in Kosovo for instance, the international legal basis for it was even unclear.[375] The selectivity of such situations has been based on political interests. The risk was that such selectivity would become the practice of international responses anywhere else. As extensively discussed in the previous chapters, the support to address gross human rights violations emerged with the reinvigoration of multilateralism following the end of the Cold War. When a State would fail in its primary responsibilities towards its citizens the international community would also be responsible to intervene in extreme conflict situations. Since 2005, the norm of 'the responsibility to protect' civilians presented operational shortcomings on the ground, including unclear strategies of mandates' configuration of the Security Council supporting complementary actors fostering peace, justice and security, such as the Court. The test of the 'responsibility to protect' civilians by the international community, intervening in violent conflicts in Africa and the Middle East, has been partially left in the hands of the volatile character of global politics. Such responsibility is not legally defined and in the stage of policy formulation and still requiring implementation and harmonization. Therefore, it is required to spend a couple of words *a)* on the formulation of governance frameworks dealing with humanitarian escalations;

---

373 T. Murithi, "The African Union and the International Criminal Court: An Embattled Relationship?", *Institute for Justice and Reconciliation* (IJR), 2013, accessible at: www.africaportal.org/dspace/articles/african-union-and-international-criminal-court-embattled-relationship K. Kindiki, "The Normative and Institutional Framework of the African Union Relating to the Protection of Human Rights and the Maintenance of International Peace and Security: A Critical Appraisal", 3 *Afr. Hum. Rts. L.J.* 97 (2003).

374 See J. Mayall, *The New Interventionism: 1991–1994. The UN experience in Cambodia, former Yugoslavia and Somalia,* at 94, transferred to digital printing in 2001.

375 See D. H. Joyner, "The Kosovo Intervention: Legal Analysis and a More Persuasive Paradigm" *EJIL* (2002), Vol. 13 No. 3, at 597, accessible at: http://ejil.oxfordjournals.org/content/13/3/597.full.pdf.

*b)* on the role of complementary global regimes and the responsibilities of the States in such formulations; and *c)* on the prerequisites of their harmonization to optimize the results at domestic, regional and international levels. The international politics of mass atrocities and the governance frameworks at their disposition require with any doubt systemic changes.

### 6.2.2. THE FORMULATION OF GOVERNANCE FRAMEWORKS

At present the formulation of governance frameworks dealing with law enforcement and civilian protection duties in situations of mass atrocities is an idea not yet realized. It is clear that the current impasse in regard to the enforcement of law is troubled by the politics of double standards of the Security Council and by the shortcomings of States and regional organizations to *fully cooperate* with the Court. Despite the fact that two arrest warrants are outstanding against the President of the Sudan, Omar-Al Bashir, and despite the Court's orders and widespread calls of the international community to respect its obligations of cooperation with the Court, the visit of Omar-Al Bashir to many African States had taken place anyway since the Court's judicial orders. Furthermore, the Sudan, as a member of the UN, did not comply with the UN Resolution 1593 (2005) to arrest the perpetrators of serious violations of international humanitarian law. Obviously, the fact that the highest authorities in the country are responsible of the crimes requires an optimized use of the international tools currently at disposition. Such good use depends on the drift in global politics and on the willingness to preserve internationally law and order. The legal dichotomy between pluralism and constitutionalism, and the global regimes and institutional frameworks deriving from them, have to rely on their complementary role for their effectiveness. There is no other way to improve their good governance. This requires further efforts in regard to law enforcement, civilian protection duties and capacity-building models to be applied in conflict and post-conflict situations. It needs to be noted that in the Sudan the Security Council did not take the previous law enforcement position as in the situation in Sierra Leone. In the Charles Taylor's case before the Special Court for Sierra Leone, the Security Council, acting under Chapter VII of the UN Charter, unanimously passed the Resolution 1638 (2005) which empowered the United Nations Mission in Liberia (UNMIL) to arrest, detain, and transfer Taylor to the UN court in Sierra Leone in the event that he appeared in Liberia or in another African country. In the case of the Sudan the international politics of mass atrocities manifested the risk to undermine the credibility of a fair, impartial and independent international judiciary.[376] The problem is that

---

376 See W. A. Schabas, "The International Criminal Court and the Security Council Referral of the Darfur Situation", D. R. Black, P. D. Williams (eds.), *The International Politics of Mass*

both support and cooperation were not provided on very sensitive issues falling under the Rome Statute regime and the critics proliferate. Such trend confirms the complications characterizing the legal and political debates in regard to the emerging regime of international criminal justice, including the political convergence required for its place in the arrays of peace and security.[377]

The policy formulations of humanitarian interventions deserve some observations. After the Cold War the challenges of human security in Africa pressured the leadership for a political agenda sustained by the international actors involved in the continent. The domestic criminal regimes and the dictatorships would come across legal frameworks and renewed political approaches by African leaders themselves, western governments, international organizations and civil society. Sovereignty would finally be seen as a defined responsibility of domestic governance institutions of the nation-states towards their citizens. If it is true that the 'non-intervention' policy of African States applied in mass atrocities situations during the Cold War turned out to be only on paper on civilian protection duties and victim rights in the post-cold war phase, such policy still requires an appropriate implementation visible in the practice of civilian protection applied on the ground.[378] Moreover, after an extensive analysis of the serious shortcomings in the field operations in the last couple of decades, eminent observers demonstrated to policy-makers the necessity to review old models of conflict management performed by the UN involved in security matters and sustainable peace in African countries.[379] Finally, with the Rome Statute the majority of the African States committed themselves to put an end to the mentality of impunity of serious crimes perpetrated before, during, and after the explosion of armed conflicts. However, immediately after its establishment the Court's involvement in large scale humanitarian atrocities with investigation and prosecution in African countries, resumed in political pressure over its presence, its priorities, and the controversial relation between peace, justice and security.

Since the start of the first generation of referrals received from the States and the Security Council in the Sudan and Libya, the Court made immediately clear its prosecutorial strategy, based on judicial and not political decisions, its policy over admissibility, interest of justice and gravity, according to its treaty, the Rome

*Atrocities*, 2010, at 149.

377 M. G. Ituma, "The Crossroads of Politics and Law: The Unfinished Debate between the United States and the International Criminal Court", in *Africa Peace and Conflict Journal*, 5:2 (2012), at 79–82, accessible at: www.apcj.upeace.org/issues/APCJ_Vol_5_2_Final_Web.pdf.

378 On the failure of the responsibility to protect in Darfur, see N. Grono, "The International Community's Failure To Protect", 105 *African Affairs* 421, 2006, at 622.

379 See T. Piiparinen, *The Transformation of UN Conflict Management. Producing Images of Genocide from Rwanda to Darfur and Beyond*, (2010).

Statute, which is complementary to the UN Charter.[380] The confirmation of its complementary role to the United Nations derived from the fact that the Court did not hesitate to take over the situation in Darfur referred by the Security Council under Chapter VII of the UN Charter, extending the Court's jurisdiction to a non-State party such as the Sudan.[381] But before assessing further the ways such complementary roles have been applied in the practice, it is required to recall some background governance issues, including the methods evolving around the international responses in mass atrocity crimes. The joint task force on peace and security between the African Union and the United Nations for instance, requires further efforts facilitating cooperation on humanitarian concerns and human security on the ground, including the opportunity to enforce the arrest warrants of the Court while isolating the criminal perpetrators from the top diplomacy circles.[382] A joint task force is also required and recommended between the AU and possibly with the involvement of the Assembly of the States Parties of the ICC (ASP) interacting with the UN political institutions. Such joint task force should have a specific role in regard to the AU decision-making, possibly merging international crimes in the jurisdiction of an *African Court* complementing the work of the ICC. The idea is that the ICC would represent a model of international criminal justice to be followed by any court or tribunal at domestic, regional and international levels. Moreover, the establishment of the *African Court* by the AU should demonstrate its feasibility complementing the ICC, and this, of course, remains to be seen.[383]

---

[380] For an overview of the Policies and Strategies see the Policy Papers and Prosecutorial Strategy accessible on the web portal of the International Criminal Court (OTP): www.icc-cpi.int/Menus/ICC/Structure+of+the+Court/Office+of+the+Prosecutor/Policies+and+Strategies/.

[381] UN doc. S/RES/1593 (2005) Referring the Situation in Darfur, Sudan to the Prosecutor of the International Criminal Court, Adopted by Vote of 11 in Favour, To None Against, with 4 Abstentions (Algeria, Brazil, China, United States). See also UN doc. S/RES/1970 (2011) on Libya. This resolution represents the first time the Security Council has voted unanimously for an ICC referral.

[382] The African Union (AU), United Nations (UN) Joint Task Force (JTF) on Peace and Security held its sixth consultative meeting at the AU Headquarters, in Addis Ababa, on the margins of the 20th Ordinary Session of the AU Assembly of Heads of State and Government on 26 January 2013, the AU-UN-JTF Joint Communiqué is accessible at: www.peaceau.org/uploads/au-un-6th-jtf-meeting-26-01-2013.pdf.

[383] See M. du Plessis, "Implications of the AU decision to give the *African Court* jurisdiction over international crimes", in *Institute for Security Studies,* Paper No. 235, June 2012. It needs to be noted that the Protocol on the Statute of the African Court of Justice and Human Rights had merged the African Court on Human and Peoples Rights and the Court of Justice of the African Union into a single Court, *The African Court*, see the Draft Protocol on Amendments to the Protocol on the Statute of the African Court of Justice and Human Rights 15 May 2012, accessible at: www.peaceau.org/uploads/ex-cl-731-xxi-e.pdf.
See C. Jalloh, *The African Union and Its Discontents with the International Criminal Court*, Jurist, Forum, August 6, 2010, accessible at: http://jurist.org/forum/2010/08/the-african-union-and-the-icc-growing discontent.php See also AU doc. Assembly/AU/Dec.296(XV), *Decision on the Progress Report of the Commission on the Implementation of Decision Assembly/AU/DEC.270(XIV) on the Second Ministerial Meeting on the Rome Statute of the International*

### 6.2.3. THE ROLE OF COMPLEMENTARY GLOBAL REGIMES

In theory the role of complementary global regimes is to consolidate effective protection mechanisms of individuals in situations of war (*protective* justice), including a reliable sequence between peace negotiations and the judicial proceedings, or else, individual criminal accountability (*retributive* justice), and through reparation to the victims (*restitutive* justice). It is too soon to conclude if the mechanisms currently applied fostering peace, justice and security are capable to challenge domestic jurisdictions dealing with the devastating actions of criminal regimes on individuals and entire communities. Nevertheless, a defined common strategy and institutional architecture optimizing the end results of democratic transformation, national reconstruction and good governance at domestic levels is required. These mechanisms largely include: constitutional reforms, investigations and prosecutions, reparations, reconciliation and peace building measures, memorialization and truth commissions. The approach is intended to be case-by-case and oriented to each particular conflict scenario. As several observers point out, if the emerging regime of international criminal justice delivers results not simply in terms of effective prosecution of a few leaders who could easily be replaced, but instead, "by promoting peace in a region where little else has succeeded over the last decades, the African enthusiasm that led to the establishment of the world's first permanent international criminal tribunal will probably revive, returning even more strongly than before".[384] This is of course true, but then again, it is not only a common responsibility of complementary global regimes and their political institutions, but primarily a responsibility of the nation-states themselves, including regional organizations. After all, the African States expressed their strong political will to be part of the Rome Statute, and some of them voluntarily referred their inability to investigate and prosecute international humanitarian crimes to the Court. There are no doubts about the gaps characterizing the emerging international architecture fostering peace, justice and security. These gaps derive from the absence of a political *road map* and the determination of States to govern war and crime with multilateral and universal tools. The primary responsibility to adjust constitutional parameters in accordance with universal norms *erga omnes* lies in the hands of the States, while the role of complementary global regimes is to provide capacity-building in domestic jurisdictions. As stated by Delmas-Marty the emerging regime of international criminal justice and the rule of criminal law in general, "might found an ethic of globalization and show how to organize interactions at different levels

*Criminal Court Doc. Assembly/AU/10(XV).* Adopted by the Fifteenth Ordinary Session of the Assembly of the Union on 27 July 2010 in Kampala, Uganda.

[384] See W. A. Schabas, *supra.*

to achieve pluralist stabilisation".[385] In order to achieve this important objective the political convergence of expectations at global level is absolutely required.

It needs to be noted that during the Review Conference of the Rome Statute in Kampala the limited presence of States Parties and observer delegations in the assessment panels for the implementation of the treaty, was remarkable. There is no doubt that such educational segment of the Review Conference requires further work of researchers and practitioners. However, the attention was not prioritized on the side of the main representatives of the States Parties to probe and question the positive and negative aspects in the implementation of the Rome Statute. Accurate recommendations about the reform of the working relationship between the Security Council and the Court will need to be further addressed by relevant findings of academia and civil society organizations. The Review Conference only initiated the discussions between governmental delegations on implementation and harmonization. Hopefully, this debate will continue soon on several crucial issues such as complementing the role of peace and justice and the reform of the working methods between the Security Council and the Court. The political dialogue on these matters, between the decision-making of States either parties to the Rome Statute or only members of the UN, is fundamental. Such dialogue requires to be shaped at multilateral level neutralizing the unilateral interests of some powerful observers trying to shape the Court at their own benefit. In my view such trend needs to be completely neutralized opting for democratic reforms at national, regional and international levels in regard to the intervention in mass atrocities, individual criminal accountability of such serious crimes and the formulation of humanitarian escalations. The problem is the slow motion in realizing such reforms in the short term, while the political determinations and the actions taken in the middle and long terms have to be more concrete. Many issues have to find consensus in the UN General Assembly and in the Assembly of States Parties to the Rome Statute, however, it remains to be seen the outcome of it. Considering the challenges in the international politics of mass atrocities and the emerging architecture dealing with it, both of them deserve further discussion. These challenges represent the key issues in order to optimize the results of complementary global regimes and their interactions in conflict and post-conflict societies. Organizational improvements for a better interaction between the UN system and the Rome Statute institutions would bring more results of early warning and deterrence, while intervening for stability, reconstruction and good governance. The implementation of an interaction strategy in respect of the separation of powers would benefit the fight against the culture of impunity establishing the rule of law, while renewing the trust of citizens in governance

385 See M. Delmas-Marty, 'Le droit pénal comme étique de la mondialisation', *Revue de science criminelle* 1, 2004. See also M. Delmas-Marty, *Ordering Pluralism. A Conceptual Framework for Understanding the Transnational Legal World*, 2009, at 109.

institutions and public service. In any case, implementation and harmonization are both required and the next paragraph elucidates some of the reasons.

### 6.2.4. THE PREREQUISITES OF IMPLEMENTATION AND HARMONIZATION

In order to maximize the results on the ground, compulsory cooperation is absolutely required between relevant stakeholders. This is clear in the situations in the Sudan and with the first referral to the Court from the Security Council in regard to Darfur. Such cooperation should be based on the principle of universality. The UN members should have mandatory obligations in case of Court's referrals especially after the refusal of the Sudan to cooperate. Besides, their cooperation should undermine the fragmentation and decentralization of international law and its institutions, and prepare the grounds for a global structure of governance. The new system falling under the Rome Statute should be integrated with the old system of the United Nations in respect of its judicial independence. If we consider the gaps of support in the referral activity coming from the Security Council and also in the situations where the Court and the Security Council are both involved, such an integrated model of governance is not yet realized. It is clear that the relationship agreement between the United Nations and the Court, the Rome Statute provisions and other agreements and arrangements are not sufficient for the governance of war and crime in authoritarian regimes. An appropriate implementation is required in the immediate, middle and long terms to enhance the relationship and partnership between complementary global regimes maximizing the results in the field operations. The last resort option to fight against the impunity of serious crimes cannot be left disconnected by parallel working relationships and distant political engagements of civilian protection mechanisms at international, regional and domestic levels. Besides, the States and regional organizations should address political issues about peace and justice exclusively to the ASP, leaving the judicial proceedings entirely to the Court in accordance with the provisions of the Rome Statute and the principle of complementarity.

The priority is to solve the complexity of an *impasse* undermining the evolution to centralize individual rights in times of war, including the credibility of emerging regimes preserving universal purposes towards multilateral solutions. Until such issues are not resolved by the political organs enforcing complementary global regimes, it will be unrealistic, speculative and partial to refer to a global architecture fostering peace, justice and security. Another aspect of the international responses to the humanitarian escalations of *last resort* between political and judicial institutions is that they would not offer any preventive action of mass atrocities and this on the top of law enforcement and civilian protection gaps. The risk is that neither the cause nor the effect of war and crime in conflict and post-conflict situations would receive a reliable architecture to be dealt with. In order to give orientation with specific guidelines to regional and bilateral solutions the multilateral approaches in humanitarian escalations deserve further attention. Such escalations are characterized by the violence and severe violations of human rights and international humanitarian law and destabilize international peace and security. The next section looks at the global, regional and bilateral actors involved in mass atrocities in Africa and in the Sudan, including the impact of their policy formulations in regard to humanitarian interventions and civilian protection duties in the Sudan. Particularly, it underscores the discrepancies between the findings of international commission of inquiries, the failure of law enforcement and civilian protection duties, including the accountability mechanisms against the criminal leadership in the Sudan, which regrettably is still in power.

## 6.3. THE INTERNATIONAL, REGIONAL AND BILATERAL ACTORS IN THE SUDAN

### SECTION OUTLINE

This section explores the role of the relevant actors involved in the Sudan. It points out the unresolved issue of the working methods between peace negotiations, peace enforcement and the accountability system of mass atrocities committed in the Sudan, despite the notorious status of the criminal regime in the country. The problems incurred in monitoring the elections in South Sudan and the clashes in Abyei prior the referendum, did not neutralize the controversial governance in the mediation efforts falling under the Comprehensive Peace Agreement between the UN and the Sudanese government. This represented a sensitive issue on top of the serious divergences between the configuration of the UN mandate and the credibility of the judicial decisions released by the Court, including the current political unrest and the violence spreading in South Sudan. South Sudan is a young and independent State which has to hold accountable the perpetrators of serious crimes committed against civilians. In regard to the working methods between peace and justice, the reports of the UN activities in the North Sudanese region confirm that UNMIS provided transportation to the Court's accused Ahmed Haroun who has been considered by the UN the 'key player' to provide good offices for the Comprehensive Peace Agreement.[386] Wasn't

[386] See M. R. Lee, 'UN in Sudan Didn't Ask Security Council As Flew War Criminal Haroun to Abyei', *Inner City Press*, 12 January 2011, accessible at: www.innercitypress.com/un2harun011211.html.

the accused supposed to be brought to justice instead?[387] When questioned about this controversial issue, for the UN, the "*Governor* Haroun was critical in its role to bring the Misseriya leaders in southern Kordofan to a peace meeting in Abyei to stop further clashes and killings. In accordance with the UNMIS mandate the UN will continue to provide the necessary support to those key players in their pursuits to find a peaceful solution".[388] This matter deserves a couple of words. First of all, the UN position here creates confusion as the legalistic approach in accordance with Article 16 of the Rome Statute about the *deferral* of investigation and prosecution is only applicable with a resolution adopted by the Security Council under Chapter VII of the UN Charter and prior investigations and prosecutions would be performed by the judicial institution.[389] Such provision is not applicable in case of warlords expected to be brought to justice and without a lawful resolution of the Security Council. The following questions arise: are the Chapter VI of the UN Charter and the *soft* measures of mediation in peace processes applicable in such case? Obviously, human rights groups are critical about such controversial approach taken in the peace process. It compromises the possible accomplishments of justice. They argue that such an approach would only neutralize the truth established by the Court's judicial deliberations and they are absolutely right.[390]

The question is whether the global tools fostering peace and justice will actually work together to undermine the devastating consequences of international threats and crimes, including the credibility of their governance. The configuration of political mandates should take in consideration judicial decisions and support them. This is the only way the complementary character of international regimes could work. The option of law enforcement for the commission of mass atrocity crimes after the judicial outcomes of the Court is not settled by a reliable model of legal and political engagements. On the one hand, the law enforcement that

---

387 See ICC-02/05-01/07 Pre-Trial Chamber I, Warrant of Arrest of Ahmad Harun, accessible at:: www.icc-cpi.int/iccdocs/doc/doc279813.PDF.

388 See Questions and Answer during the UN Secretary-General Spokesperson's Daily Briefing, 12 January 2011, accessible at: www.un.org/News/briefings/docs/2011/db110112.doc.htm.

389 Article 16 of the Rome Statute about the deferral of investigation or prosecution reads: No investigation or prosecution may be commenced or proceeded with under this Statute for a period of 12 months after the Security Council, in a resolution adopted under Chapter VII of the Charter of the United Nations, has requested the Court to that effect; that request may be renewed by the Council under the same conditions.

390 Ahmad Muhammad Harun is allegedly criminally responsible for 42 counts on the basis of his individual criminal responsibility under articles 25(3)(b) and 25(3)(d) of the Rome Statute, including: Twenty counts of crimes against humanity: murder (article7(1)(a)); persecution (article 7(1)(h)); forcible transfer of population(article 7(1)(d)); rape (article 7(1)(g)); inhumane acts (article 7(1)(k)); imprisonment or severe deprivation of liberty (article 7(1)(e)); and torture (article 7(1)(f)); and Twenty-two counts of war crimes: murder (article 8(2)(c)(i)); attacks against the civilian population (article 8(2)(e)(i)); destruction of property (article 8(2)(e)(xii)); rape (article 8(2)(e)(vi)); pillaging (article 8(2)(e)(v)); and outrage upon personal dignity (article 8(2)(c)(ii)).

should characterize the compliance and accountability of universal laws does not follow the *last resort* option of justice pointing out the most responsible perpetrators of serious crimes. On the other hand, when executive and judicial authorities intervene in intra-state conflicts the civilian protection duties are characterized by multidimensional operations on the ground not coordinated between each other. The problem of coordination would also aggravate the lack of preparedness, early warnings and preventive measures of mass atrocities on the ground. In any case, the inconsistency dealing with warlords and criminals in peace processes and further negotiations with them needs to be absolutely resolved. An efficient exchange of information and intelligence between peace and justice mandates is absolutely required. Before approaching the dynamics that characterized the conflict management in the Sudan, it is necessary to spend a couple of words about the political support required in mass atrocities, considering the failure of the promise of *never again* in regard to the genocide in Darfur and the international, regional and bilateral actors involved in the Sudan. The attention goes to the interventions under the flag of humanitarianism in Africa and the political support required in mass atrocities. The next paragraphs examine how global solidarity worked in Darfur, considering the inconsistencies of legal and political engangements in mass atrocities.

### 6.3.1. THE FAILURE OF THE PROMISE OF 'NEVER AGAIN' IN DARFUR

With regard to the situation in Darfur although there was a consensus that ethnic groups had been targeted and that crimes against humanity had therefore occurred, there have been discussions about whether genocide took really place. In May 2006, the International Commission of Inquiry on Darfur organized by the United Nations (UNCOI) "concluded that the government of Sudan has *not* pursued a policy of genocide".[391] According to its conclusions "international offences such as the crimes against humanity and war crimes that have been

[391] The International Commission of Inquiry on Darfur was established pursuant to United Nations Security Council resolution 1564 (2004), adopted on 18 September 2004. The resolution, passed under Chapter VII of the United Nations Charter, requested the Secretary-General rapidly to set up the Commission. In October 2004 the Secretary-General appointed a five member body (Mr. Antonio Cassese, from Italy; Mr. Mohammed Fayek, from Egypt; Ms Hina Jilani, from Pakistan; Mr. Dumisa Ntsebeza, from South Africa, and Ms Theresa Striggner-Scott, from Ghana), and designated Mr. Cassese as its Chairman. The Secretary-General decided that the Commission's staff should be provided by the Office of the High Commissioner for Human Rights. Ms Mona Rishmawi was appointed Executive Director of the Commission and head of its staff. The Commission assembled in Geneva and began its work on 25 October 2004. The Secretary-General requested the Commission to report to him within three months, i.e. by 25 January 2005.

committed in Darfur may be more serious and heinous than genocide".[392] Scholars and practitioners have questioned the methodology of the commission neglecting the genocide in Darfur. The report of the UN Commission of Inquiry on Darfur concluded before the referral to the ICC that there was "insufficient evidence of *genocidal* intent". The serious critics referred to the reasoning of the commissioners and the failure to conduct forensic investigations at all sites of reported mass ethnic murders. In addition, "the UNCOI badly confused the issues of motive and intent, deployed evidence in a conspicuously contradictory fashion, and misrepresented the consequences of *genocidal* violence and displacement of civilians in Darfur".[393]

The US government, non-governmental organizations (NGOs) and individual world leaders have chosen to use the word 'genocide' for what was taking place in Darfur and according to the definition of genocide. The international legal definition of the crime of genocide is found in Articles II and III of the 1948 Convention on the Prevention and Punishment of Genocide. Article II describes two elements of the crime of genocide: 1) the mental element, meaning the "intent to destroy, in whole or in part, a national, ethnical, racial or religious group, as such", and 2) the physical element which includes five acts described in sections *a, b, c, d* and *e*. A crime must include both elements to be called "genocide". Article III described five punishable forms of the crime of genocide: genocide, conspiracy, incitement, attempt and complicity.[394] In any case, despite the critics to the UNCOI, the right channels to investigate and prosecute such crimes, working on the findings to establish genocide among other crimes, which it did, was the International Criminal Court.[395] The independent judicial outcomes performed by the Court, however, extensively delayed. Following the referral from the UN Security Council in 2005, the Prosecutor received the information previously archived by the UN International Commission of Inquiry on Darfur (UNCOI). In addition, the Office of the Prosecutor requested information from a variety of sources, leading to the collection of thousands of documents. The Office also interviewed over 50 independent experts. After extensive preliminary analysis the Prosecutor concluded that the statutory requirements for initiating an investigation were satisfied. In 2010 the Appeals Chamber rendered its

392 Report of the International Commission of Inquiry on Darfur to the United Nations Secretary-General, United Nations International Commission of Inquiry on Darfur, 18 September 2004, accessible at: www.un.org/News/dh/sudan/com_inq_darfur.pdf.

393 For a critical overview see E. Reeves, *Report of the International Commission of Inquiry on Darfur: A critical analysis (Part I an II)*, 2006, accessible at: www.sudanreeves.org.

394 See W. A. Schabas, "Convention for the Prevention and Punishment of the Crime of Genocide", 2008, *United Nations Audiovisual Library of International Law*, the electronic version is accessible at: http://untreaty.un.org/cod/avl/ha/cppcg/cppcg.html.

395 The UNCOI recommended the Security Council to refer the crimes to the ICC in application of Chapter VII of the UN Charter to re-establish peace. See P. Alston, 'The Darfur Commission as a Model for Future Responses to Crisis Situations', Vol. 3 *Journal of International Criminal Justice*, Issue 3 July 2005, at 539.

judgment on the Prosecutor's appeal, reversing, by unanimous decision, Pre-Trial Chamber I's decision of 4 March, 2009, to the extent that Pre-Trial Chamber I decided not to issue a warrant of arrest in respect to the charge of genocide. The Appeals Chamber directed the Pre-Trial Chamber to decide whether or not the arrest warrant should be extended to cover the charge of genocide.

The arrest warrant of Al Bashir lists seven counts on the basis of his individual criminal responsibility under Article 25(3)(a) of the Rome Statute as an indirect (co)perpetrator including: five counts of crimes against humanity: murder, Article 7(1)(a); extermination, Article 7(1)(b); forcible transfer, Article 7(1)(d); torture, Article 7(1)(f); and rape, Article 7(1)(g); two counts of war crimes: intentionally directing attacks against a civilian population as such or against individual civilians not taking part in hostilities, Article 8(2)(e)(i); and pillaging, Article 8(2)(e)(v). Three counts of genocide: genocide by killing (article 6-a), genocide by causing serious bodily or mental harm (article 6-b) and genocide by deliberately inflicting on each target group conditions of life calculated to bring about the group's physical destruction (article 6-c). There are four cases of the Court in Darfur. The judges have issued arrest warrants *a)* against Ahmad Harun and Ali Kushayb, for crimes against humanity and war crimes; *b)* against Omar Al-Bashir for genocide, crimes against humanity and war crimes; and *c)* summonses to appear for rebel leaders Abdallah Banda, Saleh Jerbo and Abu Garda for war crimes. On the 2nd of December 2011, the Prosecutor requested the Pre-Trial Chamber I to issue an arrest warrant against the current Sudanese Defense Minister Abdelrahim Mohamed Hussein for crimes against humanity and war crimes committed in Darfur from August 2003 to March 2004.[396]

## 6.3.2. WHAT KIND OF LAW ENFORCEMENT STRATEGY?

The critics about the Court's investigation and prosecution in the Darfur case did not take long. As far as the critics are constructive they deserve to be mentioned and digested. In fact, eminent scholars and practitioners argued that "if the Court's investigations were serious about prosecuting Al Bashir, the office of the Prosecutor should have issued a sealed request and asked the judges to issue a sealed arrest warrant to be made public only once Al Bashir traveled abroad, instead of publicly requesting the warrant, allowing him to avoid his arrest simply by remaining in the Sudan, or allowing him to prepare his political campaign with African States Parties to the Rome Statute against the Court" and based on

[396] See ICC-02/05-01/09, Case *The Prosecutor v. Omar Hassan Ahmad Al Bashir*, accessible at: www.icc-cpi.int/Menus/ICC/Situations+and+Cases/Situations/Situation+ICC+0205/ See ICC-OTP-20111202-PR750, *ICC Prosecutor Presents New Case in Darfur*, accessible at: www.icc-cpi.int/NR/exeres/D6519D05-76EC-4EFC-AE37-E02FBD346D7A.htm.

the assumptions of new colonialism in the continent.[397] Furthermore, for some observers, the indictment only to Sudan's president excluding the other members of the political and military leadership that together with him planned, ordered, and organized the massive crimes in Darfur, was considered partial and still controversial for several reasons. In any case any mistake in such prosecutorial strategy "may harden the Sudanese government's position, endanger the survival of the peacekeeping forces in Darfur, and even induce Al Bashir to take revenge by stopping or making even more difficult the flow of international humanitarian assistance for the two million displaced persons in Darfur".[398] On the top of that, as further emphasized by Cassese, such prosecutorial strategies "might further alienate the Great Powers (China, Russia, and the United States) and the African Union which are hostile to the ICC".[399]

The compulsive behavior by the alleged criminal perpetrators after the Court's indictments became soon evident. The President of Sudan Al Bashir warned again aid agencies in South Darfur that the camps were under the full authority of his government and that any of the parties involved on the ground, whether from UNAMID, the AU or NGOs, would be expelled if they disrespected the government authority. The Sudanese government announced the expulsions of the humanitarian agencies shortly after the Court issued an arrest warrant for President Al Bashir for war crimes and crimes against humanity, and only later genocide in Darfur. Civil society organizations called on the government to reinstate immediately the license to operate and to facilitate all humanitarian agencies providing assistance in the Sudan but without success.[400] Such scenario took shape under the eyes of the US and other superpowers of the Security Council, which were not engaged to take any action fulfilling the hope of police and law enforcement after the arrest warrants issued by the international judicial authority.[401] This, of course, confirmed that the emerging regime of international criminal justice falling under the Rome Statute would function without any police enforcement.

---

397 See A. Cassese, *Flawed International Justice for Sudan*, 2008, accessible at: www.project-syndicate.org See also A. Abdelrahman, "Bashir's Last Part of Genocide Plan", *Sudan Tribune*, August 8, 2010, accessible at: www.sudantribune.com/spip.php?article35892 See also K. H. Mohmmad, "Sudan, Chad Offered the ICC as a Precious Advance of Goodwill Between Them", *Sudan Vision*, August 8, 2010, accessible at: www.sudanvisiondaily.com.

398 See A. Cassese, *supra*.

399 See A. Cassese, *supra*.

400 See Human Rights Watch, *Sudan: Expelling Aid Agencies Harms Victims*, March 5, 2009, accessible at: www.hrw.org/node/81326.

401 See XI Report of the Prosecutor of the International Criminal Court to the Security Council Pursuant to UNSC 1593 (2005), 17 June 2010, accessible at: www.icc-cpi.int/NR/rdonlyres/A250ECCD-D9E5-433B-90BB-76C068ED58A3/282160/11thUNSCReportENG1.pdf.

### 6.3.3. THE INTERNATIONAL, REGIONAL AND BILATERAL ACTORS

The practice examined in the Sudan demonstrates that the maintenance and restoration of peace, justice and security come along closer in the policy debates by means of controversial issues.[402] At multilateral level, international organizations both make international law and are governed by it, but a consistent legal framework of interactions between complementary governance institutions is scarce.[403] At bilateral level, the policy of governments on retributions and sanctions has been extremely important in regard to genocide and mass atrocities committed in the Sudan. Most notably in passing the Darfur Peace and Accountability Act of 2006, the US government codified specific economic and legal sanctions on the Sudanese government as a result of its findings of genocide.[404] The sanctions continue to underscore the US efforts to end the suffering of the millions of Sudanese affected by the crisis in Darfur. The US also organized a multinational team of investigators, the so called 'Darfur Atrocities Documentation Team' (ADT). The task received by this team of experts was to collect data from the refugees in Chad coming from the Darfur region of Sudan in order to enable the US to determine whether the mass violence being directed against African tribes (Fur, Massaleit, and Zaghawa) constituted undeniably genocide.[405]

Moreover, looking back also at the policy formulation of some other relevant States and international actors a Commission for Africa also known as the 'Blair Commission for Africa' was established by the UK government to examine and provide impetus for stability and development in Africa. The Commission's report acknowledged that "much more must be done to prevent conflict in Africa if development in the continent is to be provided and accelerate". The report called for practical means to implement 'agreed criteria for humanitarian intervention and the use of force drawing on the principles of the 'responsibility to protect' human life which some years later was simply discharged to the African Union (AU) in the Sudan.[406] The same policy trend of the US, the UK and France and further political distance taken by Russia and China characterized, of course, the actions taken by the Security Council in the Sudan and the reduction of level of

---

402 See the reference of the debate over the 'Rule of Law and the International Criminal Court' in the statements released by Member States of the Security Council (29 June 2010). UN doc. S/PRST/2010/11.

403 For an extensive overview of international organizations see M. P. Scharf, *The Law of International Organizations*, 2007, accessible at: www.cap-press.com/pdf/1608.pdf.

404 For an overview of the sanctions see 'The United States-Sudan Relations', *Embassy of the US Karthoum-Sudan*, accessible at: http://sudan.usembassy.gov/ussudan_relations.html.

405 For an overview of the ADT project see S. Totten, E. Markusen, *Genocide in Darfur: Investigating the Atrocities in the Sudan*, 2006.

406 The Commission for Africa, *Our Common Interest: Report of the Commission for Africa*, 2006 accessible at: http://allafrica.com/sustainable/resources/view/00010595.pdf.

diplomatic representations advocating for a unified action. The Security Council Committee established pursuant to Resolution 1591 (2005) was established to oversee the relevant sanctions measures and to undertake the tasks set out by the Security Council in sub-paragraph 3 (a) of the same resolution. The Security Council first imposed an arms embargo on all non-governmental entities and individuals, including the *Janjaweed*, operating the States of North Darfur, South Darfur, and West Darfur with the adoption of Resolution 1556 (2004). The regime of sanctions was modified and strengthened with the Resolution 1591 (2005), which expanded the scope of the arms embargo and imposed additional measures including a travel ban and freeze of assets of individuals designated by the Committee.[407]

Since 2006 the reports of the Court addressed to both the UN General Assembly and Security Council contained detailed information on the criminal findings in Darfur.[408] Furthermore, the lack of cooperation by Khartoum and by the international community was constantly emphasized by the Court's officials when addressing the UN political institutions. The EU, NATO, and the US as important key international players also remained silent after such reports on specific criminal findings. As indicated by Grono of the International Crisis Group "the EU approach has been largely to stand behind the African Union (AU). The EU has made it clear that it considers the AU as the lead international player in Darfur and that the EU's role is primarily to support "an African solution to an African problem" by partly funding the AU mission in the Sudan. Shortly after such political engagement coming from the EU, its support consistently decreased as the EU also pressured for a UN transfer to the AU mission. With regard to the NATO, it was initially a strategic competitor of the EU in Darfur. However, NATO has only been providing expertise and logistics without putting troops on the ground in any significant numbers. Between 2005 and 2007 NATO helped the AU expanding its peacekeeping mission in Darfur by providing airlift for the transport of additional peacekeepers into the region and by training AU personnel. The support provided by NATO however, did not imply the provision of military troops but only logistics. The NATO support ended when AMIS was transferred to the United Nations/African Union Mission in Darfur (UNAMID). One year later NATO has expressed its readiness to consider any requests for support to the new UN-AU hybrid peacekeeping force, made up of peacekeepers

[407] The Security Council Committee established pursuant to resolution 1591 (2005) concerning the Sudan which sanctions measures currently in effect are summarized in the table accessible at: www.un.org/sc/committees/1591/ For an overview of the peacekeeping deployments in Darfur see UN doc. S/RES/1672 (2006); UN doc. S/RES/1706 (2006).

[408] See *XI Report of the Prosecutor of the International Criminal Court to the UN Security Council Pursuant to UNSC 1593 (2005)* accessible at: www.icc-cpi.int/NR/rdonlyres/A250ECCD-D9E5-433B-90BB-76C068ED58A3/282160/11thUNSCReportENG1.pdf For the chronology of the *Court Reports and Statements* see the electronic version of the documents accessible at: www.icc-cpi.int/Menus/ICC/Reports+on+activities/Court+Reports+and+Statements/.

and civilian police officers, but without showing a consistent engagement on the ground.[409] We all know how different the approach of such global actors was in the situation in Libya considering the military operations deployed against the regime.[410]

In regard to the situation in Darfur it needs to be noted that the US abstained and did not use its veto power in the Security Council on the referral to the Court. For some observers this could be seen as a new direction of the US policy regarding the emerging regime of international criminal justice established by the Rome Statute and its previous distant political position.[411] Despite different policy interpretations a concrete engagement by the Obama administration is still to be politically and legally verified. An important aspect from the analysis of its policy is that the US was not prepared to commit its troops on the ground in the Sudan but only pressuring for an African solution through the African Union (AU). China is the largest importer of oil from the Sudan and was ready to block any deployment of troops in Darfur. In general terms, China and Russia are quite distant from the UN engagement in civil wars for humanitarian reasons. Both governments may well fear possible international judicial interventions on their own territories deriving from serious human rights breaches. Besides, in 2008 the UN Security Council statement calling for the Sudanese government to comply with the Court by handing over two men suspected of war crimes in Darfur, has been scrapped due to the opposition from China and Russia.[412] The Arab League, and most of its member States, was opposed to a Western-led intervention in Africa, and strongly protective of one military intervention of its own. The last and most important actor remains the African Union (AU) which in a way undermined the outcomes

409 See Press Release, *NATO Supporting AU's Mission*, 1 February 2008, accessible at: www.nato.int/cps/en/natolive/news_8306.htm?selectedLocale=en.

410 See UN doc. S/RES/1973 (2011).

411 In November 2009, the US participated as an observer to the eighth session of the Assembly of States Parties (ASP) in The Hague with a delegation comprised by State and Defense Department officials and headed by the Ambassador at large for War Crimes, Steven Rapp. One year later the US has been an observer at the Review Conference of the Rome Statute in Kampala. According to the statement of Harold Hongju Koh, Legal Advisor of the US Department of State "the outcome in Kampala demonstrates again principled engagement that can protect and advance our interests, it can help the States Parties to find better solutions, and make for a better Court, better protection of our interests, and a better relationship going forward between the US and the ICC". For a policy overview of the US 'engagement strategy' with the Court see the speeches of Harold Hongju Koh Legal Advisor U.S. Department of State and Stephen J. Rapp Ambassador-at-Large for War Crimes Issues, "US Engagement With The International Criminal Court and The Outcome Of The Recently Concluded Review Conference", June 15 2010, accessible at: www.state.gov/s/wci/us_releases/remarks/143178.htm.

412 UN doc. S/PV.5905 (2008), the electronic version of the document is accessible at: http://daccess-dds-ny.un.org/doc/UNDOC/PRO/N08/367/43/PDF/N0836743.pdf?OpenElement See K. Glassborow, 'China, Russa quash ICC efforts to press Sudan over Darfur crimes', *Sudan Tribune*, 12 January 2008, accessible at: www.sudantribune.com/spip.php?article25544.

of the emerging regime of international criminal justice neglecting a permanent institutional liaison with the Court on African grounds.[413]

The AU was operating in Darfur with the consent of the government of Sudan and was reluctant to push too hard. The AU feared of being further marginalized by the Sudanese authorities in its economic relations. The AU had also been desperately trying to prove that it could resolve one of Africa's most destructive conflicts even when all the evidence demonstrated that it could not do it". These motivations, as further emphasized by Grono, confirm that "the international community shies away from effective intervention" in Darfur. Instead, the international community should have focused its efforts to solve at least the priority of humanitarian aid "thereby addressing the effects but not the causes of mass atrocities in Darfur".[414] From the documents of recorded interviews performed by International Crisis Group is remarkable to emphasize what a senior UN official noted about the UN humanitarian intervention under the flag of the responsibility to protect: "we are only keeping people alive with our humanitarian assistance until they are massacred".[415] This was indeed the reality for the refugees in Darfur. The obvious conclusion is that despite the humanitarian interventions in mass atrocities by international, regional and bilateral actors an architecture dealing with the causes of war and crime is still under construction.

### 6.3.4. CONCLUSIONS

The governance institutions of complementary character should initiate effective strategies of interactions particularly around country-specific situations where the States are not fulfilling their treaty obligations on cooperation, as in the case of the Sudan. The accountability of criminal perpetrators should be the priority in peace processes. After all, an effective architecture fostering peace, justice and security requires to keep alive the political dialogue between regional and international realities, while marginalizing criminal domestic regimes. The international community did not respond properly to early warnings of threats and crimes in Darfur. In such situations the establishment of mechanisms of early warnings should have been the priority. There are no doubts that these are required steps in the configuration of the mandates of the Security Council. As pointed out in the next section the hybrid solutions of peace enforcement and the *last resort* options

---

413 See T. Murithi, "The African Union and the International Criminal Court: An Embattled Relationship?" Institute for Justice and Reconciliation (IJR) *Policy Brief*, Number 8, March 2013, accessible at: www.ijr.org.za/publications/pdfs/IJR%20Policy%20Brief%20No%208%20 Tim%20Miruthi.pdf.

414 See N. Grono, "Briefing Darfur: The International Community Failure To Protect", 105/421 *African Affairs*, 2006, at 628.

415 See N. Grono, *supra*.

of justice in Darfur did not work. The struggle is to find mechanisms to prevent war and crime and maximize the results on the ground. This struggle however, still focuses on the effect more than having a real impact on the causes of such conflicts. Besides, the democratization process between political, executive and judicial global mandates are still waiting to be digested. The AU reaction is a clear reflection of such divergence. The lead international actors and the leadership at regional level addressed serious issues. Darfur has been a test case for the AU and for the international community as a whole, and their shortcomings have being cruelly exposed. The situation in Darfur represented the failure to speak and act with one voice and one arm on peace, justice and security.

The lesson learned is that the international norm or the 'right' to intervene under the flag of the responsibility to protect civilians should be explicitly based on law enforcement and civilian protection duties under the paradigm of international criminal justice and accountability. In less than a decade the responsibility to protect civilians in situations of war and crime became the centrepiece of the efforts to reform the UN. Since 2005 the doctrine of the responsibility to protect was embraced by the key quarters of the international community, notably the UN Secretariat, the EU and the AU. It culminated with the endorsement of the UN General Assembly at the World Summit stating that: "each individual State has the responsibility to protect its population from genocide, war crimes, ethnic cleansing and crimes against humanity. This responsibility entails the prevention of such crimes, including their incitement through appropriate and necessary means. The international community through the United Nations has the responsibility to use appropriate diplomatic, humanitarian and other peaceful means, in accordance with Chapters VI and VIII of the Charter to help protect populations from genocide, war crimes, ethnic cleansing and crimes against humanity". This is now widely accepted as providing the criteria for international responses to armed conflict and large scale atrocities.[416] It remains to be seen which are the main requirements applied in the mandate configurations on the ground and the support provided to international criminal justice in the context of the responsibility to protect civilians. The current struggle is to find possible ways civilian protection duties would be implemented and harmonized through the configuration of complementary mandates on the ground enabling peace and justice to complement with each other.

The fight against the impunity of serious crimes is undermined not only by political standpoints but also by legal issues such as the implications of the AU decision to give the *African Court* jurisdiction of international crimes. We have seen how the *ratio* of Article 16 of the Rome Statute results to be problematic on

416 UN doc. A/RES/60/1, 24 October 2005, articles 138 and 139, accessible at: http://unpan1.un.org/intradoc/groups/public/documents/un/unpan021752.pdf.

peace and justice priorities causing the political *impasse* in the AU. Article 16 demonstrates the gaps in the governance of peace and justice. The Court does not obtain any cooperation but only a deep-rooted political deadlock coming from the African States as parties to the treaty. The Assembly of the States Parties to the Rome Statute has an important role in such context. Such sensitive issues deserve a strong involvement by the political body and not by the judicial organ of the Rome Statute, such as the Court. In order to solve urgent issues in the quest for peace, justice and security in Africa, the UN and the Rome Statute regimes need the implementation of agreements and arrangements between peace enforcement and *retributive* justice, including civilian protection measures, and thus, implementing measures of *protective* and *restitutive* justice in a comprehensive manner. The preventive diplomacy and the competence of complementary governance institutions of early warnings is an important requirement. In order to offer a comprehensive overview of the unresolved issues, the next section debates both the conflict management and the civilian protection duties in the Sudan claimed by civil society organizations. It further underscores the need of a political *road map* defining the complementary character of global regimes fostering peace, justice and security with an integrated model of governance. The international community should either prevent or respond immediately to the commission of mass atrocity crimes. The good timing of humanitarian interventions would safe many more human lives. In other words, locating possibilities to transform bureaucratic constraints is the direct responsibility of international governance institutions of complementary character.[417]

## 6.4. THE MANAGEMENT OF THE INTRA-STATE CONFLICT IN THE SUDAN

### SECTION OUTLINE

The intent of this section is to offer some comprehensive views of the conflict management in the Sudan using the UN political mediation, peace agreements, negotiations and peace operations. It debates about the configurations of both peacekeeping operations and civilian protection duties of the United Nations and the African Union (AU). Despite the *last resort* involvement of the Court in the severe violations committed against civilians in Darfur and referred from the Security Council, the situation did not reach any stage of peace building and sustainable solutions for civilians. As anticipated in the previous section, with the UNAMID mandate deployed on the ground there should have been a clear

[417] See T. Piiparinen, "Bureaucratic Mechanisms", *The Transformation of UN Conflict Management*, 2010, at 118. See also H. Wiseman, "The UN and International Peacekeeping: A Comparative Analysis", in UNITAR (eds.), *The UN and the Maintenance of International Peace and Security*, 1987 at 263.

duty of peacekeeping troops to enforce the Court's arrest warrants irrespective of the consent of the Sudanese government. This was absolutely not the case. On top of that, with the Resolution 1996 (2011), the Security Council determined that the situation in South Sudan also constitutes a threat to international peace and security in the region.[418] The Security Council established the mission in South Sudan (UNMISS) to consolidate peace and security.[419] Unfortunately, the management of the conflict did not provide sustainable solutions for peace and civilian protection in North and South Sudan. There is currently further escalation of violence against civilians. This section emphasizes the evolution of the UN peacekeeping mandate and the UN-AU hybrid solutions which did not undermine the urgent and undoubtedly legitimate concerns of civil society organizations about civilians. This section provides some guidelines for the relevant actors involved in multiple situations to reach sustainable peace. The arrays of peace and security should hold accountable the most responsible of the crimes. The emerging regime of international criminal justice as an important tool to protect civilians in situations of war and crime should have received support with every means after the referral of jurisdiction in the situation in Darfur. Regrettably, this was not the case.

### 6.4.1. THE BACKGROUND OF THE UN-AU CONFLICT MANAGEMENT

As previously anticipated, the conflict management and the peace enforcement by the UN have been fragmented in the Sudan prior the *last resort* option to refer to justice in Darfur. This is only one aspect characterizing the international humanitarian intervention performed on the ground. Immediately after the failure of the peace negotiations with the Sudanese authorities, the configuration of the UN mandate on the ground was characterized by the political intent to handover the violence in Darfur to the African Union. A brief background of the conflicts in the Sudan is necessary in order to have an understanding of the African Union mission (AMIS), including *a)* the evident intolerance of the Sudanese government allowing the initial deployment of the AU mission in Darfur, *b)* the shortcomings of the UN-AU hybrid mission (UNAMID), and later the unacceptable government's closure of corridors for humanitarian assistance and *c)* its continuous attacks on peacekeepers.[420]

418 UN doc. S/RES/1996 (2011).

419 On 9 July 2011 South Sudan became the newest country in the world. The birth of the Republic of South Sudan is the culmination of a six-year peace process. The mandate of UNMIS ended following the completion of the interim period set up by the Government of Sudan and SPLM during the signing of the Comprehensive Peace Agreement (CPA) in 2005.

420 See J. Flint, A. de Waal, *Darfur: A short history of a long war,* (2005). See also, A. de Waal, ed., *War in Darfur and the Search for Peace* (2007).

The political background in the country demonstrates that for decades, from 1983 to 2005 and since its independence, the government of the Sudan, the Sudan People's Liberation Movement/Army (SLM/A) and the Justice and Equality Movement (JEM), as the main rebel movements in the South of Sudan, fought in a civil war over resources, power, religion, including self-determination.[421] The country has been divided along the lines of Arab-Muslims in the North, and Africans in the South. Even though the North has enjoyed relative economic, social and political development, the South of the country has been constantly marginalized. Southern rebellion began in the 50s. Before the independence in 1956, the conflict erupted as a result of fears that independence would not only result in northern domination but could also mark the return to the Arab enslavement of the Africans in the south.[422] The war ended in 1972 with the signing of the Addis Ababa peace agreement and resumed again in 1983 when the agreement was broken by the central government. In the course of that period until now, more than two million people have died, four million displaced internally, and thousands of civilians have fled the country as refugees in Chad, and in the Kalma camp for internally displaced persons, or so called IDPs in Nyala, in the south of Darfur.[423]

The attempts for stability in the country by major regional and international actors such as the Inter-Governmental Authority on Development (IGAD), the Organization of African Unity (OAU) at the time, and shortly later, the hybrid solution offered by the AU and the United Nations (UNAMID), achieved little success. In regard to the peace process several agreements were signed between the government and the various factions. These agreements centred on the principles of governance, the transitional process and the structures of government, as well as on the right of self-determination for the people of South Sudan, currently a new State. Other agreements were taking place on security arrangements including wealth- and power-sharing. Finally, the Comprehensive Peace Agreement (CPA), which is a blend of six agreements, was signed in January 2005 which paved the way for the establishment of the UN Advance Mission in Sudan (UNAMIS) to oversee the implementation of the peace agreement in its entirety in accordance with the Resolution 1547 (2004). UNAMIS was mandated to facilitate contacts with the parties concerned and to prepare for the introduction of an envisaged UN peace support operation. The Secretary-General appointed Jan Pronk as his Special Representative for the Sudan and head of UNAMIS, who led the UN

421 For more on the history of the conflict in Darfur, see A. de Waal, 'Who are the Darfurians? Arab and African Identities, Violence and External Engagement', *African Affairs*, 104/415, 2005, at 181.

422 See F. Deng, 'Sudan at the Crossroads', MIT Centre for International Studies, *Audit of the Conventional Wisdom Series*, 07–05, March 2007, accessible at: http://web.mit.edu/CIS/pdf/Audit_03_07_Deng.pdf.

423 A. M.S. Bah, I. Johnstone, 'Peacekeeping in Sudan: The Dynamics of Protection, Partnerships and Inclusive Politics', *Centre on International Cooperation*, Occasional Paper, 2007.

peacemaking support to the IGAD-mediated talks on the North-South conflict, as well as to the African Union-mediated talks on the conflict in Darfur.[424]

## 6.4.2. FAILED UN HANDOVER OF PEACEKEEPING OPERATIONS

Several shortcomings characterized the UN mission in Darfur. The interest of international engagement became visibly weak if we look at the deployments of multinational forces by the UNMIS. The configuration strategy of the Security Council of its peace enforcement mandate was to handover the situation in Darfur even prematurely, to the African Union (AMIS). Soon it became clear that the lack of international engagement in Darfur displayed the configuration of the UN-AU hybrid option (UNAMID) combined with the failure of the peace agreements of the Sudanese authorities. On the top of that, the sequence of the Security Council's mandates in the Sudan has been characterized by the following negative elements: *a)* the political and diplomatic failure pressuring the Sudanese authorities to stop the violence; *b)* the weak multilateral engagement followed by hybrid solutions between the African Union and the United Nations, while the Security Council would pressure the AU for the feasibility to take over the main peacekeeping operations in Darfur; and *c)* the serious shortcomings of civilian protection duties in such multidimensional operations.

In order to emphasize the failure of protecting civilians during peace enforcement operations the analysis of the mandates' configuration of the UN Security Council is required. UNAMIS or so defined 'advance mission' had a political and diplomatic purpose monitoring the peace agreements, while UNMIS was expected to be operational on the ground in Darfur with scarce deployments of peacekeepers. As a response to the escalating crisis in Darfur, the Security Council, with its Resolution 1556 (2004) assigned some additional tasks to the United Nations Mission in Sudan (UNMIS) relating to Darfur.[425] At the same time, the United Nations and a group of non-governmental organizations advocating in the region launched a massive humanitarian operation in Darfur, constantly expanding activities to respond to the needs of an increasing number of people displaced by the violence. As a result of these developments the UN Special Representative and UNAMIS were deeply engaged in Darfur, particularly in supporting the African Union and its mission in the Sudan by, among other things, participating in the Abuja peace talks and establishing a United Nations

424 See UN. Doc. S/RES/1547 (2004).

425 For an overview see the UNMIS mandate and its challenges, accessible on the UN portal of Peacekeeping operations at: www.un.org/en/peacekeeping/missions/unmis/mandate.shtml.

assistance cell in Addis Ababa which supported deployment and management of the African Union Mission in the Sudan (AMIS).

Having determined that the situation in Sudan continued to constitute a threat to international peace and security, the Security Council decided to establish the United Nations Mission in the Sudan (UNMIS).[426] The Security Council with its Resolution 1706 (2006) decided to expand the UNMIS mandate to include its deployment to Darfur without prejudice of the existing mandate and operations. The Security Council invited the consent of the Sudanese Government of National Unity, called on Member States to ensure expeditious deployment and requested the Secretary-General to ensure additional capabilities to enable UNMIS to deploy in Darfur. The Security Council decided that the mandate of UNMIS would be to support implementation of the peace deployments and the N'djamena Agreement on Humanitarian Ceasefire of the conflict in Darfur by performing a number of specific tasks. The Security Council decided that UNMIS would be strengthened by up to 17,300 military personnel and by an appropriate civilian component including up to 3,300 civilian police personnel and up to 16 Formed Police Units.

By further terms of the text of its resolutions the Security Council requested the Secretary-General to consult jointly with the African Union on a plan and timetable for a transition from AMIS, visibly failing and not equipped to contrast the widespread violence in Darfur, to a United Nations operation in Darfur (UNMIS). In the following steps, however, UNMIS was not able to deploy to Darfur due to the government of the Sudan's steadfast opposition to a peacekeeping operation undertaken solely by the United Nations as envisaged in Security Council Resolution 1706 (2006). The UN then embarked on an alternative approach to try to stabilize the region through the phased strengthening of AMIS, before transfer of authority to a joint AU/UN peacekeeping operation. Following prolonged and intensive negotiations with the government of the Sudan and significant international pressure, the government accepted the peacekeeping operation in Darfur. As soon as such operations were guaranteed from the Sudanese government, the Security Council with its Resolution 1769 (2006) authorized the establishment of the United Nations-African Union Hybrid Operation in Darfur (UNAMID). On its part, UNMIS continued to support the implementation of the Comprehensive Peace Agreement (CPA) providing good offices and political support to the parties, monitoring and verifying their security arrangements and offering assistance in a number of areas, including governance, recovery and development. The mission had focused on the commitments between the parties, including *a)* the redeployment of forces, *b)* the resolution of the dispute over the oil-rich Abyei region, and *c)* the preparations for national elections in 2010 and

426 UN doc. S/RES/1590 (2005).

the referenda in 2011, which decided the political stand of self-determination of South Sudan.

The analysis of the mandate's configuration of UNAMID and UNMIS indicates, however, that no electoral assistance had been planned with serious consequences on the result of the presidential elections. The Sudan presidential and parliamentary elections were held in the Sudan from 11 April to 15 April 2010 (extended from the original end date of 13 April 2010) to elect the President and the National Assembly of the Sudan. The election brought to the end the transitional period which began when the decades-long second Sudanese civil war ended in 2005. Early results on 20 April 2010 showed that President Omar Al Bashir's party National Congress was well ahead the opposition. On 26 April 2010, full results were announced and Al Bashir was confirmed as the winner by having received 68.24% of the votes.[427] Such result in the political transition of the country was characterized by the non-cooperation of the international community to follow up on the judicial indictments of the Court against President Al Bashir and few other Sudanese top leaders responsible of genocide, crimes against humanity and crimes of war. Despite the international presence into the country the criminal regime was re-established and would not cooperate with any of the international governance institutions, including civil society organizations. The humanitarian crisis would take larger proportions.

### 6.4.3. DARFUR AND THE FAILURE OF THE RESPONSIBILITY TO PROTECT

On paper, the civil war in the South Sudan concluded with the signing of the Comprehensive Peace Agreement (CPA) in 2005. Despite such an agreement, which was pressured by the international community and led by the US, the conflict continued in the Darfur region. According to the Secretary-General, "a stable Sudan requires a peaceful Darfur".[428] In this regard, it was essential that the work of the United Nations and the African Union in the Sudan had to be complementary. The simple question was: *how*? In the meantime, the AU was pressuring the Security Council to defer the situation in the Sudan and was consistently against the Court's decisions about President Al Bashir. Moreover, the practice of the conflict management applied on the ground in Darfur undermined the effectiveness of the AU hybrid mission and the UN operational peacekeeping role with the mandate to protect civilians for several reasons.[429]

---

427 See IRIN, *Sudan: Elections in a volatile climate*, humanitarian news and analysis, 19 February 2010, accessible at: www.irinnews.org/report.aspx?ReportID=88167.

428 See UN doc. S/2006/591, 28 July 2006, Report of the Secretary-General on Darfur.

429 See A. de Waal, "Darfur and the failure of the responsibility to protect", 83 *International Affairs* 6 (2007), at 1039–1054. See Human Rights Watch, *They Shot at Us as We Fled: Government*

As previously anticipated, in addition to the African Union Mission in the Sudan (AMIS) there was an African Union (AU) peacekeeping force operating primarily in the country's western region of Darfur with the aim of performing peacekeeping operations related to the Darfur conflict. Originally founded in 2004, with a force of 150 troops, by mid-2005 its numbers were increased to about 7,000.[430] Under the United Nations Security Council Resolution 1564/2004, AMIS was to "closely and continuously liaise and coordinate at all levels" its work with the United Nations Mission in Sudan (UNMIS).[431] AMIS was the only external military force in Darfur until UNAMID was established. As previously said, it was not able to effectively contain the violence in Darfur. A more sizable, better equipped UN peacekeeping force was originally proposed in 2006, but due to Sudanese government opposition, it was not implemented at that time. AMIS' mandate was extended repeatedly throughout 2006, while the situation in Darfur continued to escalate. After terrible shortcomings to stop the violence in Darfur, AMIS was finally replaced by UNAMID in 2007.[432]

In May 2007, the African Union officially declared that AMIS was on the point to collapse. In previous months seven Nigerian peacekeepers had been killed, while lack of funding had caused soldiers' salaries to go unpaid for several months. The internal chaos in the country and its serious consequences would be externally visible to the still inactive international actors. Both Rwanda and Senegal warned that they would withdraw their forces if the UN members did not live up to their commitments of funding and supplies. On the top of that, the financial assistance promised over the last decade by the Americans and the Europeans to AMIS was not provided. In 2007, the United Nations Security Council finally approved the mandate of UNAMID with Resolution 1769 (2007) which was to take over operations from AMIS.[433] AMIS was finally merged into UNAMID but civilian protection did not characterize the configuration of peace enforcement operations on the ground. As emphasized by de Waal, "the pursuit of the responsibility to protect in Darfur has not achieved its goal". Contrary to

*Attacks on Civilians in West Darfur,* 2008, accessible at: www.hrw.org See also, Human Rights Watch, *No One To Intervene: Gaps in Civilian Protection in Southern Sudan*, 2009, accessible at: www.hrw.org.

430 See AU doc. Assembly/AU/Dec.68 (2005), *Decision on the Situation in the Darfur Region of Sudan,* (2005), accessible at: www.africa-union.org/DARFUR/homedar.htm.

431 UN doc. SC/RES/1590 (2005). UN doc. SC/9649 Security Council Extends UNMIS mandate until 30 April 2010. See also UN doc. SC/RES/1870 (2009).

432 On 31 March 2006 the mandate of AMIS would have run out, with the African Union force already on the ground to be incorporated into a UN peacekeeping mission. Nevertheless, during a March 10, 2006 meeting of the African Union's Peace and Security Council, the Council decided to expand the mission for six months until 30 September 2006. On August 31, after United Nations Security Council Resolution 1706 failed to see the implementation of its proposed UN peacekeeping force of 20,000 due to opposition from the government of Sudan, on October 2 the AU extended AMIS' mandate further, until December 31, 2006, and then again until June 30, 2007.

433 UN doc. SC/9089 (2007).

the position taken by the most ardent advocates of the responsibility to protect, de Waal argues that "this failure owes much to the inadequate conceptualization of protection duties of civilians. The inflated expectation that physical protection by international troops is indeed possible, within the limits of the military strength envisaged, including the confused advocacy around the issue, has created the premises for its failure in Darfur. It is possible that more concerted international pressure could have brought a bigger and better-equipped international force to Darfur much earlier. That would, in itself, have been a positive development. But the expectation that such a force could have 'saved' Darfur is erroneous".[434] According to the chronology and evidence of all steps in such tentative handover from the UN to the AU, and back to the UN mission in Darfur (UNAMID) the shortcomings on the ground are clearly visible. Once again early warnings were not followed and applied in such mandate's configurations. The lessons learnt by the global actors of complementary character should be clear. Hopefully, there would be a gradual expansion in the interpretation of the Security Council of what constitutes a threat to the peace, breach of the peace, or act of aggression and the commission of mass atrocity crimes. In Darfur the promise of '*never again*' in regard to genocide has not been maintained.

## 6.5. THE LESSONS LEARNED

This case study arguing about peace, justice and security in the Sudan demonstrates that the recognition of the doctrine of the responsibility to protect civilians in situations of war and crime requires further multilateral efforts. The implementation of such doctrine is proving to be a real test for the international politics of interventions in mass atrocities. Such politics are strictly related to the old promise of designing a democratic reform of the governance system of peace and security and their maintenance, management and restoration.[435] The same considerations are valid for the complementary regime of the Rome Statute preserving the interests of justice. Besides, complementary global regimes must guard their mission "to ensure that they are not subverted, or perceived to have been subverted, as a pawn for great power use, to merely target weak and or defeated adversaries in less influential regions of the world".[436] This is not the case considering the findings in the case study which underscore: *a)* the failure of the peace processes between the Sudanese government and the UN; *b)* the lack of cooperation by the Sudanese government with the international efforts; and *c)* the

434 See A. de Waal, *supra*.

435 See P. Hilpold, 'The Duty To Protect and the Reform of the United Nations. A New Step in the Development of International Law?', 10 *Max Planck Yearbook of United Nations Law*, 2006, at 35.

436 See C. C. Jalloh, *Regionalizing International Criminal Law?*, 2009, Working Paper 2009–20, accessible at: http://ssrn.com/abstract=1431130.

extreme violence perpetrated against civilians in the country, despite the judicial outcomes of the Court. The global political engegements to protect civilians failed in North Sudan including the criminal accountability of its leadership.

### 6.5.1. SOLVING THE GAPS IN THE WORKING METHODS

In this chapter dealing with the criminal regime in North Sudan several issues arise between the 'interests of peace' having exclusively a political nature and the 'interests of justice' characterized by a legal and jurisdictional character. In the triggering mechanisms falling under Article 16 for instance, the Rome Statute does not exclude the constant deception of political processes undermining the judicial and neutral role of the Court. Moreover, the last resort option of international criminal justice does not receive any kind of mandatory engagements by the UN political and executive premises and its members. This became clear with the referral of the situation in Darfur from the Security Council to the Court, right after the failure of hybrid operations of peacekeeping forces provided by the United Nations and the African Union which were supposed to protect civilians, while working with all possible means on sustainable peace. Many African States, as relevant parties to the Rome Statute, reveal serious inconsistency of compliance in their legal obligations deriving from the treaty. At regional level the AU recalls political standpoints waiting to be resolved in the UN premises and related to the membership and permanent representation of African States in the Security Council. Their pressure to obtain clarification on the *deferral* activity from the Security Council does not receive any political follow up at the expenses of the Court as a judicial and not political institution. It is clear that the compromised regime of the permanent members of the Security Council resumed in Article 16 of the Rome Statute is not working and creates controversial politicization. The ASP needs to keep abreast on such sensitive political issues. If at provisional level Article 16 of the Rome Statute has not been used by the Security Council it still creates political shortcomings in the AU undermining the important meaning of justice and accountability.

Besides, it would also be appropriate to develop a set of criteria for the methods applied by the Security Council to make a *referral* to the Court: *a)* using the reports of human rights violations in a particular situations monitored by the UNHRC, *b)* understanding the relation between the commission of core crimes under international law and the existence of threats to international peace and security, and *c)* using preliminary information about the commission of core crimes susch as the outcomes of the preliminary situation analysis of the Prosecutor. The development of such set of criteria would help the decision-making of the Security Council to offer law enforcement capacities, and would also provide civil society and other stakeholders with a set of principles that they could also apply in order to put pressure on the Security Council to make referrals to the Court.[437] The referral of the situation in the Sudan should have been characterized by law enforcement capacity considering the criminal regime in the country. In that way, the deterrent effect of peace and justice would have increased sustainable solutions. Unfortunately, with the Rome Statute and the establishment of the Court there is no further progress of law enforcement measures. The Court still functions without police. The practice indicates several shortcomings in the fight against the impunity of domestic criminal regimes violating fundamental individual rights. This is the case in the Sudan and the criminal leadership still in power in the country, which is politically advocating with all its partners against the Rome Statute system.[438]

The situation in Darfur indicates primarily the failure of early warnings. On top of that, the international intervention required law enforcement and civilian protection mandates deployed on the ground immediately after the failure of the peace process initiated by the UN, avoiding any manipulation from the domestic criminal regime in power in the country. The problem is still the weak political determination to fight against the impunity regime in North Sudan. For the States partners of such criminal regime the priority has been given to their own economic interests characterizing their relationship with the Sudanese leadership and its resources at the expenses of civilians. In conclusion, it is clear that for a reliable architecture fostering peace, justice and security the enforcement of public international authorities and the definition of their complementary character should be appropriately reviewed in both documents: the UN Charter and the Rome Statute. Such an effort in combination with a political *road map* based on an integrated approach of governance would influence further the design of reliable architecture dealing with conflict and post-conflict situations, and with the fight against international threats and crimes destabilizing peace and security.

The solutions in the short and middle terms have to be found in an integrated approach of governance of peace, justice and security operations on the ground. In the long term a political *road map* is necessary in order to deal with situations where criminal leaders are still in power and civilians are victimized. Such

---

437 See H. Mistry, "Developing consistency", in *The UN Security Council and the International Criminal Court*, International Law Meeting Summary with Parliamentarians for Global Action, Chatham House, 16 March 2012, at 4, accessible at: www.pgaction.org/pdf/activity/Chatham-ICC-SC.pdf.

438 A group led by the AU chair with representatives from Africa's five regions pressures the Security Council to defer proceedings against Kenya's leadership and the Sudanese president, Omar Hassan al Bashir, who faces charges of genocide. See African Union (AU) Decision on Africa's Relationship with the ICC, African Union Ext/Assembly/AU/Dec.1 (Oct.2013). The AU decision is accessible at: http://summits.au.int/en/sites/default/files/Ext%20Assembly%20AU%20Dec%20&%20Decl%20_E_0.pdf.

political *road map* would strengthen the credibility of global regimes fostering peace, justice and security and their complementary character. In conclusion of this case study it is clear that the consensus of systemic reforms, if reached, would preserve further the international legal order strengthening its legal and political institutions. Such process of building political consensus on substantive reforms represents the main challenge for complementary global regimes. We have clearly seen that the practical dilemma on the ground indicates an insufficient implementation and harmonization of the interactions between such complementary mandates involved in the same field operations, such as in the Sudan. These gaps reflect the standards of cooperation applied on the ground which are inconsistent and not sufficient to maximize the results to *prevent*, *react* and *rebuild* in situations of war and crime. Substantive reforms are required between governance frameworks particularly in the working relationship between the Security Council and the International Criminal Court.

# 7. MULTIDIMENSIONAL OPERATIONS AND THE ISSUE OF COOPERATION IN THE DEMOCRATIC REPUBLIC OF CONGO (DRC)

## PRELIMINARY REMARKS

The DRC has the size of Western Europe and gained formal autonomy from Belgium in 1960. Since the country's decolonization the current updated empirical data on governance show that the human development index is lower now than in 1975 and the GDP pro capita roughly one-third of what it was back in 1960. The World Bank has currently put the DRC as fourth worst-administrated State after Somalia, Iraq and Myanmar.[439] The DRC has been classified as the second most unstable country after the Sudan, and the fifth most corrupted African State. An estimated 5.4 million people have died because the war and its after-effects since 1998. In spite of the end of the civil war since 2002, millions of Congolese continue to die each year. Arguably considered as the world's most deadly crisis after WWII, its intra-state instability receives more attention than many of the past and recent crises such as Bosnia, Iraq and Ukraine.[440] Since its independence the DRC has been the subject of cross-border incursions, including the interference of neighbouring States in its domestic affairs. The illegal exploitation of natural resources has emerged as the primary means of financing the civil war including the illicit trade of corporations. Such intrusions demolished any institutional heritage in the fragile domestic apparatus of the country. The internal political transition in the DRC is characterized by extreme violence and crime to retain power on civilians, territories and resources. The last elections in 2011 marked the second vote held since the Kivu Conflict that killed more than five million people. The electoral process was characterized by voting difficulties as some voting materials arrived late, or did not arrive at all. The presidential election involved 11 candidates, although the victory of President Joseph Kabila received claims of intimidation and vote-rigging. With regard to the delicate situation

---

439 See The World Bank World Development Indicators respectively in 2012, 2013, 2014, accessible at: http://data.worldbank.org/sites/default/files/wdi-2014-book.pdf.

440 For an overview of the causes and the effects of the conflict in the DRC see I. Samset, 'Conflict of Interests or Interests in Conflict? Diamonds and War in the DRC', 2002 *Review of African Political Economy* 29, at 463.

affecting the civilian population including the concerns related to democratic transitions in the country, this case study puts forward important elements to be taken in consideration by the decision makers on reconfigurations, cooperation standards and interactions, including the alternative between 'comprehensive' and 'narrowly focused' international mandates able to complement with each other on the ground.

This case study advocates for more significant political engagement coming from the African Union, the European Union, the United Nations and the peacekeeping missions in the LRA-affected region where the International Criminal Court is still involved. This chapter highlights the need for more financial and technical support of early warning networks, sensitization and demobilization efforts, including long-term rehabilitation for returnees and ex-combatants. These activities, of course, also require a well-functioning domestic accountability system. In fact, the statements released by the Congolese government that the LRA threat no longer exists in the DRC is a claim strongly disputed and requires international attention. After all, the instability in the DRC is directly linked to the causes of mass atrocity crimes committed in the region, especially by the genocide in Rwanda and the criminal activity of the LRA in the South of Sudan and Central African Republic. This case study explores the evolution of multidimensional responses in an environment of violent conflicts, volatile sites, mass atrocities, poverty and the complete absence of the State able to safeguard civilian lives.

This chapter examines the challenges of international responses fostering peace, justice and security and the opportunities, to prevent, or reduce, deadly conflicts, while protecting civilian lives.[441] It offers recommendations to implement the relationship between the global regime preserving human rights and sustainable peace, through the UN presence in the country, and the criminal accountability emerging regime of the Rome Statute, including the enforcement of arrest warrants, judicial decisions, operational assistance and protection of civilians *in situ*. It reports about sensitive fact-findings by non-governmental human rights organizations on the issue of civilian protection and massive humanitarian violations, which are offering information, guidelines and recommendations for the international governance institutions of complementary character involved in the DRC. The intersection between peace enforcement, international justice and human security requires a model of governance falling under the paradigm of accountability. The DRC case confirms such necessity. This chapter demonstates that the fight against the impunity of international crimes at domestic and

441 See H. F. Weiss, 'The DRC: A Story of Lost Opportunities to Prevent or Reduce Deadly Conflicts', in R. H. Cooper, J. Kohler (eds.), *Responsibility To Protect. The Global Moral Compact for the 21st Century*, 2009, at 115.

international levels in the DRC is characterized by the gaps in the configurations of international mandates of complementary character requiring partnerships on the ground in order to maximize the results in accordance with the human security doctrine. The section below clarifies the case study objectives. It offers an overview of the background, analysis, issues and purpose of the case study in the DRC.

## 7.1. THE CASE STUDY OBJECTIVE: WHAT KIND OF CONFIGURATIONS IN THE FIELD OPERATIONS?

### SECTION OUTLINE

This case study demonstrates that the harmonization of complementary efforts deployed in the field operations is an idea not yet realized. The Rome Statute, as a multilateral treaty, requires a balance between the *retributive*, *restitutive* and *protective* aspects of international criminal justice, while the United Nations struggles with its credibility of civilian protection duties in conflict and post-conflict situations. In devastated societies characterized by conflicts, crimes, corruption and instability the interaction between complementary global regimes represents an opportunity to maximize the results on the ground. Ending the impunity of serious crimes is an urgent priority in the DRC. Confronting the judiciary lacuna where judicial corruption is pervasive is essential in this country. Violence against civilians is largely motivated by the exploitation of resources, while gender crimes are used as a weapon of war. The current disarmament, demobilization and reintegration efforts in the DRC do not produce sufficient results. Militia groups are opposing such process of stabilization in the country. The Congolese civilians face extreme violence and insecurity caused by the presence of armed groups characterizing the current political transition. The MONUC/MONUSCO[442] mandate to protect civilians has a negligible impact for several reasons.[443] Furthermore, the impunity regime normalized "predation as the principal *modus operandi* by the Congolese military, by various militia groups and by self-defense forces across the east of the country. The UN peacekeepers have done little to halt this practice".[444] Moreover, some of the warlords targeted

[442] See UN docs. S/RES/1925 (2010), S/RES/2053 (2012).

[443] See H. Edstrom, D. Gyllensporre (eds.), "Mission in Central Africa: MONUC/MONUSCO", in Political Aspirations and Perils of Security. Unpacking the Military Strategy of the United Nations, 2013.

[444] E. B. Rackley, 'Predatory Governance in the DRC: Civilian Impact and Humanitarian Response', March 2005 *Humanitarian Exchange Magazine* 29, at 3, accessible at: www.odihpn.org.

by the ICC were extremely dangerous for the local populations and could be even a risk for the victims and witnesses screened by the judicial institution.[445]

With regard to security the international responses should as much as possible intervene when the crisis has dramatic consequences on acceptable standards of human security. The international responses, rather than being exclusively militarily, should be 'narrowly focused' and serve the right actors on the ground. There is consensus that the concept of security only approached by military means may work as combustible on the flame of such violent conflicts in the DRC. The military operations by the AU authorized by the UN failed to raise acceptable standards of human security. Therefore, the efforts focusing on the preservation of lives and their protection are the priority of planning whatever security mandate. The struggle of the UN on institution-building supporting the reform of the army, police and justice systems in the corrupted domestic reality of the DRC should complement and prioritize the activity of the ICC. Police and law enforcement following supranational criminal decisions are both necessary. The priority is also to safeguard the safety of victims and witnesses. The warlords still active in the army have to be immediately targeted by the domestic judicial system with judicial proceedings *in situ*. After all, the DRC has a legal obligation to cooperate in accordance with the Rome Statute. The political organs of both the UN and the Rome Statute regime should pressure the local authorities while also working on the configuration of their complementary mandates on the ground. The exchange of information and intelligence operations are still absolutely required, including investigations and the extension of prosecutions until the domestic ability to take over would be unquestionably proven by the local authorities.

This section offers an overview of the background, the issues and the purpose of international mandates in the DRC supposed to receive complementary configurations and cooperation raising the standards of human security. It emphasizes the importance of justice in securing peace and the role that international criminal justice could play in facilitating the peace process and democratic transitions with support, assistance and cooperation. The recommendations on cooperation are addressed to the high representatives and policy makers which have considered the issue of cooperation in a number of occasions. This assessment complements the recommendations set out by the report of the Bureau on Cooperation (ASP) and by the Court in the ICC-ASP8/44 and annex 1. These relate respectively, with the cooperation with the United

[445] On 22 March 2013, Bosco Ntaganda surrendered himself voluntarily and is now in the ICC's custody. Two warrants of arrest have been issued by the ICC for Bosco Ntaganda for seven counts of war crimes and three counts of crimes against humanity allegedly committed in Ituri in the DRC between 1 September 2002 and the end of September 2003. See for a general overview M. Eriksson Baaz, M. Stern, 'Making Sense of Violence: Voices of Soldiers in the Congo (DRC)', 2008, *Journal of Modern African Studies*, 46, 1, at 57.

Nations and on the consideration of the present situation, including the ways in which such cooperation can be developed in the DRC. The report of the Court on international cooperation and assistance notes, in paragraphs 6 and 7, that although cooperation with the Court has generally been forthcoming, "public and diplomatic support remains a priority in the galvanization of arrest efforts, as does the conclusion of more agreements for the enforcement of sentences, the relocation of witnesses and interim release. Attention might be drawn to the fact as well that such agreements would cover any situation of a release from custody".[446]

## 7.1.1. THE BACKGROUND

With regard to the international responses in the aftermath of the presidential elections in 2006 and the DRC constitution several concerns and critics followed respectively, on the political transition in the country, on the widespread humanitarian violations, and on the corruption in the domestic institutions. Scholars, human rights activists and practitioners claim that international actors have given little attention to the grave human rights breaches of the first two years of the Kabila government. This brought as a result the failure to hold accountable the perpetrators of these abuses. Although the UN presence took some steps to ensure political space for the opposition during the electoral transition, the institution-building assistance provided by the UN failed to check on the executive power, even though some Congolese analysts were voicing concerns about the authoritarian shift well in advance. In 2007, some Congolese media ran an opinion about the brutal behavior of the government. Questioning the electoral process and its bloody aftermath in Kinshasa and Bas Congo, the author lamented without releasing his identity "we were ardently searching to become a democracy, but we are on our way to becoming an absurd dictatorship".[447] According to human rights activists, the elections themselves cannot bring democracy. Both the "Congolese and international actors must work to establish an independent judiciary and a vibrant parliament with an effective opposition to improve human rights, hold the executive to account for its actions, and counterbalance the restriction of political convergence. The failure to establish such counterweights will endanger the slight chance of Congo's young democracy. The same kind of focus and international cooperation that brought about the

---

446 ICC-ASP/8/44, Annex I.

447 An amnesty law was signed by President Kabila on 7 May 2009. For the debate and lack of trust to Kabila after the elections and the instable political situation for the next electoral round in 2011 see, 'Sortir de la politique du pire: Une exigence pour le chef de l'Etat', May 18, 2007, Kinshasa, *Le Potentiel* Congolese Newspaper. For an overview of the political transition in the country and the peace and justice constraints see, T. Carayannis, 'The peace and justice dilemma in the DRC', The *Challenge of Building Sustainable Peace in the DRC*, (July 2009), Centre for Humanitarian Dialogue, Background Paper, accessible at: www.hdcentre.org/files/DRC%20paper.pdf.

elections must be replicated in the cause of improving human rights and opening up democratic space, if the hopes for stability and improved governance for this war-torn nation are to be fulfilled".[448]

One of the biggest negative aspects of reliance on the ICC in the DRC is that the Court's temporal jurisdiction means that it cannot address all of the crimes committed during the civil wars in the DRC. This has been heavily criticized. The obvious expectation is that the domestic judicial capacity would arrange proceedings *in situ* undermining the regime of impunity in the country. The wars began in 1996 and the ICC's jurisdiction extends back only to 2002. Whatever the ICC mandate brings in the DRC, its jurisdictional and resource constraints limits a 'full service' justice solution. Another critic is that focusing primarily on Ituri, the ICC takes in hand only one part of the history of the Congo wars. This, and the combination with the case against Thomas Lubanga and the arrest of popular opposition leader, Jean-Pierre Bemba in 2008, for crimes allegedly committed in the Central African Republic, has eroded much of the goodwill enjoyed by the ICC initially in the DRC. Bemba's arrest prompted outrage in the DRC with accusations that the ICC is a political instrument of Kabila, or Western powers, or both. Increasingly, Congolese human rights lawyers favour a special chamber inside the Congolese judicial system supported by external donors, aware of the limitations of the ICC and the very expensive option of *ad hoc* tribunals. While this would help rebuild the DRC's justice system and allow for local ownership of justice, both elements being critical in building a durable peace, the ICC has neither the mandate nor the resources to accomplish such goals. In conclusion these are the enduring issues which current and future mediation efforts will have to contend.[449] The reality is that Kabila has the power in this country. The DRC is rich of mineral resources and this appeals different parties with negative consequences on democratic governance.

In accordance with its constitution the DRC held presidential elections in 2011 which were followed by local elections in 2012–2013. In 2010, the Congolese government, through a letter to the UN Secretary-General, requested international assistance for the organization of the entire electoral process. Earlier than that and to respond to the conflicts in the country, MONUC (*Mission de l'Organisation des Nations Unies au Congo*) was established by the United Nations Security Council in *Resolutions 1279 (1999)* and *1291 (2000)* to monitor the peace process of the Second Congo War, though much of its focus subsequently turned to the Ituri conflict, the Kivu conflict and the Dongo conflict. In 2010 MONUC was

---

448 See Human Rights Watch, *We Will Crush You. The Restriction of Political Space in the Democratic Republic of Congo*, November 2008, accessible at: www.hrw.org/en/node/76188/section/9#_ftn314.

449 See for the devate P. Clark and N. Waddell, 'Courting Conflict? Justice, Peace and the ICC in Africa', in *The International Journal of Transitional Justice*, March 2008, at 40.

renamed the *United Nations Organization Stabilization Mission in the Democratic Republic of the Congo* (MONUSCO) to reflect the new phase reached in the DRC and the inability of peace keeping to address the human security dilemma. In August 2010, the Mai Mai rebels ambushed a base of the 19th Kumaon Regiment of the Indian Army, killing three Indian peace-keepers. The attack renewed the Indian government decision to decrease the military presence in the DRC due to growing conflict in the region. It should be noted that the UN Security Council Resolution 1925 (2010) provides that MONUSCO has the mandate, *inter alia*, "to provide technical and logistical support for the organization of national and local elections, upon explicit request from the Congolese authorities and within the limits of its capabilities and resources". In 2010, a timetable of the UN missions was prepared covering until June 2012 and still subject to the decision of the Security Council regarding the extention of the missions in 2013–2014 giving absolute priority to the protection of civilians.[450]

With regard to justice, since the entry to force of the Rome Statute, the DRC authorities referred to the International Criminal Court to investigate and prosecute international crimes of common concern allegedly committed anywhere in the country. On 26 January 2009, the ICC opened its first trial in the case against Congolese warlord Thomas Lubanga Dyilo. Lubanga was the first person charged in the DRC situation as well as the Court's first detainee. The trial marks a turning point for the Rome Statute. The Lubanga proceedings represent the first test of formal victim participation in an international criminal trial. The case highlights the gravity of recruitment, enlistment and conscription of child soldiers.[451] The trial in the case of *The Prosecutor v. Germain Katanga and Mathieu Ngudjolo Chui* started on 24 November 2009. Trial Chamber II found German Katanga guilty, as an accessory, within the meaning of article 25(3)(d) of the Rome Statute, of one count of crime against humanity (murder) and four counts of war crimes (murder, attacking a civilian population, destruction of property and pillaging) committed on 24 February 2003 during the attack on the village of Bogoro, in the Ituri district of the DRC. On 23 May 2014, Trial Chamber II sentenced Germain Katanga to a total of 12 years' imprisonment. The time spent in detention at the ICC, between 18 September 2007 and 23 May 2014, will be deducted from the sentence.[452]

---

450 The authorization and further extention of the UN mission in the DRC is to be found in the Security Council Resolution 1991 of 28 June 2011 and so forth, accessible at: www.un.org/ga/search/view_doc.asp?symbol=S/RES/1991(2011).

451 ICC-01/04-01/06-2901, *Case The Prosecutor v. Thomas Lubanga Dyilo,* Decision on Sentence pursuant to Article 76 of the Statute, accessible at: www.icc-cpi.int/iccdocs/doc/doc1438370.pdf.

452 In the situation in the DRC, five cases have been brought before the relevant Chambers: *The Prosecutor v. Thomas Lubanga Dyilo*; *The Prosecutor v. Bosco Ntaganda*; *The Prosecutor v. Germain Katanga*; *The Prosecutor v. Mathieu Ngudjolo Chui*; *The Prosecutor v. Callixte Mbarushimana*; and *The Prosecutor v. Sylvestre Mudacumura.* Thomas Lubanga Dyilo,

Considering the international political engagements and the governance background in the DRC, the United Nations electoral assistance was provided through an integrated team that includes the MONUSCO Electoral Division and the UNDP's Project in Support of the Electoral Cycle (PACE). The electoral assistance was provided throughout the creation of an Independent National Electoral Commission (CENI). The organization, functioning and promulgation of laws of the Independent National Electoral Commission (CENI) by Congolese President Joseph Kabila certainly marked a significant step in the electoral process and deserved international attention. It needs to be noted that millions of Congolese went to the polls in November 2011 to cast their votes in presidential and parliamentary elections. Since its independence in 1960 this is only the second time that the country held democratic elections. Earlier in 2011, the UN issued a report that detailed numerous human rights violations during the pre-electoral period in the DRC, and warned that such incidents could threaten the democratic process and could escalate in further post-electoral violence. The report documented 188 violations apparently linked to the electoral process that occurred between 1 November 2010 and 30 September 2011, including acts of intimidation, threats, incitement, arbitrary arrests and violence. The violations most frequently infringed individuals' freedom of expression, the right to physical integrity and the right to liberty and security of the person, as well as the right to freedom of peaceful assembly.[453]

## 7.1.2. THE ANALYSIS

This case study deals with the multidimensional operations fostering peace, justice and security and the issue of cooperation in the DRC. It discusses the links between comprehensive and narrowly focused mandates encompassing a range of civilian protection tasks. In particular, it argues about the implementation of peace agreements and the actions undertaken to consolidate peace, including the reforms strengthening the institutions of the State and the rule of law, while fighting against the impunity of serious crimes. In other words, the multidimensional peace-keeping and peace-building operations supposed to contribute to the formation, recovery and democratization of the domestic jurisdiction in the DRC.[454] In this situation the intents have fallen on

---

Germain Katanga and Bosco Ntaganda are currently in the custody of the ICC. Sylvestre Mudacumura remains at large. See ICC » Situations and Cases » Situations » ICC-01/04.

453 See the report of the Joint Human Rights Office in the DRC accessible at: www.ohchr.org/Documents/Countries/ZR/ReportDRC_26Nov_25Dec2011_en.pdf For an overview of the situation during the national elections, see the UN News Centre, *Deploring election-related violence in the DRC, top UN official appeal for calm*, 1 December 2011, accessible at: www.un.org/apps/news/story.asp?NewsID=40580&Cr=democratic&Cr1=congo.

454 See C. T. Call, E. M. Cousens, "Ending Wars and Building Peace", in Coping with Crisis Working Paper Series, International Peace Academy, March 2007, at 4. For some views of

the political transitions following the authorization of the Congolese authorities involving international governance institutions, such as the UN missions and the Rome Statute institutions. In accordance with the three essential tasks set out in the Security Council *Resolution 1279 (1999)* and *Resolution 1906 (2009)*, the activities of MONUC (*Mission de l'Organisation des Nations Unies au Congo*) and later re-named MONUSCO (*Mission de l'Organisation des Nations Unies pour la stabilization en République Démocratique du Congo*)[455] should centralize *a)* the post-election peacekeeping and peacebuilding in the protection of civilian populations; *b)* the disarmament, demobilization and repatriation and reintegration of armed Congolese and foreign armed groups; *c)* the support provided to the government in security sector reform (SSR), respectively the reform of the army, police and judiciary. As part of its mandate and compared with the new peace-keeping and peace-building operations, MONUC had the following tasks: *a)* establish contact with the signatories to the Ceasefire Agreement; *b)* liaise with the Joint Military Commission, provide technical assistance and investigate ceasefire violations; *c)* provide information on security conditions; *d)* prepare for the observation of the ceasefire and disengagement of military forces; *e)* maintain contacts with signatories of the Ceasefire Agreement, facilitate the delivery of humanitarian aid and protect human rights.

While other approaches are conceivable, considering that the European Union might be operationally involved again on the ground, the UN primacy among external actors in the DRC especially in the (human) security arena, including its long-lasting presence on the ground, makes MONUC/MONUSCO the principal point of analysis. MONUSCO expresses deep concern about the renewed fighting between rival groups in Rutshuru and Masisi territories, in North Kivu, and the subsequent consequences on the civilian population.[456] Moreover, the impact of the Rome Statute in the justice system of the DRC as the complementary capacity

experts in African politics and the politics of 'collapsing State' such as DRC see, W. Reno, 'Sovereignty and the Fragmentation of the DRC', *Warlord Politics and African States*, (1998), at 147.

455 See UN doc. S/RES/1925 (2010) Adopted by the Security Council at its 6324th meeting, on 28 May 2010, accessible at: www.un.org/ga/search/view_doc.asp?symbol=S/RES/1925(2010).

456 "The situation on the ground is extremely precarious and civilians are being exposed to an unacceptable threat," said Moustapha Soumare, Deputy Special Representative of the Secretary-General, Humanitarian Coordinator and acting Head of MONUSCO. "MONUSCO troops are risking their own lives to fulfill their mandate. See latest press release, 2 March 2013, *MONUSCO expresses deep concern about the escalation of violence in North Kivu*. The UN documents on MONUSCO are accessible at: www.un.org/en/peacekeeping/missions/monusco/documents.shtml For an overview of the crisis in North Kivu, the Human Rights Watch 86-page report details crimes against civilians by Congolese army soldiers, troops of renegade general Laurent Nkunda, and combatants of a Rwandan opposition force called the Forces for the Liberation of Rwanda (FDLR). The report documents an 18-month pattern of conflict where civilians bear the brunt of the abuses. See HRW, 'The Role of the International Community', *Renewed Crisis in North Kivu,* October 2007, the report is accessible at: www.hrw.org/en/reports/2007/10/22/renewed-crisis-north-kivu.

on the ground is also debated. This case study offers an overview of the actors involved in the DRC where the public authority of state-building are partly in the hands of the subsidiary body of the UN Security Council. In this case study the following relationships are argued, namely the issues of evolution, coordination and coherence within the MONUC's mandate; MONUC's cooperation with the Congolese authorities; MONUC's coordination with the UN agencies and humanitarian NGOs; including the implementation, harmonization and coordination between MONUC and the ICC. The arrest warrants against warlords should be enforced by MONUSCO due to the State not cooperating with the Court. This case study argues that the reconfiguration of the security forces should provide support to the ICC. In order to deliver results in the context of sustainable peace-building, global mandates have to find clear interaction strategies of law enforcement and humanitarian protection in the fight against the impunity of serious breaches of human rights. The multidimensional presence of international actors in the DRC and the necessity of implementing their interactions is the purpose of this case study. The concerns arise about the lack of preparedness and accountability in the reconfiguration of the civilian protection and peace building mandate of MONUSCO. Serious concerns are particularly raised about *a)* the victims and witnesses protection and relocation programs; *b)* about the delimitation of competences between such mandates; *c)* including the option of law enforcement at disposition of the judicial outcomes of the Court, which are still in motion. In other words, both options fighting the impunity at international and domestic levels in the DRC are analysed.

### 7.1.3. THE ISSUES

With regard to the international mandates active on the ground and the enduring struggle of sustainable peace and stability several issues arise due to the lack of coherence and coordination. Mainly on the nature of the 'comprehensive' mandate of peacekeeping characterized by the militarized approach, while dealing with the responsibility to protect civilians, humanitarian assistance and preservation of human rights. The Security Council members should have a better understanding of the mission's status in the DRC and not rely exclusively on the unilateral position of the DRC government. First, considering the range of actors involved in the country, second, assessing the progress made by the military operations against armed groups, and third, deploying security forces to assume UN's protection tasks, including the establishment of State authority in the areas freed by the armed groups. These issues should have received an appropriate assessment before extending or revising the MONUC's mandate, initiating a substantive model of reconfiguration and preparedness to support complementary actors on the ground with MONUSCO serving to such purpose. The support of the electoral activities in the country should have been combined with investigations and prosecutions and with law enforcement against the most dangerous criminal perpetrators. The State apparatus in the DRC is still not able to safeguard its citizens by war and crimes, while international responses lack of interaction strategies to maximize the results in such devastated society.

The idea behind this work is to stimulate the debate on governance strategies and unresolved gaps, recommending an appropriate interrelation between civilian protection, peace and security enforcement, crime prevention and international criminal justice mandates on the ground. Such mandates need to be planned jointly and in full compliance with human rights, international humanitarian law and refugee law. This case study debates on the overall impact of such mandates in the domestic institutional reality of the DRC, enabling its governance institutions to safeguard human security. This obviously depends on the sovereign responsibilities of the DRC authorities, but not exclusively, since the international community has specific responsibilities as well. The implementation, harmonization and coordination of complementary mandates are indispensable. These aspects require urgent consensus including the know-how of global organizations operating on the ground and supporting with each other. The results about peace, justice and security in the country depend on the way the States Parties, including the non-States Parties to the Rome Statute and formal UN members would take delivery of precise guidelines of cooperation with regard to the DRC, extending the challenge of cooperation in the whole African region. In other words, what kind of practical measures would finally be applied pressuring the DRC authorities to take care about civilians?

The challenges incurred by the multidimensional operations on the ground in the DRC are extensively debated. The first option refers to the implementation of cooperation agreements, memoranda, and other legal tools either at bilateral (e.g. ICC-State) or at multilateral levels (e.g. MONUSCO-ICC). The extreme situation in the country, characterized by serious threats and crimes, shows the inevitability to implement, harmonize and coordinate the international responses. According to the rule of law as one of the most important requirements of governance, all feasible ways deserve to be analysed. The harmonization of governance of resources and competences of global mandates 'narrowly focused' means to influence the State formation and self-sufficiency of the institutional apparatus in such complex situation. The challenges incurred by multidimensional operations need to dwell on the fragility of the State, keeping away from the risk of political manipulation by the DRC government from such international presence in the country. Global actors need to harmonize their work on the ground to maximize the results. The ideal would be a deep determination to act on the causes such as corruption, militarization, resource exploitation and criminal behaviour reducing the devastating effects on the civilian population. In the quest of the State fulfilling its own responsibilities, the change of regime undermining human security in the country is the only way for this community to profit from development programs. Challenging such aggressive regime requires the harmonization of international mandates with law enforcement actions, enhancing the role that international criminal justice can play in facilitating peace processes, domestic institution reforms and democratic transitions in the country. Despite the several approaches in such debate there seems to be only one way out from war and crime in the DRC. This can obey result from a stronger unity of intents between the relevant stakeholders to make sure that the domestic institutions start working in favor of civilians affected by war and crime.

### 7.1.4. THE PURPOSE

The modest purpose of this case study is to examine the challenges of the interaction between complementary mandates on the cluster of cooperation between peace and justice in a 'failed' State, with appropriate implementation of 'arrangements and agreements' between complementary global tools. It addresses the enduring challenge for the Court made only more difficult in the absence of adequate diplomatic and political support such as the need for increased international cooperation towards arrests, including the protection of affected communities and individuals during violent hostilities. The need of political support for international criminal justice risks constant tension with other important diplomatic objectives, including peacekeeping and peace negotiations which may undermine the credibility of the international judiciary. The UN 'comprehensive' mandate active on the ground fostering peace, justice and security and the pressure for democratic political transitions in the country, requires specific arrangements between all actors involved in the field, including the Court. There is an opportunity on the ground to establish 'narrowly focused' mandates based on the rule of law. Such mandates need high cooperation standards undermining the risks for the country to fall back in the regime of war and mass atrocities.

The concern addressed in this case study questions the extent in which the governance of 'comprehensive' international responses may challenge the complex reality in a 'failed' State such as in the DRC, without raising appropriately the international standards of cooperation between complementary mandates and the Congolese authorities. This study also measures the level of cooperation provided by the DRC to the Court where the most dangerous criminal perpetrators are still at large and around. The problem in the DRC is a lack of responsibility by the government to design acceptable security sector reforms protecting the affected communities and civilians by war and crime. The justice system, including army and police are still unable to function in acceptable ways. The membership of the DRC of the Rome Statute system does not show any consistent check against the impunity, with genuine investigations by the State itself, including the delivery of meaningful justice to the victims. Furthermore, being a party to the Rome Statute is not serving as a deterrent of serious crimes.[457] Another problem derives from the temporal jurisdiction of the Court which leaves uncovered serious crimes committed in the country. The DRC leadership launched amnesties for crimes previously committed not applicable to serious human rights breaches and humanitarian violations falling under the Rome Statute. There seems to be a hole to be covered in the country for sustainable order and stability. In any case the violence can be put to an end only finding an appropriate balance between the 'interests of peace' and the 'interests of justice' and only by vigorous interactions improving responsibility and cooperation while providing such balance. The practice applied shows several problems of legal and political nature. The DRC situation has been characterized by the failure of democratic elections, retention of internal power by the political élite, and the limited impact of international responses.[458]

## 7.2. THE PROBLEM OF OPERATIONAL COHERENCE AND COOPERATION

### SECTION OUTLINE

In the DRC the Court delivered arrest warrants against warlords which the State is not entirely enforcing. The humanitarian violations continue and the law enforcement of judicial decisions does not receive appropriate follow up. This section argues about the absence of coherence in the context of governing peace, justice and security operations in the DRC. It debates about the possible evolution of international operations performed by executive and judicial mandates,

457 Lately, 50 Congolese NGOs and Human Rights Watch lodge a formal complaint against Colonel Innocent Zimurinda. The complaint was addressed to General Amuli Bahigwa, the officer in command of Congolese army operations in eastern Congo. The Congolese groups said that abuses were continuing under Zimurinda's command, including with his direct involvement: "We have taken this unusual step of jointly lodging a formal complaint against Colonel Zimurinda because we can no longer tolerate the abuses he continues to commit against civilians", said Joseph Dunia of *Promotion de la Démocratie et Protection des Droits Humains* (PDH). "We fear these attacks on civilians will continue unless there is urgent action by the authorities to suspend and investigate him". See HRW, '*Complaint Against Colonel Innocent Zimurinda*' 1 March 2010, accessible at: www.hrw.org/en/news/2010/03/01/complaint-against-lt-col-innocent-zimurinda.

458 For an overview of the causes and the effects of the conflict in the DRC see I. Samset, 'Conflict of Interests or Interests in Conflict? Diamonds and War in the DRC', 2002 *Review of African Political Economy* 29, at 463. For an extensive overview of the local governance in Eastern DRC see also the contributions by way of working papers of K. Vlassenroot, H. Romkema, 'War and Governance in the DRC', in *Local Governance and Leadership in the DRC*, (2007) Oxfam-Novib, accessible at: www.psw.ugent.be/crg/publications/working%20paper/localgov_rapport_eng_def.pdf.

providing security and law enforcement assistance, including planning and support between interdependent operations in the field. The common goal should be the preservation of law and order including a democratic transition in the country through a coherent strategy of interactions between domestic and global actors. A clear interaction strategy would have a positive impact on the rule of law, institutional building and justice in the DRC for the following main reasons. First of all, far from politicized actions and in respect of the judicial independence of the Court, such coherent efforts of governance would persuade global consent to the Court as equal, independent and enforced international judicial tool, dissolving the friction with the political and executive authority of the Security Council. Second, a coherent support to the Court would develop the ability of peace enforcement serving judicial mandates on the ground, offering more credibility to the peace operations on humanitarian protection and human rights defence in the country. Third, it would expedite the cooperation of the State to take over its own responsibilities against the impunity of serious crimes, while offering higher degree of deterrence, stability and democratic transition at both national and regional levels. Fourth, it would offer directions and guidelines of cooperation also for non-States Parties to the Rome Statute furthering positive engagement from them, including legal and political legitimation of multilateral involvement by regional organizations. The judicial outcomes of the Court would also serve as a signal of action required by the non members of the treaty and their future ratification of the Rome Statute.

The UN is a key actor in the DRC but not the only one engaged in the post-conflict peace-building. In general terms, the UN has the political legitimacy and the capacity to convene parties and should strengthen cooperation and cohesion with the multiple regional and international actors involved on the ground. This section recognizes that cooperation is first and foremost a responsibility of the government in the DRC but also requires the support from regional and international actors. Such actors can optimize the results on the ground through appropriate interactions and complementing with each other. With regard to the Court, the current phase of investigative and prosecutorial activities in the DRC requires cooperation with the UN mission on the ground. Such multilateral cooperation should become the priority. Only relying on the bilateral cooperation with the State and its domestic authorities is not sufficient for the Court and neither for the UN. The DRC authorities should be pressured in accordance with the respective peace and justice mandates. They should start their own judicial proceedings *in situ* challenging visibly the impunity regime of international crimes. The analysis of the UN legislative history in the DRC shows that the governance of peace operations focusing on the responsibility to protect does not take in consideration as much as necessary the presence of the ICC, neither providing support with law enforcement assistance, victims' protection and relocation, or securing assets, infrastructures and facilities.

Moreover, the modernization of the operations on the ground by the Security Council require awareness about the responsibilities of the military hierarchy and criminal accountability of all parts involved in the civilian protection duties. In order to have a spectrum of governance of such operations on the ground which are characterized by the lack of coherence and coordination, and by the limited support provided to the Court, this section offers an overview of the Security Council activity in the DRC and the cooperation standards practiced with the ICC in the field operations.

### 7.2.1. THE PROSPECT OF COHERENCE

In 2004 the UN Security Council provided "*inter alia* that MONUC will have the mandate, in support of the government of national unity and transition of the DRC, to investigate human rights violations to put an end to impunity, and to continue to cooperate with efforts to ensure that those responsible for serious violations of human rights and international humanitarian law are brought to justice, while working closely with relevant agencies of the UN".[459] Apparently, it was early to consider the ICC presence in the planning of the UN mission in 2004. In 2005 the memorandum of understanding between MONUC and the ICC regulating such interaction finally entered into force but waits for further implementation (MoU).[460] The ideal would be to reach consensus in the Security Council on the reconfiguration of its mandate. The security of the operations regarding victims' relocation and protection may also fall in the civilian protection already foreseen in such comprehensive mandate of the UN.

The investigation of the Court in the DRC situation involves allegations of thousands of deaths by mass murder and summary execution occurred since 2002, as well as large-scale patterns of rape, torture and the use of child soldiers.[461] Numerous armed groups active in the DRC were allegedly involved in these crimes. Given the scale of the situation, the investigation of the cases would proceed in sequence. Some cases selected on the basis of gravity were prioritized in

---

459 UN doc. S/RES/1565 (2004).

460 UN Treaties Vol. 2221, I-39500 No. 1292, 8 November 2005, MoU between the UN and the ICC concerning cooperation between the MONUC and the ICC (with annexes and exchange of letters), accessible at: http://untreaty.un.org/unts/144078_158780/5/3/12842.pdf.

461 The Office of the Prosecutor has been closely analyzing the situation in the DRC since July 2003, initially with a focus on crimes committed in the Ituri region. In September 2003 the Prosecutor informed the Assembly of the States Parties that he was ready to request authorization from the Pre-Trial Chamber to use his own powers to start an investigation, but that a referral and active support from the DRC would assist his work. In a letter in November 2003 the government of the DRC welcomed the involvement of the ICC and in March 2004 the DRC referred the situation in the country to the Court. See ICC doc. ICC-01/04 Situation and Cases in the Democratic Republic of the Congo, accessible at: www.icc-cpi.int/menus/icc/situations%20and%20cases/situations/situation%20icc%200104/.

2005, while others would be developed subsequently. The first investigations and the collection of evidence brought the prosecutorial activity in The Hague with judicial proceedings. The Office of the Prosecutor and the Registry established a field office in Kinshasa and a field presence in Bunia and concluded a cooperation agreement with the government of the DRC. However, because of logistical challenges and the lack of effective control of many areas the government's ability to cooperate with the Office of the Prosecutor remains a great challenge for the current investigative and prosecutorial activity. The State indeed did not show any willingness and ability to take over the criminal proceedings *in situ*. With regard to the prosecutions and the indictments to warlords by the Court, the State failure about acceptable standards of cooperation should attract further the attention of the international community. The Security Council including non-States Parties like the US should offer political and diplomatic assistance, pressuring the DRC government to follow up on the ICC judicial decisions. In this way the critics about double standards and about the controversial US position towards the Court would be neutralized by legitimized cooperation efforts.

Despite the lessons learned after the genocide in Rwanda the DRC is still one of those that missed early intervention. Many projects have been devoted to the development of early-warning indicators about State failure, and many books and policy papers have been written about how to create the political wills for early conflict prevention, but success has been limited. In the DRC situation, early intervention has not been performed and the UN mandate in the country showed a lack of preparedness for several reasons.[462] As far as the situation escalated at such violent extent in the country, and no early-warning had good effect, consensus is now necessary on narrowly focused operations between complementary mandates fostering peace, justice and security. The law enforcement on the ground of some of the Court's arrest warrants against Congolese warlords requires immediate action. When the State cooperation fails, the Security Council should be engaged in law enforcement operations. The question is whether in the practice there would be at least the determination to act with human security parameters in such violent situations, or the search of measures to *prevent*, *react* and *rebuild* would only remain theoretical assumptions.

---

462 For an overview of the challenges incurred by MONUC supporting multidimensional operations in the country such as humanitarian protection, conflict management and peace enforcement see, V. K. Holt, T. C. Berkman, *The Impossible Mandate? Military Preparedness, the Responsibility to Protect and Modern Peace Operations*, (2006), at 155. For the broad range of issues arising from the fact that the UN mission in the DRC, MONUC, is an integrated mission mandated, among other things, to protect civilians and humanitarian aid workers and to improve the security conditions under which humanitarian assistance is provided and the failure to reach coherent standards of assistance on the ground see T. Mowjee, 'Coherence: Integration Missions in Theory and in the DRC', *Humanitarian Agenda 2015 DRC Case Study*, (2007), at 15.

## 7.2.2. THE STANDARDS OF COOPERATION

In the previous chapters the structural and normative challenges embodying the emerging regime of international criminal justice based on international cooperation upraised several concerns. In accordance with the treaty provisions, Article 87(6) of the Rome Statute addresses the relationship between the Court and intergovernmental organizations in providing that: "...the Court may also ask for other forms of cooperation and assistance which may be agreed upon with such an organization, and which are in accordance with its competence and mandate". Article 54(3)(d) leaves space to 'arrangements or agreements' to facilitate such cooperation. While at provisional level the Rome Statute clarifies in detail the obligation of the States Parties to cooperate with the Court, including the cooperation with non-parties under *ad hoc* agreements, international organizations such as the UN are not bound by such obligations. There is no provision in the Rome Statute defining the level of involvement of multinational forces in the arrest of individuals indicted by the Court in case the State does not take its own responsibilities. Further action is left to the political interest of the international community and to the international cooperation capacity-building of the Court towards 'arrangements or agreements' with other international organizations.

As explained above, the 'multidimensional' operations in a 'failed' State, such as in the DRC, typically require the participation of several organizational entities engaged in state-building operations. In order to ensure the coherence as a whole of such complementary activities it is necessary to harmonize, integrate and coordinate their respective mandates and operations. Article 18 of the relationship agreement between the UN and the ICC clarifies that the UN "undertakes with due regard to its responsibilities and competence under the Charter of the United Nations and subject to its rules, to cooperate with the Prosecutor of the Court and to enter with the Prosecutor into such arrangement or agreements as may be necessary to facilitate such cooperation, in particular when the Prosecutor exercises his duties and powers with respect to investigation and seeks the cooperation of the UN under Article 54 of the Statute".[463] In 2005 an important memorandum of understanding has been established between the UN and the ICC concerning cooperation between the MONUC and the ICC (MoU). Chapter III and particularly Article 10 on cooperation and legal assistance has been used for such governance, and will need further attention on facilitating exchange of information between the organizations including substantive and operational assistance (MoU).

---

[463] For the provisions on cooperation between the organizations see respectively Article 18 of the Relationship Agreement between the United Nations and the International Criminal Court and Article 54 of the Rome Statute.

When the Security Council decided to extend its mission in the DRC the reason was to respond to continued attacks against civilians, respectively, the widespread sexual violence, the recruitment of child soldiers and the extrajudicial executions. The Security Council emphasized that the protection of civilians must be given first priority in the allocation of available capacity and resources of any other tasks. In the context of civilian protection, the Security Council urged the Congolese government to establish sustainable peace in the eastern part of the country, to ensure respect for human rights and put an end to impunity, reforming the justice system and the security sectors as fundamental requirements to restore the rule of law. Furthermore, the ongoing debate in the Security Council on a strategic review of the situation in the DRC, including the reconfiguration of its mandate, was based first "to determine, in close cooperation with the Congolese government and troop- and police-contributing countries, the modalities of a reconfiguration of the UN mandate, in particular the critical tasks that must be accomplished before the mission could envisage".[464] In such debate the Security Council does not mention the role of the Court and the support expected by its peace operations thereof. It will be up to the Secretary-General to emphasize again the standards of cooperation to be provided in the UN mandate configuration to complementary partners involved on the ground such as the ICC. The next paragraph examines the evolution of the comprehensive mandate of the Security Council on the ground, its reconfiguration and the necessity of 'narrowly focused' operations fostering peace, justice and security in the DRC.

### 7.2.3. THE UN MISSION IN THE DRC

The necessity of a coherent model of interaction and support of the Security Council to the ICC is obvious. Some adjustments should have been considered in the reconfiguration of the new deployment of the UN mandate in the country (MONUSCO). In the first place the Security Council decided that MONUC will have the mandate, in close cooperation with the Congolese authorities and the United Nations country team and donors, to support the strengthening of democratic institutions and the rule of law and, to that end, to: *a)* provide advice to strengthen democratic institutions and processes at the national, provincial, regional and local levels; *b)* promote national reconciliation and internal political dialogue, including through the provision of good offices, and support the strengthening of civil society and multi-party democracy, and give the necessary support to the Goma and Nairobi peace processes; *c)* assist in the promotion and protection of human rights, with particular attention to women, children and vulnerable persons, investigate human rights violations and publish its findings, as appropriate, with a view to putting an end to impunity, assist in the development

[464] UN doc. S/RES/1906 (2009).

and implementation of a transitional justice strategy, and cooperate in national and international efforts to bring to justice perpetrators of grave violations of human rights and international humanitarian law; *d)* in close coordination with international partners and the United Nations country team, provide assistance to the Congolese authorities, including the national independent electoral commission, in the organization, preparation and conduct of local elections; *e)* assist in the establishment of a secure and peaceful environment for the holding of free and transparent local elections; *f)* contribute to the promotion of good governance and respect for the principle of accountability; *g)* in coordination with international partners, advise the government of the DRC in strengthening the capacity of the judicial and correctional systems, including the military justice system. The further evolution of the UN mission in the field and its impact on humanitarian protection, security issues and accountability in the DRC in the post-election phase will be discussed in the next session. The next session concludes with some remarks on the presence of the Court in the DRC which confirms the need of cooperation to be settled in the configuration on the ground by a narrowly focused mandate of the Security Council.

### 7.2.4. THE ICC PRESENCE IN THE DRC

The DRC is one of the situations that the ICC is currently investigating and prosecuting falling under the 'self-referral' category of the States Parties to the Rome Statute. The government of the DRC referred the situation to the Court which focused its attention on atrocities committed in the Ituri province. The Ituri militia leaders have been charged with crimes against the humanity and war crimes, including the involvement in the murder in February 2005 of nine Bangladeshi peacekeepers, ambushed during a MONUC patrol near Lake Albert.[465] As previously anticipated, between 2006–2008 the ICC secured the arrest of Thomas Lubanga, the political and military leader of the rebel *Union des Patriotes Congolais* (UPC), Germain Katanga, commander of the *Force de Résistance Patriotique en Ituri* (FRPI) and Mathieu Ngudjolo, former leader of the *Front des Nationalistes et des Intégrationnistes* (FNI). They were arrested by Congolese authorities during military training in Kinshasa and transported to The Hague. In total four arrest warrants have been issued for the DRC situation. The accused Thomas Lubanga Dyilo, Germain Katanga, Mathieu Ngudjolo Chui are currently in the custody of the ICC. The suspect Bosco Ntaganda is now also

465 Thomas Lubanga was arrested and imprisoned in the DRC, following the killing of nine Bangladeshi peacekeepers in the gold-rich Ituri region. The military arm of Lubanga's Union of Congolese Patriots, UPC, was implicated in the killings of the Bangladeshi peacekeepers. See Ayesha Kajee, 'Lubanga Case Signals Hope for Child Soldiers', 29 March 06 *Institute for War and Peace Reporting*, No.58, accessible at: www.iwpr.net/?p=%3Cp%3ENo%20item%20 found.%3C/p%3E&s=f&o=260591&apc_state=henh.

in custody. The situation of the DRC has been assigned to Pre-Trial Chamber I, which is composed by three judges. The Court has charged Lubanga with three counts of war crimes: enlisting children under the age of fifteen years, conscripting them to the armed forces of the UPC and using them to participate actively in the hostilities. Katanga and Ngudjolo have both been charged with six counts of war crimes and three of crimes against humanity, including murder, sexual slavery and conscription of children, all stemming from an alleged joint FRPI-FNI attack on the village of Bogoro in Ituri in 2003.

### 7.2.5. CONCLUSIONS

For many human rights experts involved in the DRC the recommendations to the Security Council regarding its mandate refer to the lack of clarity of its comprehensive strategy in the country. According to the UN Special Advisor on Sexual Violence in the DRC, Dahrendorf, "the mandate to protect civilians, to monitor human rights abuses and to enforce the arms embargo has been renewed. However, since then, it is not clear how far the UN mission in the DRC will remain involved in promoting and safeguarding the remaining agendas of the peace process, such as judicial reform, devolution of central government powers to provincial assemblies and anti-corruption legislation. The UN political role will have to be re-defined by the Security Council in line with the recommendation made by the Secretary-General and with regard to the Congolese institutions. The security sector reform (SSR) in the DRC is not an isolated process, but it has to take place at different levels simultaneously and in combination with other reform processes. The SSR has to be incorporated into ongoing efforts aimed at strengthening governance, such as an effective legislature and other oversight bodies, financial management, human rights and civilian protection. There is a lack of conceptual clarity amongst all actors involved on the way the SSR is coupled with a lack of expertise and appropriate human and financial resources dedicated to these efforts. The UN's approach to SSR in the DRC has been marred at structural, conceptual and management level, and a lack of dedicated strategic capacity at the level of the UN mission to assist in the coordination of SSR".[466] The security sector reform in the DRC must be viewed in the broader spectrum of the development of domestic institutions and capacity-building. The Security

466 The focus of the UN integrated mission in Security Sector Reform (SSR) is an examination of the army, police and judicial institutions in the DRC. For an analysis of the key elements and obstacles of the SSR, a brief overview of MONUC involvement in SSR activities, and final recommendations see, N. Dahrendorf, 'MONUC and the Relevance of Coherent Mandates: The Case of the DRC', in H. Hänggi, V. Scherrer (eds.), *Security Sector Reform and UN Integrated Missions*, (2008), at 98.

Council needs to take such recommendation in consideration while adjusting appropriately its mandate.[467]

This section argued on the challenges in the governance of international responses in a failed State characterized by constant instability between the conflict and post-conflict phases. The conflict in eastern DRC is in part incited by the overflow of the genocide ideology from Rwanda, and it has involved up to seven African nations in the Great Lakes region, including Uganda. The conflict is characterized by the deliberate targeting of the civilian population which has suffered mass murder, rape, torture and mutilation. The situation continues to cause a threat to international peace and security in the whole region and it still requires appropriate consideration of peace enforcement and international criminal justice. The international community did not have the resources, the political will, or the know-how to take early action in the region. The genocide in Rwanda confirmed such trend. The international failure to take seriously the initial massacres of 1994 in Rwanda, which ultimately led to genocide became four years later a major cause of war in the DRC. The empirical data of peace enforcement at disposition in the country, since its colonial independence struggling with social, economic, and political State formation, confirm the failure of governing early signs of State failure through comprehensive international responses. However, the current struggle of the international governance institutions is not only worth it for the DRC, but for the whole region, where the needs of sustainable peace, justice and security are interrelated and their operations should be more coherent and complement with each other.

Questions and concerns arise on the governance of international responses, cooperation standards and their interaction thereof. There are urgent adjustments to be made considering the evolution of executive mandates on the protection of civilians with militarized operations, combined with the lacuna of supporting judicial decisions with law enforcement, police operations and protection of victims and witnesses. It is premature to establish if the membership of the DRC to the Rome Statute system and the support provided by the UN on democratic transition in the country would influence further the developments in the domestic governance institutions. The priorities remain the fight against the regime of impunity of massive crimes in the country, where the process of demilitarization, civilian protection, law enforcement and police, good governance of courts and tribunals, including the welfare of individuals and victimised communities, can be optimized by an interaction strategy of global governance institutions. These global efforts would surely reflect on the State at micro level offering at least a model of governance to be followed by the domestic institutions in the country. There is the need to avoid the militarized approach which instead should turn their

[467] See N. Dahrendorf *supra*.

support to law enforcement and police operations to an international judiciary, including civilian protection duties extended to the victims of international humanitarian crimes. Moreover, the main important element is to hold all actors involved accountable for their actions without any exclusion.

## 7.3. FIGHTING THE IMPUNITY AT INTERNATIONAL AND DOMESTIC LEVELS

### SECTION OUTLINE

This section explores the problems of 'inability' and 'unwillingness' of the DRC government investigating and prosecuting the perpetrators of serious international crimes; its domestic justice system; the impact of the Rome Statute in the judicial apparatus of the country, including other alternatives dealing with the regime of impunity falling outside the temporary jurisdiction of the ICC. In the DRC the justice system is completely unable to preserve the rule of law. Its domestic governance institutions, courts and tribunals do not have any meaning for the populations in the chaotic scenario of impunity and commission of serious crimes. The ability of domestic courts to deliver justice for victims of rape and sexual violence is almost inexistent. The prisons do not retain such violators. The majority of the criminals easily escapes and commits the same crimes over and over again. Entire communities have been victimized in the DRC and victim rights are not recognized.

Thomas Lubanga was the first to be arrested by the ICC on charges for the recruitment and use of child soldiers. This indictment drew considerable attention about the issue of child soldiers and hopefully also from other rebel leaders in the country, the majority of which had children among their forces. On the positive side, Lubanga's arrest had an enormous educational impact, making clear what was not previously understood that "recruiting, enlisting, and using children to fight, is a war crime".[468] It may seem surprising that the use of child soldiers was not considered to be a crime. Instead child soldiers had been part of the entourage of every senior armed leader in the DRC, and this indeed for years. Laurent Kabila's Kadogo troops were probably the best known example. In some places in the East, parents have even 'donated' their children to an armed group

[468] Such unawareness of crimes in time of conflicts is empirically confirmed, according to the finding of a survey which respondents were interviewed and assessed in Ituri, North Kivu, and South Kivu. See P. Vinck, P. Pham, S. Baldo, R. Shigekane, *Living with Fear: A Population-based Survey on Attitudes about Peace, Justice, and Social Reconstruction in Eastern Democratic Republic of Congo*, Human Rights Center of the University of California Berkeley, Payson Center for International Development, and ICTJ, August 2008.

to help protect the community.[469] More commonly the conscription of children in the army was forced by kidnapping them from their villages. In those cases militia, warlords and army commanders were so familiar with such practice that they considered this being normal in time of conflict.

The views of Hayner and Davis on the demobilization of children, their rehabilitation and care after conflict are completely shared. In principle, there is no apparent procedural way to release the child soldiers into a formal system of demobilization. Children's rights advocates began to see a new pattern emerge. After Lubanga's arrest, armed groups entering demobilization programs and sites no longer brought children with them. Instead, according to NGOs involved in child demobilization, the children were abandoned, left behind in the forest or perhaps in a village. In a few cases the armed group would return the children to their families. Only a small proportion of the abandoned children would find their way to the UN or other children's service agencies, whose programs are designed on the assumption that child soldiers would be released through the official demobilization process. In addition, demobilization benefits are generally available only to those demobilized through formal entry points.[470] For this reason international rehabilitation programs have been very weak either for girls as victims of sexual crimes or for child soldiers, or for both. This is another reason why the coordination between complementary actors on the ground is extremely important. This section reflects on the impact of complementary global regimes fighting against the impunity in domestic governance systems with the scope to maintain, preserve and restore the rule of law. The new inspiration comes from the principles to be applied to reparations for victims in the context of the case against Lubanga, who was found guilty by the ICC and sentenced to a total imprisonment of 14 years. Hopefully the DRC authorities will take over *in situ* very soon the judicial proceedings against other criminal perpetrators.

In order to offer an assessment of the justice system in the DRC, this section contains the finding of the report entitled *Rebuilding courts and trust: An assessment of the needs of the justice system in the Democratic Republic of Congo* (DRC) of the International Bar Association's Human Rights Institute (IBAHRI), in conjunction with the International Legal Assistance Consortium (ILAC). The report includes recommendations to the government of the DRC at both central and regional levels; the most notable of which is for the government to increase

469 Practice not acceptable under international standards. The donation of children was more common among local Mayi Mayi groups, which were initially conceived as community-based protection forces. This practice is also not acceptable under international standards.

470 See L. Davis, P. Hayner, 'The ICC's Impact on Children', *Difficult Peace, Limited Justice: Ten Years of Peacemaking in the DRC*, March 2009, International Center for Transitional Justice, at 30, accessible at: www.ictj.org/static/Africa/DRC/ICTJDavisHayner_DRC_DifficultPeace_pa2009.pdf.

funding of the judicial system and fight corruption within the judiciary. The report follows the IBAHRI-ILAC delegation visit to the DRC to undertake an examination of the current state of the country's justice system. The IBAHRI and ILAC experts found ongoing conflicts, serious violations of human rights, violence against women and international crimes, which have added sensitive challenges of a justice system already struggling to meet the basic demands of the population. Further, the report states that the judicial system in the DRC continues to suffer from underinvestment, corruption, and a severe lack of resources and infrastructure. The frequent disregard or delay in compliance with court orders by members of the executive and the overall difficulty for individuals to access justice and have judgments enforced, is deplored by the IBAHRI and ILAC. The two non-governmental organisations and eminent think-tanks are concerned that legal aid is not easily accessible in the DRC, and that tribunals are not present in all regions, which contributes to the feeling of injustice for victims and a sentiment of impunity for perpetrators. Christian Ahlund, Executive Director of ILAC said, right after releasing such important findings, "we wish to offer our contribution to the ongoing effort to improve the justice system in the DRC, particularly in areas that are in great need of assistance. The report includes recommendations for specific projects in areas that the delegation has visited and that are still relatively untouched by international intervention". "The current situation of the administration of justice in the DRC is of grave concern" said Justice Richard Goldstone, IBAHRI Co-Chair. "The Government must make the improvement of the justice system as a priority. This is the only way to fight impunity and restore the rule of law in the country".[471]

Extremely useful for a legal overview is also the case study and the recommendations delivered by *Avocats sans frontières*, on the application of the Rome Statute by the courts in the DRC.[472] Another important legal, political and institutional overview of the current state of justice in the DRC comes from an evaluation of the sensitive security system reform in the country.[473] This section contains an

471 The International Bar Association's Human Rights Institute (IBAHRI) and the International Legal Assistance Consortium (ILAC) organised an international delegation of jurists to visit the Democratic Republic of Congo (DRC) in February 2009. The IBAHRI and ILAC mission was aimed at conducting a needs assessment of the Congolese judicial system in order to assess where expertise can be most constructively applied, both geographically and thematically, to assist the reconstruction of the justice system. See International Bar Association's Human Rights Institute (IBAHRI), the International Legal Assistance Consortium (ILAC), *Rebuilding Courts and Trust: An Assessment of the Needs of the Justice System in the Democratic Republic of Congo,* August 2009, OSISA and Swedish Ministry for Foreign Affairs, accessible at: www.ibanet.org/Article/Detail.aspx?ArticleUid=6c2be523-f512-48c1-b09c-fc9a8b1d0aab.

472 Avocats Sans Frontières, 'Summary of Recommendations relating to the Application of the Rome Statute by the Congolese Courts', DRC Case Study, March 2009, at 125, accessible at: www.asf.be/publications/ASF_CaseStudy_RomeStatute_Light_PagePerPage.pdf.

473 L. Davis, 'The Current State of the Security System in the DRC', *Justice-Sensitive Security System Reform in the DRC,* February 2009, International Centre for Transitional Justice, accessible at: www.initiativeforpeacebuilding.eu/pdf/Justice_Sensitive_Security_System_reform_in_the_

overview of the emerging regime of fighting the impunity in the DRC through the application of Rome Statute provisions in local courts, which are limited by the problems facing the judicial system (deprived judicial budget; shortage of judges and deficiencies in training; corruption; lack of independence; prisons conditions and infrastructure; poor means of communication; geographical restraints). It reports on the cases before the ICC, including limits and critics of its impact fighting the impunity in the DRC (not targeting the highest-level perpetrators; limited geographic reach in the country; unwillingness to prosecute crimes committed by government forces; limited charges on the crimes committed; limited information and outreach activity in the country). In order to complete the assessment this section also explores other alternatives dealing with impunity. It explores the evolution of the jurisprudence of domestic courts; the impunity regime of sexual violence, the international assistance for institution-building currently present in the country which lacks of coherence and cooperation.

## 7.3.1. THE IMPACT OF THE ROME STATUTE

As briefly clarified above, several problems characterize the governance of the domestic system in the DRC, respectively *a)* the justice system structure, *b)* the lacuna in the national legislation, and *c)* the application of the Rome Statute provisions in domestic courts.

### *a) Implementing legislation*

The ICC has become an important factor in the DRC following the referral by the Congolese government of the situation on its territory on 3 March 2004. The DRC's ratification of the Rome Statute instituting the ICC dates back to 11 April 2002.[474] Despite its ratification, the DRC has yet to actually adopt the bill formally incorporating the Rome Statute into Congolese law. The legal experts of IBAHRI-ILAC met in 2009 with representatives of the Permanent Commission of Congolese Law Reform, who explained that they had prepared a draft law at the government's request upon ratification of the Rome Statute. The acting President of the Commission said that the draft had been handed to the government two years ago. The delegation was informed that a draft law could be presented again before the National Assembly at its next session. The draft law has been a matter of debate for several years, and some speculate that certain government officials are resisting the legislation because of fears that they may themselves end up being

DRC.pdf C. Aptel, 'Challenges Facing Domestic Justice in the DRC', *Domestic Justice Systems and the Impact of the Rome Statute*, September 2009, International Center for Transitional Justice, at 6, accessible at: www.internationalcriminaljustice.net/experience/papers/session7.pdf.

474 Décret-loi No 13 of 13 March 2002.

prosecuted.[475] In its current format, the draft law involves changes to the Penal Code in order to include war crimes, crimes against humanity and genocide, and in order to replace the sentence of capital punishment with life imprisonment. Amendments would also be required to the Military Penal Code in order to move war crimes, crimes against humanity and genocide under the exclusive jurisdiction of the civilian Courts of Appeal. The draft legislation would also clarify the definition of these crimes, as there are currently discrepancies between the definitions found in the Military Penal Code and in the Rome Statute. This anticipated transfer of jurisdiction is the cause of debate as to the prudence of removing jurisdiction from military courts over military personnel in cases of international crimes, in light of the present state of the civilian justice system. The current draft law provides for the transfer of jurisdiction to the Courts of Appeal, but it also introduces a military judge in the composition of the five judge bench which will hear these infractions.

*b) Application of the Rome Statute provisions in domestic courts*

Given the monistic nature of the Congolese legal system, the Rome Statute is already part of domestic law even in the absence of an implementing law.[476] The Constitution provides at Article 153 that courts can apply ratified international instruments as long as these are not contrary to law and custom.[477] Local courts have started invoking the provisions of the Rome Statute in their judgments since 2006.[478] The *Tribunal militaire de garnison* of Mbandaka was the first one to do so in the cases of Mutins de Mbandaka[479] and Songo Mboyo.[480] In these two cases, the tribunal used the definition of crimes against humanity found in the Rome Statute. In Songo Mboyo, the tribunal used the definition of rape as a crime against humanity as outlined in the Rome Statute, which is wider than the

475 The Permanent Commission of Congolese Law reform modified the text before submitting it to the then Minister of Justice. Human Rights First has issued comments, jointly with Human Rights Watch, on the draft, stressing remaining concerns and suggesting alternative language, in particular with regard to the death penalty and cooperation procedures. It is now for the Minister of Justice in the current transitional government to take the legislation forward. For the comments of HRF and HRW see document accessible at: www.humanrightsfirst.info/cah/ij/icc/implementation/imp_dem_rep_congo.aspx.

476 In a *monistic system*, ratified international treaties become directly applicable national law, while a *dualistic* system requires an additional act of the legislature to transform the ratified treaty into national law.

477 While Article 156 of the 2006 Constitution of the DRC limits the jurisdiction of military justice to members of the armed forces and of the police.

478 A recent publication by Avocats Sans Frontières analyses the jurisprudence of Congolese military courts applying the Rome Statute. See ASF, *Etude de jurisprudence. L'application du Statut de Rome de la Cour Pénale Internationale par les Jurisdictions de la RDC*, March 2009, accessible at: www.asf.be/index.php?module=publicaties&lang=fr&id=51.

479 Military Court of the Garrison of Mbandaka, *Affaire Mutins de Mbandaka*, 12 Januery 2006, RP 86/05.

480 Military Court of the Garrison of Mbandaka, *Affaire Songo Mboyo*, 12 April 2006, RP 84/05.

one found in the Military Penal Code. Recently, the trial of Mai Mai militia chief Gédéon Kyungu Mutanga showed another example of the application of the Rome Statute by domestic courts. In March 2009, the *Tribunal militaire de garnison* of Haut-Katanga found Gédéon guilty of crimes against humanity. The court applied the definition of crimes against humanity as found in the Rome Statute. The jurisprudence of domestic courts as regards the application of the Rome Statute provisions is still limited not only in the number of decisions, but also in the strength of the legal reasoning found in the judgments. In its study, *Avocats sans frontières* notes the weakness of the decisions and explains that judges often omit to point out the constitutive elements of the crime or the evidence on which they are founding their decision.[481] Challenges to the proper functioning of the judiciary also influence the application of the Rome Statute by domestic courts. Magistrates have rarely been adequately trained and investigative capacities are very limited. The lack of qualified magistrates and judicial personnel also poses a challenge to proper application of the Rome Statute domestically.[482]

### c) *Cases before the ICC in the DRC*

Following the referral by the Congolese government, the Prosecutor opened an investigation in 2004 which led to warrants of arrest being issued against four Congolese nationals. There are currently three pending cases before the ICC for the crimes committed in the DRC. Thomas Lubanga Dyilo, accused of war crimes and crimes against humanity in relation to the use of child soldiers, was arrested in 2006 and his trial began in January 2009.[483] In the joint case of Germain Katanga and Mathieu Ngudjolo Chui, charges were confirmed on 26 September 2008 and the trial started in September 2009.[484] In addition, a warrant of arrest was issued against Bosco Ntaganda, the alleged Deputy Chief of the General Staff of the *Forces Patriotiques pour la Libération du Congo* (FPLC) and alleged Chief of Staff of the *Congrès National pour la Défense du Peuple* (CNDP), an armed group active in North Kivu. In addition to the three above mentioned cases, the ICC has charged another Congolese national, former opposition leader Jean-Pierre Bemba, with crimes against humanity and war crimes committed in the Central African Republic.[485]

The strategic approach and the prosecutorial policy of the ICC in the DRC have been both criticized by several scholars, human rights activists and observers

[481] Avocats Sans Frontières, *supra* note 482.
[482] Avocats Sans Frontières, 'Criminal Responsibility, Grounds for exclusion of Responsibility and Extenuating or Aggravating Circumstances', *DRC Case Study*, March 2009, at 64, accessible at: www.asf.be/publications/ASF_CaseStudy_RomeStatute_Light_PagePerPage.pdf.
[483] ICC-01/04-01/06.
[484] ICC-01/04-01/07.
[485] ICC-01/04-01/08.

on different issues. Some of them argue that the Court is not targeting the perpetrators at the highest-level. Many of the militia groups in eastern Congo have operated with the direct support of the political leadership in neighbouring countries. Human rights organizations argue that the ICC prosecutor has shown no intention to investigate this higher level of involvement. In 2006 Human Rights Watch on this issue stressed that the: "Chief prosecutor should also investigate those who armed and supported militia groups operating in Ituri, including key players in power in Kinshasa, Kampala and Kigali. The crimes committed in Ituri are part of a broader conflict in the Great Lakes region, and the Court should finally pierce the veil of impunity that stretches beyond Congo's borders".[486]

## 7.3.2. THE LIMITS AND CRITICS OF THE ICC

A variety of limits and critics have characterized the impact of the ICC in the DRC. First of all, the Court's geographic reach within DRC is considered too limited. Some scholars and practitioners regret that the unilateral focus on Ituri during the Court's first years in the country has raised questions about its role and impact. According to Davis and Hayner, "the fighting in Ituri is less connected to the ruling elite and least implicates the government, compared to events in the Kivus and elsewhere. The judiciary is considered to be stronger in Ituri more than in other areas of conflict because of intensive international engagement. Partly because local authorities had done some substantive investigation of the cases that the ICC selected for prosecution, these are generally considered the easier cases. The density of international peacekeeping troops was the highest in Ituri, and so it is possible that the prosecutor chose the location safest for his investigating staff as well as for the witnesses. An obvious aspect of its intervention is that the ICC became active when the conflict was calming down in Ituri. The more-entrenched, politically more complex, and longer-term conflict was centred in North and South Kivu".[487] Another issue is that the Court seems unwilling to prosecute crimes committed by government forces. For many commentators this is particularly unfortunate, "since the national army has often been cited as the worst offender in serious rights abuses".[488] Some observers believe that the Court is acting in a partial manner, perhaps worried that it might put at risk the political support and collaboration it currently receives from the government.[489]

486 See R. Dicker, Human Rights Watch, "D.R. Congo: ICC Arrest First Step to Justice," press release, March 17, 2006; www.hrw.org.

487 See L. Davis, P. Hayner, 'The Role and Impact of the ICC', *Difficult Peace, Limited Justice: Ten Years of Peacemaking in the DRC*, March 2009, International Center for Transitional Justice, at 25, accessible at: www.ictj.org/static/Africa/DRC/ICTJDavisHayner_DRC_DifficultPeace_pa2009.pdf.

488 See L. Davis, P. Hayner *supra*.

489 See P. Clark, N. Waddell 'Law, Politics and Pragmatism', *Courting Conflict? Justice, Peace and the ICC in Africa*, March 2008, at 40.

The ICC prosecutor's actions in Uganda, where arrest warrants only targeted the armed opposition, reinforced this impression, as did the arrest of Jean-Pierre Bemba, President Kabila's main political rival, for crimes allegedly committed in the Central African Republic. For these groups of observers the charges are too limited. In the Court's very first case, the charges against Thomas Lubanga focused on the use of child soldiers but made no mention of killings, sexual crimes, and other severe atrocities of which Lubanga is also widely suspected. Such limited criminal charge is considered to 'undermine the credibility of the ICC' as well as limiting victims' participation, as international human rights organizations argued in an open letter to the prosecutor in 2006.[490] Local human rights groups and women's organizations were especially critical of the failure to include sexual crimes in the charges against Lubanga, given the continued high occurrence of, and general impunity for such crimes, especially after later arrests involved much broader charges, including sexual crimes. Some NGOs strongly urge the prosecutor to broaden her investigations. Another critic is that the Court has done modest national outreach. The main consequence is the fact that the affected communities have many misconceptions about the Court's role and its powers. Although this reflects a lack of resources and insufficient in-country staff, the prosecutor said that the limited outreach was initially intentional to avoid jeopardizing the peace process and to protect the safety of witnesses. Local human rights advocates strongly criticized this approach and it appeared that the Court was planning a more proactive public education program in the future.[491] There are no doubts that these issues are all related to the necessity to improve the cooperation, assistance and support to the Court on the ground. The Court is in urgent need of securing its sites, the staff, the protection of witnesses, potential witnesses or victims identified or contacted in the course of the investigative activity, including their participation in the proceedings and relocation programs.

### 7.3.3. THE ALTERNATIVES TO THE ICC

The ICC's jurisdiction is limited not only in terms of time, as it only covers crimes committed after the entry into force of the Rome Statute on 1 July 2002, but also in terms of the number of individuals it may prosecute. The prosecution strategy of the ICC is to carry out targeted investigations and trials, and to prosecute those bearing the greatest responsibility. The ICC operates according to the principle of complementarity with the national justice system, taking over when the latter lacks

---

490 See HRW joint letter to the Chief Prosecutor of the International Criminal Court, July 31, 2006, accessible at: www.hrw.org.

491 See F. Petit, *Sensibilisation à la CPI en RDC: Sortir du Profil Bas*, ICTJ, March 2007, accessible at: www.ictj.org According to the Court's outreach report which addresses many of these concerns, see Public Information and Outreach Unit of the ICC, *Outreach Report 2009*, accessible at: www.icc-cpi.int.

the will or the capacity to judge perpetrators of the most serious crimes.[492] On this basis, it remains the responsibility of the Congolese courts to try perpetrators of serious violations of human rights and international humanitarian law. However, the present weakness of the Congolese justice system makes this difficult. As described in the sections above, judicial institutions, civil as well as military, face numerous challenges in their day-to-day operations. Moreover, the prosecution of international crimes requires extensive investigative capacities. There is also the need to strengthen current investigation capacities of the judicial police. The lack of witness protection programmes in the DRC is another obstacle to the investigation and prosecution of international crimes.[493]

### a) *The 'Mapping Project'*

Years of conflict, notably during the wars that took place in the country between 1995–1997 and 1998–2002, caused massive human rights violations and violations of international humanitarian law, many having been committed prior to the DRC's ratification of the Rome Statute. Potential solutions to put an end to impunity for these crimes will need to be examined. An important step in that process is the Justice Mapping Project. Originally a MONUC initiative, the project was established by the Office of the High Commissioner for Human Rights (OHCHR), in close collaboration with MONUC. The Justice Mapping Project covers the most serious violations of human rights and international humanitarian law committed in the DRC between March 1993 and June 2003 (until the implementation of the transitional government). The project is divided into three steps. It aims first at establishing an inventory of human rights violations committed between 1993 and 2003. This portion of the project does not involve forensics or any formal investigation as the project's team members use a 'reliable body of evidence' established by cross-referencing sources, reports and witness statements. In this way the Congolese justice system is examined to determine its capacity to deal with the human rights violations inventoried. On this point, the director of the project noted the strong need to reinforce the country's legal aid system. Finally, the project's report proposes options for transitional justice to deal with impunity and makes suggestions to deal with related issues such as memorial, vetting and compensation.

---

492 Article 17, Rome Statute. See the OTP-ICC public policies and strategies accessible at: www.icc-cpi.int.

493 See International Bar Association's Human Rights Institute (IBAHRI), the International Legal Assistance Consortium (ILAC), *Rebuilding Courts and Trust: An Assessment of the Needs of the Justice System in the Democratic Republic of Congo,* August 2009, OSISA and Swedish Ministry for Foreign Affairs, accessible at: www.ibanet.org/Article/Detail.aspx?ArticleUid=6c2be523-f512-48c1-b09c-fc9a8b1d0aab.

#### b) *The Truth and Reconciliation Commission*

It should be recalled that the DRC made an attempt at a truth and reconciliation commission. Created by the Sun City Accord of 16 December 2002, the commission was then established by law in 2004.[494] Faced since the beginning with issues related to its credibility and independence, the DRC's Truth and Reconciliation Commission was never successful and was dissolved in December 2006, without having heard a single case. However, the idea is still alive and the former head of the Truth and Reconciliation Commission presented a proposal to the Senate in 2008 for the establishment of a new commission. The issue of amnesty will need to be examined by a future transitional justice mechanism in the DRC. Amnesty appears to be still used as a method in peace negotiations, as illustrated by the recent amnesty law covering crimes committed from June 2003 to May 2009 in the regions of North and South Kivu.[495] This law does not apply to acts of 'genocide, war crimes and crimes against humanity'.

### 7.3.4. THE GENDER CRIMES

Rape and sexual violence are now internationally recognised as crimes against humanity, war crimes and genocide. The DRC, throughout its long running conflict, has witnessed some of the highest levels of sexual violence in the world.[496] Rape has been used as a weapon of war by all sides involved in the conflict, and an estimated 200,000 women and girls of all ages have been assaulted over the past 12 years.[497] While sexual violence is rampant and prevalent throughout the DRC, the most affected areas have been in north-eastern provinces (for example Ituri, North Kivu, South Kivu and Maniema).[498] The victims were very young in part

---

494 Loi No /04/018 du 30 Juillet 2004 portant sur l'organisation, attributions et fonctionnement de la Commission Vérité et Réconciliation (Law on the organisation of the Truth and Reconciliation Commission).

495 Loi No 09/003 du 7 mai 2009 portant amnistie pour faits de guerre et insurrectionnels commis dans les provinces du Nord-Kivu et du Sud-Kivu Law on amnesty for acts of war and insurrection committed in the eastern provinces of North and South Kivu).

496 UN doc. S/RES/1820 (2008) on Women and Peace and Security. In the resolution, passed on 19 June 2008, the Security Council noted that "women and girls are particularly targeted by the use of sexual violence, including as a tactic of war to humiliate, dominate, instill fear in, disperse and/or forcibly relocate civilian members of a community or ethnic group". The resolution demanded the "immediate and complete cessation by all parties to armed conflict of all acts of sexual violence against civilians".

497 According to the statistics compiled by the United Nations Children Fund (UNICEF) see UN News Service, 28 February 2009, available at: www.unhcr.org/refworld/docid/49aff7bc1e.html.

498 For an assessment of programmatic responses see, M. Pratt, L. Werchick, 'Sexual Terrorism: Rape as a Weapon of War in Eastern Democratic Republic of Congo. An assessment of programmatic responses to sexual violence in North Kivu, South Kivu, Maniema, and Orientale Provinces', (2004), accessible at: www.osisa.org/resources/docs/PDFs/Sexual_Terrorism.pdf.

due to the erroneous belief that raping a virgin girl is a remedy against HIV and AIDS.[499] Unfortunately, despite the adoption of laws against sexual violence in the country,[500] this crime is perpetrated at an alarmingly high rate, with many acts committed by those charged with protecting the general public (the FARDC and the PNC). The struggle of the domestic courts to apply the law properly does not show sufficient results, with most of the sexual violence cases remaining under investigation for years. Even if a perpetrator is tried and convicted, the sentence is rarely enforced. The law on sexual violence requires the courts to conclude a case within three months after the case is brought to the justice system, but this is hardly ever possible due to the fact that the justice sector is severely under-resourced and under-staffed.[501] The absence of an effective criminal justice delivery system has led to an increase in the number of out-of-court settlements based on traditional justice and often leading to forced marriages, to the detriment of the victim's rights and in violation of the various laws on sexual violence. The problem is two-fold. On the one hand, the major problem encountered by the victims, often leading to the perpetrators' impunity, is the difficulty to prove the crime in court, or even bring the matter to court. This is all the more difficult issue in addition to the absence of any witness protection programme. On the other hand, even if the victim can bring the matter to court and have the perpetrator(s) arrested and convicted, there is no certainty that reparation will be paid. This is because victims may not be able to afford to pay the legal fees required for judgment enforcement, or because the perpetrator will not have sufficient resources to pay. Also, due to very deficient security in most of the prisons, it is not uncommon that the perpetrators are able to escape and become once again a threat to victims and witnesses. The inability of the justice system to handle such crimes has had the adverse effect of creating a sentiment of impunity for witnesses and victims. Unfortunately, and as a direct result of the many crimes remaining unpunished and the general sense of impunity, rape and sexual violence in the DRC is increasing at an alarming rate and is now being committed by ordinary citizens, in addition to the armed and military groups. The international community has reacted to some extent on the brutality of sexual violence committed in DRC, particularly in the east of the country. However, the efforts to fight impunity need to be re-directed in the whole region. Next paragraph has the purpose to analyse the strategies of international responses on such sensitive issues.

---

499 See *Report of the Special Rapporteur on violence against women*, (2009), 14, at 16.

500 Loi No 06/018 modifiant et complétant le Décret du 30 janvier 1940 portant Code Pénal Congolais (Law amending the Congolese Penal Code).

501 Loi No 06/019 de 2006 sur les violences sexuelles (Law on sexual violence), Art 1, adding art 7*bis* to the Code de procédure pénale (Penal Procedure Code).

## 7.3.5. THE INTERNATIONAL ASSISTANCE

The MONUC Rule of Law Section was first set up in 2004 as a small unit to advice on a range of rule of law issues and has since expanded to support wider security sector reform, including civilian and military justice and reform of the penitentiary system. The Rule of Law Section has adopted a three-tiered approach to the support of the justice system, providing, first, immediate assistance to enable existing DRC capacity to be fully maximised. Second, the section supports DRC authorities in designing mid-term coordinated strategic plans to reform justice sub-sectors, such as legislation, military justice, prisons and courts. Third, the section supports short-term implementation of urgent elements of longer-term reform strategy, including building capacity to investigate and try cases involving international crimes. Closely attached to MONUC is the Office of the Senior Adviser and Coordinator on Sexual Violence for DRC. The Office was created in March 2008 as an answer to increasing international reaction against the extent and brutality of sexual violence in the DRC, particularly in the war-torn eastern part of the country. The Office has been set up with the support of UN Action Against Sexual Violence in Conflict, a conglomerate of 12 UN agencies and sections (including UN DPKO), and the UNDP Bureau for Crisis Prevention and Recovery (UNDP BCPR). On 18 March 2009, in consultation with UN agencies and MONUC sections, international NGOs, the Sexual Violence Task Force and the DRC's ministries of justice, defence, interior and gender, the Office launched a 'Comprehensive strategy on combating sexual violence in the DRC'.[502] This strategy consists of four pillars: i) fighting impunity; ii) prevention and protection; iii) security sector reform (reforming the Congolese army and police); and iv) coordinated medical, mental-health, legal and reintegration assistance to victims. The aim of this strategy is, according to the office, to provide a practical framework for action.

---

[502] UN. Doc. S/RES/1794 (2007). In response to this UNSC resolution MONUC with the support of the UN Action Against Sexual Violence in Conflict Network, would implement the Comprehensive Strategy on Combating Sexual Violence in the DRC. The Comprehensive Strategy is made up of 5 components each led by a specialist UN agency. An Operational Plan that put the strategy into action was then developed. It highlighted the fifth and final pillar dedicated to the collection and analysis of data on sexual violence. The enormity and importance of this task will not simply improve the understanding of the dynamics of this violence but offer insight into the most effective responses that may end it. Each of the five components is led by a UN agency or MONUC section: 1. Protection and prevention (UNHCR); 2. Ending impunity for perpetrators (Joint Human Rights Office – MONUC/OHCHR); 3. Security sector reform (MONUC, SSR); 4. Assistance for victims of sexual violence (UNICEF); 5. Data and mapping (UNFPA). The total appeal for the implementation of the Operational Plan in the next two years is US $56million. At national level, the Operational Plan and costing was endorsed by the government of the DRC in November 2009. The prioritization and implementation of the activities of the Comprehensive Strategy will be coordinated by UN agencies and their governmental counterparts for each of the five components. For a detailed overview see, *The Comprehensive Strategy on Combating Sexual Violence in DRC: Executive Summary*, Final Version, 18 March 2009, accessible at: http://monuc.unmissions.org/Default.aspx?tabid=4073.

There is a growing consensus in the UN system and beyond that the rule of law is a precondition for sustainable peace and development at both international and national level. It is also recognized that security and justice are essential stepping stones in achieving the rule of law. Neither can be left unattended in preventing conflict, nor in responding to or recovering from the same. At the international level, the achievement of peaceful relations will eventually be determined by the commitment to resolving conflict and disputes on the basis of the UN Charter. At the national level, conflict prevention and recovery, democratic governance, poverty reduction, gender equality and the Millennium Development Goals (MDGs) will depend on the capacity to prevent and manage conflict, while also advancing political, social and economic aspirations. According to the principles of global democratic governance the rule of law is both the vehicle and its manifestation. Its evolution however, depends from the political convergence on specific issues of capacity-building and international assistance.

As a programmatic development agency, the United Nations Development Program (UNDP) responds to requests by host-governments for capacity development support. Technical assistance to national efforts in the justice and security sector is provided by UNDP within its framework of Crisis Prevention and Recovery and Democratic Governance. In doing so, UNDP recognizes the centrality of national ownership and early foundations towards long-term investments. The Global Programme outlines UNDP's services to rule of law programming in conflict- and post-conflict situations within its Crisis Prevention and Recovery mandate. It is a living document and will continuously be reviewed and updated on the basis of best practices and lessons learned from the field. The following terms are usually referred to: 'the rule of law', 'access to justice', 'justice and security sector reform', and 'security and sector reform'. The UNDP is an active member and important founder of the *Comité Miste de Justice* (CMJ) and contributor to the Action Plan in the DRC. In 2008, UNDP launched a US$390 million governance programme with the DRC. The programme, which ran throughout 2012, consists of five components, one of which, the legal and security governance component, worked towards judicial reform, capacity-building in the security forces, efforts to combat corruption in public administration, and action to strengthen internal and external audit institutions. Within the framework of the Action Plan of the CMJ, UNDP supports the drafting of organic laws for the justice system, the upgrading of equipment and the training of judges. UNDP also supports the *Conseil Supérieur de la Magistrature* (CSM) and has contributed US$36,000 to its secretariat during the first three months of 2009. In early 2009, the UNDP Bureau for Crisis Prevention and Recovery (BCPR) decided to contribute an additional US$2 million to reform activities in the judicial system.[503]

[503] For an detailed overview see, UNDP, 'A Global UNDP Programme for Justice and Security 2008–2011', *Strengthening the Rule of Law in Conflict and Post-Conflict Situations*, (2008), accessible at: www.undp.org/cpr/documents/jssr/rule_of_law_final.pdf.

### 7.3.6. CONCLUSIONS

The DRC is a country where history, geography and recent political developments present huge challenges to establish the rule of law. A number of countries, the UN, the ICC, other international and regional organisations, including NGOs, are assisting the DRC in its task to build a judicial system.[504] As clarified by Davis, "the inability of the justice and penal systems to deliver justice exacerbates violations committed against the civilian population, worsens public security (especially of vulnerable groups) and strengthens impunity. To be successful, the reform of the police, judiciary and penal systems must necessarily be seen as interrelated and approached in a coordinated manner".[505]

It appears that most of the ongoing rule of law reforms in the country is either targeting the central institutions in Kinshasa, or has been developed in response to the atrocities and human suffering in the eastern part of the DRC. As a consequence, and despite the combined efforts by the DRC government and the international community, it seems that vast areas of the country are still largely untouched by any reform activities. Against this background the reports examined recommend projects of assistance with two different approaches: one which focuses on central institutions in Kinshasa, which may or may not yet have been targeted by the current reform activities; and one which targets two important regional centres, Kisangani and Lubumbashi. For Kisangani the reports propose a holistic approach with practical projects designed to support the current objectives of the Congolese Ministry of Justice and to fit in with the priorities identified in the Ministry of Justice's Roadmap matrix. In Lubumbashi, IBAHRI's reports propose a more target-driven project to support the already well established Lubumbashi bar association. The IBAHRI, with its particular expertise, is well positioned to implement activities in that regard, which could be extended to other bar associations. It is hoped that in the near future the benefits derived from these projects could provide a foundation for similar projects within

---

504 The main international actors involved in providing assistance in the security system in the DRC have been the UN (MONUC has been on the ground since 1999 and is now the largest peacekeeping operation in the world), World Bank, US, EU (and its Member States), Angola, South Africa and, increasingly, China. For an overview of the EU engagement in the country or test case in the field of coordination and coherence between the EU and Member State of the Security Sector Reforms programmes (SSR) see, L. Davis, 'European Engagement in Security System Reform in the DRC', *Justice-Sensitive Security System Reform in the DRC,* February 2009, International Centre for Transitional Justice, at 24, accessible: www.initiativeforpeacebuilding.eu/pdf/Justice_Sensitive_Security_System_reform_in_the_DRC.pdf For a more detailed discussion, see H. Hoebeke, S. Carette and K. Vlassenroot, *EU support to the Democratic Republic of Congo*, Centre d'Analyse Stratégique, (2007), accessible at: www.egmontinstitute.be/papers/07/afr/EU_support_to_the_DRC.pdf.

505 L. Davis, 'Transitional Justice and Security System Reform', *Justice-Sensitive Security System Reform in the DRC,* February 2009, International Centre for Transitional Justice, at 24, accessible: www.initiativeforpeacebuilding.eu/pdf/Justice_Sensitive_Security_System_reform_in_the_DRC.pdf.

other parts of the country. Also, and particularly because of the way violence and injustice are being directed towards women, a theme that infiltrates most of the following recommendations refers to gender issues. This includes the protection of women's rights, in law and practice, and the promotion of women's participation at all levels of the judiciary, bar, government and civil society. All training programmes should include women and all access-to-justice programmes should target women.[506]

## 7.4. THE ABSENCE OF COORDINATION, COHERENCE AND LAW ENFORCEMENT

This chapter argued that multidimensional operations fostering peace, justice and security in the DRC lack of coherence and preparedness including also strategies of cooperation between complementary mandates. The struggle of such international responses to deliver results on the ground between conflict and post-conflict is enormous. The problem in the DRC is that international mandates active on the ground are disconnected between them. With regard to the UN mission the political nature of the MONUC/MONUSCO mandate including its operational purpose is broad and shows unfeasible expectations. The UN mandate needs a re-configuration which should think about the actors struggling *in situ* which are complementary mandates in purpose and nature. Moreover, the UN mission can provide *a)* appropriate diplomatic dialogue *vis-à-vis* the DRC government engaging police enforcement actions against criminals; *b)* assisting on the reform of the army, police and justice domestic systems; *c)* avoiding that the military demobilization does not preclude impunity of international crimes; and *d)* securing civilians with relocation and rehabilitation programs.

For the international responses involved in the protection of civilians, on the preservation of the rule of law, justice and human rights, including the maintenance of stability and conflict management characterized by 'zero tolerance' in peace enforcement, it is important to reach preparedness and flexibility of re-configurations and re-conceptualizations serving complementary mandates on the ground with appropriate arrangement and agreements of cooperation. Challenges exist at different levels for the UN mission in the DRC: at conceptual and structural levels and ultimately also on coherence and

---

506 For the research findings, conclusions and legal recommendations delivered by the International Bar Association's Human Rights Institute (IBAHRI), the International Legal Assistance Consortium (ILAC), see *Rebuilding Courts and Trust: An Assessment of the Needs of the Justice System in the Democratic Republic of Congo*, August 2009, research supported by the Open Society Initiative for Southern Africa (OSISA) and the Swedish Ministry for Foreign Affairs, at 45, accessible at: www.ibanet.org/Article/Detail.aspx?ArticleUid=6c2be523-f512-48c1-b09c-fc9a8b1d0aab.

coordination characterizing such mandates. The conceptual level relates to *a)* the nature, purpose or scope and preparedness of the mandate's deployments; *b)* the organizational structure defining the channels of communications, the level of responsibility, accountability and chain of command including the decision making on each operation; *c)* the coherence and coordination refers to the ability to assist complementary actors, showing flexibility and preparedness of operational reconfigurations in order to deliver visible results.

The Court on its side needs to spread investigations and prosecutions, giving the priority to participation and reparation of victims including arrangements and agreements on relocation of witnesses. The DRC State must take full responsibility of its obligations falling under the Rome Statute initiating genuine criminal proceedings on the ground. The main findings of this study demonstrate that international criminal justice is not an isolated process. It has to take place at different levels simultaneously and in tandem with other global actors, as an important part of the peace-building process. Despite the critics, the limits and the few resources at disposition, international criminal justice remains a priority. The cause of some sensitive problems is found in the difficulties on consensus and lack of flexibility to reconfigure the UN mandate on the ground, preparing its mission to serve the range of actors involved *in situ*, shifting from a 'comprehensive' unfeasible mandate to a narrowly focused one, much less costly but surely more efficient.

Political and diplomatic expertise pressuring the DRC government on its obligations is necessary. Criminals and warlords need to be released to justice with judicial proceedings on the ground. At domestic level, the effectiveness of security structures can be measured by three cornerstones: *a)* the ability to protect the national territory against aggression and internal threats, *b)* the adherence to the rule of law, and *c)* the ability of security services to protect and respect citizens' rights (army, police and justice). The domestic justice system relates to these clusters. As clarified by eminent experts involved in the UN engagement in the DRC, security forces and its governance institutions are seriously deficient in all these aspects in the country. Such malfunctioning institutions pose a security threat themselves on the communities due to corruption and bad governance.

This chapter argued that international responses are an essential cornerstone to influence the domestic governance institutions and the future stability of the DRC. Army, police and justice are the most vulnerable to corruption and graft and have been neglected aspects by the UN and by the involvement of donors. According to the UN experts directly involved on these issues the "*problematique* consists of the entangled history of a factionalised army, with major access to and control of vast natural resources, the lack of division of powers between police and army, and the political control exerted over the judiciary. Regulatory bodies such as courts, parliament, and anti-corruption and auditing institutions remain ineffective and are themselves prone to corruption".[507]

Another problem is the lack of balance between the bilateral cooperation with the DRC government and the multilateral cooperation standards of global mandates involved on the ground. This chapter argued that due to the situation in the country the centrality of cooperation should raise the standards of multilateral cooperation, avoiding unilateral and opportunistic consensus with the leadership of the country. After all, the involvement of global mandates is to centralize the interests of individuals more than the interests of the government. These are enduring issues with which political mediation efforts will have to contend raising the international standards of cooperation between complementary mandates deployed on the ground, in order to challenge criminal, aggressive and violent regimes victimizing entire communities. After all, these communities are supposed to receive development and humanitarian aid but they only experience war and death without a well-functioning domestic accountability system.

## 7.5. THE NECESSITY OF STRENGTHENING PARTNERSHIPS ON THE GROUND

At provisional level and pursuant to Article 2 of the Rome Statute, on 4 October 2004 the Secretary General of the United Nations and the President of the International Criminal Court signed an agreement that provides for the structure of the relationship between these institutions. The relationship-building between the organizations is still at its initial stage. In order to deliver better results on the ground in conflict and post-conflict situations under investigation or prosecution, high level of political and diplomatic engagement is required. In order to preserve the rule of law, human rights and justice, the implementation of partnerships between the actors engaged to bring stability in failed States, is an important requirement of global governance. The Court needs to rely on the multidimensional operations of the UN. Such pragmatic support would translate the political determination expressed in the Preamble of the Rome Statute recognizing the link between peace and justice and that "grave crimes threaten the peace, security, and well-being of the world". Cooperation is fundamental in order to contribute to the prevention of these crimes, and put an end to impunity for the perpetrators of such crimes. As stated by the UN Secretary General in his remarks to the Sixth Assembly of States Parties to the Rome Statute of the International Criminal Court, "there are no easy answers to this morally and

[507] See N. Dahrendorf, 'MONUC and the Relevance of Coherent Mandates: The Case of the DRC', in H. Hänggi, V. Scherrer (eds.), *Security Sector Reform and UN Integrated Missions*, (2008), Chapter 3, Introduction, at 67.

legally charged balancing act. However, the overarching principle is clear: there can be no sustainable peace without justice. Peace and justice, accountability and reconciliation are not mutually exclusive. To the contrary, they go hand in hand".

In the absence of a self sufficient domestic system of governance in the DRC, 'narrowly focused' mandates have to work together, complementing each other in order to challenge the criminal regime of impunity. The role of the Court is quite limited, and in most scenarios primary activities will remain with States, international organizations and civil society. The issue of cooperation is at the core of the Rome Statute. An important cluster of cooperation as recognized by the Assembly of States Parties to the Rome Statute is the one with the UN system. The UN can provide documents and information, it can supply logistical and other technical support to Court field operations, and it can even accommodate the Court in its security arrangements. The implementation of such cluster of cooperation is urging if we consider the multidimensional operations taking place in a 'failed' State such as in the DRC. The legal obligations of the States Parties, including the important support from international, regional organizations, States non-Parties and other stakeholders, are also important clusters of cooperation interrelated between them, and on which the ICC needs to rely.

The role and limitations of the UN in the DRC with regard to the security sector reform (army, police and judiciary) have to be clearly defined as well as the reconfiguration of the comprehensive range of tasks received by MONUC/ MONUSCO. In order to strengthen partnerships on the ground between complementary mandates: reconfiguration, cooperation standards, sharing knowledge, expertise and lessons learned are all areas in need of implementation. The general recommendations, as the explicit outcome of this case study, are addressed to the UN Security Council, General Assembly, the Secretary General, including the Assembly of the States Parties of the Rome Statute. The MONUC (MONUSCO) mandate, to protect civilians, monitoring human rights abuses and enforcing arms embargo, needs to be re-defined. Political and diplomatic pressure on the DRC government to fulfil its obligation is mandatory. The important feature of enforcing the judicial decisions of the ICC, including providing support for the protection and relocation of victims and witnesses would be a serious engagement strengthening partnerships on the ground.

The general provisions in the memorandum of understanding (MoU) concerning cooperation between the UN mission in the field and the Court need to be revisited. Particularly its *purpose*: Article 1 (MoU) should set out modalities of cooperation not only on investigations but also on prosecutions and enforcement of arrest warrants, due to the State not performing its duties; *cooperation*: Article 2 (MoU) should clarify in detail the modalities of cooperation and law enforcement. Furthermore at structural level, the UN Rule of Law section, which is supporting short-term implementation of urgent elements of longer-term strategy of reforms, including building capacity to investigate and try cases involving international crimes, may use the ICC expertise including cooperation with the Office of the Senior Adviser and Coordinator on Sexual Violence for the DRC.[508] Such liaisons between the UN mission deployed on the ground and the ICC would facilitate the flow of information and legal assistance in order to speed up the judicial proceedings challenging the criminal regime in the country. At operational level, specific arrangements of law enforcement cooperation after prosecutions of war criminals need to be put in place. Such arrangements would complement the demobilization activity of combatants in lower ranks which must be prosecuted by the local authorities.

The Assembly of the States Parties to the Rome Statute should facilitate legal assistance on the implementation of legislation and criminal law in the DRC, in line with other UN channels and donors involved in the security sector reform (army, police, and justice). To make the Rome Statute system work effectively, the interaction with an important partner such as the UN is fundamental. In order to accomplish visible results, States, international organizations, civil society and other actors have to cooperate and interact with unity of intents, implementing a system of international justice based on democratic governance. This chapter offered an overview of the challenges in the framework of cooperation in a failed State. It proposed an urgent implementation of the relationship of complementing mandates involved in peace-making, peace-keeping, peace-building, security sectors reforms, law enforcement, criminal and restorative justice, including the challenges to preserve further the rule of law and human rights as important prerequisites of democratic governance.[509] In other words, it offered an overview of the actions required by the political premises enforcing global governance institutions of complementary character.

---

508 The Office was created in March 2008 as an answer to increasing international reaction against the extent and brutality of sexual violence in the DRC, particularly in the war-torn eastern part of the country. On 18 March 2009, in consultation with UN agencies and MONUC sections, international NGOs, the Sexual Violence Task Force and the DRC's ministries of justice, defence, interior and gender, the Office launched a 'Comprehensive strategy on combating sexual violence in the DRC' consisting of four pillars: i) fighting impunity; ii) prevention and protection; iii) security sector reform (reforming the Congolese army and police); and iv) coordinated medical, mental-health, legal and reintegration assistance to victims. The aim of this strategy is to provide a practical framework for action.

509 For the UNDP programmatic approaches see, 'Role of UNDP in Crisis and Post-Conflict Situations', DP/2001/4 of 27 November 2000. UNDP Strategic Plan 2008–2011/DP/2007/43, 16 July 2007, paragraphs 84 and 102. See also the UNDP global programme on 'Strengthening the Rule of Law in Conflict and Post-Conflict Situations 2008–2011. A Global UNDP Programme for Justice and Security', accessible at: www.undp.org/cpr/documents/Rule_of_Law_Global_Programme.pdf.

The next chapter offers the concluding assessment and provides the answers to the research questions addressed in this work. The examination of the case studies selected point out many challenges which will surely need further investigation. The governance of complementary global regimes depends from both the States and the international community, including the strategies of interactions between themselves. The political convergence about the systemic changes required is still to be found. We have seen that the governance of justice and its impact on sustainable peace in conflict and post-conflict situations cannot be assessed on its own. It depends from several factors. Besides, there are difficulties to uphold the idea of an international architecture of governance based on human security and fostering peace and justice in conflict and post-conflict situations. In principle, an understanding of the past is fundamental to determine the way forward in the global fight against war and crime.[510] The current devastating effects on civilians in conflict and post-conflict situations require, without any doubt, the attention of decision-makers. First of all, they have to find political convergence at domestic, regional and international dimensions. The actions required are the reforms in both systems of the United Nations and the Rome Statute in accordance with their complementary nature. In this way the results of their actions would be maximized and their role amplified.

[510] J. Muravchik, *The Future of the United Nations: Understanding the Past to Chart a Way Forward*, 2005.

# 8. CONCLUDING ASSESSMENT

## The governance architecture dealing with individuals in situations of war and crime

> "If you want to understand the causes that existed in the past, look at the results as they are manifested in the present and if you want to understand what results will be manifested in the future, look at the causes that exist in the present."
> The Writings of Nichiren Daishonin, *The Opening of the Eyes*, 1272, Part I, p. 279

### PRELIMINARY REMARKS

The meaning of complementary global regimes fostering peace, justice and security depends on the ways they are governed in accordance with humanitarian principles. The international governance institutions deriving from such regimes have to meet the highest standards of accountability, effectiveness and quality management, including cooperation and support between them in order to protect civilians. The presence of the International Criminal Court and the United Nations involved in the same situations is not characterized by an integrated model of governance. The practice of saving human lives and alleviating the sufferings of civilians in conflict situations requires political convergence of expectations of decision-makers. This study debates the global humanitarian policy to intervene in conflict situations and the preparedness of international governance institutions dealing with mass atrocity crimes and aggression, including their public authority, delimitation of competence and responsibility. It contributes to the contemporary visions for the preservation of the international legal and political order, including the capacity-building of the international community governing intra- and inter-state conflicts on the ground, much more than as distant observers, or with militarized international responses deriving from the ideology of hazardous solutions. The dilemma of human security requires further policy efforts and a political *road map* to promote the extention of international complementarity between both legal and political frameworks of governance of the international community. The policy formulation of interaction strategies between multilateral premises of universal character dealing with international threats and crimes deserves debate for several reasons. Their complementary character depends on the political forces involved in the preservation of law and order and is considered absolutely necessary.

In this study the search of a definition of complementary global regimes is advocated *a)* for further progress of a universal jurisdiction of the world community; *b)* for the evolution of international governance institutions centralizing fundamental individual rights; and *c)* for systemic changes in the prevention, response and reconstruction of situations of war and crime. The complementary nature of global regimes needs further political responsibilities and legal accountabilities if the national, regional and international realities have to benefit from such models of governance, including their resources and expertise. After all, the fight against the impunity of international crimes requires the ability to offer applicable models of domestic governance for the protection of civilians in domestic legislations and national consitutions. In this study the preservation of basic individual rights upholds the requirement to empower the links between sustainable peace, justice and human security necessary to the concept of *global justice* and its debates. Such debate challenges the assumption of established legal theory in which the normative framework of criminal justice can be abstracted from actual power relations. It offers elements of a new doctrine between power and the rule of law.[511] The open question is whether the challenges between statehood, sovereignty and international governance are seriously managed throughout complementary global regimes and by the governance structures deriving from them. The progress of a global society dealing with legal and political frameworks preserving human security in the current transition of the world order requires constant verification. Even with the advent of the Rome Statute system the dilemma of human security in conflict and post-conflict situations still remains. The preservation of the rule of law as a principle of governance in multilevel jurisdictions; the constellation of multilateral institutions of complementary character; the collective responsibility to intervene in humanitarian emergencies; the global solidarity and the mutual accountability indicate serious interaction gaps fostering peace, justice and security with a comprehensive model of governance. The political convergence and a *road map* solving the dilemma between capacity-building or only symbolic politics of law enforcement is required in the international responses in both intra- and inter-state civil wars. The *quo vadis* of civilian protection measures requires, without any doubt, a political *road map* compatible with the current times of violent political transitions characterized by criminal acts against civilians, disintegration of nation-states and destabilation of international peace and security.

[511] See H. Köchler, *Global Justice or Global Revenge? International Criminal Justice at the Crossroads*, 2003.

## 8.1. THE LONG WAY AHEAD OF COMPLEMENTARY GLOBAL REGIMES

### SECTION OUTLINE

In this study the emerging regime of international criminal justice is interpetred as complementing the role of other universal actors in the constellation of treaty-based bodies and institutions fostering human security, but most importantly by the challenges occurred in the democratization of the international society, in the governance of international threats and crimes and in the preservation of human rights standards. Its presence in the international legal order requires deeper responsibilities and systemic changes of international governance institutions of complementary character. Today the delimitation of competence between international humanitarian interventions in conflict and post-conflict situations and State sovereignty indicates that 'the States have a responsibility to protect their own citizens from avoidable humanitarian catastrophe, but when the States are unwilling or unable to do so, that responsibility must be borne by the broader intervention of the international community and its global governance institutions'.[512] Following the 'humanitarian' collective intervention performed in Darfur and Libya and the controversial political positions about Syria, the argument is that the responsibility to protect civilians operates in a contested doctrinal framework. Some observers would see such norm as a 'progress', while others as an 'empty promise' or only as a 'license for humanitarian intervention' or 'inaction'.[513] Another view is that the responsibility to protect norm addresses the international community's failure to prevent mass atrocity crimes. This responsibility can be interpreted as a new principle of international collective security not being legally defined.[514] It introduces the concept of shared responsibility and compliance with international law which theorists need to address at the present and in the years to come.[515]

The multidisciplinary topics proposed in this study including the debates found in the literature require the attention of relevant decision-makers on important issues. The main political challenges for the Assembly of the States Parties to the

---

512 See UN doc. A/RES/60/1, 2005 World Summit Outcome, para. 138–139.

513 G. Evans, 'Delivering on the Responsibility to Protect: Four Misunderstandings, Three Challenges and How to Overcome Them', Address to SEF Symposium 2007, *The Responsibility to Protect: Progress, Empty Promise or a License for Humanitarian Intervention*, accessible at: www.crisisgroup.org.

514 The responsibility to protect norm (R2P or RtoP in the UN circles) did not receive binding character. For an overview of the strategic and tactical choices to develop and to accept the R2P norm see, E. C. Luck, 'Building a Norm: The Responsibility to Protect Experience', in R. I. Rotberg (ed.), *Mass Atrocity Crimes. Preventing Future Outrages*, 2010, at 108.

515 See for an overview G. W. Downs, A. Trento, 'The Compliance Gap: Some Conceptual Issues', in E. C. Luck and M. W. Doyle (eds.), *International Law and Organization: Closing the Compliance Gap*, 2004, at 19.

Rome Statute and its institutions; the implementation of the Rome Statute and cooperation with the United Nations; the role of the Rome Statute institutions in international governance systems; and the promotion of the universality of the Rome Statute are the main issues deserving further debate. The global efforts to protect human rights and to promote the rule of law, to maintain and restore international peace and security, as well as to prevent and punish serious international crimes are common objectives for the Rome Statute institutions and the United Nations. The recognition that international criminal justice is an integral element of conflict resolution would in concrete mean that it should receive support on the ground to be more effective. After all, within the cycle of maintenance and restoration of peace and security, justice is an important component upholding the doctrine of human security, but how is such 'cosmopolitan' idea dealt with in the practice? Moreover, is there a new impulse, moral, legal, political, based on the human security doctrine for the progress of the constitution of the world community? Are multilateral treaties linked to a *road map* of governance considering the controversial reality in world politics, the impasse in the democratization of global institutions and the collapse of governance systems at domestic, regional and international levels? According to the principles of the rule of law, multilateralism, collective responsibility, global solidarity and mutual accountability a systemic change in the governance of international humanitarian escalations in conflict and post-conflict societies is required. The governance of justice punishing the perpetrators of serious crimes is still waiting for implementation. Such governance does not include any law enforcement engagements and hopefully a strategy for victim rights will arise soon integrating the rehabilitation of communities victimized by war and crime to development programs, reconstruction and domestic capacity-building.

### 8.1.1. THE LAST RESORT OPTION OF JUSTICE

Since the end of the cold war the threats to international peace and security include both inter-state and intra-state conflicts, including the commission of international crimes deriving from such conflicts. The legal and political developments to govern globally international threats and crimes resumed in forcible and non-forcible actions by the Security Council in several situations. Unfortunately, in the majority of the international humanitarian escalations, the causes and the effects of war and crime have not been diminished in sustainable ways. The engagement of the international community to formulate a system of governance protecting civilians in situations of war and crime is an on-going process. However, the severe violations of international humanitarian law have been treated as serious threats to international peace and security and would require a reliable structure of governance. The 'test' of the Security Council using subsidiary tools without fully supporting them does not bring any result. The notion that international criminal justice is a tool of the Security Council and a *last resort* instrument in the policy framework of the 'responsibility to protect', rather than the paradigm of *retributive* and *reparative* justice deserve further discussions. This study attempted to verify what is missing in the construction of a global architecture of governance fostering peace, justice and security which requires advocacy and political consensus.

First of all, a couple of concluding remarks deserve to be made about the international dimensions of internal conflicts and the strategic trends in the resolutions of the Security Council applied during intra-state civil wars. In the last decade the challenging resoluteness of the Security Council demonstrated that even in purely internal armed conflicts, "the deliberate targeting of civilian populations or other protected persons and the committing of systematic, flagrant and widespread violations of international humanitarian and human rights law in situations of armed conflict may constitute a threat to international peace and security".[516] This trend has been controversial in the situation in Darfur (Sudan) referred to the Court. The rise, fall, and stabilization, including the selectivity of the resolutions of the Security Council dealing with specific civil wars over the past twenty years, can be explained with the following considerations, respectively: *a)* the trends in conflict patterns in civil wars, *b)* the humanitarian violations of laws internationally recognized and *c)* the considerations whether mass atroctities would spread at larger scale. Moreover, when addressing a larger portion of internal civil wars, the Security Council engaged in the civil war in Uganda under the agenda item entitled *'The situation in the Great Lakes Region'* which also addressed the internal wars in the Sudan, Burundi, in the DRC, and Rwanda.[517] Unfortunately, the fact that the Court was involved in the same region since the advent of the Rome Statute system in accordance with the positive complementarity principle did not mean any support from the Security Council. Furthermore its working methods with the Court are inconsistent since the configuration of its mandates on the same grounds.[518]

An accurate examination of the use of Chapter VII of the UN Charter after the cold war indicates an increased number of resolutions of the Security Council falling under its security provisions. The referral of the situation in Darfur (Sudan)

516 UN doc. S/RES/1296, (April 19, 2000).

517 UN doc. S/RES/1653, (January 27, 2006).

518 For an overview of the current debate on the working methods of the UNSC, on the cooperation and follow-up to UNSC referrals to the Court, including the search of mechanisms to ensure timely and coordinated support to the Court, see ICC-OTP-20141024-PR1055, *Justice plays a "crucial role" in maintaining international peace and security: ICC Prosecutor briefs the United Nations Security Council,* 24 October 2014. The ICC Prosecutor Statement to the United Nations Security Council on the Subject of "Working Methods of the Security Council", 23 October 2014, is accessible at: www.icc-cpi.int/en_menus/icc/press%20and%20media/press%20releases/Pages/pr1055.aspx.

and in Libya to the Court corresponds to such nature of the Security Council's resolutions addressing internal civil wars spreading at local, regional and international levels. One may expect that such an activity would have been rapidly aligned to the quest of justice in these countries, but this was not the case. Besides, the political strategy of mandate's configuration of the Security Council was constantly oriented to opt out for hybrid solutions of peace enforcement in intra-state conflicts. In the DRC and in the Sudan for instance, the political settlements of the Security Council would pressure (regional) authorities such as the AU to take over with military operations on the ground. Such security shifts carried out devastating consequences on civilians and on the humanitarian situation as a whole due to the gaps of resources. On top of that, the criminal offenders would rely on the regime of impunity in these countries despite international judicial proceedings initiated by the Court. The practice applied through the Security Council indicates that mass atrocity crimes have been left in the limbo of impunity in several African situations, including the devastating consequences affecting civilians in such violent conflict zones. The risk is that such trend would persist even with the presence of the Court. The interrelation between the lack of support from the Security Council to the Court and its mandate configurations have been discussed during the case studies selected in this work. The conclusion is that the arrangements and agreements of *last resort* on the ground between them are not self-sufficient. They do not strengthen the engagements on the ground for the sake of civilians. Therefore, the mandate configurations should promote that peace and justice would work in parallel for the sake of individuals, giving a stronger deterrent signal of criminal activities in these countries, while pressuring for security sector reforms and judicial proceedings *in situ*.

### 8.1.2. THE CONFIGURATIONS OF INTERNATIONAL MANDATES

The case studies selected demonstrate the necessity of an integrated model of governance of peace, justice and security for the sake of civilians in times of war and crime. At this moment in time the Court struggles to receive a better place in the arrays of international peace and security maintenance. The global efforts to maximize the results on the ground have to be fulfilled applying an integrated approach of governance which is absolutely not the case. The case studies offered an insight of the Security Council involvement in internal civil wars and mass atrocities such as in the DRC with the presence of the Court in the country, including the 'test' of referral activity to the Court from the Security Council in the Sudan and Libya, and the failure of consensus building with regard to the dangerous situation in Syria, and the violence spreading at regional level in the whole Middle East. The quantitative research findings of relevant analysts consulted in this study explicitly demonstrate that a capacity-building and a model of international assistance applicable into intra-state civil wars 'did not develop evenly over time'.[519] The same assumption is valid in the case of inter-state conflicts and the crime of aggression. Such accountability system is still in transition in global politics. There is not yet any agreement about its governance between the legal frameworks dealing with State responsibility and the individual accountabilities.[520] The involvement of international complementary tools fostering peace and justice in inter-state conflicts will be the next 'test' of global governance. However, it remains to be seen how it will work between the responsibility of nation-states and the individual accountabilities of criminal perpetrators.

In order to complete this assessment some final observations about the mandate configurations of the Security Council in African civil wars are required. In accordance with the accurate data available on the trends in how the Security Council has engaged in civil wars, some conclusions are possible about the variations in *where* and *when* the Security Council chose to engage, including the gradual evolution of its response strategies in such conflicts. The combination of political and security settlements with the parties involved in the conflicts and the peace enforcement deriving from them surely influenced the responses of the Security Council. These responses were visible in its resolutions and in the UN legislative history since the end of the cold war. The analysis performed of the activity of the Security Council indicates that its demands to civil war parties were increasingly adopted in the context of multidimensional peace operations (deployment of peacekeeping, targeted sanctions, police and military law-enforcement operations, while providing access to humanitarian assistance).[521] These capacities and competences have not been put at disposition of international justice. It also needs to be noted that some of the factors characterizing the conflict management of the Security Council, such as: *a)* the political and strategic interests characterizing its engagements; *b)* the selectivity of its peace enforcement; *c)* the delay of sanctions about the exploitation of natural resources and embargos and *d)* the longstanding trend of exonerating criminal behaviors in the majority of the situations for the sake of managing conflicts and war parties.[522]

---

519 For a quantitative analysis of the patterns of the Security Council engagement in civil wars and the understanding of compliance of its resolutions in (intra-state) armed conflicts see J. Cockayne, C. Mikulaschek, C. Perry, *The United Nations Security Council and Civil War: First Insights from a New Dataset*, 2010.

520 See F. Rosenfeld, "Individual Civil Responsibility for the Crime of Aggression", *Journal of International Criminal Justice*, Oxford Journals Law, 2012, Volume 10, Issue 1, 249–265. See also M. Vesterdahl, "Re-defining the Crime of Aggression: The Evolution of an Outdated Ideal to Include Non-State Actors", 2010, available at: http://works.bepress.com/matthew_vesterdahl/1.

521 See M. Malitza, "The Improvement of Effectiveness of UN Peacekeeping Operations", in UNITAR, *The UN and the Maintenance of International Peace and Security*, 1987, at 246.

522 See J. Cockayne et al, *supra*.

The configurations of its security mandates on the ground are still disconnected from the activities of complementary mechanisms such as international investigations, prosecution and the management of protection duties of civilians. The analysis of the cases dealt with in this study (DRC, Sudan), were limited to the peace operations characterized by the multidimensional component of the Security Council operations and the lacuna thereof found in its mandates' configuration in situations of genocide, crimes of war and crimes against humanity. The configuration of the respective mandates deployed in the field operations indicates that the Security Council increasingly addressed the political aspects of post-conflict peace-building without succeeding in the majority of the situations in Africa. Another problem also derives from the fact that shortly after its security settlements would be in place, they became soon volatile in the majority of the situations, with conflict and violence recurring again, and requiring further engagements often shifted to domestic violent and criminal regimes. This is the case in the DRC, where the attacks of the M23 rebel group against civilians and also against the UN peacekeeping mission pose still serious threats. The consequences are also well known in the crises in Rwanda, Somalia, Angola, Sierra Leone, Uganda, Burundi, Mali, Kenya, Central African Republic and Sudan and at regional level in the main African Great Lakes Region.

In general, when the Security Council engaged in civil wars it did not merely seek to end an armed conflict, but rather it encouraged civil-war parties to reach and implement political and governance arrangements that could sustain peace and prevent conflicts deteriorate again. One of the tasks frequently performed during peace operations was to monitor compliance between civil-war parties, which was already in place between the belligerents, with security demands trying to destabilize conflict and violence.[523] The UN executive organ should absolutely be careful and avoid negotiating peace agreements with war criminals. The configuration of its mandates in the field operations should integrate justice and support the activity of the Court in accordance with its findings. Unfortunately, in both case studies selected this was not the case.

### 8.1.3. THE COURT'S SUPPORT TO MAXIMIZE THE RESULTS

The evident political compromise characterizing the Rome Statute system limits in some ways the use of international justice in the arrays of peace and security. This study offered an overview of both limits and opportunities. The States Parties themselves recognized the complementarity character of the Rome Statute system to the UN in the quest of sustainable peace in conflict and post-

523 See J. Cockayne et al, *supra*.

conflict situations. It is recommended that the Security Council would support the Court's investigations and prosecutions, including programs of relocation of witnesses and victims combined with the mobilization and de-militarization of child soldiers and rehabilitation of ex-combatants. The configuration of the Security Council's mandates in the field operations where the Court is involved need to provide support and assistance to the Court, especially in the Sudan, Libya, Uganda and DRC and in other current and future situations. The ideal would be to provide the configuration of the Security Council's mandates under the flag of the 'responsibility to protect' with the demands of the Court to protect, demobilize, relocate and rehabilitate victims and witnesses, including law enforcement actions on the ground following the judicial outcomes of the Court. The ideal would be that the concept of 'responsible' sovereignty required by the nation-states protecting their citizens cannot be separated by the responsibilities of international governance institutions implementing political configurations between their mandates when intervening in domestic criminal regimes. The Court needs support before, during, and after the humanitarian escalations and referral activity coming from the Security Council would take place. There is, however, a long way to go.

We have seen that the 'responsibility to protect' (RtoP or R2P) is a norm or set of principles based on the idea that State sovereignty is not a privilege but a responsibility of the nation-states. Furthermore, in the international legal order the RtoP is a global policy directive, it is not a law. The RtoP provides a framework towards political engagements using tools that already exist to prevent mass atrocities, like mediation, early warning mechanisms, economic sanctioning, and Chapter VI powers. Civil society organizations, States, regional organizations, and international governance institutions have a role to play in the operationalization of the RtoP. The authority to employ the *last resort* options and intervene with military operations rests solely with the UN Security Council (Chapter VII) and the General Assembly. Full implementation of the RtoP is hindered by the perception that it is being used by western countries to serve their interests when justifying violations of sovereignty of other countries in developing regions. The same political standpoints are visible in the groundless critics addressed to the Court of targeting exclusively African countries. Besides, the UN easily underscored that the best way to discourage States or groups of States from misusing the responsibility to protect for inappropriate purposes would be to develop fully the UN strategy, standards, processes, tools and practices. The overview of the UN three pillar strategy implementing the RtoP, respectively, Pillar I: the Protection Responsibilities of the States; Pillar II: the International Assistance and Capacity Building; Pillar Three: Timely and Decisive Response, demonstrates that the Court is only seen as an effort of dissuasion and deterrence which role in the UN report is limited to the protection responsibilities of the State to become part of it, instead of emphasizing also global governance issues and interaction strategies in the second and third pillars: international assistance and capacity building, including timely and decisive response.[524] Therefore, it will be relevant to see in this regard the future developments in the political positions of the African Union (AU), Arab League and UN political institutions about the Rome Statute system. It is too soon to speculate whether the idealistic vision of merging civilian protection duties between complementary global regimes would find its place in the policy formulation at global level, after the first rejections of such governance approach by the permanent members of the Security Council and by the AU. These issues deserve further attention. The configuration of mandates on the ground considering the presence and the activities of the Court would be the most appropriate and cannot wait any longer. Another problem of different nature refers to the political impasse to extend the jurisdiction of the Court with a range of other crimes.

Although the concept of sovereignty, statehood and international governance are currently in the work-in-progress, the political convergence and a *road map* dealing with the responsibilities towards civilians in extreme situations of war and crime are absolutely required. Such a *road map* should be visible *a)* in the interaction strategies between global regimes of complementary character and their political institutions, *b)* in the progress of their further empowerment, and *c)* in the decision-making enforcing them. The politics of international criminal justice will have to find solutions on these matters. Hopefully, the permanent members of the Security Council such as the US, Russia and China will join the Rome Statute system soon. Their role as distant observers undermines multilateral systems for the sake of fundamental individual rights. It still remains to be seen how far they will take over their global responsibilities towards individuals in times of war and crime. The place of international criminal justice and accountability in the arrays of peace and security maintenance raises many concerns. In order to offer sustainable peace in conflict and post-conflict situations, the challenges and opportunities require constructive debate in the Assembly of the States Parties of the ICC, in the UN General Assembly, in the regional political realities and in national parliaments and constitutions.

[524] See the Report of the UN Secretary-General, *Implementing the responsibility to protect*, 12 January 2009, UN doc. A/63/677.

## 8.2. AN INTEGRATED APPROACH OF GOVERNANCE

### SECTION OUTLINE

It can be concluded that there is still a long way ahead for an integrated approach of governance applicable on case-by-case basis in situations of mass atrocity crimes. The role of complementary global regimes to prevent mass atrocity crimes through timely intervention requires implementation. The peace operations should support law enforcement and civilian protection which should serve the quest of justice and accountability. The capacity-building offering reliable and sustainable models of governance in domestic and regional realities affected by war and crime require further efforts. The determination to fight against the impunity of international crimes requires without any doubt systemic changes. It is suggested to establish a joint vision of governance with early warnings. The international governance institutions of complementary character have to optimize their relationship and partnership jointly at global level and in the field operations. Solutions are expected *inter alia* on the protection of victims and witnesses of serious crimes by way of: *a)* developing appropriate alternative protective measures before the Court, *b)* the possible establishment of a joint international authority dealing with civilian protection activities and deployments of international humanitarian police, and *c)* the adoption of a joint approach to negotiate relocation agreements. In this respect, the States adapting to the Rome Statute and implementing their legislation need to pay particular attention to the protection of victims and witnesses. After all, the Rome Statute's provisional character and its interpretation require such an effort at global, regional and domestic levels upholding human security measures. There are no doubts that multilateral systems require further progress on these delicate issues affecting the lives of civilians in situations of war and crime. This study addresses the emergence of an international architecture of governance fostering peace, justice and security which requires systemic changes at structural, normative and functional levels and an integrated model of governance.

### 8.2.1. THE INTERSECTION BETWEEN POLICY, LAW AND INSTITUTIONS

This study offers an overview of the evolution of international law and its institutions dealing with civilians in situations of war and crime. It highlights the necessity to get closer to the individuals during mass atrocities (with peace operations and civilian protection mechanisms, international criminal investigations and prosecutions, including fair trials based on the preservation of human rights standards). The interaction between peace and justice in the field operations represents an important paradigm shift for international governance and its institutions. It can be affirmed that such interaction is characterized by institutional, normative and policy decentralization which are centered around the *political question* related to the definition of international threats and crimes, and the jurisdictional authority to decide when such crimes occur or the main *legal question*, including the *operationalization* of the international responses on the ground when massive crimes would occur.[525] The challenges, obstacles and concerns in such legal and political decentralization have been analysed in details. Firstly, in order to verify the global trends governing peace, justice and security, this study looked at the current interaction between complementary global regimes including their meaning in international relations and international law. In other words, this study focused on the theoretical fundaments for the creation of an architecture fostering peace, justice and security in accordance with the challenges of the time.

The main conclusion is that the areas of collective security, human rights and the rule of law still suffer from the impasse of democratic reforms of the UN political institutions and bodies.[526] Such an impasse has an impact on the further relationship between complementary regimes which also require appropriate reviews such as the Rome Statute system. Their complementary role ultimately results from such reforms based on an integrated approach of governance.[527] The approach in this study contained two dimensions of governance: one relates to the struggle of complementary institutions of universal character cooperating with each other in their respective areas of competence, and the other, refers to the political determination to enforce them with appropriate institutional reforms, know-how, resources and cost-effective capacity-building. In conclusion, the governance of complementary global regimes requires a *road map* of interactions based on reforming activity, systemic change and an extention of complementarity at international level between complementary international mandates. The political forces need to design a *road map* of interaction, partnerships and relationships between international governance institutions dealing with mass atrocity crimes and other international threats and crime. The responsibility 'not to veto' would require the permanent five members of the Security Council to urgently agree

525 See H. Köchler, *supra*.

526 See UN Watch Report, *Dawn of a New Era? Assessment of the United Nations Human Rights Council and its Year of Reform*, presented at UN Headquarters, May 7, 2007, accessible at: www.unwatch.org/site/apps/nl/content2.asp?c=bdKKISNqEmG&b=1330819&ct=3842825 See also Yale Center for the Study of Globalization, *Reforming the United Nations for Peace and Security*. Proceedings of a workshop to analyze the Report of the High-level Panel on Threats, Challenges, and Change, 2005, accessible at: www.ycsg.yale.edu/core/forms/Reforming_un.pdf.

527 See R. Thakur, *The United Nations, Peace and Security. From Collective Security to the Responsibility to Protect*, 2006. See also R. Thakur, *Making States Work: State Failure and the Crisis of Governance*, 2005.

not to use their veto power to block action in response to genocide and mass atrocities. The Rome Statute institutions are still struggling to identify themselves in the global order delivering a visible impact in the local realities affected by war and crime, including their relationship with the United Nations and regional institutions. Therefore, the domestic, regional and international responsibilities to protect civilians in times of war and crime require harmonization in universal laws in the UN Charter and in the Rome Statute.

The governance of the emerging regime of international criminal justice in the context of human security and sustainable peace in *intra* and inter-State civil wars represents a 'paradigm in the making' in modern international relations and international law. The rhetoric offered in this context is that in a world of global threats, security depends from an effective multilateral system based on well-functioning international governance institutions and a rule-based international order. However, there seem to be problems in reaching political convergence on such sensitive issues. Although extensive literature exists on international criminal justice, the relationship between threats and crimes, and the ideal direction crime control should take in world politics, must still be verified. Such relationship and its governance depends on too many factors, including the complex process of crime definition through the tools at disposition in the international legal and political order, characterized by the absence of a supranational organization, institutional fragmentation and a customized treaty-based jurisdiction dealing with individuals. Therefore, a political *road map* to govern global regimes of complementary character is absolutely required.

In order to accomplish a supranational order as emphasized by Delmas-Marty, it is required to return to politics "determining wheter legal and other symbolic system share common values".[528] The interaction between complementary global regimes represents a paradigm in the making, whether or not the concept of collective security and the use of peace enforcement would receive the exclusive purpose to protect individuals during violent conflicts. In any case, for human security experts international governance institutions have to promote an integrated approach when dealing with international threats and crimes affecting individual lives. International lawyers, political analysts and criminologists will increasingly have to become multidisciplinary in their vision and strategic planning, flexible enough in their ability to form working groups, teams and alliances. They have to construct methods to interact with each other and develop their own networks while deflating those of criminal groups.[529]

---

528 M. Delmas-Marty, *Ordering Pluralism. A conceptual Framework for Understanding the Transnational Legal World*, 2009 at 165.

529 See W. Bruggeman, 'The ICC as an Important Partner in Enhancing Global Justice', *International Summit on Democracy, Terrorism and Security*, 8–11 March 2005 Madrid,

## 8.2.2. THE CURRENT INTERACTION STRATEGIES

In the preamble of the Rome Statute the States Parties established the Court in relationship with the United Nations system with the jurisdiction over the most serious crimes. Such relationship is too weak to destabilize criminal and violent regimes and requires additional arrangements and agreements in the field operations on a case-by-case basis, while it also requires the formulation and the harmonization of the humanitarian policy at global level in order to benefit the conceptual framework of the human security doctrine. The ideal would be to configure multidimensional peace operations under the flag of the responsibility to protect which would serve to safe and relocate civilians in extreme conflict environments. In this context, the Assembly of the States Parties to the Rome Statute not only struggles to find a defined political identity but also on the ways it would provide assistance to fragile domestic realities of its members. The struggle to strengthen national capacities on victims and witnesses protection programmes for instance, need to be directed through the Assembly and the multilateral partners active in the area such as the UN specialized agencies. These issues of capacity-building need solutions on the top of the civilian protections and law enforcement dilemma of the judicial decisions of the Court against warlords, when States or global actors do not cooperate, including the accountability of State and non-State actors in intra- and inter-state conflicts.

The findings of this study clearly demonstrate that the international governance of global regimes of complementary character can be more efficient and effective if they work together. An interaction strategy upholding human security measures between them is required at two levels: either between the political forces empowering them with consensus and political convergence of expectations, or between themselves with arrangements and agreements applied in the field operations in accordance with the treaty provisions of the Rome Statute. We have seen that mass atrocity crimes represent serious offences deteriorating human security and sustainable peace not only locally, but at larger scale. The case of Rwanda revealed how the gravity of such offences spread at regional level. It is clear that the judicial role of the Court is not sufficient to obtain the deterrent effect initially hoped in the fight against the impunity of international crimes. Many of the judicial outcomes of the Court still wait to be enforced. Its operations should receive further support on the ground. The configuration of international mandates of the Security Council should support the activity of the Court deriving from all type of referrals. After all, the quest of justice offers valuable orientation and guidelines applicable in peace negotiations. Nevertheless, after years of divergence in the debate of peace *versus* justice the regime of international

---

the document is accessible at: http://english.safe-democracy.org/confronting/the-icc-enhancingglobaljustice.html.

justice falling under the Rome Statute has still an ambiguous place in the arrays of international peace and security. This is also true in regard to the controversial position taken by the African Union against the Court, after the investigation and prosecution of crimes committed during violent political transitions and against criminal perpetrators still in power (Sudan, Kenya). With the advent of the Rome Statute, however, it should be clear that any political compromise with criminal domestic regimes and their impunity during peace processes must be absolutely avoided.

The practice applied on the ground in conflict and post-conflict situations gives rise to the pessimistic view that the rule of law as a principle of governance is not self-sufficient. Multilateralism is characterized by serious political deadlocks and by the impasse of democratic institutional reforms of international governance institutions regulating their complementary roles. Collective and shared responsibilities to protect civilians in conflict environments and mass atrocity situations do not receive appropriate legal frameworks and normative regulations towards compulsory cooperation. Instead, such responsibilities may result on volatile military engagements with negative consequences on civilian populations. Global solidarity is characterized by several gaps in the governance of international threats and crimes and contains the risks of militarization under the flag of humanitarianism. Mutual accountability is still at its embryonic stage considering the gaps of jurisdiction of *last resort* and the accountability system falling under the Rome Statute. On the top of all these serious concerns, the main phenomena requiring action is to provide models of governance retaining the shortcomings, disintegration and systemic failure of governance in both nation-states, regional and international realities. Therefore, the governance of complementary global regimes in an integrated, harmonized and consolidated ways is further required with an extention of complementarity between the tools at disposition of the international community.

### 8.2.3. THE LESSONS LEARNT

This study is partly based on case studies of international humanitarian escalations in case of failure to secure individuals during difficult political transitions of nation-states and the commission of mass atrocity crimes. It focuses on the impact of international governance institutions for the preservation of law and order. It offers an analysis of the regime of international criminal justice which depends on international cooperation without any assurance of police and law enforcement. It debates the difficulties of international governance institutions of complementary nature in the absence of appropriate interactions. It emphasises the particularities of context between the governance of international humanitarian interventions, civilian protection duties and the possible definition of global justice. In order to accomplish results a political *road map* fostering peace, justice and security in collapsed societies is required. The case studies demonstrate that international peace, justice and security are absolutely interdependent and cannot work in parallel with conflicting priorities. This is particularly true looking at the practice applied in the configuration of international mandates on the ground in the case studies selected. In order to implement the links between *a)* investigating and prosecuting serious violations of international humanitarian law, *b)* improving human security and *c)* offering sustainable peace in conflict and post-conflict situations, the relationship between the Rome Statute institutions and the United Nations needs implementation on the following clusters in the immediate, middle and long term: a) *structural*: interactions between policy decision-makers on several clusters of governance, deployments in the field of multinational police forces, inter-institutional liaisons *in situ*, political configurations and knowledge sharing on protection mechanisms of victims and witnesses (relocation, reparation and rehabilitation); b) *normative*: legislative harmonization, cooperation agreements of binding character, common projects of legal and security assistance to domestic governance institutions; c) *functional*: working methods, reporting activity and resource sharing of civilian protection duties.

This work concludes emphasizing the interactions required between the Court and its institutional partners in the UN system. In order to develop a global vision of humanitarian protection duties the networks with the UN specialized agencies are very important. The institutional partners identified are among others: the Children's Rights & Emergency Relief Organization (UNICEF), the United Nations High Commissioner for Refugees (UNHCR), the United Nations Office for Drugs and Crimes (UNODC), and the United Nations High Commissioner for Human Rights (UNHCHR). Furthermore, important interactions are expected to improve the relationship between the Assembly of States Parties to the Rome Statute, the key UN departments and specialized agencies dealing with the rule of law issues, NGOs providing rule of law assistance and working on ICC issues, the UN development agencies and the Trust Fund for Victims (TFV), the United Nations Human Rights Council (HRC) recommending the Security Council to refer situations to the Court. The relationship agreement between the ICC and the UN, the memorandum of understanding with MONUC in the DRC falling under such agreement (later renamed MONUSCO); the New York liaison office of the Court with the UN as institutional link, the focal points and working groups and the reporting activity of the Court with the UN political institutions, represent only the initial stage of governance systems and further definition of their complementary nature. The political organs of both organizations will have to meet in the middle somewhere. The Assembly of the States Parties needs to build up mechanisms of assistance and capacity-building providing models of governance in domestic judicial systems. This is valid for the rest of the security sectors in domestic institutions sharing knowledge and preparing fragile States to reform police, army and judiciary under the UN flag, while monitoring the relevant development programs and donors. This approach of governance would require common projects of UN character including dissemination and awareness of the activities of the Court which are not only *retributive* but also *protective* and *restitutive*. In this way the ratification campaign of the Rome Statute would surely benefit from such integrated approach of governance strenghtening the relationship between peace, justice and security for the sake of individuals.

## 8.3. CONCLUSIONS

This study argues for the paradigm shift of international law and international public institutions as the global tools for the protection of individuals in situations of war and crime. This concept is relatively new in both doctrines. International mandates have to be as close as possible to individual citizens.[530] This is the common target expressed in both the Rome Statute and the UN Charter and the reason for their necessary harmonization at normative, structural and functional levels. From an institutional perspective the Court cooperates already with the UN in many different areas, including the exchange of information and logistical support. The Court reports to the UN each year on its activities, and some meetings of the Court's governing body, the Assembly of States Parties (ASP), are held in the UN facilities. The relationship between the Court and the UN is governed by a relationship agreement between the International Criminal Court and the United Nations which will need further implementation on cooperation issues.[531] Despite such institutional liaisons the first generation of referrals addressed to the Court by the Security Council (Sudan, Libya) did not receive appropriate support from the UN institutional apparatus, including the important role of the General Assembly on the issue of resource sharing. The first Review Conference of the Rome Statute considered some amendments to the Rome Statute as the

530 See J. Dugard, 'The Future of International Law: A Human Rights Perspective. With Some Comments on the Leiden School of International Law', (2007) LJIL 20, 729 at 739. For an overview of the debate over the protection of the individual under international law, the 2007 special issue of the *Leiden Journal of International Law* is presented as a tribute to John Dugard and his contribution to international law. See T. Skouteris, A. Vermeer-Kunzli, 'Editor's Introduction: John Dugard and the Protection of the Individual in International Law', (2007) LJIL 20, 741 at 744.

531 See the Negotiated Relationship Agreement between the International Criminal Court and the United Nations www.icc-cpi.int/library/asp/ICC-ASP-3-Res1_English.pdf For some literature on Cooperation Agreements and Enforcement see, G. A. Knoops, *Surrendering to International Criminal Courts: Contemporary Practice and Procedures*, (2002). V. P. Oosterveld and J. M. McManus, 'The Cooperation of States with the International Criminal Court', (March 2002) 25 *Fordham International law Journal* 3, at 767. Han-Ru Zhou, 'The Enforcement of Arrest Warrants by International Forces: from the ICTY to the ICC', 2006 *Journal of International Criminal Justice* 4, no. 2, 202 at 218. H. Zsolt, 'The Making of the Basic Principles of the Headquarter Agreement', (March 2002) 25 *Fordham International Law Journal* 3, 625 at 637.

treaty made specific reference to review the list of crimes within the Court's jurisdiction.[532] The main recommendation addressed to the decision-makers in this study is to find consensus on the harmonization of the treaty law, with provisions implementing the relationship between complementary mandates, respectively in the UN Charter and in the Rome Statute.

This is particularly true considering the increasing number of nation-states which leaders retain power during internal political transitions at the expenses of civilians. These leaders claim their positions from 'democratic' outcomes of general elections as in the situation in Kenya or Ivory Coast, where the unrest between political factions resumed in post-electoral violence requiring the involvement of the Court, and this on the top of ethnic, religious and power related conflicts. The main responsible should face international criminal justice. These situations are very complex as indeed in the Sudan. The leaders in this country retain domestic power whether the international community proved the commission of serious international crimes against their own people. In the DRC the political élite should focus on good governance of security sectors (army, police and judiciary) and perform judicial activity *in situ*. The criminal perpetrators abusing civilians should be isolated, captured and put to trial. The victims cry for justice. The governance of the emerging regime of international criminal justice in the context of peace and security during intra-state conflicts is characterized by several overlaps. The mandate configurations of the UN political organs and the multidimensional operations in the field where the Court is involved are not yet designed to provide authority, engagement and support to international judicial decisions. This emerged repetitively *in situ* in the Sudan, in Uganda, in Kenya and in the DRC, just to name a few situations reported in this study. Unfortunately, such trend might be repeated again. The risk is that violence remains the norm during political transitions of domestic regimes characterized by massive crimes. At present, the Court's arrests warrants are outstanding against eight suspects, including four alleged commanders of the LRA in the situation in Uganda. They are still free for years by now and this has devastating consequences on civilians. In regard to the Sudan, the Court informed several times the Security Council and the Assembly of States Parties about the non-cooperation in the arrest and surrender of Omar Al Bashir (Sudan) who is still travelling in several African States (DRC, Malawi, South Africa), but without success.

---

532 Any amendments to the Rome Statute require the agreement of two thirds of member countries to be adopted and the ratification of 87.5% for the amendment to come into force. However, amendments relating to the definition of crimes apply only to those member countries that ratify the amendment. After the adoption of the 2010 Kampala Amendments the crime of aggression is adopted on the basis of Article 121.5 of the Rome Statute. See for an overview, R. E. Fife, 'Review Conference: scenarios and options', 2006-11-21, accessible at www.icc-cpi.int/library/asp/ICC-ASP-5-INF2_English.pdf.

These are only some of the reasons why the Court's existence cannot be considered as the panacea for the "*malum mundus*". Furthermore, there are still no mechanisms in place for the deterrence of unilateral intervention policy of the nation-states in the affairs of sovereign States for humanitarian reasons falling under the flag of the responsibility to protect civilians. Peace and justice are still characterized by tensions in the short and middle terms and judicial decisions of *last resort* are not followed. It is expected that the UN would support the judicial mandate of the Court with appropriate configurations of its peace enforcement mandates at least in situations referred to the Court by the Security Council. The view expressed in this study is that support should be provided in all situations where peace operations are deployed on the ground. In Darfur the Court received jurisdiction from the Security Council without any guarantee of enforcement assistance and basic resources. On top of that the Court did not receive any operational or political support. Such parameters of governance deserve discussions also in the current practice applied in the Democratic Republic of Congo and in other situations where such international complementary institutions are both involved. This study underscores the importance of the humanitarian escalations of *last resort* between complementary international mandates and their governance in the field operations. It argues about the notion that the Court would be part of the maintenance and restoration of peace and security as *last resort* option rather than being purely based on the paradigm of international justice and accountability. The majority of the situations where complementary governance institutions are involved swift from weak stability falling back easily into the conflict. Therefore, they should be prepared to complement and support with each other defining their mutual interests at all levels (political, legal, structural and operational). This requires the political committment from decision-makers.

This study offers an analysis of the interactions required in accordance with the ideal of global justice in the international society. In other words, it examines the ways international regimes of complementary and universal nature may preserve the international order in accordance with the challenges of the post-cold war era. In order to guarantee law enforcement and individual protection mechanisms on the ground, the formulation of policy and law needs to give priority to applicable measures of human security. This study argues that there is a moral and legal case for intervention on humanitarian grounds where crimes internationally recognized have been committed, but that at such, military intervention and the authorization of the use of force under the flag of the responsibility to protect need to be shared in a context of balancing powers, if not such frameworks would be constantly compromised in the absence of a reliable accountability system, including the negative consequences on civilians. It is hoped that the embryonic regime of international criminal justice would have a deterrent function in the commission of crimes during political transitions in African countries and in other regions of the world.[533] At this moment in time, however, its enforcement is still more of a vision considering the weak interaction between the relevant international actors and their legal and political engagements. In such context there is also the necessity to develop more coherent theories of global governance in accordance with the current challenges of the time and the current intersection between politics and law on such sensitive issues.[534]

In summary, this study provides verification on the following global issues which require urgent solutions:

### 8.3.1. IS THERE ANY PROGRESS IN THE DEMOCRATIZATION OF AN INTERNATIONAL 'SYSTEM'?

At international level the requests of democratization are related to the reform of the permanent membership of the UN Security Council and its veto powers; on the protection of civilians and peace enforcements mandates; on the proposals for global peoples assemblies giving voice to civil society in the UN General Assembly on matters of international mutual concern; and also with regard to the provisions of the Rome Statute centralizing the victims' role in judicial proceedings with participation, protection and reparation, including the dialogue between such global institutions and regional and non-governmental organizations. Such open dialogue with regional inter-governmental organizations and civil society symbolizes the emerging regime of international criminal justice and needs to be kept alive. After all, it has been the strength of the advocacy of both civil society and regional organizations that brought the Rome Statute to become a reality.

In general, the idea of international democracy was centred on a broader participation in decision-making by under-represented States, regional political realities and civil society which is still struggling for concrete accomplishments. An important aspect of such democratization efforts is to focus on the interaction of complementary global regimes and the ways they contribute to the progress of an 'open' global society. This interaction is important to build up a democratic global system of governance fostering peace, justice and security in accordance with the principle of their inter-dependence. The preservation of peace, justice and security is not worthy if it functions within conflicting regimes. Considering the theory and the practice of humanitarian escalations and serious human rights

---

533 See A. Cassese, "International Criminal justice: Is it Needed in the Present World Community?" in G. Kreijen *et al* (eds), *State, Sovereignty, and International Governance*, 2002, Part II, Practical Manifestations.

534 See K. Dingwerth, P. Pattberg, 'Global Governance as a Perspective on World Politics', in 12 *Global Governance*, 2006, at 194.

breaches, this study argues the necessity of global strategies preserving law and order in conflict and post-conflict societies. It addresses structural, normative and functional challenges in the intersection between complementary international regimes. It offers an overview of the international legal and political order dealing with international threats and crimes. It explores the complementary role of international criminal justice at both domestic and international levels in the quest of sustainable peace and human security in conflict and post-conflict societies.

In other words, the interaction of complementary global regimes is also important to define further constitutional measures in the new order, including human security mechanisms applicable in conflict and post-conflict situations such as protection, relocation and rehabilitation of victims and witnesses including reparation measures, which deserve to be associated to development programs in domestic governance systems, once judicial proceedings have been performed.

### 8.3.2. THE PROMOTION OF GLOBAL INTERACTIONS AND DEMOCRATIC GOVERNANCE

This study wants to shed some light on what global interactions between complementary regimes would entail for the maintenance of peace, justice and security, from legal, political and institutional perspectives. Normative, structural and functional analysis of the emerging regime of international justice reveals that an appropriate interaction between the Rome Statute institutions and the United Nations system is still in progress. Recommendations are necessary for policy makers on normative and institutional reforms for further progress of democratic global governance institutions, preserving peace, justice and security in conflict and post-conflict societies. The purpose of this study is to stimulate the debate on such interaction through an assessment of international governance institutions, including recommendations of democratic adjustments preserving international relations, international law and order. There is the necessity of a global engagement in the democratization process preserving peace, justice and security in affected communities by war and crime. Only through such democratization process decision makers would enable complementary global mandates to rehabilitate dysfunctional domestic institutions in case of humanitarian escalations and serious violations of international law.

Following a referral by the Security Council to the Court the use of resources should be also supported by an appropriate law enforcement strategy. Attention is also needed on the political and legal relationship between the UN institutions and the ASP-ICC (Assembly of the States Parties and International Criminal Court), implementing further the project of universal jurisdiction. Considering the main organizational, operational and institutional issues, the attention in this study focuses on the current status of global governance in criminal matters in the absence of powers of enforcing compliance, or *supranational* organization. The 'triggering mechanisms' need attention according to the promotion of '*checks and balances*' of public powers in the international legal order. In the context of finding effective mechanisms of governance between the ICC and the UN the controversy has been whether the Security Council, the International Court of Justice or the General Assembly would declare the criminal responsibility of a State, with the Court determining the criminal individual responsibility of perpetrators. The Security Council received a specific legal and political role within the regime of international criminal justice falling under the Rome Statute, which deserves some reflections after the first decade of its existence.

### 8.3.3. ARE THERE FURTHER DEFINITIONS OF INTERNATIONAL CRIMES OF COMMON CONCERN?

The governance model proposed in this study between the United Nations and the Rome Statute institutions (the Assembly of States Parties, the International Criminal Court and the Trust Fund for Victims) supports the fight against international threats and crimes and the rehabilitation of affected communities, promoting study groups on the definition of crimes, including legal and institutional matters. The purpose of this research is also to stimulate the debate on international crime definitions (terrorism, corruption, trafficking of drugs and weapons of mass destruction). The first involvement of the Court to end the impunity of humanitarian crimes which are harming civilians considers rape and other grave sexual violence against women and children as a war crime. The treaty law considers up to six grave violations against children in situations of armed conflict which are characterizing the Court's charges in the DRC and Uganda (killing or maiming of children; recruitment or use of children as soldiers; attacks against schools or hospitals; denial of humanitarian access for children; abduction of children; rape and other grave sexual abuse of children).[535]

With regard to the universality principle of the Court's jurisdiction and war crimes, my view is that the Rome Statute should rectify the crime settlement over the use of arms of mass destruction and the use of nuclear weapons not sufficiently mentioned in the provisions of the Rome Statute, and which are also related to the extension of war crimes, and the definition of the crime of

[535] See ICC-02/04-01/05, Situation in Uganda and related Cases, *The Prosecutor v. Joseph Kony, Vincent Otti, Okot Odhiambo and Dominic Ongwen.* See ICC-01/04-01/06, Situation in Democratic Republic of the Congo, *The Prosecutor v. Thomas Lubanga Dyilo.*

aggression and leadership crimes. But would this help to set the US and other powerful States to come on board of the Rome Statute system? This will depend by the trend in global politics and from the UN-ASP promotion of the universality of the Court's jurisdiction. The amendment proposals of the Rome Statute addressed by the States Parties to the ASP and their policy positions expressed during the first review conference in Kampala recall the necessity of further debate. For some observers, the danger is that the Rome Statute would always encounter limits according to the political consensus to be reached by the States Parties, especially on issues strictly related to their legislation and approximation mechanisms. The ASP inputs on cooperation and the UN expertise with regard to the international threats are the keys to overcome the political obstacles of further jurisdictional improvements of the Rome Statute. Another problem is to safeguard the independent role of the Court in the contemporary international order characterized by the executive priorities of the Security Council. This is in fact related to the issue of the crime of aggression which focuses on the use of force, on the Security Council's powers and the interaction with the Court. The crime of aggression was mentioned in the founding treaty even if political consensus over its definition was never reached at UN level and later in the ASP-ICC. The nuclear issue was left completely outside the Statute's provisions, as well as terrorism and drug trafficking. The developments since the establishment in Rome of the treaty and its first review conference in Kampala have been extensively debated and indicate the lacuna of such regime dealing with crimes characterizing inter-state conflicts.

### 8.3.4. APPROACH

This study explores the emerging regime of international criminal justice and its governance which is by definition complementary to the duty of the United Nations. In order to assess contemporary models of international responses in conflict and post-conflict societies this study examines the broadening conceptions of governance in the absence of a *supranational* body. It considers the growing nexus between the studies of governance offering mechanisms of sustainable peace, justice and security in fragile and so-called 'failed' States. It reflects on the evolution or devolution of democratic processes of interactions between complementary global institutions fostering civilian protection duties which cannot be looked separately in situations where international peace and security are both at risk. It offers an assessment of the models proposed by international governance institutions getting closer to individuals during and after armed conflicts, while exploring the ability of the international society in the definition of threats and crimes, getting closer to the idealistic approach of a world government engaged in both intra-state and inter-state conflicts in accordance with a universal constitution.

The international legal order is based on the respect for the personality, sovereignty, and independence of States, and "the faithful fulfillment of obligations derived from treaties and other sources of international law". Human rights and international humanitarian law are either the archetype of internal affairs or a matter of international concern, especially in the area where "the faithful fulfillment of obligations derived from treaties and other sources", impacts daily on the relations between the State and individuals under its jurisdiction.[536] As cited by Cassese, "human rights have by now become a *bonum commune humanitatis,* a core of values of great significance for the whole of humankind. It is logical and consistent to grant the courts of all States the power and also the duty to prosecute, to bring to trial, and to punish persons allegedly responsible for unbearable breaches of those values and norms. National courts would operate not on behalf of their own authorities but in the name and on behalf of the whole international community".[537] An effective model of international governance of justice monitors at domestic level the faithful fulfillment of obligations derived from the treaties.[538] The majority of the situations where the Court is involved display the requirement of capacity-building to domestic governance systems, including the political support at regional level among other specific needs to protect individuals in situations of war and crime.

In the absence of *supranational* organization appropriate governance between the competent international mandates defending fundamental rights in conflict and post-conflict societies is indispensable in order to rehabilitate communities after war and crime. An effective model of international governance is necessary in order to maximize results during *peace-building* operations and post-conflict justice. This model of governance of justice would destabilize criminal regimes that represent the main cause of intra-state civil wars, avoiding the risks for

536 See F. Kalshoven, "State Sovereignty versus International Concern in Some Recent Cases of the Inter-American Court of Human Rights", in G. Kreijen 'et al' (eds.), *State, Sovereignty and International Governance*, (2004), at 259.

537 See A. Cassese, *The International Criminal Court: An End to Impunity?* Crimes of War Project, 2003, accessible at: www.didierbigo.com/students/readings/IPS2011/13/cassese2003.pdf Considering another perspective, which complements the empirical approach in post-conflict societies in order to examine the necessity of international investigations and prosecutions and the impact of international Courts on domestic criminal proceedings, it is important to consider the current interaction between national and international Courts, involved in prosecuting individuals in mass atrocity situations, in combination with an analysis of the problems presented by the limited response of the international community to mass atrocity situations. This approach of justice governance entails original case studies, and comparisons of their interactions between the different legal systems, domestic, regional, and international, and makes recommendations for optimizing the complementary nature of international and national Courts. This is the purpose of the research project, *Impact of International Courts on Domestic Criminal Procedures in Mass Atrocity Cases.* See DOMAC (2008) research project funded under the Seventh Framework Programme for EU Research (FP7), accessible at: www.domac.is.

538 For a legal analysis of the Court's relationship with domestic jurisdiction see C. Stahn and G. Sluiter, *The Emerging Practice of the International Criminal Court*, (2009), at 208.

these communities of going back to the regime of war, shortly after the UN intervention. Both mandates (ICC-UN) allow fragile States to rebuild their own executive, legislative and judicial powers. Moreover, in the long term this model of governance would influence the project of universal jurisdiction and the judicial empowerment of competence allocation *vis-à-vis* the executive power of the Security Council. At strategic level, as shown by the legal reports of the Secretary-General, in order to maximize results in the peace operations: "international security, rule of law and justice must go hand in hand". The problem is to solve the dilemma of judicial empowerment towards a well-defined enforcement strategy with the executive powers of the Security Council *(checks and balances)* supporting the *ex-ante* nature of the Court and its involvement in ongoing conflicts.

In the model of governance proposed, the escalation of human rights violations threatening international peace and security should be followed by a mechanism of *horizontal* nature: *judicial referral* (Security Council – International Criminal Court) and *law enforcement referral* (International Criminal Court – Security Council), in order to maximize results in the field on a case-by-case basis in the situations referred to the Court.[539] The United Nations and the Rome Statute institutions have a universal mandate. In fact the definition of universal organizations applies for both systems. There is the necessity of building consensus, consolidating the responsibility to protect individuals with the determination of ending the impunity of international crimes, towards an appropriate interaction between these organizations. The right of intervention of the international community (in case the State is unwilling or unable to protect civilians – *responsibility to protect)* must follow up on the judicial decisions of the International Criminal Court (when the State is unwilling or unable of starting judicial proceedings – *complementarity*). The model of governance proposed in this study refers to the enforcement on a case-by-case basis: *a)* maximizing the results in the Security Council operations and referral activity to the Court; and *b)* ending the impunity of serious international crimes with the Court's presence in the conflict and post-conflict phase. In conclusion, the responsibility to protect deserves some progress in order to serve the main activities of the Court.

### 8.3.5. MOTIVATION

The motivation in this study is to verify whether there is a genuine political determination of harmonization between the United Nations and the International Criminal Court in solving some of the tensions between peace

[539] The *vertical referrals*: nation-states – International Criminal Court and *proprio motu* powers in accordance with Article 15 of the Rome Statute.

and justice, cooperation and complementarity, including the long term impact of their presence in the field operations on victims and affected communities. The intent of this study is to verify whether these complementary global entities are just left by means of parallel and distant working relationships, reflecting an improper hierarchy between political and judicial international authorities, which would only create undesired frictions and disputes, or if they work together with unity of intents, providing assistance and cooperation in the field operations of one another, improving the capacity-building of regional and domestic systems. Further consensus will be necessary for democratic reforms which would allow the implementation of international cooperation standards, including international and shared responsibilities of cooperation between complementary global regimes and regional and domestic systems. An overview of the shortcomings occurring during humanitarian escalations of *last resort*, from peace processes to transitional justice, and their impact on the ground, have been approached in the case studies dealing with conflict and post-conflict situations in African countries, where the United Nations and the Rome Statute institutions are both currently involved. The policy debates and the legislation of the UN institutions, regional organizations and Rome Statute institutions have been extensively examined.

The motivation for this research also refers to the new steps in the law-making process and the treaty law to implement the defence of human rights; to enhance further the fight against international crimes; and to put an end to the impunity regime of serious human rights offences. This research offers a model implementing the governance of justice, at a time where the completion strategies of the International Criminal Tribunals for Rwanda and the Former Yugoslavia are well under way, while the operation of a new mixed tribunal by the Security Council (Special Tribunal for Lebanon) brings new concerns of fragmented and multilevel jurisdictions.[540] The International Criminal Court was created as a demonstration by the international community's commitment to put an end to impunity of serious crimes internationally recognized establishing new policies

[540] In this context is important to consider the adoption of the Security Council Resolution 1757 (2007) 30 May 2007 (UN doc. S/RES/1757) over the establishment of the Special Tribunal for Lebanon, the so-called Hariri Tribunal. This "hybrid" international court is mandated to try those suspected of assassinating former Lebanese Prime Minister Rafik Hariri, who was murdered in February 2005. Several human rights organizations such as Human Rights Watch had argued that the tribunal should have been given jurisdiction over 14 other attacks perpetrated in Lebanon since October 1, 2004, that it is to be a "tribunal of an international character based on the highest international standards of criminal justice" and that several issues need to be addressed during the negotiations between the United Nations and the Lebanese government in order to ensure that the "highest international standards of criminal justice" are attained. The tribunal marks the first time that an UN-based international criminal court will be trying a "terrorist" crime committed against a specific person. See HRW, *Establishing the Hariri Tribunal, Letter to the Secretary-General Kofi Annan*, 2006 (April), accessible at http://hrw.org/english/docs/2006/05/01/lebano13297.htm.

based on justice and the rule of law.[541] The Court's presence provides high judicial standards for other courts and tribunals, while its *ex-ante* role of permanent tribunal is unique and requires global support.

This study defends the necessity of applying the doctrine of *checks and balances* in the international legal order between universal organizations and *vis-à-vis* the States, consolidating complementary regimes dealing with serious human rights breaches. It debates the necessity for the judicial power to operate in the context of a global law enforcement strategy and a compulsory cooperation regime. It offers a model of governance between the humanitarian intervention under the UN umbrella and the field operations to gather information and evidence of international crimes by the investigative channels of the Court. It considers the judicial proceedings of post-conflict justice (rehabilitation and reparation) as necessary operational steps of nation building and reconstruction. The existence of a permanent and independent international organization with jurisdiction over individuals accused of committing serious international crimes, in particular, genocide, crimes against humanity and war crimes, signifies the establishment of a judicial power independent from power politics, from the *selective justice* performed by the Security Council and from the unilateral national security policy of its members. There is an important impetus to analyse the interaction of complementary international mandates in the context of *complementarity* with the States. Studies and reports on these global issues are extremely important, considering the solutions to be found in the current transition of international relations, characterized by the crisis in international democracy, and by the disintegration of the nation-state even in Western societies with a difficult momentum of political unrests, shifts of power, civil wars and serious violations against the dignity of individual lives. From a legal perspective further research will be necessary in order to define the criminal responsibility of corporations and other non-state actors, giving new insight to the application of accountability and universal reach of crimes by a permanent International Criminal Court.

### 8.3.6. COUNTRY-SPECIFIC SITUATIONS

The political breakdowns and the failure of newly established nation-states is evident in civil wars which create situations where domestic institutions are deprived of their capabilities, triggering a constant crisis of basic governance parameters. In the majority of these situations, characterized by economic decline

541 See UN doc. A/63/323, Fourth Report of the International Criminal Court to the United Nations for 2007/08, Address to the United Nations General Assembly Judge Philippe Kirsch, President of the International Criminal Court, 30 October 2008, accessible at: www.icc-cpi.int/Menus/ICC/Reports+on+activities/Court+Reports+and+Statements/Court+Reports+and+Statements.htm.

and dependent upon natural resources, domestic authorities become unable to control violence on their own, or persist in the unwillingness to investigate or prosecute international crimes of serious concern. Such breakdowns of nation-states are well recorded in Africa, where their inability to initiate judicial proceedings after and during violent conflicts proves the necessity of institutional-capacity building at international level. Since the establishment of the Court there have been State referrals from the governments of the Democratic Republic of Congo, Uganda, Central African Republic,[542] Ivory Coast,[543] Mali and and the Union of the Comoros, two referrals from the Security Council regarding the situation in Darfur and Libya. In 2010 Pre-Trial Chamber II granted the Prosecutor's request to open an investigation *proprio motu* in the situation in Kenya, which is a State Party to the Rome Statute since 2005.[544] It needs to be noted that the Kenyan parliament did not agree on the establishment of a special criminal tribunal of their own to take care of the crimes committed during the political transition in the country. The Kenyan parliament voted twice negatively to have a special criminal tribunal looking into the criminal responsibility for the 2007–2008 post-election violence. There was no other option for the ICC intervention.[545] The Office of the Prosecutor has also received thousands communications since July 2002 about multiple country-situations and performs daily preliminary examinations.[546]

The obvious consequence in the majority of conflict and post-conflict societies is the presence of authoritarian criminal regimes which have serious repercussions on individual lives and which are left to international interventions of last resort. Considering the UN intervention in the DRC conflict, or so-called the 'Kivu Conflict' which was generated by an explosive mix of power-hungry militias and ethnic tensions, fuelled by a violent tug of war for control over mineral resources. The conflict is taking place between the Congolese armed forces (FARDC) and the Rwandan Hutu militia group, the Democratic Forces for the Liberation of Rwanda (FDLR) in the mountainous provinces of North and South Kivu. After

542 See ICC-OTP-20140924-PR1043, 24 September 2014, *Statement of the Prosecutor of the International Criminal Court, Fatou Bensouda, on opening a second investigation in the Central African Republic.* See also Situation in the Central African Republic II, Article 53(1) Report, 24 September 2014.

543 Ivory Coast had accepted the jurisdiction of the ICC on 18 April 2003. On both 14 December 2010 and 3 May 2011, the Presidency of the country reconfirmed the acceptance of the Court's jurisdiction. On 15 February 2013 Ivory Coast deposited its instrument of ratification and became State Party to the Rome Statute.

544 ICC-01/09, 31 March 2010, Decision Pursuant to Article 15 of the Rome Statute on the Authorization of an Investigation into the Situation in the Republic of Kenya, accessible at: www.icc-cpi.int/iccdocs/doc/doc854287.pdf.

545 See G. M. Musila, "Options for Transitional Justice in Kenya: Autonomy and the Challenge of External Prescriptions", *IJTJ* (2009) 3 (3), at 445–464.

546 For an up-to-date overview see ICC portal, Communications and Preliminary Examinations, accessible at: www.icc-cpi.int ICC » Structure of the Court » Office of the Prosecutor » Preliminary Examinations.

a dramatic shift in political alliances, in January 2009 the DRC and Rwanda launched joint military operations in eastern Congo against the FDLR, some of whose leaders had participated in the Rwandan genocide, and which had targeted Congolese civilians in these areas over the previous 15 years. Peace and security has been compromised in the African Great Lakes region including the regime of impunity of mass atrocity crimes.

Seventy years since the end of WWII and the creation of the United Nations the events in the DRC remind us that the system of collective security based around the UN is still unable to save the lives of innocent civilians caught up in armed conflict. Even worse, the United Nations itself is facing accusations of complicity in violations of international law. MONUC was given the mandate to support and participate in military operations with the Congolese armed forces against the FDLR in December 2008, as long as such operations were conducted in accordance with the laws of war. But according to human rights activists MONUC disregarded crucial elements of formal legal advice given by the UN Office of Legal Affairs (OLA) in 2009 and did not establish conditions for respecting international humanitarian law, as required by its mandate, even before it began to support the operations on the ground.[547]

Serious concerns emerge from the empirical research findings of such interventions in conflict prevention and conflict management and which do not seem to be prepared to act on the causes and on the effects of humanitarian atrocities. "There are many tasks which UN peacekeeping forces should not be asked to undertake and many places they should not go. But when the UN does send its forces to uphold the peace, they should be prepared to confront the persistent forces of war and violence with the ability and determination to defeat them." This important guideline was part of the comprehensive review of the whole question of peacekeeping operations in all their aspects in the UN.[548] The Brahimi Report offered an in-depth critique about the conduct of UN operations and made specific recommendations for a change. Only "by making such changes", the Panel argued, "would the UN be able to meet the critical 21st century peacekeeping and peacebuilding issues presented by its member States" The Brahimi Report was drafted during the May-June 2000 peacekeeper hostage crisis in Sierra Leone, with that crisis very much in mind. Experience in the 1990s had also amply demonstrated that undersized and under-equipped forces with weak or unclear mandates could neither deter political factions nor

[547] See Human Rights Watch, "MONUC and Civilian Protection" in *You Will Be Punished. Attacks on Civilians in Eastern Congo,* Report of Human Rights Watch (HRW), December 2009, pp. 134–153, accessible at: www.hrw.org/sites/default/files/reports/drc1209web_1.pdf.

[548] See A/55/305, S/2000/809, *Report of the Panel on United Nations Peace Operations,* known as the "Brahimi Report" after the Panel chair, UN Under-Secretary-General Lakhdar Brahimi, August 2000.

contain the well-armed gangs that arise in the power and legitimacy vacuums following civil wars. Such was the case, for example, in Angola, Somalia, Bosnia and Rwanda between 1991 and 1994.

In the comprehensive UN review of the whole question of peacekeeping operations in all their aspects and inter-institutional communication between the president of the UN General Assembly and the president of the Security Council, the paragraph 62 reads "Peacekeepers (military troops or police) who witness violence against civilians should be presumed to be authorized to stop it, within their means, in support of basic United Nations principles and, as stated in the report of the Independent Inquiry on Rwanda, with 'the perception and the expectation of protection created by the UN operational presence".[549] Military ethics experts took the Panel to task for the "presumed to be authorized" language, arguing that, if protecting civilians is not part of an operation's mandate, then the Panel has potentially invited soldiers who witness atrocities to violate lawful national orders not to intervene. But they also note that *force majeure* "in the sense of a collision of duties," where "the necessity of choice is inevitable," may offer a path by which peacekeepers, in specific emergency circumstances, may act outside their mandate, drawing on the ethical imperative to protect civilians that is implied or imposed by international humanitarian law.[550] The International Criminal Court, however, is still kept out of any forces to be deployed on the ground.

The mission in the DRC illustrates the difficulties that characterize such an approach,[551] and suggests that the United Nations and its member States do not yet have the expertise and commitment to deal effectively with complex humanitarian emergencies.[552] In 2004, the government of DRC referred the situation of crimes

---

549 'Brahimi report', UN Doc. A/55/305, para. 62.

550 The distinction drawn is between an implicit, blanket authority to act and an emergency imperative that is justified case by case. See T. Van Baarda and F. Van Iersel, 'The Uneasy Relationship between Conscience and Military Law: The Brahimi Report's Unresolved Dilemma', (2002) 9 *International Peacekeeping* 3, 25 at 50.

551 Experts in peacekeeping and peacemaking in Africa discussing the history of UN efforts since post cold war era in DRC, Sierra Leone conclude that the UN is still struggling to find a case by case approach in such humanitarian disasters. See A. Bariagader, 'United Nations Peace Operations in Africa: A Cookie-Cutter Approach?', 2006 *Journal of Third World Studies* 23, 2, 11 at 29. In DRC, the UN Security Council Resolution 1843, UN doc. S/Res/1843 (2008), November 20, 2008, increased the number of troops from nearly 17,000 troops to just fewer than 20,000 though not all of the new troops have yet arrived. As of August 2009, 18,638 uniformed personnel were physically deployed, including 16,844 troops, 705 military observers, and 1,089 police. The mission also includes 1006 international civilian personnel, 2,539 local civilian staff and 615 United Nations Volunteers. See MONUC facts and figures, accessible at: www.un.org/Depts/dpko/missions/monuc/facts.html.

552 According to empirical case studies performed by African experts on the DRC, the massive conflict lasting from 1996 to 2003 that drew in seven African countries and led to about three million deaths, the greatest number of fatalities in any war since World War II, started as a direct consequence of the Rwandan genocide in 1994. See G. Prunier, *From Genocide to Continental War: The "Congolese" Conflict and the Crisis of Contemporary Africa* published in

within the jurisdiction of the International Criminal Court allegedly committed anywhere on its territory, since the entry into force of the Rome Statute, on 1 July 2002. The DRC government asked the Prosecutor of the Court to investigate in order to determine whether one or more persons should be charged with such crimes, and the authorities committed to cooperate with the Court. In January 2009 the first trial of the Court started against the most accountable Congolese 'warlords' with some of them still at large (Sylvestre Mudacumura). In the Sudan it is even worse. The political *élite* responsible of mass atrocities in Darfur are still in charge of the leadership in the country. President Al-Bashir travels all over in Africa. Such trend has divided the international community and many African States are not cooperating in accordance with their legal obligations falling under the Rome Statute.

### 8.3.7. FROM REJECTION TO POLITICAL SUPPORT

This study has also the scope to address the Court's political rejection considering the American position and also by other permanent members of the Security Council, such as Russia and China. The United States signed under the Clinton administration and then rejected the Court under the Bush administration. For a while it even became its public enemy together with other powerful States which followed their own strategic intervention policy, delivering a governance model of justice sometimes even outside the multilateral premises of the UN. The Obama Administration has stated its intent to cooperate with the International Criminal Court. In response to a question from the Senate Foreign Relations Committee, former Secretary of State Clinton remarked that the US will end its 'hostility' towards the Court. In addition, Susan Rice, US Ambassador to the United Nations, in her first address to the Security Council, expressed the US support for the Court's investigation in the Sudan. These statements coupled with the removal of the sanctions and the realization of the negative impact of the Bilateral Immunity Agreements (BIAs), represent a positive shift for those who believe in the US cooperation with the Court and which may lead to greater participation with it. The Obama Administration however, has made no formal policy decision yet on the ICC membership, neither on the status of the Bilateral Immunity Agreements (BIAs).[553]

---

the US as *Africa's World War: Congo, the Rwandan Genocide, and the Making of Continental Catastrophe*, (2009).

553 See "The United States and the International Criminal Court", *Wikipedia* the free encyclopedia, accessible at: http://en.wikipedia.org/wiki/United_States_and_the_International_Criminal_Court See also L. Di Cicco, "The Non-Renewal of the 'Nethercutt Amendment' and its Impact on the Bilateral Immunity Agreement (BIA) Campaign", April 30 2009, accessible at: www.amicc.org/docs/Nethercutt2009.pdf For an overview of the hearing of the US Senate Foreign Relations Committee see J. Kerry, "*Toward a Comprehensive Strategy for Sudan*" 2009, accessible at: http://kerry.senate.gov/cfm/record.cfm?id=316485.

The expectations on the Court's role seem very high notwithstanding its opposition if we consider the limited resources given by the Assembly of States Parties (ASP), the political and governing body of the ICC, and the lack of support by the Security Council following the Darfur referral. The debate ended on March 31, 2005 with the Security Council finally approving the *Resolution 1593* granting the ICC jurisdiction to investigate ongoing atrocities in Darfur. The Resolution passed by a vote of 11–0, with four countries abstaining. This was an extraordinary result considering the complex politics involved. Algeria and the United States cited their preference for an African tribunal as the reason for their failure to support the referral. But the reluctance of the US was compounded by their ideological opposition to the ICC itself. The fact that they did not exercise the veto was due in part to the inclusion in the Resolution of a provision exempting nationals of States not Parties to the ICC Statute who are involved in peacekeeping from the jurisdiction of the Court. At the other end of the scale of views, Brazil withheld its vote precisely to object the compromised language introduced by the US. China justified its failure to support the resolution by saying that a political process for peace should be prioritized over the quest for justice.[554] Yet it did not cast a veto, but abstained.

Taking in consideration the international relations issues, this study approaches the support received by the European Union and NGO coalitions as important channels to solve the controversial positions with other regional organizations, such as the Arab League and the African Union. The analysis focuses on the peace enforcement configurations of the Security Council on the ground, where the Court is also involved with investigations and prosecutions, including the escalations of *last resort* addressed to the emerging regime of international criminal justice. The argument is the lack of support to the Court, including a detached interaction between complementary global regimes, alongside the policy formulation of global humanitarianism and civilian protection duties in conflict and post-conflict situations.

554 See, UN doc. S/RES/1593 (2005).

# EXECUTIVE SUMMARY

## PROBLEM STATEMENT

In this study the governance of complementary global regimes fighting against war and crime is based on the principles of the rule of law, multilateralism, collective responsibility, global solidarity and mutual accountability. These principles of governance promote social progress, human rights and the achievement of sustainable peace. In the current international legal and political order urgent solutions are required in the short, middle and long term balancing the '*right*' of humanitarian intervention and its transition to the '*responsibility*' to protect civilians with every means. Legal frameworks are required preserving fundamental individual rights while extending the criminal accountabilities equally when dealing with the international crimes characterizing conflict and post-conflict situations. The preservation of the rule of law has the potential to impact order and stability in transition societies while also retaining universal values shared by the world community. However, the ways international humanitarian law and human rights law may provide a relevant legal framework applicable in situations not qualifying as an armed conflict is still not clear, including the accountability mechanisms, law enforcement, and civilian protection measures in conflict and post-conflict situations. The historical, political and legal factors of such lacuna are extensively examined in the struggle to achieve a democratic global architecture of governance dealing with war and crime and based on human security. In order to measure the aspects of democratic governance, further research would still be required per situation, keeping in mind that a perfect analytical formula does not exist, while the theory offers valuable principles for the policy formulation to *prevent*, *react* and *rebuild* the devastation in conflict and post-conflict situations.

In the last decade the inquiries of legality of the '*right*' of humanitarian intervention in international law received valuable and extensive scholarly analysis. The risk of unilateral humanitarian intervention derived from the failure of the collective security system established after WWII was characterized by the delegating role of the UN Security Council to military *ad hoc* coalitions as the only alternative to the inaction in case of mass atrocity crimes. In the post-cold war era and with the adoption of the Rome Statute, the shift of civilian protection duties deserves discussion in order to centralize individuals in conflict and post-conflict situations, extending the accountabilities of the criminal leaderships and major perpetrators, while monitoring the impunity regime of domestic jurisdictions in the conflict and post-conflict phases. The paradigm shift between the concept of international security and human security is in transition and deserves attention, including the serious shortcomings of law enforcement after the judicial outcomes based on supranational rules. The practice of the responsibility to protect civilians on the ground deserves assessments, not only for the military responses authorized and for the forces deployed in the field such as peacekeepers, but also for other *complementary* actors of the United Nations such as the International Criminal Court, which also struggles with protection measures of witnesses and victims of serious humanitarian breaches of international law. For the International Criminal Court and in accordance with its *ex-ante* character, the ideal would be receiving support before, during, and after the human security concerns would arise in violent conflict and post-conflict situations. But this is an idea not realised, and probably it will never do. If we look at the political distance taken by some relevant States and regional entities from the Rome Statute, it would be accurate to refer to an *impasse* in the design of a governance structure of complementary character. This study analyses the strengths and weaknesses of *complementary* international regimes and proposes reforms in order to respond to the spreading of intra-state conflicts and the commission of serious crimes deriving from them, including the international responses in inter-state armed conflicts which governance is still in a state of uncertainty (e.g. aggression).

The legal frameworks based on cooperation are characterized by several shortcomings of compliance and require responsibilities in the political configurations of mandates deployed in the field operations including their legal accountabilities. The *complementarity* principle intended to delimit domestic and international responsibilities is not applied in the delimitation of competence between international public authorities involved in the humanitarian escalations so-called of '*last resort*'. The international responsibilities and the forms of accountabilities of non-state actors are not yet defined when intervention in mass atrocities occurs and since international crimes are committed. In many situations, the political configuration of mandates on the ground takes in consideration, on the one hand, only the compromised position of the local government without even verifying whether the peace negotiations are taking place with the individuals most responsible of the crimes. On the other hand, the judicial activity in the field should not be paralyzed by peace processes and negotiations. In the majority of these situations the right timing and the unity of intents of global actors involved in mass atrocities are seriously compromised. Moreover, victim rights and civilian protection duties are still waiting for reliable models applicable on the ground. Another issue, which is not considered a marginal one, refers to the internal regime of accountabilities in the UN when peace forces deployed would also commit unlawful acts. Thus, international political responsibilities and legal accountabilities are in transition and require both legal and political debate based on accurate findings provided by research projects in the field of international law, international relations and peace and security studies.

This study explores the quest of complementarity and the dilemma of human security between the pluralist, liberal and constitutional views of legal and policy frameworks governing international threats and crimes. It attempts to verify the challenges and opportunities in the governance of complementary global regimes fostering peace and justice in societies in transition from conflict to reconstruction offering reliable models of governance and capacity-building. It examines the dynamics of the humanitarian escalations of *last resort* between international governance institutions and their impact in the field operations: *a)* establishing the facts about violations of fundamental individual rights; *b)* investigating and prosecuting the perpetrators of international crimes; *c)* providing relocation, rehabilitation and reparation to the victims of international crimes; *d)* solving the tensions between peace and reconciliation against justice and accountability in the transition of conflict societies; and *e)* recognising sustainable national reconstruction and development using peace and justice as interdependent and universal mechanisms. In order to maximize the results when dealing with the devastation of communities affected by war and crime, this study advocates for further progress of an architecture of governance fostering peace and justice. The current place of justice in the arrays of peace and security maintenance should be challenged *a)* preparing the ground for humanitarian international responses, *b)* maximising the results in the field operations and *c)* centralising civilian protection duties.

## TOPIC

This study emphasizes the meaning and preservation of the rule of law in international relations through complementary governance institutions shifting from collective security to human security applying civilian protection duties. It introduces the challenges in the field of international law and its institutions which have repercussions in the governance of peace and justice. The practice indicates the difficulties thereof in both conflict and post-conflict situations. Therefore, the definition of the complementary character of global institutions for the pursuit of human security represents an important opportunity. This study debates the intersection between policy and law for an implementation of complementary global regimes able to influence national governance systems worldwide when dealing with threats and crimes destabilizing peace and security. The United Nations and the origins of the International Criminal Court as an independent judicial institution have been analysed in detail. In theory, their relationship depends on the intersection between law and politics, and particularly on the will of the nation-states to implement the regime of international criminal justice in national legislations, on the fight against threats and crimes at global level, on the establishment of a democratic balance of powers flexible enough to adjust the configuration of mandates in the field operations. The three parts of this study make specific reference to the situations where both the United Nations and the International Criminal Court are currently involved.

This study debates the shortcomings of international responses in situations of humanitarian violations of massive proportions and the systemic change of governance required between the gaps of early warnings, inaction, selectivity and political engagements in countries devastated by war and crime. The path of such systemic change of governance is based simultaneously on specific responsibilities for the nation-states and the international community for the sake of civilians in situations of war and crime. This study examines the challenges, obstacles and concerns characterizing the current governance of international criminal justice as a tool to achieve sustainable peace in situations of war and crime. It focuses on the compliance gaps of such governance and possible democratic solutions towards the interaction between complementary global tools. It analyses the legal mechanisms regulating the relationship between the United Nations and the Rome Statute system and the necessity of harmonisation of their partnerships in the treaty law of both organizations. All parts of this study focus on the structural, normative and functional issues and the necessity of adjustments and institutional reforms introducing systemic changes in the governance of complementary global regimes fostering human security.

## RESEARCH QUESTIONS

In order to improve human security in situations where the dignity of civilian lives has been heavily compromised this study considers the current interaction between complementary global regimes and provides some recommendations. Emphasis is given in finding measures to maximise the results in the preservation of law and order at global level and in the field operations. This study underscores the requirement of an accountability system that would retain political responsibilities and legal accountabilities at the same extent for all parties involved in conflict and post-conflict situations including non-state actors. In this way the rule of international law will surely progress.

The issues approached in this study are addressed through the following questions:

*Do we witness the emergence of an international architecture of governance fostering peace and justice, including measures of human security applicable in conflict and post-conflict situations?*

*What kind of challenges, obstacles and concerns characterize the governance of complementary global regimes?*

*How do the referrals addressed to the International Criminal Court and their governance in the field operations currently work?*

This study examines the challenges and opportunities characterizing the governance of complementary global regimes and the role of the relevant stakeholders involved. It advocates for appropriate interaction strategies in order to maximise the results in the devastation of war and crime and the *protective, retributive,* and *reparative* aspects of justice. A *road map* of interactions between complementary global regimes is absolutely required. The global architecture fostering peace, justice and security depends from an integrated model of governance strengthening compliance with international law and all its branches, humanitarian, criminal and human rights law among other fields of study.

## OBJECTIVE

The objective of this study is to promote an effective interaction strategy between complementary global regimes in accordance with the human security doctrine and its links with international law. In this study the humanitarian approach of human security is interpreted as the paradigm shift from the centralisation of the State to the protection of civilians in case of unwillingness or inability of governments and political élites to take care of their own citizens. Human security has the potential to shift fundamental issues in international law such as statehood, sovereignty and international governance, including the role of non-state actors in international legal frameworks. Human security measures, such as civilian protection, relocation, rehabilitation and reparation are absolutely required in situations of war and crime. The shift of security with a human face should be used strengthening global efforts to prevent the commission of mass atrocity crimes, prepare the ground for humanitarian intervention and rebuild situations of war and crime. This study wants to shed some light on what global interactions between complementary regimes would entail for the maintenance of peace, justice and security, from legal, political and institutional perspectives. It recommends further implementation, reforms and democratic adjustments. In the absence of a *supranational* organization the debate about the future of international criminal justice between prevention and accountability raises the concern about the fragmentation and proliferation of decentralised judicial international mandates. Namely, the UN Security Council political compromise establishing *ex post* judicial mandates falling outside the jurisdiction of the International Criminal Court; the problems of universal ratification of the Rome Statute; including the lacuna of accountability of humanitarian interventions falling under the policy of the responsibility to protect civilians in armed conflicts. This study argues that for an implementation of a global system of international criminal justice able to influence law and order, including *'l'état de droit'*, or institutional capacity-building in domestic realities, it is necessary to organise: competence allocations, delimitation of competences, institutional reforms, mutual and complementing support between complementary institutions. All of these are fundamental preconditions of democratic global governance and would provide a pragmatic definition of the complementary character of international governance institutions.

The objective of this study is to examine the challenges of complementary global regimes, their institutional structure and the political convergence required in order to maximize the results in situations of war and crime. This study explores the institutional 'contours' in the emerging regime of international criminal justice complementing the implementation of human rights protection mechanisms at global level. The case study objectives focus on the necessary configuration of complementary mandates *in situ*, their responsibilities of early warnings between political failure, chaos, corruption, bad governance and mass atrocity crimes. The presence of complementary mandates is characterized by problems of operational coherence and cooperation standards. The impact of the UN mission on the ground between humanitarian protection, security issues and criminal accountability is extensively analysed, including the results to fight against the impunity at all levels with the utmost vigilance of both the United Nations and the International Criminal Court, including regional intergovernmental actors, practitioners, academics and civil society.

## OUTLINE

The introduction offers an overview of the research questions, the methodology applied and the structure of the topics. It attempts to contribute to the challenging conceptual debate about statehood, sovereignty and governance between the maintenance of peace and security and the paradigm shift of international justice and accountability. It clarifies the origins of the International Criminal Court and its complementary nature with the United Nations. It analyses the emerging regime of international criminal justice and the dilemma of post-conflict enforcement of law considering the origins and development of such regime and the need to solve both policy and normative gaps in order to protect civilians in situations of war and crime. Furthermore, the introduction addresses the problem and possible solutions on controversial governance issues, the purpose and motivation of the multidisciplinary approach, including the research questions, the methodology and the core structure of the analytical work in the field of study proposed.

The first part of the study argues for the quest of complementarity and the dilemma of human security. It analyses the evolution of legal and political frameworks centralizing the fundamental rights of individuals damaged by civil wars and the role of international criminal justice. It focuses on the transition of complementary global regimes dealing with human security in conflict and post-conflict situations and recommends an integrated approach of governance of peace and justice as tools of human security.

The second part analyses the challenges, obstacles and concerns in the emerging regime of international criminal justice and also some of the opportunities deriving from an integrated approach of governance of peace and justice. It discusses the international responses during intra-state conflicts and mass atrocity crimes and their escalations; the intersection between policy and law for an implementation of international regimes of complementary character involved in societies devastated by war and crime; the prospects of international criminal justice and the evolution of a universal jurisdiction through the promotion of the human security doctrine. It emphasises the important requirement of political consensus on several issues and offers an overview of the governance structure of complementary global regimes and their competence.

The third part proposes two case studies where complementary interventions are currently performed, particularly in the Sudan (Darfur) and in the DRC. It debates the humanitarian escalations of *last resort* and their governance in the field operations since the presence of new institutions under the Rome Statute regime complementing the United Nations. This part underscores the requirement of appropriate synergies. It suggests an integrated model of governance and an extension of complementarity between global regimes fostering peace and justice. Unfortunately, the emerging regime of justice based on the complementarity principle only towards its States Parties is not self-sufficient. The ratification of the treaty was compromised by no compulsory cooperation with the UN Security Council in all categories of referrals addressed to the International Criminal Court.[555] The extension of complementarity between global regimes sharing humanitarian escalations of serious crimes of common concern is absolutely required, including the policy formulations of international threats and international crimes and further jurisdictional extensions. This, of course, depends on the political convergence to empower governance institutions in accordance with the contemporary challenges occurring in the international society and their capacity to deal with mass atrocity crimes. The definition of complementary global regimes depends on the political determinations to get closer and work together standing on the side of individuals in conflict and post-

555 See Article 13, Article 14, Article 15 and Article 16 of the Rome Statute.

conflict situations. It remains to be seen how far the political forces will further evolve on this path.

## RESEARCH OBJECTIVE

The aim of this study is to offer some clarifications on sensitive governance issues such as: *a)* the humanitarian interventions upholding peace and justice; *b)* the preservation of the rule of international law and its harmonisation; *c)* the evolution of the human security doctrine and international law; *d)* the configuration and balance of powers between political, judicial and executive international public authorities; *e)* the meaning of complementary governance institutions; *f)* the law enforcement dilemma and the relationship and partnership of complementary international mandates in the field missions and their multidimensional operations performed on the ground. This study debates the ability of global features to maintain, preserve and restore the rule of law, while offering capacity-building in situations characterized by international threats and crimes. Human security centralizing the fundamental rights of individuals in such legal and political frameworks is the priority. Complementary global regimes should be governed in accordance with such priority. This study provides an assessment of the governance of justice in the context of human security and sustainable peace in intra- and eventually inter-states conflicts. It selects a couple of country situations and examines the dynamics of the modern humanitarian escalations between complementary regulatory frameworks dealing with intra- and eventually inter-state conflicts.

## CONCLUSIONS

In the current legal and political order the meaning of complementary global regimes is to outline the responsibilities around statehood, sovereignty and international governance, upholding the preservation of human rights and further evolution of the human security doctrine. The findings in this study clearly indicate that the eventual progress of global frameworks of complementary character would have an impact on the governance of humanitarian escalations in situations of war and crime. Their complementary nature is based on the responsibilities of States and the international community to centralize the fundamental rights of individuals in situations of war and crime. The debate on the delimitation of statehood, sovereignty and international governance are central for the evolution of contemporary international law. Such debate deserves to remain open through democratic dialogue in parliaments, national constitutions and between the different legal systems and traditions of the world community while promoted by the multilateral premises enforcing complementary global regimes. There are serious gaps in either identifying mechanisms of early warnings or configurations of operational mandates before, during, and after mass atrocity escalations would occur, while the regional realities are not fully supportive, at least providing the political support required to international governance institutions, also among the legal obligations of their members according to international treaties such as the Rome Statute (e.g. African Union and the League of Arab States). Besides, the current standards of interactions between the Rome Statute institutions and the United Nations should evolve for an appropriate mobilisation of reparations once the judicial outcome will decide on affected communities in multiple situations and for the sake of reconstruction and development. In conclusion, this study associates the governance of justice in the context of state-building and sustainable peace.

The governance of humanitarian escalations between complementary global regimes does not yet include appropriate configurations of civilian protection, police and law enforcement during investigations and prosecutions, including the assistance after the arrest warrants addressed against dangerous warlords. This study takes in consideration the major issues currently under scrutiny within the maintenance of peace, justice and security, particularly the peace enforcement operations and their configurations in the quest of international justice and accountability. Such issues also reflect the poor implementation of arrangements or agreements in the field missions and operations on the ground. The concerns are the weak human security strategies and insufficient mechanisms of interaction between international governance institutions. Such challenges have an impact at several levels, domestic, regional and international, political and legal, historical and ethical, humanitarian and economic. There is evidence to suggest that the systemic failure in the governance of complementary global regimes, as well as the 'test' of civilian protection duties in the African Union and in the League of Arab States and their political distance currently taken from the Rome Statute regime requires political convergence and a *road map* of interactions. The interaction and the involvement in state-building activities at domestic, regional and international levels are at the core of such challenges. Hopefully, such interactions will offer models of governance developing further the existence of the international society in the current shift from modernity to post-modernity standing on the side of individuals with systemic reforms.

This study considers both law and policy challenges occurring globally for the preservation of national, regional and international stability towards complementary global regimes. It debates the humanitarian interventions according to the duty to protect civilians in situation of war and crime with old models of conflict management and the preservation of human security in conflict and post-conflict situations. In the power-reality of international relations a reliable accountability system based on the principles of neutrality, integrity and universality is still opposed by some of the permanent members of the UN Security Council (US, China and Russia). This study outlines some of the reasons behind by looking into the past and current challenges for international governance institutions. These institutions of complementary character should be well-suited in order to respond to the challenges and complexity of international threats and crimes. Unfortunately, the emerging regime of international criminal justice is still marginalized in the arrays of peace and security.

The cooperation standards currently applied remain a controversial issue in international relations and international law. The question arising is whether complementary global regimes would ever be able to have an impact on the causes of threats characterizing intra- and inter-state conflicts finding measures for the prevention of mass atrocity crimes. Prevention and reaction should be treated as the two faces of the same coin focusing on reconstruction and capacity-building. As extensively discussed, the pending issues are the responsibility to protect norm, the authorization of the use of force and the political engagements to advocate for *checks and balances* systems based on the accountability of States and individuals at the same extent. The open question is whether the emerging regime falling under the Rome Statute would ever benefit from the humanitarian engagements of international police and law enforcement capacities. The urgent priority is to implement civilian protection duties with protection, relocation, rehabilitation and reparation among other measures. Such important activities require a place in the configuration of peace and justice mandates on the ground, in the field operations. The complementary duties of international governance institutions would influence the international legal order of being further constitutionilised: strengthening the global fight against the impunity in situations of war and crime, persuading the domestic jurisdictions to do so and enabling their governance of security sectors and civilian protection duties.

# APPENDICES

# TREATIES, LEGAL TEXTS AND SOURCES

## PRIMARY LAW

### *The Charter of the United Nations – Excerpts*

The Charter of the United Nations was signed on 26 June 1945, in San Francisco, at the conclusion of the United Nations Conference on International Organization, and came into force on 24 October 1945. The Statute of the International Court of Justice is an integral part of the Charter.

Amendments to Articles 23, 27 and 61 of the Charter were adopted by the General Assembly on 17 December 1963 and came into force on 31 August 1965. A further amendment to Article 61 was adopted by the General Assembly on 20 December 1971, and came into force on 24 September 1973. An amendment to Article 109, adopted by the General Assembly on 20 December 1965, came into force on 12 June 1968.

The amendment to Article 23 enlarges the membership of the Security Council from eleven to fifteen. The amended Article 27 provides that decisions of the Security Council on procedural matters shall be made by an affirmative vote of nine members (formerly seven) and on all other matters by an affirmative vote of nine members (formerly seven), including the concurring votes of the five permanent members of the Security Council.

The amendment to Article 61, which entered into force on 31 August 1965, enlarged the membership of the Economic and Social Council from eighteen to twenty-seven. The subsequent amendment to that Article, which entered into force on 24 September 1973, further increased the membership of the Council from twenty-seven to fifty-four.

The amendment to Article 109, which relates to the first paragraph of that Article, provides that a General Conference of Member States for the purpose of reviewing the Charter may be held at a date and place to be fixed by a two-thirds vote of the members of the General Assembly and by a vote of any nine members (formerly seven) of the Security Council. Paragraph 3 of Article 109, which deals with the consideration of a possible review conference during the tenth regular session of the General Assembly, has been retained in its original form in its reference to a "vote, of any seven members of the Security Council", the paragraph having been acted upon in 1955 by the General Assembly, at its tenth regular session, and by the Security Council.

*Chapter VI: Pacific Settlement of Disputes*

**Article 33**

1. The parties to any dispute, the continuance of which is likely to endanger the maintenance of international peace and security, shall, first of all, seek a solution by negotiation, enquiry, mediation, conciliation, arbitration, judicial settlement, resort to regional agencies or arrangements, or other peaceful means of their own choice.
2. The Security Council shall, when it deems necessary, call upon the parties to settle their dispute by such means.

**Article 34**

The Security Council may investigate any dispute, or any situation which might lead to international friction or give rise to a dispute, in order to determine whether the continuance of the dispute or situation is likely to endanger the maintenance of international peace and security.

**Article 35**

1. Any Member of the United Nations may bring any dispute, or any situation of the nature referred to in Article 34, to the attention of the Security Council or of the General Assembly.
2. A state which is not a Member of the United Nations may bring to the attention of the Security Council or of the General Assembly any dispute to which it is a party if it accepts in advance, for the purposes of the dispute, the obligations of pacific settlement provided in the present Charter.
3. The proceedings of the General Assembly in respect of matters brought to its attention under this Article will be subject to the provisions of Articles 11 and 12.

**Article 36**

1. The Security Council may, at any stage of a dispute of the nature referred to in Article 33 or of a situation of like nature, recommend appropriate procedures or methods of adjustment.
2. The Security Council should take into consideration any procedures for the settlement of the dispute which have already been adopted by the parties.

3. In making recommendations under this Article the Security Council should also take into consideration that legal disputes should as a general rule be referred by the parties to the International Court of Justice in accordance with the provisions of the Statute of the Court.

**Article 37**

1. Should the parties to a dispute of the nature referred to in Article 33 fail to settle it by the means indicated in that Article, they shall refer it to the Security Council.
2. If the Security Council deems that the continuance of the dispute is in fact likely to endanger the maintenance of international peace and security, it shall decide whether to take action under Article 36 or to recommend such terms of settlement as it may consider appropriate.

**Article 38**

Without prejudice to the provisions of Articles 33 to 37, the Security Council may, if all the parties to any dispute so request, make recommendations to the parties with a view to a pacific settlement of the dispute.

*Chapter VII: Action with Respect to Threats to the Peace, Breaches of the Peace, and Acts of Aggression*

**Article 39**

The Security Council shall determine the existence of any threat to the peace, breach of the peace, or act of aggression and shall make recommendations, or decide what measures shall be taken in accordance with Articles 41 and 42, to maintain or restore international peace and security.

**Article 40**

In order to prevent an aggravation of the situation, the Security Council may, before making the recommendations or deciding upon the measures provided for in Article 39, call upon the parties concerned to comply with such provisional measures as it deems necessary or desirable. Such provisional measures shall be without prejudice to the rights, claims, or position of the parties concerned. The Security Council shall duly take account of failure to comply with such provisional measures.

**Article 41**

The Security Council may decide what measures not involving the use of armed force are to be employed to give effect to its decisions, and it may call upon the Members of the United Nations to apply such measures. These may include complete or partial interruption of economic relations and of rail, sea, air, postal, telegraphic, radio, and other means of communication, and the severance of diplomatic relations.

**Article 42**

Should the Security Council consider that measures provided for in Article 41 would be inadequate or have proved to be inadequate, it may take such action by air, sea, or land forces as may be necessary to maintain or restore international peace and security. Such action may include demonstrations, blockade, and other operations by air, sea, or land forces of Members of the United Nations.

**Article 43**

1. All Members of the United Nations, in order to contribute to the maintenance of international peace and security, undertake to make available to the Security Council, on its call and in accordance with a special agreement or agreements, armed forces, assistance, and facilities, including rights of passage, necessary for the purpose of maintaining international peace and security.
2. Such agreement or agreements shall govern the numbers and types of forces, their degree of readiness and general location, and the nature of the facilities and assistance to be provided.
3. The agreement or agreements shall be negotiated as soon as possible on the initiative of the Security Council. They shall be concluded between the Security Council and Members or between the Security Council and groups of Members and shall be subject to ratification by the signatory states in accordance with their respective constitutional processes.

**Article 44**

When the Security Council has decided to use force it shall, before calling upon a Member not represented on it to provide armed forces in fulfilment of the obligations assumed under Article 43, invite that Member, if the Member so desires, to participate in the decisions of the Security Council concerning the employment of contingents of that Member's armed forces.

**Article 45**

In order to enable the United Nations to take urgent military measures, Members shall hold immediately available national air-force contingents for combined international enforcement action. The strength and degree of readiness of these contingents and plans for their combined action shall be determined within the limits laid down in the special agreement or agreements referred to in Article 43, by the Security Council with the assistance of the Military Staff Committee.

**Article 46**
Plans for the application of armed force shall be made by the Security Council with the assistance of the Military Staff Committee.

**Article 47**
1. There shall be established a Military Staff Committee to advise and assist the Security Council on all questions relating to the Security Council's military requirements for the maintenance of international peace and security, the employment and command of forces placed at its disposal, the regulation of armaments, and possible disarmament.
2. The Military Staff Committee shall consist of the Chiefs of Staff of the permanent members of the Security Council or their representatives. Any Member of the United Nations not permanently represented on the Committee shall be invited by the Committee to be associated with it when the efficient discharge of the Committee's responsibilities requires the participation of that Member in its work.
3. The Military Staff Committee shall be responsible under the Security Council for the strategic direction of any armed forces placed at the disposal of the Security Council. Questions relating to the command of such forces shall be worked out subsequently.
4. The Military Staff Committee, with the authorization of the Security Council and after consultation with appropriate regional agencies, may establish regional sub-committees.

**Article 48**
1. The action required to carry out the decisions of the Security Council for the maintenance of international peace and security shall be taken by all the Members of the United Nations or by some of them, as the Security Council may determine.
2. Such decisions shall be carried out by the Members of the United Nations directly and through their action in the appropriate international agencies of which they are members.

**Article 49**
The Members of the United Nations shall join in affording mutual assistance in carrying out the measures decided upon by the Security Council.

**Article 50**
If preventive or enforcement measures against any state are taken by the Security Council, any other state, whether a Member of the United Nations or not, which finds itself confronted with special economic problems arising from the carrying out of those measures shall have the right to consult the Security Council with regard to a solution of those problems.

**Article 51**

Nothing in the present Charter shall impair the inherent right of individual or collective self-defence if an armed attack occurs against a Member of the United Nations, until the Security Council has taken measures necessary to maintain international peace and security. Measures taken by Members in the exercise of this right of self-defence shall be immediately reported to the Security Council and shall not in any way affect the authority and responsibility of the Security Council under the present Charter to take at any time such action as it deems necessary in order to maintain or restore international peace and security.

## *The Rome Statute of the International Criminal Court*

**Table of Contents***

**Preamble:**

**The States Parties to this Statute, Conscious** that all peoples are united by common bonds, their cultures pieced together in a shared heritage, and concerned that this delicate mosaic may be shattered at any time,

**Mindful** that during this century millions of children, women and men have been victims of unimaginable atrocities that deeply shock the conscience of humanity,

**Recognizing** that such grave crimes threaten the peace, security and well-being of the world,

**Affirming** that the most serious crimes of concern to the international community as a whole must not go unpunished and that their effective prosecution must be ensured by taking measures at the national level and by enhancing international cooperation,

**Determined** to put an end to impunity for the perpetrators of these crimes and thus to contribute to the prevention of such crimes,

**Recalling** that it is the duty of every State to exercise its criminal jurisdiction over those responsible for international crimes,

**Reaffirming** the Purposes and Principles of the Charter of the United Nations, and in particular that all States shall refrain from the threat or use of force against the territorial integrity or political independence of any State, or in any other manner inconsistent with the Purposes of the United Nations,

**Emphasizing** in this connection that nothing in this Statute shall be taken as authorizing any State Party to intervene in an armed conflict or in the internal affairs of any State,

**Determined** to these ends and for the sake of present and future generations, to establish an independent permanent International Criminal Court in relationship

* This Table of Contents is not part of the text of the Rome Statute adopted by the United Nations Diplomatic Conference of Plenipotentiaries on the Establishment of an International Criminal Court on 12 July 1998. It has been included in this publication for ease of reference.

with the United Nations system, with jurisdiction over the most serious crimes of concern to the international community as a whole,
**Emphasizing** that the International Criminal Court established under this Statute shall be complementary to national criminal jurisdictions,
**Resolved** to guarantee lasting respect for and the enforcement of international justice,

**Have agreed as follows:**

**Part I Establishment of the Court**
Article 1 The Court
Article 2 Relationship of the Court with the United Nations
Article 3 Seat of the Court
Article 4 Legal status and powers of the Court

**Part II Jurisdiction, admissibility and applicable law**
Article 5 Crimes within the jurisdiction of the Court
Article 6 Genocide
Article 7 Crimes against humanity
Article 8 War Crimes
Article 9 Elements of Crimes
Article 10 Nothing in this Part shall be interpreted as limiting or prejudicing in any way existing or developing rules of international law for purposes other than this Statute.
Article 11 Jurisdiction *ratione temporis*
Article 12 Preconditions to the exercise of jurisdiction
Article 13 Exercise of jurisdiction
Article 14 Referral of a situation by a State Party
Article 15 Prosecutor
Article 16 Deferral of investigation or prosecution
Article 17 Issues of admissibility
Article 18 Preliminary rulings regarding admissibility
Article 19 Challenges to the jurisdiction of the Court or the admissibility of a case
Article 20 Ne bis in idem
Article 21 Applicable law

**Part III General principles of criminal law**
Article 22 Nullum crimen sine lege
Article 23 Nulla poena sine lege
Article 24 Non-retroactivity ratione personae
Article 25 Individual criminal responsibility
Article 26 Exclusion of jurisdiction over persons under eighteen
Article 27 Irrelevance of official capacity

**Part VI The trial**
Article 62 Place of trial
Article 63 Trial in the presence of the accused
Article 64 Functions and powers of the Trial Chamber
Article 65 Proceedings on an admission of guilt
Article 66 Presumption of innocence
Article 67 Rights of the accused
Article 68 Protection of the victims and witnesses and their participation in the proceedings
Article 69 Evidence
Article 70 Offences against the administration of justice
Article 71 Sanctions for misconduct before the Court
Article 72 Protection of national security information
Article 73 Third-party information or documents
Article 74 Requirements for the decision
Article 75 Reparations to victims
Article 76 Sentencing

**Part VII Penalties**
Article 77 Applicable penalties
Article 78 Determination of the sentence
Article 79 Trust Fund
Article 80 Non-prejudice to national application of penalties and national laws

**Part VIII Appeal and revision**
Article 81 Appeal against decision of acquittal or conviction or against sentence
Article 82 Appeal against other decisions
Article 83 Proceedings on appeal
Article 84 Revision of conviction or sentence
Article 85 Compensation to an arrested or convicted person

**Part IX International cooperation and judicial assistance**
Article 86 General obligation to cooperate
Article 87 Requests for cooperation: general provisions
Article 88 Availability of procedures under national law
Article 89 Surrender of persons to the Court
Article 90 Competing requests
Article 91 Contents of request for arrest and surrender
Article 92 Provisional arrest
Article 93 Other forms of cooperation
Article 94 Postponement of execution of a request in respect of ongoing investigation or prosecution

Article 127 Withdrawal
Article 128 Authentic texts

| Table of Selected Contentious Cases of the International Court of Justice | |
|---|---|
| **Application instituting proceedings** | **Topic** |
| 23 June 1999<br>02 July 1999<br>03 February 2015 | Armed Activities on the Territory of the Congo (*Democratic Republic of the Congo v. Rwanda*)<br>Application of the Convention on the Prevention and Punishment of the Crime of Genocide (*Croatia v. Serbia*)<br>Application of the Convention on the Prevention and Punishment of the Crime of Genocide (*Croatia v. Serbia)* |
| 17 October 2000 | Arrest Warrant of 11 April 2000 (*Democratic Republic of the Congo v. Belgium*) |
| 24 April 2001 | Application for Revision of the Judgment of 11 July 1996 in the Case concerning Application of the Convention on the Prevention and Punishment of the Crime of Genocide (*Bosnia and Herzegovina v. Yugoslavia*), Preliminary Objections (*Yugoslavia v. Bosnia and Herzegovina*) |

## SECONDARY LAW

### *Negotiated Relationship Agreement between the International Criminal Court and the United Nations*

ASP Resolution: ICC-ASP/3/Res.1
Adoption: 04.10.2004,
Entry into Force: 22.07.2004
Source: ASP/UN

The International Criminal Court and the United Nations,

*Bearing in mind* the Purposes and Principles of the Charter of the United Nations,
*Recalling* that the Rome Statute of the International Criminal Court reaffirms the Purposes and Principles of the Charter of the United Nations,
*Noting* the important role assigned to the International Criminal Court in dealing with the most serious crimes of concern to the international community as a whole, as referred to in the Rome Statute, and which threaten the peace, security and well-being of the world,
*Bearing in mind* that, in accordance with the Rome Statute, the International Criminal Court is established as an independent permanent institution in relationship with the United Nations system,
*Recalling* also that, in accordance with article 2 of the Rome Statute, the International Criminal Court shall be brought into relationship with the United Nations through an agreement to be approved by the Assembly of the States

Parties to the Rome Statute and thereafter concluded by the President of the Court on its behalf,
*Recalling* further General Assembly resolution 58/79 of 9 December 2003 calling for the conclusion of a relationship agreement between the United Nations and the International Criminal Court,
*Noting* the responsibilities of the Secretary-General of the United Nations under the provisions of the Rome Statute of the International Criminal Court, Desiring to make provision for a mutually beneficial relationship whereby the discharge of respective responsibilities of the United Nations and the International Criminal Court may be facilitated,
*Taking into account* for this purpose the provisions of the Charter of the United Nations and the provisions of the Rome Statute of the International Criminal Court,

Have agreed as follows:

**I. General provisions**

**Article 1**
**Purpose of the Agreement**

1. The present Agreement, which is entered into by the United Nations and the International Criminal Court ("the Court"), pursuant to the provisions of the Charter of the United Nations ("the Charter") and the Rome Statute of the International Criminal Court ("the Statute"), respectively, defines the terms on which the United Nations and the Court shall be brought into relationship.
2. For the purposes of this Agreement, "the Court" shall also include the Secretariat of the Assembly of States Parties.

**Article 2**
**Principles**

1. The United Nations recognizes the Court as an independent permanent judicial institution which, in accordance with articles 1 and 4 of the Statute, has international legal personality and such legal capacity as may be necessary for the exercise of its functions and the fulfillment of its purposes.
2. The Court recognizes the responsibilities of the United Nations under the Charter.
3. The United Nations and the Court respect each other's status and mandate.

**Article 3**
**Obligation of cooperation and coordination**

The United Nations and the Court agree that, with a view to facilitating the effective discharge of their respective responsibilities, they shall cooperate closely, whenever appropriate, with each other and consult each other on matters of mutual interest pursuant to the provisions of the present Agreement and in conformity with the respective provisions of the Charter and the Statute.

## II. Institutional relations

### Article 4
### Reciprocal representation

1. Subject to the applicable provisions of the Rules of Procedure and Evidence of the Court ("the Rules of Procedure and Evidence"), the Secretary-General of the United Nations ("the Secretary-General") or his/her representative shall have a standing invitation to attend public hearings of the Chambers of the Court that relate to cases of interest to the United Nations and any public meetings of the Court.
2. The Court may attend and participate in the work of the General Assembly of the United Nations in the capacity of observer. The United Nations shall, subject to the rules and practice of the bodies concerned, invite the Court to attend meetings and conferences convened under the auspices of the United Nations where observers are allowed and whenever matters of interest to the Court are under discussion.
3. Whenever the Security Council considers matters related to the activities of the Court, the President of the Court ("the President") or the Prosecutor of the Court ("the Prosecutor") may address the Council, at its invitation, in order to give assistance with regard to matters within the jurisdiction of the Court.

### Article 5
### Exchange of information

1. Without prejudice to other provisions of the present Agreement concerning the submission of documents and information concerning particular cases before the Court, the United Nations and the Court shall, to the fullest extent possible and practicable, arrange for the exchange of information and documents of mutual interest. In particular:
   (a) The Secretary-General shall:
      (i) Transmit to the Court information on developments related to the Statute which are relevant to the work of the Court, including information on communications received by the Secretary-General in the capacity of depositary of the Statute or depositary of any other agreements which relate to the exercise by the Court of its jurisdiction;
      (ii) Keep the Court informed regarding the implementation of article 123, paragraphs 1 and 2, of the Statute relating to the convening by the Secretary-General of review conferences; (iii) In addition to the requirement provided in article 121, paragraph 7, of the Statute,

circulate to all States Members of the United Nations or members of specialized agencies or of the International Atomic Energy Agency which are not parties to the Statute the text of any amendment adopted pursuant to article 121 of the Statute;

(b) The Registrar of the Court ("the Registrar") shall:

(i) In accordance with the Statute and the Rules of Procedure and Evidence, provide information and documentation relating to pleadings, oral proceedings, judgments and orders of the Court in cases which may be of interest to the United Nations generally, and particularly in those cases which involve crimes committed against the personnel of the United Nations or that involve the improper use of the flag, insignia or uniform of the United Nations resulting in death or serious personal injury as well as any cases involving the circumstances referred to under article 16, 17, or 18, paragraph 1 or 2, of the present Agreement;

(ii) Furnish to the United Nations, with the concurrence of the Court and subject to its Statute and rules, any information relating to the work of the Court requested by the International Court of Justice in accordance with its Statute;

2. The United Nations and the Court shall make every effort to achieve maximum cooperation with a view to avoiding undesirable duplication in the collection, analysis, publication and dissemination of information relating to matters of mutual interest. They shall strive, where appropriate, to combine their efforts to secure the greatest possible usefulness and utilization of such information.

**Article 6**
**Reports to the United Nations**

The Court may, if it deems it appropriate, submit reports on its activities to the United Nations through the Secretary-General.

**Article 7**
**Agenda items**

The Court may propose items for consideration by the United Nations. In such cases, the Court shall notify the Secretary-General of its proposal and provide any relevant information. The Secretary-General shall, in accordance with his/her authority, bring such item or items to the attention of the General Assembly or the Security Council, and also to any other United Nations organ concerned, including organs of United Nations programs and funds.

**Article 8**
**Personnel arrangements**

1. The United Nations and the Court agree to consult and cooperate as far as practicable regarding personnel standards, methods and arrangements.
2. The United Nations and the Court agree to:
   (a) Periodically consult on matters of mutual interest relating to the employment of their officers and staff, including conditions of service, the duration of appointments, classification, salary scale and allowances, retirement and pension rights and staff regulations and rules;
   (b) Cooperate in the temporary interchange of personnel, where appropriate, making due provision for the retention of seniority and pension rights;
   (c) Strive for maximum cooperation in order to achieve the most efficient use of specialized personnel, systems and services.

**Article 9**
**Administrative cooperation**

The United Nations and the Court shall consult, from time to time, concerning the most efficient use of facilities, staff and services with a view to avoiding the establishment and operation of overlapping facilities and services. They shall also consult to explore the possibility of establishing common facilities or services in specific areas, with due regard for cost savings.

**Article 10**
**Services and facilities**

1. The United Nations agrees that, upon the request of the Court, it shall, subject to availability, provide on a reimbursable basis, or as otherwise agreed, for the purposes of the Court such facilities and services as may be required, including for the meetings of the Assembly of States Parties ("the Assembly"), its Bureau or subsidiary bodies, including translation and interpretation services, documentation and conference services. When the United Nations is unable to meet the request of the Court, it shall notify the Court accordingly, giving reasonable notice.
2. The terms and conditions on which any such facilities or services of the United Nations may be provided shall, as appropriate, be the subject of supplementary arrangements.

**Article 11**
**Access to United Nations Headquarters**

The United Nations and the Court shall endeavor, subject to their respective rules, to facilitate access by the representatives of all States Parties to the Statute, representatives of the Court and observers in the Assembly, as provided for in article 112, paragraph 1, of the Statute, to United Nations Headquarters when a meeting of the Assembly is to be held. This shall also apply, as appropriate, to meetings of the Bureau or subsidiary bodies.

**Article 12**
**Laissez-passer**

The judges, the Prosecutor, the Deputy Prosecutors, the Registrar and the staff/officials of the Office of the Prosecutor and the Registry shall be entitled, in accordance with such special arrangements as may be concluded between the Secretary-General and the Court, to use the laissez-passer of the United Nations as a valid travel document where such use is recognized by States in agreements defining the privileges and immunities of the Court. Staff of "the Registry" includes staff of the Presidency and of the Chambers, pursuant to article 44 of the Statute, and staff of the Secretariat of the Assembly of States Parties, pursuant to paragraph 3 of the Annex of Resolution ICC-ASP/2/Res.3.

**Article 13**
**Financial matters**

1. The United Nations and the Court agree that the conditions under which any funds may be provided to the Court by a decision of the General Assembly of the United Nations pursuant to article 115 of the Statute shall be subject to separate arrangements. The Registrar shall inform the Assembly of the making of such arrangements.
2. The United Nations and the Court further agree that the costs and expenses resulting from cooperation or the provision of services pursuant to the present Agreement shall be subject to separate arrangements between the United Nations and the Court. The Registrar shall inform the Assembly of the making of such arrangements.
3. The United Nations may, upon request of the Court and subject to paragraph 2 of this article, provide advice on financial and fiscal questions of interest to the Court.

**Article 14**
**Other agreements concluded by the Court**

The United Nations and the Court shall consult, when appropriate, on the registration or filing and recording with the United Nations of agreements concluded by the Court with States or international organizations.

## III. Cooperation and judicial assistance

**Article 15**
**General provisions regarding cooperation between the United Nations and the Court**

1. With due regard to its responsibilities and competence under the Charter and subject to its rules as defined under the applicable international law, the United Nations undertakes to cooperate with the Court and to provide to the Court such information or documents as the Court may request pursuant to article 87, paragraph 6, of the Statute.
2. The United Nations or its programs, funds and offices concerned may agree to provide to the Court other forms of cooperation and assistance compatible with the provisions of the Charter and the Statute.
3. In the event that the disclosure of information or documents or the provision of other forms of cooperation would endanger the safety or security of current or former personnel of the United

Nations or otherwise prejudice the security or proper conduct of any operation or activity of the United Nations, the Court may order, particularly at the request of the United Nations, appropriate measures of protection. In the absence of such measures, the United Nations shall endeavour to disclose the information or documents or to provide the requested cooperation, while reserving the right to take its own measures of protection, which may include withholding of some information or documents or their submission in an appropriate form, including the introduction of redactions.

**Article 16**
**Testimony of the officials of the United Nations**

1. If the Court requests the testimony of an official of the United Nations or one of its programs, funds or offices, the United Nations undertakes to cooperate with the Court and, if necessary and with due regard to its responsibilities and competence under the Charter and the Convention on the Privileges and Immunities of the United Nations and subject to its rules, shall waive that person's obligation of confidentiality.
2. The Secretary-General shall be authorized by the Court to appoint a representative of the United Nations to assist any official of the United Nations who appears as a witness before the Court.

**Article 17**
**Cooperation between the Security Council of the United Nations and the Court**

1. When the Security Council, acting under Chapter VII of the Charter of the United Nations, decides to refer to the Prosecutor pursuant to article 13, paragraph (b), of the Statute, a situation in which one or more of the

crimes referred to in article 5 of the Statute appears to have been committed, the Secretary-General shall immediately transmit the written decision of the Security Council to the Prosecutor together with documents and other materials that may be pertinent to the decision of the Council. The Court undertakes to keep the Security Council informed in this regard in accordance with the Statute and the Rules of Procedure and Evidence. Such information shall be transmitted through the Secretary-General.

2. When the Security Council adopts under Chapter VII of the Charter a resolution requesting the Court, pursuant to article 16 of the Statute, not to commence or proceed with an investigation or prosecution, this request shall immediately be transmitted by the Secretary-General to the President of the Court and the Prosecutor. The Court shall inform the Security Council through the Secretary-General of its receipt of the above request and, as appropriate, inform the Security Council through the Secretary-General of actions, if any, taken by the Court in this regard.
3. Where a matter has been referred to the Court by the Security Council and the Court makes a finding, pursuant to article 87, paragraph 5 (b) or paragraph 7, of the Statute, of a failure by a State to cooperate with the Court, the Court shall inform the Security Council or refer the matter to it, as the case may be, and the Registrar shall convey to the Security Council through the Secretary-General the decision of the Court, together with relevant information in the case. The Security Council, through the Secretary-General, shall inform the Court through the Registrar of action, if any, taken by it under the circumstances.

**Article 18**
**Cooperation between the United Nations and the Prosecutor**

1. With due regard to its responsibilities and competence under the Charter of the United Nations and subject to its rules, the United Nations undertakes to cooperate with the Prosecutor and to enter with the Prosecutor into such arrangements or, as appropriate, agreements as may be necessary to facilitate such cooperation, in particular when the Prosecutor exercises, under article 54 of the Statute, his or her duties and powers with respect to investigation and seeks the cooperation of the United Nations in accordance with that article.
2. Subject to the rules of the organ concerned, the United Nations undertakes to cooperate in relation to requests from the Prosecutor in providing such additional information as he or she may seek, in accordance with article 15, paragraph 2, of the Statute, from organs of the United Nations in connection with investigations initiated *proprio motu* by the Prosecutor pursuant to that article. The Prosecutor shall address a request for such information to the Secretary-General, who shall convey it to the presiding officer or other appropriate officer of the organ concerned.

3. The United Nations and the Prosecutor may agree that the United Nations provide documents or information to the Prosecutor on condition of confidentiality and solely for the purpose of generating new evidence and that such documents or information shall not be disclosed to other organs of the Court or to third parties, at any stage of the proceedings or thereafter, without the consent of the United Nations.
4. The Prosecutor and the United Nations or its programs, funds and offices concerned may enter into such arrangements as may be necessary to facilitate their cooperation for the implementation of this article, in particular in order to ensure the confidentiality of information, the protection of any person, including former or current United Nations personnel, and the security or proper conduct of any operation or activity of the United Nations.

**Article 19**
**Rules concerning United Nations privileges and immunities**
If the Court seeks to exercise its jurisdiction over a person who is alleged to be criminally responsible for a crime within the jurisdiction of the Court and if, in the circumstances, such person enjoys, according to the Convention on the Privileges and Immunities of the United Nations and the relevant rules of international law, any privileges and immunities as are necessary for the independent exercise of his or her work for the United Nations, the United Nations undertakes to cooperate fully with the Court and to take all necessary measures to allow the Court to exercise its jurisdiction, in particular by waiving any such privileges and immunities in accordance with the Convention on the Privileges and Immunities of the United Nations and the relevant rules of international law.

**Article 20**
**Protection of confidentiality**
If the United Nations is requested by the Court to provide information or documentation in its custody, possession or control which was disclosed to it in confidence by a State or an intergovernmental, international or non-governmental organization or an individual, the United Nations shall seek the consent of the originator to disclose that information or documentation or, where appropriate, will inform the Court that it may seek the consent of the originator for the United Nations to disclose that information or documentation. If the originator is a State Party to the Statute and the United Nations fails to obtain its consent to disclosure within a reasonable period of time, the United Nations shall inform the Court accordingly, and the issue of disclosure shall be resolved between the State Party concerned and the Court in accordance with the Statute. If the originator is not a State Party to the Statute and refuses to consent to disclosure, the United Nations shall inform the Court that it is unable to provide the requested information or documentation because of a pre-existing obligation of confidentiality to the originator.

## IV. Final provisions

### Article 21

**Supplementary arrangements for the implementation of the present Agreement**

The Secretary-General and the Court may, for the purpose of implementing the present Agreement, make such supplementary arrangements as may be found appropriate.

### Article 22

**Amendments**

The present Agreement may be amended by agreement between the United Nations and the Court. Any such amendment shall be approved by the General Assembly of the United Nations and by the Assembly in accordance with article 2 of the Statute. The United Nations and the Court shall notify each other in writing of the date of such approval, and the Agreement shall enter into force on the date of the later of the said approvals.

### Article 23

**Entry into force**

The present Agreement shall be approved by the General Assembly of the United Nations and by the Assembly in accordance with article 2 of the Statute. The United Nations and the Court shall notify each other in writing of the date of such approval. The Agreement shall thereafter enter into force upon signature.

**In witness thereof**, the undersigned have signed the present Agreement.

**Signed** this __________ day of __________ at United Nations Headquarters in New York in two copies in all the official languages of the United Nations and the Court, of which the English and French texts shall be authentic.

| **Resolutions adopted by the United Nations Security Council referring to the International Criminal Court (Sudan, Darfur)** | | |
|---|---|---|
| **S/RES/1564** | **18 September 2004** | The Security Council threatened the imposition of sanctions against Sudan if it failed to comply with its obligations on Darfur, and an international inquiry was established to investigate violations of human rights in the region (International Commission of Inquiry on Darfur). |
| **S/RES/1593** | **31 March 2005** | The situation concerning Sudan adopted after receiving a report by the International Commission of Inquiry on Darfur, the Security Council referred the situation in the Darfur region of Sudan to the International Criminal Court (ICC) and required all States to co-operate fully. |

| List of United Nations Security Council resolutions concerning Sudan (1996–2012) | | | |
|---|---|---|---|
| - S/RES/1044 | S/RES/1665 | S/RES/1919 | S/RES/2075 |
| - S/RES/1054 | S/RES/1672 | S/RES/1922 | |
| - S/RES/1070 | S/RES/1679 | S/RES/1923 | |
| - S/RES/112 | S/RES/1706 | S/RES/1935 | |
| - S/RES/1372 | S/RES/1709 | S/RES/1945 | |
| - S/RES/1547 | S/RES/1713 | S/RES/1978 | |
| - S/RES/1556 | S/RES/1714 | S/RES/1982 | |
| - S/RES/1564 | S/RES/1755 | S/RES/1990 | |
| - S/RES/1569 | S/RES/1769 | S/RES/1997 | |
| - S/RES/1574 | S/RES/1779 | S/RES/1999 | |
| - S/RES/1585 | S/RES/1784 | S/RES/2003 | |
| - S/RES/1588 | S/RES/1812 | S/RES/2024 | |
| - S/RES/1590 | S/RES/1828 | S/RES/2032 | |
| - S/RES/1591 | S/RES/1841 | S/RES/2035 | |
| - S/RES/1593 | S/RES/1870 | S/RES/2046 | |
| - S/RES/1627 | S/RES/1881 | S/RES/2047 | |
| - S/RES/1651 | S/RES/1891 | S/RES/2057 | |
| - S/RES/1653 | S/RES/1913 | S/RES/2063 | |

| Resolution adopted by the United Nations Security Council referring to the International Criminal Court (Libya) | | |
|---|---|---|
| **S/RES/1970** | **26 February 2011** | The Security Council condemned the use of lethal force by the regime of Muammar Gaddafi against protesters participating in the Libyan civil war, and imposed a series of international sanctions in response. The resolution marked the first time a country was unanimously referred to the International Criminal Court by the Security Council. |
| **S/RES/1973** | **17 March 2011** | The resolution formed the legal basis for military intervention in the Libyan civil war, demanding "an immediate ceasefire" and authorizing the international community to establish a no-fly zone and to use all means necessary short of foreign occupation to protect civilians. |

| List of United Nations Security Council resolutions concerning Libya (1955–1994) |
|---|
| - S/RES/109 |
| - S/RES/1192 |
| - S/RES/1506 |
| - S/RES/1970 |
| - S/RES/1973 |
| - S/RES/2009 |
| - S/RES/2016 |
| - S/RES/2017 |
| - S/RES/2022 |
| - S/RES/2040 |
| - S/RES/731 |
| - S/RES/748 |
| - S/RES/883 |
| - S/RES/910 |
| - S/RES/915 |
| - S/RES/926 |

| Selected Security Council resolutions about the Democratic Republic of Congo (DRC) | |
|---|---|
| **Resolution No.** | **Topic** |
| A/RES/2098 | 28 March 2013 – This resolution renewed MONUSCO's mandate, including an intervention brigade to neutralise rebel groups in eastern DRC, until 31 March 2014. |
| A/RES/2078 | 28 November 2012 – This resolution renewed DRC sanctions and the mandate of the Group of Experts supporting the sanctions committee until 1 February 2014. |
| A/RES/2076 | 20 November 2012 – The Security Council condemned the M23's actions and external support given to the group and expressed its intention to consider additional targeted sanctions against the leadership of the M23 and those providing it with external support. |

| ICC – Assembly of States Parties (ASP) – Sessions & Resolutions |
|---|

## ICC – ASP – 2014/2015 – 13th Session – Resolutions

| Resolution No. | Date | Meeting | Docs | Subjects |
|---|---|---|---|---|
| **ICC-ASP/13/Res.1** | 17.12.2014 | 12h plenary meeting | E F S A R C | Programme budget for 2015, the Working Capital Fund for 2015, scale of assessments for the apportionment of expenses of the International Criminal Court, financing appropriations for 2015 and the Contingency Fund |
| **ICC-ASP/13/Res.2** | 17.12.2014 | 12th plenary meeting | E F S A R C | Permanent premises |
| **ICC-ASP/13/Res.3** | 17.12.2014 | 12th plenary meeting | E F S A R C | Cooperation |
| **ICC-ASP/13/Res.4** | 17.12.2014 | 12th plenary meeting | E F S A R C | Victims and affected communities, reparations and Trust Fund for Victims |
| **ICC-ASP/13/Res.5** | 17.12.2014 | 13th plenary meeting | E F S A R C | Strengthening the International Criminal Court and the Assembly of States Parties |

## ICC – ASP 2013/2014 – 12th Session – Resolutions

| Resolution No. | Date | Meeting | Docs | Subjects |
|---|---|---|---|---|
| **ICC-ASP/12/Res.1** | 27.11.2013 | 12h plenary meeting | E F S A R C | Programme budget for 2014, the Working Capital Fund for 2014, scale of assessments for the apportionment of expenses of the International Criminal Court, financing appropriations for 2014 and the Contingency Fund |
| **ICC-ASP/12/Res.2** | 27.11.2013 | 12th plenary meeting | E F S A R C | Permanent premises |
| **ICC-ASP/12/Res.3** | 27.11.2013 | 12th plenary meeting | E F S A R C | Cooperation |
| **ICC-ASP/12/Res.4** | 27.11.2013 | 12th plenary meeting | E F S A R C | Complementarity |
| **ICC-ASP/12/Res.5** | 27.11.2013 | 12th plenary meeting | E F S A R C | Victims and affected communities, reparations and Trust Fund for Victims |
| **ICC-ASP/12/Res.6** | 27.11.2013 | 12th plenary meeting | E F S A R C | Independent Oversight Mechanism |
| **ICC-ASP/12/Res.7** | 27.11.2013 | 12th plenary meeting | E F S A R C | Amendments to the Rules of Procedure and Evidence |

## ICC – ASP – 2012/2013 – 11th Session – Resolutions

| Resolution No. | Date | Meeting | Docs | Subjects |
|---|---|---|---|---|
| **ICC-ASP/11/Res.1** advance version | 21.11.2012 | 8th plenary meeting | E F S A R C | Programme budget for 2013, the Working Capital Fund for 2013, scale of assessments for the apportionment of expenses of the International Criminal Court, financing appropriations for 2013 and the Contingency Fund |
| **ICC-ASP/11/Res.2** advance version | 21.11.2012 | 8th plenary meeting | E F S A R C | Amendment of the Rules of Procedure and Evidence |
| **ICC-ASP/11/Res.3** advance version | 21.11.2012 | 8th plenary meeting | E F S A R C | Permanent premises |
| **ICC-ASP/11/Res.4** advance version | 21.11.2012 | 8th plenary meeting | E F S A R C | Independent Oversight Mechanism |
| **ICC-ASP/11/Res.5** advance version | 21.11.2012 | 8th plenary meeting | E F S A R C | Cooperation |
| **ICC-ASP/11/Res.6** advance version | 21.11.2012 | 8th plenary meeting | E F S A R C | Complementarity |
| **ICC-ASP/11/Res.7** advance version | 21.11.2012 | 8th plenary meeting | E F S A R C | Victims and Reparations |

## ICC – ASP 2011/2012 – 10th Session – Resolutions

| Resolution No. | Date | Meeting | Docs | Subjects |
|---|---|---|---|---|
| **ICC-ASP/10/Res.1** | 20.12.2011 | 7th plenary meeting | E F S A R C | Amendments to the rule 4 of the Rules of Procedure and Evidence |
| **ICC-ASP/10/Res.2** | 20.12.2011 | 7th plenary meeting | E F S A R C | Cooperation |
| **ICC-ASP/10/Res.3** | 20.12.2011 | 7th plenary meeting | E F S A R C | Reparations |
| **ICC-ASP/10/Res.4** | 21.12.2011 | 9th plenary meeting | E F S A R C | Programme budget for 2012, the Working Capital Fund for 2012, scale of assessments for the apportionment of expenses of the International Criminal Court, financing appropriations for 2012 and the Contingency Fund |
| **ICC-ASP/10/Res.5** | 21.12.2011 | 9th plenary meeting | E F S A R C | Strengthening the International Criminal Court and the Assembly of States Parties |
| **ICC-ASP/10/Res.6** | 21.12.2011 | 9th plenary meeting | E F S A R C | Permanent premises |

## ICC – ASP 2010/2011 – 9th Session – Resolutions

| Resolution No. | Date | Meeting | Docs | Subjects |
|---|---|---|---|---|
| **ICC-ASP/9/Res.1** | 10.12.2010 | 5th plenary meeting | E F S A R C | Permanent premises |
| **ICC-ASP/9/Res.2** | 10.12.2010 | 5th plenary meeting | E F S A R C | Establishment of a study group on governance |
| **ICC-ASP/9/Res.3** | 10.12.2010 | 5th plenary meeting | E F S A R C | Strengthening the International Criminal Court and the Assembly of States Parties |
| **ICC-ASP/9/Res.4** | 10.12.2010 | 5th plenary meeting | E F S A R C | Programme budget for 2011, the Working Capital Fund for 2011, scale of assessments for the apportionment of expenses of the International Criminal Court, financing appropriations for 2011 and the Contingency Fund |
| **ICC-ASP/9/Res.5** | 10.12.2010 | 5th plenary meeting | E F S A R C | Independent Oversight Mechanism |

## ICC – ASP – 2010 – Review Conference – Resolutions

| Resolution No. | Date | Meeting | Docs | Subjects |
|---|---|---|---|---|
| **RC/Res.1** | **08.06.2010** | 9th plenary meeting | E F S A R C | Complementarity |
| **RC/Res.2** | **08.06.2010** | 9th plenary meeting | E F S A R C | The impact of the Rome Statute system on victims and affected communities |
| **RC/Res.3** | **08.06.2010** | 9th plenary meeting | E F S A R C | Strengthening the enforcement of sentences |
| **RC/Res.4** | **10.06.2010** | 11th plenary meeting | E F S A R C | Article 124 of the Rome Statute |
| **RC/Res.5** | **10.06.2010** | 12th plenary meeting | E F S A R C | Amendments to article 8 of the Rome Statute |
| **RC/Res.6** | **11.06.2010** | 13th plenary meeting | E F S A R C | The Crime of Aggression |

## ICC – ASP – 2009/2010 – 8th Session – Resolutions

| Resolution No. | Date | Meeting | Docs | Subjects |
|---|---|---|---|---|
| **ICC-ASP/8/Res.1** | 26.11.2009 | 7th plenary meeting | E F S A R C | Establishment of an independent oversight mechanism |

| | | | | |
|---|---|---|---|---|
| **ICC-ASP/8/Res.2** | 26.11.2009 | 8th plenary meeting | E F S A R C | Cooperation |
| **ICC-ASP/8/Res.3** | 26.11.2009 | 8th plenary meeting | E F S A R C | Strengthening the International Criminal Court and the Assembly of States Parties |
| **ICC-ASP/8/Res.4** | 26.11.2009 | 8th plenary meeting | E F S A R C | Family visits for indigent detainees |
| **ICC-ASP/8/Res.5** | 26.11.2009 | 8th plenary meeting | E F S A R C | Permanent premises |
| **ICC-ASP/8/Res.6** | 26.11.2009 | 8th plenary meeting | E F S A R C | Review Conference |
| **ICC-ASP/8/Res.7** | 26.11.2009 | 8th plenary meeting | E F S A R C | Programme budget for 2010,<br>the Working Capital Fund for 2010,<br>scale of assessments for the apportionment of expenses of the International Criminal Court,<br>financing appropriations for the year 2010,<br>the Contingency Fund,<br>conversion of GTA psychologist post to an established one,<br>Legal aid (defence) and<br>the Addis Ababa Liaison Office |
| **ICC-ASP/8/Res.8** | 25.03.2010 | 10th plenary meeting | E F S A R C | One-time payments for the permanent premises |
| **ICC-ASP/8/Res.9** | 25.03.2010 | 10th plenary meeting | E F S A R C | Review Conference |

## ICC – ASP – 2008/2009 – 7th Session – Resolutions

| Resolution No. | Date | Meeting | Docs | Topic |
|---|---|---|---|---|
| **ICC-ASP/7/Res.1** | 21.11.2008 | 7th plenary meeting | E F S A R C | Permanent premises |
| **ICC-ASP/7/Res.2** | 21.11.2008 | 7th plenary meeting | E F S A R C | Venue of the Review Conference |
| **ICC-ASP/7/Res.3** | 21.11.2008 | 7th plenary meeting | E F S A R C | Strengthening the International Criminal Court and the Assembly of States Parties |
| **ICC-ASP/7/Res.4** | 21.11.2008 | 7th plenary meeting | E F S A R C | Programme budget for 2009, the Working Capital Fund for 2009, scale of assessments for the apportionment of expenses of the International Criminal Court, financing appropriations for the year 2009 and the Contingency Fund |
| **ICC-ASP/7/Res.5** | 21.11.2008 | 7th plenary meeting | E F S A R C | Amendment to the Financial Regulations and Rules |
| **ICC-ASP/7/Res.6** | 21.11.2008 | 7th plenary meeting | E F S A R C | Amendment to the Rules of Procedure of the Assembly of States Parties |
| **ICC-ASP/7/Res.7** | 21.11.2008 | 7th plenary meeting | E F S A R C | Amendment to the Rules of Procedure of the Committee on Budget and Finance |

## ICC – 2007/2008 – 6th Session – Resolutions

| Resolution No. | Date | Meeting | Docs | Topic |
|---|---|---|---|---|
| **ICC-ASP/6/Res.1** | 14.12.2007 | 7th plenary meeting | E F S A R C | Permanent premises |
| **ICC-ASP/6/Res.2** | 14.12.2007 | 7th plenary meeting | E F S A R C | Strengthening the International Criminal Court and the Assembly of States Parties |
| **ICC-ASP/6/Res.3** | 14.12.2007 | 7th plenary meeting | E F S A R C | Amendment to the Regulations of the Trust Fund for Victims |
| **ICC-ASP/6/Res.4** | 14.12.2007 | 7th plenary meeting | E F S A R C | Programme budget for 2008, the Working Capital Fund for 2008, scale of assessments for the apportionment of expenses of the International Criminal Court and financing appropriations for the year 2008 |
| **ICC-ASP/6/Res.5** | 14.12.2007 | 7th plenary meeting | E F S A R C | Amendment to the Financial Regulations and Rules |
| **ICC-ASP/6/Res.6** | 14.12.2007 | 7th plenary meeting | E F S A R C | Amendments to the pension scheme regulations for judges of the International Criminal Court |
| **ICC-ASP/6/Res.7** | 06.06.2008 | 9th plenary meeting | E F S A R C | Funding of the disability pension of a former judge of the International Criminal Court |
| **ICC-ASP/6/Res.8** | 06.06.2008 | 9th plenary meeting | E F S A R C | Review Conference |

## ICC – ASP – 2006/2007 – 5th Session – Resolutions

| Resolution No. | Date | Meeting | Docs | Topic |
|---|---|---|---|---|
| ICC-ASP/5/Res.1 | 01.12.2006 | 7th plenary meeting | E F S A R C | Permanent premises |
| ICC-ASP/5/Res.2 | 01.12.2006 | 7th plenary meeting | E F S A R C | Strategic planning process of the Court |
| ICC-ASP/5/Res.3 | 01.12.2006 | 7th plenary meeting | E F S A R C | Strengthening the International Criminal Court and the Assembly of States Parties |
| ICC-ASP/5/Res.4 | 01.12.2006 | 7th plenary meeting | E F S A R C | Programme budget for 2007, the Working Capital Fund for 2007, scale of assessments for the apportionment of expenses of the International Criminal Court and financing appropriations for the year 2007 |
| ICC-ASP/5/Res.5 | 01.02.2007 | 9th plenary meeting | E F S A R C | Procedure for the nomination and election of judges, the Prosecutor and Deputy Prosecutors of the International Criminal Court: amendment to operative paragraph 27 of resolution ICC-ASP/3/Res.6 |
| ICC-ASP/5/Res.6 | 01.02.2007 | 9th plenary meeting | E F S A R C | Conditions of service and compensation of judges of the International Criminal Court: amendment to the pension scheme regulations for judges of the International Criminal Court |

## ICC – ASP – 2005/2006 – 4th Session – Resolutions

| Resolution No. | Date | Meeting | Docs | Topic |
|---|---|---|---|---|
| ICC-ASP/4/Res.1 | 02.12.2005 | 3rd plenary meeting | E F S A R C | Code of Professional Conduct for counsel |

| | | | | |
|---|---|---|---|---|
| **ICC-ASP/4/Res.2** | 03.12.2005 | 4th plenary meeting | E F S A R C | Permanent Premises |
| **ICC-ASP/4/Res.3** | 03.12.2005 | 4th plenary meeting | E F S A R C | Regulations of the Trust Fund for Victims |
| **ICC-ASP/4/Res.4** | 03.12.2005 | 4th plenary meeting | E F S A R C | Strengthening the International Criminal Court and the Assembly of States Parties |
| **ICC-ASP/4/Res.5** | 03.12.2005 | 4th plenary meeting | E F S A R C | Procedure for filling vacancies in the Board of Directors of the Trust Fund for Victims |
| **ICC-ASP/4/Res.6** | 03.12.2005 | 4th plenary meeting | E F S A R C | Procedure for filling vacancies in the Committee on Budget and Finance |
| **ICC-ASP/4/Res.7** | 03.12.2005 | 4th plenary meeting | E F S A R C | Amendment regarding the term of office of members of the Board of Directors of the Trust Fund for Victims |
| **ICC-ASP/4/Res.8** | 03.12.2005 | 4th plenary meeting | E F S A R C | Programme budget for 2006, the Working Capital Fund for 2006, scale of assessments for the apportionment of expenses of the International Criminal Court and financing appropriations for the year 2006 |
| **ICC-ASP/4/Res.9** | 03.12.2005 | 4th plenary meeting | E F S A R C | Pension scheme for judges |

| | | | | |
|---|---|---|---|---|
| **ICC-ASP/4/Res.10** | 03.12.2005 | 4th plenary meeting | E F S A R C | Amendments to the Financial Regulations and Rules |
| **ICC-ASP/4/Res.11** | 03.12.2005 | 4th plenary meeting | E F S A R C | Transfer of funds from Major Programme III to Major Programme V under the 2005 programme budget |
| **ICC-ASP/4/Res.12** | 27.01.2006 | 7th plenary meeting | E F S A R C | Interim Premises |

## ICC – ASP – 2004/2005 – 3rd Session – Resolutions

| Resolution No. | Date | Meeting | Docs | Topic |
|---|---|---|---|---|
| **ICC-ASP/3/Res.1** | 07.09.2004 | 3rd plenary meeting | E F S A R C | Negotiated Draft Relationship Agreement between the International Criminal Court and the United Nations |
| **ICC-ASP/3/Res.2** | 09.09.2004 | 5th plenary meeting | E F S A R C | Amendment to rule 29 of the Rules of Procedure of the Assembly of States Parties |
| **ICC-ASP/3/Res.3** | 10.09.2004 | 6th plenary meeting | E F S A R C | Strengthening the International Criminal Court and the Assembly of States Parties |
| **ICC-ASP/3/Res.4** | 10.09.2004 | 6th plenary meeting | E F S A R C | Programme budget for 2005, Contingency Fund, Working Capital Fund for 2005, scale of assessments for the apportionment of expenses of the International Criminal Court and financing of appropriations for the year 2005 |

| | | | | |
|---|---|---|---|---|
| **ICC-ASP/3/Res.5** | 10.09.2004 | 6th plenary meeting | E F S A R C | Travel of members of the Committee on Budget and Finance |
| **ICC-ASP/3/Res.6** | 10.09.2004 | 6th plenary meeting | E F S A R C | Procedure for the nomination and election of judges of the International Criminal Court |
| **ICC-ASP/3/Res.6 Consolidated version** | 10.09.2004 | 6th plenary meeting | E F S A R C | Procedure for the nomination and election of judges, the Prosecutor and Deputy Prosecutors of the International Criminal Court (ICC-ASP/3/Res.6) – Consolidated version |
| **ICC-ASP/3/Res.7** | 10.09.2004 | 6th plenary meeting | E F S A R C | Establishment of the Secretariat of the Trust Fund for Victims |
| **ICC-ASP/3/Res.8** | 10.09.2004 | 6th plenary meeting | E F S A R C | Intensifying dialogue between the Assembly of States Parties and the International Criminal Court |

## ICC – ASP – 2003/2004 – 2nd Session – Resolutions

| Resolution No. | Date | Meeting | Docs | Topic |
|---|---|---|---|---|
| **ICC-ASP/2/Res.1** | 12.09.2003 | 5th plenary meeting | E F S A R C | Programme budget for 2004, Working Capital Fund for 2004, scale of assessments for the apportionment of expenses of the International Criminal Court and financing of appropriations for 2004 |
| **ICC-ASP/2/Res.2** | 12.09.2003 | 5th plenary meeting | E F S A R C | Staff regulations for the International Criminal Court |

| | | | | |
|---|---|---|---|---|
| **ICC-ASP/2/Res.3** | 12.09.2003 | 5th plenary meeting | E F S A R C | Establishment of the Permanent Secretariat of the Assembly of States Parties to the International Criminal Court |
| **ICC-ASP/2/Res.4** | 12.09.2003 | 5th plenary meeting | E F S A R C | Travel and subsistence expenses of members of the Committee on Budget and Finance |
| **ICC-ASP/2/Res.5** | 12.09.2003 | 5th plenary meeting | E F S A R C | Term of office of the members of the Committee on Budget and Finance |
| **ICC-ASP/2/Res.6** | 12.09.2003 | 5th plenary meeting | E F S A R C | Establishment of a trust fund for the participation of the least developed countries in the activities of the Assembly of States Parties |
| **ICC-ASP/2/Res.7** | 12.09.2003 | 5th plenary meeting | E F S A R C | Strengthening the International Criminal Court and the Assembly of States Parties |
| **ICC-ASP/2/Res.8** | 11.09.2003 | 4th plenary meeting | E F S A R C | Recognition of the coordinating and facilitating role of the NGO Coalition for the International Criminal Court |
| **ICC-ASP/2/Res.9** | 12.09.2003 | 5th plenary meeting | E F S A R C | Role of the United Nations in the establishment of the International Criminal Court |

## ICC – ASP – 2002/2003 – 1st Session – Resolutions

| Resolution No. | Date | Meeting | Docs | Topic |
|---|---|---|---|---|
| **ICC-ASP/1/Res.1** | 09.09.2002 | 3rd plenary meeting | E F S A R C | Continuity of work in respect of the crime of aggression |
| **ICC-ASP/1/Res.2** | 09.09.2002 | 3rd plenary meeting | E F S A R C | Procedure for the nomination and election of judges, the Prosecutor and Deputy Prosecutors of the International Criminal Court |
| **ICC-ASP/1/Res.3** | 09.09.2002 | 3rd plenary meeting | E F S A R C | Procedure for the election of the judges for the International Criminal Court |
| **ICC-ASP/1/Res.4** | 03.09.2002 | 1st plenary meeting | E F S A R C | Establishment of the Committee on Budget and Finance |
| **ICC-ASP/1/Res.5** | 03.09.2002 | 1st plenary meeting | E F S A R C | Procedure for the nomination and election of members of the Committee on Budget and Finance |
| **ICC-ASP/1/Res.6** | 09.09.2002 | 3rd plenary meeting | E F S A R C | Establishment of a fund for the benefit of victims of crimes within the jurisdiction of the Court, and of the families of such victims |
| **ICC-ASP/1/Res.7** | 09.09.2002 | 3rd plenary meeting | E F S A R C | Procedure for the nomination and election of members of the Board of Directors of the Trust Fund for the benefit of victims |
| **ICC-ASP/1/Res.8** | 09.09.2002 | 3rd plenary meeting | E F S A R C | Provisional arrangements for the secretariat of the Assembly of States Parties |

| | | | | |
|---|---|---|---|---|
| **ICC-ASP/1/Res.9** | 09.09.2002 | 3rd plenary meeting | E F S A R C | Permanent secretariat of the Assembly of States Parties |
| **ICC-ASP/1/Res.10** | 09.09.2002 | 3rd plenary meeting | E F S A R C | Selection of the staff of the International Criminal Court |
| **ICC-ASP/1/Res.11** | 03.09.2002 | 2nd plenary meeting | E F S A R C | Relevant criteria for voluntary contributions to the International Criminal Court |
| **ICC-ASP/1/Res.12** | 03.09.2002 | 2nd plenary meeting | E F S A R C | Budget appropriations for the first financial period and financing of appropriations for the first financial period |
| **ICC-ASP/1/Res.13** | 03.09.2002 | 2nd plenary meeting | E F S A R C | Working Capital Fund for the first financial period |
| **ICC-ASP/1/Res.14** | 03.09.2002 | 2nd plenary meeting | E F S A R C | Scales of assessments for the apportionment of the expenses of the International Criminal Court |
| **ICC-ASP/1/Res.15** | 03.09.2002 | 2nd plenary meeting | E F S A R C | Crediting contributions to the United Nations Trust Fund to Support the Establishment of the International Criminal Court |
| **ICC-ASP/1/Res.16** | 21.04.2003 | 10th plenary meeting | E F S A R C | Commencement of functions by the Committee on Budget and Finance; election of two members from the Eastern European States; and deferment of drawing of lots |

# BIBLIOGRAPHY

Abdelrahman, A. (2010), 'Bashir's Last Part of Genocide Plan', in *Sudan Tribune*, August 8, 2010, accessible at: www.sudantribune.com/spip.php?article35892

African Press Releases (2010), *'Congo Kinshasa: US, UN Accuse Governmental Forces of Crimes Against Humanity'*, 12 March 2010, accessible at: http://allafrica.com/stories/201003120819.html

Africa Recovery, United Nations, (2000), 'Key provisions of the Lusaka cease-fire agreement', (April 2000), in *Africa Recovery*, 14–1: 19.

African Union, (2009), *Report of the AU High Level Panel on Darfur (AUDP)*, 29 October 2009, the electronic version of the report is accessible at: www.africa-union.org/root/ar/index/Communiqu%20on%20Darfur%20_eng.pdf

Aguirre, M. and Abrisketa, J. (2009), 'Pressing Issues for UN Peacekeeping Operations in the DRC', September 2009, *Transnational Institute*, accessible at: www.tni.org/article/pressing-issues-un-peacekeeping-operations

Akaki, S. (2008), "Is Africa a Cold War Battleground?", in *Global Research*, July 23, 2008, accessible at: www.globalresearch.ca/index.php?context=va&aid=9648

Aksar, Y. (2004), 'The Matter of Protection of Humanitarian and Human Rights Law', *Implementing International Humanitarian Law. From the Ad Hoc Tribunals to a Permanent International Criminal Court*, Routledge, 2004: 33.

Al-Bulushi, S. And Branch, A. (2010), 'Review Conference of the Rome Statute. In Search of Justice: The ICC and Power Politics', 23 June 2010, Egypt, accessible in Arabic at: www.almasryalyoum.com

Al-Bulushi, S. and Branch A., (2010), *In Search of Justice: The ICC and Power Politics*, 2010: 4, accessible at: www.almasryalyoum.com

Ali, N. (2014) Bringing the Guilty to Justice: Can the ICC be Self-Enforcing? Chicago Journal of International Law, vol. 14, iss. 2 (2014): 408–452.

Allen, S.G. (2004), 'From Peace-keeping to Peace-building: The United Nations and the Challenge of Intrastate War', in *The United Nations and Global Security*, ed. Richard M. Price and Mark W. Zacher, Palgrave Macmillan, 141–60.

Alston, P. (2005), 'The Darfur Commission as a Model for Future Responses to Crisis Situations', *Journal of International Criminal Justice* 3–3: 600–607.

Ambos, K., Large J. and Wierda, M. (2009), *Building a Future on Peace and Justice: Studies on Transitional Justice, Peace and Development. The Nuremberg Declaration on Peace and Justice*, Springer: Berlin Heidelberg.

AMICC (2010), 'Analysis of the Backgrounder Published by the Heritage Foundation: An Inconvenient Founding: America's Principles Applied to the ICC', accessible at: www.amicc.org/docs/AMICC_analysis_of_Heritage2010.pdf

Amnesty International, (2009), *DRC: Submission to the Universal Periodic Review. Sixth Session of the UPR Working Working Group of the Human Rights Council (HRC),*

Report November-December 2009, the report is accessible at: www.amnesty.org/en/library/info/AFR62/009/2009/en
Annan, K. (2004), *A More Secure World: Our Shared Responsibility*, UN report of the Secretary-General's High-level Panel on Threats, Challenges and Change, United Nations (2004: 7–131).
Annan, K. (2004), *Report of the Secretary General on The Rule of Law and Transitional Justice in Conflict and Post-Conflict Societies*, UN Doc. S/2004/616 (August 23, 2004: 8).
Annan, K. (2004), *The Rule of Law Remains Elusive*, addressed at the opening of the general debate of the fifty-ninth session of the General Assembly New York, 21 September 2004, the statement is accessible at: www.un.org/Pubs/chronicle/2004/issue3/0304p4.asp
Aptel, C. (2009), '*Case Study 1: The DRC, Challenges in Building Judicial Capacity in a Post-Conflict Context*', Conference Working Paper, New York, September 9–11, 2009, Session 7: 6, Transitional Justice and Domestic Justice Systems, ICTJ, accessible at: www.internationalcriminaljustice.net/experience/papers/session7.pdf
Aptel, C. (2009), 'Challenges Facing Domestic Justice in the DRC', in *Domestic Justice Systems and the Impact of the Rome Statute*, September 2009, International Center for Transitional Justice, 2009: 6, accessible at: www.internationalcriminaljustice.net/experience/papers/session7.pdf
Arfi, B. (2005), *International Change and the Stability of Multiethnic States: Yugoslavia, Lebanon and Crises of Governance*, Indiana University Press: Bloomington.
Armstrong, E. (2005), "Integrity, Transparency and Accountability in Public Administration", in *Ethics, Transparency and Accountability*, United Nations source: DESA, UN Department of Economic and Social Affairs, accessible at: http://unpan1.un.org/intradoc/groups/public/documents/un/unpan020955.pdf
Arnold, J. (2007), 'Protection of Human Rights by Means of Criminal Law: On the Relationship between Criminal Law and Politics' in Kaleck W., Ratner M., Singelnstein T. (eds.), *International Prosecution of Human Rights Crimes*, Springer.
Arsanjani, M.H. and Reisman, W.M. (2005), 'The Law-in-Action of the International Criminal Court', in *The American Society of International Law* 99–2: 385–403.
Avocats Sans Frontières (2009), *Etude de jurisprudence. L'application du Statut de Rome de la Cour Pénale Internationale par les Jurisdictions de la RDC*, March 2009, accessible at: www.asf.be/index.php?module=publicaties&lang=fr&id=51
Avocats Sans Frontières, (2009), *The Application of the Rome Statute of the International Criminal Court by the Courts of the Democratic Republic of Congo*, Case Study: March 2009.
Avocats Sans Frontières, (2009), 'Summary of Recommendations relating to the Application of the Rome Statute by the Congolese Courts', DRC Case Study, March 2009, at 125, the ASF publication is accessible at: www.asf.be/publications/ASF_CaseStudy_RomeStatute_Light_PagePerPage.pdf
Bah, Alhaji M.S. and Johnstone, I. (2007), 'Peacekeeping in Sudan: The Dynamics of Protection, Partnerships and Inclusive Politics', *New York Centre on International Cooperation*, Occasional Paper, 2007: New York, accessible at: www.cic.nyu.edu/internationalsecurity/docs/CIC_paper2_sudan_final.pdf

Baimu, E. and Sturman, K. (2003), 'Amendement to the AU's Right To Intervene: A Shift from Human Security to Regime Security?' in *African Security Review* 12–2: 56–63

Baldor, L.C. (2009), 'Obama: US Choosing Words Carefully in Terror War', *Associated Press*, 2009, February 3, the article is accessible at: http://abcnews.go.com/Politics/wireStory?id=6798802

Barber, R. (2009), 'Reflections on the Peacekeeping Failure in Darfur: Is There Any Substance to the Responsibility to Protect?' *Journal of International Peacekeeping* 13–33: 294.

Bariagader, A. 2006, 'United Nations Peace Operations in Africa: A Cookie-Cutter Approach?', *Journal of Third World Studies* 23–2: 11–29.

Barnett, M.N. (1997), 'Bringing in the New World Order: Liberalism, Legitimacy, and the United Nations', in *World Politics* Volume 49, Number 4: 526–551.

Bassiouni, M.C. (2014) Surrender to International Tribunals, in Bassiouni, M.C. *International Extradition: United States Law and Practice,* (New York: Oxford University Press, 2014), at 44–49.

Bassiouni, M.C. and Guellali A. (2010), 'Jihad: Challenges to International and Domestic Law', in T.M.C. Asser Press: 273.

Bassiouni, M.C., (2008), *The Pursuit of International Criminal Justice: A World Study on Conflicts, Victimization, and Post-Conflict Justice,* Intersentia: Mortesel.

Bassiouni, M.C. (2009), *A Guide to Documents on the Arab-Palestinian/Israeli Conflict: 1897–2008,* Bril: Martinus Nijhoff Publishers.

Bassiouni, M.C. (2008), *The Chicago Principles on Post-conflict Justice,* International Human Rights Law Institute.

Bassiouni, M.C. (2008), I *International Criminal Law: Sources, Subjects, and Contents,* 3rd rev. ed. Brill: Martinus Nijhoff Publishers.

Bassiouni, M.C. (2008), II *International Criminal Law: Multilateral and Bilateral Enforcement Mechanisms,* 3rd rev. ed. Brill: Martinus Nijhoff Publishers.

Bassiouni, M.C. (2008), III *International Criminal Law: International Enforcement,* 3rd rev. ed. Brill: Martinus Nijhoff Publishers.

Bassiouni, M.C. (2006), 'The Perennial Conflict Between International Criminal Justice and Realpolitik', in *Georgia State University Law Review* 22: 541–553.

Bassiouni, M.C. (2005) I *The Legislative History of the International Criminal Court: Introduction, Analysis, and Integrated Text of the Statute, Elements of Crimes and Rules of Procedure and Evidence,* Brill: Martinus Nijhoff Publishers.

Bassiouni, M.C. (2005) II *The Legislative History of the International Criminal Court: An Article-By-Article Evolution of the Statute from 1994–1998,* Brill: Martinus Nijhoff Publishers.

Bassiouni, M.C. (2005) III *The Legislative History of the International Criminal Court: Summary Records of the 1998 Diplomatic Conference,* Brill: Martinus Nijhoff Publishers.

Bassiouni, M.C. (2003), 'Justice and Peace: The importance of Choosing Accountability Over Realpolitik', in *Case Western Reserve Journal of International Law,* 35–2: 191–204.

Bassiouni, M.C. and Ferencz, B.B. (2008), '*The Crime Against Peace and Aggression: From its Origins to the ICC*', in International Criminal Law (3 ed. in Transnational/Brill), 1:

1–45, accessible at: http://law.cwru.edu/lectures/files/2008-2009/20080926_CWRU-08-Bassiouni_Ferencz_Peace_Aggression.pdf

Bassiouni, M.C. and. Blakesley, C.L. (1992), 'The Need for an International Criminal Court in the New International World Order', *Vanderbilt Journal of Transnational Law* 25: 151.

Baylis, J. Smith, S., and Owens, P. (2007), 'International and global security in the post-cold war era', in *The globalization of world politics: an introduction to international relations*, 2007: 253–273.

Bedjaoui, M. (1994), *The New World Order and the Security Council: Testing the Legality of Its Acts*, Martinus Nijhoff Publishers, 1994: 56–90.

Beigbeder, Y. (2005), *International Justice against impunity. Progress and New Challenges*, Martinus Nijhoff Publishers.

Belasco, A. (2010), 'The Cost of Iraq, Afghanistan, and Other Global War on Terror Operations Since 9/11', July 16, 2010, *US Congressional Research Service, Prepared for Members and Committees of Congress*, RL33110, accessible at: www.fas.org/sgp/crs/natsec/RL33110.pdf

Bellelli, R. (ed.) *International Criminal Justice: Law and Practice from The Rome Statute to Its Review*, Ashgate 2010.

Berdal, M. and Malone, D.M. (eds.), *Greed and Grievance: Economic Agendas in Civil Wars*, Boulder, Co.: Lynne Rienner 2000.

Berdal, M. (2004), 'The United Nations after Iraq', in *Survival* 46(3): 83.

Bertucci, G. (2008), 'Recent Terrorist Acts and Emerging Governance Challenges' in *World Public Sector Report: People Matter. Civic Engagement in Public Governance*, 2008, ST/ESA/PAD/SER.E/108, United Nations, Department of Economic and Social Affairs, 2008: 40, the report is accessible at: http://unpan1.un.org/intradoc/groups/public/documents/un/unpan028608.pdf

Bertucci G. and Alberti A. (2001), 'Globalization and its impact on the State: The role of the State in domestic and international governance' in *World Public Sector Report: Globalization and the State*, ST/ESA/PAD/SER.26, 2001, United Nations, Department of Economic and Social Affairs, at 29, the report is accessible at: http://unpan1.un.org/intradoc/groups/public/documents/UN/UNPAN012761.pdf

Bevir M. (2009), *Key Concept of Governance*, Sage Publications.

Black, D.R. and Williams, P.D (2010), *The International Politics of Mass Atrocities: The Case of Darfur*, Security and Governance, Routledge.

Black, D.R. and Williams, P.D (2010), 'Solidaristic Openings', *The International Politics of Mass Atrocities*, Security and Governance, 2010: 259.

Blokker, N. (2010) 'International Organisations as Independent Actors: Sweet Memory or Funtionally Necessary?', in *Accountability for Human Rights Violations by International Organisations*, J. Wouters, E. Brems et al (eds.), International Law, Intersentia.

Blokker, N. (2007), 'The Crime of Aggression and the United Nations Security Council', in *Leiden Journal of International Law* 20: 867.

Blokker, N. and Schermers, H.G. (2001), *Proliferation of International Organizations: Legal Issues*, 2001: 200, Kluwer Law International.

Blokker, N. (2000), 'Is the Authorization Authorized? Powers and Practice of the UN Security Council to Authorize the Use of Force by Coalitions of the Able and Willing', in *European Journal of International Law* 11–3: 541–568.

Blockmans, S., Wouters J. and T. Ruys (eds.), (2010), *The European Union and Peacebuilding. Policy and Legal Aspects,* The Hague, T.M.C. Asser Press, xxvi-499.

Boas, G. and Oosthuizen G. (2010), 'Suggestions for Future Lessons-Learned Studies: The Experience of Other International and Hybrid Criminal Courts of Relevance to the International Criminal Court', in *International Criminal Law Services*: January 2010.

Bobbitt, P. (2008), *Terror and Consent: The Wars of the Twenty-First Century,* Penguin Group.

Boister, N. (2005), 'Reflections on the relationship between the duty to educate in humanitarian law and the absence of a defence of mistake of law in the Rome Statute of the International Criminal Court', in R. Burchill, N. D. White and J. Morris (eds.), *International Conflict and Security Law. Essays in Memory of Hilaire McCoubrey,* 2005: 10, Cambridge University Press.

Bolton, J. (1999), 'Reject and Oppose the International Criminal Court', *Toward an International Criminal Court?: Three Options Presented as Presidential Speeches,* US Council on Foreign Relations, 1999: 37.

Booth, C. and du Plessis, M. (2009), 'Africa's Obstruction to Justice', *The Guardian,* 18 July 2009, accessible at: www.guardian.co.uk/commentisfree/2009/jul/18/darfur-bashir-african-union-icc

Bosco, D. (2014) *Rough Justice: the International Criminal Court in a World of Power Politics.* (New York: Oxford University Press, 2014) at 312.

Broomhall, B. (2005), *International Justice and the International Criminal Court: between Sovereignty and the Rule of Law,* Oxford Monographs in International Law, Oxford University Press.

Brown, M. (1997), 'The Causes of Internal Conflict: An Overview', in *Nationalism and Ethnic Conflict* edited by Michael Brown et al., Cambridge, MA: The MIT Press, 1997: 3–26.

Bruggeman, W. (2005), 'The ICC as an Important Partner in Enhancing Global Justice', *International Summit on Democracy, Terrorism and Security,* 8–11 March 2005 Madrid.

Buchanan, A. (2004), *Justice, Legitimacy and Self-Determination: Moral Foundation for International Law,* Oxford University Press.

Burgess, S.F. (2007), 'UN Conflict Management in Africa under Secretary General Kofi Annan, 1997–2006', in *International Studies Association,* 2007, accessible at: www.isanet.org/publications/

Burke-White, W. (2005), 'Complementarity in Practice: The International Criminal Court as Part of a System of Multi-level Global Governance in the DRC', in *LJIL* 18–3: 557.

Buzan, B. and Hansen L. (2009), *The Evolution of International Security Studies,* Cambridge: Cambridge University Press.

Call, C.T. (2007), ed., *Constructing Justice and Security After War* (Washington, D.C.: United States Institute of Peace Press, 2007: 405.

Call, C.T. and Cook S. eds (2003), 'Governance After War: Rethinking Democratization and Peacebuilding', in *Global Governance,* 9(2).

Caplan, R. (2005), *International Governance in War Torn Territories: Rule and Reconstruction,* Oxford University Press: New York.

Carayannis, T. (2009), 'The peace and justice dilemma in the DRC', in *The Challenge of Building Sustainable Peace in the DRC,* (July 2009), Centre for Humanitarian Dialogue, Background Paper, accessible at: www.hdcentre.org/files/DRC%20paper.pdf

Carothers, T. (2003), 'Promoting the Rule of Law Abroad: The Problem of Knowledge', in *Carnegie Endowment for International Peace, Rule of Law Series* 34: 9.

Carothers, T. (1998), 'The Rule of Law Revival', *Foreign Affairs* 77: 95.

Casper, G. (Aug. 9, 2003), *Rule of Law? Whose Law?* note Address, 2003 CEELI Award Ceremony and Luncheon, San Francisco, Cal. quoting Martin Krygier, International Encyclopedia of the Social & Behavioral Sciences 13404 (Smelser & Baltes eds., 2001), accessible at: http://iis-db.stanford.edu/pubs/20677/Rule_of_Law.pdf

Cassese, A. (2007), *The Human Dimension of International Law. Selected Papers,* Oxford University Press.

Cassese, A. (2007), 'On some Problematical Aspects of the Crime of Aggression', in *Leiden Journal of International Law* 20: 841–849.

Cassese, A. (2008), *Flawed International Justice for Sudan,* accessible at: www.project-syndicate.org

Cassese, A. (2004), 'et al' "Failure of International Sanctions against Serious State Delinquencies" in *State, Sovereignty and International Governance,* Brus, Dugard, Duursma, Kreijen, Oxford University Press, (2004: 240).

Cassese, A. (2003), 'A Big Step Forward for International Justice', in *The ICC: An End to Impunity? Crime of War Project Magazine,* (December 2003).

Cassese, A. (1998), 'Reflections on International Criminal Justice', in *Modern Law Review,* 61–1: 1–10.

Cassese, A. (1990), 'Remarks on Scelle's Theory of Role Splitting in International Law' *EJIL* 1: 210.

Cassese, A. (1978), *United Nations Peacekeeping. Legal Essays,* Brill: Martinus Nijhoff Publishers.

Chadwick, F. A., Lyons, G. M., Trent J. E. (eds.) 1995, *The United Nations System: The Policies of Member States,* UNU Press.

Chandler, D. (2004), 'Imposing the 'rule of law': the lessons of bih for peacebuilding in Iraq', in *International Peacekeeping* 11(2): 312–333.

Chapman, P. F (2009), 'Ensuring Respect: United Nations Compliance with International Humanitarian Law', 17 *Human Rights Brief* 1, 2009, at 2, Center for Human Rights and Humanitarian Law, American University Washington College of Law, accessible at: www.wcl.american.edu/hrbrief/17/171.pdf?rd=1

Chesterman, S. (2008), '*The UN Security Council and The Rule of Law: The Role of the Security Council in Strengthening a Rules-based International System*', Final Report and Recommendations from the Austrian Initiative, 2004–2008', Federal Ministry for European and International Affairs.

Chesterman, S. Ignatieff M. and Thakur R. eds (2005), *Making States Work: State Failure and the Crisis of Governance,* United Nations University Press: New York.

Chossudovsky, M. and Marshall A.G. (2010), 'The Global Economic Crisis: The Great Depression of the XXI Century', *Global Research*: Centre for Research on Globalization.

Chesterman, S. (2001), *Just War or Just Peace? Humanitarian Intervention and International Law*, Oxford Monographs in International Law.

Chiomenti, C. (2006), 'Corporations and the International Criminal Court', in O. De Schutter (ed.), *Transnational Corporations and Human Rights*, Palgrave Macmillan, 2006: 287–312.

Choudhary, K. (2007), 'Globalisation, Modernity and Nation-building', in Choudhary (ed.), *Globalisation Governance Reforms and Development in India*, Sage, 2007: 523.

Cilliers, J., Malan, M. (2001), *Peacekeeping in the DRC. MONUC and the Road to Peace*, South African Institute for Security Studies, Monograph n. 66, accessible at: www.iss.co.za/Pubs/Monographs/No66/CONTENTS.HTML

Clapham, C. (2002), 'Problems of Peace Enforcement: Lessons to Be Drawn from Multinational Peacekeeping Operations in Ongoing Conflicts in Africa', in *Africa in Crisis: New Challenges and Possibilities*, ed. Tunde Zack-Williams, Diane Frost, and Alex Thomson, Macmillan, 2002: 196–215.

Clark, J.N. (2010), 'The ICC, Uganda and the LRA: Re-Framing the Debate', in *African Studies* 69–1: 141–160, Routledge.

Clark, P. (2009), 'Grappling in the Great Lakes: The Challenges of International Justice in Rwanda, the DRC and Uganda' in Bowden, B., Charlesworth, H., Farrall, J. (eds.), *The Role of International Law in Rebuilding Societies After Conflicts. Great Expectations*, 2009: 244.

Clark, P. and Waddell N. (2008), 'Law, Politics and Pragmatism', *Courting Conflict? Justice, Peace and the ICC in Africa*, in *The International Journal of Transitional Justice*, Royal African Societies, March 2008: 40.

Cook, R.C. (2009), 'The Nature of the current Financial Crisis: The System is designed to exert Total Control over the Lives of Individuals', *Global Research*: Centre for Research on Globalization.

Cornwell, D.J. (2007), *Doing Justice Better. The Politics of Restorative Justice*, Waterside Press.

Cornwell, D.J. (2006), 'New Horizons: International Perspectives on Restorative Justice', in *Criminal Punishment and Restorative Justice. Past, Present and Future Perspectives*, Waterside Press, 2006: 108.

Cryer, R. (2005), *Prosecuting International Crimes: Selectivity and the International Criminal Regime*, Cambridge University Press: Cambridge.

Culbertson, R. and Pouligny B. (2007), 'Re-imagining Peace After Mass Crime: A Dialogical Exchange Between Insider and Outsider Knowledge', in Pouligny, et al., *After Mass Crime: Rebuilding States and Communities*, Tokyo/New York/Paris: United Nations University Press, 2007: 271–287.

Dagne, T. (2010), 'The Democratic Republic of Congo: Background and Current Developments' in *CSR Report for Congress*, US Congressional Research Service, February 2010, accessible at: http://fpc.state.gov/documents/organization/139252.pdf

Dahrendorf, N. (2008), 'Experience of MONUC in Security Sector Reform (SSR). 'MONUC and the Relevance of Coherent Mandates: The Case of the DRC', in Hänggi, H. and

Scherrer, V. (eds.), *Security Sector Reform and UN Integrated Missions*, Lit Verlag Press: 2008, Chapter 3: 76.

Dahrendorf, N. (2008), 'MONUC and the Relevance of Coherent Mandates: The Case of the DRC', in Hänggi and Scherrer (eds.), *Security Sector Reform and UN Integrated Missions*, (2008), Lit Verlag Press, 2008: 98.

Dahrendorf, N. (2005), *Mirror Images in the Congo: Sexual Violence and Conflict*, Open Democracy, 26 October 2005, accessible at: www.opendemocracy.net/democracy-resolution_1325/congo_2964.jsp

Damrosch, L.F. (1998), 'Enforcing International Law through Non-forcible Measures', *Recueil De Cours/Collected Courses*, Académie de Droit International de La Haye: 202.

Deflem M. (2009), 'Review of Governing Through Globalized Crime: Futures for International Criminal Justice', in *Contemporary Sociology*, 38: 153.

D'Aspremont J. (2007), 'Abuse of the Legal Personality of International Organizations and the Responsibility of Member States', in *International Organizations Law Review* 4-1: 91–119.

Davis, L. (2009), 'European Engagement in Security System Reform in the DRC', *Justice-Sensitive Security System Reform in the DRC*, February 2009, International Centre for Transitional Justice, 2009: 24, accessible: www.initiativeforpeacebuilding.eu/pdf/Justice_Sensitive_Security_System_reform_in_the_DRC.pdf

Davis, L. (2009), 'Justice-Sensitive Security System Reform in the DRC', in *Initiative for Peacebuilding in the Democratic Republic of Congo*, International Centre for Transitional Justice, February 2009, accessible at: www.initiativeforpeacebuilding.eu/pdf/Justice_Sensitive_Security_System_reform_in_the_DRC.pdf

Davis, L. and Hayner, P. (2009), 'The Role and Impact of the ICC', *Difficult Peace, Limited Justice: Ten Years of Peacemaking in the DRC*, March 2009, International Center for Transitional Justice, 2009: 25, accessible at: www.ictj.org/static/Africa/DRC/ICTJDavisHayner_DRC_DifficultPeace_pa2009.pdf

Davis, L. and Hayner, P. (2009), 'The ICC's Impact on Children', in *Difficult Peace, Limited Justice: Ten Years of Peacemaking in the DRC*, March 2009, International Center for Transitional Justice, 2009: 30, accessible at: www.ictj.org/static/Africa/DRC/ICTJDavisHayner_DRC_DifficultPeace_pa2009.pdf

Day, G. and Freeman, C. (2005), 'Operationalizing the Responsibility To Protect. The Policekeeping Approach', in *Global Governance* 11-2: 139.

De Lint, W., Marmo, M. and Chazal N. (2014), *Criminal Justice in International Society*, Abingdon: Routledge, 2014, at 320.

Delmas-Marty M. (2009), *Ordering Pluralism: A Conceptual Framework for Understanding the Transnational Legal World*, Hart Publishing, Portland, USA.

Deng, F.M. 'Sudan at the Crossroads', in MIT Centre for International Studies, *Audit of the Conventional Wisdom Series*, 07-05: March 2007, Cambridge, accessible at: http://web.mit.edu/CIS/pdf/Audit_03_07_Deng.pdf

De Waal, A. (2010), *Making Sense of Darfur*, August 4 2010, accessible at: http://blogs.ssrc.org/sudan/author/dewaala/

De Waal, A. (2007) ed., *War in Darfur and the Search for Peace*, Global Equity Initiative, Harvard University Press: Cambridge.

De Waal, A. (2007), 'Darfur and the failure of the responsibility to protect', in *International Affairs* 83–6: 1039–1054.

De Waal, A. (2005), 'Who are the Darfurians? Arab and African Identities, Violence and External Engagement', in *African Affairs*, 104–415: 181.

De Wet, E. (2010), 'The constitutionalization of public international law', in Michel Rosenfeld and Andras Sajo (eds), *The Oxford Handbook of Comparative Constitutional Law* (Oxford University Press, forthcoming).

De Wet, E. (2009), 'Holding the United Nations Security Council accountable for human rights violations through domestic and regional courts: a case of 'be careful what you wish for'?', in Jeremy Farrall and Kim Rubenstein (eds), *Sanctions Accountability and Governance in a Globalised World* (Cambridge University Press, Cambridge), 143–168.

De Wet, E. (2008), 'The Relationship between the International Criminal Court and ad hoc Tribunals: Competition or Companionship?', *Die Friedenswarte* 83: 33–57.

De Wet, E. (2007), 'The Emerging International Constitutional Order: the Implications of Hierarchy in International Law for the Coherence and Legitimacy of International Decision- Making', in *Potchefstroom Electronic Law Journal*, 2–1: 2–27.

De Wet, E. (2006), 'The International Constitutional Order', in *International and Comparative Law Quarterly* 55: 53–76.

De Wet, E. (2004), *The Chapter VII Powers of the United Nations Security Council Habilitationsschrift*, Hart Publishing Ltd., Oxford: 413.

De Wet, E. and Nollkaemper A. (2003) eds. *Review of the Security Council by Member States*, Intersentia, Antwerp, 160.

De Wet, E. and Nollkaemper A. (2003) eds. 'The Role of Human Rights in Limiting the Enforcement Power of the Security Council: A Principled View', in Erika de Wet and De Zeeuw, J. (2008), *From Soldiers to Politicians. Transforming Rebel Movements After Civil War*, Lynne Rienner Publishers: Boulder (Colorado).

Dieng, A. (2001), 'Africa and the Globalization of Justice: Contributions and Lessons from the International Criminal Tribunal for Rwanda', *Justice in Africa*, document and outcome of the conference 30 July – 2 August 2001.

Dingwerth, K. and Pattberg, P. (2006), 'Global Governance as a Perspective on World Politics' in *Global Governance* 12: 185–203.

Dobbins, J. (2005) 'et al.', 'The UN's Role in Nation-Building: From the Congo to Iraq', Rand, 2005. available at: www.rand.org/publications/MG/MG304/

Doctors Without Borders/Médecins Sans Frontières (2010), 'DRC: Thousands of displaced civilians trapped by conflict, wounded unable to reach hospitals in Hauts Plateaux, South Kivu', Press Release March 11, 2010, accessible at: www.doctorswithoutborders.org/press/release.cfm?id=4306&cat=pressrelease&ref=related-sidebar

Doyle, M. and Sambanis, N. (2006), 'War-Making, Peacebuilding, and the United Nations', in *Making War and Building Peace: United Nations Peace Operations*, Princeton University Press: Princeton and Oxford, 2006: 23.

Dugard, J. (2007) 'The Future of International Law: A Human Rights Perspective. With Some Comments on the Leiden School of International Law', LJIL 20, 729 at 739.

Dugard, J. (2007) 'The Human Rights Council: Different Perspectives on Palestine', in *LJIL* 20: 729–739.

Dugard, J. (2004) et al, *State, Sovereignty and International Governance*, Oxford University Press, 2004: 5.

Dugard, J. (2001), 'Judicial Review of Sanctions', in Gowlland-Debbas V. (ed.), *United Nations Sanctions and International Law*, Kluwer Law International, 2001: 83.

Du Plessis, M. and Ford, J. (2008), *Unable or Unwilling? A Five-Country Study on African Implementation of the Rome Statute of the International Criminal Court*, Institute for Security Studies,Monograph Series, 141: 5–149, accessible at: http://cigj.anu.edu.au/cigj/link_documents/Ford_Pubs/Ford_Unable_Unwilling_2008.pdf

Du Plessis, M. (2005), 'Africa and the International Criminal Court', *Centre for the Study of Justice and Reconciliation*, Criminal Justice Conference 7–8 February 2005, accessible at: www.csvr.org.za/wits/confpaps/duplessis.htm

Du Plessis, M. and Pete, S. (2004), 'The ICC and serious crimes committed by the UN peacekeepers in Africa. Who Guards the Guards?', 2004: 13–4, *African Security Review*, accessible at: www.iss.co.za/pubs/ASR/13No4/FduPlessis.htm

Eboe-Osuji C., (2010), 'Healing the Rift: The Impasse between the African Union and the International Criminal Court', in *Reflexions in International Criminal Law*, March 20, 2010: 7, accessible at: http://ceboe-osuji.blogspot.com/2010/03/healing-rift-impasse-between-african.html

Eboe-Osuji C., (2007), 'The Role of the Security Council in Prosecuting the Crime of Aggression: an African Perspective' in *The Monitor-Journal of the Coalition for the International Criminal Court* 34–8.

Egeland, J. (2005), *Eastern DR of Congo surpasses Darfur as biggest, most neglected emergency - UN relief official*, UN News Centre, 16 March 2005, accessible at: www.un.org/apps/news/story.asp?NewsID=13675&Cr=democratic&Cr1=congo

Eriksson Baaz, M. and Stern, M. (2008), 'Making Sense of Violence: Voices of Soldiers in the Congo (DRC)', in *Journal of Modern African Studies*, 46–1: 57.

European Commission under the Sixth Framework Research Program (EU), *Defining Terrorism: Citizens and Governance in a Knowledge-Based Society*, (2008), accessible at: www.transnationalterrorism.eu/tekst/publications/WP3%20Del%204.pdf

Evans, G. (2008), *The Responbility to Protect: Ending Mass Atrocity Crimes Once and for All*, Brookings Institution Press: xiv-348, Washington DC.

Evans, G. (2008), 'Operationalising R2P in Coercive Peace Operations', 2008 ICG, accessible at: www.crisisgroup.org/home/index.cfm?id=5658&l=1

Evans, G. (2007), 'Delivering on the Responsibility to Protect: Four Misunderstandings, Three Challenges and How to Overcome Them', Address to SEF Symposium, *The Responsibility to Protect: Progress, Empty Promise or a License for Humanitarian Intervention*, Bonn, 30 November 2007.

Evans, G. and Sahnoun M. (2002), 'The Responsibility to Protect', in *Foreign Affairs*, November/December 2002, 81–6: 99.

Everest, L. (2004), 'Oil Power and Empire: Iraq and the US Global Agenda', in *Common Courage Press*, accessible at: www.worldcantwait.net/materials/OPE-CHAPTER%20ONE.pdf

Falk, R. (2007), "An Ethos of Accountability and Responsibility", *The Costs of War: International Law, the UN, and World Order After Iraq*, at 104.

Fassbender B. (2009), *The United Nations Charter as the Constitution of the International Community*, Martinus Nijhoff Publishers.

Fassbender, B. (2009), 'Universality and the Problem of Sovereignty' in *The United Nations Charter as the Constitution of the International Community*, Martinus Nijhoff, 2009: 136.

Fassenberg, B. (2005), 'The Meaning of International Constitutional Law', in Macdonald, R. St. J. D. and Johnston, M. (eds.), *Towards World Constitutionalism: Issues in the Legal Ordering of the World Community*, Martinus Nijhoff Publishers, 2005: 837.

Fassenberg, B. (2003), 'An Illusion Shattered? Looking Back on a Decade of Failed Attempts to Reform the UN Security Council', in *Max Planck UNYB* 7: 183–218.

Fassenberg B. (1998), *UN Security Council Reform and the Right of Veto: A Constitutional Perspective*, Kluwer Law International.

Fassbender, B. (1998), 'The United Nations Charter as Constitution of the International Community', in *Columbia Journal of Transnational Law* 36: 529.

Fearon, J. and Laitin, D. (2003), 'Ethnicity, Insurgency and Civil Wars', in *American Political Science Review* 97–1: 75–90.

Ferstman, C., Goetz M., Stephens A. (2009), *Reparations for Victims of Genocide, War Crimes and Crimes Against Humanity: Systems in Place and Systems in the Making*, Bril Martinus Nijhoff Publishers.

Findlay, M. (2009), 'International and Comparative Criminal Justice Network', in *International Criminal Justice and Global Governance*, Research Theme I, University of Sidney.

Finkelstein, L.S. (1995), 'What is Global Gocernance?', in *Global Governance* 1995–1: 367–372.

Flint, J. and de Waal, A. (2005) *Darfur: A short history of a long war*, (2005), International African Institute, Zed Books: London and New York.

Foreman, S. 'Dix ans de Cour pénale internationale: avancées et limites', in *La justice pénale internationale face aux crimes de masse: Approches critiques*, Edited by R. Nollez-Goldbach and J. Saada. (Paris: Editions Pedone, 2014), at 145–165.

Frick, M.L. and Oberprantacher A. (2009), *Power and Justice in International Relations: Interdisciplinary Approaches to Global Challenges*, Essays in Honour of Hans Köchler, Ashgate: Farnham (Surrey), UK.

Friman, H. (2001), 'The Democratic Republic of Congo: Justice in the aftermath of peace in DRC?' in *African Security Review* 10–3: 63–77.

Fukuyama, F. (2004), *State-Building: Governance and World Order in the 21st Century.* Ithaca, NY: Cornell University Press.

Gaer, F.D. (2003), 'Human Rights NGOs in UN Peace Operations', in *International Peacekeeping* 10 (1): 73–89, 25.

Gaeta, P. (2009), 'Does President Al Bashir Enjoy Immunity from Arrest?', in *Journal of International Criminal Justice*, 7–2: 315–332, Oxford Journals.

Gaeta, P. (2009), *The UN Genocide Convention. A Commentary*, Oxford Commentaries on International Law, Oxford University Press.

Gallant, K. S. (2003), 'The International Criminal Court in the System of States and International Organizations', (September) 16 *LJIL* 03: 553- 591.

Gallavin, C. (2003), 'Article 53 of the Rome Statute of the International Criminal Court: In the Interests of Justice', 14 *KCLJ* 03: 179–198.

Gallavin, C. (2005), 'The Security Council & the ICC: Delineating the Scope of Security Council Referrals and Deferrals', 5 *New Zealand Armed Forces Law Review* 05: 19–38.

Galtung, J., Gosovic, B., Khosla, A., Zammit, A., (2008) 'The Millennium Development Goals: Missing Goals and Mistaken Policies' in *MDGs: A Costly Diversion from the Road to Sustainable Development,* 2008: 20–37, accessible at: www.transcend.org/tri/downloads/the_mill.pdf

Galtung, J., Jacobson, C.G. and Frithjof Brand-Jacobson K. (2002), *Searching for Peace: The Road to Trascend,* 2nd Edition Pluto Press: London.

Galtung, J. and Fisher, D. (2002) *To End Terrorism, End State Terrorism,* in Transcend Research Institute Publications, accessible at: www.transcend.org/tri/

Galtung, J. and Ikeda, D. (1995), *Choose Peace,* Pluto Press: London.

Glasius,M.(2009)'TheICCandtheGazaWar:legallimits,symbolicpolitics',accessibleat:www.opendemocracy.net/article/the-icc-and-the-gaza-war-legal-limits-symbolic-politics

Glassborow, K. (2008) 'China, Russa quash ICC efforts to press Sudan over Darfur crimes', in *Sudan Tribune,* 12 January 2008, accessible at: www.sudantribune.com/spip.php?article25544

Gates, S. and Reich, S. (2009) *Child Soldiers in the Age of Fractured States,* (eds.), University of Pittsburg Press 2009: 143.

Gevers, C. (2009), 'South Africa Bold Proposal Shows Up the Flaws in the Rome Statute', in *BusinessDay,* 29 December 2009, accessible at: www.businessday.co.za/articles/Content.aspx?id=90453

Goldstone, R. (2007), 'International Criminal Court and Ad Hoc Tribunals', in T. Weiss, S. Daws (eds.), *The Oxford Handbook on the United Nations,* Oxford University Press, 463–474.

Goldstone, R. and Smith, A., (2008), *International Judicial Institutions: The Architecture of International Criminal Justice at Home and Abroad,* Global Institutions, Routledge.

Goucha, M. (2000), 'First International Meeting of Directors of Peace Research and Training Institutions. Foreword' *What Agenda for Human Security in the Twenty-first Century?* UNESCO 2001–2005: 11, web document accessible at: www.unesco.org/securipax/whatagenda.pdf

Gowlland-Debbas V. (2004), 'Human Rights and Humanitarian Law: Are there some Individuals Bereft of all Legal Protection? The Relevance of Paragraph 25 of the ICJ's Advisory Opinion on Nuclear Weapons', in *Mapping New Boundaries,* Proceedings of the American Society of International Law, 98th Annual Meeting, Washington D.C., 2004: 358–363.

Gowlland-Debbas, V. (2002), 'The Relationship between Political and Judicial Organs of International Organisations: The Role of the Security Council in the New International Criminal Court', International Organisations and International Dispute Settlement: Trends and Prospects, in Laurence Boisson de Chazournes, Cesare Romano and Ruth Mackenzie (eds.), Transnational Publishers, 2002: 195–218.

Gowlland-Debbas, V. (2001), 'The Role of the Security Council in the New International Criminal Court from a Systemic Perspective', in Boisson, de Chazournes, L. and Gowlland-Debbas, V. (eds.), *The International Legal System in Quest of Equity and Universality,* Martinus Nijhoff Publishers, 2001: 629–650.

Gray, C. (2004), *International Law and the Use of Force* (2d ed.), Oxford University Press.

Gray, C. (2001), 'Peacekeeping after the Brahimi Report: Is There a Crisis of Credibility for the UN?', *Journal of conflict and Security Law* 6(2): 267.

Grono, N. (2006), 'Briefing Darfur: The International Community Failure To Protect', *African Affairs* 105–421: 621–631.

Guehenno J.M. (2002), 'On the Challenges and Achievements of Reforming UN Peace Operations', in *International Peacekeeping* 9–2: 69–80.

Gueye, L. (2010), 'Congo under Increased Pressure from the US to Deliver on Justice', in *Global Policy Forum*, 25 March 2010, accessible at: www.globalpolicy.org/component/content/article/164icc/48872congounderincreased-pressure-from-the-us-to-deliver-on-justice-.html

Guiora, A.N. (2005), 'Counter-terrorism and the rule of law', Case Legal Studies Research Paper No. 05–15, *Istanbul Conference on Democracy and Global Security*, accessible at: http://ssrn.com/abstract=759605

Hagan, J. and Rymond-Richmond, W. (2009), *Darfur and the Crimes of Genocide*, Cambridge University Press.

Hagedorn, A. (2010), 'UN-immunity disregards fundamental human rights: A decision by the Court of Appeals at The Hague in the case of the Mothers of Srebrenica', in *The Hague Justice Portal*, 2010, the article is accessible at: www.haguejusticeportal.net/eCache/DEF/11/659.html

Haggard, S. (1987), 'Theories of International Regimes', in *International Organizations* 41: 491.

Hall, C.K. (2007), 'Universal Jurisdiction: Developing and Implementing an Effective Global Strategy' in W. Kaleck, M. Ratner, T. Singelnstein, (eds.), *International Prosecution of Human Rights Crimes*, 2007: 85, Springer.

Harrington, J., Milde, M., and Vernon, R. (2006) eds., *Bringing Power to Justice? The Prospects of the International Criminal Court*, McGill-Queen's University Press: Quebec

Hathaway, O.A. (2002), 'Looking Ahead: Can Treaties Make a Difference?' *The Yale Law Journal* 111–8: 1935.

Hasenclever, A., Mayer, P., Rittberger, V. (1997), *Theories of International Regimes*, Cambridge Studies in International Relations: Cambridge.

Helman, G.B. and Ratner, S.R. (1993), 'Saving Failed States', in *Foreign Policy* 89–3.

Hope, K.R. (2003), *The UNECA and Good Governance in Africa*, Harvard International Development Conference: Governance and Development in a Dynamic Global Environment, Boston, accessible at: www.uneca.org/dpmd/Hope_Harvard.doc

Hills, A. (2001), 'The Inherent Limits of Military Forces in Policing Peace Operations', in *International Peacekeeping* 8–3: 79–98.

Hilpold, P. (2006), 'The Duty To Protect and the Reform of the United Nations. A New Step in the Development of International Law?', *Max Planck Yearbook of United Nations Law* 10: 35.

Hoebeke, H., Carette, S. and Vlassenroot, K. (2007), *EU support to the Democratic Republic of Congo*, Centre d'Analyse Stratégique, accessible at: www.egmontinstitute.be/papers/07/afr/EU_support_to_the_DRC.pdf

Hoile, D. (2014), *Justice Denied: The Reality of the International Criminal Court*, London: The Africa Research Centre, 2014, at 609.

Holt, V.K. and Smith, J.G. (2008), 'Halting Widespread or Systematic Attacks on Civilians: Military Strategies and Operations Concepts', in *Future of Peace Operations Program*,

The Henry L. Stimson Center, Kofi Annan International Peacekeeping Training Center, Human Security Program: Foreign Affairs and International Trade Canada.

Holt, V.K. and Berkman, T.C. (2006) *The Impossible Mandate? Military Preparedness, the Responsibility to Protect and Modern Peace Operations*, The Henry L. Stimson Center, 2006: 155.

Hughes, B. and Hunt, C. (2009), 'The Rule of Law in Peace and Capacity Building Operations: Moving beyond a Conventional State-Centred Imagination', in *Journal of International Peacekeeping* 13, 3–4: 267.

Human Rights Watch (2010), *Democracy On Hold*, Summary, June 29, 2010, accessible at: www.hrw.org/en/reports/2010/06/29/democracy-hold

Human Rights Watch (2010), *'Trail of Death. LRA Atrocities in Northeastern Congo'*, March 2010 Report, accessible at: www.hrw.org/node/89324

Human Rights Watch (2010), *'Complaint Against Colonel Innocent Zimurinda'* 1 March 2010, accessible at: www.hrw.org/en/news/2010/03/01/complaint-against-lt-col-innocent-zimurinda

Human Rights Watch (2009), *Selling Justice Short. Why Accountability Matters for Peace,* July 2009, accessible at: www.hrw.org

Human Rights Watch (2009), 'DR Congo: Civilian Cost of Military Operation is Unacceptable', 13 October 2009, www.hrw.org/en/news/2009/10/12/dr-congo-civilian-cost-militaryoperationunacceptable

Human Rights Watch (2009), "MONUC and Civilian Protection" in *You Will Be Punished. Attacks on Civilians in Eastern Congo,* 12–2009: 134–153, Report of Human Rights Watch (HRW) December 2009, the report is accessible at: www.hrw.org/sites/default/files/reports/drc1209web_1.pdf

Human Rights Watch (2009), *Sudan: Expelling Aid Agencies Harms Victims,* March 5, 2009, accessible at: www.hrw.org/node/81326

Human Rights Watch (2008), *They Shot at Us as We Fled: Government Attacks on Civilians in West Darfur,* accessible at: www.hrw.org

Human Rights Watch (2008), *No One To Intervene: Gaps in Civilian Protection in Southern Sudan*, 2009, accessible at: www.hrw.org

Human Rights Watch (2008), *We Will Crush You. The Restriction of Political Space in the Democratic Republic of Congo*, November 2008, the report is accessible at: www.hrw.org/en/node/76188/section/9#_ftn314

Human Rights Watch (2007), 'The Role of the International Community', in *Renewed Crisis in North Kivu*, October 2007, accessible at: www.hrw.org/en/reports/2007/10/22/renewed-crisis-north-kivu

Human Rights Watch (2007), *Ten Steps for Darfur: Indicators for Evaluating Progress in the HRC Group of Experts Process*, September 24, 2007, accessible at: www.hrw.org/en/reports/2007/09/24/ten-steps-darfur

Human Rights Watch (2006), 'Joint letter to the Chief Prosecutor of the International Criminal Court', July 31, 2006, accessible at: www.hrw.org

Humanitarian news and analysis by the Integrated Regional Information Networks (IRIN), (2010), *Sudan: Elections in a volatile climate*, 19 February 2010, accessible at: www.irinnews.org/report.aspx?ReportID=88167

Humanitarian news and analysis by the Integrated Regional Information Networks (IRIN), (2006), *Justice for a Lawless World? Rights and reconciliation in a new era of international law. GLOBAL: Justice Unfettered? Internationalising Justice in the human rights era*, the article is accessible at: www.irinnews.org/IndepthMain.aspx?IndepthId=7&ReportId=59464

Hunt, C.T. and Bellamy, A.J. (2010), 'Mainstreaming the Responsibility to Protect in Peace Operations', *Asia-Pacific Centre for the Responsibility to Protect*, Program on the Protection of Civilians, Working Paper N. 3, 2010, Asia-Pacific Centre for the Responsibility to Protect, University of Queensland, Australia.

Hurwitz, A. (2005), 'Toward Enhanced Legitimacy of Rule of Law Programs in Multidimensional Peace Operations', in European Society of International Law (SEDI): Geneva Research Forum, ESIL Web Publications.

Hurwitz, A. (2008), 'Introduction: Civil War and the Rule of Law: Toward Security, Development, and Human Rights', in *Civil War and the Rule of Law: Toward Security, Development, and HumanRights*, eds. Agnes Hurwitz and Reyko Huang, Boulder and London: Lynne Rienner, 2008: 2.

ICISS, Report referring to "Human Rights, Human Security and Emerging Practice", in *The Responsibility to Protect*, Report of the International Commission on Intervention and State Sovereignty, International Development Research Centre, Ottawa, Canada, 2001: 14–18.

Idonor, D. (2010), 'Africa: Nigeria, France Want Africa on UN Security Council Seat', *Vanguard*, 1 June 2010, accessible at: http://allafrica.com/stories/201006010076.html

Ikenberry, G.J., and Deudney, D. (1999), 'The Nature and Sources of Liberal International Order' in *Review of International Studies* Volume 25, 1999: 179–96.

Ikenberry, G.J. (2001), *After Victory: Institutions, Strategic Restraint, and the Rebuilding of Order AfterMajor Wars*, Princeton, NJ: Princeton University Press.

Ikeda, D. (2001), *For the Sake of Peace*, Middleway Press: Santa Monica.

Ingadottir, T. and Romano, C. (2000), *The Financing of the International Criminal Court. A discussion Paper*, ICC Discussion Paper N. 2, accessible at www.pict-pcti.org/publications/ICC_paprs/FinancingICC.pdf

International Bar Association's Human Rights Institute (IBAHRI-2009), the International Legal Assistance Consortium (ILAC), *Rebuilding Courts and Trust: An Assessment of the Needs of the Justice System in the Democratic Republic of Congo*, August 2009, accessible at: www.ibanet.org/Article/Detail.aspx?ArticleUid=6c2be523-f51248c1b09cfc9a8b1d0aab

International Center for Transitional Justice (2009), '*Focus: 2009 DRC Amnesty Law. Amnesty Must Not Equal To Impunity*' 2009 ICTJ, accessible at: www.ictj.org/static/Factsheets/ICTJ_DRC_amnesty_fs2009.pdf

International Crisis Group (2009), 'Conflict Risk: DR Congo', 27 January 2009 accessible at: www.crisisgroup.org/home/index.cfm?id=5897&l=1

International Crisis Group (2003), 'The Kivus: The Forgotten Crucible of the Congo Conflict', in *Africa Report* 56, (24 January 2003), accessible at: www.crisisgroup.org/home/index.cfm?id=1630&l=1

International Crisis Group (2000), 'Scramble for the Congo. Anatomy of an Ugly War', (December 20, 2000), ICG Africa Report No. 26, at 3.

International Crisis Group (1999), 'The Agreement on a Ceasefire in the Democratic Republic of Congo. An Analysis of the Agreement and Prospects for Peace', (August 20, 1999), ICG DRC Report No. 5, at 18.

International Rescue Committee (2008), 'Mortality in the Democratic Republic of Congo: An Ongoing Crisis', 22 January 2008, accessible at: www.theirc.org/special-report/congo-forgotten-crisis.html

Jalloh, C.C. (2010), 'The African Union and Its Discontents with the International Criminal Court', in *Jurist Forum*, 6 August 2010, accessible at: http://jurist.org/forum/2010/08/the-african-union-and-the-icc-growing discontent.php

Jalloh, C.C. (2009), 'Regionalizing International Criminal Law?', in *International Criminal Law Review* 9: 445–466.

Jalloh, C.C. (2009), 'A Win-Win for the International Criminal Court', in *International Criminal Law Review* 9: 467–499.

Jensen, E. (2003), 'The Rule of Law and Judicial Reform: The Political Economy of Diverse Institutional Patterns and Reformers' Responses' in E. Jensen and T. Heller, *Beyond Common Knowledge: Empirical Approaches to the Rule of Law*, Stanford University Press, 2003: 336–345.

Johnson, S. (2003), 'The Jurisdiction Debates: The Security Council and the ICC', in *Peace Without Justice. Hegemonic Instability or International Criminal Law?* Ashgate, 2003: 80.

Justino, P. (2009), *The Impact of Armed Conflicts on Household Welfare and Policy Responses*, Micro Conflict Research Working Paper 12, (Microcon) accessible at: www.microconflict.eu/publications/RWP12_PJ.pdf

Kajee, A. (2006), 'Lubanga Case Signals Hope for Child Soldiers', *Institute for War and Peace Reporting*, No. 58, the report is accessible at: www.iwpr.net/?p=%3Cp%3ENo%20item%20found.%3C/p%3E&s=f&o=260591&apc_state=henh

Kaleck, W. (2006), 'et al', *International Prosecution of Human Rights Crimes*, Springer.

Katayanagi, M. (2002), *Human Rights Functions of United Nations Peacekeeping Operations*, Martinus Nijhoff Publishers.

Kelsen, H. (1948), 'Collective Security and Collective Self-Defense Under the Charter of the United Nations', *The American Journal of International Law* 42–4: 783.

Keohane, R.O. (1998), 'International Institutions: Can Interdependence Work?', in *Foreign Policy*, Frontiers of knowledge, (Spring 1998) 110: 82–96.

Keohane, R.O. (1989), *International Institutions and State Power: Essays in International Relations Theory*, Westview Press: Boulder.

Keppler, E. and Dicker, R. (2007), 'Trading Justice for Peace in Uganda Won't Work', in *Uganda Daily Monitor*, 2 May 2007, accessible at: www.hrw.org/en/news/2007/05/02/trading-justice-peace-uganda-won-t-work

Kerr, R. and Mobekk, E. (2007), *Peace and Justice. Seeking Accountability after War*, Polity Press.

Kingah, S. (2006), 'The Revised Cotonou Agreement between the European Community and the African, Caribbean and Pacific States: Innovations on Security, Political Dialogue, Transparency, Money and Social Responsibility', *Journal of African law* 50: 59.

Kiiver, P. (2007), 'Constitutions in the Age of Internationalization: Towards Transnational Constitutional Standards', in *HiiL Rule of Law Inventory Report: Discussion Paper for High Level Expert Meeting on the Rule of Law*, accessible at: www.hiil.org

Kiyani, A. (2010), 'Africa and the ICC: Resistance or Cooperation?', *Liu Institute of Global Issues,* 2010, accessible at: http://blogs.ubc.ca/ligi/2010/05/25/africa-and-the-icc-resistance-or-cooperation/

Kiyani, A. (2010), 'Article 16: Peace, Justice and Political Interference in the Court', in *Institute for Global Issues,* Reports From the Field, 2010, accessible at: http://blogs.ubc.ca/ligi/2010/06/03/article-16-peace-justice-and-political-interference-in-the-court/

Knight, A. (2000), *A changing United Nations. Multilateral Evolution and the Quest for Global Governance,* Palgrave.

Köchler, H. (2010), *Security Council Reform: A Requirement of International Democracy,* forthcoming.

Köchler, H. (2009), *Global Justice or Global Revenge? The ICC and the Politicization of International Criminal Justice,* Lecture delivered at the World Conference for International Justice, "United against the politicization of justice" organized by the General Sudanese Students Union, Khartoum, Sudan, 6 April 2009, accessible at: http://i-p-o.org/IPO-Koechler-ICC-politicization-2009.htm

Köchler, H. (2009), 'The Politics of Global Powers', in *The Global Community. Yearbook of International Law and Jurisprudence,* forthcoming.

Köchler, H. (2008), The Global War on Terror and the Question of World Order, Studies in International Relations, XXX, International Progress Organization: Vienna.

Köchler, H. (2006), 'The Use of Force in International Relations. Challenges to Collective Security', Studies in International Relations, XXVIII, International Progress Organization: Vienna.

Köchler, H. (2005), 'The Collapse of the Power Balance of the Cold War and the Crisis of the United Nations. Quo Vadis, United Nations?' in *Law Review*: 49–65.

Köchler, H. (2005), 'Security Council Refer Darfur crimes to the International Criminal Court, but No Impunity for Peacekeepers', in *Amnesty International Press Release,* AFR 54/032/2005, News Service No: 74, (29 March 2005).

Köchler, H. (2005), *Double Standards in International Criminal Justice: The Case of Sudan,* Studies in International Relations, XXVIII, International Progress Organization: Vienna.

Köchler, H. (2004), 'The Iraq Crisis and the United Nations. Power Politics vs. the International Rule of Law', in Memoranda and declarations of the International Progress Organization (1990–2003), Studies in International Relations, XXVIII, International Progress Organization: Vienna.

Köchler, H. (2003), *Global Justice or Global Revenge? International Criminal Justice at the Crossroad,* Springer: New York.

Köchler, H. (1997), *The United Nations and International Democracy. The Quest for UN Reform,* Studies in International Relations, XXII. Studies in International Relations, XXVIII, International Progress Organization: 9–15.

Koh, H.H. and Rapp, S.J. (2010), 'US Engagement with the International Criminal Court and the Outcome of the recently concluded Review Conference', June 15 2010, accessible at: www.state.gov/s/wci/us_releases/remarks/143178.htm

Koh, H.H. (2007), 'Repairing America's Human Rights Reputation', in *Cornell Int'l L.J.* 40: 635

Komarnicki, T. (1952), 'The Problem of Neutrality under the United Nations Charter', in *Transactions of the Grotius Society,* Vol. 38: 77.

Knoops, G.A. (2004), *The Prosecution and Defense of Peacekeepers Under International Criminal Law*, Martinus Nijhoff Publishers.

Knoops, G.A. (2002), *Surrendering to International Criminal Courts: Contemporary Practice and Procedures*, Transitional Publishers.

Kleffner, J.K. (2008), *Complementarity in the Rome Statute and National Criminal Jurisdictions*, Oxford University Press.

Kleffner, J.K. (2003), 'The Impact of Complementarity on National Implementation of Substantive International Criminal Law', *Journal of International Criminal Justice* 1: 86.

Kooijmans, P. (2000), *Internationaal Publiekrecht in Vogelvlucht* (2000: 359), translation from Dutch by M. Brus 'et al', 'Bridging the Gap between State Sovereignty and International Governance: The Authority of Law', in *State, Sovereignty and International Governance*, Oxford University Press, (2004: 3).

Kramer, R.C., Michalowski, R.J. (2005), "War, Aggression and State Crime. A Criminological Analysis of the Invasion and Occupation of Iraq", *The British Journal of Criminology* 45: 446, accessible at: http://homepages.wmich.edu/~kramerr/BJC.pdf

Krasner, S.D. (1983), 'Structural Causes and Regime Consequences: Regimes as Intervening Variables', in *International Regimes*, S.D. Krasner (ed.) Ithaca, NY: Cornell University Press.

Krause K., Knight, A. (1995), *State, Society, and the UN System: Changing Perspectives on Multilateralism*, UNU Press.

Krisch, N. and Kingsbury, B. (2006), 'Introduction: Global Governance and Global Administrative Law in the International Legal Order', in *EJIL* 17–1: 1–13.

Krisch, N., Kingsbury B. and Stewart, R.B. (2005), 'The Emergence of Global Administrative Law', in *Law and Contemporary Problems* 15: 68.

Ladeur, K.H. (2004), *Public Governance in the Age of Globalization*, Ashgate.

Lakoff, G. And Frisch E. (2006), *Five Years After 9/11: Drop the War Metaphor*, accessible at: www.rockridgeinstitute.org/research/rockridge/fiveyearsafter911/

Laitin, D. and Fearon, J.D. (2004), 'Neotrusteeship and the Problem of Weak States', in *International Security* 28–4: 5–43.

Lambourne, W. (2010), 'Transitional Justice and Peacebuilding After Mass Violence', in *International Journal of Transitional Justice* (forthcoming).

Lambourne, W. (forthcoming), 'Justice After Genocide: The Rwandan Experiment with Gacaca Community Justice', 2010 in proceedings from the conference "Social Justice and Human Rights in the Era of Globalisation: Between Rhetoric and Reality", Katholieke Universiteit Leuven, Belgium, 21–23 August 2006.

Lambourne, W. (2007), "Peacekeeping and Peacebuilding" in United Nations Association of Australia, *Australia and the United Nations*, UNAA, 2007: 27–32.

Lambourne, W. (2004), 'Post-Conflict Peacebuilding: Meeting Human Needs for Justice and Reconciliation', in *Peace, Conflict and Development Journal*, 2004: 4, accessible at: www.peacestudiesjournal.org.uk/docs/PostConflictPeacebuilding.PDF

Laurenti, J. and Robichaud, C. (2007), *Breaking the Nuclear Impasse. New Prospects for Security against Weapons Threats*, Century Foundation Press, International Relations, Arms Control, 2007: 100.

Lee, R.S.K. (2005), *States' Responses to Issues Arising from the ICC Statute: Constitutional, Sovereignty, Judicial Cooperation, and Criminal Law*, Transnational Publishers, 2005: 215.

Legro, J.W. (2005), *Rethinking the World: Great Power Strategies and International Order* Ithaca, NY: Cornell University Press, 2005: 24–49 and 161–189.

Leonard, E.K. (2005), 'Discovering the New Face of Sovereignty: Complementarity and the International Criminal Court' in *New Political Science*, 27: 87–104.

Leonard, E.K., *The Onset of Global Governance: International Relations Theory and the International Criminal Court,* Ashgate.

Leonard, E.K. (2005), 'Preventing Selective Justice', in *The Onset of Global Governance: International Relations Theory and the International Criminal Court,* Ashgate, 2005–47.

Lepard, B.D. (2002), *Rethinking Humanitarian Intervention. A Fresh Legal Approach Based on Fundamental Ethical Principles in International Law and World Religions,* 2002: 456, The Pennsylvania State University Press.

Lewis, B. (2004), *The Crisis of Islam: Holy War and Unholy Terror,* Random House Trade Paperback: New York.

Lyck, M. (2009), *Peace Operations and International Criminal Justice. Building Peace After Mass Atrocities*, Routledge: New York.

Linklater, A. and Suganami, H. (2006), *The English School of International Relations. A Contemporary Reassessment*, University of Wales, Aberystwyth, Cambridge University Press: 8.

Luck C. and Doyle M. W. (2004), *International Law and Organization: Closing the Compliance Gap*, Lanham, MD.

MacDonald, Ronald St. John and Johnston, Douglas M. (eds.) 2005, *Towards World Constitutionalism: Issues in the Legal Ordering of the World Community*, Martinus Nijhoff Publishers: Leiden, Boston.

Mamdani M. (2001), *When Victims Become Killers: Colonialism, Nativism and Genocide in Rwanda*, Princeton: Princeton University Press.

Mani, R. (2005), 'Balancing Peace with Justice in the Aftermath of Violent Conflict', *Development* 48–3: 28.

Mearsheimer, J. (1994), 'The False Promise of International Institutions', *International Security*, 19–3, 1994–95: 5–49.

Mærli, M.B. and Lodgaard, S. (2007), 'Encountering Proliferators, Real or Potential' in *Nuclear Proliferation and International Security*, Routledge Global Security Studies 2007: 71.

Martin, L.L. and Simmons, B.A. (1998), 'Theories and Empirical Studies of International Institutions', in *International Organization* 52–4, Autumn 1998: 729–757.

Martin Martinez, M. M. (1996), *National Sovereignty and International Organizations,* Kluwer Law International.

Maxwell, S. (2005), 'How to Help Reform Multilateral Institutions: An Eight-Step Program for More Effective Collective Action', *Global Governance* 11: 415.

Mays, T.M. (2002), *Africa's First Peacekeeping Operation: The OAU in Chad, 1981–1982,* Praeger Publishers.

Méndez, J.E. (2010), 'The Importance of Justice in Securing Peace', in *Review Conference of the Rome Statute*, ICC doc. RC/ST/PJ/INF.3, 30 May 2010, accessible at: www.icc-cpi.int/iccdocs/asp_docs/RC2010/Stocktaking/RC-ST-PJ-INF.3-ENG.pdf

Méndez, J.E. (2010), "Facing the short term tensions and integrating a 'justice track' to mediation efforts", in *The Importance of Justice in Securing Peace*, Review Conference of the Rome Statute, ICC doc. RC/ST/PJ/INF.3, 30 May 2010: 4.

Milliken, J. (2003), *State Failure, Collapse and Reconstruction*, Blackwell Publishing.

Mobekk, E. (2009), 'Security Sector Reform and the UN Mission in the Democratic Republic of Congo: Protecting Civilians in the East', in *International Peacekeeping* 16–2: 273–286.

Mobekk, E. (2005), 'Identifying Lessons in UN International Policing Missions', November 2005, *Geneva Centre for the Democratic Control of Armed Forces (DCAF)*, Policy Paper 9, accessible at: www.dcaf.ch/_docs/pp09_united-nations-international_policing.pdf

Mohamad, R. (2014) 'International Criminal Court in the Development of International Rule of Law: a Reflection of Asian-African Views', in *Institutional Supports for the International Rule of Law*, Edited by C. Sampford and R. Thakur, London: Routledge, 2014, at 59–73.

Moreno-Ocampo, L. (2008), 'The International Criminal Court: Seeking Global Justice', in *Case W. Res. J. INT'L L.* 40:215–225.

Moreno-Ocampo, L. (2005), XI Report of the Prosecutor of the International Criminal Court to the Security Council Pursuant to UNSC 1593 (2005), 17 June 2010, the report is accessible at: www.icc-cpi.int/NR/rdonlyres/A250ECCD-D9E5-433B-90BB-76C068ED58A3/282160/11thUNSCReportENG1.pdf

Mowjee, T. 'Background and Conflict Details', in *DRC Case Study*, 2007, at 4, Feinstein International Center, Briefing Paper, accessible at: https://wikis.uit.tufts.edu/confluence/display/FIC/Publications

Müller, J. (2006), *Reforming the United Nations. The Struggle for Legitimacy and Effectiveness*, Brill, Martinus Nijhoff Publishers.

Munck, G.L. and Verkuilen, J. (2002), 'Conceptualizing and Measuring Democracy: Evaluating Alternative Indices', in *Comparative Political Studies* February 35–1–5 :34.

Mutua, M. (2008), 'The Quest for a Democratic Constitution', in *Kenya's Quest for Democracy*, Lynne Rienner Publishers, 2008: 145–278.

Naarden, G.L. and Locke, J.B. (2004), 'Peacekeeping and Prosecutorial Policy: Lessons from Kosovo', in *American Journal of International Law* 98(4): 727–743.

Nabulsi, K. (2001), 'Evolving Conceptions of Civilians and Belligerents. One Hundred Years After The Hague Peace Conferences', in *Civilians in War*: 9.

Naldi, G.J. and Magliveras ,K.D.(2002), 'The African Union. A New Dawn for Africa?' in *International & Comparative Law Quarterly*, Cambridge University Press 51: 415–425.

Naldi, G.J. (1999), *The Organisation of African Unity: An analysis of its role*, 2nd edition, Cambridge University Press.

Nollkaemper (eds.), *Review of the Security Council by Member States*, Intersentia, Antwerp: 7–30.

Normand, R. and Zaidi, S. (2007), *Human Rights at the UN The Political History of Universal Justice*, Indiana University Press. For other scholars' publications involved on the UN Intellectual History Project see the list accessible at: www.unhistory.org/

Nye J.S. Jr. (2004), *Power in the Global Information Age,* Routledge: London.

O'Brien, P. (2008), 'The International Criminal Court 10 Years After the Rome Statute. Successes Achieved and Challenges Ahead', 12 July 2008, *International Society for the Reform of Criminal Law,* Dublin, the research paper is accessible at: www.isrcl.org/Papers/2008/OBrien.pdf

O'Hanlon, M. and Singer, P.W. (2004), 'The Humanitarian Transformation: Expanding Global Intervention Capacity', in *Survival* 46(1): 77–100.

Okouma, G.O. (2007), 'Security Council Reform: a Transitional Approach', in *United Nations Chronicle Online Edition*, 2007, web-article accessible at: www.un.org/Pubs/chronicle/2007/webArticles/120307_security_council_reform.html

Olasolo, H. (2009), *The Criminal Responsibility of Senior Political and Military Leaders as Principals to International Crimes*, Hart Publishers.

Okumu, W. (2003), 'Humanitarian International NGOs and African Conflicts', in *International Peacekeeping* 10–1: 120–137.

Oosterveld V.P. and McManus, J.M. (March 2002), 'The Cooperation of States with the International Criminal Court', in *Fordham International law Journal* 25–3: 767.

Oswald, B. (2004), 'Model Codes for Criminal Justice and peace operations: some legal issues', in *Journal of Conflict and Security Law* 9(2): 253.

Ottaway, M. (2002), 'Rebuilding State Institutions in Collapsed States', in *Development and Change* 33–5, 2002:1001–1023.

Paris, E. (2008), "The New World Order" in *The Sun Climbs Slow: Justice in the Age of Imperial America*, Knopf Canada: 35–51.

Paris, R. (2004), 'International Peacebuilding and the 'Mission Civilisatrice', in *Review of International Studies*, 28–4: 637–56.

Paris, R. (2002), *At War's End: Building Peace After Civil Conflict*, Cambridge University Press.

Paris, R. (2001), 'Human Security. Paradigm Shift or Hot Air?' in *International Security*, 26–2: 87–102.

Petit, F. (2007), *Sensibilisation à la CPI en RDC: Sortir du Profil Bas,* ICTJ, March 2007, accessible at: www.ictj.org

Piiparinen, T. (2009), 'Bureaucratic Mechanisms', in *The Transformation of UN Conflict Management. Producing images of genocide from Rwanda to Darfur and beyond,* Routledge, 2009: 118.

Piiparinen, T. (2007), 'The Lessons of Darfur for the Future of Humanitarian Intervention', in *Global Governance* 13–3: 365.

Pirozzi, N. and Ronzitti, N. (2011), 'The EU and the Reform of the UN Security Council: Toward a New Regionalism?', in *IAI Working Papers*, 12–12, May 2011, at 9, accessible at: www.iai.it/pdf/DocIAI/iaiwp1112.pdf

Posen, B. (1993), 'The Security Dilemma And Ethnic Conflict', in *Survival* 35–1, 1993:27–47.

Pouligny, B. (2003), 'UN peace operations, INGOs, NGOs, and promoting the rule of law: exploring the intersection of international and local norms in different postwar contexts', in *Journal of Human Rights* 2–3: 372.

Pratt, M. and Werchick, L. (2004), 'Sexual Terrorism: Rape as a Weapon of War in Eastern Democratic Republic of Congo. An assessment of programmatic responses to sexual violence in North Kivu, South Kivu, Maniema, and Orientale Provinces', accessible at: www.osisa.org/resources/docs/PDFs/Sexual_Terrorism.pdf

Proulx, V. J. (2009), 'Rethinking the Jurisdiction of the ICC in the Post-September 11 Era: Should Act of Terrorism Qualify as Crimes Against Humanity?' Working Paper, McGill University Faculty of Law.

Prunier, G. (2009), *From Genocide to Continental War: The "Congolese" Conflict and the Crisis of Contemporary Africa*, published in the US as *Africa's World War: Congo, the Rwandan Genocide, and the Making of Continental Catastrophe*, Oxford University Press.

Rackley, E.B. (2005), 'Predatory Governance in the DRC: Civilian Impact and Humanitarian Response', in *Humanitarian Exchange Magazine,* March 2005: 29–3, accessible at: www.odihpn.org

Rajagopal, B. (2008), 'Rule of Law and Security, Development and Human Rights: International Discourses, Institutional Responses" in Agnès Hurwitz (ed.) *Rule of Law and Conflict Management: Towards Security, Development and Human Rights,* Boulder and London: Lynne Rienner.

Rama, S.A. (2006), "Nationalism, Civil Wars, and Genocide', in *Order and Change in the Contemporary International System,* New York University Press.

Ramsbotham, O., Woodhouse T., Miall H. (2005), *Contemporary Conflict Resolution,* Polity Press: Cambridge.

Rapp, S.J. (2010), 'Statement by Stephen J. Rapp, US Ambassador-at-Large for War Crimes, Regarding Stocktaking at the Eighth Resumed Session of the Assembly of States Parties of the International Criminal Court', in *Briefing US Ambassador-at-Large for War Crimes*, 23 March 2010, US mission to the UN, accessible at: http://usun.state.gov/briefing/statements/2010/138999.htm

Rastan, R. (2008), 'Testing Co-operation: The ICC and National Authorities', in *Leiden Journal of International Law* 431–21: 456.

Ratner, S.R., Abrams, J.S. and Bischoff, J.L. (2009), *Accountability for Human Rights Atrocities in International Law: beyond the Nuremberg Legacy,* 2nd Ed. Oxford University Press.

Reeves, E. (2006), *Report of the International Commission of Inquiry on Darfur: A critical analysis (Part I an II),* accessible at: www.sudanreeves.org

Reilly, B. (2001), 'Democracy, Ethnic Fragmentation, And Internal Conflict', in *International Security* 25–3, 2001: 162–185.

Reisman, W.M. (July 2005), 'On Paying the Piper: Financial Responsibility for Security Council Referrals to the International Criminal Court', in *The American Journal of International Law* 99–3: 615–618.

Reno, W. (1998), 'Sovereignty and the Fragmentation of the DRC', in *Warlord Politics and African States,* Lynne Rienner Publishers 1998: 147.

Reus-Smit, C. (1997), 'The Constitutional Structure of International Society and the Nature of Fundamental Institutions', in *International Organization* 51–4, 1997: 555–589.

Reychler, L. (2010), 'Coordination de la politique étrangere de l'Union Européenne', in *Revue de la chaire de dynamique sociale, Kinshasa, R.D.C., Mouvements et enjeux sociaux,* numéro spécial- avril 2010: 13–27.

Reychler, L. (2010), Sustainable peace building architecture, in N. Young (Red.), International Encyclopedia of Peace, Oxford University Press: Oxford.

Reychler, L. (2009), 'Peacemaking, Peacekeeping and Peacebuilding', in R. A. Denemark (Red.), The International Studies Compendium Project, Wiley-Blackwell Publishing: Oxford.

Reychler, L. and Migabo Kalere, J. (2009), 'R.D. Congo Pays de l'avenir. Questions pour construire une paix durable', *Cahiers of the Center for Peace Research and Strategic Studies* (CPRS), 84: 107.

Reychler, L. (2007), 'Preventing war crimes and genocide: a look from the balkony', in J. Bec-Neumann (Red.), Darkness at Noon. War Crimes, Genocide and Memories: 226–241, Center for Interdisciplinary Postgraduate Studies: Sarajevo.

Reychler, L. (2006), 'Challenges of Peace Research', in *International Journal of Peace Studies, Volume* 11: 1–16.

Reychler, L. (2004), 'Strengthening the United Nations System with Peace Research', in *The Journal of Peace Studies* 11(1): 169–206.

Richmond, O. (2001), 'Human Security, the Rule of Law, and NGOs: Potentials and Problems for Humanitarian Intervention' in *Human Rights Review*, 2(4) (July–September 2001).

Roach, S.C. (2009), "Global Governance in Context", *Governance, Order, and the International Criminal Court. Between Realpolitik and a Cosmopolitan Court*, Oxford University Press: Oxford, (2009: 1).

Roach, S.C. (2009), "Justice of Peace? Future Challenges and Prospects for a Cosmopolitan Court", *Governance, Order, and the International Criminal Court. Between Realpolitik and a Cosmopolitan Court*, Oxford University Press: Oxford, (2009: 225–235).

Roach, S.C. (2005), 'Arab States and the Role of Islam in the International Criminal Court', in *Political Studies* 53: 143.

Roberts, A. and Zaum, D. (2008) *Selective Security: War and the United Nations Security Council since 1945*, International Institute for Strategic Studies, London, Abingdon: Routledge, 2008.

Robertson, G. (2002), *Crimes Against Humanity: The Struggle for Global Justice*, The New Press: New York.

Romano, C.P.R. (1999), 'The Proliferation of International Judicial Bodies: The Pieces of the Puzzle', in *International Law and Politics*, 31: 709.

Roth, K. (2010), 'Stocktaking of International Criminal Justice. Peace and Justice', in *Review Conference of the Rome Statute*, RC/ST/PJ/1, 7 June 2010.

Rotberg, R.I. (2010), Mass Atrocity Crimes. Preventing Future Outrages, (Rotberg ed.), World Peace Foundation, Cambrdidge.

Rotberg, R.I. (2003), 'Failed States, Collapsed States, Weak State: Causes and Indicators', in *State Failure and State Weakness in a Time of Terror*, The World Peace Foundation, Brookings Institution Press, 2003: 101.

Rotberg, R.I. (2005), *Battling terrorism in the Horn of Africa*, Brookings Institution Press.

Rotberg, R.I. (2002), 'The New Nature of Nation-State Failure', *The Washington Quarterly* 2002: 25–86.

Rothenberg, D. and Bassiouni, M.C. (2007), 'Facing Atrocity: The Importance of Guiding Principles on Post-Conflict Justice', in *The Chicago Principles on Post-Conflict Justice*, International Human Rights Law Institute, Chicago Council on Global Affairs, Istituto Superiore Internazionale di Scienze Criminali, Association Internationale de Droit Pénal, 2007: 6.

Roscini, M. (2007), 'Great Expectations: The implementation of the Rome Statute in Italy', in *Journal of International Criminal Justice* 5: 493.

Ryngaert, C. (2009), *The Effectiveness of International Criminal Justice*, Intersentia.

Rytter, J.E. (2001), 'Humanitarian Intervention without the Security Council: From San Francisco to Kosovo and Beyond', Nordic Journal of International Law 70-1-2: 121.

Sadat, L.N. (ed.) 2011, *Forging a Convention for Crimes Against Humanity*, Cambridge University Press, forthcoming.

Samset, I. (2002), 'Conflict of Interests or Interests in Conflict? Diamonds and War in the DRC', in *Review of African Political Economy* 29: 463.

Schabas, W.A. (2010), 'The International Criminal Court and the Security Council Referral of the Darfur Situation', in Black, D.R. and Williams, P.D. (eds.), *The International Politics of Mass Atrocities*, 2010: 149.

Schabas, W.A. (2009), *Genocide in International Law*, 2nd ed., Cambridge University Press: Cambridge.

Schabas, W.A. (2008), "Convention for the Prevention and Punishment of the Crime of Genocide", *United Nations Audiovisual Library of International Law*, the electronic version is accessible at: http://untreaty.un.org/cod/avl/ha/cppcg/cppcg.html

Schabas, W.A., Sthan, C. and El Zeidy, M.M. (2008), 'The International Criminal Court and Complementarity: Five Years On', in *Criminal Law Forum*, 2008: 3, accessible at: www.springerlink.com/content/n86h134236147107/

Schabas, W.A. (2007), *An Introduction to the International Criminal Court*, 3 rd ed. Cambridge University Press: Cambridge.

Schabas, W.A. (2006), *The UN International Criminal Tribunals: Former Yugoslavia, Rwanda and Sierra Leone* Cambridge University Press: Cambridge.

Scharf, M.P. (2010), *The International Criminal Court After Kampala: Should the United States Change its Relationship with the International Criminal Court?*, International and National Security Law Practice Group, 12 July 2010, National Press Club: Washington, DC.

Scharf, M.P. (2007), *The Law of International Organizations*, Carolina Academic Press: Durham, North Carolina, accessible at: www.cap-press.com/pdf/1608.pdf

Scharf, M.P. (1998), 'Results of The Rome Conference for an International Criminal Court', in *The American Society of International Law Insights*, August 1998.

Scharf, M.P. and Sadat L. (1996), 'The Proposed Permanent International Criminal Court: An Appraisal', in *Cornell Int'l L. J.* 29: 665.

Scharf, M.P. (1996), 'The Politics of Establishing an International Criminal Court', in *Duke Journal of Comparative and International Law* 6: 167–173.

Scharf, M.P. (1994), 'Symposium: Should there be an International Tribunal for Crimes Against Humanity' in *Pace International Law Review* 6: 87–91.

Scelle, G. (1936), 'Théorie et pratique de la fonction exécutive en droit international', *Recueil des Cours* 55: 91.

Scheffer, D. (2010), 'States Parties Approve New Crimes for International Criminal Court', in *American Society of International Law* 2010: 14–16, accessible at: www.asil.org/insights100622.cfm#_edn1

Scheffer, D.J. (1999), 'The United States and the International Criminal Court' in *The American Journal of International Law*, American Society of International Law, 93-1: 12–22.

Scheltema, M. (2005), *Hague Institute for the Internationalization of Law. National Law in a Global Society*, Hague Academic Press.

Schrijver, N.J. (2010), *Development without Destruction. The UN and Global Resource Management* , Bloomington: Indiana University Press.

Schrijver, N.J. (2009), 'Final Observation: The Role and Nature of Public International Law in the Pursuit for Sustainable Development', *The Evolution of Sustainable Development in International Law: Inception, Meaning and Status*, Collected Courses of the Hague Academy of International Law 329, 2009 (October), Chapter VII: 383–386, Martinus Nijhoff Publishers.

Schrijver, N.J. (2009), 'The EU's common development cooperation policy', in Telò, M. (Ed.) *The European Union and Global Governance* (2009: 176–191). Routledge: Oxford.

Schrijver, N.J. and Herik L. van den, (2009) 'Eroding the primacy of the UN system of collective security: The Judgment of the European Court of Justice in the cases of Kadi and Al Barakaat', *International Organizations Law Review*, 5 (2): 329–338.

Schrijver, N.J. (2008), 'International Organisations, Democracy and Good Governance: do they practice what they preach?' in Berendsen B. (Ed.), *Democracy and Development*, Amsterdam: KIT Publishers, (2008: 225–235).

Schrijver, N.J. and Dekker I.F. (2008), *Katern Volkenrecht* (a review of current developments in international law), *Ars Aequi*, 57 (6): 6051–6053.

Schrijver, N.J. (2008), 'Many Roads Lead to Rome, How to Arrive at a Legally Binding Instrument on the Right to Development?' in Kirchmeijer F. (Ed.), *Implementing the Right to Development: The Role of International Law*, Geneva: Friedrich-Ebert-Stiftung, (2008: 127–129).

Schrijver, N.J. (2007), 'De Verenigde Naties in de 21ste eeuw' in Jansen, T. Nijman, J., Sap, J.W. (Eds.), *Burgers en barbaren. Over oorlog tussen recht en macht.*, Amsterdam: Boom (2007: 149–162).

Schrijver, N.J. (2007), 'Reforming the UN Security Council in Pursuance of Collective Security', *Journal of Conflict & Security Law*, 12 (1): 127–138.

Schrijver, N.J. (2007), 'The Future of the Charter of United Nations: a new 'society of the committed' or just old wine in new bottles?', *Leiden Journal of International Law*, 20 (4): 809–823.

Schrijver, N.J. (2006), 'Les valeurs générales et le droit des Nations Unies' in Chemain, R. & Pellet, A. (Eds.), *La Charte des Nations Unies, constitution mondiale*, Paris: Pendone, (2006: 85–89).

Schrijver, N.J. (2006), "The Future of the Charter of the United Nations", *Max Planck Yearbook of United Nations Law*, 10: 1–34.

Scrijver, N.J. (2006), 'Clearing Away the Dead Wood in the Charter', in "The Future of the Charter of the United Nations", *Max Planck Yearbook of United Nations Law*, 10: 30.

Schrijver, N.J. and als (2006), *The United Nations of the Future. Globalisation with a Human Face*, Amsterdam: KIT Publishers.

Schrijver, N.J. (2005), 'Challenges to the Prohibition to Use Force: Does the Straitjacket of Article 2(4) UN Charter Begin to Gall Too Much', in Blokker, N.M. & Schrijver, N.J. (Eds.) *The Security Council and the Use of Force, Theory and Reality – A Need for Change? Bevriend boek van Meijers-reeks*, Leiden/Boston: Martinus Nijhoff Publishers, (2005: 31–45).

Schrijver, N.J. (2005), 'L'Article 2, paragraphe 4: la prohibition du recours à la force', in Cot, J.P., Pellet A. (eds.), *La Charte des Nations Unies*, (2005), Economica, para 35.

Schrijver, N.J. (2005), 'Les études sur les Nations Unies: Tendances et perspectives' in Cot, J.P. & Pellet, A. (Eds.), *La Charte des Nations Unies. Commentaire article par article* (II), Paris: Economica, (2005: 2241–2251).

Schrijver N.J. (2005), 'UN Reform: A Once-in-a-Generation Opportunity?' in *International Organizations Law Review*, 2 (2): 271–275.

Schrijver, N.J. (2004), 'September 11th and Challenges to International Law', in Boulden J. and. Weiss T.G (eds.), *Terrorism and the UN: Before and After September 11*, Indiana University Press, 2004: 55–73.

Schwartz, E.P. (2005), 'UN Peacekeeping Reform: Seeking Greater Accountability and Integrity', in *Council on Foreign Relations*, US Senate Publications, accessible at: www.cfr.org/publication.html?id=8113

Schweller, R. (2001), 'The Problem of International Order Revisited', in *International Security* Volume 26, Number 1 2001: 161–186.

Schwöbel, C., Marks, S. (2011), *Global Constitutionalism: An Idea with Radical Potential?*, Martinus Nijhoff Publishers.

Seybolt T.B. (2007), 'Controversies about Humanitarian Military Intervention', in *Humanitarian Military Intervention: The Conditions for Success and Failure*, Oxford University Press, 2007: 294.

Shiner, P. and Williams A., (2008), *The Iraq War and International Law*, Hart Publishing: Oxford, Portland, Oregon.

Shultz, R.H. (1995), 'State Disintegration and Ethnic Conflict: A Framework for Analysis', *The Annals of the American Academy of Political and Social Science* 541–75: 88.

Sieff, M. and Vinjamuri Wright, L. (1999), 'Reconciling Order and Justice? New Institutional Solutions in Post-Conflict States', in *Journal of International Affairs* 52, no. 2 (Spring 1999): 757–779.

Singer, P.W. (2004), 'War, Profits, and the Vacuum of Law: Privatized Military Firms and International Law', *Columbia Journal of Transnational Law*, 42: 2, at 521.

Singh, S. and Mishra, S. (2004), *International Criminal Court: Politics Of The "Unlike-Minded" Nations*, PL WebJour 8, accessible at: www.ebc-india.com/lawyer/articles/813.htm#Ref1

Slaughter, A.M. and Burke-White, W. (2006), 'The Future of International Law is Domestic (or, The European Way of Law)', in *Harvard Journal of International Law* 47: 327.

Slaughter, A.M. (2004), *A New World Order: Government Networks and the Disaggregated State*, Princeton University Press, 2004: 8.

Slaughter, A.M. (2000), 'Governing Through Government Networks', in Byers, M. (ed.), *The Role of Law in International Politics*, Oxford University Press, 2000: 177.

Slaughter, A.M., Tulumello, A., Wood, S. (1998), 'International Law and International Relations Theory: A New Generation of Interdisciplinary Scholarship', *The American Journal of International Law* 92–3: 367.

Smith, M. (2010), 'An Inconvenient Founding: America's Principles Applied to the ICC', in *The Heritage Foundation*, February 2010, accessible at: www.heritage.org/Research/InternationalOrganizations/bg2370.cfm

Song, S.H. (2010), President of the International Criminal Court, *Opening Remarks of the Review Conference*, ICC Statements, 31 March 2010.

Sriram, C.L. (2004), *Confronting Past Human Rights Violations: Justice vs Peace in Times of Transition,* Franc Cass: New York.

Sriram, C.L. (2008), *Peace as governance. Power-Sharing, Armed Groups and Contemporary Peace Negotiations,* Palgrave Macmillan.

Stahn, C. and van den Herik L. eds. (2010), *Future Perspectives on International Criminal Justice,* TMC Asser Press/CUP.

Stahn, C. and Sluiter G. (2009), eds. *The Emerging Practice of the International Criminal Court,* Brill: Martinus Nijhoff Publishers.

Stahn, C. and Kleffner J. K. eds. (2008), Jus *Post Bellum. Towards a Law of Transition from Conflict to Peace,* TMC Asser Press.

Stahn, C., El Zeidy, M., Olasolo, H. (2005), 'The International Criminal Court's Ad Hoc Jurisdiction Revisited', in *American Journal of International Law* 99–421.

Sterio, M. (2008), 'The Evolution of International Law', in *International and Comparative Law Review,* 2008 (March) Cleveland-Marshall Legal Studies Paper No. 08–150, accessible at: http://ssrn.com/abstract=1104723

Sunderland, M. (2010), 'Kenya and Sudan in the Spotlight as ICC Conference Opens in Uganda', in *Sudaneseonline,* 31 May 2010, accessible at: www.sudaneseonline.com/en3/publish/Latest_News_1/Kenya_and_Sudan_in_the_Spotlight_as_ICC_Conference_Opens_in_Uganda.shtml

Sunga, L.S. (1997), 'Aggression, Threat of Aggression, Intervention and Colonial Domination' in *The Emerging System of International Criminal Law: Developments in Codification and Implementation,* 1997: 31, Kluwer Law International: The Hague.

Sunga, L.S., 'The Role of Humanitarian Intervention in International Peace and Security: Guarantee or Threat?' in H. Köchler (ed.), *The Use of Force in International Relations. Challenges to Collective Security',* Studies in International Relations, XXVIII, International Progress Organization: Vienna, 2006: 41–83.

Tadjbakhsh, S. and Chenoy, A. M. (2007), *Human Security. Concept and implications,* 2007, Routledge Advances in International Relations and Global Politics.

Taft, W.H. and Buchwald, T.F. (2003), 'Preemption, Iraq, and International Law', in *The American Journal of International Law* 97–3: 557, accessible at: www.jstor.org/stable/3109840

Tallgren, I. (1998), "Completing the International Criminal Order", *Nordic Journal of International Law* 67–2: 107.

Thakur, R. and Weiss T.G. (2010), *United Nations and Global Governance: An Unfinished History,* UNIP, Indiana University Press.

Thakur, R. (2007), 'The Responsibility To protect, and To Prosecute?" in *Addressing International Governance Challenges* (CIGI).

Thérien J.P. (2009), 'The United Nations and Global Democracy: From Discourse to Deeds', *Cooperation and Conflict* (December 2009), Sage Journals, 44–4: 355–377.

Tolbert, D. and Wierda M. (2010), 'Stocktaking Peace and Justice' in *The Rome Statute Review Conference,* International Center for Transitional Justice, ICTJ Briefing, Thematic Case Study, May 2010, accessible at: www.ictj.org/static/Publications/ICTJ_RSRC-PeaceandJustice_bp2010.pdf

Tolbert, D. and Solomon A., (2006), 'What is the Rule of Law, Which Rule of Law?', in *United Nations Reform and Supporting the Rule of Law in Post-Conflict Societies,*

*Harward Human Rights Journal* 19: 29, accessible at: www.law.harvard.edu/students/orgs/hrj/iss19/tolbert.shtml#fn10

Tomuschat, C. and Thouvenin, J.M. (2006), *The Fundamental Rules of the International Legal Order: Jus Cogens and Obligations Erga Omnes,* Martinus Nijhoff Publishers at 236–471.

Totani Y. (2008), *The Tokyo War Crimes Trial. The Pursuit of Justice in the Wake of World War II,* Harvard University Press.

Totten, S. and Markusen E. (2006), *Genocide in Darfur: Investigating the Atrocities in the Sudan,* Routledge.

Trent, J.E. (2008), *How to Reform the United Nations: A Proposal,* Centre on Governance, University of Ottawa.

Tuck, R. (1999), *The Rights of War and Peace: Political Thought and the International Order from Grotius to Kant,* Oxford University Press, (1999: 234).

Turns, D. (2007), 'The Court's Judgment on the Merits: The Jurisdictional Question' in "Application of the Convention on the Prevention and Punishment of the Crime of Genocide: Bosnia and Herzegovina v Serbia and Montenegro', in *Melbourne Journal of International Law* 8(2): 398.

Udombana, N.J. (2006), 'Pay Back in Sudan? Darfur in the International Criminal Court', in *Tulsa Journal of Comparative and International Law* 13–56: 1–57.

UNDP (2005), 'Violent Conflict: Bringing the Real Threat into Focus', in *International cooperation at a crossroads: Aid, trade and security in an unequal world,* Human Development Report Chapter V: 151–181, accessible at: http://hdr.undp.org/en/media/HDR05_chapter_5.pdf

UNDP (2008), 'A Global UNDP Programme for Justice and Security 2008–2011', *Strengthening the Rule of Law in Conflict and Post-Conflict Situations,* (2008), accessible at: www.undp.org/cpr/documents/jssr/rule_of_law_final.pdf

UNESCO (2005), *What Agenda for Human Security in the Twenty-first Century,* UNESCO: Paris.

UNESCO (2008), Human *Security: Approaches and Challenges,* UNESCO: Paris.

Unger, T. and Wierda, M. (2009) , 'Pursuing Justice in Ongoing Conflict: A Discussion of Current Practice' in *Building a Future on Peace and Justice,* Springer, 2009: 263.

United Nations Peacebuilding Commission, Working Group on Lessons Learned (UN PBC – WGLL), *Comparative lessons from the United Nations Rule of Law Assistance,* reports delivered on 20 October 2008: 2.

United Nations Press release, 2 August 2010, *Secretary-General Saddened by Death of Four Peacekeepers in South Darfur,* the electronic version of the press release is accessible at: www.un.org/News/Press/docs/2010/sgsm13033.doc.htm

Van Baarda, T. and Van Iersel, F. (2002), 'The Uneasy Relationship between Conscience and Military Law: The Brahimi Report's Unresolved Dilemma', in *International Peacekeeping* 9–3: 25–50.

Van den Herik, L. and Schrijver N.J. eds. (2013), *Counter-Terrorism Strategies in a Fragmented International Legal Order. Meeting the Challenges.* Cambridge University Press.

Van den Herik, L. (2007), 'The Security Council's Targeted Sanctions Regimes: In Need of Better Protection of the Individual', in *LJIL* 20: 797–807.

Verrijn Stuart, H. (2008), 'The ICC in Trouble', in *Journal of International Criminal Justice* 6–3: 409, accessible at: http://jicj.oxfordjournals.org/content/6/3/409.short

Pella, V.V. (1950), 'Towards and International Criminal Court', *American Journal of International Law*, 44: 37.

Vinck, P., Pham, P., Baldo, S., Shigekane, R. (2008), *Living with Fear: A Population-based Survey on Attitudes about Peace, Justice, and Social Reconstruction in Eastern Democratic Republic of Congo*, Human Rights Center of the University of California Berkeley, Payson Center for International Development, and ICTJ, August 2008.

Vlassenroot, K. and Romkema, H. (2007), 'War and Governance in the DRC', in *Local Governance and Leadership in the DRC*, Oxfam-Novib, accessible at: www.psw.ugent.be/crg/publications/working%20paper/localgov_rapport_eng_def.pdf

Voorhoeve, J. (2007), 'From War to the Rule of Law. Peace Building after Violent Conflicts', in WRR, *Dutch Scientific Council for Government Policy*, accessible at: www.wrr.nl/content.jsp?objectid=4143

Wald, M.P. (2009), *Tyrants on Trial. Keeping Order in the Courtroom*, Open Society Institute: New York.

Washburn, J. (2003), *Background on Peacekeeping and the ICC: Existing Safeguards for Peacekeepers*, AMICC, accessible at: www.iccnow.org/documents/FS-AMICC-Peacekeeping.pdf

Webel, C. and Galtung, J. (2007), *Handbook of Peace and Conflict Studies*, Routledge: New York.

Weiss, T.G. (2004), 'The Sunset of Humanitarian Intervention? The Responsibility to Protect in a Unipolar Era', in *Security Dialogue* 2: 135.

Weiss, T.G. (2003), 'The Illusion of UN Security Council Reform', in *The Washington Quarterly* 26: 147–161.

Weiss, T.G. (2000), 'Governance, good governance and global governance: Conceptual and actual challenges', in *Third World Quarterly* 21–5: 795–814.

White, N.D. (2009), 'Empowering Peace Operations to Protect Civilians: Form over Substance?' *Journal of International Peacekeeping* 13, 3–4: 327.

White, N.D. (2002), 'The Legal Organs: Accountability and the rule of Law', in *The United Nations System. Toward International Justice*, 2002: 111, Lynne Rienner Publishers.

White, N.D. (2001), 'Comment on the Report of the Panel on UN Peace Operations (The Brahimi Report)', *Journal of Conflict and Security Law* 6(1): 127.

The White House, *The National Security Strategy of the United States of America*, September 2010, Washington DC.

Williams, G.H. (2005), *Engineering Peace: The Military Role in Postconflict Reconstruction*, United States Institute of Peace Press: Washington DC.

Williamson, R. (2003), 'Peacebuilding: the UN playing a constructive role', in *Seton Hall Journal of Diplomacy and International Affairs* 4(1)-15.

Willson, B. (2000), 'US Aggression Against Iraq: Historical and Political Context', 1st January 2000, accessible at: www.brianwillson.com/u-s-aggression-against-iraq-historical-and-political-context/

Wimmer, A. (1997), 'Who Owns the State? Understanding Ethnic Conflict in Post-Colonial Societies', in *Nations and Nationalism* 3–4, 1997: 631–666.

Wirth, S. (2002), 'Immunity for Core Crimes? The ICJ's Judgment in the Congo v. Belgium Case', in *European Journal of International Law* 4–13: 877.

Wolff, S., eds. Wichmann N., Mounier N. (2009), *The External Dimension of Justice and Home Affairs: A Different Security Agenda for the European Union?*, Routledge.

Yusuf, A. A. (2003) 'The right of intervention by the AU: A paradigm shift in regional enforcement action?', *African Yearbook of International Law*, vol. 11, pp. 3–21.

Zacklin, R. (2004) 'The Failings of Ad Hoc International Tribunals', in *Journal of International Criminal Justice* 2-2: 541–545.

Zalman, A. and Clarke, J. (2009), 'The Global War on Terror: A Narrative in Need of a Rewrite', in *Ethics & International Affairs* 2009: 2–23, accessible at: www.cceia.org/resources/journal/23_2/essays/002#_footnote16

Zhou, H.R. (2006) 'The Enforcement of Arrest Warrants by International Forces: from the ICTY to the ICC', in *Journal of International Criminal Justice* 4-2: 202–218.

Zifcak, S. (2006), 'Globalizing The Rule of Law: Rethinking Values and Reforming Institutions', in *Globalization and the Rule of Law*, 2006: 32–62.

Zsolt, H. (March 2002), 'The Making of the Basic Principles of the Headquarter Agreement: The Twenty-Fifth Memorial Issue. The Eve of the International Criminal Court: Preparations and Commentary. Completing the Work of the Preparatory Commission', in *Fordham International Law Journal* 25-3: 625–637.

Zwanenburg, M. (2004), *Accountability of Peace Support Operations*, Martinus Nijhoff.

# ABOUT THE AUTHOR

In this book the author analyses the intersection between law and politics in particular the progress achieved and achievable by the formulation of the global humanitarian policy and by the legal frameworks responding to international threats and crimes. His multidisciplinary work provides an assessment of the international tools currently at disposition by the world community for the governance of international criminal justice in the context of human security and sustainable peace, dealing with intra- and eventually inter-state civil wars caused by autocratic, totalitarian and criminal regimes.

His areas of expertise cover international law and international relations, law of international organisations, European policy, law and institutions, human security and global affairs. He holds a MA in European Law, Economics and Politics from the European College of Parma where he was, among other duties, in charge of drafting policy and research addressing practitioners, academics, public institutions and civil society strengthening the EU framework for research and innovation. He also holds a MA in Political Science and International Relations from the University Orientale of Naples and he performed the Erasmus program at La Sorbonne University of Paris.

His previous research and analysis focused on the prospects of reforms of the United Nations institutional framework fostering peace and security. He also performed policy research in the field of conflict studies, conflict prevention, preventive diplomacy and peace-building, focusing in particular on the protection of civilians in extremely violent conflict zones addressing a broad audience of policy-makers and practitioners.

In previous years he addressed EU institutions providing recommendations to the decision-making on programming activities in fragile States and conflict affected country-situations, enabling development and capacity-building in the context of the EU Foreign Affairs and Security Policy.

Since 2004 he is employed in the Office of the Prosecutor of the International Criminal Court, the first permanent and treaty-based international judicial institution established to help end impunity for the perpetrators of the most serious crimes of concern to the international community.

Lightning Source UK Ltd.
Milton Keynes UK
UKOW01f1449071117
312355UK00006B/204/P

9 781780 68402